MADAME BLAVATSKY

Also by the Author

STEALING HEAVEN: THE LOVE STORY OF HELOÏSE AND ABELARD
ELEANOR OF AQUITAINE
FREE WOMAN: THE LIFE AND TIMES OF VICTORIA WOODHULL

MADAME BLAVATSKY

The Woman Behind the Myth

MARION MEADE

G.P. PUTNAM'S SONS
NEW YORK

Acknowledgments

This book would not have been written without the inspiration and encouragement of William Targ, who must be given credit for believing that H.P.B.'s story deserved to be told one more time.

Many organizations assisted me in the gathering of information. Foremost I am indebted to the New York Public Library for granting me the privilege of working in the Frederick Lewis Allen Room. I am also grateful for help given by staff members of the following libraries: the Butler Library of Columbia University; Monica Schulzetenberg of the Yale Divinity School Library; Kathleen Jacklin of the Cornell University libraries; the Olcott Library and Research Center of the Theosophical Society in America; the library of the New York Theosophical Society; Wayne Norman of the Eileen J. Garrett Library of the Parapsychology Foundation; the library of the Association for Research and Enlightenment; and the Department of Manuscripts of the British Library.

I am equally indebted to those individuals who have helped me in various ways: J. Gail Cayce of the Edgar Cayce Foundation, Dr. Gideon Panter, Martha Hollins, Jerome Rainville, Diane Matthews, Thetis Powers, Two Worlds Publishing Co. of London, Hanna Loewy, Mary E. Sidhu, Nancy Sommershield, Julie Coopersmith, Karen Dent, the staffs of Samuel Weiser's Bookstore, and Quest Book Shop in New York City, and Norman Goodman, County Clerk of the New York County Court House.

Library of Congress Cataloging in Publication Data

Meade, Marion, date.
    Madame Blavatsky, the woman behind the myth.

    Bibliography: p.
    Includes index.
    1. Blavatsky, Helene Petrovna Hahn-Hahn, 1831–1891.
2. Theosophists—Biography. I. Title.
BP585.B6M42   1980   299'.934'0924 [B]   79–29648
ISBN 0-399-12376-8

PRINTED IN THE UNITED STATES OF AMERICA

Contents

Acknowledgments 4
Preface 7
Horoscope 10

RUSSIA *1831–1849*

I The Fadeyevs and the von Hahns 15
II Lelinka 24
III Visions and Voices 35
IV The Plumeless Raven 47

THE VEILED YEARS *1849–1873*

I The Hindu at Ramsgate 61
II Agardi Metrovitch 68
III Yuri 76
IV Russia for the Last Time 93

NEW YORK *1873–1878*

I Immigrant 101
II "John King" and Other Spooks 132
III The Theosophical Society 147
IV *Isis Unveiled* 158

INDIA *1878–1884*

I Bombay 193
II The Mahatmas 217
III The Astral Post Office 234
IV Adyar 260

EUROPE *1884*

I Paris 285
II London 304
III Elberfeld 312
IV Homeward Bound 321

THE SECRET DOCTRINE *1884–1887*

I The Investigation 335
II Würzburg 353
III Ostend 370

LONDON *1887–1891*

I Priestess of Lansdowne Road 389
II Sweet Mango 418
III Twilight 441

Epitaph 456
Appendixes
  A The Question of H.P.B.'s Psi Faculties 461
  B The Mahatma Papers 464
  C Parallel Cases 467
Notes and Sources 469
Bibliography 499
Index 512

Preface

When Helena Petrovna Blavatsky was forty-five, she looked back on four-and-a-half turbulent decades and observed, "One cannot remake one's past, one can only efface it according to one's strength." Actually she took pains to do both, and given her boundless energy, such efforts at revision were not entirely unsuccessful. For the last fifteen years of her life, she worked strenuously to re-create herself, erasing what she regretted having done, inserting new material, continually editing herself into the person she would have liked to have been. Thus at the age of fifty-four, in spite of two husbands, an indeterminate number of lovers and a child, she solemnly insisted she was a virgin.

Because she was an eccentric who abided by no rules except her own, she had excellent reasons for trying to conceal a history scandalously inappropriate for a religious teacher who wished to be taken as seriously as Jesus or Buddha. As the originator of modern Theosophy and cofounder of the Theosophical Society, she saw her mission as sublimely messianic: to save the world. Theosophy, literally interpreted from the Greek, means divine wisdom or knowledge of God, and, pre-Blavatsky, had been associated with the Christian Gnostics, Hebrew Cabalists and the teachings of Jakob Bohme and Paracelsus. Madame Blavatsky's Theosophy was nothing less than an attempt to synthesize Brahmanism, Buddhism and Occultism into a new religion. It advocated a universal brotherhood of humankind and postulated the existence of Mahatmas or Masters, wise men of superhuman knowledge who lived in the Himalayas. It was her conviction that these men had trained her and then sent her out into the world with permission to disclose some of the secret knowledge that could light up a pitiless and incomprehensible universe.

In this she failed, even though it was failure on a grand scale. Theosophy changed nothing, nor was it for that matter taken very seriously. Blavatsky's attempt to bring Eastern wisdom to a West corrupted by materialism was doomed to failure, and probably no other individual, no matter how dedicated, could have succeeded where she failed. Madame Blavatsky misjudged the Western mind. It was not only the intelligentsia who rejected her doctrine, but also ordinary folk of common sense. Who could accept a philosophy marbled with parlor magic and the suspicious incense of hallucination, whose

7

saints were invisible supermen hiding in Tibet and whose miracles were letters falling from the air? Although the nobility of her message remained inviolate, the grandeur was gone.

If she failed as Buddha or Jesus, she succeeded in other roles she considered beneath her. The significance of the Theosophical movement in restoring to colonial India its own spiritual heritage and, eventually, its independence as a nation, should not be overlooked. At a time when few nonacademics placed any value on Eastern scriptures, it was the Theosophical Society that gave Gandhi his first English translation of the *Bhagavad-Gītā,* which would virtually become his bible.

Not only did Madame Blavatsky inspire Hindus to respect their own roots but, more than any other single individual, she was responsible for bringing to the West a knowledge of Eastern religion and philosophy that paved the way for contemporary Transcendental Meditation, Zen, Hare Krishnas; yoga and vegetarianism; karma and reincarnation; swamis, yogis and gurus.

Interestingly enough, her impact on our culture was not limited to religion and occultism. It also revitalized the European literary heritage by contributing to the "Irish Renaissance." Writers such as Yeats and "A.E." (George Russell) became members of the Theosophical Society, and their creativity was stimulated by Madame Blavatsky's visions of the ancient wisdom-traditions. Even Joyce, who was less than enchanted with her philosophy, read her works and could not resist drawing upon them in *Ulysses:* "Yogibogeybox in Dawson chambers. *Isis Unveiled* . . . Crosslegged under an umbrel umbershoot he thrones an Aztec logos, functioning on astral levels, their overshoul, mahamahatma. The faithful hermetists await the light, ripe for chelaship, ringroundabout him . . . Hesouls, shesouls, shoals of souls."

And yet, even if Madame Blavatsky had sparked none of this, she might still have captured a place in history as an extraordinary woman. When I embarked on this biography, I believed it necessary to decide whether she was truly a great person or not, one that I liked or did not. Before my research had progressed very far, it became clear that such an approach was doomed to fail. Like most people, H.P.B., as she was called, was a mixture of greatness and weakness. Only in that light is an appraisal possible. Regrettably, elements of her character are difficult to admire. But after careful study we can understand why she behaved as she did and can even sympathize without condoning her actions. At the same time, she possessed a genuine daring and a vastness of body and soul that compels admiration. In every way, she was an immense person. She weighed more than other people, ate more, smoked more, swore more, and visualized heaven and earth in terms that dwarfed any previous conception.

One simply cannot make an informed judgment about her paranormal abilities. Madame Blavatsky lived in a markedly different world from ours, where the wall between reality and unreality was at least transparent, sometimes even nonexistent. For that reason, her fifty-nine years could more correctly be termed an experience rather than a life. From childhood, she exhibited mediumistic abilities: she heard voices, glimpsed unseen presences, and faced a variety of difficulties that the average person does not meet. In an earlier period, she would have had to use every bit of her considerable ingenuity to avoid ending up at the stake or in prison. As it was, she suffered her entire life from the jeers of those who believed her a liar or psychotic. It is to her credit that she tried to make sense of the puzzle that was Helena Petrovna Blavatsky. If all the pieces refused to fit into a coherent picture, surely she could not be blamed. Perhaps this inability to understand herself was the reason she preferred to be called H.P.B. rather than her given name, which she said was only a label for her physical body.

There have been a number of biographical treatments of her. The first was by her friend Alfred Sinnett, with whom she cooperated after her fashion: she put at his disposal a body of "facts" freshly minted for the occasion, but later disowned these "memoirs." Posthumously, her interpreters have invariably fallen into one of two categories: those who approached her with hostility and ended by depicting her as a publicity-seeking charlatan, which at times she did seem to be, and those adherents of Theosophy who regarded her as a saint with a few minor failings. As for myself, I see Madame Blavatsky as an extremely intelligent woman trying to grapple with experiences that were inexplicable. My approach has been to collect the accessible facts about her, to weigh them as honestly as I could, and to present my conclusions, even though I am fully aware that those conclusions may not please every reader.

It was H.P.B.'s ill luck to live in the nineteenth century when aggressive women were judged by harsher standards than today. More than once during the writing of this book, I have pondered whether her success as a religious teacher might have been greater had she been a man. The fact that she sometimes provoked the most intense outbursts of hatred very likely can be attributed to her sex, but ultimately this sort of conjecture is futile and very much beside the point. She herself refused to abide by sexual stereotypes. Indeed, she ostentatiously thumbed her nose at them unless, of course, it suited her purpose to do otherwise. And I suspect she would have regarded this line of investigation as "flapdoodle," to use her favorite expression.

She used to say that even though her contemporaries did not appreciate her, she would be vindicated in the twentieth century when her teachings and her person would finally be understood. While that prophecy has not been totally fulfilled, there is no doubt that we can understand her better than did the Victorians. Perhaps a final assessment of her must wait until the twenty-first century.

NATAL HOROSCOPE OF H. P. BLAVATSKY

Place of birth: Ekaterinoslav, Russia
35:01 E. Longitude; 48:27 N. Latitude
Date of birth:
   July 31, 1831, according to Julian calendar
   August 12, 1831, according to Gregorian calendar
Local Time: 1:42:00 A.M.
G.M.T.: 11:21:56 P.M. (August 11)
Sid. Time: 23:00:43
Adjusted Calculation Date: February 2, 1831

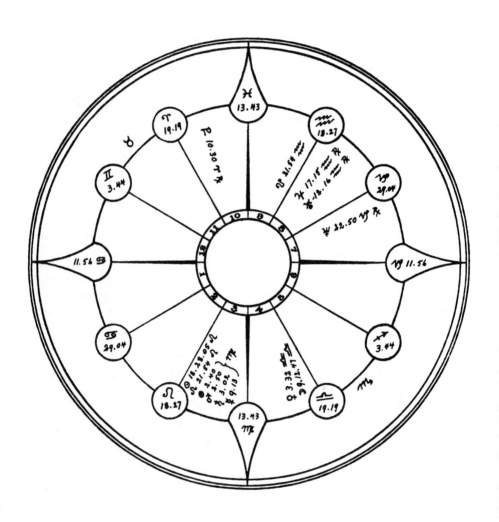

Magnifying and applying come I,
Outbidding at the start the old cautious hucksters,
Taking myself the exact dimensions of Jehovah,
Lithographing Kronos, Zeus his son, and Hercules his grandson,
Buying drafts of Osiris, Isis, Belus, Brahma, Buddha,
In my portfolio placing Manito loose, Allah on a leaf, the
    crucifix engraved,
With Oden and the hideous-faced Mexitli and every idol and
    image,
Taking them all for what they are worth and not a cent more,
Admitting they were alive and did the work of their days,
(They bore mites as for unfledg'd birds who have now to rise
    and fly and sing for themselves.)
Accepting the rough deific sketches to fill out better in myself,
    bestowing them freely on each man and woman I see,
                    * * *
I too am not a bit tamed, I too am untranslatable,
I sound my barbaric yawp over the roofs of the world.

                              Walt Whitman, *Song of Myself*

RUSSIA

1831–1849

I

The Fadeyevs and the von Hahns

In the fall of 1878, soon after she had become the first Russian woman naturalized as a citizen of the United States, Helena Petrovna Blavatsky fired off one of her periodic attempts to establish the truth about herself.

"To begin with," she wrote caustically to a French journal, "I am not a *Countess* so far as I know. Without overlooking the fact that it would be more than ridiculous—it would be *unconstitutional*—in a citizen or citizeness of the Republic of the United States—who abjures all titles of nobility upon being naturalized—to claim one, above all which never belonged to him or her—I am too democratic, and I love and respect the people sufficiently, having devoted all my sympathy to them, and this without distinction of race or color, to trick myself out in any kind of title!"[1]

This wordy, not entirely insincere, protest was delivered with the self-assurance of one whose predecessors are so respectable that she need not descend to vulgar social-climbing. She was not a countess; she was, however, the granddaughter of a princess, and her family, prominent in Russian history since the High Middle Ages, had produced its share of warriors, saints, and rascals.

The noble family of Dolgorukov could trace its lineage back to the twelfth century canonized prince St. Mihail Vsevolodovich of Chernigov, and through him to the semilegendary Rurik, the first prince of Novgorod.[2] St. Mihail's great-greatgrandson Prince Konstantin Ivanovich, ruled over the town of Obolensk and founded the renowned Obolensky family. It was his fiery grandson Prince Ivan who won the nickname "Dolgorukoy," which meant "long-handed" or "far-reaching"—a tribute to his talent for detecting hidden enemies.

Until as recently as the early eighteenth century, the elder line of the Dolgorukovs continued to produce notable, and sometimes notorious, individuals: Prince Gregory, ambassador to Poland; Prince Yakov, the favorite of Peter the Great; Princess Katherine, who was betrothed to Czar Peter II and whose destiny was thwarted when Peter was poisoned on the eve of their marriage; Prince Serguey, executed for forgery and sundry political intrigues in 1739.

Apart from Princess Katherine, whose fame lay in the dubious distinction of having failed to reach the throne, the achievements the Dolgorukovs had

15

always centered on the male side of the line. But by the nineteenth century the energies of the men seemed to have lapsed into comparative sluggishness, and whatever prestige the family could boast of was to be found only on the female side, a fact of some relevance in the life of Helena Petrovna Blavatsky.

In the 1830s, Lady Hester Lucy Stanhope, the Englishwoman who roved the world dressed as a man, remarked about her travels in Russia:

> In that barbarian land I met an outstanding woman-scientist, who would have been famous in Europe, but who is completely underestimated due to her misfortune of being born on the shores of the Volga River, where there was none to recognize her scientific value.[3]

Not withstanding Lady Stanhope's British chauvinism and her mistake about the woman's birthplace, the scientist had not been totally unrecognized. Princess Helena Pavlovna Dolgorukova, H.P.B.'s maternal grandmother, would have been an unusual person in any nation or century. A noted botanist, a scholar who spoke five languages fluently, an excellent artist, she possessed endowments rare for a woman of her time. Even more unusual was the fact that she succeeded in exercising her talents. While natural science was her chief interest, she was also proficient in archaeology and numismatics, and during her lifetime accumulated valuable collections in these areas. For many years she carried on correspondence with European scientists, among them geologist Sir Roderick Murchison, who founded the Royal Geographic Society. A fossil shell, the Venus-Fadeef, was named in her honor.

The roots of Princess Helena's scientific interests are unclear. Her father, Prince Paul Dolgorukov, had little interest in orthodox science. On the contrary, he spent most of his time on his estate at Rzishchevo, in the Province of Kiev, addicted to his library of works on alchemy and magic, and was considered somewhat odd by his neighbors.

Having been born into an atmosphere of privilege and blessed with outstanding intelligence, it was the misfortune of the Princess to have an irregular family life. Her mother, Henrietta, was of French descent. A beauty with a reputation for flightiness, she married Prince Paul in 1787, produced two daughters in less than two years, and promptly abandoned him, leaving her infants behind. Twenty years later, shortly before Henrietta's death, she returned to her husband, but by that time Princess Helena was well past the age when she might have benefited from a mother's nurturing.

At the advanced age of twenty-four, the Princess opposed her father by expressing her intent to marry a young man her own age, Andrey Mihailovich Fadeyev. Fadeyev was a bright, ambitious fellow, as much in love with Helena as she was with him, but he happened to be a commoner—a fact of considerable importance to her father, Prince Paul, but of none whatever to his daughter. Eventually the Prince relented, and the marriage took place in

1813. Their first child, Helena Andreyevna, the mother of II. P. Blavatsky, was born the following year.

After the birth of Helena Andreyevna, the Fadeyevs moved to Ekaterinoslav, a Southern Russian city on the Dnieper River now called Dnepropetrovsk, where Andrey joined the Czar's bureaucracy as an officer in the Foreign Department of Immigration. Ekaterinoslav, in the words of a German visitor, seemed "partly like a portion of a great plan not completed, and partly like a town which has fallen from its former greatness."[4] Originally founded by Catherine the Great as a summer residence, it was abandoned, along with other royal retreats, when she began to concentrate her architectural efforts on Tsarskoe Selo, near St. Petersburg. In the meantime, however, her lover Prince Gregory Potemkin had already laid out wide boulevards, built a palace which in luxury and Oriental splendor surpassed anything then known in Russia, and created a magnificent park stretching along the rocky banks of the Dnieper. A city planned on a gigantic scale, built to accommodate a million souls, it was actually inhabited by only a few thousand.

By the time of the Fadeyevs' arrival, Catherine's palace had fallen into ruins and, due to sand deposits, the Dnieper was navigable for only six weeks in the spring. In this provincial town, the Princess pursued her scientific studies and raised her daughter. Hers was an unusually happy marriage and the family was close knit. She had little taste for social calls on her neighbors, although apparently she responded cordially when they came to her. She paid no attention at all to fashionable modes of child-rearing. Generally Russian parents of the upper classes had little contact with their offspring, beyond morning and evening greetings, but the Princess, despite a retinue of serfs, refused to hand over her daughter to the care of nurses. Later, in a story which may be considered autobiographical, her daughter would write: "If I had to tell you that our mother was our nourisher, our caretaker, our teacher, and our guardian-angel, that, still, would not describe all her sacrificial, endless, selfless attachment, by which she constantly gladdened our lives." Remembering Princess Helena's own motherless childhood, it is unnecessary to look further for an explanation of her passionate attachment to her firstborn, Helena Andreyevna, and later, to her younger children: Katherine, Rostislav, and finally Nadyezhda, who was born when the Princess was thirty-nine.

Until the age of thirteen, Helena Andreyevna was educated by her mother, under whose supervision she studied history, language and literature. An ardent reader, she became a great admirer of French, German and Russian writers, whom she read in their own languages. Books induced in her visible emotional reactions. She could be found laughing and weeping over their pages. At an early age, she mastered the techniques of poetical composition and struggled to write her own verse, although at times she found this form of expression inadequate. "The thoughts would rush to her brain, powerless to be expressed in mere words, which only impeded their powerful and invisible flight, and she had to impatiently throw aside her impotent pen."

A graceful, dreamy girl, delicate in health and indulged by her mother, she found plenty in books to fuel her imagination. She had a tendency to measure the heroic figures and settings of literature against her own surroundings: the barren steppes stretching on all sides to the horizon, the dry, blackish-gray soil with its parched grass and thistles, Ekaterinoslav itself with its unsophisticated residents. "My attention," she recalled, "was taken up by historical events, by the aspirations, passions and actions of outstanding people who have contributed to the spiritual elevation of mankind." In comparison, her everyday life "looked pale and insignificant as an ant-hill."

Determinedly intellectual, she held herself aloof from the other young ladies of Ekaterinoslav, whose interests and goals were more commonplace. "I reached with my mind everywhere," she later said of herself as she had been at fifteen. "I felt with my heart everything." There is a portrait of Helena Andreyevna, whose date is unknown but appears to be from the period of her teens. Her dark hair is pulled back smoothly behind the ears and curled under; the filmy white gown, tight at the elbows in the current fashion, reveals a slim, childish figure; and around her neck is knotted, somewhat rakishly, a small scarf. The perfect oval face, with its button mouth and dreamy eyes, gives an impression of elegant hauteur. It is a pretty face, evidently composed demurely for the portrait, but it fails to give the smallest indication of the banked fires smoldering beneath the surface.

She had her share of admirers among the young men of the town, and would have had more if she had not clung to her impossibly lofty expectations about men. No doubt influenced by her parents' loving relationship, she was also affected by her reading, and she fantasized herself the heroine of a romantic literary tale in which love and marriage were synonymous. As a result, she nourished dreams about "the possibility of eternal changeless love between two people." There was nothing abstract about this conviction: "I had profound faith in it, I hoped for it, I waited for its realization, lovingly carrying in my heart the germ of the sacred fire." Her love would be reserved for someone special: "I did not waste any of its sacred flame on temporary infatuations. No—I guarded it as a celestial gift, which I hoped would bring me happiness once and forever."[5] Such was the idealistic concept on which she planned to base her marriage.

At sixteen, she encountered Captain Peter Alexeyeivich von Hahn of the horse artillery. Recently decorated in the Turkish Campaign[6], von Hahn was twice her age, well educated, good-looking and charming, with the splendid masculinity that could be found among uniformed officers of Czar Nicholas's regiments. That Helena felt dazzled by this heroic visitor is easily understandable. The captain, who was not based permanently in Ekaterinoslav, was immediately smitten by the refined Helena and set about courting her in the manner of a man who knows how to charm and amuse an inexperienced young woman.

For a person addicted to plumbing the depths of her own emotions, Helena Andreyevna does not seem to have submitted the dashing Captain von Hahn to a thorough examination. Swept away, she evidently had no clear sense that marriage would mean leaving home and following the army from one barracks and backwater town to the next, many far worse than Ekaterinoslav. The power of physical attraction prevailed and when he proposed, she enthusiastically accepted.

There is no record of von Hahn's feelings. However, he does not seem to have been an unusually sensitive man, and it would not be unfair to surmise that he, like any other professional soldier, failed to take women seriously. If he noticed at all that Helena Andreyevna's view of men was foggy with illusions, he must have dismissed it as girlish romanticism that she would soon outgrow.

Von Hahn's pedigree seemed sufficiently impressive for a daughter of a Dolgorukov. His solidly military family was descended from an old Mecklenburg family—the Counts Hahn von Rotternstern-Hahn, one branch of which had migrated to Russia a century earlier. Peter's father, Alexis Gustavovich von Hahn, was a well-known general in the army of Field Marshal Alexander Suvorov and had won a decisive battle in the Swiss Alps. For a time he had been commandant of the city of Zurich. Peter von Hahn's mother had been a countess before her marriage; one of his brothers was Postmaster General of St. Petersburg; and other members of the family were sprinkled in high positions throughout the army and civilian government.[7]

It is not surprising that Princess Helena, despite a natural reluctance to part with her favorite child, should have reacted favorably to her daughter's choice of a mate. The couple was married toward the end of 1830, and by Christmas, Helena Andreyevna was pregnant.

A thousand miles to the north of Ekaterinoslav, at the Winter Palace in St. Petersburg, Czar Nicholas I was seething with frustration—if a man known for his outward detachment could be described as seething. More than six feet tall, utterly humorless, he ruled with an iron rod the fifty-five million souls— nearly half of them slaves—who populated an immense empire that stretched from eastern Poland to the Pacific Ocean. Once, in a letter to Empress Alexandra, he protested, "I am not your salvation, as you say. Our salvation is over there yonder where we shall all be admitted to rest from the tribulations of life."[8] Yet to his subjects, the thirty-four-year-old monarch appeared only slightly less awesome than the Almighty, a fact of which Nicholas was all too clearly aware.

Despite his philosophic acceptance of life's inevitable pain, Nicholas was gripped by alarm in 1830. Europe, in his opinion, had gone mad. Earlier that year he had been outraged by the French revolution, which had overthrown

Bourbon King Charles X in favor of Louis Philippe. The kindest words he could find for the usurper were "traitor" and "scoundrel." In what seemed to him an epidemic, a revolution in Belgium had won that country its independence from the Netherlands. Now, on the heels of these ominous events, Nicholas was forced to contend with a major insurrection in his own domain. A man who struck people as autocracy personified, he was deeply worried and, although he had once lamented, "I was born to suffer," the "Iron Czar" did not welcome needless aggravation.

Among the peoples who Nicholas detested, such as Jews, Greeks, and Poles, the Poles had stood first on the list since their 1829 assassination attempt during his coronation in Warsaw. To be sure, the Poles had no reason to love him: in 1795 the kingdom of Poland had been partitioned between Russia, Austria and Prussia and its name erased from the map of Europe in one stroke. Token moves to do something for the unfortunate Poles had been attempted by Napoleon, and even by Nicholas's elder brother, Alexander I, who had given his eastern slice of Poland a constitution and a parliament. Nevertheless, rumbles of discontent persisted.

On November 29, 1830, a military revolt erupted in Warsaw. It was sparked by student cadets at the officers' training school, who murdered several senior officers loyal to the Russian government. Army regiments and masses of civilians were quick to join the uprising. The Russian viceroy and commander-in-chief, Nicholas's brother Grand Duke Constantine, did nothing to stanch the momentum and within weeks the Russian army was forced to flee the country. At first, Nicholas observed helplessly. But by January 1831, in a belated move to grab back his lost property, he began mobilizing troops and shipping them to the Polish border. Peter von Hahn's battery was among them.

During these unforeseen events, Helena Andreyevna returned home with her family. She continued her studies as before, but now she was pregnant. In addition to her fear that Peter might be killed in combat, she had another anxiety: a cholera epidemic of serious proportions broke out that winter, accounting for more deaths among the regiments than the Poles. Grand Duke Constantine was its most notable victim.

This was an interlude of national terror that did not confine itself to any single area of the country. In villages and cities, among peasants and royal families, the disease swept away its victims with startling rapidity. At St. Petersburg, in the belief that the government was deliberately poisoning the water, citizens mobbed Haymarket Square. The Emperor, driving up in an open carriage, rose to his feet. "Wretches," he screamed, "is this your gratitude? The Almighty looks down upon you. On your knees, wretched people, on your knees."[9] Ten thousand fell to the cobbles, crossed themselves, and went home, abandoning questions about the provisions he was making to check the epidemic.

In Ekaterinoslav, where the plague did not strike until summer, hardly a day went by without news of somebody dead or dying. Inevitably, tragedy knocked on the Fadeyevs' door and a number of serfs fell ill. The disease began with convulsions, stomach pains and vomiting, and ended a few days later with coffins and funerals. Once cholera entered a house, it generally spread rapidly, making no distinction between servant and master.

It was in this morbid atmosphere that Helena Andreyevna gave birth to a premature child during the night between July 30 and 31, 1831.[10] Not only did the infant girl arrive weeks ahead of schedule, but she appeared to be far from healthy. Plans were immediately made for baptism, lest she be carried off by natural causes or cholera with the burden of original sin on her soul. Hasty though the baptism may have been, it was conducted with all the customary paraphernalia of the Greek Orthodox ritual: lighted tapers, three pairs of godparents, participants and spectators standing with consecrated candles during the lengthy ceremony. In the center of the room stood the priest with his three assistants, all in golden robes and long hair, as well as the three pairs of sponsors and the household serfs.

In the first row behind the priest was the baby's child-aunt, Princess Helena Pavlovna Dolgorukova's three-year-old daughter, Nadyezhda. She must have grown weary of standing in the hot, overcrowded room for more than an hour and, unnoticed by the adults, had sat down on the floor and begun to play with her candle. As the ceremony drew to a close, while the sponsors symbolically renounced Satan by spitting three times at an invisible enemy, the flames of Nadyezhda's candle lit the bottom of the priest's robe. Nobody noticed until it was too late: the priest and several bystanders were severely burned.[11] For this reason among others, it would be remarked that Helena Petrovna Blavatsky had been born under exceedingly bad omens. Indeed, according to the superstitious beliefs of orthodox Russia, she was doomed from that day forward to a life of trouble and vicissitude.

In the short run, precisely the opposite seemed to be the case. The cholera infection died out in the Fadeyev household without having stricken a single member of the family, and as the summer of 1831 ended, the tide of war had already turned against Poland. However, it was not until the following summer that Peter von Hahn returned home to the bride he had left eighteen months earlier and the daughter he had never seen.

By eighteen, Helena Andreyevna von Hahn had plunged into married life with a man who was still virtually a stranger to her. Their first home was the small garrison town of Romankovo, whose single advantage was its proximity to the Fadeyevs. But just as Madame von Hahn was struggling to accustom herself to her new surroundings and friends, the captain was transferred to Oposhnya, a tiny community in the Province of Kiev. The stay in Oposhnya proved equally brief, and over the next two years there was a succession of further moves. During that time, Helena Andreyevna gave birth to her second child, a son named Alexander, nicknamed Sasha.

In the early years with Peter, Helena Andreyevna must have made an effort to adjust, but an army wife's rootless mode of life was not to her taste. Russian cavalry officers, as a group, were known neither for their intellect nor even for their serious interest in military strategy. Trained to serve with blind obedience, they were not encouraged to display initiative, and most of them frittered away their time drinking and gambling. How closely Captain von Hahn fit into the general ambience is unknown, but his wife found the existence empty and unimaginative, and decried the boring dinner parties and the endless conversations about horses, dogs and guns. One imagines that these provincial towns were the sort Chekhov depicted in *The Three Sisters* and that like Masha, whose knowledge of three languages was an unnecessary luxury, Helena Andreyevna found she knew "a lot too much" to fit in.

Nineteenth-century Russia was a land of aristocratic indolence, where no patrician did anything for himself that a serf could do for him. A husband asked nothing from his wife but that she be pretty, dress with taste, and appear elegantly attired the first thing in the morning. For the remainder of the day, her sole function was to sit in a stately pose upon the sofa while sewing, reading a novel, or receiving guests. If she needed the cushions rearranged or her cigarette lit, she was expected to call for a servant. No Russian "lady" would dream of violating polite rules of conduct by entering the kitchen or attending to her children's daily needs. Intellectual stimulation of the type sought by Helena Andreyevna did exist, but certainly not in an army town. Still, such lofty deprivations might have been tolerable had there not been other problems in her marriage.

What Helena Andreyevna may have suspected in the first weeks after the wedding, she knew for certain after her reunion with Peter in 1832: Peter was less spiritual than she; in fact, he professed to be something of an agnostic. But even more distressing to the strong-willed young woman was the realization that her husband had no respect for her. The low status of women in Russian society could not have completely escaped her notice, but she had persisted in envisioning her spouse as a friend and companion who would echo her own aspirations. Now she had to deal with the consequences of her error, for Peter had no patience with her. "The fine, sharp and fast mind of my husband," she recalled, "as a rule accompanied by a cutting irony, smashed every day one of my brightest, my most innocent and pure aspirations and feelings." Worse, he ridiculed her:

All that I admired, all that I aspired to from my childhood, all that was sacred to my heart was either laughed at, or was shown to me in the pitiless and cynical light of his cold and cruel reasoning.

Whenever she expressed feelings or opinions, he either belittled them or, yawning, turned the subject to dinner menus and other domestic trivia. In time she was able to pretend indifference to his disdain but her apparent submission really derived from lack of an alternative: she was still totally unaware of how to extricate herself from the situation. As his insensitivity wounded her ever more deeply, she grew increasingly disenchanted by both her husband and marriage.

It should be remembered that Peter von Hahn's treatment of his wife was neither deliberately cruel nor unusual. He behaved like a typical Russian husband of his class. It was Helena Andreyevna who was different. She insisted upon making demands that a man could not possibly fulfill, even if he had wanted to, and it was these demands that made her a misfit. Interestingly, she did not use that insight against herself. Instead of feeling guilty, she tried to cope with the outrage of a woman of sensitive temperament for whom there was no place in the world. Like countless other women, she directed her rage toward her husband; unlike them, she did not stop at the obvious source of her discontent but went on to aim her anger at society. What is to be marveled at is that the nineteen-year-old woman was able to rise above commonplace marital anguish by looking beyond the personal to the universal. It seemed clear to her that a woman's intelligence and talents "are in vain before the crowd; she will be like a criminal rejected by Society," and she posed a question:

Why, then, does Nature endow her so lavishly with her penetrating mind, her abilities and talents, her perceptions of higher purposes of life, her deep feeling for beauty?

And she answered it:

It is not Nature who hinders her . . . but man—man-made laws and social conditions.[12]

In the 1830s few women asked such questions, let alone answered them, and those who wrote about them were fewer still: George Sand in France and the Countess Ida Hahn-Hahn[13] in Germany.

The first three or four years of Helena Andreyevna's marriage may be summed up as the radicalization of a Russian wife. It was a self-administered process that offered no solutions or remedies and would leave her more miserable than before. Not surprisingly, the chronic tension in the von Hahn household was escalating rapidly. Toward the middle of 1834, Helena Andreyevna and Peter returned to Romankovo where she became pregnant for the third time. Shortly after their arrival, their son Sasha fell ill and died, contributing a fresh sorrow to her already acute sense of despair.

Two dominant moods emerge from this period of Helena Andreyevna's life: a deepening resentment toward her marriage and a rapidly developing feminist consciousness. She appears to have been a dutifully conscientious mother but lacking in the fierce affection and self-sacrificing disposition of her own mother. But then, the Princess was happily married while her daughter was not. In any event, Helena Andreyevna got off to a poor start in the profession of parenthood: her firstborn, little Helena Petrovna, or "Lelinka," proved to be a child who would tax the patience of the most devoted mother.

II

Lelinka

H.P.B.'s failure to mention her mother in later years, with the notable exception of the false remark that Helena Andreyevna had died when H.P.B. was a baby, was evidence of deep hostility. With few exceptions, H.P.B.'s general view of her own sex was unmistakably contemptuous: women lacked concentration and precision, they could not control their tongues, and above all, they could not be trusted. Some of this negativism undoubtedly derived from the general misogyny of the period, but she rejected women as could only one who had passionately loved a female and been rebuffed.

One of H.P.B.'s earliest memories is that she was perpetually ill: "sick and ever dying till seven or eight," is the way she phrased it, although family lore gives no evidence that she was ever in mortal danger. Her second memory was of being "spoilt and petted on one side, punished and hardened on the other,"[14] and in this, her recollection is amply supported. From the beginning, Lelinka was a nervous, high-strung infant, a colicky baby designed to drive to distraction a woman like Helena Andreyevna.

Her volatile temperament aside, Helena's appearance was somewhat less than irresistible. Her frequent illnesses did not prevent her from eating with gusto; she was a lumpish little girl who all her life would be struggling—not terribly hard at times—against obesity. Within the family, opinion about her was divided, as public opinion would be for the next sixty years. The more polite members said that Lelinka must have inherited her curly hair and vivacity from Peter von Hahn's mother, but, in reality, her kinky mop of pale brown frizz could never be called curly, and her vivacity could often have passed for demonic possession. Her most striking features were her prominent azure eyes, which seemed to observe her surroundings with an intensity that was hypnotic to many and frightening to some. Nobody who ever met H.P.B. forgot her eyes.

In the midnineteenth century, the typical Russian child was given its own way to a degree that shocked European visitors from the West who thought them undisciplined brats. But even in this permissive context, Helena Petrovna was an unusually willful and independent child. Badly behaved to the point of being unmanageable, Helena never hesitated to throw a temper tantrum when she could not get her way. The slightest contradiction, recalled her Aunt Nadyezhda, "brought on an outburst of passion, often a fit of convulsions."[15] Her habit of automatically defying authority may well have resulted from a nervous constitution and a naturally aggressive temperament, but it was also a by-product of being spoiled by the Fadeyevs and by the superstitious serf nurses into whose care she was placed. While the household was devoutly Christian—icons hung in every room—alongside the priests and the Orthodox sacraments, the Empire's pagan religion persisted and retained popularity, particularly among the servants. Old Russia, a hothouse of superstition, abounded in tales of wolves, monsters, ghosts, leshies, brownies and goblins, all of which were believed to manipulate human lives. *Roussalkas*, beautiful water spirits, were believed to be the souls of the unchristened who returned to entice the unwary to watery graves. Every house had its *domovoy*, a goblin in the form of an old man who lived behind the stove and played pranks when displeased.

According to legend, these supernatural beings could be placated or even controlled by individuals who, like H.P.B., had been born between the thirtieth and thirty-first of July. Furthermore, the Fadeyev serfs called Lelinka a *sedmitchka*, a word difficult to translate but meaning one connected with the number seven—a reference to H.P.B.'s having been born during the seventh month of the year. On the night of her birthday, they would carry her around the house and stables, sprinkling holy water and repeating mystical incantations to appease the *domovoy*. This ritual was supposedly conducted without the knowledge of her mother or grandparents. More likely, they simply refused to assign the slightest importance to it. There was too much superstition to pay attention to, and it governed every aspect of daily life: a baby must never look in the mirror or see its own shadow; a cradle mustn't be rocked unless the infant was in it; if a child moaned in its sleep, the nurse must make the sign of the cross to ward off evil spirits.

Believing that Helena Petrovna possessed special magical powers, the house serfs revered her, and she must have relished the attention, which she was not getting from her mother or father. But while she reveled in the backstairs admiration, she also saw that the servants feared her. A strange incident had taken place on a visit to Ekaterinoslav during the years when the von Hahns were living at various army bases, and it was legend among the servants. One day on an outing along the Dnieper, Helena, accompanied by a nurse and a fourteen-year-old serf named Pavlik who was pulling her in a cart, apparently set out to frighten the boy. "I will have you tickled to death by a *roussalka!*" she threatened. Then, pointing to a willow, she yelled, "There's one coming down from that tree. Here she comes . . . see, see!"[16]

Whether Pavlik actually thought he saw the dreaded nymph or whether he was merely fed up with the abuse of a miniature tyrant, he promptly ran off and the nurse had to return home without him. Several weeks later, his body was found by fishermen who caught it in their nets. Although the police verdict was "accidental drowning," the serfs had no doubt that Pavlik had died because Lelinka had withdrawn her magical protection and delivered him to some watchful *roussalka*. The family, however, disapproved of this superstitious interpretation and grew even more displeased when they heard Helena Petrovna corroborating the story, indignantly insisting that she had indeed handed over the boy to her faithful servants, the water nymphs.[17]

This particular incident was not so much brought on by an overactive imagination as by Helena's firm belief in an invisible world of supernatural beings whose lives were inextricably blended with those of mortals. Hard put to distinguish between fact and fiction, she was convinced that *roussalkas* sat in every tree. Didn't she see them with her own eyes? Hadn't Pavlik drowned? She felt herself powerful and invulnerable, and became increasingly convinced that mighty forces would carry out her wishes.

That her family recognized her abnormalities is clear; that they were at a loss to deal with them is equally obvious. H.P.B. would later recall that during her childhood she had been exorcised by countless priests and drenched in enough holy water to float a ship. At that time, when exorcism failed to eradicate outrageously unacceptable behavior, it was believed that beating might succeed. But although she received a good many scoldings and punishments, they failed to have the desired effect.

In these critical early years, H.P.B.'s mind was being formed not entirely by the superstitions of the peasants, which influenced all Russian children. There was also a general instability, presumably in part inherited, but enhanced by unconscious psychological conflicts about her parents. To Helena Andreyevna von Hahn, the troublesome child represented merely one problem out of many, undoubtedly not the most serious. Slowly, perhaps without realizing it, she was devising the only reasonable method of dealing with her foundering marriage: removing herself whenever the opportunity arose. At first this meant frequent trips home to Ekaterinoslav, but in 1834, soon after she found herself pregnant for the third time, she was able to arrange a more extended absence. In that year, Andrey Fadeyev became a member of the Board of Trustees for the Colonizers and moved his family to Odessa, on the Black Sea. Shortly afterward, Helena Andreyevna followed with Lelinka. She remained in Odessa until the spring of 1835 when her second daughter, Vera, was born.

After this separation, she rejoined her husband and resumed the wandering existence of an army wife, first in the Ukraine and later in the provinces of Tula and Kursk. The southern steppes, in winter, only deepened Helena Andreyevna's basic sense of loneliness. When the hurricanes known as *metels* swept down in furious, whirling gusts, the snow fell so thickly that houses disappeared, whole flocks of sheep froze, and people had to dig paths through six-foot drifts to reach their neighbors. At those times when the thermometer hanging between the double glass windows read sixteen degrees below zero, there would be nothing to do but huddle near the stove and listen to the bubbling samovar. Helena Andreyevna's discontent continued to fester until the spring of 1836, when her life suddenly took an unexpected turn. After four years of boring provincial towns, her husband's battery was temporarily assigned to the most exciting place in the Empire—the capital city of St. Petersburg.

The first railroad had been built only the previous year, and it still did not reach southern Russia. The von Hahns must have made the journey in a caravan of horse-drawn carts that transported coachmen, maids, nurses, household belongings and food provisions. The family itself would have ridden in a *dormez*, a cumbersome, high-wheeled wagon covered with leather and lined with straw and featherbeds. Since lying down was more comfortable than sitting, one usually made a journey stretched out on a featherbed, surrounded by roast chickens and other edibles, which were hung from the roof.

Travelers entering St. Petersburg from the south had to ride through the triumphal arch called Moscow Sastawa, an excellent vantage point from which to view the canals and gilt of the cupola churches of the "Venice of the North." It was obligatory to drive across Isaac Square, past the magnificent statue of Peter the Great, the Admiralty and Isaac Church, and then to turn down the city's main thoroughfare, Newsky Perspective. Along this artery flowed a constant stream of life: throngs of men on foot and horseback, bundled women sporting the latest French gowns under their furs, four-horse carriages and the smaller, faster *droschkis*. The street's immense width contained a double line of carriageways floored with wood and sidewalks a dozen feet broad. Flanking either side of the boulevard were palaces, elegant townhouses and luxurious shops whose windows were frosted with the clearest glass and illuminated at night with floods of gaslight.

St. Petersburg, the center of all that was "smart," was an intellectual and cultural aphrodisiac to Helena Andreyevna. Her position as the daughter of Princess Dolgorukov guaranteed her entry to a high level of society, and although the "season" was almost over, she plunged into a strenuous round of suppers, receptions, operas and concerts. The city's real socializing, however, took place at private gatherings where guests would arrive at 8 P.M. and immediately sit down at tables of whist, Boston, ombre and preference—the latter, played for money, was highly popular with the women. Conversation, in French, was plentiful and varied—the women gossiping and exchanging news of the latest plays, novels, and fashions; the men discussing business and politics. By midnight, the rooms would be thick with tobacco smoke, both men and women having adopted the fashionable cigarette habit, and the card games would continue until two in the morning, after which dinner was served. Nobody thought of leaving before 4 A.M., and sometimes they stayed until dawn.

In the drawing rooms of St. Petersburg, Helena Andreyevna would inevitably meet artists and writers, Alexander Pushkin among them, and she could not avoid comparing them to her husband. She discovered the obvious: that there were people to whom she could relate; people who shared her interests and respected her opinions. Predictably, as the gulf between herself and Peter widened, she began to dread the thought of returning to her old life with him, whenever his temporary assignment to St. Petersburg was terminated.

Early in her stay in the capital, she met a man who provided her with an opportunity for making changes in her life. O. I. Zenkowsky was editor of *The Readers' Library*, a conservative publication that sounds a good deal like a Russian version of the *Reader's Digest*. Only two years old, it was already enjoying success among provincial readers for its original fiction and condensations of contemporary novels. Zenkowsky asked her if she would like to attempt a condensation of *Godolphin*, a new work by the best-selling English novelist Edward Bulwer-Lytton. Pleased with the results, he then suggested that she write an original story for his magazine. His admiration of her creative talent no doubt fed Helena Andreyevna's determination to free herself from Peter von Hahn and, more important, showed her the avenue by which she might achieve that end. Encouraged by the prospect of earning a living by her pen, she immediately set to work on a novel which she planned to call *The Ideal*.

When springtime arrived in St. Petersburg, the ice on the Neva began to break up, furs disappeared from the streets, and the nobility began its annual exodus to country estates with their servants, horses and dogs. No one lingered, by choice, much past the end of May, when the heat, dust and stench of the canals made life unpleasant. About this time, Helena Andreyevna's father appeared in the city with her eight-year-old sister, Nadyezhda. Andrey Fadeyev, rising in the bureaucracy, had just been appointed Trustee for the nomadic Kalmuck tribes in the Province of Astrakhan. Before taking up his new position, he came to the capital on business and when he departed for Astrakhan in June, Helena Andreyevna and her daughters were with him. Peter von Hahn returned to the Ukraine alone. How definite a break she made with her husband is unclear; possibly she tried to disguise her departure as merely another of her jaunts to visit her family. More likely, since divorce was virtually impossible to obtain, she took matters into her own hands and divorced herself.

* * *

Astrakhan, in summer, baked under temperatures that rarely fell below a hundred degrees. At night people had to wrap themselves in gauze as protection against swarms of gnats. Situated on the shores of the Caspian Sea, at the mouth of the Volga, the city was a long-established trading center that had pretensions to being cosmopolitan. It boasted 146 streets, 3,883 houses, forty-six squares, a public garden, thirty-seven churches and fifteen mosques. People subscribed to French magazines from Brussels; they read de Lamartine, Balzac, Dumas, Sand and de Musset; they drank champagne and danced the quadrille. The music of Donizetti, in high vogue then, was performed at Astrakhan's theater—a tiny cramped hall whose orchestra contained a half-dozen trumpets and a single violin.[18]

While "society" consisted solely of Russians and Germans, one could walk down Astrakhan's unpaved streets and see more Oriental faces than Caucasian. There were Persians, Armenians, and Kalmucks; and some years earlier Indian merchants had established a colony but by the time H.P.B. arrived, they were mostly gone. Years later she would claim that her disgust for Christianity and her admiration for the eastern races had their origins during this period of her life. "I was myself brought up with the Buddhist Kalmucks," she wrote in a letter. "I was living in the steppes of Astrachan [Caspian Sea] till the age of ten."[19] This statement is an example of the surprisingly uneven nature of H.P.B.'s memory, as well as of her habit of rearranging her past to suit present convenience. Although she lived in Astrakhan for only about ten months during her fifth year, it obviously left a vivid impression. For the rest of her life she insisted on describing her broad face as resembling a Kalmuck peasant woman. And since she made the boast proudly, she must have remembered the Kalmucks with some fondness; although possibly she was also unconsciously acknowledging how little she took after her dainty mother.

Helena Andreyevna settled down in Astrakhan anxious to pursue her writing career. Self-confidence still shaky, she was acutely aware that a successful book could mean the difference between returning to Peter von Hahn and continuing life as an independent woman. Moreover, she may have felt uneasy about the subject of her novel, for it was a thinly disguised saga of her marital traumas and the hazards of being female. She could not, during these months of writing, have been the most attentive of mothers. Conscious of her children's presence, she was nonetheless living far away in a world of ideas and words, where two little girls under the age of five could only be distracting. In any case, her presence, or lack of it, was perhaps of less importance in those days of extended families.

Life within the Fadeyev household was lively and bustling, largely owing to the nature of Andrey's position. As second in command of the province and curator-general of the Kalmucks, he was able to reside in an aura of privilege and aristocratic sumptuousness. Aside from balls, soirées and dinners for foreign visitors, diplomatic relations had to be maintained with the Kalmuck chieftains. The wealthiest and most influential of the chieftains was a Prince Tumene, who owned an island a short distance up the Volga. The Prince, during the Napoleonic war of 1815, had raised a regiment at his own expense and led it to Paris, for which service the Czar had rewarded him with numerous decorations. Now he lived in a white palace that was half-Chinese, half-"Arabian Nights" in decor, but passed much of his day praying in a Buddhist temple he had erected nearby.

There was nothing about Tumene's little enclave that was either Russian or Kalmuck; rather it suggested the court of a rich Asiatic nabob. An imaginative child like H.P.B. could easily be transported into a land of fairies and mysterious legends. Lost in a perfect playland, Helena observed with wonder the water-encircled palace—its exterior fretted with balconies and fantastic ornaments, its interior filled with tapestries and crystals—giving the appearance that a touch of a wand had produced this preposterous mirage from the bosom of the Volga. To complete the mystical illusion, the author of these marvels was supposedly a half-savage tribesman, a worshiper of Buddha, and a believer in reincarnation. It is doubtful that anyone took the trouble to explain Buddhism to Helena, but it is certain that the shaven-headed lamas and the painted effigies of Buddha stirred her a great deal more than the rituals and icons of the Russian Orthodox Church.

Excellent horsemen who delighted in reckless displays of agility, the Kalmucks disported themselves by lassoing a wild stallion, springing upon the horse's back, and trying to keep from being thrown. Sometimes rider and horse rolled together on the grass; sometimes they skittered through the air with the speed of an arrow. These violent rodeo maneuvers, performed by women as well as men, impressed H.P.B. and it was most likely at this time that she first learned to ride. Clearly, her model of equestrianism was that of the Kalmuck daredevils. Ten years later, when conventional young ladies were sedately riding sidesaddle, she would still be straddling a horse like a tribesman, having near-fatal accidents, and causing her worried family to gnash their teeth. They could not deny, however, that she was a superb horsewoman.

While moving in the greater world as the curator-general's granddaughter, H.P.B. was simultaneously drawing closer to her mother's family and coming to think of it as her own. Her younger sister Vera held little interest for her; she was far more attracted to her uncle and aunts whose ages made it possible for her to regard them as older siblings. Her Aunt Katherine, seventeen and still unmarried, had no patience with Helena's peculiar makeup, and never would. But it was a different story with twelve-year-old Uncle Rostislav who was almost as wild as H.P.B. herself. Highly talented since childhood, he was particularly interested in science, history, and the lives of famous generals. By the age of ten he had memorized long poems, by Russian and foreign writers. When H.P.B. lived with the family, Rostislav was being tutored privately, in preparation for his entry two years hence into the College of Artillery at St. Petersburg.

While Rostislav could understand his niece, it was the Princess's youngest daughter, Nadyezhda, who adopted Helena as friend and sister— one for whom no sacrifice was too great. Lelinka, even at the age of five, was like no other person Nadyezhda had ever met. Her reckless defiance of adults astonished her well-brought-up aunt. But her good points did not go unrecognized: she was merry, quick minded, had an affectionate nature, and when no one opposed her she could be an extraordinarily delightful child. The family was making a mistake, Nadyezhda thought,

> to regard and treat her as they would any other child. Her restless and very nervous temperament, one that led her into the most unheard-of, ungirlish mischief; her unaccountable—especially in those days—attraction to, and at the same time fear of, the dead; her passionate love and curiosity for everything unknown and mysterious, weird and fantastical; and foremost of all, her craving for independence and freedom of action—a craving that nothing and nobody could control; all this, combined with an exuberance of imagination and a wonderful sensitiveness, ought to have warned them that she was an exceptional creature, to be dealt with and controlled by means as exceptional.[20]

But it did not warn them and the quality most frequently noticed by the family was her genius for being exceptionally naughty. Still, H.P.B. had found a loyal ally in Nadyezhda, and their friendship must have compensated for the lack of sympathy she met elsewhere in the family.

By the spring of 1837, Helena Andreyevna had completed *The Ideal*, under the pseudonym "Zenaida R-va," had seen it published in *The Readers' Library* and had been invited to become a regular contributor to the magazine. At once she began collecting material for a novella, *Memoirs of Gelesnobodsk*. However, her health was poor and in May her parents took her, with the two children, for treatment at Zheleznovodsk—a hot spring spa in the Caucasus. There her condition must have improved because her literary output was copious: she finished the novella; began a second major novel, *Umballa*, about Kalmuck life; and began planning yet another story which would be set in the Caucasus.

Instead of returning to Astrakhan, Helena Andreyevna and her daughters settled at Poltava, a Ukrainian town famous only as the site of a battle in the reign of Peter the Great. It was there that she met and befriended a Russianized German woman, Antonya Christianovna Kuhlwein. The unmarried daughter of a Lutheran minister, Antonya Kuhlwein was an educated woman who had made her way without a man. Presumably she saw the logic in Helena Andreyevna's feminist theories. As the two women became close friends, Antonya could not help but notice that Madame von Hahn was too frail both to work like a Trojan and to tutor her children. Now she offered to take charge of the education of Helena Petrovna and Vera.

The position of nursery governess required no skills other than elementary mastery of the three R's, a smattering of geography, the basics of painting, and the obligatory piano. Given Madame von Hahn's theories on the importance of education in attaining women's rights, Antonya Kuhlwein was probably better qualified than the average governess. She must also have possessed a stouter than average character. When, several months later, the von Hahns left Poltava, Antonya accompanied them.

By now it was clear that Helena Andreyevna had contracted tuberculosis. On the advice of her physicians, she sought the milder climate and mineral-water treatments available in Odessa, although the city hardly offered ideal weather for an invalid: in winter, temperatures dropped to twenty-five degrees below zero, but still the Russians regarded Odessa as a Miami Beach. For Helena Andreyevna, the additional compensation of Odessa was the many well-known intellectuals who made their homes there. Despite her illness, she continued to work at a breakneck pace, and to provide the semblance of a home for her girls.

Facing the fact that her two daughters were too much for one governess to handle, she hired a second—Augusta Sophia Jeffries, an Englishwoman from Yorkshire. Even though Fräulein Kuhlwein remained in her position for at least ten years, she left little impression on H.P.B., or at least none that she later thought worth mentioning. But Miss Jeffries, who H.P.B. dubbed the "Yorkshire spinster," would always be remembered as the one responsible for teaching her to speak English with a marked Yorkshire accent.[21] Given this information, H.P.B.'s claim that she could not write and could barely speak English until the age of forty is unpersuasive.[22] Impatient as Miss Jeffries must have been with her intractable pupil, she must nevertheless have been successful in imparting the rudiments of the language in which virtually all of H.P.B.'s vast literary output would be written.

How much seven-year-old Lelinka knew of her parent's estrangement is unclear, but it must have been enough to cause her pain. By this time she was already experiencing somnambulism and somniloquence, and, recalled her aunt, conducting in her sleep "long conversations with unseen personages, some of which were amusing, some edifying, some terrifying for those who gathered around the child's bed."[23] These nocturnal disturbances, in addition to nightmares, spontaneous trancelike states and psychosomatic illnesses, would continue to plague H.P.B. for years to come. Her unconscious mind had grasped the fact that the exciting figure who was her father had abandoned her, while her mother, too, "died when I was a baby."[24] In a sense, this was true, for Helena Andreyevna, always remote, had become even more inaccessible, abandoning H.P.B. this time to the Kuhlweins and Jeffries with their continual admonishments about self-control and decorum.

H.P.B.'s determination to kill her mother prematurely reveals something about her attitude toward her father. She could not have been shielded from the knowledge that Helena Andreyevna did not love Peter von Hahn; that indeed he had made her unhappy. She must have overheard a great deal in the small household at Odessa—all of it, naturally, from her mother's side. Despite what she heard, however, her sympathies continued to lie with her father. The high points of her youth were the times spent with him. Life with the artillery battery, so distasteful to her mother, took on for her the colors of grand adventure. The masculine atmosphere with its hard drinking, outspoken talk and coarse humor seemed admissible in a girl who had all the bad qualities of an energetic boy and the men accepted her for what she was.

One of the men, whom she later identified only as D———, went out of his way to play with her, showing her family portraits and allowing her to ransack his drawers and scatter his belongings. Once D——— showed her a miniature painting of his aunt, Tekla Lebendorff—an elderly woman in a cap and white curls, wearing a green shawl. When Helena declared that the woman was old and ugly, he teased her, saying that one day she would be just as old as his aunt. The episode, seemingly insignificant, stuck in her mind and would emerge several years later in a most curious form.

The eighteen-month interlude in Odessa abruptly terminated with the return of Peter von Hahn who made a sufficiently serious attempt at reconciliation to result in Helena Andreyevna's fourth pregnancy. No sooner was she aware of the pregnancy, however, than she fled to be with her family, now living on the Volga at Saratov, where Andrey Fadeyev had been promoted to Governor of the Province. While living in Odessa, Helena Andreyevna had completed a third major novel, *Djelaleddin*, as well as a novella, *Medallion*. At Saratov she wrote her most important work, *The World's Judgment*. It was quickly followed by a sequel, *God's Judgment*, which she did not consider worthy of publication. In June, 1840, she gave birth to a son whom she named Leonid, and promptly went to work on *Theophania Abiadjio*, the novel which was to bring her recognition as a major writer.

By this time the novels of "Zenaida R-va" were being hailed as extraordinary events in the Russian literary world. She was called Russia's George Sand and the feminine equal of the great poet Michael Lermontov. She was perused by Russia's most influential literary critic, Vissarion Belinsky, a radical who had no use for timid bourgeois thinkers, and who once wrote of himself: "For me, to think, feel, understand and suffer are one and the same thing."[25] Belinsky could not bear to see the cruelties human beings inflicted upon one another, whether in the name of government, religion or matrimony. The humiliation suffered by women at the hands of men lacerated him. It is little wonder that he adored the novels of Helena Andreyevna von Hahn:

There are writers who live apart from their books, and there are others whose lives are closely bound to their writings. While reading the former we delight in their God-given talents, but reading the latter, we delight in conception of the beautiful human individuality that interpenetrates the written word; we love it and aspire to meet it face to face; we long to know the details of their own lives. Zenaida R-va belongs to the latter class of writers.[26]

In Helena Andreyevna's work, the humiliations of being female in a male-dominated society constitute a persistent theme—a theme drawn from the circumstances of her own life. And if there is one particularly dominant motif, it is the plight of the woman artist who wants desperately to break out of what society decrees to be her proper place and to use her talents productively. Every outstanding woman, observes the heroine of *The Ideal*, "especially a writer, will be persecuted by the world. In its eyes she will only be a monstrous caprice of Nature, a feminine monster." Accordingly, the women Helena Andreyevna depicted lead double lives—searching for their psychic identity in their inner world, on the one hand; seeing their reflection in the mirror of public opinion, where their strivings are viewed as grotesque and unnatural, on the other. But as much as her characters wanted freedom, they also wanted love. Like Helena Andreyevna, they did not find it. "In vain will she look around for another soul, mutual in understanding," but the men her heroines find are Peter von Hahns.

It is not difficult to reconstruct von Hahn's feelings about his wife's literary success and especially her conspicuous airing of their marital woes. It was shocking to him for a woman to write about the intimate details of her life, even under a pseudonym, and the rift between them widened further. When Helena Andreyevna speaks of the "hundred-headed monster of public opinion" that declared her heroines "immoral"[27] and spatters them with mud, she may have been referring to public opinion in general, but she was certainly including the reactions of her husband. Nevertheless, in the spring of 1841, von Hahn made a final attempt to reunite his family, and Helena Andreyevna agreed to visit him in the Ukraine with the three children. Perhaps she allowed herself to be persuaded for the sake of her son; perhaps she was simply too frail and weary to care. "I am not only ill in my body," she wrote, "but in my soul also. I will not last long now."[28]

The winter of 1842 was unusually mild, so mild that in St. Petersburg the Neva twice thawed and refroze—something that had not happened within memory. At Odessa, alone again with her children and the two governesses after the failed reconciliation with Peter, Helena Andreyevna was attended full-time by Dr. Vassily Benzenger, but there was little he could do for her. When her parents arrived in May, they found her at work on a new book, which she was calling *The Flowergirl*, but she had no illusions about completing it. She died in the arms of her mother on June 24, just twenty-eight years old.

Shortly before their mother died, Vera recalled, she looked pityingly at ten-year-old Helena Petrovna.

* * *

Ah well, perhaps it is best that I am dying, so at least I shall be spared seeing what befalls Helene. Of one thing I am certain: her life will not be as that of other women, and she will have much to suffer.[29]

The remark, Vera saw in retrospect, had the ring of true prophecy.

III

Visions and Voices

During the last six of her first ten years, Helena Petrovna von Hahn had lived with her father for a total of less than twelve months. And if she entertained hopes that her mother's death might mean his return, they were quickly dashed. After the funeral, Peter returned at once to the Ukraine while Helena, Vera and Leonid accompanied their grandparents to Saratov. There is no indication that another arrangement was considered, and it was doubtless Helena Andreyevna's wish to have her children raised by her own family.

At Saratov, Andrey Fadeyev, like all provincial governors, played the role of a petty king with courtiers, orderly officers and ostentatious protocol modeled on that of the Czar's household at St. Petersburg. Socially, although the Fadeyevs were the most distinguished members of local society, Princess Helena preferred the seclusion of her study to the banal gossip of the drawing room, and her eldest granddaughter would have been miserable anywhere at that point.

For a girl about to enter puberty, the death of her mother must have come as a great emotional shock. However, the Princess, no matter how benevolent she may have been, was not about to tolerate her grandaughter's nonsense. She warned that fits of temper would not be permitted; nor would Helena be allowed to do as she pleased. Intimidated by her dignified grandmother, H.P.B. tried hard to behave, but her self-restraint did not last long. One day she slapped a serf nurse who had been with the family all her life and news of the incident quickly reached the Princess.[30]

Physical violence toward serfs was so common a practice that even the young Tolstoy had struck a serf in anger, but the Princess did not subscribe to such behavior. She ordered the mansion's bells to be rung and the household servants to assemble in the main hall. There she announced that Lelinka, by unjustly striking a serf, had violated the codes of good manners and common decency, and she commanded her to beg the nurse's pardon and kiss her hand to show sincerity. Red-faced with shame, H.P.B. obstinately refused.

The Princess, countering with deliberate severity, told her that if she did not obey instantly, she would be sent away in disgrace. No noble lady would refuse to apologize for wronging a servant, especially one who had given her masters a lifetime of faithful service. Helena Petrovna's defiance crumbled at once, and she burst into tears and knelt before the nurse. However extreme the Princess's method—certainly her threat must have been an empty one—it served its purpose. H.P.B. herself would remember it as a valuable lesson, for it taught her the principle of doing justice to those incapable of defending themselves. Her sympathies would always be with the underdog.

H.P.B.'s existence between 1842, when she arrived at Saratov, and 1849, when she married Nikifor Blavatsky, was defined by commonplace routines, which she rebelled against, and a sense of security, which she refused to acknowledge. No one could compensate for the neglect of her father, whom she adored. She was not alone in her feeling of abandonment: Leonid, as it later turned out, would also be scarred by the suspicion that his father had not loved him. Only Vera seems to have been relatively indifferent to Peter's absence.

Still, life for the von Hahn children was undeniably comfortable and far from uninteresting. The first floor of the governor's mansion was a series of vast reception halls where the official business of the province—the Czar's business—was conducted. A section of the ground floor had been requisitioned by the Princess, who turned it into a museum to house her historical antiquities and zoological collection. From behind the glass panes of gigantic cupboards, peered lifelike stuffed animals and birds, including an alligator, a silvery seal, and a flamingo with scarlet-lined wings. Every day at dusk the von Hahn children and their Aunt Nadyezhda passed through the museum to say their ceremonial good nights to the Princess, who could always be found in an adjoining study. Afterward the head nurse would shepherd her charges, followed by serfs with trays of food and coals, up flight after flight of stairs to the top-floor nursery. From the windows of their eyrie they could glimpse snow-covered rooftops. Around the fire, rounds of bread were toasted while the children listened to a serf nurse—whose "memory retained every idea connected with superstition"—regale them endlessly with fairy-tale people: the wicked magician Gray Wolf, Princess Meletressa, Ivan Zarewitch. Vera, a practical child, thought it ridiculous that her sister

thoroughly took to heart all the troubles of the heroes, and maintained that all their most wonderful adventures were quite natural. People *could* change into animals and take any form they liked, *if they only knew how;* men *could* fly, if they only wished so *firmly.*[31]

* * *

And when the children laughed at her gullibility, H.P.B. heatedly voiced her assurance that "such wise men had existed in all ages, and existed even in our own days, making themselves known, of course, only to those who were worthy of knowing and seeing them, and who believed in them."

By now, the two-governess staff had expanded. Antonya Kuhlwein was still on the scene; Miss Jeffries had been replaced by a mousy young Englishwoman to whom none of the children paid any attention; and a Swiss woman joined the teaching staff. All the governesses, it was said, regarded themselves as martyrs. Helena Petrovna found the lessons tedious and had to be kept under surveillance lest she slip out of the house to play with uncouth street boys. "All of our teachers," Vera said, "had exhausted their patience with Helene, who would never conform to fixed hours for lessons but who, notwithstanding, astonished them by the brilliance of her abilities,"[32] especially the ease with which she mastered foreign languages and played the piano.

In summer, everything changed. With the first hint of mild weather, the whole household would pile into wagons for the annual emigration to the governor's country villa outside Saratov. This exodus included not only the Fadeyev family with upwards of a hundred serfs, but also the family of Princess Helena's daughter Katherine, who had recently married an obscure agronomist named Yuli Witte. The Wittes were Dutch Lutherans from the Baltic Provinces but Princess Helena insisted that Yuli convert to Russian Orthodoxy as a condition for the marriage—a small price to pay for marrying the daughter of a Dolgorukov princess. Drawn into the Fadeyev family circle, Witte had no objection to making his home with his in-laws, especially now that Katherine was pregnant.

Helena's Uncle Rostislav, too, was back home. His hot temper had led to the termination of his studies at the Artillery College, from which he was asked to leave after a year. College was followed by a short, unhappy career in the army and even though he had finally passed the examination to become an officer, he returned to Saratov where he promptly resigned his commission and devoted his time to studying science. Helena Petrovna had great respect for Rostislav, despite his unrelieved succession of failures, and she was apparently more receptive to his advice than to anyone else's.

In the country, everyone rode cossack horses, explored an abandoned park full of crumbling kiosks and pagodas, and delighted in nocturnal expeditions into the forest to catch night butterflies for the Princess's entomological collection. Helena's greatest joy was stealing off to visit Baranig Bouyrak, an old man frequently covered from head to foot with bees and said to be a sorcerer. The villa itself could fire any child's imagination. Resembling a medieval castle more than an eighteenth-century house, it was a rambling building full of subterranean galleries, turrets, abandoned passages and weird nooks and crannies that offered unparalleled hiding places. The former residence of the Pantchoolidzef family, governors of Saratov for several generations, it apparently came gratis with the position of governor. Along with the mansion also came a fourth tutor—Madame Henriette Peigneur, who had been governess for the Pantchoolidzef family for twenty-five years. In her youth, during the French revolution, she had been chosen a "Goddess of Liberty" and ridden in processions through the streets of Paris. Now, a bent old woman, she was given to reminiscing about her former glory as a beauty queen and did not demand very much work from her pupils. She was also a veritable anthology of hair-raising legends about the villa. Vera wrote:

> Our heads were full of stories about the ghosts of martyred serfs seen promenading in chains during nocturnal hours; of the phantom of a young girl, tortured to death for refusing her love to an old master, which was seen floating in and out of the little iron-bound door of the subterranean passage at twilight; and other stories that left us children and girls in an agony of fear whenever we had to cross a dark room or passage.[33]

The exception, of course, was Lelinka who had no fear, but boundless curiosity to know more. The Princess finally gave permission to the children to explore the underground labyrinths, accompanied by no less than a half-dozen men servants carrying torches and lanterns. Finding more broken wine bottles than human bones, however, they quickly lost their fascination with the dungeons and went back to their usual games. To Helena, however, the subterranean corridors offered the perfect refuge from the governesses. In a corner, under a barred window, she built a kind of tower from old broken chairs and tables. She would stay in this snug spot for hours at a time reading books, including one of popular legends called *Solomon's Wisdom*. Eventually her hiding place was discovered, and then Andrey Fadeyev periodically would have to send a deputation of servants, headed by a police officer, to drag H.P.B. upstairs.

Undaunted and unrepentant, Helena Petrovna insisted that she was not afraid in the cellar and, in any case, had not been alone. Her companions were beings she called "playmates," one of whom was a hunchbacked little boy.[34] It was true that whenever the escort found her, she was usually deep in conversation with someone, but the someone was invisible. The family was loath to consider the possibility that anything more than imagination might have been operating. Actually, it is as common now as then for lonely youngsters to conjure up imaginary playmates. Reflecting a desire for companionship, or perhaps for someone to whom a child can transfer anger or blame, the invisible playmate is not necessarily evidence of emotional instability. On the contrary, it may be an indication of problem-solving, and in an ordinary child, one might perceive it as a struggle toward mental health.

But Helena Petrovna was not ordinary, and her family knew it. Vera, in *Juvenile Reflections Compiled for My Children*—a book based on her childhood diary—admits that her sister "was the strangest girl one has ever seen,"[35] though later, in less guarded moments, she disparagingly referred to her as "crazy Helena."[36] It is more than probable that Helena was called "crazy" by the other children, and by the adults, and it was not without ample justification.

However fearless she might have been, Helena was now experiencing terrifying hallucinations in which she was pursued by the "terrible glaring eyes" of inanimate objects.

> She would shut her eyes tight during such visions, and run away to hide from the ghostly glances thrown on her by pieces of furniture or articles of dress, screaming desperately, and frightening the whole household. At other times she would be seized with fits of laughter, explaining them as the amusing pranks of her invisible companions.[37]

That winter, back in Saratov, she would be discovered under the roof, amid nests of pigeons. When asked what she was doing, she explained that she was "putting them to sleep," according to the rules set forth in *Solomon's Wisdom*. At other times she would escort Vera, Leonid and Nadyezhda into the Princess's museum at twilight and, straddling the seal, "narrated to us the most inconceivable tales about herself, the most unheard-of adventures of which she was the heroine," Vera recalled. Each of the stuffed animals, Helena claimed, had taken her into its confidence and divulged the history of its life in previous incarnations. Where, Vera wondered later, could she have learned about "the superstitious mysteries of metempsychosis" in a family so Christian as theirs? Still, as a child, Vera believed every word that her sister uttered.

> Never can I forget the life and adventures of a tall white flamingo . . . He had been ages ago, she told us, no bird, but a real man. He had committed fearful crimes and a murder, for which a great genius had changed him into a flamingo, a brainless bird, sprinkling his two wings with the blood of his victims, and thus condemning him to wander for ever in deserts and marshes.

After that, when Vera came into the museum, she closed her eyes and ran past quickly to avoid seeing the blood-covered murderer.

H.P.B.'s marvelous evocative powers carried away her audiences to the point where, even if vaguely, they saw what she saw. As a child, she frightened her sister "very nearly into fits." Vera remembered that near the summer estate there was a sandy tract of land which appeared to have at one time been the bottom of a lake, since its soil yielded petrified relics of fishes and shells. Helena would stretch out on the ground, her elbows buried in the sand, and conjure underwater battles of long-dead sea monsters. Then she would abruptly switch her narrative from past to present tense. Suddenly the earth was opening. Around them the air was condensing into waves. Water surrounded them. They were standing on the bottom of the sea, amid coral reefs and caves with stalactites. She could feel the velvety water caressing her body. Then suddenly the sea was engulfing them; they were drowning. Helena could see it all.[38]

During the drama, her audience would be sure they were drowning. Afterward, they would feel abused and regard Helena Petrovna as quite mad. A notable exception to this critical view was held by her Aunt Nadyezhda who argued that H.P.B. was superior to everyone else in the family, and simply not appreciated. She spoke of the "envy and animosity of all those who, in their trivial inferiority, felt wounded by the splendor of the faculties and talents of this really marvellous"[39] niece of hers. There is apparently much truth in Nadyezhda's words, for Helena unquestionably had a superior intelligence. Her aversion to formal instruction notwithstanding, she had the facility of grasping and assimilating the most difficult subjects with speed and ease, subjects that took other people years of study to master. This is confirmed by independent testimony from other members of the family who were decidedly hostile to H.P.B., but who recall being "impressed by the extraordinary facility with which she acquired skill and knowledge of the most varied description. Her abilities in this respect verged on the uncanny."[40]

Forty years later people on several continents would be arguing whether Helena Petrovna Blavatsky was a genius, a consummate fraud, or simply a lunatic. By that time, an excellent case could have been made for any of the three. To a great extent, the truth was confused by H.P.B. herself. Far from trying to pass herself off as a genius or a scholar, she went out of her way to insist that she had only normal intelligence and, furthermore, a relatively poor education. If Nadyezhda's statements can be trusted—and in this instance it appears that they can be—her niece received the typical superficial education given to a girl of good family: she studied Russian, French and English. Afterwards, during her travels, she would pick up a smattering of Italian. As far as serious academic study was concerned, "there was no shadow of it, not even the least promise thereof." Then where did Helena get her knowledge of hieroglyphics, of Hebrew, Sanskrit and Greek? "She never saw them even in a dream," would declare Nadyezhda in 1881. "I can swear to it."[41]

Forty years hence, when Nadyezhda would make that declaration, H.P.B. was flatly refusing to take any credit whatsoever for the complex philosophies coming from her pen. Rather, she insisted that she was but the passive instrument of others wiser and greater than herself. But in the 1840s, her brilliance was so obvious that the Fadeyevs did not view her abnormal behavior with excessive alarm. Helena was unquestionably strange, but, given her extraordinary intelligence, they must have hoped that she would outgrow her eccentricities, as children outgrow stammering or bed-wetting.

Maturity often does bring an end to such difficulties, but sometimes the problems simply take a different form. For several years, Helena had been receiving nightly visitations from an elderly woman who chose to make known her presence through H.P.B.'s handwriting. She called herself Tekla Lebendorff and gave a detailed account of her life, including her birthplace (Revel, in the Baltic Provinces), her marriage, the history of her daughter Z——— and her thrilling romance, and her son F——— who had committed suicide, and who in fact sometimes appeared in person to lament his sufferings. Tekla went on to describe her death and to give the name and address of the Lutheran pastor who had administered the last sacrament. In case that was not proof enough, she also reproduced a petition that she had presented to the Czar, writing it out verbatim and even including a remark Nicholas had written in the margin.

Tekla Lebendorff, it will be remembered, was the aunt of D———, an officer in Peter von Hahn's regiment who had befriended H.P.B. This was the woman whose portrait Helena had thought so ugly, but she had forgotten all that by then. All she knew was that when she sat down with paper and pen, she could produce pages of manuscript in Tekla's "clear, old-fashioned, peculiar handwriting and grammar, in German (a language I had never learnt to write and could not even speak well) and in Russian." The fact that some of the writing was in German and all of it clearly not in Helena's own hand caught the Fadeyevs' attention and led them to predictable conclusions.

"From the first," Helena explained, "all around me were impressed with the belief that the spirit possessing me must be that of a dead person,"[42] and H.P.B. agreed. The Fadeyevs knew nothing about mediumship or automatic writing, nor did they believe in séances and disembodied spirits as did some trendy intellectuals of that era. In their opinion, the writing was a by-product of possession and they sent for the family priest who attended the sessions, sprinkling holy water from an aspergillum. The priest unhesitatingly declared the messages to be devil's work, but since Tekla insisted that she saw God, the Virgin Mary and a host of angels, he could not object strongly enough to halt the proceedings.

Despite their horror and disapproval, it seems likely that the Fadeyevs could not help being intrigued by the writing. One imagines, too, that they regarded the sessions as a diverting parlor game for the long winter evenings. Inadvertently, of course, they were encouraging Helena to produce further communiqués from Tekla Lebendorff by providing her with the attention she craved. Even if the attention was negative, it was welcomed by Helena.

In addition to seeing entities that no one else saw, she also heard the voices of pebbles, trees, and pieces of decaying timber. To Helena, all of nature seemed animated with a life of its own—visible and audible to herself alone. Without discounting the possibility that some sensitive individuals might very well communicate with trees, it is undeniable that Helena sometimes had a distorted concept of her environment. That she confused daydreams with reality is at once an obvious and insufficient explanation. More exactly, she seemed to find life in its natural state flat and tepid, and felt a compulsion to exaggerate and embroider her surroundings. She also wanted to dramatize Helena Petrovna.

Yet some small part of H.P.B. always managed to retain a grip on the real world, even if it came and went in flashes. At the age of twelve, she must have felt herself in a struggle to maintain her sanity. Although the writings of her relatives give the impression that she fully accepted her bizarre experiences, this is highly unlikely. She was, it must be emphasized, an intelligent, hypersensitive girl who undoubtedly tried to understand herself. Given her orthodox religious environment, she must have been secretly burdened with despair, a suspicion that she was headed for madness, and a sense of having sinned grievously.

Like the Irish-born medium Eileen Garrett who also had invisible playmates as a child and was called "liar" and "crazy," H.P.B. must have been deeply hurt by the reactions of her family. Bewildered by accusations of dishonesty, resentful because her inner experiences were not considered valid, she withdrew to the catacombs or the attic where she found peace in being alone. There she could speak freely with children who accepted and loved her for what she was, and for what she was not. If she was forced to invent them, it did not much matter.

At this point, it might be instructive to pause and further examine the experiences of Eileen Garrett,[43] since her childhood bears a number of striking similarities to H.P.B.'s. Both of Garrett's parents committed suicide within a few weeks of her birth, although she was not aware of this until some years later. She was raised by an aunt and uncle. At the age of four, she first saw "the children," two invisible girls and a boy, and soon afterward discovered that she could avoid suffering by retreating into episodes of amnesia. This technique of escape, she stated, seemed to come naturally to her from earliest childhood and "may well have prepared the way for the later development" of her clairvoyance. Later, as an adult, Garrett spent many years bouncing from one psychiatrist to another in an attempt to learn more about the nature of her psychic experiences. She was always quite open in admitting that she herself did not know whether they were rooted in mental illness or in genuine supernormal powers. Garrett, of course, was a child of the twentieth century, while H.P.B. was born before psychoanalysis was practiced.

Even though Eileen Garrett finally came to believe that "the entities are formed from spiritual and emotional needs of the person involved," the psychiatric establishment did not offer her much enlightenment, doubtless because the answers to her questions cannot be answered with any degree of surety. Traditionally, psychologists have viewed psi capabilities as evidence of neurasthenia, pathological daydreaming, multiple or disintegrated personality, or *grand hysterie*. Sigmund Freud refused to take the subject seriously, while Carl Jung, the psychologist most intrigued by the supernormal, started out attributing psi facilities to pathology, but seems to have been in the process of changing his mind shortly before his death.

Tormented by doubts as H.P.B. must have been, she did not discuss them, except perhaps with Nadyezhda. Early on, she became convinced that confiding in people was useless and, given her stubborn nature, she must have decided to brazen it out by confidently insisting that her visions and voices were without a doubt real. Either way, the Fadeyevs never let her forget they were the doings of "the evil one."

Curiously, a kind of vicious-circle effect now began to operate. In dodging the pain of her mother's death and her father's absence, she was able to dream herself into a state of altered consciousness where another kind of reality held sway. At the same time, her belief in an invisible world of supernatural beings predated the traumatic parental experiences. By the age of thirteen, her defenses seemed to be reinforcing each other and pulling her even further from facing the problem. Now, instead of *roussalkas* and invisible children, she saw an adult male—handsome, virile, wise, protective and . . . invisible. A psychiatrist might have contended that she had devised a father figure, but Helena had a completely different interpretation of the events that began to take place.

The first of these incidents happened before the family portraits in the reception hall of the governor's mansion. One particular painting, hung far up near the ceiling and covered by a curtain, intrigued Helena, but when she asked to see it, she was refused. Waiting until the room was empty, she dragged a table over to the wall, set a smaller table on it, then placed a chair atop both. Mounting this unstable platform, she leaned one hand against the dusty wall and jerked aside the curtain with the other. The movement threw her off balance and as she began to fall, she felt herself losing consciousness.

When she awakened she found herself lying on the floor, unhurt. The tables and chair were back in their usual places, and the curtain again covered the portrait. Had she not left a hand print on the dusty wall, she might have thought she had dreamed the whole incident. To Helena, this was evidence of the intervention of supernatural agencies, capable of coming to her aid during times of crisis.

A similar kind of rescue occurred during the summer that she turned fourteen. A horse that she was riding in her usual reckless style suddenly bolted, and she fell with her foot entangled in the stirrup. Under normal circumstances, she might easily have been killed. But there was what she described as "a strange sustaining power"[44] around her that seemed to hold her up in defiance of gravity, and the horse was mysteriously brought under control.

Both of these episodes happened at times when Helena Petrovna was engaged in some activity for which she could have expected a scolding. Obviously, such fine distinctions between good and bad behavior were not important to her invisible guardian.

Even after living with her grandparents for three years she never gave up on Peter von Hahn. In 1886, looking back on that summer of 1845, when she became fourteen, she wrote that "father brought me to London to take a few lessons of music."

* * *

Took a few later also —from old Moscheles. Lived with [von Hahn] somewhere near Pimlico . . . Went to Bath with him, remained a whole week, heard nothing but bell-ringing in the churches all day. Wanted to go on horseback astride in my Cossack way; he would not let me and I made a row I remember and got sick with a fit of hysterics. He blessed his stars when we went home; travelled two or three months through France, Germany and Russia. In Russia our own carriage and horses making twenty-five miles a day.[45]

There was, however, another version of the reunion with her father.[46]

That summer, according to Vera's diary, von Hahn visited his children for the first time since his wife's death. They were shocked to find they had difficulty recognizing him because he had aged so considerably. According to Helena's account of the events, Peter immediately whisked her away, leaving Vera and Leonid behind, even though in reality a journey from Saratov to London would have meant a major sacrifice of von Hahn's time and money. Helena boasted that he thought enough of her musical ability to arrange for lessons with Ignaz Moscheles, the renowned conductor, composer and teacher of Mendelssohn. Actually, her studying with Moscheles that summer would not have been impossible, since he had in fact returned from Germany in March, 1845, to conduct the London Philharmonic.

Despite that, Helena's lessons fall into the same fantasy category as her later boast to Henry Olcott that, while in London, she played a charity concert with Clara Schumann and Arabella Goddard, performing a Schumann piece for three pianos.[47] The only note of realism in her London story is that von Hahn would not tolerate her maverick behavior and "blessed his stars" when he could return her to the Fadeyevs.

The most significant experience of Peter von Hahn's visit that summer was observing Helena's mediumship and making the acquaintance of Tekla Lebendorff. His reaction was far more negative than the Fadeyevs' but for different reasons. Unlike them, he was not a pious man who objected on religious grounds; rather, he considered the idea of spirits an affront to his reason.[48] What he could not shrug off was the fact that Helena was not only writing in German, but also in a handwriting quite unlike her own. Subsequent to the events, he asked one of his brothers, a government official, to compile a dossier on Tekla Lebendorff. In the course of a business trip to Revel, the brother was able to establish that there certainly had been a Madame Lebendorff who, owing to her son's dissolute behavior, had left the city and gone to live with relatives in Norway, where she died. The statistics Helena's uncle uncovered about the woman—her age, number of children and so forth— corroborated all of his niece's statements.

When my uncle returned to St. Petersburg he desired to ascertain, as the last and crucial test, whether a petition, such as I had written, had ever been sent to the Emperor. Owing to his friendship with influential people in the Ministère de l'Intérieur, he obtained access to the Archives; and there, as he had the correct date of the petition, and even the number under which it had been filed, he soon found it and comparing it with my version sent up to him by my aunt, he found the two to be *facsimiles,* even to a remark in pencil written by the late Emperor on the margin, which I had reproduced as exactly as any engraver or photographer could have done.[49]

However, crucial as this test may have seemed to Helena, the skeptical Peter von Hahn was still not completely satisfied.

For all three von Hahn children, seeing their father again was anticlimactic. He looked older than his forty-seven years and no longer cut such a dashing figure. His abortive marriage had left him weary and unsettled, and, unknown to the children, he was considering remarriage. After an uneasy month among the strangers who were his children, he departed.

In January of 1846, the viceroy of the Caucasus, Prince Mihail Vorontzov, appointed Helena's grandfather Director of State Lands in Trans-Caucasia. As Imperial Russia continued to expand its frontiers, the Caucasus became the scene of a long, drawn-out war of conquest. After fifteen years of campaigning, the mountains still held unsubdued Daghestan guerrillas and Circassian tribesmen. Proper administration of newly acquired lands exceeded the capabilities of the Russian government and, while Fadeyev's promotion was prestigious and reflected his rising importance in the civil service, the job would bring its share of frustrations. Since his new assignment did not take effect immediately, the family remained in Saratov for the winter and spent the summer, as usual, at the country villa.

In mid-August, Andrey, Princess Helena, and Nadyezhda moved to Tiflis, in Georgia, but the von Hahn children did not accompany them. Instead they were left with their aunt and uncle Katherine and Yuli Witte and the couple's two young sons, Andrey and Alexander. The Wittes had taken a summer house on the other side of the Volga, near the village of Pokrrovskoye, and did not return to Saratov until December.

Leaving Helena behind was not the wisest step the Princess could have taken, since Katherine, though well meaning, had absolutely no sympathy with her niece and no interest in psychic phenomena. It quickly became evident that she would have to contend with sleepwalking, Tekla Lebendorff, and other weird happenings which took place with alarming regularity.

One of the governesses then with the family had a habit of keeping fruit in her bureau until it rotted, a quirk that disgusted Katherine. The woman became seriously ill and once she was confined to bed, the first thing Katherine did was to order the bureau cleaned out and the fruit thrown away. She did not anticipate that the sick woman, on the point of death, might ask for one of her "nice ripe apples." In a quandary, Katherine went to the servants' quarters to send someone out for a rotten apple. While there, she received news that the woman had just died. Katherine rushed upstairs, trailed by Helena Petrovna and the servants, and as they passed the open door of the governess's room, they saw her eating an apple. That is, at least, what Helena claimed. Presumably she did see such a sight and described it so vividly that Katherine "shrieked with horror." Recounting this incident in 1884, H.P.B. said that the vision "disappeared at once, and we rushed into the bedroom. There she lay on the bed, and the nurse was with her, having never left her one minute for the last hour. It was her last thought made objective."

Then she added, as if fearing that nobody would believe her: "A perfectly true story, one witnessed by myself."[50]

Thanks to Andrey Fadeyev's connections, Yuli Witte was able to get a bureaucratic job in Tiflis as director of the Department of State Property. At the beginning of May, 1847, as soon as the snow had melted, the Wittes took the von Hahn children and Antonya Kuhlwein to join the Fadeyevs. With no railroads or paved roads, the journey to Tiflis was a rather complicated venture. Leaving Saratov, they cruised down the Volga on the SS *St. Nicholas,* stopping for two days at Astrakhan. There they took passage aboard the SS *Teheran,* and followed the coastline of the Caspian Sea as far as Baku, which they reached on May 21. The next day they started out in carriages for Shemaha, where the Fadeyevs and Nadyezhda had come to meet them, and where they stayed for about a month. Then, at a leisurely pace they headed northwest to Tiflis, crossing the Shemaha pass and the Kura River, which they forded at Minguichaur, stopping for a day at Elizabethpol'.

The magical vistas of the Caucasus—its mountain peaks snowcapped year-round while lemon trees bloomed in the subtropical river valleys—inspired great literature from Pushkin, Tolstoy and Lermontov. It is puzzling that Helena, who had a passion for travel, recorded nothing about this first long trip of her life. If it were not for Vera's diary, we would have known nothing of their itinerary.

At the end of June, eight weeks after leaving Saratov, the traveling party reached Tiflis, a city set in the mountain valley of the Kura River. Having come under Russian control only forty-five years earlier, Tiflis had an unusual ambience. The Russian sector, where the Fadeyevs lived, looked perfectly European: stately avenues, rows of modern houses, cafés, milliners, even a bookseller. A few blocks away, however, the scene gave way to a rich spectacle of Asiatic bazaars, caravansaries and streets full of open shops where smithies and shoemakers carried on their crafts in view of the passersby. Although one saw plenty of Russian military uniforms and French frock coats, the town overflowed with dark-skinned Persians in loose flowing dresses, fierce-eyed Kurds, horse-peddling Circassians, and beautiful Georgian women in long veils and high-heeled slippers.[51] Tiflis, like Astrakhan, contained diverse nationalities and Asiatic Russia infected Helena Petrovna with an incurable passion for exotic peoples. European Russia, with its fussy decorum and manners imitative of the French, held so little charm for her that she would later abandon it without noticeable qualms.

The family had not been at their new home a month before they embarked on one of those summer processions that aristocratic Russians were so fond of. First they went to Borzhom, a resort on the estate of Grand Duke Mihail Nikolayevich, and then to the hot baths of Abbas-Tuman, stopping to take the curative waters. Life during the summer social season was easy and informal, and the prominence of the Fadeyevs assured their welcome at picnics, horseback-riding excursions for the children, suppers and balls for the adults. At the end of August, they returned to Tiflis and settled down at the Sumbatov mansion.

IV

The Plumeless Raven

During that first winter at Tiflis, Helena led a life which, even if not to her liking, could not be described as uneventful. Around this time she received a shock that rocked her self-confidence and forced her to rethink her belief in the supernatural. The officer who had first introduced Helena to Tekla Lebendorff at her father's military camp when she was five, came to Tiflis and called on the Fadeyevs. In the intervening years, Helena had lost all memory of the connection between D—— and his Aunt Tekla, and she remembered him only as a warm man who had shown her kindness. When D—— invited the von Hahn children to visit him at his military quarters, they accepted enthusiastically and were sent off by the Princess in the company of a governess. Entering his room, the first thing that Helena noticed was the miniature of Tekla sitting on a table. Overcome by the sight, she screamed, "It is, it is the spirit. It is Mrs. Tekla Lebendorff."

D—— was, to say the least, astonished. "Of course it's my old aunt," he replied, expressing surprise that she remembered the portrait, not to mention his aunt's name. When Helena began to explain that his dead aunt and sometimes her son who had committed suicide were in the habit of visiting her at night, she was interrupted by an outburst of laughter. His aunt was not dead, D—— assured her; she was living in Norway and, in fact, he had just received a letter from her. As for the unfortunate son, it was true that he had once attempted suicide, but he had recovered and now was employed in a Berlin bank.

When these startling revelations were conveyed to the Fadeyevs, H.P.B. recalled, "Never were people more taken back than were my venerable aunts." For if it was not Tekla who had dictated petitions to the Czar and rhapsodized over angels and archangels, who was it? Exasperated by the whole business, her family concluded that it was the Devil. And it was insinuated that Lelinka had somehow tricked them.

Innocent of deception, Helena also apparently rejected the devil theory. But she was helpless to come up with anything remotely approaching a satisfactory explanation. It would be many years before she would be able to account for the writing, describing it as "the work of my mind," and calling the facts relayed by Tekla "the objective reproduction of what my own mind read and saw in the astral light."[52] At the time, however, her sense of chagrin and confusion must have been acute. Only one thing was certain: the writing career of Tekla Lebendorff was finished.

If Helena's belief in spirits was somewhat battered by that experience, it was not completely demolished and she continued to indulge her passion for the mystical in other ways. For all her distaste of lessons, no scholar was more ardent a reader. According to Vera, "she could not be prevailed to give up her books, which she would devour night and day as long as the impulse lasted. The enormous library of her grandparents seemed then hardly large enough to satisfy her cravings."[53] Judging by the breadth of references in H.P.B.'s adult writings, the Fadeyev library must have been filled with works on science, history and philosophy. But what Vera does not mention is that it also included the occult collection that belonged to their great-grandfather Prince Paul Dolgorukov.

On Dolgorukov's death in 1837, the library had been inherited by his daughter, Princess Helena, and while it is safe to assume that she had no interest in this type of literature, her granddaughter had a passion for it. Undoubtedly it was in the Prince's collection that Helena found *Solomon's Wisdom,* the book that inspired her hypnotic experiments with pigeons. Altogether the library contained hundreds of books on alchemy, magic, and occult sciences, and H.P.B. conceded that she "had read them with the keenest interest before the age of fifteen. All the devilries of the Middle Ages had found refuge in my head and soon neither Paracelsus, Kunrath, nor C. Agrippa would have had anything to teach me."[54]

H.P.B.'s admission that she was strongly influenced by the medieval alchemists, whose works she regarded as sources of revelation equal to the Bible, sheds an interesting light on the development of her philosophy. Significantly, she made that statement in a letter written in 1882 to a friend of her youth, Prince Alexander Dondoukoff-Korsakoff, which was not made public until 1951. She would not have willingly publicized this bit of information, for she was generally reluctant to admit where she had learned things, preferring to give the impression that they came to her by mysterious means. The fact is, she seems to have acquired information from the same places as most of us—books.

At fifteen and sixteen years old Helena's escape into the absorbing world of alchemy must have proved a comfort, for in these volumes, she at last encountered individuals with mental powers similar to her own. Nevertheless, she still had to spend most of her waking hours with the Fadeyevs who by this time had made it abundantly clear that they expected more from her than she seemed willing to concede. They pressured her to behave like a well-bred young lady and to participate in the social life appropriate for a girl of her age and station. Throughout the winter season, young ladies displayed themselves at weekly assemblies dubbed "brides' fairs," where predatory mothers paraded arm in arm with their daughters, hoping to catch the eye of an eligible young gentleman. In addition, there was an endless succession of balls, private parties and midnight suppers, to most of which Helena Petrovna received invitations.

Princess Helena must have had premonitions about launching into society a granddaughter who not only shunned parties, but who also displayed a marked aversion for ribbons, and silks, and all other female accoutrements. It would be another six years before Paris introduced horsehair crinolines, but styles were already moving toward billowing skirts, tight-laced wasp waists, and extremely low décolletage. This particular fashion, so feminine and utterly impractical for normal activity, was clearly not created with girls like Helena Petrovna in mind. In a photograph dating from this period, we see her looking like a baby lamb in a rumpled bathrobe. She is wearing an obviously expensive, well-made gown, but with her wooly hair, her thick waist and a strand of pearls slung over her left breast in what is perhaps a calculated gesture of defiance, she appears the very model of what a fashionable Russian girl was not supposed to look like. She is not smiling.

Throughout her life, H.P.B. was to regard social duties lightly and often scornfully, avoiding formal functions when she could, and, when she could not, behaving so outrageously that her hosts wished she would go home. The contrived rituals of the drawing room and the ballroom struck her as the worst sort of hypocrisy, "ergo, I ran amuck against society and the established proprieties." At sixteen, however, she was proving most trying to her grandmother and her Aunt Katherine, who were facing the fact that Peter von Hahn could not be counted on to shape Lelinka's future and that they, therefore, must assume this responsibility themselves. Helena Petrovna did not appreciate their efforts: "I hate dress, finery, and civilized society. I despise a ballroom, and how much I despise it will be proved . . . by the following:

When hardly sixteen I was forced one day to go to a dancing party, a great ball at the Viceroy's. My protests were not listened to by my parents [*sic*], who told me they would have me dressed up — or rather, according to fashion, undressed—for the ball by servants by force, if I did not go willingly. I then deliberately plunged my foot and leg into a kettle of boiling water, and held it there till it nearly boiled raw. Of course I scalded it horribly, and remained at home for six months.[55]

* * *

Of course this assault upon her body effectively put an end to dancing that winter, and the months she spent recuperating from the burns were undoubtedly devoted to her alchemy books. Still, while entry into the world of young men and marriage might be postponed by boiling an appendage, it could not be permanently canceled. And the prospect was frightening to Helena. Many years later, she said:

> "There is nothing of the woman in me. When I was young, if a young man had dared to speak to me of love, I would have shot him like a dog who bit me."[56]

Yet there were exceptions. The following summer, in 1848, a young man named Constantine Petrovitch Kauffmann "used to make vain declarations of love to me on a heap of potatoes and carrots at Abaz-Touman," the vacation resort near Tiflis. Since she referred to him, in 1881, as "my poor innocent red-nosed friend,"[57] there seems to have been no question of shooting him. Perhaps she was feeling sorry for her tepid cavalier, or perhaps she was merely boasting: Constantine had become General Petrovitch Kauffmann, whose daring exploits in the conquest of Turkestan made him a national hero.

H.P.B. cannot be taken at her word on the subject of men. In her adult letters, she liked to present herself as non-sexual—there are frequent references to her being frigid, unfeminine and sexless. "Never—physically speaking—has there ever existed a girl or woman colder than I. I had a volcano in constant eruption in my brain and—a glacier—at the foot of the mountain."[58] But glacial as she might have felt at the age of fifty, when those words were written, it would be a mistake to assume that she experienced none of the normal adolescent's yearning for romantic love. In her letters to Prince Alexander Dondoukoff-Korsakoff, one is struck by a gushing tone so far removed from her normal tartness that it suggests she may have unconsciously regressed to her manner of speaking in those distant days in Tiflis, when she first knew the Prince. She is at once flirtatious, coy, sycophantic, silly and simpering; she repeatedly quotes a Russian proverb: "The prettiest girl in the world cannot give more than she has."[59] She playfully alludes to the Prince's virility, calling him "Don Juan" and "sinner"; and she signs her name Elena, instead of her customary and much more masculine signature H. P. Blavatsky.[60] All of this is so unlike H.P.B., that it seems to be another person speaking. And in a sense it was—Helena Petrovna von Hahn.

But, buried in her anti-male, anti-sex diatribes, there was an important nugget of self-awareness. Even as a young girl, she had an aversion to the traditional female preoccupations with home, husband, adornment and children. Not only had she had a firsthand view of marital failure in her own family, but those ten years with her mother had also infected her. While she never admitted to having read Zenaida R-va's books—she rarely mentioned that her mother was an author, much less a well-known one—she must have perused those nine volumes of feminist despair with more than passing interest. H.P.B. never marched in a suffragist parade, nor did she throw even verbal support behind the flourishing nineteenth-century women's movement. Still, she absorbed the message. There may have been, as she remarked, "nothing of the woman in me" in the Victorian definition, but there was a greal deal of Helena Andreyevna von Hahn in her.

The spring and summer of her seventeenth year, H.P.B. and Vera accompanied Nadyezhda and the Wittes first to Pyatigorsk and Kislovodsk for water cures, on the way to which they narrowly escaped injury from an avalanche. A few weeks after her birthday, they moved on to the German colony of Elizabethal' to join her grandparents and they wound up, finally, at the water resort of Ekatarinenfeld. This summer holiday at the spas had a serious purpose, for Princess Helena, now fifty-nine, was in poor health and had possibly already suffered the first of several crippling strokes that would eventually confine her to a wheelchair.

In the early autumn, back in Tiflis, the Fadeyevs moved to a luxurious old mansion that had once belonged to the Chavchavadze princes. One visitor recalled that it was a melancholy place, "carrying the imprint of something weird or peculiar about it—something that carried one back to the epoch of Catherine the Great."[61]

The deep gloom of the new house must have added to Helena's uneasiness. She later described herself as living, during that time, "a *double* existence, mysterious, incomprehensible even to myself,"[62] in which she spent "the day in my physical body and my nights in my astral body." She could not define what she was seeking any more precisely than as "the *unknown.*" But she may well have sensed, by that time, that her whole life would be devoted to a ceaseless investigation of "the powers of nature that are inaccessible to our reason."[63] Such unorthodox ambitions obviously required the complete freedom her grandparents were never likely to grant.

The tradition of female intellectuality in her family notwithstanding, Helena was expected, sooner or later, to marry. Despite her weight problem, her widely proclaimed anti-male sentiments, and her general unconventionality, she was not unattractive to men. Even as a young woman she was an indefatigable conversationalist who always had something interesting to say—a refreshing change from the usual adolescent inanities and one that appealed to a number of young men in her social set. The red-nosed Constantine Petrovitch, with whom she had dallied at Abbas-Tuman the previous summer, must have been intrigued, as was Prince Alexander Dondoukoff-Korsakoff— however much they also may have teased her to her face, laughed behind her back, and called it all magical superstition and humbug. What other girl of their acquaintance expounded on philosophers' stones,[64] sibyls and Red Virgins? Who else would dare sneak off to visit Maria Solomonovna Babuna, in whose home congregated the sorcerers of Tiflis with their "love potions and other horrors"?[65]

Prince Alexander Golitsyn, who often visited the Fadeyevs, appreciated

Helena Petrovna's originality from a very different perspective than the others. While little is known about this young man, an acquaintance of the Fadeyevs would later describe him as "either a Freemason or a magician or a fortune-teller"[66] and given his family background, the Prince's interest in the occult was natural. The Prince's grandfather, also named Alexander Golitsyn, was an aristocrat who had been a favorite of Alexander I. In the 1820s, the elder Golitsyn had been strongly affected by certain mystical and pietistic trends then current in Europe and, rejecting Orthodoxy as irrelevant, he had formed a Bible Society which embraced the idea that spiritual forces ruled the world and that a new universal church would spring up in Russia. So persuasive was Golitsyn that Alexander I gave him the unprecedented title of Minister of Education and Spiritual Affairs. Some years later, however, when a schism in the Orthodox Church was imminent, Golitsyn fell from the Czar's grace and his Bible Society was suppressed. Nevertheless, his interest in the occult persisted and became shared by the grandson who was so taken with Helena Petrovna.

Not only did young Prince Golitsyn talk knowledgeably about mediumship and clairvoyance, he must also have discussed his grandfather's dream of a universal occult church. This concept, albeit somewhat distorted, would stay in Helena Petrovna's mind and become one of the many strands influencing her life's work.

Despite Golitsyn's impressive lineage, the Fadeyevs could not have approved of his growing influence on Helena. While it is impossible to determine the exact nature of their relationship, the evidence indicates that he was not a romantic suitor. In any case, he suddenly left Tiflis in that winter of 1849, to Helena's dismay and probably to the Fadeyevs' relief. In 1874, twenty-five years later—Helena would claim that she had been betrothed to the Prince, but that he had died.[67]

In the meantime, another gentleman had appeared on the scene who, from the Fadeyevs' point of view, was more suitable. Engrossed in Golitsyn, Helena Petrovna had not paid much attention to Nikifor Blavatsky, an old friend of her grandparents. He came from the landed gentry of Poltava and had started his career as a clerk—first in the office of the civil governor of Poltava and then of the Caucasus. There followed a succession of bureaucratic jobs with the military and civil government of Trans-Caucasia. From 1840 to 1842, he had been Inspector of Police at Shemaha, in the Caucasus, near Baku, and, immediately before meeting Helena, he had lived in Persia. Now, in the winter of 1848–1849, he had settled temporarily in Tiflis, before taking up the most prestigious assignment of his career: vice-governor of the newly formed Province of Erivan, which lay directly to the south of Tiflis.

During the winter months, Nikifor Blavatsky called frequently on the Fadeyevs, and as time wore on it became apparent, even to Helena, that she was the main attraction. In those days, a man became designated a beau by the frequency of his visits and the length of time he spent chatting with a young woman. Nikifor was unquestionably a serious suitor, even though Helena, by then preoccupied by the loss of Golitsyn, failed to take him seriously.

At the same time, Helena was struggling to absorb another disturbing piece of news: her father had married again, to a Baroness von Lange. In view of his neglect of her during the previous years, she must have regarded the marriage as a second abandonment. Her temper and disposition, recalled Nadyezhda, were decidedly foul. When Blavatsky falteringly made advances, she spurned them. She told Nadyezhda and Vera that she did not love him and did not even like him. She found him old and physically unappealing, and nicknamed him "the plumeless raven,"[68] because of his receding hairline or premature baldness.

However, Helena's initial response to Nikifor Blavatsky failed to end matters between them. When her governess declared that she was too vile-tempered to ever find a husband, even one like "the plumeless raven," Helena took up the challenge to prove her wrong. Three days later, prompted by the same impetuous madness that had led her to boil her foot, she wrung a marriage proposal out of Nikifor. Confused as he must have been, he was also pleased, because he loved her. The Fadeyevs must have breathed a deep sigh of relief over the engagement of their wild granddaughter to a mature, sensible bureaucrat who would put up with her varied aberrations.

"Then," recalled Nadyezhda Fadeyev, "frightened at what she had done, she sought to escape from her joking acceptance of his offer. But it was too late."[69] Was it really too late to break the engagement? Had she really consented in jest? Whatever her later opinion of Blavatsky may have been, the truth was that at the time, he interested her. She found in him what she had found in no man except Golitsyn: he did not laugh at her belief in the occult. On the contrary, he seems to have shared it.

> Whereas all the young men laughed at "magical" superstitions, he believed in them! He had so often talked to me about the sorcerers of Erivan, of the mysterious sciences of the Kourds [*sic*] and Persians, that I took him in order to use him as a latch key to the latter.[70]

Whether or not Nikifor genuinely shared her enthusiasms is debatable. It must have been apparent to him that an expression of belief was the only way to her heart.

Nikifor's unwavering persistence, when he must have known how little Helena cared for him, is puzzling. Helena would later claim that she felt ashamed of being Madame Blavatsky, although the reasons are not readily apparent. Nikifor loved her, he had a kind disposition, and eventually he would support her, emotionally and financially, in socially untenable situations. According to Vera, he was "in all respects an excellent man, with but one fault"[71]—his insistence on marrying a girl who did not respect him.

Helena's shame would come later. In the spring of 1849, she experienced panic. She must have realized that it was not marriage she wanted, but rather freedom from her grandparents' authority and the unhindered pursuit of her occult studies. As it was, she would merely be exchanging one guardian for another. And, as the wife of a vice-governor, she would be obliged to perform the kinds of social duties she had always abhorred. She realized that she would be making a mistake, well before she made it. Why a person of such strong will could not have corrected it in time remains a mystery.

In 1886, she wrote to her biographer, Alfred Sinnett:

Details about my marriage? Well, now they say that I wanted to marry the old whistlebreeches *myself*. Let it be. My father was four thousand miles off. My grandmother was too ill. It was as I told you. I had engaged myself to spite the governess, never thinking I could no longer *disengage* myself. Well, Karma followed sin.[72]

It turned out that Helena could not disengage herself without seriously entangling her family, which was already under a great deal of strain. The Princess, apparently too ill to give the matter her undivided attention, left it to Katherine and Andrey, neither of whom would listen to Helena's "prayers and supplications not to be married to old B———."[73] In their view, she had made her choice and now must stick by it. Many harsh words passed between Helena and the rest of the family in this battle of wills: Vera accused Helena of slandering their mother; there were quarrels between Vera and Nadyezhda, who had never liked each other, when Nadyezhda took Lelinka's side. The betrothal brought out the worst in everyone.

Taking matters into her own hands, Helena finally appealed to Nikifor himself, warning him that he was making a mistake. However, instead of openly stating her feelings, she apparently tried to force him to break off the engagement. She told him, according to Vera, that the only reason she had chosen him over other suitors was that she would feel fewer compunctions about making him miserable. "You make a great mistake in marrying me," she said to him before the marriage. "You know perfectly well that you are old enough to be my grandfather. You will make somebody unhappy, but it won't be me. As for me, I am not afraid of you, but I warn you that it is not you that will gain anything from our union."[74] Vera's secondhand account of this conversation perpetuates H.P.B.'s misleading claim that Nikifor was a doddering old man who, though close to seventy, was reluctant to acknowledge being older than about fifty. In fact, he was thirty-nine at the time.

Unmoved, Nikifor refused to break the engagement. A few weeks later, when he had departed for Erivan, Helena ran off in search of Prince Golitsyn. Where she went, and whether or not she actually located him, were unrecorded. However, if she did find him, their encounter must have been unsatisfying, because she returned home shortly.

While news of her escapade may not have immediately reached Blavatsky, unpleasant stories circulated in Tiflis. One day, on Princess Lydia Gagarin's balcony, Alexander Dondoukoff-Korsakoff gave Helena a lecture on morality. The Fadeyevs, shaken by her flight and aware that she was gaining a reputation for looseness, were now doubly anxious to get her safely married and proceeded hastily with preparations for the wedding.

At the end of June of 1849, Helena was escorted to her wedding by the whole family, including Katherine who only ten days earlier had given birth to her third son—Sergei Yulyevich[75]. The only absent relative—the one most important to Helena—was her father, who did not make the long journey from St. Petersburg, where he was living with his new wife. This impressive family cavalcade was organized less for the sake of appearances than for security reasons, since it was not in Helena's nature to yield gracefully and she continued to entertain strategies for escape. Seized by a "great horror,"[76] she felt as if she were being swept toward the threshold of mortal danger. But even though her instinct warned her to run, a kind of paralysis prevented her from taking any action.

Leaving Tiflis, the wedding party rode south along the Kura River and then began to climb up into the mountain ranges of the southern Caucasus where the scenery was breathtaking: sharp peaks, romantic valleys watered by torrential streams, the forest-encircled Blue Sea. The area was popular with residents of Tiflis, who flocked there in summer for their holidays. Halfway to Erivan, the party reached the small town of Gerger (now Armansky Gerger), and then headed toward the settlement of Dzhelal-ogli (now Kamenka), where Nikifor was to join them for the nuptials on July 7 (Old Style).

Much later in her life, H.P.B. became quite censorious about sex. At seventeen, it can be assumed that she was merely ignorant and scared. Young girls were invariably uninformed about the sexual side of marriage. It was not uncommon for new brides to rush home after their wedding night, declaring that their husbands had been rude. Helena, however, was more fortunate than most. On the day of her wedding, either her grandmother or her Aunt Katherine made "a distinct attempt to impress her with the solemnity of marriage, with her future obligations and her duties to her husband and married life."[77] Instead of assuaging her dread, however, this last-minute lecture merely heightened it. A few hours later, standing at the altar with Nikifor, when she heard the priest say, "Thou shalt honour and obey thy husband," the word "shalt" proved to be the proverbial last straw. Forgetting where she was, she flushed angrily and breached every code of manners by muttering in a perfectly audible voice: "Surely, I shall not."[78]

Puzzled as Nikifor Blavatsky may have been by his bride's extraordinary outburst, he seems to have spared no effort or expense to make the honeymoon pleasant. Immediately after the ceremony, the couple set off for Darachichag—a fashionable mountain resort whose name means "valley of flowers"—where he planned for them to spend July and August, before he had to take up his duties at Erivan.

There is no question that the marriage was a disaster from the start. Despite their romantic surroundings, the couple "came into violent conflict from the day of the wedding—a day of unforeseen revelations, furious indignation, dismay and belated repentance." With all due consideration for a bride's natural modesty, Nikifor naturally wished to assert his marital rights. To his bewilderment, Helena would not allow him to touch her.[79]

H.P.B. adamantly insisted that: "*I never was his wife,* I swear it up to the hour of my death. NEVER have I been WIFE Blavatsky although I lived for a year under his roof."[80] The marriage actually lasted for three months, but there is small doubt that it was ever consummated. During those months when Blavatsky repeatedly attempted to initiate a sexual relationship, he must at last have understood the true meaning of Helena's threat that he would get nothing from the marriage. She was equally unwilling to give anything outside the bedroom and their relationship soon deteriorated into a battlefield devoid of ordinary civility. Whatever pretenses Nikifor had formerly made about interest in the occult quickly evaporated. He no longer had patience for lengthy metaphysical discussions and it became clear to Helena that he knew nothing about the sorcerers of Erivan. All he wanted was a normal marriage with a normal wife. "What I wanted and searched for," H.P.B. wrote, "was the subtle magnetism that one exchanges, the human 'salt,' and father Blavatsky did not have it." As far as her occult studies were concerned, "this did not suit the old man, hence quarrels, nearly battles."[81]

Toward the end of August, they received a visit from her family, which had remained in the vicinity vacationing. While nothing was said about the true state of affairs, her relatives could not have supposed the marriage happy. At the end of the month, the Fadeyevs accompanied the newlyweds to Erivan, stopping on the way to visit the monastery of Echmiadzin—the headquarters of the Armenian Church—with its Tibetan bell inscribed *Om Mani Padme Hum*; they gawked at Mount Ararat, on whose summit Noah was supposed to have landed his ark; and they visited the nearby ruins of Bashgarni. It was all very interesting and educational, but it did not succeed in alleviating Helena's misery. The Fadeyevs went back home, and she was left alone with her husband.

The Armenian city of Erivan was old and Asiatic in character, with only a few newly built houses and occasional Russian soldiers in the streets. After Helena had strolled about the town, visiting the dozens of canals and the bazaar where merchants sat with tame falcons on their wrists, there was little to do. Preoccupied by fantasies of escape, she persuaded Nikifor to allow her to take horseback trips around Mount Ararat and the neighboring countryside. Rightfully wary, Nikifor designated a Kurd named Safar Ali Bel Ibrahim Bek Ogli to be her personal escort, but in reality, he was to function as her guard. Apparently unaware of Safar Ali's real job, Helena confided to him her plans for escape, which he promptly reported to his employer. By this time, it must have been painfully clear to Nikifor that only a full-time police officer could keep his wife from running away, and it could hardly have come as a surprise when she suddenly disappeared one day.

H.P.B. liked to give the impression that she rode through the mountains back to Tiflis all alone. Such a journey would have been difficult for an eighteen-year-old girl unfamiliar with the trails, no matter how expert a horsewoman she may have been. But she may have felt her situation desperate enough to warrant a few risks in fleeing from what she considered imprisonment. If she had disliked Nikifor at the beginning of the marriage, she now despised him.

I, hating my husband, N. V. Blavatsky (it may have been wrong, but still such was the nature *God* gave me), left him, abandoned him—a *virgin* (I shall produce documents and letters proving this, although he himself is not such a swine as to deny it).[82]

He was not at all a swine. In fact, for the rest of his life, he tactfully refrained from making any public comment whatsoever about the woman who would make his name world famous.

The Veiled Years

1849–1873

I

The Hindu at Ramsgate

In Tiflis, Helena Petrovna went noisily to pieces, swearing that "I would kill myself if I was forced to return"[1] to Erivan. Her grandfather was embarrassed, unnerved, and finally, furious. Helena's flight was not only an affront to his friend, it was also a social disgrace. With her indiscreet pursuit of Prince Golitsyn—a scandal narrowly averted by marriage—still fresh in his memory, he could now foresee a whole chain of headaches looming ahead. Fadeyev decided that he could no longer be responsible for his troublesome granddaughter.

The problem, however, was what to do with her. An eighteen-year-old woman, married or not, could not be permitted to run loose. Shipping her back to Blavatsky seemed out of the question, and the ailing Princess Helena was in no condition to supervise her. By process of elimination, Helena's father became the only alternative. Writing to von Hahn at St. Petersburg, Fadeyev outlined both the situation and the proposed solution in terms that did not brook refusal. Von Hahn, finally settled at fifty-one with his second wife, the Baroness von Lange, who was expecting their first child, could hardly have welcomed the news. But after a further exchange of letters, it was agreed that Fadeyev would have Helena sent overland to Poti, a port on the Black Sea, and from there she would travel by steamer to Odessa, where von Hahn would collect her. Having no trust in Helena, Fadeyev placed her in the custody of four serfs— one of them his personal steward—and dispatched this convoy, amounting to nothing less than an armed guard, in a capacious four-in-hand.

Helena left Tiflis feeling "sick at heart."[2] After years of phantasizing a reunion with her father, she realized that it was, of course, too late. If he had not wanted her before, she now discovered that she no longer wanted him. She felt sure that he would begin by moralizing and end by returning her to Nikifor. These were not unrealistic fears and by the time they approached Poti, her mind was hard at work on schemes to slip away from her escort.

On the westward trip through Georgia, she had caused sufficient delays to make the party miss the steamer for Odessa at Poti. In the harbor was an English vessel, the SS *Commodore*, from whose skipper Helena learned it was headed first for Kerch in the Crimea, and from there would sail north-east-ward to Taganrog on the Sea of Azov, before turning south again for Constantinople. She devised a two-stage plan: she would book passage to Kerch for the servants, and to Constantinople for herself. When she proposed this idea to the skipper, he at first refused to have anything to do with it. She succeeded in convincing him, she claimed, by a liberal outlay of rubles. But there were also other reasons for his change of mind.

Kerch, viewed from the steamer, was an extremely pretty town which rose like an amphitheater surrounding the bay: the church cupolas were painted green and topped with immense gilded crosses, and on a steep hill to the left stood a museum modeled after a Greek temple. Telling them that she would join them in the morning, Helena sent the serfs ashore to find lodgings for their layover while they allegedly would await a ship to Odessa.

That night the *Commodore* slipped quietly out of the harbor and Helena Petrovna Blavatsky finally managed to shake free of all restrictions. Hungry for life, she could plunge into the adventures and travels she had dreamed about. "My soul needed space,"[3] as she put it, but she did not bargain for the steep price she would have to pay. No sooner had they reached Taganrog than the skipper suggested it would be best if the harbor police, who would be coming aboard, did not see her. The reason remains obscure: either she had not paid for her passage, or there was some irregularity in her papers, or perhaps, as an unchaperoned female minor, she was a "suspicious person." The skipper instructed her to conceal herself in a coal bin and, when she balked, he had her dress as a cabin boy and huddle in a bunk feigning illness.

It should have been clear by now that more than respectful regard was motivating the captain to perform these services for a stowaway, and one wonders if she naively believed he would smuggle her into Turkey without asking recompense. She told Alfred Sinnett that "further embarrassments developed" once the *Commodore* dropped anchor in Constantinople harbor, and she was forced to "fly ashore precipitately in a caique with the connivance of the steward to escape the persecutions of the skipper."[4] Thus, with uncharacteristic delicacy, she surmounted this final obstacle to her freedom. She was not the least bit daunted by having to enter Constantinople in a rowboat; nor, apparently was she concerned about the livid, outwitted men she had left in her wake—least of all the amorous skipper of the *Commodore.*

Working to earn one's living was socially unacceptable for upper-class women in the 1840s. The fact that only the meanest kinds of employment were open to them served as further discouragement. Indeed, it was commonly accepted that if a woman worked, she was making a statement: either her father had provided insufficiently for her support, or that she had failed to find a husband. In a foreign country, the odds against finding employment were vastly increased.

How Helena supported herself after she left Russia remains a mystery. Not only did H.P.B. provide no illumination, she did her best to add to the confusion. Her biographer dutifully set down what she told him: that she "communicated privately with her father and secured his consent to her vague programme of foreign travel." Von Hahn, according to Sinnett, "supplied his fugitive daughter with money, and kept her counsel in regard to her subsequent movements."[5] Yet, from everything that is known of Peter von Hahn, left fuming at the Odessa docks, this account seems wildly out of character. The unromantic fact was she found herself stranded in Turkey with little or no funds, and she had to live by her wits. Even for a person as clever as H.P.B., income-producing activities were limited to three: governess, lady's companion, or mistress—being kept by a man. Helena could never have endured the restricted life of a governess and, although she was not really suited for the remaining two "careers" either, these appear to be among those that she eventually settled for.

First, however, she apparently tried to capitalize on the only talent of which she was then aware—horseback riding. Gossip reported much later, some of it by her own relatives, has her joining the circus as a bareback rider. H.P.B. herself admitted that she did have an experience with horses at Constantinople, but she gave a rather different account:

At Constantinople I was in need of money and I wanted to earn the 100 offered to the one who won the *steeplechase*— eighteen hedges to jump with a wild horse which had just killed two grooms. I jumped sixteen but at the seventeenth my horse reared, fell backwards and *crushed* me. It was in 1851. I came to myself six weeks later; but before entering my *Nirvana* (for it was fully one), I saw a man, a giant, dressed differently from the Turks, who lifted my tattered and bloody garments from under the horse and—nothing more, nothing but the memory of a face I had seen somewhere.[6]

Allowing for exaggeration, and understanding that the main point of this tale is that unseen forces protected her, it is still possible to extract a few nuggets of plain truth from it: that she rode for money in Constantinople and, in the course of this activity, suffered an injury which left her with a chest scar that would still be troubling her twenty years later.

There is evidence that most of Helena's time for the next two years was spent as companion to various wealthy old women. She soon attached herself to the Russian community living in Constantinople. Such enclaves of Slav expatriates—temporary transplants or permanent residents—flourished in London, Paris, Rome and in nearly every large European city. They gathered around the samovar, smoked cigarettes and engaged in interminable discussions about God, politics and music, all of them tinged with nostalgia for the homeland they had abandoned in favor of the palmy lobbies of first-class European hotels. Given Helena's family background, it was natural for her to gravitate toward this group, and equally natural for them to befriend her.

H.P.B. was fortunate to meet in Constantinople a Countess Kiselev, an eccentric woman in her sixties who happened to be well connected in Russia. Her husband, Count Paul Kiselev, was both a liberal reformer who had devoted most of his life to the unsuccessful cause of serf liberation, and an intimate of Czar Nicholas—seemingly incompatible roles, but this was nevertheless a fact. The countess's interests ran, evidently, to the more exotic, and in particular, to the occult. H.P.B. would later waggishly declare that when the countess died, she left "millions and all her medium apparatuses, writing tables and *tarots* to the Church of Rome."[7] The countess took on Helena as her companion, dressed her in trousers because she thought it to be chic to be seen with "a gentleman student,"[8] and the two of them moved on to Egypt.

Once she became famous, Madame Blavatsky would contend that she had spent twenty years wandering the globe in pursuit of esoteric knowledge. However, only a handful of individuals came forward to support her claim, stating they had encountered her during this period. One of them was Albert Leighton Rawson, a young American artist, scholar and traveler who was just as fascinated by the mysteries of the East as was Helena. A native of Chester, Vermont, who had once disguised himself as a Moslem divinity student and joined a caravan making the annual pilgrimage to Mecca, Rawson had a weakness for wild ventures, disguises, and colorful women. In 1850, when he met Helena in Cairo, he found her "charming," "companionable," and "almost irresistible" (later adding the qualification that she was all those things "when not 'possessed' ")[9] and he offered to squire her around the city.

Somewhere between Tiflis and Cairo, Helena had blossomed into a highly attractive young woman. Having shed her extra weight, she described herself as "very thin then,"[10] and Rawson commented admiringly on her "full, moon-shaped" face, a figure that was "supple, muscular and well rounded, fit to delight an artist," and her small, delicately molded hands and feet. He declared that "she could win at a single interview the admiration of any man who had ever lived outside of himself long enough to discover that he was not three-quarters of the universe," obviously including himself in this unchauvinistic group. He hurried to add, however, that male admiration of her womanliness meant little to Helena—it was for her mind that she wanted to be appreciated.

Helena took pains to create an interesting image of herself for Rawson. She told him that she was the widow of a Russian general and that she had come to Cairo with a friend to study the relics of an ancient civilization. Having "killed" Nikifor and widowed herself in one imaginative stroke, she proceeded to enjoy her visit. Rawson, an obliging tour guide, made no objection when she suggested taking lessons from a snake charmer, although he warned her that "persons in European dress would be sure to be molested as hated infidels, if not actually put in danger of life or limb by crazy fanatics." Disguising themselves as Moslems, with H.P.B. in male attire, they visited the chief of the Cairo snakemen, Sheik Yusaf ben Makerzi, and learned how to handle the serpents without getting bitten. Back at Shepheard's Hotel, where Helena was staying with the countess, she gleefully informed her employer that she had solved one of Egypt's mysteries—and she proved it by loosing a snake from a bag she had hidden in the folds of her skirt.

Having mastered snake charming, Helena was ready for further challenges. She had heard of a Coptic magician, Paulos Mentamon, who was reputed to be a respository of astrological formulas and magical incantations. Rawson somehow wrangled an introduction and, once again in disguise, they set off for the native quarter. Rawson flatteringly told the Coptic: "We are students who have heard of your great learning and skill in magic, and wish to learn at your feet." Mentamon did not beat around the bush: "I perceive that you are two Franks in disguise," he snorted, "and I have no doubt you are in search of knowledge—of occult and magical lore. I look for coin."[11]

While this callous demand for money was a big letdown, Rawson fortunately had ample funds that he was willing to part with, not without noting sarcastically that Mentamon had indeed discovered the secret whereby the philosophers' stone could turn anything into gold. Later, H.P.B. would mention studying with Mentamon, but she dismissed his teachings as unimportant and inferior. To know how much of the magician's repertory she actually mastered might help to throw important light on her later career, but this apparently was not information she wished to advertise.

In Cairo, as always, Helena had a recurrent need to get out of her body, and one way to do this, she had already discovered, was by smoking tobacco. There was nothing extraordinary about her adopting this habit; many fashionable Russian women now smoked. But apparently she found special advantages in it that others did not. It seemed to tranquilize her, to lift her up off the earth: "I close my eyes and float on and on, anywhere or wherever I wish," she said.[12] Less conventionally smoked among her social peers, but more commonly used as a means to out-of-body experiences, was hashish, to which she was then introduced by Rawson. Twenty-five years later, along with opium, she was still taking hashish, and there is some evidence that she was addicted to the drug.[13] Among its varied physiological effects, hashish produces visions. Helena thought it "a wonderful drug" that enabled her to lift the veil and solve various "profound mysteries." She told Rawson that her hashish dreams "are as real as if they were ordinary events of actual life."[14] The hypnotic states that she achieved artifically were not totally unlike those that she could induce naturally in herself without hashish, but undoubtedly they were far more spectacular with the drug.

Whatever else hashish did for her, it succeeded in bringing to consciousness ideas that may have seemed fanciful, even absurd, to others but completely plausible to her. One day she told Rawson and the countess that she had forty years to construct a more enduring fame than the builder of the Great Pyramid. "Who was he, anyway?" she demanded of them. "Only a name, an oppressor of his fellow men." And she added cryptically, "I will bless mankind by freeing them from their mental bondage." The megalomania of such statements evoked sarcasm from Countess Kiselev: "That is sublime, Helene, but how do you propose to go about this little task?"

Helena could not elaborate at that point, because she had no notion of what she wished to accomplish, much less how to go about it. While her private vision of herself as a religious teacher was still far from formed, she did have a fear of being inconsequential—she did not want to be a person whom posterity could ignore. She insisted to Rawson and Kiselev: "I know I was intended to do a great work."[15]

After three months in Egypt, Helena followed the countess to Greece and "other parts of Eastern Europe." At this point, Kiselev may have returned to Russia, or perhaps she simply had had enough of Helena's role as her "gentleman student." Helena would later speak vaguely of traveling with "an English lady of rank,"[16] and also of visiting Paris in 1850 or early 1851 where, according to the account she gave to Alfred Sinnett, she met literary celebrities and her psychic gifts were brought to the attention of a famous mesmerist who expressed eagerness to use her as a sensitive. Also, while in Paris, she met another elderly Russian woman—Princess Bagration-Muhransky—whose family was among the oldest and most eminent in Georgia and who was also probably acquainted with the Fadeyevs. When the Princess and her retinue set off for London in the spring of 1851, Helena went with them.

London was offering at that time the most spectacular tourist attraction of the century: The Great Exhibition of the Works of Industry of All Nations. Referred to simply as the Great Exhibition, it was to be a showpiece for contemporary science and invention. To house the exhibit, there had been erected in Hyde Park a dazzling glass building measuring 1,848 feet in length. If the 13,000 exhibits—ranging from McCormick reapers to the enormous Koh-i-noor diamond— did not lure the visitors from all over the world, the Crystal Palace itself did. From May, when it was officially opened by Queen Victoria, until October, when the exhibit closed, some 6,009,948 visitors filed through the hall. They arrived in their best plaid silk bonnets and pot hats, drank Schweppes ginger beer and soda, ate nearly 2,000,000 buns, and bought untold millions of souvenirs—iron door stops, tortoise-shell glove boxes with the Crystal Palace painted on their lids, and little ladies' handbags called reticules, which were just coming into style.

A visit to London, even in years when there was no Great Exhibition, always offered a diversity of entertainment. There were the churches, the Marble Arch, the Tower of London; there were theaters and concerts, and the fashionable Cremorne Gardens along the Embankment in Chelsea, where the smart set went to dance and drink and be amused after the theater. Just how much leisure time Helena had for sight-seeing is unclear, but she gave the impression that life with Princess Bagration was rigorously confining. Unlike Countess Kiselev, who did not mind snakes and probably enjoyed hearing about her companion's jaunts to visit magicians, Princess Bagration demanded service from her employees and H.P.B. recalled that she "held me confined in Mivart's Hotel, making me read the *Chitaminyi* and the Bible."[17] Reading aloud from Scripture was not Helena's idea of freedom— or fun. On August 12, she celebrated her twentieth birthday by taking a seven-by-eleven-inch sketchbook she had recently purchased, plus pencils, pen and ink, and fleeing to Ramsgate, a new seaside resort that was rapidly becoming popular with pleasure-seeking Londoners.

On warm days, the beach at Ramsgate was so crowded that it was difficult to pick one's way through the throng. Women lay on their backs at the water's edge and let the waves fling their bathing dresses over their heads, "so that as far as decency is concerned," reported the London *Observer,* "they might as well be without any dresses at all." More shocking to the *Observer,* gentlemen equipped themselves with opera glasses to better view the opposite sex and the women stared back "without so much as a blush or a giggle."[18]

This was just the sort of atmosphere that a cooped-up young woman might adore on her birthday. Helena spent the day and evening there, sketching on the first page of her book a scene of water and sailboats, and after she returned to the hotel, she wrote under the picture in French:

Memorable night! On a certain night by the light of the moon that was setting at Ramsgate on August 12, 1851,* when I met the Master of my dreams!!

The identity of this man of her dreams is far from clear. Years later H.P.B. would revise the sketchbook and insist that it was the first fleshly manifestation of Mahatma Morya. However, since she also claimed to have first seen him in a London crowd, one gets confused. The person she actually saw may have been the novelist Edward Bulwer-Lytton, whose Rosicrucian tale *Zanoni* would influence her own work.[20] Perhaps, after all, the evening at Ramsgate had been topped off by a particularly vivid hallucination. Still, it is entirely possible that she met a real man who aroused romantic feelings in her. On the second page of the sketchbook she wrote of a man and woman, out of doors on a beautiful summer night, "flowers of fire strewn over the sky," the man saying to the woman "I love you—words formed of a divine perfume of the soul."[21] But she added that he would later regret having uttered them.

Those sensuous lines would seem to indicate a romantic interlude with a living man, although later she altered some of the words to imply that she had been speaking of her Mahatma. Nonetheless, by the time she got around to writing on page three, the affair, if it was one, had proved disillusioning. Love, she wrote bitterly, "is a vile dream, a nightmare"[22] and happiness lay only in the acquisition of supernatural powers. Page four contains a few scrawls and

*August 12 is July 31 in Russian style, the day of my birth—*Twenty years!*[19]

the address of a Captain Miller, Dragoon-guards, Aldershot, but whether Captain Miller had anything to do with her disillusionment is impossible to know because the pages are undated and by page five she was drawing a poodle sitting on a table.

Whatever emotional ordeals she was passing through that summer, life as a lady's companion did not make them more endurable. Severely depressed, she was tired of the Princess and "sick of everything." In two years away from Russia, she had learned a few conjuring tricks and the useless knack of calming snakes. She felt a failure. "I escaped on to Waterloo Bridge, for I was seized with a strong desire to die. I had long felt the temptation approaching. This time I did not seek to resist it and the muddy water of the Thames seemed to me a delicious bed."[23] At the last moment, however, she was turned back from suicide by the opportune appearance of her invisible protector who promised a great destiny lying in wait.

Princess Bagration left London, and for a short while Helena stayed on at Mivart's with another woman who had also been in the Princess's employ. After that, she moved about—to a hotel in the Strand and then to a furnished room in Cecil Street. London had nothing to offer her. There was virtually no interest in psychic phenomena in England, although unknown to her some young men at Cambridge had formed earlier that year a society to conduct "a serious and earnest enquiry into the nature of the phenomena vaguely called supernatural."[24] In 1852, an American medium, Mrs. Hayden, would visit London and charge a guinea a sitting, and by 1853 a craze for table-tilting would sweep in from the Continent, even Queen Victoria and Prince Albert having a go at it. But all that still lay in the future. Even if Helena had wished to support herself as a professional medium—which she definitely did not— no market for such wares then existed.

Afterward, those last weeks in London would become hazy. Having no money, no friends, and nothing to do, it was a melancholy time of her life, which she preferred to forget.[25]

II

Agardi Metrovitch

Since H.P.B. was hard put to account for the next seven years of her life, her description of this period sounded so far-fetched that even her biographer conceded "the obvious embarrassments of my task."[26] Sinnett excused himself, and his subject, by saying that Helena had kept no diary and had a poor memory. Actually, she did her best to be quite specific about her itinerary.[27] In July, 1851, she allegedly went to Canada to study the Indians, moved on to the United States where she spent a year and bought land (but lost the title papers) and drifted around in Central and South America. Some time in 1852, then in the West Indies, she wrote to "a certain Englishman" whom she had known in Germany, asking him to join her on a trip to the Orient. With the Englishman and a Hindu, she sailed via the Cape to Ceylon and from there to Bombay, where the party split up. Determined to enter Tibet, Helena set out alone for Nepal but the British resident would not allow her to cross the border. She departed for Southern India, then on to Java and Singapore before returning to England.

The year was now 1853 and preparations were under way for the Crimean War, altogether an unfortunate time for a Russian to be living in England. Once again Helena crossed the Atlantic, visiting New York and Chicago before slogging across the Rocky Mountains in a covered wagon. At San Francisco, she boarded a ship bound for India via Japan and landed at Calcutta. In 1856, for a second time, she tried to get into Tibet. At Lahore she encountered the father of her old governess Antonya Kuhlwein and his two companions, the brothers N————, all of whom planned to penetrate Tibet under various disguises. Accompanied by a Tartar shaman, they traveled through Kashmir to Leh, the chief city of Ladak, but the brothers were picked up and deported before they had walked sixteen miles into the forbidden territory: Mr. Kuhlwein came down with fever and had to return to Lahore. Helena, wearing a disguise provided by the shaman, successfully crossed the frontier and passed "far on into the generally inaccessible country."[28] After a number of supernatural experiences, some of a frightening nature, she was rescued by a party of twenty-five Lamaist horsemen and swooped back to the frontier.

In India once more, she was warned by her invisible protector that the Sepoy Rebellion would soon begin and she was advised to leave the country. Sailing aboard a Dutch vessel, she made her way from Madras to Java, arriving in Europe in 1858.

Unfortunately, hardly a word of this seems to be true. In order to credit H.P.B.'s version, it is necessary to believe that an unaccompanied young woman with no visible income was able to circumnavigate the earth twice in eight years. Forty years later, journalist Elizabeth Cochrane ("Nellie Bly") would race around the globe in seventy-two days, six hours, eleven minutes and fourteen seconds, but her trip was a publicity stunt sponsored by the New York *World*. No matter how daring and resourceful a woman may have been, and certainly Madame Blavatsky possessed those qualities in abundance, it was still an impossible feat in the 1850s.

Especially implausible are H.P.B.'s visits to Tibet. Natural mountain barriers and a harsh climate had always made the "Roof of the World" inaccessible, and few Europeans were tempted to drop in. In 1792, however, harassed by Gurkha invasions and missionaries peddling Christianity, Tibet officially closed its doors to foreigners. You could not get a passport for Tibet, and if somehow you did, the Tibetans refused to honor it. Nevertheless, in 1846 two French priests, Abbe Evariste Huc and his friend Father Gabet, did manage to slip in, although not without difficulty. While Huc was not the first European to visit Tibet, he was the first to write a detailed account of the country and its people. In *Recollections of Travel in Tartary, Tibet and China,* a book with which H.P.B. incidentally was familiar, Huc painted a formidable picture of the hardships of travel: snow storms in June, avalanches, robbers, travelers freezing by the roadside and eaten by vultures. Any explorer setting out for Tibet would need to equip herself with baggage ponies, tents, stoves, an escort of native bearers, an interpreter, and—most crucial—food, water and fuel for the entire trek. Surviving without them, as H.P.B. implied she had done, would be not far from a miracle.

Finally, there is the matter of Madame Blavatsky's sex. The Tibetans were inhospitable to all strangers, man or woman, but there is small likelihood that they would admit a white woman to their religious ceremonies, as H.P.B. claimed she had been admitted. In fairness, however, it should be pointed out that other women have succeeded in penetrating Tibet. From 1850 to 1852, a Mrs. Hervey (who delicately withheld her first name) traveled in Kashmir, Tibet and China, and wrote a three-volume description of her adventures. Mrs. Hervey's travels, however, seem to have been confined to the frontier and to Balistan, known as Little Tibet, and she was accompanied by a sizable retinue of coolies and guides. Around the turn of the century another Englishwoman, Dr. Susie Carson Rijnhart, spent four years living on the border and claimed to have made a few trips over it, and in the twentieth century, the French explorer Alexandra David-Neel spent fourteen years there. A practicing Buddhist, David-Neel spoke and wrote fluently all the Tibetan dialects and eventually was made an honorary lama. So while the occurrence of women going to Tibet is not completely unknown, what we do know about such trips makes H.P.B.'s account seem all the more unpersuasive. There is no evidence, except her own word, that she ever stepped foot inside Tibet.[29]

H.P.B.'s account of how she spent her twenties obscures a large portion of the truth, or so the evidence suggests. Her deliberate falsification of the facts apparently represented an effort to cover up a mode of living that was not only unacceptable to her contemporaries, but totally objectionable in an ascetic who believed she had a mission to "save the world from despair."[30] There remains the interesting question: If she was not leaping continents, what was she doing?

In 1850, soon after arriving in Constantinople, she met a middle-aged opera singer with whom she formed an off-and-on relationship that would last twenty years. Agardi Metrovitch, a man in his late forties and the illegitimate son of the Duke of Lucea, had been brought up in the Hungarian town of Metrovitz (now Sremska Mitrovica in Yugoslavia) whose name he adopted as his stage name. H.P.B.'s claim that he was a hothead— "*a Carbonaro,* a revolutionist of the worst kind, a fanatic rebel"—indicates that his politics were far left. According to Helena, their first encounter took place one evening when, returning to Missire's Hotel, she stumbled over his seemingly dead body. "He had received three good stabs in his back from one, or two, or more Maltese ruffians, and a Corsican, who were paid for it by the Jesuits."[31] She had to guard him four hours with a revolver before finding someone to assist her. According to her cousin Sergei Witte, Agardi Metrovitch fell in love after seeing her perform in the circus.[32]

Since Helena spent the rest of 1850 and also 1851 in Egypt, France and England, she could not have been intimately involved with him during that period. But after finding herself footloose in London, she joined Metrovitch and accompanied him to various cities and towns where he had singing engagements. That she should have been attracted to a musician is understandable, for she herself was an ardent lover of music and a talented pianist. An opera singer's mode of life with its constant traveling and its theatricality would have appealed to Helena, even if she had to be a backstage mistress. She could not abide dullness, and life with Metrovitch offered compensations that being the wife of the vice-governor of Erivan had not.

In the same sketchbook that H.P.B. began at Ramsgate there is a sketch of Metrovitch in a scene from *Faust* but it is difficult to determine how much is Mephistopheles' makeup and how much Metrovitch. His features are sharp, almost emaciated, with a high brow, long nose, and thin-lipped mouth. Helena's cousin claimed that as one of the most celebrated bassos of the time he enjoyed a brilliant career until his voice began to deteriorate. If that is true, he escaped the notice of nineteenth-century music historians because none of the biographical dictionaries compiled at the time mention his name.

Even though H.P.B. liked to paint herself as passionless, there is no doubt that she loved Metrovitch, and he, her. He is supposed to have written several letters to Andrey Fadeyev announcing that he had married Helena and calling himself "grandson." Apparently he did not realize that his "wife" had another husband, or if he did know, it does not seem to have troubled him.

One of H.P.B.'s more refreshing traits was her utter disregard for the Victorian code of morality; she did as she pleased when she pleased, even if it meant a bigamous or common-law marriage, or simply "free love" as it was then termed. However, it would be a mistake to assume that she was never troubled by pricks of conscience, for later she would moan that "just because the devil got me into trouble in my youth, I really cannot go and rip up my stomach now like a Japanese suicide."[33] She could not have condoned Metrovitch's indiscreet letters to her grandfather, and H.P.B.'s temper being what it was, their life together must often have been stormy. She may not have been sexually faithful to him either, because her cousin stated that, several years after the Fadeyevs heard from Metrovitch, they received mail from a second man. "A certain Englishman from London informed them in a letter bearing an American stamp that he had been married to Mme. Blavatski, who had gone with him on a business trip to the United States."[34] If this occurred at all, it must have been an unimportant interlude because Helena returned to Metrovitch.

These years of apparently aimless wandering would prove an embarrassment to H.P.B.'s followers, who offered by way of apology the theory that the 1850s were "a preparation for discipleship, then discipleship itself."[35] Technically this was true, although certainly not in the sense meant by the Theosophists. She was constantly preparing herself, though for what end she could not say. In 1888, in a prospectus for *The Secret Doctrine,* she would state that "the author of this work has devoted more than forty years of her life to the study and acquisition of this knowledge,"[36] adding that it had been acquired in various secret schools of wisdom. This mysterious assertion cannot completely disguise the fact that esoteric knowledge was contained in books, which were available to any scholar who troubled to visit the major libraries of Europe. Not only was H.P.B. an insatiable reader, she also had a bloodhound's nose for sniffing out obscure works known mainly to librarians and curators, books that had lain dust-covered for decades.

As a student she loved anything that moved her soul and forced her to plunge into thought. Interested mainly in science and theology, she familiarized herself with the standard works in these areas, not because she accepted conventional ideas, but the better to pick them apart. Her passion, however, was for hidden or occult knowledge, either that rejected by the Establishment, or knowledge that voluntarily exiled itself because it had to be hidden from the eyes of the profane. The secret meaning of everything fascinated H.P.B.; myths and traditions she took for actual history, and those who viewed them as fantasies she dismissed as superficial thinkers. It is not surprising that a person as defiant of convention as H.P.B. should dote on knowledge that was rejected and subversive.

In the midnineteenth century, no student of Masonic, Hermetic, Cabalistic or Rosicrucian literature could have missed an idea that repeated itself constantly: namely, that there exists a secret tradition, also called the Ancient Wisdom, Secret Doctrine, and a dozen other names, which explains the great plan of the universe and mankind's place in God's scheme. Although no two interpretations of the secret wisdom were the same, one thread weaving through them all was the idea that the keys to the secrets have been entrusted to a brotherhood of supermen. This intriguing notion was, of course, the basis of the Rosicrucian order whose founder, Christian Rosenkreutz, sought the wise men in their Arabian home, learned the secrets of the Book M, and in turn became himself a keeper of the wisdom.

Years later, Helena would tell a Russian compatriot that, before the age of thirty, she had been a materialist who did not believe in God,[37] a curious admission for one who was to insist that Theosophy was not *a* religion, it *was* religion. Nevertheless, even in her twenties, she was obsessed by God and His divine plan, and would remain so for the rest of her life. Why this should be so is easily understandable in terms of her background for even though she had abandoned Russia, it had not abandoned her, and at heart she remained quintessentially Russian. Atheist though she may have considered herself at times, she was soaked in the mysticism of the Russian people, their eagerness to grasp the intricate and subtle questions of life, their addiction for all-encompassing philosophic systems. Her religious training as a child had been conventionally pious, even rigid, and in alienating herself from the Fadeyevs, she not only rejected the gorgeous pomposity of the Byzantine Church but Christianity as well, which left her with the problem of finding a more compatible system. There were, after all, other religions she might have embraced, but none of them truly satisfied her. In the end she would be obliged to tailor Hinduism and Buddhism to her own needs.

While Helena's life with Metrovitch left ample time to pursue her occult studies, it did not rule out other activities and interests. According to her cousin, the Fadeyevs learned from the newspapers that Helena was giving piano concerts in London and Paris and, for a time, managed the Serbian royal choir, all of which might have been possible considering the musical circles in which she traveled. At the same time, according to Witte, she also became "the right hand"[38] of the renowned medium Daniel Dunglas Home. Toward the end of her life, Helena vehemently denied knowing Home, let alone working for him, but the denials contradict her own earlier claims.

"In 1858," she told the New York *Daily Graphic,* "I returned to Paris and made the acquaintance of Daniel Home. He had married the Countess Krohle,* a sister of the Countess Koucheleff Bezborrodke, a lady with whom I had been very intimate in my youth. Home converted me to Spiritualism."

Spiritualism, an essentially American religious movement, held that human personality survives death as a discarnate, who can demonstrate individual survival by communications such as raps and various other materializations. It was necessary, however, for psychically gifted individuals such as Home to act as intermediaries between the two spheres of existence.

Asked the reporter, "Did you ever see any of his levitations?"

"Yes, but give me a light. [Puff, puff.] Thanks. Yes, I have seen him carried out of a four-story window."[39]

Home, born in Scotland but raised in the United States, returned to Europe in 1855 where he became the darling of high society. A tall slim youth of twenty-two with an elegance of bearing and fastidious taste in dress, he was not, strictly speaking, a professional medium because he did not charge fees for his sittings. Yet there were certain gifts from royalty which cannot be refused without boorishness, and Home rapidly became a rich man. Even

*Countess Alexandrine (Sasha) de Kroll

though he possessed considerable talent as a mental medium, Home's most astounding feats, not yet satisfactorily explained, were physical phenomena—partial materialization, psychokinetic effects, bodily elongation and levitation—all demonstrated in full light as contrasted to virtually every other physical medium's requirement for darkness.

Home was able to levitate tables, chairs, and himself. It was nothing for him to drift to the ceiling, leave a pencil mark, and slowly descend to the ground; on one occasion, the entranced Home floated out a bedroom window, hovered seventy feet above the ground, and bobbed back into a drawing-room window. Or so his awed witnesses claimed. Although Robert Browning, attending a séance with Elizabeth, thought Home a charlatan and savagely portrayed him in *Mr. Sludge, the "Medium,"* his wife was greatly impressed, and so was almost everyone else who saw him. Certainly Home was no Mr. Sludge using tacky mediums' tricks. Despite numerous attempts to discover fraud in his mediumship (he was investigated by such distinguished scientists as Sir William Crookes), Home is alone among the principal physical mediums in never having been detected in the use of trickery or devices. His mediumship remains the most impressive instance of physical phenomena on record; skeptics, however, claim mass hypnosis as the explanation. By coincidence, Madame Blavatsky has also been charged with using mass hypnotism to achieve some of her phenomena, so perhaps she owed a greater debt to Home than she wished to admit.

The effete, consumptive Home was personally offended by anyone lacking refinement. At Paris, he did not find the earthy Helena to his taste. "I took no interest in her," he said, and it was "most repulsive to me that in order to attract attention she pretended to be a medium."[40] His harsh assessment is not remarkable, for he was jealous of all other mediums and denounced all psychic phenomena that did not exactly correspond to his own. The real reason for his attacks on H.P.B. was that he believed her coarse and immoral.

Whatever her relationship with Home and the rest of the Spiritualist crowd in Paris, Helena did not find the atmosphere congenial. She remained long enough to pick up the fine points of conducting séances, table-turning, and so forth, and she learned, too, how a medium could parlay a little genuine talent into a fashionable drawing-room attraction. But, as an insider, she noticed that even genuine mediums were not above using a judicious bit of trickery now and again to bolster their feats, and she began to develop a low opinion of them, and of the mediumistic abilities that she herself possessed. She did not like to think of herself as a medium if it meant admitting that discarnate entities could "guide" and speak through her. The idea of being manipulated by anyone, dead or alive, was abhorrent to her, and for that reason alone she always bristled when anyone called her a medium.

By 1858, Helena was twenty-seven; nearly nine years had sped by since she had left Russia and she was experiencing homesickness for her country and family. At least she felt sufficiently nostalgic to write to Nadyezhda Fadeyev and cautiously explore the possibility of returning for a visit. She wondered, too, if there would be trouble from Nikifor Blavatsky, who might try to reclaim her as his legal wife.

Changes had taken place in Russia since her departure. Czar Nicholas had died after suddenly contracting influenza from Count Paul Kiselev, the husband of Helena's old traveling companion. Everybody was talking about Czar Alexander's plan to liberate the serfs, but nobody seriously believed that such an epochal event would come to pass. Much had changed, too, within Helena's family. The year after she had left, her father's second wife died, leaving him with an infant daughter, Liza, and that same year Peter von Hahn had retrieved his two children from the Fadeyevs. Eleven-year-old Leonid had been placed in a St. Petersburg school; negotiations were begun for Vera, then sixteen, to eventually marry a son of General Nikolay de Yahontov.

Vera would later say that she had completely lost track of Helena and believed her dead.[41] Possibly what she actually meant was that the Fadeyevs counted Helena as one who is dead, just as any respectable family at that time would have shied away from acknowledging their relationship with a notorious black sheep. Nobody, however, believed for a moment that Helena had died, not with the letters from Metrovitch, the unpleasant tales carried home by the Kiselevs and Bagrations, the newspaper clippings sent by Russian friends traveling abroad (or possibly by H.P.B. herself) about her musical activities. No, they did not think her dead, but on the other hand they never expected her to have the nerve to come back.

Sometime during the summer or early autumn of 1858, Helena parted from Metrovitch and traveled to Russian territory, but the city in which she temporarily halted is unknown. Apprehensive, unsure of what sort of welcome she might expect from her family, she turned to Nadyezhda for help in smoothing the way. In October, Nadyezhda wrote to Nikifor at Erivan, informing him of his wife's return and asking him not to bother Helena. In a stoic, rather bitter response of November 13 (Old Style), he wrote that Helena "ceased to interest me long ago. Time smooths out everything, even every memory."[42]

He had no intention of causing unpleasantness for his wife:

You may assure H.P. on my word of honor that I will never pursue her. I wish ardently that our marriage be annulled, and that she may marry again. It is possible that I too may marry again, from calculation or inclination, feeling myself not yet unsuited to family life. So make every effort, by exerting your forces, and let her also do her best to annul the marriage. I did my best, but Exarch Isador refused to do it. Therefore I do not intend to start a new lawsuit any more, or even to obtain the divorce by applying to the Emperor.

Repeating that he would not contact Helena, or make inquiries as to her whereabouts, he went on to call his marriage "a misfortune" and for him it no doubt was. Now nearly fifty, he had no wife or family, and after his futile attempts to obtain a divorce, no longer even the hope of either.

One can become accustomed to anything. So I have got used to a joyless life in Erivan. Whatsoever may happen I shall remain unaffected. My plan is to retire entirely from active service. I would then go to my estate, in that hidden corner which nobody knows of, and live there surrounded by the delights of a lonely life.[43]

Nadyezhda had less luck with the Fadeyevs. Andrey absolutely refused to have his granddaughter in Tiflis; in the end, Nadyezhda had to send Helena the address of her sister. In February, Vera's thirty-one-year-old husband had died suddenly, leaving her utterly distraught over the loss of "he who loved me more than anyone on this earth."[44] She had a four-year-old son, Feodor, and an infant, Rostislav, who had been born posthumously. While her late husband had left her some property, temporarily Vera was living with her father-in-law at Pskov, in northwest Russia near the Baltic.

Writing to Vera, Helena announced that she planned to travel after the first of the year, but at the last minute, perhaps reluctant to spend the holidays alone, she moved up her schedule by several weeks and turned up at Pskov on Christmas Day.

III

~~~~~~~~~~

Yuri

Aside from Christmas, the Yahontovs were celebrating the marriage of their daughter that evening. There was a stream of guests and even though the wedding banquet had begun, the doorbell continued to ring every few minutes. Just as the bridegroom's best man rose, champagne glass in hand, to begin the ritual toasts, the bell was heard again. Something about the impatience of the last ring must have alerted Vera for, despite the many servants and to the astonishment of the guests, she jumped up from the table and rushed to open the door. "Overcome with joy," Vera forgot the wedding and took Helena to her room. Almost immediately unusual happenings began to occur for, Vera recalled, "that very evening I was convinced that my sister had acquired strange powers." (See Appendix A.) To be sure, she had always associated strangeness with Helena but now the happenings were so startling, so flamboyant, that they could not be easily dismissed. Awake or asleep, her sister "was constantly surrounded with mysterious movements, strange sounds." Distinct little taps came from the furniture, windowpanes, floors and walls, and it did not take Vera long to discover that the knocks possessed an intelligence of their own. When asked a question, "they tapped three times for 'yes,' twice for 'no.' "[45]

Successfully upstaging the bridal couple, Helena quickly became the center of attention with her rappings and poltergeist effects. Now, as later, H.P.B. would bolster temporary insecurities by overwhelming people with phenomena, an attention-getting device that usually worked well. On this occasion, however, it was not the Yahontovs that she wished to impress but Peter von Hahn, who was attending the wedding with her brother Leonid and half-sister Liza.

During the next few weeks the drawing room of Vera's prominent in-laws was full of visitors, playing cards or singing around the piano, but most of the guests surrounded Helena Petrovna, who sat quietly in an armchair with her embroidery. Even in provincial Russia, people had heard about Spiritualism, and while there had been reports of mediums in St. Petersburg, none had penetrated so far as Pskov. Certainly nobody had ever actually heard the rappings of a so-called spirit, and for this reason Helena became an overnight sensation.

To Helena's disappointment, her most enthusiastic detractors were her father and brother. Peter von Hahn, perhaps remembering Tekla Lebendorff, would have nothing to do with the rapping sessions, remarking that such nonsense was beneath the concern of serious people. Leonid, now eighteen, and a law student at the University of Dorpat, proclaimed himself a believer "in no one and nothing." One evening, when Helena was describing how mediums could make light objects become so heavy they could not be lifted, Leonid hovered behind his sister's chair. "And you mean to say that you can do it?" he demanded.

Helena's answer was guarded. "I have done it occasionally, though I cannot always answer for its success."

When the guests pressed her to try, she agreed, but warned that she promised nothing. A three-legged table was positioned in the center of the room. Helena fixed it with an intense stare and then, still staring, she motioned one of the young men present to remove it. Even though he seized it with both hands, the table could not be moved and finally he gave up.

Suspecting collusion, Leonid approached the table; he tugged, he kicked, he shook until the wood began to splinter. But the table refused to budge. "How strange," was his only concession.

Finally, Helena asked him to try again. Leonid gave a tremendous pull, this time almost dislocating his arm because the table was light as a feather. Years later, H.P.B. explained the feat, saying that it could be produced by the exercise of her own will directing the magnetic currents, or by the aid of unseen beings from Tibet, but she did not specify which method she had used at Pskov. (It should be noted that similar phenomena have been performed by hypnotists who have good subjects.)

While Leonid had been grudgingly won over, Helena wanted badly to impress her father. Winning his respect was important to her but nothing seemed to work, not her thought-reading, not her Latin prescriptions for the treatment of various diseases, not even the excitement when Liza's governess, Leontine, wanted to know what had happened to a young man who had jilted her, and she found the answer in a letter locked inside a trunk in her room. Von Hahn ignored all of it. Secretly, Helena could not blame him because she, too, had little respect for mediums. When anyone at the Yahontovs was indiscreet enough to call her one, she indignantly denied it, declaring that she was a mediator between mortals and beings they knew nothing about. "But I could never understand the difference,"[46] confessed Vera, and neither could anyone else.

Meanwhile, Vera was in the midst of organizing her affairs and trying to adjust to widowhood. Her late husband, shortly before his death, had purchased a village of a hundred serfs at Rougodevo, in the Province of Pskov. The place had been bought sight unseen through an agent. There was, however, a sizable mansion on the property and Vera proposed to settle there with her sons, her father and half-sister Liza. Now, of course, Helena Petrovna was invited to join the ménage. Before settling in their new home, they spent a few weeks in St. Petersburg where Peter von Hahn had business to look after.

Their first weeks in the capital, at the Hôtel de Paris, were lived at a highly accelerated pace. In the mornings von Hahn was occupied with his business affairs; in the afternoons and evenings everyone made and received social calls. "There was," Vera recalled, "no time for, or even mention of, phenomena," which suggests that Helena had managed to restrain the rapping. This moratorium lasted, however, until the evening when two old friends of her father's came to visit. Having heard about Spiritualism, they were anxious to see something and Helena obliged. The old gentlemen professed amazement at her powers and later they began to castigate von Hahn because, while the rapping and "mind-reading" had been going on, he had been engrossed in his game of patience. "Old women's superstition," he barked. Nonetheless, his friends convinced him to participate in an experiment. He must go into the next room, write a message on paper, and place it in his pocket. Then they would see whether Helena's spirits could spell out the message.

In hopes of proving his friends wrong, von Hahn did as requested and then returned to his cards. "What shall you say, old friend," asked one of his cronies, "if the word written by you is correctly repeated? Will you not feel compelled to believe in such a case?"

If that happened, von Hahn replied scathingly, "you may prepare to offer me as an inmate of a lunatic asylum."

The raps produced only one word, *Zaitchik,* but that word, Vera reported, left her father trembling. Showing them the paper, he read, "What was the name of my favourite war-horse which I rode during my first Turkish Campaign?" and below, in parenthesis, he had written Zaitchik.[47] As a consequence, von Hahn did a complete about-face and after that he "became passionately fond of experimenting with his daughter's powers. Once he inquired of the date of a certain event in his family that had occurred several hundred years before. He received it. From that time he set himself and Madame Blavatsky the difficult task of restoring the family chronology."[48] The entire genealogical tree of the counts of Rotternstern and the Hahn-Hahn family had to be traced back to the first crusade, a task which occupied his attention until finally in the early summer they departed for Rougodevo, 132 miles from St. Petersburg.

The days when the gentry could buy a village with its inhabitants was quickly running out, but in the summer of 1859, Vera and her family were still able to live in feudal style. The imposing country house, surrounded by lakes and pine forests, offered a sweeping view of the countryside for 20 miles around. A suite of rooms on the ground floor was given to von Hahn, while the rest of them occupied the ten large rooms on the first floor, and the servants lived at the back. The second or third evening after their arrival, Vera and Helena were strolling through the flower gardens at the front of the house. Helena kept smiling furtively through the windows into some empty rooms and finally told Vera that she could see people inside: a long-haired German student in a velvet blouse, a fat old woman in a frilled cap, an old man with extraordinarily long nails that looked like claws.

Vera, unamused, began to shriek aloud about the Devil and when Helena said they were only lingering reflections of those who had once inhabited the rooms, she was not a bit comforted and worried about the spirits loitering in the children's rooms. Helena suggested that she send for two old serfs and give them a description of the ghosts. As it turned out, the peasants knew exactly who was meant and assured their mistress that a German student from Göttingen and a fat housekeeper had once lived there. The man with the long nails was their former master, who had contracted a skin disease in Lithuania and could not cut his nails without bleeding to death.

That matter taken care of, the household settled down to normal, if any house in which H.P.B. lived could be termed normal. "All the persons living on the premises," recalled Vera, "saw constantly, even in full noonday, vague human shadows walking about the rooms, appearing in the gardens, in the flower beds in front of the house, and near the old chapel."[49] More mysteriously, Mademoiselle Leontine discovered in her locked drawers letters containing family secrets known only to herself. Evidently Helena was having a busy time because hardly a day passed without some unexplained event: a locked piano hammering out a march, lamps suddenly extinguished as though a gale wind had blown through the house, objects ripping through the air, sofas and tables performing somersaults. Traditionally, these acoustical and kinetic effects have been attributed to a noisy, boisterous spirit called a poltergeist; today, however, they are termed Recurrent Spontaneous Psychokinesis or RSPK by parapsychologists who theorize that in certain unstable persons, or places, intense reservoirs of energy dam up. When, or if, these reserves are released, energy is transmitted from the psychical to the physical plane.

It is difficult, as usual, to pin down Madame Blavatsky's own views on these manifestations. According to Vera, Helena made a distinction between two kinds of invisible entities: brainless elementals, the shells of departed beings whom she mockingly referred to as spooks; and superhuman men with whom she was in constant communication and who visited her in their astral bodies. But whether she actually made this distinction at Rougodevo in 1859 is doubtful, since she evolved her theories gradually and in a piecemeal fashion. Moreover, H.P.B. translated Vera's recollections of this period and she did not hesitate to correct and revise the material as she went along, claiming that Vera did not know what she was talking about.

Poltergeists aside, daily life at Rougodevo was generally quiet, perhaps too quiet for a restless person like H.P.B. She spent her time reading and studying, and working with her father on the family genealogy. After supper the family would gather around the dining table and read aloud, Helena chain-smoking cigarettes, her father puffing on cigars or a long Turkish pipe. Occasionally one of these soporific evenings would be interrupted by author-spirits who obligingly made additional comments on the text being read. One night Alexander Pushkin appeared to recite a very bad poem and generally to make a fool of himself.

One afternoon when the local superintendent of police came to the house to investigate the murder of a man in a gin shop, von Hahn suggested that Helena might help locate the murderer. The name Samoylo Ivanof was rapped out, plus a few details about the criminal and his current hiding place. As a result, the man was eventually arrested. Unfortunately, the St. Petersburg police questioned Madame Blavatsky's sources of information, and it took von Hahn quite a while to convince them his daughter had had no part in the crime.

A year dragged by and toward the spring of 1860, Helena fell ill. As with all her illnesses, the nature of this one remains unclear. Below her heart the wound from Constantinople occasionally reopened, bringing on intense agony, convulsions and a deathlike trance for three or four days. Possibly this wound had not resulted from the riding accident, for H.P.B., as we shall see, gave various explanations at different times. A doctor was sent for, but when he stepped into Helena's room, he was attacked by a bombardment of poltergeist noises, which terrorized him into complete uselessness. Without his aid, Helena's wound healed as suddenly as it had reopened.

"The quiet life of the sisters at Rougodevo," Vera wrote, "was brought to an end by a terrible illness which befell Mme. Blavatsky."[50] It was also ended by the news that Princess Helena Pavlovna Fadeyev was dying. Even before H.P.B. had left Russia, her grandmother had been partially paralyzed, but her brain was still active at seventy-one. She taught religion and reading to Katherine Witte's three sons, and the youngest, Sergei, recalls that "as she could not move, I would kneel by her with a primer in my hands."[51]

Helena had not seen her grandmother for eleven years, and it had been almost that long since Vera had left Tiflis; both of them wanted to return, and under the circumstances, Andrey Fadeyev could hardly refuse Helena the wish to see her grandmother one last time. The two women left Rougodevo in the spring, journeying first to Moscow, then embarking on a grueling three-week trip to Tiflis in a coach with post-horses. At one of the stations where they stopped to change horses, a surly stationmaster declared that he would have no fresh ones for several hours. Worse yet, they would have to wait outside, for the travelers' waiting room was locked.

"Well, this is fine!" Helena fumed. Flattening her face against the window, she exclaimed, "Aha! That's what it is. Very well, then, and now I can force the drunken brute to give us horses in five minutes."

Ten minutes later, Vera remembered, the stationmaster led up three strong post-horses and politely waved them on their way. The next day Helena revealed that she had told the man of seeing in the waiting room the ghost of his dead wife, who would remain there until he had given the sisters fresh horses.[52]

In certain situations, Vera realized, Helena's mediumistic talents could come in handy, but that was not the case at Zadonsk, a shrine in cossack country, where they paused to rest a few days. Naturally Vera was eager to hear mass in the church, while Helena was not, until she learned that services were to be conducted by Isadore, the Metropolitan of Kiev. During their childhood, when Isadore had been Exarch of Georgia, he had frequently dined at the Fadeyevs, and after services, they sent him a note asking for an audience. On the way to the Archbishop's residence, Vera warned Helena to "please take care that your little devils keep themselves quiet while we are with the Metropolitan."[53]

Helena laughed and promised to try, but reminded her sister that she could not control the poltergeists. So Vera "was not astonished, but all the same suffered agonies when I heard the tapping begin as soon as the venerable old man began to question my sister about her travels. One! Two! One! Two! Three!" The chandelier began to swing, their teacups rattled, even the Metropolitan's amber rosary beads were jumping. Vera was both horribly embarrassed and annoyed because "my irreverent sister's embarrassment was tempered with a greater expression of fun than I would have wished for." When Isadore asked which of them was the medium, Vera "hastened to fit the cap on my sister's head."

Isadore spent an hour with them, asking questions about Spiritualism. While he certainly recalled the von Hahn sisters from his days in Tiflis, he had an even better reason to be interested in Helena Petrovna. For years Nikifor Blavatsky had been pestering him to grant a divorce, which he had refused. Now he did not allow the opportunity to pass without mentioning Madame Blavatsky's irregular marital status. What he probably did was advise her to return to her husband, although Vera, all discretion, only mentions Isadore admonishing H.P.B. to use her gifts wisely and dismissing the two of them with a blessing.

Princess Helena died on August 24. Shortly after, Vera must have returned to Rougodevo, but Helena remained behind in Tiflis. The reason was not at all owing to Andrey Fadeyev's sudden amicability toward his granddaughter, but rather to the fact that it had become impossible for Helena to share her sister's life. Probably during their visit to St. Petersburg, Vera had met Vladimir Ivanovich Zhelihovsky, a first cousin on the von Hahn side. Being a practical young woman of twenty-six with two small children, she decided to marry him. Obviously Helena could not tag along; she might have returned to her father and stepsister, but this prospect must have seemed dull compared to life in Tiflis, where young bluebloods from Moscow and St. Petersburg were suddenly flocking in pursuit of pleasure and adventure.

It was during the summer of 1860 that Helena became acquainted with her first cousin, Sergei Yulyevich Witte, and vice versa. Katherine's third son, an infant when she left Russia, was now twelve years old and Andrey Fadeyev's pet. A great future lay in store for Sergei, because, as Minister of Finance under Alexander III and Nicholas II, he would become the chief architect of Russia's industrial revolution, the man who changed the face of the empire and brought her to the threshold of the twentieth century. Count Witte was not a particularly lovable person; he was said to be cold, boastful, treacherous and capable of extreme pettiness. On the more attractive side, however, the statesman shared with H.P.B. many of the Fadeyev-Dolgorukov traits. Both of them were gifted with brilliant intellects, stupendous energy, and visions that they believed would transform society. Both had their passions and romantic dreams; both, alas, were unstable at times.

Writing his memoirs in 1911, at the age of sixty-two, Count Witte had little that was flattering to say of his kinswoman, but it is curious all the same that he devotes a major portion of the chapter on his childhood to Helena Petrovna. In an otherwise uneventful boyhood, she must have stood out as the most exciting figure he had encountered up to that point, and he could not, evidently, resist telling what he knew of her, both personal and hearsay. His account, enraging to H.P.B.'s followers, is, nevertheless, exactly what he said it was—"stories current in our family," "family tradition"—and as such too valuable to disregard. True, he did not know her intimately, true also that he had some facts wrong about her later career, but he was privy to the same information as the rest of the Fadeyevs and Wittes. No doubt Nadyezhda and Vera, had they been more candid, could have told similar stories; for that matter, Vera, speaking privately to friends, would be far more vicious than Sergei.

Helena, at the age of twenty-nine, was in the eyes of her pubescent cousin a great disappointment, despite the wild tales he had heard about her amatory adventures. Expecting some glamorous courtesan, he found her fat, frumpy,

> a ruin of her former self. Her face, apparently once of great beauty, bore all the traces of a tempestuous and passionate life, and her form was marred by an early obesity. Besides, she paid but scant attention to her appearance and preferred loose morning dresses to elaborate apparel. But her eyes were extraordinary. She had enormous, azure colored eyes, and when she spoke with animation, they sparkled in a fashion which is altogether indescribable. Never in my life have I seen anything like that pair of eyes.

As Witte recalled the sequence of events, Helena won their grandfather's permission to remain in Tiflis by promising "to go back to her legitimate husband."[54] Nikifor Blavatsky, faithful to his word, had not attempted to contact Helena and was currently in Berlin seeking medical treatment for an unidentified ailment. By November, however, he had suddenly resigned his post in Erivan and returned to Tiflis where he got a job as an attaché to the viceroy, and he moved into a house. Presumably he made this drastic downward career change for a good reason, about which H.P.B. was explicit. "Blavatsky and I were reconciled and I lived for one year in the same house as he; but I lacked the patience to live with such a fool and I again went away."[55]

What H.P.B. surrendered by returning to Nikifor provides some measure of her desperation. Generally able to land on her feet, she found herself at Tiflis in the humiliating position of having no means of support. Bending to her grandfather's will for survival, she seethed with the resentments that would provoke her to indiscretion during the coming year. Blavatsky remained to her "a fool" who taxed her patience to the limits, and he himself must have soon realized that his sacrifice of job and home in Erivan were all for nothing. Helena may have agreed to live with Nikifor, but one gets the impression that she spent precious little of her time in his company. Most evenings she could be found at the Fadeyev mansion where the importance of the older generation was inevitably giving way to the younger. The Princess was gone, her herbarium had been donated to the University of St. Petersburg, her collection of antiquities and artifacts bequeathed to Nadyezhda. At seventy-one, Andrey Fadeyev was serving as a member of the viceroy's Board of the Caucasus, but he had begun to feel his age, physically and mentally. As befitted an eminent civil servant with a fifty-year career behind him, he began to compose the obligatory memoirs. By the time Helena appeared on the scene, it was Nadyezhda and Rostislav, both unmarried, who did the entertaining and upheld the Fadeyev reputation as being one of the most socially sought-after salons in the city.

After a faltering beginning, Rostislav had resumed his military career and had gone on to distinguish himself during the conquest of the Caucasus and the Turkish wars. Now a colonel, he had been appointed an aide to the viceroy and was also writing a history, *Sixty Years of the Caucasian War*. And Nadyezhda, too, had not been idle. In her private apartment in the mansion, she had established a remarkable museum: arms and weapons from all over the world, ancient crockery, Chinese and Japanese idols, Byzantine mosaics, Persian carpets, not to mention statues, paintings, petrified fossils and a library of rare books. Both Nadyezhda and Rostislav cherished Helena and welcomed her back, allowing her to do as she pleased even when it meant going against their father's wishes.

"Every evening," remembered Sergei Witte, "the Tiflis society folks would foregather in our house around Yelena Petrovna," and the reason of course was that everybody wanted to attend a séance. In the 1860s, Russian intellectuals were just beginning to interest themselves in the paranormal and, even though the waves of Spiritualism that had spread over western Europe would not strike them until a decade hence, still they were fascinated by such phenomena. Helena's séances, wrote Witte,

> would last the whole evening and oftentimes the whole night. My cousin did not confine the demonstrations of her power to table rapping, evocation of spirits and similar mediumistic hocus-pocus. On one occasion she caused a closed piano in an adjacent room to emit sounds as if invisible hands were playing upon it. This was done in my presence, at the insistence of one of the guests.

His boyhood attitude toward these performances he describes as "decidedly critical."[56]

All knowledge of the séances was kept from Andrey. Each night, at precisely fifteen minutes before eleven, he would say goodnight to the assemblage, one of whom retained a memory of the old man "brushing along the parquets with his warmly muffled-up feet."[57] Once Andrey had retired, the servants would rush in silently with supper trays and close the doors of the drawing room to signal the animated talk to begin.

At the Fadeyevs, as elsewhere in the 1860s, intellectual aristocrats chewed over deep philosophical and political issues as enthusiastically as they downed kvass and tea. Although the emancipation of fifty-two million serfs was only a few months away, these men much preferred to ruminate over the meaning of history, art and life itself. They meditated as well upon Russia's cultural separateness and special political destiny, and these meditations would come to be the Pan-Slavism of which Rostislav Fadeyev was a leading advocate.

An odd mixture of types participated in the discussions in the Fadeyev drawing room; sunburned officers from the Caucasus battlefields, Freemasons, attachés and generals, foreign visitors, and the intellectual counts and princes who had never found an adequate profession. Once Helena Petrovna made her entrance,

> the conversation would be sure to turn suddenly upon the mystic subjects and she herself commence to "evoke spirits." And then the tall candles would begin to burn low, hardly flickering toward the end, the human figures on the Gobelin tapestry would seem to awaken and move, and each of us feel queer from an involuntary creeping sensation; and this generally lasted until the eastern portion of the sky began itself to pale, on the dark face of the southern night.[58]

In the darkened room, along with a good sampling of the smart set, was a handsome young baron from Estonia who found Helena absolutely delightful. Nicholas Meyendorff was an enthusiastic Spiritualist and, as it happened, a close friend of D. D. Home, who had recently married a wealthy Russian woman and settled in Russia. So intimate had the two men become, that Home regarded Meyendorff as a brother; therefore, it was natural for Meyendorff, when he became Helena's lover, to confide the details of the affair to his friend. Probably this was owing less to lack of chivalry than to the fact that Helena was in the habit of bragging about her connection with Home. In response, Home wrote a blistering condemnation and warned Meyendorff against having anything to do with her. However, Home reported regretfully, "he did not follow my advice."[59] Later, full of malice, Meyendorff would tell people that H.P.B. had some mediumistic abilities, but that she cheated. At the time of their liaison, however, he was so much in love with her that he insisted she divorce Blavatsky in order to marry him, or so Helena claimed.[60]

The affair with Meyendorff, a meaningless alliance at best, must have presented a few problems for Helena because she was living in Nikifor Blavatsky's home, but if the logistics of living with one man and sleeping with another were not unsettling enough, matters were complicated further by the unexpected arrival of Agardi Metrovitch. Sergei Witte claimed that "one fine morning she was accosted in the street" by her former companion, who "apparently had no doubts as to his rights to my cousin, and did not hesitate to assert his claims."[61] He could not have asserted them too vigorously, because Helena continued to live with Blavatsky, at least for a time, but Witte may have been euphemistically referring to a resumption of their sexual relationship.

That Metrovitch visited Tiflis we know from H.P.B. herself. She wrote to Alfred Sinnett in 1886 that her family "knew him well and he was friends with my cousins Witte."[62] She insisted, however, that he had come there with his wife, also a singer, and the pen drawing of him in *Faust* shows him whispering seductions into the ear of a praying Marguerite. Under this drawing, there is a penciled caption: "Teresina Sigñora Metrovitch (Faust)."[63] H.P.B. could never keep straight her stories about Metrovitch's having a wife, because elsewhere she referred to the woman as Nathalie. Most likely the picture was of a singer in the Tiflis opera company, the caption added at a much later date when Helena was determined to thwart "the slanderous and venomous mad-dogs who poke their noses under cover of the night into every family's and every individual's private lives."[64]

Metrovitch, almost sixty in 1861, was declining both artistically and otherwise, and his pursuit of Helena was due to economic as much as emotional needs. He had wrangled an engagement with the Italian opera of Tiflis, undoubtedly a bit of a comedown since the city's opera company was less than ten years old and scarcely on a par with even the worst of European companies, but he also wanted Helena back. For a short period she was able to juggle (one wonders how) her husband, her former lover, and her current lover, until she was struck by a catastrophe of major proportions. She found herself pregnant.

This type of ghastly accident was, of course, the nightmarish hazard for any Victorian woman reckless enough to indulge in premarital or extramarital sex. If marriage was out of the question, the most common solution was to find some secluded spot where nobody knew her, give birth secretly, and then discreetly arrange for adoption. With few exceptions did a woman think of openly bearing an illegitimate child and raising it as her own. Perhaps H.P.B. might have, for she had less regard for the proprieties than most women, but the social position of the Fadeyevs precluded any such avant-garde flaunting of one's individuality. Indeed, the pregnancy posed a major scandal not only for the Fadeyevs and Wittes, but also for Nikifor Blavatsky, who was obviously not the father, and for Nicholas Meyendorff, whom Helena bluntly claimed was. Meyendorff, denying paternity, asserted that Agardi Metrovitch was responsible. In short, the situation rapidly disintegrated into a complete mess, with accusations and counter-accusations, wringing of hands and general consternation for all parties concerned.

When the pregnancy could be hidden by neither hoopskirts nor the baggy getups Helena favored, she left Tiflis for the Province of Mingrelia where running into people she knew would be unlikely. The region was covered with dense primeval forests of beeches, oaks, chestnuts and cherry trees, whose branches were festooned with bunches of wild red grapes, sour and inedible. There were no roads, only trails for horses, and it was possible to travel all day without seeing a village. Here and there, where the forest had been cleared, one might come upon an isolated log house surrounded by a few acres of millet and maize. The single-room dwellings had two doors, but no windows or chimney, and furniture was rare. Even the palace of the ruling prince boasted only a few badly made tables and chairs.[65]

Along the major trails, at intervals of ten to twelve miles, there were military posts manned by cossack soldiers. While invariably the men had samovars, their diet was a frugal one limited to what they could raise, in addition to eggs, milk and a poor quality wheat bread. It was to the settlement at Ozurgety that Helena retired for her accouchement and bought a house. Unlike other posts, Ozurgety had in residence an army surgeon, undoubtedly the reason she chose it for her confinement. Even though she had four servants to care for her and a monthly allowance from Nikifor Blavatsky, she felt miserably alone. More disturbing, the privacy she expected was not forthcoming, since word of her presence spread quickly. "Public opinion," wrote Vera, "became furious, and society . . . made an open levee of arms against one of its own members who dared to defy its time-hallowed laws, and act as no *respectable* person would. The whole country was talking of her."[66] The outraged Mingrelians objected to Helena, her sister claimed, because she preferred the peasants and their smoky huts to the "brilliant drawing rooms"[67] of the nobility. Since drawing rooms, brilliant or otherwise, did not exist in Mingrelia, this account is fanciful, to say the least. The real objection, one surmises, was her sister's pregnancy.

Disgraced and banished, a pariah not only in Tiflis but also among the crude Mingrelians, Helena grew increasingly depressed. Her cries for help and understanding were ignored because when she wrote to Katherine Witte for additional money, she received a cutting reply: "One could believe that you have not a kopeck, like other poor people. And one would be very much surprised learning that you receive one hundred roubles every month. Because I am *quite sure* you are receiving them, with the exception of one of the winter months when Blavatsky did not get his salary either."[68]

The exact date of Yuri's birth is unknown. Since there exists a passport, dated August 23 (Old Style), 1862, and designating him as an infant, he must have been born in 1862, or possibly in late 1861. The infant was deformed, owing either to a birth defect or the clumsy obstetrical handling of an army physician unaccustomed to delivering babies; the exact nature of the handicap is not clear, but H.P.B. referred to him as "that poor cripple child" and relatives of Meyendorff explained that he had a hunchback.[69] Helena reacted with a breakdown in which she seems to have disseverred herself from the corporeal world.

Whenever I was called by name, I opened my eyes upon hearing it, and was myself, my own personality in every particular. As soon as I was left alone, however, I relapsed into my usual, half-dreamy condition, and became *somebody else.*[70]

Refusing to eat, she soon "was reduced to a living skeleton." Fevers were prevalent in Mingrelia, particularly among those unaccustomed to the climate, but Helena later insisted that she had not been delirious.

* * *

When awake and *myself*, I remembered well *who I was* in my second capacity, and what I had been and was doing. When *somebody else*, i.e., the personage I had become, I know I had no idea of who was H. P. Blavatsky! I was in another far-off country, a totally different individuality from myself, and had no connection at all with my actual life.[71]

Probably a cluster of factors contributed to her dissociative state: a difficult birth or postpartum complications, the shock of bearing a deformed child, and her normal tendency to escape pain by withdrawing into an alternate reality. By putting these elements together, one can perhaps make a more educated guess about her debilitated condition than, for instance, Vera who described it to Alfred Sinnett as "one of those mysterious nervous diseases that baffle science," or even than Madame Blavatsky herself, who said that she began "to lead a double life" at Mingrelia.[72] Both of them, understandably, avoided any reference to the tragedy of Yuri as having played a role in H.P.B.'s collapse.

The doctor at Ozurgety, feeling unqualified to deal with the situation, "packed her off to Tiflis. Unable to go on horseback, owing to her great weakness, and a journey in a cart being deemed dangerous, she was sent off in a large native boat along the river."[73] During the four-day journey to Kutais, down a narrow, barely navigable river, Helena began to hallucinate. She had the sensation that she had somehow seeped out of her physical body, which she left at the bottom of the boat, while she glided across the water into the forest. At Kutais, three of the servants disappeared; only the butler remained with Yuri and her until the carriage and escort dispatched by the Fadeyevs showed up to collect them. By the time they reached Tiflis, she had to be carried into the house more dead than alive.

In the calming atmosphere of her aunt's apartment, nursed by Nadyezhda and Rostislav, Helena's psychic and physical health began gradually to return. She would lie on the sofa while Nadyezhda sat near by, writing. Once, opening her eyes, she saw Rostislav "bending over me with so much sadness and pity in his face that I jumped to my feet and actually burst into tears."[74] The time was approaching when she had to make decisions about herself and the child: where they would live and, more important, how. Whether at H.P.B.'s request or for other reasons, Agardi Metrovitch had returned to Europe. As for Nikifor, he had done more than his duty by sending her money in Mingrelia and even afterward he continued to show compassion for her plight. Sometime during the summer of 1862 he filed a petition for the previously mentioned passport, which enabled Madame Blavatsky "accompanied by their infant ward Yury,"[75] to visit the provinces of Tauris, Cherson and Pskov. The curious wording of the petition was meant to give the illegitimate child some semilegal status, short of adoption.

In fact, it did no such thing. No one, including Helena herself, really tried to palm off Yuri as someone else's child. And yet, later on, she would insist that she had never borne a child, since she was incapable of either sexual relations or reproduction owing to "a congenital crookedness of the uterus." As if that were not frightful enough, "I am lacking something and the place is filled up with some crooked cucumber."[76] Yuri, she declared, was the illegitimate son of Nicholas Meyendorff and a friend of hers: H.P.B. adopted the child to protect her friend's reputation. Her explanations were so mind-boggling that Sinnett got smothered in their tricky turns and twists and ended by not mentioning Yuri at all.

In the meantime, Helena was facing up to reality. Her baby, not only deformed but suffering poor health in general, required more medical attention than a normal child. Thinking about his welfare, as well as her own, she asked Meyendorff for financial support. After consulting with his brothers, he again protested that he was not the father,[77] but in the end he agreed to pay. Whether he ever saw Yuri is impossible to say, but, according to his sister-in-law's report, H.P.B. sent him photographs of herself with the baby.[78]

There is no doubt that she loved the crippled child who, by some terrible irony, resembled the little hunchback invisible that she had played with in her own childhood at Saratov. Yuri was "the only being who made life worth living, a being whom I loved according to the phraseology of Hamlet as 'forty thousand fathers and brothers will never love their children and sisters.' "[79] The boy brought out in her the deep compassion that she reserved for those suffering from any kind of disadvantage, those who for one reason or another could not protect themselves.

She might have hidden Yuri, but she did not. In 1862 or '63, using the passport that Nikifor had obtained for her, she took Yuri to visit her father, who was then living in the Province of Pskov. She told him that Yuri had been adopted but von Hahn was nobody's fool and "even my own father suspected me." There must have been agitating scenes about Yuri's true paternity, because finally Helena felt compelled to consult two Pskov physicians, professors Bodkin and Pirogoff, who obligingly provided her with a certificate affirming her inability to bear a child. "Had it not been for the doctors' certificate [father] would never have forgiven me, perhaps. After, he loved and pitied that poor cripple child."[80] Perhaps she went through this farce more for Yuri's sake than her own. As much as she valued her father's goodwill, she had done without it before and might have done so now. What she could not endure was that anyone should bear ill will toward her son.

It is a pity that Victorian morals forced her to tell so many lies about Yuri. In spite of her frenzied denials, in spite of her protests that she "never bore a weazel [*sic*],"[81] she was, nonetheless, a mother and an exceedingly good one, adoring her child and making her life subservient to his. She had never found in the love of a man that ecstasy of happiness that lifts one out of one's self. She later would say, referring presumably to Metrovitch, "I loved one man deeply but still more I loved occult science,"[82] but the one she loved "more than anyone else in all the world," or anything, was Yuri. He was frequently ill and, even when well, needed constant attendance. What this responsibility did was force her to focus outwardly instead of habitually retreating into trances, and now she began a struggle to overcome "every trance of mediumship *outside her will*, or beyond her direct control." This transformation did not take place overnight, however, and it was not until several years later that she would be able to write Vera, "Now I shall never be subjected to external influences."[83]

During this period, no more is heard of poltergeists or high-gloss society séances. After returning from Pskov, she settled in Tiflis, living quietly with Rostislav, who, still unmarried, had his own residence. It was a domestic, stable interlude unlike any she had experienced before or would afterward, one limited mainly to "Yuourotita," Rostislav and Nadyezhda. Nikifor Blavatsky continued to live in Tiflis but in December, 1864, he resigned his position and retired to a small estate he owned in the Province of Poltava. It is doubtful, however, that H.P.B. had anything to do with him before his departure.

In 1864 or '65, she and Yuri joined Agardi Metrovitch in Italy. How or why this came about is impossible to reconstruct. She was never content, to remain in one place long, and perhaps she merely needed a change of scenery; perhaps Metrovitch had been seeking a reconciliation for some time, for despite lengthy separations and her flings with other men, there remained a strong bond between them.

Metrovitch's life, now as before, was composed of steamers, trains and coaches, of hotels and theaters, of conductors, composers and singers. But unlike the 1850s, his touring was now confined to second-rate companies in third-rate towns of eastern Europe. A glimpse of H.P.B.'s life with him is gleaned from a sort of diary she kept during the winter and spring of 1867 when Metrovitch was touring the Austro-Hungarian Empire. The two-and-a-half by four-inch notebook, purchased at a chemist in Budapest, is hardly a record of travel impressions kept by an ordinary tourist, as some of Helena's biographers would claim. Rather, the notations are those made by a person deeply involved in the music world with its petty jealousies and rivalries, and nearly all the people H.P.B. met or mentions have something to do with music: "Adolf Benedict, Hungarian Jew, pretending to be the foremost baritone of the world" [Karlsburg]; "Philipovich M. Heksh, the hissed baritone" . . . "the last day of the Terreur of *Robespierre*" [Klausenburg]; "Mme. Kirchberger, prima donna and admirable Lucretia. Baritone Malechevsky. Tenor Rossi. German Opera" [Temesvár].

They always sought clean, reasonably priced hotels, but very often they were obliged to settle for "expensive and bad" ones. In Belgrade their accommodations were downright "dirty and disgusting." In Debrecen, which had "the most beautiful theatre in Hungary,"[84] she went to two balls; in Oberstadt, she was delighted when people on the street said a friendly hello without knowing her, but more often the towns were "small, dirty and boring." Much of their time was spent traveling, but she did some sightseeing, and socialized briefly with locals she met at the theaters. Mainly, the life was boring, especially since they had no money to waste. It was often abysmally cold in the coaches and sleazy hotels, and the constant moving about could not have been ideal for a sickly five-year-old. In fact, Yuri's health took a turn for the worse, if not during this tour, then shortly afterward. In the autumn, "I took the poor child to Bologna to see if I could save him." Metrovitch accompanied them,

> doing all he could for me, more than a brother. Then the child died; and as it had no papers, nor documents, and I did not care to give my name in food to the kind gossips, it was he, Metrovitch who undertook all the job, who buried the *aristocratic Baron's* child—*under his, Metrovitch's,* name saying "he did not care," in a small town of Southern Russia in 1867.

Regardless of her very vocal disdain for Russia at times, she had deep roots in her homeland and could not conceive of her son's burial in foreign soil. The macabre journey ended in an unidentified town in the south, probably near Kiev. "After this," she wrote,

> without notifying my relatives of having returned to Russia to bring back the unfortunate little boy whom I did not succeed to bring back alive to the governess chosen for him by the Baron, I simply wrote to the child's father to notify him of this pleasant occurrence for him and returned to Italy with the same passport. Then comes Venice, Florence, Mentana.[85]

At the time she wrote those words, in 1886, she had been saying for a dozen years that she had fought with Giuseppe Garibaldi's army at the battle of Mentana,[86] which had taken place thirteen miles northeast of Rome on November 3, 1867, and claimed that she had been wounded five times: her left arm was broken in two places by a saber stroke, she had a musket bullet embedded in her right shoulder and another in her leg. Finally she had been left for dead in a ditch. The far-fetched story of her mutilation must have been how she experienced Yuri's passing, distorting it into her own symbolic death as a punishment for having denied she had borne him.

Actually, after Yuri's death, she and Metrovitch settled in Kiev where, under Helena's guidance, he learned enough Russian to succeed in such operas as *Life for the Tzar* and *Rusalka*. At that time the most powerful person in town was Prince Alexander Dondoukoff-Korsakoff, Helena's girlhood friend, now governor-general of Kiev. Never shy about requesting favors from influential friends, she asked Alexander to exert his influence on Metro-

vitch's behalf. Sergei Witte insinuates their relationship was more than platonic, but whatever its nature, they soon quarreled over Helena's poems lam-
pooning the Prince which were posted on doors and telegraph posts. As a
result, she and Metrovitch, in the words of her cousin, "had to clear out."[87]
Thirteen years later she wrote to the Prince from Bombay, again to ask a
favor, and begged: "Let us not talk of that dreadful time and I *implore you* to
forget it forever,"[88] reminding him that she had just "lost all that was dear to
me in the world and nearly became insane."

In letters to friends and family, she would allude to her breakdown after
Yuri passed away, mentioning her mental suffering, guilt, and the persistent
sense of having been punished for her sins. In her mind there was no doubt
that she had "covered with shame the heads of . . . the whole family." After
returning home to Tiflis and going to confession and communion, she had
thought that one sin more or less would not matter and "I still continued to
stain my soul." In 1877, confiding to Nadyezhda her rejection of Christianity,
she wrote that the Russian Orthodox god had died for her on the day of Yuri's
death. Even though she had never truly felt at home with Christianity, still
"there were moments when I believed deeply that *sins can be remitted by the
Church,* and that the blood of Christ has redeemed me, together with the
whole race of Adam." And then look what happened. "No! It is bitter and
painful to remember this past. You know at what facts I am hinting."[89] For a
long while Helena could neither accept her son's death nor forgive the God
who had permitted him to perish.

Meanwhile, she and Metrovitch had to live, but his days as a money-earner
seemed at an end. She was faced with the grim necessity of supporting both of
them. But how? By holding séances? By reading cards and telling fortunes?
There were plenty of gypsies who could do it for a few kopecks. Write? It
never occurred to her. Having no one to fall back upon except herself, she
began to hunt for business ventures that might produce ready cash. She later
described the years 1868–1870 as the time when she went to India and finally
to Tibet, where she met Master Koot Hoomi for the first time and lived in the
house of his sister at Shigatse.[90] But there is no documentation of such a trip,
and from Sergei Witte's memoirs it appears that what happened was, in truth,
very different.

By 1869 the Fadeyev and Witte families had shrunk; Andrey Fadeyev had
died and so had Yuli Witte, and with them had disappeared the opulent mode
of life in which Helena had grown up. After the Emancipation, Andrey had
kept his eighty-four domestic serfs by paying them wages, something he could
not really afford, and he had also invested heavily in the Caucasian oil and
mineral deposits that would enrich future generations but not his own. At his
death, the estate was in ruins; Witte, of course, had never been anything but a
salaried civil servant. Katherine Witte and Nadyezhda Fadeyev pooled their
assets and moved to Odessa, where they enrolled Sergei and Boris in the
university. Helena and Agardi, who soon joined them, appeared to Sergei

Witte's twenty-year-old eyes "a rather sorry sight, he a toothless lion, perennially at the feet of his mistress, an aged lady, stout and slovenly."[91] There was no question that they were in exceedingly poor financial straits. Helena (and Agardi as well one supposes) would come to her aunts' house for dinner, then spend the evening quarreling with Katherine about religion.

Helena's insecurity is evident from the haphazard way in which she went about trying to earn a living; she would start one thing, then drop it when something better came along. First she somehow came upon a cheap process for manufacturing ink and opened a retail shop to distribute her product. From there she jumped to making and selling artificial flowers, and still later she imported various woods from Mingrelia. According to Vera, all of these short-lived commercial enterprises were great successes. Sergei Witte remembered them as "dismal failures."[92] Witte's account rings somewhat truer, if only because the difficulties facing any woman who tried to engage in trade were virtually insurmountable. In the summer of 1871, Helena suddenly abandoned business. Agardi, still trying to make a comeback, had succeeded in obtaining an engagement with the Italian opera of Cairo, and the two of them hurriedly left for Egypt.

IV

~~~~~~~~~~~~~~

Russia for the Last Time

The SS *Eumonia,* bound for Alexandria, carried four hundred passengers and a cargo of gunpowder and fireworks. On July 4, 1871, in the Gulf of Nauplia just off the island of Spetsai, the ship's powder magazine exploded. Only seventeen passengers survived, H.P.B. among them; Agardi Metrovitch lost his life. Her mind dazed with the horror of limbs and heads raining about her, Helena was hauled from the water and taken ashore with the other lucky survivors. Medical care and shelter were provided by the Greek government and, finally, an offer of free passage to their destinations or back to their homes. H.P.B., baggageless and penniless, chose to continue to Egypt.

Witte heard that Metrovitch had drowned while trying to save Helena's life. Whatever the exact circumstances, she must have felt that he would have wanted her to go on, and there is evidence to suggest that she transported his remains to Alexandria for burial. In an 1884 letter to Henry Olcott, she made a brief reference to Agardi's burial there.[93] It may also be the factual basis for her fanciful, totally disjointed tale of how Metrovitch had been poisoned by agents of the Pope by drinking a glass of lemonade. She claimed to have buried him near Alexandria "under a tree on the sea shore."[94]

From Alexandria, she drifted south to Cairo in October. Since her visit twenty years earlier, the city had changed; ancient ruins and the quaint old latticework houses were being replaced by modern buildings, boulevards and mosaic sidewalks, and all day long the chipping and hammering of the masons could be heard. Soon Helena made friends with a French woman, Madame Sebir, who happened to be a medium. Although it was comforting to find someone with whom she had something in common, Helena quickly discovered that Madame Sebir's resources were more meager than her own. For economy's sake, they took an apartment together in Sekke el Ghamma el harmar (The Street of the Red Mosque) and H.P.B., needing something as an outlet for her affection, bought several monkeys, one of whom she named Koko.

Hooking up with a medium was the worst thing she could have done, though at the time it must have seemed logical. Convinced that mediumship was abnormal, she had learned to control her tendencies through a tremendous act of will. Now, however, she found herself gravitating toward the city's amateur French mediums who were, she felt, "mostly beggarly tramps when not adventuresses in the rear of M. de Lesseps' army of engineers and workmen on the canal of Suez."[95] Unwilling to be identified with these women, she decided to organize a society for the investigation of Spiritualistic phenomena, which would be based on the doctrines of Allan Kardec, a French metaphysical theorist who believed that the soul, after death, becomes a spirit that reveals itself through certain privileged beings (mediums) who are capable of receiving its messages.

Following Kardec's rule manual, Helena emphasized that her society would be a serious study group. Curiosity seekers, skeptics and potential troublemakers would not be admitted to membership. At the séances, during which concentration and respectful silence were mandatory, the spirits were questioned on the subjects of history, philosophy and science. Notes were taken. The proceedings were orderly and high-toned, at least they would have been if she had been able to follow Kardec's instructions. As it was, she had no decent mediums, which Kardec had listed as an essential, and trouble was not long in following.

In the meantime, however, Helena had widened her circle of acquaintances. She renewed her contacts with the Coptic magician Paulos Mentamon, and she also struck up a warm friendship with Lydia Paschkoff, the Russian explorer and traveler who would one day make explorations in the regions of the Upper Nile and become St. Petersburg correspondent for Le Figaro. Eccentric and worldly, Madame Paschkoff was an ardent feminist and, like Helena, a lover of the weird and fantastical. A decidedly less vivid personality was Emma Cutting, a young Levantine woman of English extraction, who until recently had been working as a nursery governess in an Egyptian family. Dismissed, she had found a menial position at the Hôtel d'Orient. She spoke Italian and French and knew some English, but was otherwise of limited intellectuality, at least she was not the type of sophisticated woman whom H.P.B. ordinarily found compatible.

Emma met Madame Blavatsky accidentally. While walking one day along the Street of the Red Mosque, she was almost knocked over "by something that brushed by me very swiftly" and upon inquiry learned that she was "that Russian Spiritist who calls the dead and makes them answer your questions." At that time Emma was feeling depressed over the death of her only brother who had killed himself. While she was an orthodox Christian who had never so much as dabbled along the shores of Spiritualism, "the idea of being able to hear his voice was for me heavenly delight," she thought. In any case, she had heard of H.P.B.'s *Société Spirite* [*sic*] from a Greek acquaintance who happened to be its secretary, and she asked for an introduction to the Madame.

Dazzled, Emma decided that Madame Blavatsky was "very interesting and very clever," but the séance she attended at Helena's apartment in Abdeen Street turned out to be a disappointment. Expecting her brother's voice, she got only a few raps. The secretary told her that the spirits preferred to appear in a room that had been especially purified and set aside for them; the Madame was now preparing such a séance chamber and if Emma returned in a few days, she would see wonders.

I called again when the closet was ready, but what was my surprise when, instead of finding the kind spirits there to answer our questions, I found a room full of people, *all alive,* and using most offensive language towards the founder of the Society, saying that she had taken their money and had left them only with this, pointing at the space between the wall and the cloth, where several pieces of twine were still hanging which had served to pull through the ceiling a long glove stuffed with cotton, which was to represent the materialized hand and arm of some spirit. I went away, leaving the crowd red as fire, ready to knock her down when she came back.

Soon afterward Emma ran into Madame Blavatsky and asked why she had pulled such a lousy trick. Helena, looking "very unhappy,"[96] blamed it on Madame Sebir.

Writing to Nadyezhda, she castigated the Society's amateur mediums who stole her money, drank too much "and now I caught them cheating most shamefully our members who come to investigate the phenomena by bogus manifestations. I had very disagreeable scenes with several persons who held me alone responsible for all this."[97] During one of these episodes, it seems that a Greek man, "possessed, I suppose, by some vile spook," rushed into her apartment with a revolver, "and finding me in the breakfast room, declared that he had come to shoot me but would wait till I had done with my meal." Fortunately, she assured Nadyezhda, she had been able to wrest away the pistol and "he is now shut up in a lunatic asylum." Despite the jocular tone of the letter, she was upset enough to swear off séances. "They are too dangerous and I am not practised and strong enough to control the wicked spooks that may approach my friends during such sittings."[98]

She was, in fact, extremely discouraged. News of the fraudulent séance must have spread because attendance at the Society's meetings dropped off sharply. So did her only source of income. Emma, evidently harboring no ill feelings, dropped around to see her. "On hearing that she was really in want I gave her pecuniary help, and continued doing so for some time."[99]

Throughout the winter of 1872, Helena found herself in increasing difficulties. She and Madame Sebir moved to a cheaper apartment in Kantara el dick Street. A sympathetic Emma continued to lend her money, even though she herself had little to spare and H.P.B. warned her that she was in no position to repay the loans. One cannot escape the impression that Emma felt fond of Madame Blavatsky and that it was a reciprocated affection. Later Emma would make the mystifying remark that she had known Agardi Metrovitch in Cairo, but it was only talk. She and Helena were confidantes, and what she knew of Agardi was what the Madame had told her, no doubt with characteristic exaggeration: how they had been secretly married and performed together on the stage, how Yuri had died, in short the whole litany of her woes. And why should Helena have not poured out her troubles to Emma? She had nothing to hide, and she had, after all, lost her child, and her lover/husband, the only family of her own that she would ever have.

"My famous Société Spirite," she wrote Nadyezhda, "has not lasted a fortnight—it is a heap of ruins,"[100] but it was not so short-lived as she implied. When the American Spiritualist James M. Peebles visited Cairo the following year, he was heartened to learn that "Madame Blavatsky, assisted by other brave souls, formed a society of Spiritualists . . . with fine writing mediums and other forms of manifestations."[101] Noting that even though Madame herself was no longer in Egypt, he reported that the Society continued to hold weekly séances during the winter months.

In April, 1872, Helena had returned to Odessa with Madame Sebir and the monkeys, but neither Russia nor her family restored her spirits. It was not merely a matter of feeling bored with her aunts—although she certainly must have been—but rather an inchoate longing for something that Russia did not provide. Away, she remembered her relatives with nostalgic craving; with them, there were quarrels because they did not understand her.

Restive and unhappy, Helena began to think of moving on, and in March or April, 1873, she visited an old friend, Madame Popesco, in Bucharest. From there she wandered on to Paris, where her brother and one of her von Hahn cousins had temporarily settled. It was her intention to make her home indefinitely with Nicholas von Hahn, the son of her Uncle Gustave, at 11 rue de l'Université, but apparently this was not his intention because after two months she moved in with Leonid and his friend M. Lequeux in the rue de Palais. About this time she met an American physician, Dr. Lydia Marquette, who was in Paris studying hospitals and attending lectures. Dr. Marquette, who spent all her free time with Helena, gives a lonely and somewhat pathetic picture of H.P.B.: "She passed her time in painting and writing, seldom going out of her room. She had few acquaintances, but among the number were M. and Mme. Leymarie."[102]

As followers of Allan Kardec, the Leymaries were active in Spiritualist circles and had all the current news on the movement. It was from them or their friends that H.P.B. must have heard about the popularity of Spiritualism in the United States. For anyone interested in psychic phenomena or even simple spirit-rapping, America was unquestionably the place to be, the Mecca of all that was exciting and avant-garde. In June, seemingly on impulse, Helena counted the last of her cash, headed for the port of Le Havre, and purchased a steamship ticket for New York.

What happened in Paris that brought her to this spur-of-the-moment decision? It was, she would say, "my mysterious Hindu" who ordered her "to embark for North America, which I did without protesting."[103] And if there was no mysterious Hindu, there were equally pressing reasons. In a few weeks she would be forty-two. Her youth behind her, she had yet done nothing with her life. She wanted to be world famous, but the world so far had failed to acknowledge her. The bitter irony was that in Russia she had become too well known; she was notorious. She knew that she had intelligence and ability, perhaps a service to render humanity, but that her past would pursue her "like the brand of the curse on Cain."[104]

Desperation brought her to Le Havre. Nevertheless, she was fond of recounting how at the docks she had met a German peasant woman, weeping because she and her children had been sold bogus tickets in Hamburg. Jauntily, H.P.B. exchanged her deluxe passage for steerage berths for all of them.[105] In reality, Madame Blavatsky traveled steerage because it was all she could afford. Like millions of other penniless emigrants, the rebellious aristocrat regarded the United States as a land of opportunity and hope, as a second chance. She meant to grab it.

New York

1873–1878

I

~~~~~~~~~~~~~~~~~

Immigrant

Madame Blavatsky arrived in New York most probably on July 5, 1873, on the French steamer *St. Laurent* out of Le Havre. During the fifteen-day crossing, the *St. Laurent* experienced extremely heavy westerly gales and head seas, causing both damage to the engine and a four-day delay at sea.

On emigrant ships, steerage could only be reached by climbing down a ladder through a hole in the hatchway deck. These hatches provided almost no ventilation and, in rough weather when air was most needed, they were kept shut. Two weeks of airlessness, overcrowding, lack of sanitary facilities, contamination of food and water, as well as the ever-present possibility of shipwreck, added up to downright misery. Remembering H.P.B.'s traumatic experiences aboard the SS *Eumonia,* one can only assume that the Atlantic crossing was a nightmare.

Steaming past The Narrows, she must have pressed against the ship's rail with the other passengers and scanned New York harbor: the surrounding rural landscape dotted with white cottages; the steeple of Trinity Church in the distance; and off the tip of Manhattan Island the circular stone structure, Castle Garden, once a music hall featuring Jenny Lind and Barnum's midgets, now a landing depot, where passengers lined up to register with the Emigration Commission before being herded back to the dock to collect their baggage. If a person had friends or relatives, she was whisked away; if there was no one, she walked to one of the many boardinghouses in the vicinity of Greenwich Street while trying to get her bearings, or she consulted one of the immigrant-aid societies who provided housing information for English, Irish, French, German and Hebrew aliens. (None existed for the few Russians who had arrived.) For Helena, as for most new arrivals, it was a lonely and bewildering moment in a land of strangers and strange customs.

On Saturday the fifth, New Yorkers were recuperating from their Fourth of July celebrations. The holiday weekend had been marred for many sections of the country by hurricanes, tornadoes and floods, but New York escaped the storms, and at 4 P.M. on Saturday the thermometer at Dickinson's Drug Store, 3 Park Row, read ninety degrees, ten above normal. Helena quickly discovered that New York was a difficult city in which to navigate if one was a single woman, even in the simple matter of finding a place to live. First-class hotels refused to admit unescorted women, and even the lesser hotels and boardinghouses tended to regard them with suspicion unless accompanied by a male relative. Of course all these types of accommodations were far beyond Helena's means, a predicament in which she was not alone.

In 1873, New York had about forty thousand women who found it necessary to support themselves. As the typewriter had not yet been invented and women were generally few and far between in the business world, they were limited to working as shop clerks, telegraphers, teachers, governesses, seamstresses and factory workers, all positions offering poor wages and long hours. The fact that decent housing was virtually impossible to secure on their incomes had not gone unacknowledged; charitable organizations were making attempts to assist such women, and in a few rare cases the women had even organized to help themselves. Earlier in the year, forty women had banded together to experiment with cooperative living by renting a newly built tenement house at 222 Madison Street. What lucky tip steered Helena Petrovna to this unique women's commune we do not know, but doubtless she herself must have regarded it as a lifesaver.

At that time Madison was a street of small two-story houses occupied by owners who were proud of their shade trees and kept their front and back gardens in good order. The owner of 222 was a Mr. Rinaldo, who did not live on the premises but took a paternal interest in his women tenants by visiting frequently and personally collecting the rent. H.P.B., installed in a private room on the second floor, found herself next door to a good-humored Scot–Irish woman, Miss Parker, who immediately came over to get acquainted. All the residents of the house thought themselves a family, and neighbors were constantly visiting. Downstairs next to the street door a room had been specially set aside as an office where mail and messages were kept and the women could congregate to talk. Naturally the arrival of an extravagant personality such as Helena Petrovna was an exciting event and the women regarded her with unabashed curiosity.

Despite the cheapness and friendliness of her new quarters, H.P.B.'s financial problems kept her in a permanent state of anxiety. She had so little money that even coffee became a luxury. She boiled the grounds several times to make her supply last and worried about how she was going to survive. Within three weeks of her arrival, she took the initiative in a rather audacious manner by boldly notifying the New York *Sun* of her presence in the city. When a woman reporter, Anna Ballard, was sent to get an interview, H.P.B. was delighted to talk about herself along with other matters that she hoped would interest *Sun* readers. She told Miss Ballard that one hundred fifty aristocratic Russian women, including Czar Alexander's daughters, had been studying medicine in Zurich when the Emperor suddenly forbade such masculine endeavors and limited them to the study of midwifery; some of the women had been forced to return to Russia while others had gone to France and Germany and a small group to the United States.

This information was, of course, invented on the spot, but the *Sun* did not pause to distinguish between fact and fiction as would the *Times* or the *Tribune,* and on July 28, they ran the story as front-page news. Judging by the final sentence it is obvious that H.P.B. played her game to the hilt: "These accomplished women, polygots, travellers, scientists, nearly moneyless are able to do much and want something to do."[1]

If Helena hoped that the *Sun* would give her a free want ad, she must have been grossly disappointed. Not once did her name appear in the article; no employer contacted the paper to make inquiries as to the whereabouts of the gifted Russian women, starving and looking for work. After this setback, H.P.B. seemed uncertain as to her next step. Day after day she sat in the first-floor office and rolled cigarettes, garnering her tobacco supply from the head of some fur-bearing animal that she wore around her neck as a pouch; she chain-smoked and passed her time talking to anyone who happened by.

By this time, she was beginning to understand what it took for an unknown to succeed in New York City. It was obvious that no matter how important an individual might have been elsewhere, New Yorkers automatically considered her a nobody. One had to work at building a reputation, and then she would be taken for just what she was worth and no more. To H.P.B., this seemed a mixed blessing in that it enabled her to start fresh, but by the same token it meant there would be no easy road to recognition, much less to procuring one's daily bread. Her abortive publicity stunt in the *Sun* had not, actually, been a bad idea; it merely had not worked as planned, and she could see that in the future she would have to be a good deal more subtle.

By August, she was still in the office, rolling her cigarettes and brooding. There was little use prowling about the city because she had no money to enjoy herself and, besides, she found it somewhat intimidating. New York, in 1873, had only two visible classes, the wealthy and the poor; the middle class, who could not afford the city, lived in the suburbs and commuted to work. Most noticeable was New York's air of prosperity, the illusion that everybody had money to throw away. One had only to walk down Broadway, the city's great thoroughfare, to observe an assorted spectacle of wealth: elegantly attired gentlemen with canes, top hats and wide cravats set with diamond stickpins; sporty fellows with derbies cocked over one eye and hair roached up in bear grease or macassar oil; corseted ladies going to extremes with powder and rouge and every variety of false hair— chignons, pompadours, braids, rolls, and spit curls. Shops displayed a generous assortment of satins, jewels, toys, paintings and silverware, and one cosmetic shop advertised thirteen different varieties of skin powder and eight kinds of creams. The Fifth Avenue Hotel charged thirty dollars a day for a suite of two rooms and a parlor (supposedly a bargain), while the one-million-dollar Stevens House apartment building on the corner of Broadway and Twenty-seventh Street offered lavish eighteen-room suites with a steam elevator, frescoed walls and separate quarters for servants. Inflation had driven up prices to the point where even essentials had become luxuries: butter was fifty cents a pound, crushed sugar sixteen, fowls twenty-five, and choice cuts of beef thirty-five.

At the same time, there were ominous signs that the boom could not continue indefinitely. By the year's end, depression had already begun to rock the country; on September 18, the failure of the great banking house of Jay Cooke and Company would precipitate further disasters of the Panic of 1873, as banks collapsed, five thousand businesses failed, the iron industry cut wages, and mines and textile mills closed down. By the following year, unemployment would rocket to three million. It was not the best time for an immigrant to make her way in the United States of America.

Elizabeth Holt had spent the summer with her mother at Saratoga. In August she was sent home to New York to get ready for the opening of school, but since a proper Victorian girl could not live alone, her mother's friend Miss Parker agreed to chaperone her at 222 Madison Street. There Elizabeth met Madame Blavatsky, which was inevitable as her room was directly opposite the office where H.P.B. spent most of her time. Madame seemed to Elizabeth "an unusual figure." It was not only her cigarettes and the crinkled blond hair—she overflowed with a nonstop fund of fabulous stories about her life in Paris, where she claimed to have decorated Empress Eugénie's private apartments. Elizabeth imagined her as "dressed in blouse and trousers, mounted on a ladder and doing the actual work, and I think this is what she told us; but I cannot be sure whether she said that she did the actual painting, frescoing, etc., or whether she merely designed it." Either seemed equally marvelous.

Elizabeth knew that H.P.B. was "greatly troubled about money," which seemed peculiar because Madame was a Russian countess. Some skeptics in the house tartly suggested that Madame was, despite her stories, nothing but an ordinary adventuress. But Miss Parker, who had accompanied H.P.B. to the Russian Consulate, assured them that the consul knew of her family and had promised to contact them for money. In the meantime, however, Mr. Rinaldo had introduced Helena to two young friends of his who owned a collar-and-shirt factory and were willing to give her freelance work designing advertising cards. "Madame also tried ornamental work in leather, and produced some very fine and intricate examples, but they did not sell, and she abandoned the leather work," recalled Elizabeth Holt.

Later, when H.P.B. became well known, Elizabeth could never quite imagine her as an ethical teacher because she remembered her excitable temper and how she expressed herself "with a vigour which was very disturbing" when things went wrong. That was a genteel way of putting it, because H.P.B., angry, had a disconcerting habit of swearing like a sailor. Still, there was much about her to admire, especially her fearlessness and her instinctive response to anyone in trouble. "Undesirable people were beginning to move into the street," recalled Elizabeth Holt,

* * *

and the neighborhood was changing rapidly. One evening one of our young girls, coming home late from work, was followed and greatly frightened; she slung herself breathlessly into a chair in the office. Madame interested herself at once, expressed her indignation in most vigorous terms, and finally drew from some fold of her dress a knife (I think she used it to cut her tobacco, but it was sufficiently sharp to be a formidable weapon of defence) and she said she had *that* for any man who molested her.

While the prim Elizabeth recognized and appreciated the guttsiness that characterized the least of H.P.B.'s actions, she also acknowledged another side of Madame Blavatsky, one that Miss Parker did not, evidently, believe appropriate for a young girl to know about. H.P.B. was in the habit of relating weird tales of the supernatural, some of them so frightening that Miss Parker stayed all night with Elizabeth instead of climbing two flights of dark stairs to her own room. Apart from spooky stories, Helena amiably dispensed information about people's pasts to anyone who asked. Miss Parker, for one, was greatly startled to hear about incidents in her own life that were, she thought, known only to herself. When she asked to be put in touch with her dead mother, Helena refused—her mother, progressed beyond reach, involved herself in higher matters now. Since Madame continually claimed to be under the authority of unseen powers, Elizabeth and the others at 222 Madison assumed that she must be speaking of her spirit guides and naturally concluded that she was a Spiritualist. For her part, Elizabeth could not get excited about Madame's spirits, those "tricksy little beings" whom she called *diaki*.[2]

Entertaining her co-residents with life readings was all very well but did nothing to solve Helena's problems. As no rubles had yet appeared from Russia, her financial situation continued to deteriorate until she was reduced to relying on the generosity of others in order to live. A few blocks away in Henry Street there was a French Canadian widow, Madame Magnon, with whom Helena had grown friendly. When Madame Magnon offered to share her home until Helena's money difficulties were straightened out, she left 222 Madison. Some of the women, notably Miss Parker, kept in touch and after the two madames decided to hold Sunday evening séances, Miss Parker was an eager participant. While Elizabeth Holt was not invited—her mother would not have approved—Miss Parker told her all the news. It seemed that one morning, when Helena failed to appear for breakfast, Madame Magnon finally went to her room and found her unable to rise. Her nightgown had been sewn securely to the mattress, stitched in such a way that Madame could not possibly have done it herself, and Magnon had to cut the threads. This, Miss Parker assured Elizabeth, was the work of the *diaki*.

In early November, Helena received a letter from her half-sister with the unhappy news that their father had died on July 27 after a three-day illness;

he had been buried at Stavropol in the Caucasus. Excusing her delay in writing, Liza said that she had not known Helena's whereabouts—she enclosed a draft for Helena's portion of the estate. The amount must have been modest, at least less than H.P.B. believed she was due, because afterward she would accuse her sister Vera of withholding half her inheritance.[3]

Shortly after this, Helena rented a place of her own at the northeast corner of Fourteenth Street and Fourth Avenue. It was a musty top-floor room containing only an iron cot, a table, and a three-drawer cabinet; downstairs, a saloon occupied the ground floor. Helena, a rabid teetotaler, could not have been delighted.

To make matters worse, she had a fire in her room, perhaps as a result of careless smoking, and after the firemen had extinguished the blaze, she discovered that her watch and chain were missing. When she complained to her landlord, who happened to be the proprietor of the saloon, he scoffed that she had never owned a watch. Helena's almost paranoid reaction to the fire supplies a clue to her anguished state of mind at that period of her life; she told Elizabeth Holt that the fire had been deliberately set in order to rob her, and, referring to what Elizabeth assumed were her spirit guides, she kept talking about "they" and "them." When she had asked "them" to give her proof of the robbery, there had immediately materialized a charred piece of paper with two white spots in the shape of a watch and chain, meaning to indicate, one supposes, that the objects had been resting on the paper before the fire.[4]

If H.P.B. actually offered this "documentation" to her landlord, it failed to sway him. In response to Elizabeth's expressions of sympathy, Helena cheerfully assured her that money was no problem—she had only to ask "them" for it and would find what she needed in the drawers of her cabinet. But it was a meaningless boast. For all her outward nonchalance, "they" had evidently failed her and it was clear that she must find another place to live. Although by this time the Madison Street commune had failed financially and closed, she was able to locate a similar working woman's home at 45 Elizabeth Street. Unlike Mr. Rinaldo's house, this was a massive, six-story brick building accommodating five hundred boarders. The ground floor was given over to a parlor, reading room, laundry and restaurant, while the upper stories had been made into dormitories. Helena had to pay $1.25 a week for lodging and laundry privileges, and she could have a decent meal in the restaurant for twenty-five cents.[5]

In early 1874, Helena met Hannah Wolff, a reporter for the New York *Star* who visited the home while interviewing one of H.P.B.'s roommates. "Scantily clad," Mme. Blavatsky lay on the carpetless floor during the conversation and "rolled and smoked cigarettes with marvellous rapidity." Afterward Helena interrogated Hannah at such length about the position of women in the American press that Miss Wolff felt she was the one being interviewed. When Wolff finally got a word in and asked why she was living in a working woman's home, H.P.B. cited necessity. So a month later, meeting her again at a women's rights convention, Wolff was surprised to find Helena with money to spare. Having received, she told Wolff, a large sum of money from Russia, she had been able to move to an expensive hotel on Fourth Avenue near Twenty-third Street. "She invited half a dozen ladies to lunch with her," Wolff recalled, "and subsequently told me that her bill footed up to five dollars each."

Neither H.P.B.'s presence at a feminist convention, nor her lavish entertaining of delegates, should be construed to mean that she had any particular interest in the cause of women's rights. On the contrary, the fact that Susan B. Anthony had illegally voted in the 1872 election left her indifferent. H.P.B. herself had no desire to vote, even though she felt strongly that women deserved the right if they wanted it. As for the notorious Victoria Woodhull who had run for President in that same election (and who had actually announced that she believed in "free love"), this was the last person Helena would champion, Mrs. Woodhull's sexual liberation being much too close to home for comfort. Rather it was loneliness that sent her to the feminist conclave, just as her need for companionship made her pursue Hannah Wolff.

Highly intuitive up to a point, H.P.B. could be, nonetheless, myopic when it came to reading people's true feelings. Failing to grasp that Hannah Wolff considered her batty, she believed that she had made a friend and began dropping in frequently at Hannah's apartment where she talked compulsively about herself. In the course of these conversations, she mentioned having fought with Garibaldi but, Wolff recalled, "I was never able to hold her to the subject so as to get any succinct or lucid account of her adventures as a soldier." By professional training or by temperament, Hannah accepted nothing unquestioningly. When Helena displayed her scars, claiming them saber wounds, Hannah privately concluded that they must be marks of a knout. She found H.P.B.'s smoking a pound of tobacco a day to be offensive and her use of opium and hashish shocking. H.P.B. would ramble on enthusiastically about the relative benefits of hashish versus opium in stimulating the imagination. She considered hashish to be superior and urged Hannah to sample the drug for herself. Hannah claims to have declined.

In the spring of 1874, Helena was still moving in Hannah's circle of friends. Introduced to a Mr. W. and learning that he was a Spiritualist, she pleaded ignorance of the subject and asked him to escort her to a lecture being given by E. V. Wilson, a well-known trance medium. Afterward she told Mr. W. that it was her first experience with mediums and that she had been thoroughly impressed.

Soon after that, she met Hannah and Mr. W. on the street, and animatedly informed them that as a result of the medium's lecture, she had begun to develop occult powers. Having placed some photographs in a bureau, she found to her astonishment that spirits had tinted them like watercolor paintings. She invited Hannah and Mr. W. back to the cheap apartment she shared with three journalists. Her roommates were two men and a woman, a decidedly bohemian arrangement for the 1870s, but at least she had a small bedroom of her own off the dining room. When Hannah and Mr. W. stopped in to see the spirit art, Helena led them to a sideboard in the dining room, pulled out some colored pictures and explained that the "colouring seemed chiefly to be done in the night and when nature was in her negative mood." Hannah did not believe this for a minute. Speaking privately to the other residents of the apartment, she learned that they too, had been skeptical of Madame's occult powers and

> had laid wait for the spirit who worked in the night-watches, and had discovered it materialized in the form of Madame Blavatsky, dressed in *saque de nuit* [*sic*]; had seen it glide softly across the room, armed with lamp, colours and brushes, take the pictures from the drawers, and rapidly work upon them one after another until they were as nearly completed as could be at one sitting.

Whatever one may conclude about these shenanigans, they attest to Helena's immense need to make an impression on those around her. It was discouraging to realize that after nearly a year in New York she was still as poor and unknown, as lonely and fragmented, as the day she arrived. Despite a few superficial friendships, including a Russian couple who lived in Brooklyn, she had failed to put down any real roots in the city and simultaneously, receiving no mail from Russia, she felt cut off from her past. Sensing the constant specter of starvation at her elbow, she felt obliged to conserve what remained of her father's inheritance while making continual efforts to find additional income.

Strangely enough, she decided to become a writer, an illogical choice of professions, because while she spoke English fairly well, her command of English grammar was virtually nil; but perhaps her association with various journalists accounts for it. Asking Hannah to be her editor, she divulged that she was writing a humorous satire on the United States government and when Wolff suggested that this might be impertinent in a newcomer who had little insight into American institutions, H.P.B. forcefully declared that she should look at the manuscript before condemning it.

By this time Wolff's distrust of Madame Blavatsky had become automatic. She showed the manuscript to one of H.P.B.'s roommates, who, in turn, escorted her to the home of Helena's Brooklyn friends, Mr. and Mrs. Yule.

"Did she tell you it was original?" Mr. Yule wanted to know.

"Certainly," Hannah said. "She claimed that it was an expression of her own views of our government in satire."

From a bookcase, Yule removed a work by a celebrated Russian humorist and said, "Well, the portion of it that you have, she translated from this volume. The second volume she borrowed when she left here and has not yet returned."

Listening to Yule read aloud from the Russian text, Hannah realized that except for the substitution of "United States" for "Russia," "President" for "Czar," and so forth, the manuscript she had been given to edit was a verbatim translation. Furious, she rushed back to Helena with the manuscript and upbraided her for plagiarism. Not only did Helena not deny it, she professed not to understand what horrendous thing she had done because, she remarked, "Americans were almost entirely ignorant of Russian literature."[6] In this attitude, she was being perfectly sincere; in fact, she would never manage to understand the inviolate nature of other authors' works, saw nothing wrong in borrowing freely, with or without attribution, and regarded those who objected as nitpickers.

After this incident, Hannah Wolff would have none of her, and H.P.B. seems to have temporarily dropped her ambition of becoming a professional writer. In late June, still looking for something to do, she encountered Clementine Gerebko, a Frenchwoman whose Russian husband had once been captain of a private steamer owned by Prince Vorontzov, viceroy of the Caucasus. Meeting this couple whom she had known slightly in Tiflis, Helena promptly responded with a passionate outburst of enthusiasm such as might be expected in a sentimental expatriate pining for contact with her native land. The Gerebkos, who had been living in America several years, owned a six-acre farm in Suffolk County, Long Island. Not only did Clementine paint an idyllic picture of their property, she said that the farm produced an annual income of nearly two thousand dollars. Would Helena Petrovna consider going into partnership with her?

Helena would. "I had to give her one thousand dollars," she recalled, "and pay half of the expenses that might occur," but for this investment she was to receive half of the farm's yearly profits. Agog with visions of the profits to be made from the bucolic setting— eggs, poultry and truck-gardening—Helena handed over a portion of Peter von Hahn's bequest, signed a three-year contract, and went to live with the Gerebkos at the beginning of July.

Though it is not easy to imagine an indolent person like Madame Blavatsky feeding chickens, she was willing to give it a try. Once she got to Long Island, what stunned her was not the prospect of hard labor, but the realization that Clementine had tricked her. Far from being a profitable business, the farm was noticeably rundown and needed at least five hundred dollars' worth of building improvements, which H.P.B. claimed that she made. By the end of the month, however, she had had enough, both of farming and Clementine, and she cursed "my unlucky star that brought me in contact with her." Apparently Clementine harbored similar feelings because, after a particularly violent squabble, she "prayed to be released of the contract" and promised to return H.P.B.'s money. Agreeing to sell the farm at auction, the three of them returned to New York City, took rooms together, and decided to continue being friends. "Alas!" added H.P.B., "three days after we had taken lodging in common, on one fine afternoon, upon my returning home, I found that the fair countess had left the place, neglecting to pay me back her little bill of one thousand dollars."

Badly rattled, Helena retained the Brooklyn law firm of Bergen, Jacobs and Ivins to bring suit against the Gerebkos. Meanwhile, of course, her inheritance had evaporated.[7]

On one of those days in July when Helena was fussing over her poultry in Long Island, Henry Steel Olcott sat in his law office at 7 Beekman Street "thinking over a heavy case in which I had been retained by the Corporation of the City of New York."[8] Bored by interminable memos detailing the construction of water meters, his mind began to wander; it occurred to him that in the wake of his recent personal upheavals he had not paid much attention to current events and trends and he decided to walk around the corner to a newspaper dealer where he purchased, finally, a copy of the *Banner of Light*. Back in his office, he began leafing through the Spiritualist paper, intending to kill time until he could go uptown to his room at the Lotos Club. One item, however, immediately grabbed his attention:

> In it I read an account of certain incredible phenomena, viz., the solid-ification of phantom forms, which were said to be occurring at a farm-house in the township of Chittenden, in the State of Vermont, several hundred miles distant from New York. I saw at once that, if it were true that visitors could see, even touch and converse with, deceased relatives who had found means to reconstruct their bodies and clothing so as to be temporarily solid, visible, and tangible, this was the most important fact in modern physical science. I determined to go and see for myself.[9]

To Olcott, who was not a Spiritualist, it all seemed wonderfully new.

Nevertheless, as incredible as the apparitions may have sounded, as earth-shaking their implications for modern science, there was, in fact, nothing particularly remarkable about either William and Horatio Eddy or their materialized spirits who identified themselves exotically as Mayflower and Honto. The United States, that summer, suffered no shortage of mediums who could "materialize" a parade of ghostly figures, not only the popular John King, self-proclaimed ghost of the famous buccaneer Sir Henry Morgan, who had been "coming through" for twenty years, but also his flirtatious daughter Katie King and hundreds of lesser personalities. So there is no reason to doubt Olcott's word when he admitted ignorance about the latest developments in Spiritualism.

Another man might have taken a weekend jaunt to Vermont, satisfied his curiosity, and returned to his law office on Monday morning. Olcott, a thrifty man, saw no reason to finance the trip himself when he might wangle a newspaper assignment and get his expenses paid. Two summers earlier he had worked briefly at the New York *Sun*, filling in for the vacationing drama editor, and now he talked to his editor friends and proposed that they send him to Vermont as a special correspondent; he would spend three or four days checking out the Eddys for fraud and perhaps get an offbeat story out of it.

It was a hot, dull summer in New York. The only scandal of note, the alleged adultery of Rev. Henry Ward Beecher with one of his parishioners, had already begun to pall. The *Sun* could use a sensational ghost story and Olcott could escape for a holiday in the cool Vermont countryside.

Henry Steel Olcott would be celebrating his forty-second birthday in a few days, but despite his law practice and other trappings of middle-class success, he could not claim to be satisfied or even happy. Most decidedly he was not happy, even though he was not the sort of person to indulge in self-pity. The eldest of six children, he had been born and raised in Orange, New Jersey, where his father owned a modest, though unsuccessful, business. While there was nothing particularly distinguished about the immediate family, the Olcotts could trace their American ancestry back to the 1630s when a well-to-do Puritan named Thomas Olcott had migrated to New England, and, going back still further, perhaps to a Dr. John Alcock who had been Dean of Westminster and Bishop of Ely in the late fifteenth century. His family's genealogy fascinated Henry Olcott and, earlier in the year, he had devoted a great deal of time to revising the 1845 edition of *The Descendants of Thomas Olcott* and he had even added a new preface.

Despite impressive forebears, Henry had been obliged to struggle, and his education at the City College of New York and Columbia University was cut short when his father's business failed. Dropping out of school, he took up farming on a share basis for two years, then returned to New York where he devoted himself to the scientific study of agriculture. By the age of twenty-three, he had won recognition for his work on various model farms, particularly for his research in sorghum, and in 1858 he wrote his first book, *Sorgho and Imphee, the Chinese and African Sugar-Canes*. Finding that his expertise in agriculture provided an entry into journalism, he was pleased to become associate agricultural editor of the New York *Tribune*.

By 1859, Henry was definitely gravitating from agriculture into newspaper work. When John Brown was scheduled to be hung that December at Charlestown, Virginia, and the Virginians refused to allow Northern papers to cover the abolitionist's execution, Olcott volunteered to take the assignment for the *Tribune* and managed not only to witness the event but write an excellent story. Two years later, the Civil War put a temporary end to both of Henry's careers.

Enlisting in the Northern Army, he served in the North Carolina campaign under General Burnside, but dysentery very quickly invalided him back to New York; by the time he was recovered and ready to return to the front, his superiors had taken note of his ability and made him a special commissioner of the War Department with instructions to investigate fraud, graft and corruption at the New York Mustering and Disbursing Office. Throughout the remaining four years of the war, he proved so zealous that the Navy Department borrowed him to clean up abuses in the Navy Yards, and it was during this period that he was promoted to the rank of colonel, a title he would use for the rest of his life.

After the war, Olcott resigned his commission, but instead of returning to his former pursuits, he decided to study law. There is no record of his having attended a university; most probably he read law in someone's office and was admitted to the bar in May, 1868, as a result of his work experience. With his customary energy, Olcott began to specialize in the new field of insurance law and soon had carved out a respectable practice in customs, revenue and insurance cases. Among his clients were the City of New York and the Life Mutual Insurance Company of New York, the latter retaining him to lobby for the insurance profession in the New York State Legislature. In short, Olcott was living proof of the old American adage that ability and hard work bring rewards.

By the age of forty, he had everything he might have reasonably expected out of life: respect and success in his chosen profession, enough money to enjoy luxuries, sufficient free time to dabble now and again in freelance newspaper work and, in addition, a family. In 1860 he had married the daughter of an Episcopalian minister, Mary Epplee Morgan, and the following year they had a son, Morgan, and the year after that a second boy, William Topping. Their third son lived only four months, however, and their daughter, Bessie, less than two years. The death of Bessie must have struck Henry Olcott deeply, because when he revised the Olcott genealogy in 1874, he made a curious error. In the listing for his own family, on page 106, he stated that his daughter had been born in June 21, 1868, but he omitted the exact date of her death, writing simply February, 1870.

Perhaps the family's tragedies drove Henry and Mary apart, because not long after Bessie's death their marriage began to sour, and by 1874 they had separated. Henry had gone to live at his club in Irving Place and begun kicking up his heels like a frustrated husband just liberated after many years of confinement. Years later, looking back, he described himself as having been "a worldly man" adding that he had been "a man of clubs, drinking parties, mistresses, a man absorbed in all sorts of worldly public and private undertakings and speculations."[10] This profligate image would be confirmed by Helena who called him "a gay dog"[11] who kept mistresses and spent his time drinking in clubs.

Considering the crucial role that he was to play in H.P.B.'s life, it is important to take a close look at the man. Physically, he was slightly above medium height with a pleasant open face, brown hair, short beard and steel-rimmed spectacles. People considered him the stereotype of a prosperous, middle-aged Yankee who was unsophisticated, honest, energetic, and practical. But that was before he grew a flowing Santa Claus beard and gave up wearing shoes. Even to those who wished to prove him a liar and charlatan, he shone as a man of integrity and sincerity. As Sir Arthur Conan Doyle observed, no one can read Olcott's autobiographical *Old Diary Leaves* without sensing that this was a man "loyal to a fault, unselfish and with that rare moral courage which will follow truth and accept results even when they oppose one's expectations and desires."[12]

That he neither looked nor acted like a mystic dreamer, nor thought of himself as one, proves nothing except that appearances can deceive wildly. For all his outward normality, Henry Steel Olcott was an incomplete person seeking the missing piece that would transform him into —he could not say what. In today's pop psychology terms, what he was seeking would doubtless be called fulfillment, or perhaps psychic contentment. He had not found it with Mary, although he adored his sons, then aged thirteen and twelve, and for their sakes, as well as the stigma attached to divorce, might conceivably have returned to his family; neither had he found peace in religion, his work, or his relationships with women other than his wife. The trouble with Henry was that he could not pursue his heart's desire, simply because he had no notion of what it might be.

Seven miles north of Rutland, in a grassy valley enclosed by the slopes of the Green Mountains, lay the hamlet of Chittenden. Farmers sitting around the stove in the village store shrugged when asked about the Eddys; Olcott found that they knew little of the séances and cared less, but he also received the distinct impression that they disliked the brothers. "Their religion," he observed tersely, "is intolerant, their sect methodist."[13] Although the Vermont countryside was charming, the Eddy farmhouse itself impressed him as gloomy and uninviting. It was a large wooden rectangle two stories high, to which the brothers had recently added a two-story, L-shaped wing. The lower floor of the extension was used as a dining room and kitchen, the upper as a séance hall.

Neither was there anything about William or Horatio to inspire confidence. They were rough, uneducated men who did all the farm work, house chores and cooking. They were curt and surly to the guests—sometimes as many as forty at a time—who paid them a fairly stiff rate of eight dollars a week for room and board. When they learned Henry was a special investigator sent all the way to Vermont by a leading New York daily, they responded only with hostile disinterest.

There is no doubt that William and Horatio Eddy had some genuine psi ability. Over several generations their family had a history of psychic powers, a grandmother four times removed even having been executed at the Salem witch trials of 1692. A fanatical father tried to cure the children of their fits and spells by administering beatings, dousing them with boiling water, and placing live coals in their hands; their mother, a strong psychic herself, was apparently unable to prevent the brutality. Later, when the Fox sisters took to the stage and demonstrated that the psychic could pull in plenty of money, Zephaniah Eddy decided to exhibit his children as freaks. In their touring act, the boys were bound and gagged, pricked with needles and wires, and nailed into suffocating boxes that resembled coffins. It is not astonishing that they grew up to distrust people, but what is difficult to understand is that they courted attention by constructing a special séance hall and inviting the public. Profit does not seem to have been a motive because they did not charge for attendance; the only costs to visitors were room and board, and even then some people were poor or sponged off them.

Olcott stayed three days. Even though he had been fascinated for years by the paranormal and had read books on hypnotism and psychic phenomena, this was his first contact with Spiritualists and he found them a motley crowd: housewives, editors, divines, peddlers of magnetic salves and mysterious nostrums, mediums, clairvoyant healers, phrenologists, sickly dreamers. Some of them, he decided, were "nice, clever people whom one is glad to meet and sorry to part from" but others struck him as "people who shed a magnetism as disagreeable as dirty dish water."[14] Pursuing the marvelous, they sat all day long and hashed over what had happened at the previous night's séance, until Olcott felt surfeited.

Back in New York, he wrote up his observations in a fraud lawyer's circumspect style by presenting grave eyewitness accounts of ectoplasmic forms—the giant Indian named Santum, an Indian squaw called Honto, and dozens of other phantom men, women and children. Although to *Sun* readers Olcott must have seemed prejudiced against the psychic movement, this was not the case. In spite of his claims to being an objective investigator, he secretly believed that the Eddy materializations "must be what they seemed, viz., the 'spirits of the dead.' "[15]

Soon after the *Sun* piece appeared, the editor of the *Daily Graphic* proposed that Henry return to Chittenden with an artist to make a thorough investigation. Unhesitatingly, Olcott interrupted his law practice, and was back in Vermont by the seventeenth of September.

Upstate New York, the birthplace of Spiritualism, had been ripe for religious unorthodoxy since evangelical Christian revivals first sprung up in the early years of the century. In the spring of 1847, when two preadolescent Hydesville girls heard rapping which gave intelligent answers to questions, the match was set to the powder keg. Margaret and Kate Fox had picked up some thread of communication between this world and the next, and to many people the implications of personal immortality were staggering; the new religion spread rapidly to all parts of the country and eventually to Europe.

While some claimed that the Fox sisters produced the raps by snapping the joints of their toes,[16] others clutched at Spiritualism because it seemed to provide answers the world desperately needed. The questions, basically, were these: Have my loved ones survived physical death as individuals with whom I can communicate? Will *I* survive? That the replies appeared to be affirmative filled a great psychic need for many spiritually restless people who could not accept the modern scientific explanation that God was no longer necessary. In nearly every town of any size in America, groups formed to invoke the denizens of unseen worlds and to devise methods whereby disembodied entities could communicate with the living. In addition to the unsophisticated raps experienced by the Fox sisters, there were tinklings of bells, flashes of light, tipping tables, levitating furniture and that was only the beginning. Soon people were receiving messages through planchettes, trumpets, automatic writing, alphabet rapping, slate writing, trance inspiration, and glossolalia— and to act as human channels for these varied communications there sprang up a remarkably large supply of mediums, clairvoyants and inspirational speakers.

Predictably the movement suffered wild fluctuations in support, ranging from spectacular accolades to vehement ridicule. It was inevitable, too, that the enthusiasm of the 1850s would give way to the excesses of a lunatic fringe, to exposures of fraud, and to the opposition of churches and some segments of the intellectual community. By the late 1870s only a hard-core remnant ⟨ believers remained, but in 1874, when Helena Petrovna Blavatsky, ex-farmer took a room at 123 East 16th Street, just off Irving Place, Spiritualism was front-page news. H.P.B. was still restlessly scanning her horizons in the hope of spying something interesting to do. Bored both with New York and with herself, she proceeded to chop off her hair to just below the ears. The result seems to have resembled a blond Afro, and in contrast to the elaborate coiffures of her day, she must have looked bizarre.

Her motto, that summer, was TRY, a subtle reminder that nothing was going to happen without effort. To be sure, she had been *trying* all along, but efforts had been confined to the realm of the impractical. Perhaps it was time to attempt something different.

Laying aside her gimmicks, she found a way of meeting the much-admired Andrew Jackson Davis, the first important figure in American Spiritualism and a man whose writings were respected throughout the world. Even though the "Poughkeepsie Seer" knew nothing about Helena, he accurately gauged her true worth and extended a gracious welcome. Born in 1826, Davis had received a total of five months' schooling before being apprenticed to a Poughkeepsie, New York, shoemaker at the age of fifteen. Shortly afterward, when a tailor who had heard a series of lectures on "animal magnetism" succeeded in mesmerizing the boy, Davis's psychic powers began to emerge. While in trance, the human body became transparent to him and he could observe each organ standing out clearly unless dimmed by disease; like Edgar

Cayce a century later, he could diagnose illnesses of those standing next to him, as well as cases thousands of miles away. Aside from his medical work, he held trance conversations with Galen and Swedenborg, gave lectures tracing the evolution of the universe, described our solar system (including a fairly accurate description of the as-yet unidentified planet Neptune), and correctly portrayed the as-yet uninvented automobile, airplane and typewriter.

Davis's trance revelations—"Harmonial Philosophy" he called his system—had been transcribed and published and would eventually fill twenty-six volumes. Doubtless H.P.B. had already read some of his works; there is no question that she read all of them before writing *The Secret Doctrine* because some of her concepts, especially those relating to the origin and evolution of worlds, are reminiscent of his ideas. Davis would influence her in other ways as well, but these would not be apparent for quite some time; she could see that he disdained séance rooms and the more gaudy trappings of Spiritualism, that he was a plain man with high moral objects: the advancement of the race by purification and self-control, a return to simple life, and the establishment of a brotherhood of humankind. These would be her objectives—someday. For the moment, however, the weird still lured.

Since her friendship with Davis satisfied her craving for intelligent companionship, she fell into the habit of visiting him nearly every day. She explained her dilemma of wanting to write but not quite knowing how to go about it, and she must also have been candid about her lack of money and prospects. Eager to be helpful, Davis told her about a Russian friend of his, the translator and publisher of his works in German. Alexander Nikolayevich Aksakov was a dedicated Spiritualist who recently had begun a monthly magazine devoted to the serious investigation of psychic phenomena, but since he had encountered trouble publishing such a periodical in Russia, he had established his editorial office in Leipzig. Possibly, Davis suggested, H.P.B. might be able to write for *Psychische Studien* either by contributing original articles or translating American authors who wrote on occult subjects, and he offered to write Aksakov on her behalf.

Around the same time that she made friends with Davis, H.P.B. also met a Russian businessman of Armenian extraction, Michael C. Betanelly. A native Georgian some ten or more years her junior,[17] Betanelly had come to the United States in 1871 to improve his life and, hopefully, make a fortune. With headquarters in Philadelphia, he acted as American agent for a Tiflis import—export firm that exchanged goat skins, wool, Persian carpets and insecticides for U.S. machinery, hardware and patented goods. Although certain Theosophists have tried to paint Betanelly as "a peasant" who was "little better than a workman,"[18] he was no such thing. A graduate of the Imperial University of St. Petersburg, he could not exactly be termed illiterate. Some of his letters written in English are slightly awkward in construction, but no more so than any person struggling in a foreign language, while his Russian correspondence is as fluent as could be wished. From everything known of him, admittedly not much, he seems to have been an intelligent, ambitious young man, not without his shrewd side, however.

There is a slight possibility that Helena may have known him in Tiflis because he would claim to be acquainted with members of the Witte family, but more likely they met for the first time in New York at a sentimental gathering of Russian émigrées, and after discovering they had mutual acquaintances back home, they fell into each other's arms. Essentially Michael and Helena shared a common desire to make their marks in America, and at the very least, they shared a wish for a decent standard of living. It is obvious that there was some physical attraction, but just how deep an intimacy they formed at this time is not clear. Since the death of Agardi Metrovitch three years earlier, there had apparently been no men in her life, and at forty-three she still must have had a vigorous libido. She responded favorably to the handsome Michael Betanelly, and the fact that he was so much younger than she must have been tremendously flattering. For obvious reasons, she did not reveal her real age.

She still spent much of her time reading voraciously: books, newspapers and periodicals, and also in the leading Spiritualist journals: the *Banner of Light, Religio -Philosophical Journal* and the *Spiritual Scientist*. Since June all of these papers had been carrying stories about the Eddy brothers, some by enthusiastic tourists such as J. H. Randall of Clyde, Ohio, who rhapsodized, "Readers, you who can not believe my statements, go and see these things for yourself,"[19] others by more discriminating observers who wondered why the Indian spirits did not speak but responded only by raps. Undoubtedly Helena read these articles, and she may also have seen Olcott's piece in the *Sun*, but the possibilities had not yet jelled in her mind.

In the September 26 issue of the *Religio -Philosophical Journal*, however, there appeared an article so eye-catching that she could not possibly have overlooked it. The entire front page, plus part of an inside page, was devoted to a euphoric report headlined ASTOUNDING WONDERS THAT STAGGER BELIEF and by-lined by Colonel Henry Steel Olcott. Sounding like a publicity agent for the Eddys, Olcott described the séances in terms generally reserved for the births of messiahs and other world-shaking events and he, too, encouraged visitors by printing travel directions to Vermont. All one had to do was take the New Haven, Hartford and Springfield Railroad to Springfield, Massachusetts, then the Connecticut River and Vermont Railroad to Rutland where the rest of the trip to Chittenden could be made by wagon. The rail fare from New York to Rutland cost eight dollars, the wagon ride two.

If Helena somehow missed the *Religio -Philosophical Journal*'s article, which is unlikely, she certainly saw Olcott's *Daily Graphic* pieces that began to appear the same week. Suddenly Colonel Olcott, whoever he was, seemed to be the man of the hour.

There was something about the writer that intrigued Helena, a karmic tug some might say, certainly a sixth sense whispering that this was the man for whom she had waited forty-four years, Michael Betanelly notwithstanding. So potent was this sensation that she would later maintain a higher power had instructed her to make the trip to Chittenden[20] for the express purpose of meeting Henry Steel Olcott. Accordingly, she packed her tobacco, a scarlet shirt such as the ones worn by Garibaldi's soldiers, and, as we shall see, several other items that might prove useful at a country séance. On Tuesday, October 13, in the company of Madame Magnon, she set out for Chittenden to meet her destiny.

At noon the next day, Henry Olcott and the *Graphic* artist Kappes stood in the doorway of the Eddys' dining hall and surveyed the luncheon crowd. A lover of good food and wine, Henry had suffered through a month of the Eddys' bad cooking, not to mention having put up with the constant stream of cranks who descended on the farmhouse. Sweeping his eyes critically along the tables, he was jolted by the sight of an unusual-looking woman. "Her hair was then a thick blond mop, worn shorter than the shoulders, and it stood out from her head, silken-soft and crinkled to the roots, like the fleece of a Cotswold ewe. This and the red shirt were what struck my attention." Both the Garibaldi shirt and the hairstyle were so outrageously anti-fashion that Olcott immediately pigeonholed her as an eccentric.

"Good gracious!" he remembered whispering to Kappes. "Look at *that* specimen, will you." Boldly settling himself opposite H.P.B. and Madame Magnon, who were talking French, he proceeded to stare.

Helena, recognizing him at once, chose to pay no attention. After the meal, she and Magnon rose and went outside, where Helena began to roll a cigarette. Olcott followed them into the yard but Helena continued to ignore him, and it was not until she fumbled for a match that he saw his opening.

"Permettez moi, Madame," he said, and lit her cigarette.

Since his remark had been made in French, Helena mistakenly assumed that he was fluent in the language, which he was not, and answered in kind. She asked him how long he had been there and what he thought of the phenomena. She described herself as "greatly interested in such things" and confided that she had read about the Eddys in the *Daily Graphic*, which had been swept off the newsstands within an hour of publication; she had been obliged to pay $1 for a copy.

From flattery she made a swift detour to archness. "I hesitated before coming here, because I was afraid of meeting that Colonel Olcott."

"Why should you be afraid of him, Madame?" Olcott asked.

"Oh!" she exclaimed, and one may be sure she was enjoying every minute of the game, "because I fear he might write about me in his paper."

She needn't worry, Henry replied, because he felt quite certain that Colonel Olcott would not mention her in his articles unless she wished it, "and I introduced myself." Twenty years later, writing his memoirs, it seemed ironic to him that their first meeting should have been so "very prosaic," but he added that even though "our acquaintance began in smoke . . . it stirred up a great and permanent fire."

That afternoon, as H.P.B. and Henry strolled about the farm getting acquainted, she spoke of her travels, hinted at occult marvels she had witnessed, and complained mildly about the tendency of American Spiritualists to emphasize materialistic phenomena at the expense of spiritual philosophy. "She did not give me any hint as to the existence of Himalayan Sages or of her own powers," Henry recalled. Of course it was scarcely likely that she would have mentioned Tibetan gurus, since they had not yet occurred to her. What she did do was undertake to charm Henry Olcott and, despite her sartorial nonconformity, this was accomplished in no time. As Henry related:

> Her manner was gracious and captivating, her criticisms upon men and things original and witty. She was particularly interested in drawing me out as to my own ideas about spiritual things and expressed pleasure in finding that I had instinctively thought along the occult lines which she herself had pursued. It was not as an Eastern mystic, but rather as a refined Spiritualist that she talked. For my part I knew nothing then, or next to nothing, about Eastern philosophy, and at first she kept silent on that subject.[21]

While the chemistry on both sides was immediate, Olcott failed to respond to her as a woman, indeed would claim that he found her androgynous. "Neither then, at the commencement, nor ever afterwards had either of us the sense of the other being of the opposite sex." Of course, "some base people from time to time dared to suggest that a closer tie bound us together" but these were unimaginative folks who could not understand that there might be "the attraction of soul to soul, not that of sex to sex." Another of Olcott's remarks about Helena, that "her every look, word and action proclaimed her sexlessness,"[22] seems to defy rational interpretation. She may have been overweight at the time, but she was far from unattractive, and possessed a lush femininity, a sort of earthy sensuality, that was remarked upon by others who encountered her. That she herself was still interested in sex is evident from her relationship with Michael Betanelly and perhaps it was because of this involvement that she felt no need to project her womanly side with Olcott— suspected, in fact, that it might threaten their budding friendship.

It was one of H.P.B.'s less admirable qualities that she used men (and women to a lesser degree) to gain her objectives, and already she had become adept at manipulation. Meeting Henry she understood at once—may have, actually, sensed it from his articles—that here was an ideal candidate for management if one knew how to go about it properly. At Chittenden, moving cautiously, she carefully refrained from scaring off a person who was, as far as she knew, a married family man. It may be asked what she wanted from

Olcott that Helena had to tread so gingerly, and the answer seems to be that she herself was not completely sure. On the most mundane level, she wanted to get her name mentioned in the *Daily Graphic* because she understood the value of publicity and knew this would be a route to recognition in the Spiritualist movement. Earlier she had tried something similar with Hannah Wolff and the spirit paintings of Helena's old photographs, but the effort had failed to result in newspaper coverage. To want her name before the public was not such a despicable ambition; on the contrary, it was a means of establishing herself as an authority so that she might get her writings published and thereby support herself. Later it would be hard for some to realize that Madame Blavatsky, despite her insistence that she lived under the protection of august beings, still had to eat like everyone else.

That evening, filing upstairs to the shadowy séance hall, Helena must have felt that she had to do something startling to attract attention, much less a mention in the *Daily Graphic*, because among the twenty-five visitors were some prominent people: the Spiritualist writer and lecturer James Peebles, a Hartford music professor named Lenzburg who was with his medium wife, the Michigan medium Mr. H. A. Phillips, and a Chicago medium Mrs. M. B. Carey, who was preparing an article on the Eddys for the *Religio-Philosophical Journal*.

The room was dimly lit by a shaded kerosene lamp in the back; on the platform at the front end of the hall stood a curtained cabinet. Everyone took a seat on one of the uncomfortable straight chairs and waited until William Eddy shambled up to the platform, settled on a chair inside the cabinet and pulled a blanket across the doorway. The first thing Helena heard were sounds—faint music and a low babble of voices. Then, in the dimness, luminous hands began to flutter slowly, the disembodied fingers extending and retreating with clutching movements and seeming to reach out to touch the hair of a woman in the first row. After the hands had vanished, the shrouded figure of a crone-like woman next slithered from the cabinet and began muttering incoherently before suddenly warbling a folk ballad in a cracked voice. Backing toward the cabinet, she began to dissolve, and in her place there strutted a tiny Indian maiden who unbraided her hair and shook it over her shoulders.

As the lineup of American Indians continued, Mrs. Phillips identified one of the forms as her spirit guide Awanola, and Mrs. Carey, not to be outdone, confided aloud that she could see *her* guide, Wassa. The next person to speak up was H.P.B.'s traveling companion Madame Magnon, who pointed to what she said was her father, Zephrin Boudreau from Three Rivers, Canada. He had been about sixty when he died, she said. "Is that you, Papa?" she called out.

"Oui," the figure squeaked.[23]

When Madame Magnon began asking questions in French, the phantom would respond by rapping its hand against the frame of the cabinet. "This gentleman," Olcott remembered, "stood so that I saw him in profile against the white wall. He had an aquiline nose, rather hollow cheeks, prominent cheek-bones and an iron-gray beard upon his chin." Certain that Boudreau must be "a gentleman,"[24] Olcott could not quite make up his mind if the spirit was merely rapping or if it were replying in French. Before he could reach a conclusion, Magnon's father had disappeared, upstaged by a phantom woman holding a child and Mrs. Dunbar in the front row began to shriek, "Oh, my baby! My Charlie!"[25] The child was held over the railing so that the sobbing Mrs. Dunbar could get a better look.

So far, the spectacle had been relatively routine—American Indians and babies—and Olcott who had been watching them for the past month was feeling a bit bored with the whole business. But the next visitor made him sit up and gasp in amazement.

He was a person of middle height, well-shaped, dressed in a Georgian (Caucasian) jacket, with loose sleeves and long pointed oversleeves, an outer long coat, baggy trousers, leggings of yellow leather, and white skull-cap, or fez, with tassel.

To Olcott, who had never seen such a strange costume, here was a potentially newsworthy spook whom he hoped someone would identify. Naturally it was Helena who obliged. "She recognized him at once as Michalko Guegidze, late of Kutais, Georgia, a servant of Madame Witte, a relative, and who waited upon Mme. de Blavatsky in Kutais."[26]

Kutais, it will be remembered, was a town through which Helena passed in 1861 or 1862 when she was extremely ill after the birth of Yuri and had to be transported back to Tiflis. It is curious that images from this traumatic episode should suddenly emerge in a Vermont farmhouse among strangers (and what is more curious was that some time later she would discover Michalko to be alive).[27] Still, that evening she felt sure that the spirit must be her Aunt Katherine's servant.

When William Eddy finished, his brother Horatio turned up the lamp wick and conducted a séance in the light. Among the phenomena was a spirit-hand that wrote Helena's name on a calling card in Russian script and another disembodied hand that she swiftly identified as that of Michalko's because a string of amber beads was wound around the wrist, a custom among Georgian peasants, she explained. Whispering in French, Olcott told her to ask the spirit if he would play a song on the guitar lying on a nearby table. "She first asked him, in Georgian and Russian, if he were really Michalko, and certain other questions; to which he responded by sweeping the guitar strings once, or thrice, as he wished to indicate 'Yes' or 'No.' "

"Ilaparakey sheni tscheerimy" [*sic*] (Speak to me, my good fellow).

There was no response.

"If it is you, knock five times or five sweeps of the guitar."

Again there was silence.

But when Helena commanded, "Play the Lezguinka,"[28] the patriotic spirit overcame its shyness and obliged with a passable rendition; afterwards, it played two more Caucasian dances as an encore.

Olcott could scarcely believe his ears. At last he had found something worth writing about, positive proof as far as he was concerned that the Eddys were genuine. It would be unlikely, he decided, that a Vermont farmer would know about the strings of amber beads on the wrists of Georgian peasants, or, for that matter, be familiar with the tunes of Russian folk songs. Besides, the Madame was "a lady of such social position, as to be incapable of entering into a vulgar conspiracy with any pair of tricksters, to deceive the public."[29]

Tremendously excited, the next morning he dashed off a short piece for the *Sun* about "Madame Blowtskey" whose spirit Michalko had rapped, "not being able to speak," and whose music had been "applauded by the Madame, who is herself a musician."[30] In his semiweekly report for the *Graphic*, Olcott described the concert in considerably greater detail, and this time managed to spell H.P.B.'s name correctly.

What happened on the night of October 14 is far from clear. According to Mrs. Carey, who was taking notes for her article, something took place but it was not musical. Madame's spirit, she wrote in the *Religio-Philosophical Journal,* "was dressed as an Arab and proved to be an Arabian guide which she had known while traveling in that country. She asked him several questions in his native tongue and he replied in the same language." After the talking, non-musical Arab, the Madame had been visited by a Turk and then by a Russian whom "she recognized as her father, but as he did not come out very distinctly she was not positive."[31] It should be pointed out that what people saw and heard at séances was quite subjective and depended on their will to believe, or as the case may be, disbelieve. At the Eddys', for example, a skeptical visitor who had departed the day before Helena's arrival observed that the séance room was so "very dark" that he found it "impossible to distinguish faces;"[32] in his opinion the so-called spirits looked like nothing more than "three dollars' worth of costumes."

During the ten days that Helena stayed at the farm, she told Olcott the story of her life —with a few deletions and additions. While she did not refer to the tragic loss of her son and lover, she did mention, for example, visits to Indian temples, her search for antiquities at the base of the Pyramids, and a particularly thrilling exploration into the interior of Africa with an armed escort. Henry thought that no biographer could have written a more romantic story than Helena had lived. "In the whole course of my experience, I never met so interesting and, if I may say it without offence, eccentric a character."[33] He could not deny being terribly impressed by both her Dolgorukov ancestors and the social position of the Fadeyevs, which doubtless encouraged Helena to embroider the lives of those relatives of a somewhat lesser status; for instance, she gave Captain von Hahn the rank of general and promoted Nikifor Blavatsky from vice-governor to governor of Erivan, but it was all the same to Olcott. However, for at least one brief moment he must have been bothered by a few doubts because he asked Madame to furnish documentary proof of her identity. Helena could not have been pleased at his request, but she acted the grand dame and responded serenely by handing him her passport, her father's will, and personal letters on crested stationery from several noblemen, including Baron Nicholas Meyendorff. It seems incredible that she had carried halfway around the globe fifteen-year-old letters from a despised ex-lover, but apparently she believed they might come in handy someday. Certainly they impressed Olcott, as did her often-repeated account of having fought with Garibaldi's army.

Probably she had not meant to make a point of mentioning Mentana but it proved convenient in accounting for her ill health at Chittenden. A few days after her arrival, her old chest wound reopened slightly and while fortunately this was not accompanied by the usual pain and convulsions, it began to cause her considerable discomfort. Olcott said that she "consulted" him about her problem and even showed him the scar. To display a scar below the heart, she would have had to partially disrobe but evidently Olcott chose not to be shocked by this immodest action. And when she solemnly explained that the scar was a stiletto wound from Mentana and made him feel the musket bullet still embedded in her right shoulder and another in her leg, he accepted her story as the truth. Of course he was aware that some of her adventures sounded not quite right and if they had come from another woman, he would have laughed in her face; but he did not imagine that a lady of such distinction as Madame Blavatsky would deliberately lie to him. Gazing into her hypnotic azure eyes and listening to her discourses with open-mouthed awe, he decided that he admired her inordinately and retired to his room where he filled his *Graphic* dispatches with accolades for the wonder woman he had chanced to discover.

There was plenty to write about. Every evening at ten minutes to seven a procession of apparitions began to drift in and out of the Eddy cabinet at intervals of from one to five minutes, and although Honto and the Indians doggedly made their appearances, they were now unceremoniously pushed out of the limelight by Madame's people: "Hassan Aga," a wealthy Tiflis merchant dressed in a black Astrakhan cap and tasseled hood who said three times that he had a secret to reveal but never managed to spit it out; "Safar Ali Bek," the man who had guarded Madame for Nikifor Blavatsky in Erivan, now transformed into a gigantic Kurd warrior carrying a feathered spear; a Circassian *noukar* who bowed, smiled and said, "*Tchock yachtchi*" (all right); a huge muscular black man in white-and-gold-horned headdress, a conjurer once met in Africa, Helena said. And there were less exotic phantoms as well: an old woman in a babushka, whom Helena recognized as Vera's nurse, and a portly man in a black evening suit and frilled white shirt, around whose neck hung a Greek cross of St. Anne suspended by a red moiré ribbon with two black stripes.

"Are you my father?" Helena asked in English, later confessing that she had been trembling.

The figure advanced toward her and stopped. "*Djadja*,"[34] he answered reproachfully.

He was, Helena informed the group, an uncle, her father's brother Gustave von Hahn who had been president of the criminal court at Grodno for twelve years and who had died in 1861. The sitters' eyes were popping. In terms of dramatic interest, Madame's relatives and even her casual acquaintances certainly outclassed the grubby Indians usually encountered at the Eddy séances.

To Henry Olcott and the others, Madame appeared to be enjoying herself enormously. According to Helena, who wrote about the Eddy séances in later years, the ectoplasmic shapes filled her with disgust; it made her skin crawl to watch the Spiritualists weeping and rejoicing in happiness at the sight of those revolting phantoms. She wished that they could see what she saw, that the creatures were not papa and mama and baby Charlie, but the dregs of personalities that had once lived; all the passions, thoughts and vices that could not follow the liberated soul and spirit after physical death. More than once, she would recall, she had seen a phantom detach itself from William Eddy and pounce upon someone in the audience, "expanding so as to envelop him or her entirely, and slowly disappearing within the living body as though sucked in by its every pore."[35] It had been, she would insist, ghastly to watch. Perhaps so. It was true that she did leave the Eddys in a hurry, but more likely this sudden exit resulted from having paid the mediums eighty dollars for room and board and having little money left.

In any case, she departed with a flourish because the séance on the eve of her leaving proved to be exceptional. As soon as the sitting began, a spirit called "George Dix" wasted no time in approaching Helena and getting right down to business:

Madame, I am now about to give you a test of the genuineness of the manifestations in this circle, which I think will satisfy not only you, but a skeptical world beside. I shall place in your hands the buckle of a medal of honor worn in life by your brave father, and buried with his body in Russia. This has been brought to you by your uncle, whom you have seen materialized . . .

When Helena began to scream, somebody hurriedly struck a light. "We all saw," Olcott reported, "Mme. de Blavatsky holding in her hand a silver buckle of a most curious shape, which she regarded with speechless wonder." After she had recovered, she affirmed that the buckle had indeed been attached to a medal worn by her father, that it had been granted by the late Czar Nicholas to his officers after the victorious Turkish campaign of 1828, and that it had been buried with von Hahn.

But could she be sure, someone wondered. Of course, she snapped back—they could see that the point of the pin was broken, something she herself had done many years ago in a moment of carelessness. But if her word was insufficient, she had at home in New York a photographic copy of an oil painting in which Peter von Hahn was wearing the very medal to which the buckle had been attached.

Henry Olcott could scarcely contain himself. Writing his report for the *Graphic*, he did not bother to disguise his total acceptance of this piece of theater, which must have been meticulously staged by H.P.B. and the Eddys, and from his pen rushed a geyser of purple prose:

Was there ever a "manifestation" more wonderful than this? A token drug by unknown means from a father's grave and laid in his daughter's hand, five thousand miles away, across an ocean? A jewel from the breast of a warrior sleeping his last sleep in Russian ground, sparkling in the candlelight in a gloomy apartment of a Vermont farm-house! A precious present from the tomb of her nearest and best beloved of kin, to be kept as a perpetual proof that death can neither extinguish the ties of blood nor long divide those who were once united and desire reunion with one another![36]

The next day, October 25, Madame Magnon and a jubilant Helena Petrovna left for New York. Due to the delay in having engravings made for Kappes' drawings, Olcott's articles about her would not appear for several weeks, but in the meantime there was much to do. Altogether the colonel had had an exhilarating effect on her and suddenly she found herself brimming with hope. When he had mentioned collecting the *Graphic* articles into a book, she had thought it a wonderful idea and offered to help. At the same time it occurred to her that the stories were important enough to warrant international readership and, thinking of Davis's friend Aksakov, she suggested translating Olcott's work for *Psychische Studien* or even some Russian journal. Olcott had been thrilled by the idea.

However much she liked Henry—and she liked him a great deal—she could not really say that she respected him. He struck her as childish—"worse than a three-year-old child" was the way she would describe him to Nadyezhda—and sometimes his "ardent and gushing imagination" pushed him to heights of gullibility that were quite amazing. Had she not warned him that William Eddy's spooks were not necessarily proof of intelligent spirit-entities? If genuine, she had tactfully suggested, they must be the medium's double escaping from his body and masquerading in other costumes. But Henry, "in love with the spirits,"[37] had not believed her and continued to insist that many of the spirit forms, the babies for instance, could not possibly have come from William.

In spite of their disagreements, he had taken to calling her "Jack" and she affectionately referred to him as "Maloney." Parting the best of friends, they promised to meet when Henry returned to the city.

Two mornings after her return from Chittenden, full of optimism and self-possession, she opened the *Daily Graphic* to find catastrophe staring up at her. In a sarcastic article by Dr. George Beard, the Eddy brothers were denounced as frauds—not clever frauds, but frauds of the cheapest and most transparent kind—and Colonel Olcott called a dupe who had been blinded by a handful of bad magicians' tricks. "When your correspondent returns to New York," Beard needled, "I will teach him on any convenient evening to do all that the Eddys do."[38]

H.P.B. had heard of Dr. Beard, a well-known New York neuropathologist who had spent two days at Chittenden just prior to her arrival there. Olcott had told H.P.B. that Beard had brought with him an electric battery. He proposed that the Eddys grasp its handles while he applied sufficient current to prevent them letting go in order to use their hands for trickery. Naturally the Eddys had refused, but when H.P.B. arrived people were still laughing about the skeptical Dr. Beard and his fruitless battery.

Beard's article threw Helena into an uproar. No sooner had she achieved the public eye than her area of endeavor became suspect. She was also alarmed at the slurs on Henry, for if he were made to appear less than a serious investigator, she would never be able to sell the translations of his article. Desperate to retrieve her vanishing hopes, she drafted a stinging reply to Beard in which she defended the Eddys, citing her own experiences as proof of their honesty. Then she hand-delivered the letter to the *Graphic*.

A Spiritualist of many years' standing, I am more sceptical in receiving evidence from paid mediums than many unbelievers. But when I receive such evidence as I received at the Eddys', I feel bound on my honour, and under the penalty of confessing myself a moral coward, to defend the mediums, as well as the thousands of my brother and sister Spiritualists, against the conceit and slander of one man who has nothing and no one to back him in his assertions.[39]

If Beard believed that he could duplicate the materializations, let him make good his boast:

I now hereby finally and publicly challenge Dr. Beard to the amount of $500 to produce before a public audience and under the same conditions the manifestations herein attested, or, failing this, to bear the ignominious consequences of his proposed *exposé*.[40]

* * *

She did not have five hundred dollars of course, but she felt on fairly safe ground in calling Beard's bluff. In her opinion he was a publicity-seeking headhunter looking for a missionary to eat, a person who went around causing "flapdoodles" (a favorite word of hers) for the want of something better to do. Unfortunately he had given her no choice but to defend the Eddys, which she had never intended, because while she did not believe them frauds (at least no more fraudulent than other mediums), she certainly did not think that the phantoms were what the Spiritualists claimed them. Rather, she was inclined to believe that the apparition of her uncle, for instance, had not really been Gustave von Hahn but a picture that she had projected on William Eddy's astral body (an exact, non-physical replica of the individual physical body). It was Eddy who unconsciously assimilated her own mental projections, but the fact that he could objectify her thoughts proved nothing about life after death. It seemed ironic to her that never at any séance she had attended, the Eddys' included, had she ever seen anybody she wanted to see, like Yuri or Agardi. All she ever got were servants and the perfidious Safar Ali who had betrayed her to Nikifor.

Having done all she could to counteract Dr. Beard, Helena now redoubled her efforts on behalf of Olcott and herself. Several weeks had passed since Andrew Jackson Davis had written to Aksakov, but no reply had come. On October 28, she decided to write herself, offering exclusive translations of eminent American psychics with whom she was acquainted. As a matter of fact, the only one she knew was Olcott, who had only recently made his debut as a commentator on Spiritualism, but she was determined to impress Aksakov. "I am also working for the *Graphic* and can send my articles regularly," she said, and offered to provide an additional service—pen-and-ink illustrations. Grossly inflating the importance of the subject she was trying to peddle, she airily misinformed Aksakov that Spiritualism was "no laughing matter" in America where the number of believers had recently mushroomed to eighteen million, or almost half the population! Even the press was giving respectful attention to the movement and "attempts at ridicule, condemnation and censure are rarer and rarer,"[41] she said.

The next day, when Olcott's *Sun* article about "Madame Blowtskey" and her singing Georgian appeared, Helena found herself a minor celebrity, for twenty-four hours anyway. Knowing how fickle the public can be, she quickly looked for ways to garner additional publicity and, coincidentally, prove George Beard a liar once and for all. Obviously the situation called for someone to corroborate the identity of the Russian phantoms at Chittenden. As it happened, Michael Betanelly was in New York that day and she had no difficulty (one presumes) in persuading him to step forward as an independent witness who, of course, knew nothing about Spiritualism and who certainly had no connection with "Madame Blowtskey." Giving his address as 430 Walnut Street, Philadelphia, he wrote to Henry Olcott at Chittenden:

Dear Sir,

Though I have not the pleasure of your personal acquaintance, I take the liberty of addressing to you a few words, knowing your name from the *Daily Graphic* correspondence on Eddy's manifestations, which I read with greatest interest.

I learned from today's *Sun* that at Eddys', in presence of Mme. Blowtskey, Russian lady, a spirit of Michalko Guegidse (very familiar name to me) has materialized in Georgian dress, has spoken Georgian language, danced Lezguinka, and sung Georgian National Air.

Being myself a native of Georgia, Caucasus, I read these news with greatest astonishment and surprise, and being not a believer in spiritualism, I do not know what to think of these manifestations.

I address to-day a letter to Mrs. Blowtskey, asking some questions about materialized Georgian, and if she left Eddys' please forward it to her, if you know her address.

I also earnestly request your corroboration of this astonishing fact, materialized Georgian, if he really came out from the cabinet in Georgian dress, and in your presence. If that occurred in fact, and if anybody will regard it, as usually, trickery and humbug, then I will state to you this: There are in the United States no other Georgians but three, of whom I am the one and came first to this country three years ago. Two others whom I know came over last year. I know they are not in Vermont now and never been there before; and I know they do not speak English at all. Besides us three, no other man speaks Georgian in this country, and when I say this, I mean it to be true fact. Hoping you will answer this letter, I remain, yours respectfully,

M. C. Betanelly[42]

To Helena and Michael, the letter must have seemed like a harmless enough deception to pull on poor Olcott, who of course had nothing to lose and everything to gain if the public accepted the Eddy phenomena as real. However, it was a mistake to have mentioned the other Georgians (who were certainly fictitious), because Henry immediately asked Betanelly for their names and suggested that the three of them sign a statement swearing they had known Michalko when alive. Probably Michael had not intended to become part of an elaborate conspiracy, but now that he had put one foot into the situation, the confederate was now obliged to wriggle out as best he could. "I am perfectly willing," he replied, "to give you all information and certificates concerning materialized Georgian spirits at Eddys' " but unfortunately he had lost the addresses of his Georgian friends whom he believed were living in New York or "out West." Having admitted he did not know their whereabouts, he went on to assure Olcott that they were not in Vermont.

Then, obviously anxious to change the subject, he hurried to tell all he knew about Michalko (not much), declared that the names of Hassan-Aga and Safar Ali Bek were "also very familiar to me," and finally claimed to have known the late Andrey Fadeyev, "a tall and old Gentleman in Tiflis, who died several years ago."[43] Why he brought in Helena's grandfather is a mystery, because his apparition had not appeared at the Eddys. One would think that this second letter of Betanelly's might have aroused Olcott's suspicions, but apparently not, for he included Michael's testimony in his *Graphic* pieces and even forwarded to the paper for facsimile reproduction a Georgian newspaper that Betanelly had supplied him.

In the meantime, Helena had her hands full. Dr. Beard's comeback to her was a nine-column article reaffirming his opinion that William Eddy staged all the apparitions and that Olcott's reports were "terribly and stupendously exaggerated" and his assertions that the spirits talked "absurdly untrue." Most of the visitors at the Eddys' were "weak-minded fools" incapable "of thinking a sensible thought."[44] Shooting back a response to his reply, Helena matched sarcasm for sarcasm and reminded readers that Beard had not accepted her five-hundred-dollar challenge.

This media combat had a number of happy results: she received an admiring letter from Gerry Brown, editor of the *Spiritual Scientist* offering to publish anything she wished to write; and the *Daily Graphic* decided that she was sufficiently newsworthy to warrant an interview. At the newspaper office, she blew smoke at the reporter and narrated a life story peppered with more falsehoods than a cookie has crumbs. Knocking three years from her age, she presented herself as a former child-bride married to a doddering seventy-three-year-old whose "habits were not agreeable to me," and "as I had a fortune of my own, I decided to travel." She mentioned having lived in England and Egypt, also in the Sudan where she made a small fortune after cornering the ostrich-feather market and at Baden-Baden where she lost a fortune at the gambling tables. In fact, she declared, money meant nothing because fortunately she had received a sizable legacy from Princess Bagration.

Goggling, the reporter kept lighting Helena's cigarettes and repeating, "That's a remarkable statement," to which H.P.B. would solemnly reply, "It's true." Name-dropping constantly, she reeled off stories about Daniel Home, Charles Darwin (whose works she claimed to have translated into Russian while in Africa), Czar Alexander, and other persons likely to impress a newspaper reporter. However hard-pressed he may have been to believe her tales, the writer must have been impressed, because he described her as "handsome, with a full voluptuous figure, large eyes, well-formed nose, and rich, sensuous mouth and chin." He thought her elegantly dressed, noting that "her clothing is redolent of some subtle and delicious perfume"[45] that he assumed was Oriental. Possibly it was hashish.

When the interview appeared on November 13, Helena could not have been overly pleased; unmistakably the reporter was making fun of her, for which she had only herself to blame, and afterward she would be more careful about what she said to newsmen. Still, the last few weeks had proved successful beyond her yeastiest imaginings, for now there was hardly a newspaper reader in New York who did not know of Madame Blavatsky—and all this before Olcott's Chittenden pieces had even appeared. As Henry admitted, she generated "a blaze of publicity"[46] on her own.

Amidst the excitement, Helena found time to move twice. From East Sixteenth Street, she shifted around the corner to 16 Irving Place and then, a few days later, to 23 Irving Place, where she rented a suite of rooms in a brownstone owned by Dr. and Mrs. I. G. Atwood. The Atwoods were Spiritualists— Dr. Atwood had a successful practice as a magnetic healer—and felt honored to house the foremost defender of the faith. Helena had the entire first floor, with a front room facing on tree-shaded Irving Place and the back on a pretty garden. H.P.B. had always liked this pleasant residential neighborhood south of Gramercy Park, but her new apartment had the additional advantage of being located only a few doors down the street from the Lotos Club. It could not hurt to be Henry's neighbor when he returned from Vermont.

H.P.B.'s mood of exhilaration lasted until she learned from Andrew Jackson Davis that he had received a reply from Alexander Aksakov. Since it was written in French, he asked her to translate for him. Reaching the part about herself, she was horrified to read: "I have heard of Madame Blavatsky from one of her relatives, who told me that she is quite a powerful medium. Unfortunately her communications show the effects of her morals, which have not been of the strictest kind."[47] Unable to hide her violent agitation, Helena explained Aksakov's remarks by saying that he must have heard ugly gossip about her. Davis reacted with sympathy and reassurance and promised to write Aksakov "that he does not know you personally and that I know you."

Unnerved, she rushed back to her apartment where she broke down in despair over her folly in trying to reach Aksakov. His words had not only "awakened all the past within me and torn open all the old wounds," but made her realize that Aksakov had the power to destroy her even in America. There was nothing left but flight, to where she could not imagine. In this anguished mood, she decided to throw herself on Aksakov's mercy:

Whoever it was told you about me, they told you the truth, in essence, if not in detail. God only knows how I have suffered for my past. It is clearly my fate to gain no absolution upon earth. This past, like the brand of the curse on Cain, has pursued me all my life, and pursues me even here, in America, where I came to be far from it and from the people who knew me in my youth. You are the innocent cause of my being obliged to escape somewhere yet farther away, where, I do not know. I do not accuse you; God is my witness that while I am writing these lines, I have nothing against you in my heart, beyond the deep sorrow which I long have known for the irrevocable past.[48]

The Helena Petrovna he had heard about and the Helena Petrovna of 1874 were "two different persons." The old Helena had not believed in God, nor had she concerned herself with morality. Nevertheless, for the past ten years she had dedicated "every moment of my life" to Spiritualism, and were she rich, she would spend her last farthing to propagandize for the Divine Truth. "But my means are very poor and I am obliged to live by my work, by translating and writing in the papers." Now even this would not be possible. Thanks to Aksakov's "just but harsh judgment" of her, there was no hope but death. She had only one request to make of him:

> Do not deprive me of the good opinion of Andrew J. Davis. Do not reveal to him that which, if he knew it and were convinced, would force me to escape to the ends of the earth. I have only one refuge left in the world, and that is the respect of the spiritualists of America, who despise nothing so much as "free love."
>
> Can it give you any satisfaction to morally destroy for ever a woman who has already been thus destroyed by circumstances? Pardon this long letter and accept the assurance of the deep respect and devotion of your obedient servant.[49]

Helena remained depressed and frightened. The best antidote for such emotions is to get them out of one's system by sharing them with a friend, but she had no one in whom she could confide, not even Michael Betanelly, who was, one imagines, the last person she would tell about previous lovers and an illegitimate child. Assuming a tone of breeziness, she wrote Henry asking if he could get her a writing assignment because she would soon be "hard up." In the same rollicking style, she reported her experiences as a celebrity:

> Don't you know, the fellows of the *Graphic* bored my life out of me to give them my portrait . . . I told them that nature had endowed and gifted me with a potato nose, but I did not mean to allow them to make fun of it, vegetable though it is. They very seriously denied the fact, and so made me laugh . . .[50]

But there was little reason for laughter. Any day Aksakov might strike again and then she would be finished.

Toward the end of November, Olcott returned to New York and Michael also came in from Philadelphia. In the course of their correspondence, Michael had expressed a strong desire to meet Olcott's colleague and "talk over Spiritualism,"[51] and now the unsuspecting Henry agreed to arrange an introduction. Afterward when Betanelly confided to Henry his profound admiration of Madame Blavatsky, there was no reason for Henry to read special significance into it, especially since H.P.B. seemed indifferent to the young man's attentions. And a few days later, when Betanelly had returned to Philadelphia and Helena suddenly announced she was going there on business, Olcott still made no connection. After two months in Vermont among the apparitions, he was having difficulty adjusting to reality: his estranged wife, his two sons who were at boarding school in New Haven, Connecticut, and his neglected law practice. There were more pressing matters to think about than an unconventional Russian woman, however charming she might be.

II

"John King" and Other Spooks

Of course Helena had no intention of letting Olcott go that easily. In her mind, the colonel was the key figure in the Spiritualist movement and, as such, a person essential to her personal plans, however vague these still were. In her relations with Olcott, as with others, there was a strong element of exploitation, but it could not be called a one-way street. One of H.P.B.'s traits, amounting almost to an obsession, was fairness, and she tried to give something in return for what she took. In Olcott's case, she began translating his Chittenden articles into Russian for publication in *Psychische Studien*. (Although Aksakov received these translations, he did not, so far as is known, print them—nor did any other publication.)

Mid-December, she joined Henry at Hartford, Connecticut, where the American Publishing Company was preparing for publication his *Graphic* articles under the title *People from the Other World*. Not only did H.P.B. help read proof, she aided him in the task of making enough last-minute revisions and additions to fill a five-hundred-page book. In many of the additions it is easy to detect her influence, not only her thinking but her prejudices as well. For example, she gave Henry an earful about Daniel Home, whom she had hated ever since her affair with Nicholas Meyendorff, and she spitefully depicted him as a mentally and physically ill machine unable to control itself—and also as a fraud. Olcott, delighted to have an inside scoop, slipped the material into his manuscript without, evidently, considering that this totally unjustified attack on Home might cause unpleasant consequences for both himself and H.P.B.

After a few days at Hartford, Helena returned to Philadelphia where she settled for the winter at Mrs. Morton's private hotel, 1111 Girard Street. She bought a bird, an ordinary little hen canary, who was not much to look at or listen to, but Helena became deeply attached to Jenny. During this period she found herself in a curious frame of mind. Inwardly she felt a growing sense of discontent and anxiety, which seemed odd because within three months she had achieved more than she could reasonably have hoped for. Thanks to Olcott, and to her own efforts, she had become an overnight celebrity in both the general and Spiritualist media, a spokeswoman and leader whose activities were deemed worthy of news coverage. The *Religio -Philosophical Journal* and other papers were begging for articles; well-known Spiritualists, such as Epes Sargent, Gen. Francis Lippitt, Hiram Corson, Louisa Andrews and Robert Dale Owen wrote for her opinions; in Philadelphia, local Spiritualists flocked to her hotel room for conversation and guidance. Suddenly she found herself in possession of an item she had never owned before—standing in the world. Furthermore, Alexander Aksakov had hastened to assure her that it would give him no satisfaction to destroy her. She hardly knew how to express her gratitude for his "infinite goodness." Apologizing for having sent him an hysterical letter, she continued to thank him effusively for his kindness to "a sinner like me."[52]

In addition to her new-found celebrity, she had the continued attention and support of a man who loved her. There is no question of Betanelly's love for her and it was not the platonic admiration of Olcott, but real sexual passion. She had told him her age was thirty-six and probably claimed to be a widow, a story she had repeated so often she must have half-believed it. At any rate, when Michael pressed her to marry him, she did not reject him. He had become too important to her emotionally, probably sexually, and certainly financially, to be dismissed. What she did, however, was delay her decision for most of the winter of 1875.

Betanelly was an ingenious and ambitious businessman, but he lacked capital, so H.P.B. offered to use her contacts to arrange a loan.

As a Spiritualist, he was strictly along for the ride on her trip; he attended séances and accompanied her to experimental sittings where she tested various mediums. Probably it did not displease him to be mentioned in the New York *Daily Graphic* and the *Religio -Philosophical Journal* as a "cultured gentleman" who "seeing the falsity of the popular religions, disbelieved in all spiritual existences"[53] but who, nonetheless, had been converted after receiving messages in Russian from an old college friend. His conversion, if there was one, would prove short-lived however.

Life was going well for Helena Petrovna, but, as happened repeatedly when such a fortuitous state of events occurred, she could not cope with success and unconsciously set about wrecking it. Betanelly, who knew her well enough to notice this self-destructive trait, would write later that if only she would keep her mouth shut she could avoid all sorts of troubles. But she could not. In fact, about this time she involved herself in a rather messy scandal, which she would have done well to ignore.

At the séances of two Philadelphia mediums, Jennie and Nelson Holmes, there regularly appeared the "materialized" spirit of a pretty young woman named Katie King, who caught the fancy of Robert Dale Owen. An elderly man, a respected writer for twenty years, Owen was an honest and generally sane person, but Katie must have bewitched him; soon he was calling her "daughter" and presenting her with expensive rings and bracelets, evidently in the belief that his gifts went with her into the spirit world.

When a friend tipped off Owen that Katie was no spirit, but a living woman, he refused to believe it. He was later forced to alter his opinion when he not only got back his jewelry but also met Eliza White, the "real" Katie King. Shocked into physical illness by the fraud, Owen had the courage to announce publicly that he had been bamboozled.

Madame Blavatsky, casting herself as the Sir Lancelot of Spirtualism, leaped to the Holmes's defense by insisting she had seen no fraud. Katie King was, she declared, a spirit, and went on to attribute the scandal to a plot on the part of "the Protestant Jesuitical society called the 'Young Men's Christian Association.' "[54] It is not entirely clear why she felt compelled to defend two mediums so obviously suspect that the Spiritualist press rejected them; she must have believed that the scandal would cause incalculable damage both to the movement and to her personal credibility. Writing about the matter to Aksakov, she stated significantly that she was ready to work day and night for the cause, "so long as I have a morsel of bread, and that only because it is hard to work when one is hungry."[55] Robert Dale Owen's accusations might snatch away her bread crusts, and, coincidentally, have a disastrous effect on the sales of Olcott's forthcoming book.

The year 1874 had ended sadly for Henry, because on December 28, after fourteen years of marriage, his wife divorced him.[56] In Victorian America, where it was considered a disgrace, divorce was an unusual action for any woman, especially a clergyman's daughter like Mary. Even though Henry always refused to comment on the divorce, it must have been a piercing blow. · In later years, it would be alleged that Helena had stolen him from his wife, while Theosophists would insist he had been divorced long before he met her. Neither version is accurate. Helena and Henry had known each other for three months before his divorce, but at the time, they were still casual acquaintances. Friendship and intimacy lay in the future.

At the beginning of 1875, Helena invited Olcott to Philadelphia, booked him a room at her hotel, and began arranging test séances to rehabilitate the Holmes's reputation. Henry, acting as prosecutor and jury, assured her that he would keep an open mind and "start at the very bottom." Naturally, he did no such thing. At the first séance, the spirit John King came to his daughter's defense by rapping out an account of what really had happened. A certain Dr. Henry Child had hired Eliza White to impersonate Katie, money had passed hands, and various agents had been employed in carrying off the fraud. In short, John declared, the Holmes had been framed. The testing continued until the night before Henry's return to New York. He watched in breathless silence as the door of the Holmes's cabinet opened and out stepped "a short, thin, girlish figure, clad in white from crown to sole."[57] Obviously it could not have been Jennie Holmes, because Olcott had tied and sealed her in a sack; nor did the apparition seem to be a living confederate. Accordingly, he concluded that Jennie and Nelson Holmes were innocent.

Most people disagreed, charging collusion between Madame and the Holmes. The weight of evidence confirms this cynical conclusion as does the fact that the couple was subsequently caught in numerous other deceptions. Some years later, Jennie Holmes would admit to a founder of the Theosophical Society that Madame had arranged the spurious phenomenon for Olcott's benefit. She further insisted that H.P.B. had proposed a partnership in the "materialization show business." Henry would manage them because Madame had already so "psychologized him that he did not know his head from his heels."[58]

A few months later H.P.B. herself would repudiate the Holmes and insist to Olcott it was she who had "materialized" Katie at the test séances. Nobody, she claimed, had been more surprised to see Miss King than Jennie Holmes.

Helena's fraternization with the Holmes, honest or otherwise, had an unhealthful effect on her. Even after Yuri's death, she had continued to will herself free from hallucinations and poltergeists. Now, in Philadelphia, due either to constant contact with sensitives or to her unstable emotional state, she suffered a relapse. Once again, she began to experience visions and voices, this time visitations from the spirit John King, whom she called her only friend. A letter to Aksakov dated February 11 reveals her intense depression and inadvertently illuminates her psychic distress:

> I have quite ceased to get any letters from my aunts and sisters; they have evidently all forgotten me, and so much the better for them. I shall now *never* go back to Russia. My father is dead, nobody wants me, and I am altogether superfluous in the world. Here I am at least a human being; there, I am—Blavatsky. I know that everybody respects me here, and I am needed for spiritism. Now the spirits are my brothers and sisters, my father and mother.[59]

One person alone, she asserted, was sufficient recompense for the loss of her family; not the living man with whom she was currently involved, but the disembodied John King "with his own black beard and his white Chinese saucer-upside-down cap." He was to her "a personality, a definite, living, spiritual personality" who did her "the honour of visiting me incessantly."

So engagingly popular a personality was John King that he had been appearing to mediums for two decades. By the same token, he was so very ordinary a spook that H.P.B.'s interest is surprising. He seems to have appeared first in the early 1850s to a farmer-medium living in Ohio, and later would control the famous Italian medium Eusapia Palladino. But no matter what country or which medium, John King was always the same—a raucous phantom-about-town, a rough ex-pirate who loved recounting his adventures not only through mediums but also by Ouija Board and automatic writing. H.P.B., who disliked sharing her spirits, dismissed all the other John Kings and referred to this one as "*my* John King."[60] She certainly tried to monopolize "Johny": he wrote notes to Henry that mysteriously appeared in a notebook Olcott carried in his pocket; he also painted pictures on satin, attended Helena's séances, wrote letters to her friends, scared the servants and stole her money. There was no mistaking John's virility and dash: he was practiced at the earthy banter Helena loved in a man, and even went so far as to kiss her on the lips. She told Michael she had hated the kiss, but she still allowed King to call her "his lass Ellie," "a fine Spanish wench," and "a fancy she-dumpling."[61] Michael evidently did not regard John as a rival—yet.

In late January, H.P.B. badly injured her knee and leg. To some, she claimed she had slipped on an icy sidewalk. To Gen. Francis J. Lippitt, Boston attorney and Spiritualist, she reported she had "nearly broken my leg by falling down under a heavy bedstead I was trying to move and that fell on me."[62] The latter version may well be true since about this time she moved from Girard Street to the Holmes's former apartment at 825 North 19th Street. When her leg refused to mend as expected, Helena was forced to spend much of her time in bed where she distracted herself by reading and by writing surprisingly cheerful letters. From Andrew Jackson Davis she ordered a complete set of his works, as well as a set of Shakespeare and several books on magic. The bill came to a whopping $33.15, which she did not have and therefore neglected to pay.[63] In addition to Davis and Shakespeare, she also read Epes Sargent's *Proof Palpable of Immortality,* which fascinated her more than any other Spiritualist book she had seen. "You may tell him so if you see him," she wrote to General Lippitt, "and say to him that he has perfectly psychologized a true born Cossack and made her fall in love with him. My best leg *won't* heal and seems determined to remain lame."[64]

Despite the bravado, she sensed that all her old insecurities were waiting to pounce. Since her defense of the Holmes, the Spiritualist journals who had clamored for her work refused to buy. She felt poor, ill, and unprotected; unseen voices kept whispering in her ears.

Troubled by her inadequacies as a writer and fearful once again that she would be unable to earn a living, Helena keenly felt the need of a sponsor. The ideal person would have been Henry Olcott, but he was busy in New York and Hartford and, in any case, as she observed to Aksakov, "he is far from rich and has nothing to live on but his literary labours, and he has to keep a wife and a whole lot of children."[65] There remained only Michael, whose business, while still small, was prospering. He was even predicting that "in a few years I will be able to open a large trade between Russia and America."[66] Toward the middle of March, Helena moved into a house Michael had leased at 3420 Sansom Street in West Philadelphia and on April 3, they were married in the First Unitarian Church by Rev. William H. Furness.

H.P.B.'s ambivalences about the marriage are evident in her behavior. She even neglected to inform her houseguest, Henry Olcott, of the wedding until after the event. Stunned, Olcott called the marriage "a freak of madness" and added, "when I privately expressed to her my amazement at what I conceived to be her act of folly in marrying a man younger than herself, and inexpressibly her inferior in mental capacity,"[67] she had her defense prepared: their fates were linked by karma, and the marriage was her punishment for "awful pride and combativeness."[68] Besides, she insisted, Michael had threatened suicide if she refused him.

She was not so frank as she might have been with Henry, but certainly more candid than she was with others. She told him that Michael asked "nothing but the privilege of watching over her, that his feeling was one of unselfish adoration for her intellectual grandeur" and added "he would make no claim to any of the privileges of wedded life."[69] Why she felt compelled to convince Henry the marriage would not be consummated is unclear, for surely it was no scandal for a married woman to sleep with her own husband. Incredibly, Henry seems to have bought the story. While there is no reason to doubt Helena's account of her non-sexual marriage to Blavatsky, it is almost impossible to believe her relationship with Michael Betanelly was not physical.

Unable or unwilling to admit she had sexual needs, Helena spent the rest of her wedding day pretending that nothing out of the ordinary had taken place. She dashed off a postcard to General Lippitt telling him she was sending him a self-portrait done by John King on white satin. He must excuse the smudges because Michael had taken it to his office "and it passed through so many uncleanly hands that it lost partially its virgin purity."[70] Aside from the references to John King's non-virginal portrait, there is no allusion to having been married earlier in the day.

Ten years later she would look back on her wedding and claim that a black wizard, possibly some beast or devil, had taken possession of her body and spoken with her tongue. When she regained consciousness, she found living in her house a "handsome young Armenian" who treated her as if he were her husband. "I order him off, but he does not go, declares that I am his wife, and that he has just been legally married to me, married before witnesses, Olcott among them." She herself remembered nothing. "I turn to Olcott; imagine my horror when he confirms it. He was a witness at the wedding, and signed the register."[71] A decade hence, such a colossal mistake must have seemed to her to be due to possession.

Actually, she had simply made the conventional error of marrying for financial security. But to her dismay, she discovered almost immediately that Betanelly's business was in trouble, and that her groom was virtually bankrupt.

Michael's situation did little to improve a temper already short from pain and incapacity. She must have made her resentment obvious enough to spark reciprocal feelings in Michael. Whatever ties of affection there were binding them began at once to crumble, and within ten days, she had begun to call John King "my only friend." Claiming to be "fonder of him than of anything on earth," she praised King for having "transformed"[72] her.

By April, 1975, H.P.B. was finally beginning to develop a profile of her mission as an ethical and religious teacher. To be sure, there had for twenty-five years been fleeting glimpses of a special destiny but up until now the exact nature of this life work had eluded her. Suddenly, revelations germinating for forty-four years began to bubble into her consciousness, prompted either by the presence of John King, or by her own subconscious desires. She now felt certain that a secret Brotherhood had elected her to be its spokesperson in the world; it was she who would carry a message of Truth: that is, the secrets of the universe that lay hidden from a race ill-equipped to grasp the ungraspable. Each century, she contended, the keepers of the Truth seek someone to act as their agent; in the nineteenth century, however unsatisfactory she might appear to others, they had chosen Helena for this exalted task.

No one can know if Helena viewed the discovery of her special mission with misgivings, or whether or not she questioned the validity of her perceptions. Did she consider that the Brotherhood might be nothing more than a functional symbol of her unconscious? Or was it a sign of mental illness? Did it occur to her that these images might have been long languishing in her unconscious, waiting for the chance to break through? Even so, her doubts must have quickly been overpowered by the radiance of her vision.

As evidenced in her correspondence, Helena saw herself as a psychological cripple whose nervousness and mercurial temper revolted the sober-minded. Still, she was guiltless, since she had been born that way and could now even see how her disabilities helped qualify her for the unique future role. Her selection, she believed, was less the result of personal merit than the total willingness to sacrifice herself for the propagation of great truths. Few, if any, besides her would voluntarily accept the persecution and ridicule sure to accompany such a thankless assignment.

The secret group under whose direct command she worked, she called the Brotherhood of Luxor. Unlike John King, the Brotherhood were not entities from the cosmic plane of existence, but rather living men with headquarters somewhere in Egypt. The chief adept and supervisor was Serapis Bey, but there were seven associate brothers, among them: Tuitit Bey, Polydorus Isurenus, Robert More. Some of their names were never revealed. While she called them her "Masters,"[73] she does not seem to have conceived of herself as their servant but, rather, as their equal, as their St. Paul.

Even though the spirit John King had pointed her in her present direction, she seems to have been uncertain about how to fit him into the overall scheme. She wrote to Aksakov that "John and I are acquainted from old times"[74] before he began to materialize for every run-of-the-mill medium. For General Lippitt, she added further details: for the past fourteen years John King had been with her daily and saved her life in the shipwreck of the *Eumonia* and at the battle of Mentana. "He loves me, I know it."[75]

From these statements, it appears that she identified King with the invisible protector of her childhood. Eventually, however, John would find himself replaced by more dignified spirits, and even now she realized that John was too earthy to act as anything but messenger and servant of the Brotherhood of Luxor.

Meanwhile Henry Olcott remained at Sansom Street with H.P.B. and Michael. Their interminable discussions must have excluded Michael, and no doubt the other odd happenings in the household did not contribute to his peace of mind. Helena, in addition, did not deign to concern herself with domestic matters. Since there were only a few ragged towels in the house, Henry bought a length of toweling, which he and Helena cut into pieces. Noting that she was about to use the fabric unhemmed, he protested such shoddy housekeeping and shamed her into getting out a needle. Suddenly, kicking the table, she yelled, "Get out, you fool!" but hastily explained that her remark had been directed not at Henry, but at an invisible being who had been tugging her skirt.

"Capital," Henry joked. "Make it hem these towels."

Towels, needles and thread were locked in a bookcase. Fifteen minutes later, Henry heard a squeaky sound "like a mouse's pipe" and Helena informed him that "that nuisance" had finished the sewing. "So," Olcott reported, "I unlocked the bookcase door and found the dozen towels actually hemmed, though after a clumsy fashion that would disgrace the youngest child in an infant-school sewing class."[76] However poor the job, he could not deny that the towels were indeed hemmed.

On another day, Helena disappeared into her bedroom and did not return. Henry called her name, but there was no answer, and, when he looked in the closet and under the bed, he found no trace of her. Finally she did return and to his inquiries as to her whereabouts, she laughed and responded that she had had some occult business to attend to, and had made herself invisible."[77]

It would be years before Henry attributed these feats to hypnosis. Then, in Philadelphia, he was at least mystified, if not "psychologized," as Helena had boasted he was. For Helena, it was less a matter of conning Henry than of comprehending the true nature of his character; he was clearly an extremely suggestible man who could be influenced against his better judgment, but who was also quick to respond to any appeal to his finer self. Above all, he was tantalized by occult knowledge, and eagerly sought to become her student. Little by little, H.P.B. set about weaning him both from Spiritualism and from his family, mistresses and clubs.

By this time, while publicly portraying herself as a leading Spiritualistic supporter, she privately was beginning to break away from its orthodoxy. American Spiritualism, she decided, was a kitchen garden of spooks and ghouls; her version loftily preached the sacred truth of "spiritual spiritualism." It was her duty, she believed, "to purify the new religion from all its filthy weeds. . . . In this desire and effort I have been thitherto alone. I am only now beginning to collect adepts; I have collected half a dozen."[78]

Actually she had corraled only Henry Steel Olcott, and even of him she could not be absolutely certain. What is interesting about her subjugation of Olcott is its matter-of-factness. Before his return to New York, Helena had convinced Olcott that the two leading Spiritualist papers, *Banner of Light* and the *Religio-Philosophical Journal,* were no longer dependable and suggested instead they support the more modest Boston periodical, *Spiritual Scientist.* While its publisher, Gerry Brown, was young and open to new ideas, his operation was failing until Helena threw herself into saving him. Contributing fifty dollars of her own money, she asked friends to invest and nagged Henry to find New York subscribers. "For God's sake, do if you can. Why, they say the Lotus Club and all your numberless acquaintances can furnish hundreds and hundreds."[79]

Finally she suggested that Olcott fund and write a subscription circular for the *Scientist.* Titled "Important to Spiritualists," the piece was a simple six-paragraph plea for readers. When Olcott had finished correcting the proofs, H.P.B. suggested that, rather than signing his own name, he attribute the work to "*the Committee of Seven,* BROTHERHOOD OF LUXOR." And who, Henry demanded, was the Brotherhood of Luxor? At which point Helena revealed that her work was being supervised by a committee of seven adepts from the Egyptian branch of a universal mystic brotherhood. Henry, as usual, was impressed.

H.P.B.'s next project for Henry was the creation of a "Miracle Club" for the investigation of psychic phenomena. Club members would be entitled to attend private séances, but were forbidden to speak of their experiences or even to disclose the address of the meeting place. As club medium, H.P.B. suggested David Dana, whom she said was an upstanding young man, whose brother, Charles Dana, was editor of the New York *Sun.*

The club lasted only a few weeks, mainly because H.P.B. quarreled with David Dana, who, despite his distinguished family, demanded payment for his services. As the loyal Olcott put it delicately, "the wretch failed utterly not only as a medium, but was also reported to us as having spread calumnies against the one who had done him kindness."[80]

The failure of the Miracle Club hardly mattered to H.P.B., who was feeling increasingly unwell. John had cured her leg and ordered three days of complete rest, but she had failed to follow his instructions, the leg felt "worse than ever" and she had caught a nasty head cold.[81] No doubt John's medical advice was echoed by her human physician, Dr. Seth Pancoast, a student of the Cabbala, whose advice she customarily ignored. As if these ailments were not enough, she awoke one morning at 3 A.M. dreaming of Nikifor Blavatsky, a phenomenon she took as "a premeditated insult on the part of Providence."[82]

On April 26, despite her physical discomfort, she made her way to Riverhead, Long Island, where her case against Clementine Gerebko, the woman who had absconded with Helena's thousand dollars, finally had come to trial. For reasons known only to herself, Helena insisted upon giving her testimony in French so that an interpreter had to be rounded up, by no means an easy matter in rural Long Island. Since she planned to act as her own principal witness, her two attorneys, William Ivins and William Fales, carefully briefed her on the crucial points to make during her testimony. To their consternation, she ignored their advice once she took the witness stand, and proceeded in direct opposition to their instructions.

When the attorneys took her to task, H.P.B. casually replied that John King had been standing at her side the entire time dictating her testimony. To this, Ivins and Fales could only shake their heads.

Still, a month later, Judge Calvin E. Pratt decided in Helena's favor and ordered Gerebko to pay her $1146 plus the costs of the legal action.

In New York sometime in early May, Henry Olcott received his first letter from the Brotherhood of Luxor. Although postmarked Philadelphia, the envelope appeared to be of foreign origin, possibly Egyptian. The Brotherhood seemed to communicate only in English and French, for the black-glazed envelope inscribed in gold ink and sealed with red wax was addressed to "États-Unis d'Amérique" and also included the words "Pour Messager Spécial." Opening this exotic missive, Olcott found a thick sheet of green paper inscribed with the same gold ink:

FROM THE BROTHERHOOD OF LUXOR, Section the Vth to Henry S. Olcott.
> Brother Neophyte, we greet thee.
> He who seeks us find *us*. Rest thy mind—banish all foul doubt. We keep watch over our faithful soldiers. Sister Helen is a valiant, trustworthy servant. Open thy Spirit to conviction, have faith and she will lead thee to the Golden Gate of truth. She neither fears sword nor fire

but her soul is sensitive to dishonour and she hath reason to mistrust the future. Our good brother "John" hath verily acted rashly, but he meant well. Son of the *World,* if thou dost hear them both. TRY.

The Brotherhood strong urged Henry to "effect an opprobrious punishment" on Dr. Henry Child who had exposed the Holmeses (by what means they did not specify) and to do his best to keep the Miracle Club afloat. The communication was signed:

TUITIT BEY
Observatory of Luxor
Tuesday Morning.
Day of Mars.[83]

Subsequent letters arrived from Serapis Bey, who exhorted Henry to "Be courageous and hopeful," to "Try,"[84] and to work on Gerry Brown who suddenly had grown balky about turning his paper into Helena's and Henry's mouthpiece. According to Serapis, Brown had a sensitive nature "not unlike the Thibet Lotus—it shrinks and withdraws from the hand which tries to force open its tender petals." He advised Olcott to see him alone, to "try to make him open his heart to you,"[85] and to convince Brown to increase the paper to sixteen pages. Naturally, Helena was also growing disgusted with Brown and later she voiced her opinion with characteristic bluntness: "The man might have become a POWER, he preferred to remain an Ass."[86]

Apart from needing an outlet for her work, Helena had her reasons for boosting the *Scientist.* To her dismay, Spiritualism was falling so quickly out of vogue with the public that major papers would no longer touch the subject. Olcott blamed it on the Katie King scandal but he may simply have mistaken for a trend what was actually a fad. Even Helena had to admit that "it seems to be all over."[87] Crying disaster, she keened to Alexander Aksakov:

> Look at poor A. J. Davis; he can barely keep body and soul together, his books are not selling at all. The *Banner* has fallen from 25,000 subscribers to 12,000. Olcott is sitting on heaps of his *People from the Other World,* like Marius on the ruins of Carthage, and thinking bitter things. Not a thousand copies of his book have been sold in five months.[88]

The American economy had not yet pulled itself out of the slump of 1873, and even H.P.B. could observe the effects of depression on her own life and on Betanelly's foundering business. "There is terrible panic," she wrote. "Those who have got money hide it, and those who have not are dying of hunger." She told Aksakov that the previous year she had earned six thousand dollars by her writings, but the figure seems wildly high for a time when established writers rarely made five hundred. She went on to explain that she had spent it all on the Cause and once again faced hunger. Since she had Michael, she was being less than candid, but she still was not mentioning a husband to Aksakov. "Here, you see, is my trouble, tomorrow there will be nothing to eat. Something quite out of the way must be invented."[89]

Critical biographers of Madame Blavatsky have pounced upon those last words as evidence of crass commercialism, but this judgment seems overly harsh. Her devotion to Spiritualism had never gone much beyond lip service, and her private plans lay in a different direction. Her constant insecurity about money reflected less a preoccupation with wealth than with the assurance of subsistence. Her basic wants were restricted to food, books, travel; fashion did not interest her. What she needed more than money, however, was a new cause to sustain her, now that the prop of Spiritualism had been pulled from beneath her.

That she had gone out of fashion as swiftly as she had come in thoroughly shook Helena's confidence. In addition, her physical condition continued to deteriorate until, toward the middle of May, periostitis and partial mortification of the leg set in. When Dr. Pancoast told her the limb could not be saved, Helena consulted a clairvoyant, Mrs. Michener, who promised that amputation need not be necessary "if I do as *she* tells me."[90] Despite Mrs. Michener's treatment, Helena, in excruciating pain, saw her leg, swollen to twice its normal size, begin to turn black.

On May twenty-sixth, she again summoned Dr. Pancoast who urged amputation. Terrified and enraged, Helena began to scream that she didn't care if the leg was mortified; she would not let him cut it off. Michael's long face infuriated her further, and she insisted that he leave the house. He could come back, she shouted, "when I write that I am better or when somebody else writes him that I am gone *home,* or kicked the bucket. . . ."

Once Michael and Pancoast had left, she sent for Mrs. Michener "and had a talk with her. In short I had prepared myself to die—didn't care—but decided to die with both legs." For the next two days she cursed Michael for "a soft ninny" and the doctor as an "unclean goblin" as her maid applied cold water poultices to reduce the swelling. Unbelievably, within forty-eight hours the swollen area looked considerably better, and the person most surprised was Helena herself. Of course, she immediately invented a somewhat repellent miracle to account for it, writing to General Lippitt that "a white *pup,* a dog by night laid across the leg, cured all in no time."

Two weeks later, she was still "very weak, cross, and generally feel *mad* from 12 A.M. to 12 P.M.," but apparently had enough energy to write an entertaining letter to Lippitt: "Fancy my father's daughter— on a wooden leg; fancy my leg going in the spirit land before me . . ." Her dramatic recovery she now attributed to her own willpower or "because I am not wanted yet in the bosom of Abraham."[91] With Michael still barred from the house, she was being cared for by Madame Magnon, who had come in from New York, and by David Dana, with whom she must again have been on good terms. Her third companion, John King, had finally begun to get on her nerves. "He has his vices and considerably vicious vices, too,"[92] she complained breezily to Lippitt, rambling on to describe every occasion on which John had behaved spitefully, lied, stole, and forged people's handwritings. Obviously she was feeling better because she told Lippitt that in two or three weeks she planned to visit Hiram Corson, a Cornell professor and well-known Spiritualist with whom she had been corresponding, and after leaving Ithaca she proposed she might go to the seashore until October.

What she desperately wanted was to sequester herself in "some *isolated spot* on this globe."[93] Instead, she had to face Michael. That same day, rebelling against being locked out of his own house, he returned to force a resolution. Helena, at best ambivalent about her husband, did not want him back but dreaded losing him. She must have been profoundly shocked when Michael, at the end of his rope, threatened to return to Russia. Since his business was virtually bankrupt and his wife no longer loved him, why should he remain?

Helena responded by withdrawing into what appeared to be a trance. She lay on her bed, Michael recalled, "as one dead for two or three hours at the time, pulse and heart stopped, cold and pale as dead."[94] The next morning his distress gave way to bewilderment when he found Helena sitting up in bed, writing letters and acting as if nothing had happened. This cheerfulness continued until the pettiest household disruption would propel her into a temper, after which she lapsed into trance, seemingly oblivious to her surroundings.

According to Magnon and Dana, there was no cause for alarm when Madame appeared to be comatose; it only meant her spirit was traveling. Perhaps, Michael retorted tartly, but to him she certainly looked dead. By this point he felt sufficiently suspicious to check with the maid, who told him that Madame rose during the night and walked around on her leg; it was only during the day that she became paralyzed.

Michael must have thought himself the only sane person in a madhouse, for the following Wednesday a package of money and a letter addressed to Gerry Brown dropped on his head, along with orders from John King to take them immediately to the telegraph office. Michael protested he didn't have time to run the errand, but John refused to take no for an answer.

While the séances, materializations and deathlike trances continued as before, Helena grew increasingly morose. Racking her brain for a way to share her panic with someone, she arranged for Master Serapis to send Henry Olcott a grim letter describing Sister Helen's "bitter hours of mental agony and sorrow" over "this *crafty* youth" whom she had married. While Serapis admitted to feeling pity for Betanelly, he had no compunction about calling him a "weak and silly wretch." The letter continued:

His love for her is gone, the sacred flame has died out for want of fuel, he heeded not her warning voice; he hates *John* and worships the *Dweller* who holds with him communication. Finding himself on the brink of bankruptcy, his secret design is to sail for Europe, and leave her unprovided and alone. Unless we help him for the sake of her, our Sister, her life is doomed and for her her future will be poverty and sickness.[95]

The situation was hardly so black as Serapis painted because Helena knew that she would soon be receiving a substantial sum from the Gerebko judgment; surely Master Serapis, who seemed to know everything about her, must have been aware of her court victory. Nevertheless, he went on to inform Olcott that Michael's business had unfilled orders from foreign governments and that were he able to ship them, "there are millions in the future in store for him." Unfortunately, he added, the man "has no money and his brains are weak. Will my brother try to find him a partner?" Apparently distrusting Henry's own powers of ingenuity, Serapis suggested that Olcott approach a distant relative of his ex-wife's. "Let the transaction be executed at your discretion and pleasure. Does my good brother Henry understand me, does he realize what I mean?"[96]

Henry did. He was able to get Michael about fifteen hundred dollars from a man named Everman, but whether this person was a member of his former wife's family is unknown. By this time, Olcott had become exceedingly suggestible. On the advice of a man he had never met, whose very existence was questionable, he arranged a loan for another man whom he disliked. Judging by the letters Serapis wrote over the next weeks, Olcott did not agree straight off, and Serapis was obliged to suggest that his failure to comply would result in the loss of future occult powers: "You must not part with Helena. . . . Try to help the poor broken-hearted woman. . . . Watch over her, Brother-mine—forgive her outburstings of passion, be *patient, merciful,* and charity bestowed on another will return to thee a hundred fold nobly."[97]

But Henry was not without his pride. A few months earlier, in a fit of suspicion, he had visited the Russian Consulate to check the information Helena had given him at Chittenden about her Dolgorukov ancestors. Now he demanded from her further information about her mysterious brotherhood, flatly insisting that he communicate with them directly. "I want all my messages from them *verbatim et literatim,*"[98] he told her.

She replied sweetly: "You want too many things at once, my dear."

Of course she would be happy to comply, but, she reminded him, he would be unable to read the orders without her translation. "Now my advice to you, Henry, a friendly one: don't you fly too high, and poke your nose on the forbidden paths of the Golden Gate without some one to pilot you." With totalitarian aplomb, she advised "patience, faith, no questioning, thorough obedience and Silence."[99]

In early July, Helena, on two good legs, walked out of her marriage with Michael Betanelly. Immediately, she ran to join Henry in Boston, where, at

Aksakov's request, Olcott was auditioning mediums to go to Russia, all expenses paid. After six miserable months of trauma, Helena was delighted to be among people again. She and Henry stayed at the home of Mr. and Mrs. Charles Houghton in Roxbury and made forays into Boston for séances.

H.P.B. spent two days in Springfield at the home of Louisa Andrews, the Spiritualist author with whom she had been corresponding. Judging Madame Blavatsky on the basis of her vivacious letters, both Louisa and her sister Em felt greatly attracted to Madame and were eagerly looking forward to meeting her. The first day went beautifully, for the sisters wanted nothing more than to be friends, but at the initial séance, John King threw a pencil at Louisa, who did not have the foresight to dodge. Although he tried to make up the next day by writing her a letter, Louisa and Em were resistant to his pleas. They considered the letter an example of "very poor trickery," and even though they smiled politely, Madame "read our feelings like an open book" and indignantly accused them of thinking her a fraud.

To make matters worse, Helena exploded with a burst of true confession that further alienated her hostesses. As Louisa recalled, Madame seemed "half wild with anxiety, even terror," and blurted out "something which had occurred and which, if not *miraculous,* was *criminal* and would, if discovered, have put her into the *penitentiary.*" Whether or not Helena's secret admission was of her bigamy, it forced Louisa to conclude that her guest "was a very unprincipled woman."

H.P.B., on the other hand, deciding that Louisa and Em were being altogether hateful, refused to spend another night under their roof. After Madame left, Em suffered from nightmares during which she felt "as if she had been having her blood sucked by a vampire," and Louisa took the double precaution of destroying both John King's pencil and Madame's letters "because I felt their magnetism to be evil."[100]

Back with Olcott in Boston, Helena had to face the problem of her uncertain future. What she really wanted was to live in New York with someone else paying her bills and looking after her. The "someone" was of course Henry, but she could not bring herself to broach the subject with him. Helena had been indirectly manipulating people since childhood by claiming that *roussalkas* and invisible beings under her power were protecting her from harm. At the same time, she would deny responsibility for any mischief by laying off blame on the spirits. Accordingly, she now appointed Serapis to act as her intermediary in persuading Henry Olcott to undertake the support of a dumpy, middle-aged woman for whom he had no sexual attraction. Serapis tackled the problem by using a tone at once conspiratorial and man-to-man:

She may in her despair and present straightened [*sic*] circumstances be tempted to return to Philadelphia and her spouse. *Do not* allow her to do this, Brother mine. Tell her you are both going to Philadelphia and

instead of that take the tickets to New York City, NOT FURTHER.
Once arrived . . . find her a suitable apartment and do not let one day
pass without seeing her [there] . . . for if she finds herself once for a few
hours with that polluted mortal, her powers will suffer greatly . . . and
your own progress might be impeded . . .[101]

Naturally all this required money and also might entail some temporary
hardship for Olcott's sons, whom he had promised to support, but

if you succeed to bring her out before the world in her true light, not of
an adept but of intellectual writer and devote yourself both to work
together the articles dictated to her, your fortune will be made . . . She
must have the best intellects of the country introduced to her . . . She
will make you acquire knowledge and fame through herself.

And, Serapis cautioned: "*Try* to have her settled by *Tuesday Eve.*"[102]

III

The Theosophical Society

Back in Irving Place, Helena at last began to feel solid ground under her feet.
With Olcott down the street at the Lotos Club and a stream of guests dropping by in the evenings, she was seldom alone. Thanks to Henry's contacts,
the company was not limited to Spiritualists, mediums and crackpots, but
included, as Henry modestly described them, New York's "bright, clever
people of occult leanings."[103] They were scientists, philologists, authors, journalists, lawyers, doctors and broad-minded clergymen who made fascinating
conversation in English, French, and Russian. The salon could always be
relied upon to be lively, sometimes instructive, even extraordinarily bizarre.
According to Reverend Doctor J. H. Wiggin, editor of *The Liberal Christian,*
some of the subjects discussed on the night of his visit were the possibility of
flowers having souls, the phallic element in religion, gravitation, jugglery and
chemistry. While Madame impressed him as "a most original and interesting
woman,"[104] he could not help sympathizing with those guests who complained
about her cigarettes.

If Helena happened to be in the proper mood, visitors found their secret thoughts being read and their most intimate affairs discreetly referred to. Enthroned on the sofa, she filled the room with gusts of cigarette smoke and talked extravagantly. Only a few weeks earlier, she had lamented to Aksakov from Boston that she was "ready to sell my soul for spiritualism, but nobody will buy it."[105] Overnight, people were buying it and paying close attention. Among the most ardent of the devotees was a gangling twenty-four-year-old Irishman named William Quan Judge.

While H.P.B.'s new friends were, at the very least, comfortably off, William Judge had known both physical and financial hardship. Born in Ireland in 1851, he had suffered a sickly childhood and at the age of seven had even been pronounced dead. A few moments later, however, his bereft family saw him revive. During his year of convalescence he began reading books about magic and religion. He would later attribute the development of his life-long interest in mysticism to this period. When William was about thirteen, his mother died bearing her seventh child. Afterward the family emigrated to the United States and settled in Brooklyn, where Frederick Judge undertook the double responsibility of earning a living and caring for his family. In this he was aided by William, who secured a position clerking for an attorney and ended up by being admitted to the bar in 1872. By the time Helena met him, he worked in the office of the U.S. Attorney for the Southern District of New York, and was a married man with an infant daughter. His wife, Ella, was a strict Methodist, who disapproved when William, after reading Olcott's articles in the *Daily Graphic*, wrote to the colonel for an introduction to Madame Blavatsky. When Olcott finally got around to issuing an invitation to 46 Irving Place, Ella did not accompany him.

Instead Judge brought with him a bachelor friend from the Sandwich Islands, who was studying law in New York, with the intention of remaining there and establishing a practice. Casually, H.P.B. informed the incredulous student that within six months he would return home with a wife. During this exchange, Judge hardly spoke, although the few remarks Madame had thrown his way indicated she could read his mind. The next day, determined to test her powers, Judge unearthed an old scarab from among his possessions and asked a friend's clerk to wrap and mail it to Madame Blavatsky, making sure his own hand did not touch the package. Several days later, when he returned for a second visit to Irving Place, Helena majestically thanked him for the scarab.[106]

As people got to know H.P.B., they responded to her with awed admiration, like the captivated Judge, or dismissed her as an attention-hungry eccentric. Charles C. Massey, a friend of Henry's and a well-to-do English barrister who had given up his practice to study psychic phenomena, during a stop in New York, was naturally trotted over to Madame's salon by Olcott. During the evening, the question of whether spirits could materialize as butterflies came up for brief but zestful debate and then was dropped. Not fifteen minutes later, however, they noticed fluttering about the parlor a winged creature, which Helena and Olcott immediately hailed as a butterfly, but which Massey could see was nothing but a moth. When Helena waved toward the window and cried, "Let's have another," a second moth flew in. Pleased with herself, she asked the moths to leave; one obliged, but the other got stuck behind the draperies. Massey, unimpressed, noted in his diary that the moths "must be frequent visitors and no magic is required to account for them."[107]

Another guest who failed to find H.P.B. extraordinary was Emma Hardinge Britten, a well-known writer and lecturer of about Helena's own age. Born in England, Emma, accompanied by her widowed mother, had come to the United States with a theatrical company and remained. Initially repelled by Spiritualism, Emma soon experienced conversion when she discovered that she was a powerful medium. She turned her psychic talents to writing and public speaking and, traveling the length and breadth of the country, the pugnacious Emma soon won a reputation as the great female proselytizer of the Spiritualist movement. She was so popular an orator that people were turned away from her already packed lectures and the texts of her speeches reprinted in full by the Spiritualist papers.

Emma was an attractive woman with a round face, prominent front teeth, and braids coiled around her head. Showing up at H.P.B.'s with her husband, William, a former Universalist minister, she was immediately surrounded by a group of admirers and although Helena welcomed celebrities into her drawing room, she did not take kindly to females who upstaged her. Eying her guest warily, Helena listened while Emma talked volubly about her work-in-progress. Five years earlier she had published a hefty history of the Spiritualist movement, *Modern American Spiritualism*, and now was working on a second book, which would deal with the ancient occult sciences, the existence of adepts, and the astral light. In short, she was poaching in what H.P.B. considered her exclusive province. But what most intrigued Helena was Emma's vociferous insistence that she was not the author of *Art Magic* but only the amanuensis, or as she put it "translator," for a Chevalier Louis, whom she would only identify as a learned French adept she had met in Europe.

While Helena and Olcott might lift their brows in private, they had to admit that Mrs. Britten was a superb saleswoman for Chevalier Louis. She even distributed a handsome, printed prospectus, calculated in Olcott's opinion, to push "the most jaded curiosity to the buying-point."[108] The author, announced Mrs. Britten, would permit the printing of only five hundred copies and reservèd the right of refusing buyers whom he found undeserving. After the first edition was run, the plates were to be destroyed. Since the Brittens had found no publisher willing to go along with this arrangement, they planned to publish the work themselves at the exorbitant price of five dollars. Olcott, although committed for two copies, disdained the whole process as too precious for his taste.

Helena, keeping silent for once, began to construct personal possibilities based on the Brittens' endeavor. There was no doubt in her mind that she was destined to write a book, had once even written a few pages. Showing them to Henry she had remarked, "I wrote this last night by order, but what the deuce it is to be I don't know."[109] Since no further instructions had come from her superiors, she had thrown the writing into a drawer. Now it occurred to her that if Emma Britten could write a book, she could write a better one, and she could certainly improve on Emma's ridiculous account of her "Chevalier Louis." And didn't Helena have the entire Brotherhood of Luxor behind her?

Actually, H.P.B. had little choice but to turn to books, since she had reached an impasse with articles. Nobody except Gerry Brown would print her work and even he bought with less regularity. Ironically, Helena's English had greatly improved since the months in Philadelphia when she had been obliged to ask a neighbor to correct her copy. Despairing of finding her own editorial outlet, she began feeding ideas to Henry, who had less trouble in placing pieces. On August 30, in the New York *Tribune,* he stated that had he been familiar with the great occultists of the past such as Paracelsus, when he wrote *People from the Other World,* the book would have turned out very different. "I have looked in vain for these past twenty-five years in Spiritualist literature for anything worthy of the name of a philosophy," he declared. As if those remarks were not sufficiently insulting, he added, "Together with all other sensible men, I have deplored their puerile, absurd and often repulsive characteristics, and been shocked at the disgusting fallacies of free love and individual sovereignty to which they have given birth."[110]

Two weeks later, in the same paper, he repudiated all connection with American Spiritualism "in its present form."[111] Olcott's repeated emphasis on "free love" is amusing since, by his own admission, Henry had been having extramarital affairs and at that very moment was keeping H.P.B.

Helena and Henry's blasts drew an immediate outcry from indignant Spiritualists who protested the free-love smear and demanded to know why Olcott did not revise his book if it was inaccurate. Moreover, they pointed out derisively, how did it happen he had found answers in the Dark Ages? It was widely accepted that no intelligent person could regard medieval alchemists and magicians as authorities.

Although her days were idle, H.P.B. found her evenings fully occupied. On Tuesday, September 7, a crowd of seventeen gathered in her parlor to hear George H. Felt, an engineer and architect, give an unusually dense lecture on "The Lost Canon of Proportion of the Egyptians." This was not Felt's first appearance at Madame's, for he had been introduced by one of the regulars, Charles Sotheran, a rare book expert who was editor of the *American Bibliopolist.* Helena had found Felt interesting and asked him to give an informal lecture, which would offer her guests something out of the ordinary. Having brought with him some nicely done illustrations, Felt began somewhat ponderously by explaining his theory that the architectural proportion employed by the ancient Egyptians was actually preserved in temple hieroglyphics. The audience proceeded to yawn, but visibly perked up when Felt went on to remark that the Egyptians had been adepts in magical science and that some of their hieroglyphic figures were realistic drawings of "elementals," the messenger-spirits who pop up at séances. He himself, he added modestly, had discovered an ancient formula for evoking elementals.

Would it be possible for him to do a demonstration? Could he actually call forth an elemental? He announced that he could, if they were willing to finance the operation and to pay for his time.

"Of course," Henry wrote in *Old Diary Leaves,* "we passed an informal vote of hearty thanks for his highly interesting lecture, and an animated discussion followed." While people were chatting, it occurred to Henry "that it would be a good thing to form a society to pursue and promote such occult research." On a scrap of paper he scribbled, *"Would it not be a good thing to form a Society for this kind of study?"*[112] and handed it to William Judge to pass over to H.P.B., who read it and nodded her head. Olcott got up and presented his idea to enthusiastic murmurs, and George Felt promised he would teach them to evoke and control "elementals." Thus it was unanimously agreed that Olcott's society should be formed; Judge made a motion that Olcott be elected chairman, while Henry nominated Judge as secretary. Since it had grown late, Henry suggested they adjourn to return the following evening with sympathetic friends who might be potential members.

Years later H.P.B. would tell disciple Annie Besant that her Master ordered her to found the Theosophical Society. She claimed it was she, not Olcott, who had written down the suggestion and passed it by Judge to the colonel, but this was clearly not the case.[113] However, the true version painted H.P.B. as little more than an interested bystander, and assigns her virtually no role in subsequent events. The following Wednesday, sixteen people showed up to hear Felt deliver a second lecture, after which there was general discussion about the formation of Henry's society. Having given some thought to the matter since the previous evening, he now described the society as a study group to collect and disseminate ancient philosophies, such as the Cabbala. He also suggested founding an occult library.

It was not until the third meeting on the following Monday, that they discussed names for the new society. Among the suggestions were Egyptological, Hermetic and Rosicrucian, but none seemed appropriate. Finally Charles Sotheran picked up a dictionary and began skimming its pages until he came to the word "theosophy." Henry recalled that "after discussion, we unanimously agreed that was the best of all, since it both expressed the esoteric truth we wished to reach and covered the ground of Felt's methods of occult scientific research."[114] The group began tackling the question of bylaws, Mrs. Britten offered her home as the next meeting place, and they adjourned.

During all this activity, Helena was conspicuous by her lack of prominence. Given her fondness for the limelight, she must have been hard put to restrain herself; on the other hand, organizational details bored her, and she may have been relieved to leave them to Olcott. In her only known letter from this period, she noted matter-of-factly, to Aksakov, that "Olcott is now organizing the Theosophical Society in New York."[115] Nevertheless, it seems odd that at this critical moment she should suddenly succumb to an urge to travel; on Tuesday the fourteenth, the day after the Society's name had been selected, she left New York.

As a consequence of her writings Helena had made friends with Hiram Corson, professor of Anglo-Saxon and English literature at Cornell University, and his French wife Caroline, also a scholar. In the summer of 1874, the Corsons' only daughter died. Caroline was able to accept the loss, but Hiram had found no comfort in orthodox religion, turning instead to Spiritualism for assurance of the continued existence of his child. The couple had been begging Helena to visit Ithaca, and now she decided to accept, naturally without bothering to inform them of her decision. At the last moment Henry wrote: "I requested her to write to you herself and she promised to do so, but she is so absorbed with the things of the other world that with good intentions she may forget her duty."[116] Unfortunately, the Corsons did not catch the tactful warning hidden between the lines of Olcott's note. Since they were expecting a witty, erudite Russian woman to show off to their academic friends, H.P.B. came as a rude shock.

The city of Ithaca, New York, lies in a picturesque valley at the foot of Lake Cayuga; three hundred feet above the valley, on the east hill stood Corson's home on Huestis Street. Nearby was Cornell University with its imposing array of lecture halls, libraries and faculty homes. When H.P.B. arrived on September 17, Indian summer was in full bloom. The mornings and nights were crisp and frosty, with middays pleasantly warm; the lake was bathed in autumn haze, the hills dotted with goldenrod, the vineyards full of ripening grapes. To the Corsons' chagrin, their beautiful scenery interested Helena even less than they did. From early morning until midnight she sat in her room, frequently not even bothering to descend for meals.

In no way was Helena a normal guest. Always uncorseted, she walked about in a loose wrapper under an embroidered jacket with pockets for her cigarette papers and tobacco. Corson, who smoked himself, thought her tobacco cheap and was horrified to discover she smoked upwards of two hundred cigarettes a day. Caroline would not have cared how many cigarettes Madame smoked, if only she had used an ashtray instead of the carpets and the flowerpots.

As Corson later told his son Eugene, he had never encountered anyone so intense as Madame Blavatsky: "Nothing around her mattered; though the heavens fall she would keep on her way."[117] Nevertheless, still eager to be a good host, he suggested for the hundredth time that she might enjoy a drive around the Cornell campus. Grumbling, Helena let herself be persuaded, and also reluctantly acceded to Corson's request that she refrain from smoking in public. Ithacans looked askance at a woman smoking and such an act was sure to stir up trouble for him. Halfway through the ride, she could bear it no longer and ordered the coachman to stop so that she could get out for a smoke.

On the roadside? Corson sputtered.

Why not? she retorted. If people wanted to take her for a gypsy, let them. Leaving Corson in the carriage, she hunkered down on a rock and puffed several cigarettes in rapid succession before returning to the carriage.

At Ithaca, Helena began the book that eventually would become *Isis Unveiled.* "I am now writing a big book," she informed Aksakov on September 20, "which I call, by John's advice, *Skeleton Key to Mysterious Gates.*"[118] She was deliberately unclear about the subject, only vaguely alluding to her plans for lambasting scientists, Papists, Jesuits and other half-baked fools. She spent the rest of the letter enthusing about Egypt and the Hermetic philosophers.

Wearily Corson wrote to his son on October 2, "Mme. B. is still with us. She gives us a good deal of trouble, and we get very little from her in return, for she is occupied wholly with her own work. I had expected we should have some 'sittings' together; but she is not only not disposed, but is decidedly opposed to anything of the kind." He had come to the conclusion that "she is a smart woman, but ignorant of all the graces and amenities of life. She is a great Russian bear."[119] Aware of their disappointment, Helena relented, graciously produced a few raps, and once caused a heavy table to rise without touching it. Always on these occasions, she cautioned Corson that these phenomena were energized by her own willpower and should not be classified as ordinary mediumistic phenomena. On an evening when frost had been predicted, Caroline decided to bring in her potted plants from the porch, but H.P.B. told her not to bother because she would get "John" to carry them in. The next morning Caroline found the plants inside the house.

During her three weeks in Ithaca, Helena had emerged from the house only for the carriage ride and for an elaborate sitting with a local photographer. Pleased with the results, she ordered three dozen pictures, at a total cost of thirteen dollars. By this time she must have known the Corsons were dying to get rid of her, but as she was not yet ready to depart, she realized she had to stage a major event in order to pacify them. One morning Hiram Corson awoke to find on the table next to his bed a striking likeness of his dead daughter wearing a wreath of flowers in her hair and with gnome faces crowding the background. Most startling to Corson was the fact that the portrait had been drawn on a sheet of the expensive stationery he had noticed the previous evening while visiting the home of Andrew D. White, president of the University. Corson had admired the stationery in White's study, had even touched it during their conversation, but had not taken any away with him. Positive that the portrait had been sketched on White's stationery, he did not, evidently, stop to consider that similar notepaper might be available in local stores. Greatly excited, he rushed to his wife who took one look at the picture and screamed, "This is the work of the devil."[120] She burst into tears and threw the picture into the fire. Feeling horribly unappreciated, H.P.B. departed for New York the next day.

During her absence from the city, Henry had been busy alienating the Spiritualists, and in a lecture on September 24 he had "waved the sacred banner of the Lodge in their faces," and been generally insulting. "Things are red hot here, I tell you," he wrote Helena the next day. "Thank God I have lived long enough to sound the trumpet once for the holy Lodge." He could hardly contain his delight when, after the lecture, a woman friend of Andrew Jackson Davis's had moaned that he had just "given spiritualism its death-blow tonight." To Helena, he chortled, "It was enough to make you die of laughter."[121]

As a result of his ill-advised effervescence and her unusual comportment, H.P.B. lost the friendship of some people she valued, Corson for one. A few weeks after her return to New York she wrote plaintively, "This is the third letter I write you and not a word in response. Are you angry? Are you mad with me for anything?" She could not understand his fury over Olcott's remarks, as little as she comprehended Caroline's upset at the spirit picture of her deceased daughter. " 'Pon my word, I feel as if all was not right, as if she was kind of angry with me for something." Feeling as innocent of wrongdoing "as an unborn kitten," she enclosed fifty cents for the Corson's maid whom she had forgotten to pay for doing her laundry. "Mary," she said, "must think me mean."[122] Unwilling to offend even a servant, she was greatly disturbed when her generosity was unacknowledged and continued to send the Corsons disarming letters.

Back on Irving Place, Helena was pleased to learn of Henry's progress with the Theosophical Society. On October 16, and again on October 30, she attended meetings at Mrs. Britten's home in West Thirty-eighth Street to discuss by-laws and elect officers. William Judge and H.P.B.'s Philadelphia physician, Dr. Seth Pancoast, were present, as well as her attorneys William Ivins and William Fales with several lawyer friends, all of whom failed to take the occasion as seriously as she would have wished. One of them, James C. Robinson, who had come expecting an extremely odd crowd, was not disappointed; the Theosophists, he wrote a friend, are "the most 'pecolliar' people I have seen for many a day." He remembered that Fales took mischievous pleasure in feeding Henry irrelevant clauses and amendments, all phrased in silly but fancy jargon. Poor Olcott "loved those fine phrases, those mysterious and meaningless clauses, but the boys were pitiless . . . We had lots of sport."[123]

H.P.B. relegated herself to rolling cigarettes without commenting on the frivolity. As the evening progressed, Henry managed to draw up a constitution stating simply that the object of the Society was to collect and diffuse a knowledge of the laws which govern the universe. The Society was not a Spiritualistic schism, nor would it offer any dogma or creed, unless it be devotion to the truth. Members would be accepted without regard to race, sex, color, country or creed and were permitted to hold any religious belief they liked. Interestingly enough, there was no mention of the universal brotherhood which would eventually become the most publicized objective of the Theosophical Society.

The evening closed with the election of Olcott as president, Pancoast and Felt as vice-presidents, and Judge as counsel. Helena consented to accept the modest position of corresponding secretary.

Even though the Society was only a discreet whisper away from Spiritualism, Henry took great pains to inform the public that Theosophy was no Spiritualist offshoot. His about-face made Helena uncomfortable, enough so that she assured Aksakov that the Society "is the same spiritualism but under another name." She went on to boast that "the rules of the society are so strict that it is impossible for a man who has been in the least mixed up in any dirty matter to become a member. No free lovers or atheists or positivists are admitted. . . ."[124] Aksakov, who knew something of Madame's own past, must have puzzled over how she herself had passed the Society's strict admission requirements.

To Olcott, the Society was a serious business worthy of his time and money; accordingly, he hired a room in Mott Memorial Hall at 64 Madison Avenue where, on November 17, 1875, he delivered his presidential address. Used regularly by another club, the dim, book-lined chamber boasted a platform at one end. It was small but adequate to their needs since only a handful of "fellows" turned up. H.P.B. listened from the audience, while Henry grandiosely predicted the Theosophical Society would earn a place in history as the first group to communicate with races of unseen beings. Helena thought these were rash predictions and wrote in her scrapbook that Henry was "counting the price of the bear's skin before the beast is slain."[125] The colonel himself, rereading the speech seventeen years later, admitted that it sounded "a bit foolish."[126]

In spite of Olcott's efforts to put the Society on a dignified footing, difficulties arose immediately. George Felt failed to produce a single "elemental," not even "the tip end of the tail of the tiniest Nature-spirit."[127] Assured by Helena that he would come through eventually, Henry authorized the Society's treasurer to give Felt a hundred dollars for his experiments, but as the months passed and Felt did not even bother to turn up for scheduled lectures, he was mortified. Felt had exposed them to the mockery of every skeptic in New York. It was bad enough that the general press ridiculed the new Society while, worse yet, the Spiritualist papers ignored it, but after a few months the membership began to drop. When Charles Sotheran, one of the founders, noisily resigned, he warned people, in a letter to the *Banner of Light,* to stay away from the Theosophists. Henry tried to bolster interest by hiring clairvoyants and mesmerizers, paid for out of his own pocket, but, by the following spring, even Helena no longer bothered to attend meetings.

H.P.B. had more important concerns on her mind than the fading Theosophical Society. At the end of November, she and Henry moved together to 433 West Thirty-fourth Street, thereby relieving him of having to pay rent on two establishments. While his room was on the second floor and H.P.B.'s on the first, gossip still circulated. Olcott may have been divorced but Madame was still married and although she had tried to conceal her second marriage, too many people knew about Michael. She gave instructions to turn him away if he ever appeared at the door, but this order was gratuitous, for he desired a reconciliation no more than she. Still, her simultaneous intimacy with two men was shocking. Louisa Andrews, writing to Hiram Corson, called Madame's treatment of Betanelly shameful. "What her relationship with Olcott is, I do not know, but if it be not criminal (and I believe it is not), it is not from principle."[128]

At Thirty-fourth Street, H.P.B. planned to get down to business on her book, but she found that good intentions were hardly enough. During her stay at Ithaca, she had galloped through twenty-five pages of foolscap each day and since she remained there nearly a month, must have accumulated roughly six hundred pages. Unfortunately, little was publishable, and she knew it. Unlike many fledgling writers, Helena understood her intention: to restate the entire occult doctrine and salvage the ancient world from the modern stigma of superstition and ignorance. To reveal the traces, in ancient and medieval history, of a secret science whose principles had been lost was a formidable task. First it meant foraging through science, religion and philosophy, then correlating the findings in a book with structural unity. An encyclopedia of legends and fables would not do; rather, H.P.B. planned to digest and codify the ancient myths, retelling them in terms intelligible to the modern devotee.

So far, the bulk of her work was almost totally incoherent. Unable to admit this, she kept the manuscript hidden and made no comment on its progress. Although she had written that "I am nailed up like a slave to my chair writing all day,"[129] Olcott, who knew better, found her "not very industrious."[130] Frustrated and more than a little guilty about her poor progress, Helena informed Professor Corson on January 8, 1876, that "my book is finished,"[131] when actually she had yet to seriously begin.

For a change, money was not a problem, since Henry took care of everything, including her debt to Andrew Jackson Davis. She had at last succeeded in selling two articles to the New York *Sun,* although "A Story of the Mystical" and "The Luminous Circle" can hardly be termed journalism. H.P.B.'s own distinctive blend of fact and fiction, they were first-person occult travelogues stuffed with vampires, dervishes, and Rumanian gypsies. She was delighted to get a more than respectable thirty dollars for each story.

In fact, what she often tried to pass off in her writings as fact was so bizarre even Gerry Brown's readers protested. That sort of niggling never failed to irritate Helena, who never bothered with personal responses to readers' inquiries. Instead, Brown received a response from "Endreinek Agardi of Koloswar,"[132] who swore that he could vouch for Madame Blavatsky as he had been an eyewitness to the events described in one of her articles.

Where Helena got the name *Endreinek* is hard to say, but *Agardi* was obviously suggested by Metrovitch, and *Koloswar* was a pretty Hungarian town the two of them had visited on tour in 1867. It is amusing to note that "Endreinek Agardi's" letter found its way into H.P.B.'s scrapbook.

By early January, 1876, both Helena and Henry had begun to make changes in their daily routines. She was fond of pointing out lightly that a true ascetic did not indulge in sex, meat or alcohol. Now, to her astonishment, Henry began taking her seriously. No more was he seen at the Lotos Club bar and gave up meat and wine. Frequently he did not eat at all. Seeing him waste away, Helena regretted having nagged him; she had simply not expected him to turn into a fanatic. "I can do nothing with him," she wrote Corson, adding pointedly that Olcott lived "to purify American Spiritualism of the dirt of free love."[133]

As for herself, she had never liked alcohol. Sex was another matter, but after Michael, she had relinquished it with less regret than difficulty. Once she had even exclaimed to a friend, "To Hades with this sex love! It is a beastly appetite that should be starved into submission."[134] She had considerably less success in taming her excessive passions for tobacco and rich food. Shamed by Henry's new regime, she fasted for nine days on salad, stopped smoking, and slept on the floor. She suffered from nightmares. On the ninth night, she felt herself leaving her body, "looking at it with repulsion while it was walking, talking, getting puffed up with fat and sinning. Pheugh, how I hated myself." It was, she decided, "one of the most disgusting scenes"[135] she had ever witnessed and she resolved to change.

In spite of her good intentions, she soon slipped back into her customary excesses, although she was again making another attempt to begin her book. She remained at her desk for seventeen or eighteen hours a day, to Henry's boundless admiration, and he claimed to know of no managing editor or reporter with her "dogged endurance and tireless working capacity . . . it was seldom that either of us got to bed before two o'clock A.M." Later, he would brag that Helena did not go out of the house for six months. In any case, Henry spent his days at his law office and had no real idea what she did in his absence. When he returned after work, they would have an early dinner before settling down to their big writing table "and work, as if for dear life, until bodily fatigue would compel us to stop. What an experience!"[136]

IV

Isis Unveiled

There has been considerable controversy over how—and by whom—*Isis Unveiled* was actually written. During Madame Blavatsky's lifetime, it would be said that she could not possibly have produced it herself, the book being far too complex to have issued from the mind of a woman; instead, she had found the completed manuscript, so the story went, among the effects of a man who had died while living in Olcott's apartment. Other rumors attributed the work to Olcott himself, still others to a Platonist scholar named Alexander Wilder. Shortly after Helena's death, William Emmette Coleman, a scathing critic of Madame, spent three years studying *Isis* and her other works for the express purpose of proving her a plagiarist. In *Isis Unveiled*, he claimed, there were some two thousand passages copied from other books without credit.

> By careful analysis, I found that in compiling *Isis* about 100 books were used. About 1400 books are quoted from and referred to in this work; but, from the 100 books which its author possessed, she copied everything in *Isis* taken from and relating to the other 1300. There are in *Isis* about 2100 quotations from and references to books that were copied, at second-hand, from books other than the originals; and of this number only about 140 are credited to the books from which Madame Blavatsky copied them at second-hand. The others are quoted in such a manner as to lead the reader to think that Madame Blavatsky had read and utilised the original works, and had quoted from them first-hand—the truth being that these originals had evidently never been read by Madame Blavatsky. [Readers of *Isis*, Coleman went on to insist] had been mislead into thinking Madame Blavatsky an enormous reader, possessed of vast erudition; while the fact is her reading was very limited, and her ignorance profound in all branches of learning.[137]

While this particular conclusion may be challenged, Coleman seems to have done his homework thoroughly when he estimated that H.P.B. used about a hundred books. As Olcott admitted, "our whole working library scarcely comprised one hundred books of reference,"[138] including Joseph Ennemoser's *History of Magic*, Hargrave Jennings' *Rosicrucians*, J. S. Forsyth's *Demonologia*, and works by Eliphas Lévi, S. F. Dunlap, Louis Jacolliot, Henry Roger Gougenot Des Mousseaux, and Max Müller. Occasionally H.P.B. would borrow books from friends, but most were purchased through Andrew Jackson Davis, or discovered in out-of-the-way bookshops.

Even though Olcott acknowledged H.P.B.'s library, he believed it to be neither her only source, nor her main one. Looking at the hundreds of quotations in *Isis*, he was sure they could not all have emerged from the books on her shelf; had he not known better, he would have assumed *Isis* was written in an alcove in the British Museum. However, Olcott is not a good witness for H.P.B. because, unlike the arch-analyzer William Coleman, he had not read those hundred books, and in any case, always opted for romance over reality. It excited him to see Helena sparkling with unimaginable erudition. "Whence did she get this knowledge?"[139] he wondered, dismissing the traditional childhood governesses, universities, libraries and travel experience. The answer was simple; she received her knowledge

> *from the Astral Light*, and, by her soul-senses, from her Teachers—the "Brothers," "Adepts," "Sages," "Masters," as they have been variously called. How do I know it? By working two years with her on *Isis* and many more years on other literary work.[140]

More to the point, Henry knew not only because H.P.B. told him so but because every night as he sat opposite her, he could see she did not function in an ordinary manner. Her pen flying across the page, she would suddenly stop, stare vacantly into space, and adjust her vision as if looking at something which was invisible to him. Then she would copy down what she had just read in the astral light. The quotation complete, her eyes would resume their natural expression, and she would continue writing as before. Helena's "astral light" was the universal fluid spoken of by Eliphas Lévi; in the twentieth century, Edgar Cayce would call it "the Akashic record," God's book of life written upon the skein of time and space; and parapsychologists would hypothesize it as possibly some psychic collective memory that could be drawn upon by mediums. To Henry Olcott, who had never read Lévi, the astral light was pure magic.

Once, when he questioned a quotation he believed she had miscopied, her eyes glazed over and she pointed to a shelf in the corner: "There, there; go look for it over there!"[141] Finding two books that to his knowledge had not been in the house before, he corrected the quotation, returned the books to the shelf, and resumed his seat. However, when he looked over at the shelf a few minutes later, he was stupefied to see that the books had vanished. Of course, Helena explained serenely they were merely apports that had been "dematerialized," i.e., transported through space and material obstacles such as walls, and then "rematerialized" in their original forms.

The strongest evidence for Helena's version was the marked variation in handwriting Henry saw in the manuscript. In addition to Helena's own script, there were three or four others: one small and plain, another bold and free, still others whose queer *a*'s and *e*'s made the writing nearly illegible. There was also a great variation in the grammatical styles, for some were poor and required corrections in every line, while others were beautifully written. "Most perfect of all," he recalled, "were the manuscripts which were written for her while she was sleeping." On one particular evening, they had worked until 2 A.M. and, too exhausted for her final smoke, Helena had begun to doze off in her chair before Henry left. The next morning, at breakfast, she showed him thirty or forty pages that had been written for her by one of her Masters. "It was perfect in every respect," Olcott reported, "and went to the printers without revision."

His testimony evidences the overwhelming probability that Madame Blavatsky often wrote while in a dissociated state. It is known that trance handwriting can vary sharply from a medium's normal script and sometimes changes to approximate that of the purported entity communicating; in fact, Olcott states quite clearly that immediately prior to each change in handwriting, Helena would either fall into a trance or leave the room for a few minutes. When she returned to her desk, she would seem to be a different person with "different—very, *very* different command over her temper, which, at its sunniest was almost angelic, at its worst, the opposite." Frequently she asked him to frame in good English some ideas she had been unable to express properly, and although Olcott always tried his best, he was hard-pressed to please her. Sometimes she let his failures pass with benevolent patience, sometimes not. "For the slightest of errors, she would seem ready to explode with rage and annihilate me on the spot!" Among her favorite epithets for Henry were "idiot"—which she pronounced "ee-jut," as well as "ass" and "ass's grandfather."[142]

Not that Henry liked being called names. He attributed both H.P.B.'s nasty temper and her genius to the fact of having undergone seven years of occult training; it would be unfair to expect her to comport herself as a normal person, or write books as an ordinary writer. Of course Helena was the one who had manufactured this further excuse for her outrageous behavior. What she always failed to see was that the myths she invented for Henry's benefit were gradually turning into monsters that would turn to devour their creator. Worse yet, she gradually came to believe, or to half-believe, her own myths. About this time she wrote to her sister:

> Well, Vera, whether you believe me or not, something miraculous is happening to me. I am writing *Isis*; not writing, rather copying out and drawing that which She personally shows to me. Upon my word, sometimes it seems to me that the ancient Goddess of Beauty in person leads me through all the countries of past centuries which I have to describe. . . . I sit with my eyes open and to all appearances see and hear everything real and actual around me, and yet at the same time see and hear that which I write. I feel short of breath; I am afraid to make the slightest movement for fear the spell might be broken. Slowly century after century, image after image, float out of the distance and pass

before me as if in a magic panorama; and meanwhile I put them together in my mind, fitting in epochs and dates, and I know *for sure* that there can be *no mistake*. Races and nations, countries and cities, which have for long disappeared in the darkness of the prehistoric past, emerge and then vanish, giving place to others . . . and then I am told the consecutive dates.[143]

Although Helena began the letter attributing her sensations to the goddess Isis, she seemed confused about the real identity of her tour guide. Can it be, after all, the everyday Helena who is responsible? "Most assuredly it is not I," although possibly it could be "my Ego, the highest principle which lives in me." Finally she concluded that her information derived from "my Guru and teacher who helps me in everything. If I happen to forget something, I have just to address him" and the needed information passed before her eyes. Abruptly, however, the guru to whom she had just referred metamorphosed into a group. "They know everything. Without them, from whence could I gather my knowledge?"[144]

Remembering Helena Petrovna's vivid imagination, and her propensity for lying, Vera wrote back to say she feared for Helena's sanity. H.P.B. replied plaintively:

Do not be afraid that I am off my head. All that I can say is that someone positively *inspires me*—more than this, someone enters me. It is not I who talk and write: it is something within me, my higher and luminous Self, that thinks and writes for me. Do not ask me, my friend, what I experience, because I could not explain it to you clearly. I do not know myself![145]

To Olcott she could never confess these self-doubts without losing credibility, but with her sister she at least attempted honesty. Think of her, she suggested, as a sort of storehouse of somebody else's knowledge.

Somebody comes and envelopes me as a misty cloud and all at once pushes me out of myself, and then I am not "I" anymore—Helena Petrovna Blavatsky—but someone else. Someone strong and powerful, born in a totally different region of the world; and as to myself it is almost as if I were asleep, or lying . . . not quite conscious—not in my own body but close by, held only by a thread which ties me to it . . . I am perfectly conscious of what my body is saying and doing— or at least its new possessor. I even understand and remember it all so well that afterwards I can repeat it and even write down *his* words.[146]

These sensations were not, of course, new to her, since even in childhood she had felt the presence of a powerful male protector. Her sense of being pushed out of her body is similar to what she had experienced in Mingrelia after the birth of Yuri. But those past episodes had taken place during times of great psychic stress, while now she was living under conditions of relative well-being. For that matter, she had located a human male protector in the person of Henry Olcott; even though he was much too immature to resemble the man of her visions, nevertheless, he had rescued her from poverty and an unwanted husband and had made it possible for her to write. If she connected her earlier experiences with the intelligence who was currently "enveloping my body and using my brain," she did not mention it to Vera, or to Nadyezhda to whom she described herself as "an enigma for future generations, a Sphinx!"[147] She clearly fancied this mysterious image of herself and in letters to her aunt, who knew that she had been a brilliant student, could not resist boasting:

> Just fancy that I, who have never in my life studied anything, and possess nothing but the most superficial smattering of general information; I, who never had the slightest idea about physics or chemistry or zoology, or anything else—have now suddenly become able to write whole dissertations about them.[148]

Nadyezhda must have sputtered in astonishment at those words, particularly the claim to know nothing about zoology, for had not all of them in the Fadeyev household imbibed botany and zoology from Princess Helena? Physics and chemistry? These subjects would have presented little difficulty for her niece. As if anticipating Nadyezhda's reaction, Helena hurried to add:

> It's not a joke; I am perfectly serious; I am really frightened because I do not understand how it all happens. It is true that for nearly three years past I have been studying night and day, reading and thinking. But whatever I happen to read, it all seems familiar to me.[149]

It may be that her recent experiences did frighten her initially, but soon they began to intrigue, excite and flatter her. Actually, almost any creative writer would recognize her sensation of being inspired. Some writers might even admit to having sensed that another's hand pounded the typewriter keys from time to time. By the same token, it is also a common experience to writers of both fiction and non-fiction, reading over what they have written, to marvel at insights of which they had not believed themselves capable. But H.P.B., despite having had a writer for a mother, knew so little of the creative process that she could only conclude she must be unique.

For Helena these universal experiences were so intense as to push her into trance while writing. Or possibly the cause lay elsewhere. Among her friends during this period was her old companion from Cairo, Albert Rawson, who, now living in New York, felt delighted to see her and obligingly arranged for her to take hashish, he reported, "under the care of myself and Dr. Edward Sutton Smith." To Rawson she said nothing about voices and invisible entities, but only raved about the hashish which "multiplies one's life a thousand-fold."

There were some men, and later one woman, whom H.P.B. made no attempt to impress with her occult powers, and Rawson was one of them. He was allowed to see the side of her she generally hid—the tireless, always dissatisfied worker—and accordingly he praised her as "an intellectual wonder, a reader of enormous capacity and retentive memory." It was a pity, Rawson concluded, that her formal education had been neglected "for if she had been started aright who knows but she might have reincarnated Pythagoras or Bacon?"[150]

The idea of reincarnation was repulsive to Helena, nor was she interested in being Bacon or Pythagoras. She preferred to invent a Helena Petrovna more marvelous than any man who had actually existed, but whether this was a conscious decision is hard to determine. It was impossible for her to open her mouth without over-dramatizing or embellishing, and now with *Isis* she was clearly exaggerating her sensations. Even so, it is hard to understand how she could have forgotten the one hundred books she had combed and digested with such thoroughness.

Undoubtedly it pleased Helena to insist that she "received" much of her material, but she knew very well it was not an unprecedented claim. Aside from the silly Emma Hardinge Britten and her "Chevalier Louis," more impressive writers had made similar claims. One was the hero of her youth, Edward Bulwer-Lytton who, in *Zanoni*, stated that his story had come from an elderly Rosicrucian. In Helena's immediate circle, Andrew Jackson Davis swore that the only book he had ever read was a romantic novel, a statement seemingly contradicted by his familiarity with Emanuel Swedenborg and the sociologist Charles Fourier. Supposedly Davis had "received" the material for his two dozen books while in trance; his supporters attributed his familiarity with Swedenborg to "clairvoyance for printed matter," a term describing the ability of a sensitive to "read" word for word and cite page and line number in books hundreds of miles away. There was no doubt that Davis's claim to virtual illiteracy made his books seem marvelous, and no one was more aware of this than Helena. She too claimed this rare type of clairvoyance, although it is extremely doubtful that she actually possessed it.[151]

By the spring of 1876, work occupied Helena's attention to the exclusion of all else. She paid no attention to the steadily declining membership of the Theosophical Society nor was she much concerned when, after a quarrel, William Judge no longer attended meetings or visited her.

Although Judge and others had left, Henry refused to abandon the Society; he ordered engraved stationery, paid the rental of the meeting room out of his own pocket, and instituted a secret handshake for what were probably the handful of remaining members. Desperate to dredge up new recruits, Henry named to the Society's Council an elderly Bavarian nobleman named Joseph Henry Louis Charles, the Baron de Palm.

The baron had a distinguished manner and an impressive list of titles including Grand Cross Commander of the Order of the Holy Sepulchre and Knight of Saint John of Malta. He talked a great deal about his Spanish castles and mining properties in the Western United States, but, unfortunately, was temporarily short of funds. Since he was also obviously ill and alone, Henry brought him home and called a physician, who diagnosed nephritis and pneumonia. In gratitude, Palm decided to make a will in which he named Henry executor of his estate and designated the Theosophical Society as the beneficiary of his silver mines and real estate. In return, he asked that no clergyman officiate at his funeral and that his body be cremated. Henry agreed.

Both H.P.B. and Olcott must have calculated Palm's fortune as an eventual lifesaver of the Theosophical Society, but this pleasant prospect did not alleviate Helena's chief difficulties. For one thing, after some three months of arduous labor and eight hundred and seventy pages of manuscript, she decided the book was dreadful, threw it out, and began it over a third time. In part, this decision may have been prompted by the publication of Emma Britten's *Art Magic*, which received atrocious reviews. H.P.B. was horrified to see that reviewers were linking Emma and her foolish book to the Theosophical Society, described by the *Religio-Philosophical Journal* as "the so-called Theosophical Society, an outgrowth of the absurd religious dogmas of ancient priestcraft."[152] Even though Emma hotly denied all such connections, people continued to treat *Art Magic* as a Society publication and the T.S. (Theosophical Society) itself as a public joke. God forbid that Helena should produce something similar to *Art Magic*, especially since she knew that both Emma and herself used many of the same occult books as source material.

Personally H.P.B. was faring no better than the Society. In the *Banner of Light*, Hiram Corson, whom she considered a true friend, had called her an "imposter." This attack was not unexpected since the Spiritualists now had nothing but harsh words for her. Still, Corson's betrayal hurt; newspaper articles insinuating that she was immoral and anonymous letters accusing her of prostitution devastated her. But her biggest shock came from Daniel Dunglas Home. Home had not appreciated being called a fraud in Olcott's book *People from the Other World*, and retaliated by writing to the Boston *Herald* that Madame Blavatsky was the most notorious cheating medium he knew of. He went on to attack her private life by including a letter from Nicholas Meyendorff, who declared that he had known Madame intimately.[153] Enraged, H.P.B. wrote to Alexander Aksakov, one of whose cousins was married to Home,

> How on earth do I interfere with Home? I am not a medium, I never was and never will be a professional one. I have devoted my life to the study of the ancient cabbala and occultism. My position is very cheerless; sim-

ply helpless. There is nothing left but to start for Australia and change my name forever.[154]

She begged Aksakov to make Home hold his tongue by conveying her warning that if he persisted she would spread frightful stories about him. Despite her spirited self-defense, she felt sickened at Home's treachery.

On May 20, Baron de Palm died in Roosevelt Hospital. Olcott, already overworked and exhausted, was obliged to carry out the dead man's last wishes in regard to a funeral. Instead of arranging for the modest non-sectarian service, which Palm had requested, Henry saw an opportunity to grab publicity for the Theosophical Society, and engaged the two-thousand-seat Masonic Temple at Twenty-third Street and Sixth Avenue.

The New York papers had a field day ridiculing in advance Henry's "pagan funeral." Colonel Olcott, jeered the *World*, would appear as high priest wearing a leopard skin and carrying a roll of papyrus; Madame Blavatsky would play an ancient Egyptian instrument called a sistrum; George Felt would bear an asp purchased at a toy store on Eighth Avenue; and the procession would also include slaves carrying offerings of "early potatoes, asparagus, roast beef, French pancakes, bock-beer, and New Jersey cider." Naturally, more than a few New Yorkers turned out to see this spectacle.

That afternoon, when Helena and Henry arrived at the Masonic Temple, the police were struggling to keep order among a mob of Sunday idlers looking for amusement. Inside, where every seat was filled and the aisles jammed, nobody paid much attention to the baron's embalmed body lying in a rosewood casket on the stage.

Olcott, wearing a disappointingly conventional black robe, attempted to get the service under way with an Orphic hymn, but there was so great a commotion in the audience that he had to remind people repeatedly they were in the presence of death. Not until Emma Britten appeared to give a ten-minute oration and sprinkle the coffin with rose petals did the hecklers quiet down, but once Henry appeared the yelling and whistling started up once more. Helena, sitting quietly in the audience, was torn between laughter and tears, but when a particularly noisy spectator called Henry names, and was removed by a policeman, she stood up, pointed to the heckler, and shouted, "He's a bigot, that's what he is."[155] Her outburst drew from the audience a huge laugh in which she herself joined.

After the funeral, Henry rushed to Palm's trunk and found two of his own shirts with the name-tags ripped out, old love letters from obscure actresses, and a heap of shabby clothing. There was no money, jewelry, and certainly no manuscript of *Isis Unveiled*, as Helena's traducers would claim. There remained only the will.

Still hopeful, Helena told Aksakov that Palm owned rich silver mines and 17,000 acres of land and went on to announce that "eight of us are preparing to set off for Thibet, Siam and Cambodia"[156] after first making a side trip to Yucatán where they planned to investigate certain ruins. This, of course, was wishful thinking on a grand scale. In reality, as they learned several months later, Baron de Palm's property had been sold for taxes years earlier. "The mining shares," Olcott reported, "were good only for papering walls, and the Swiss castles proved castles in the air."[157] The baron's assets did not even reimburse Henry for the costs of the funeral and the probate. And as if that were not bad enough, they were stuck with Palm's corpse because there were no facilities for cremation in the United States. Storing Palm in carbolized clay, Henry investigated the possibilities of open-air burning only to learn that the city's sanitary laws forbade it. Not until midsummer would he read in the newspaper about a Dr. F. Julius Le Moyne who was building a crematorium for his own personal use in Washington, Pennsylvania.

Soon after Palm's funeral, H.P.B. and Olcott took an apartment together at the corner of Forty-seventh Street and Eighth Avenue. This time there was no pretense of separate quarters. Those who had come to regard them as a couple did not find this daring step hard to accept, but it served to outrage others.

The new neighborhood was too far uptown to be regarded as fashionable, but the flat itself perfectly suited H.P.B.'s needs. A sunny suite of rooms on the second-floor corner, the place boasted a large parlor, dining room, three bedrooms, kitchen and bath. In the main room Helena arranged an office for herself by using her desk and bookshelves to fence off a three-sided enclosure. Seated inside this pen, she had only to reach out an arm to get any book or paper she needed.

At the outset, she made it clear that she would not involve herself in housekeeping. After Henry saw her trying to boil an egg by laying it on the live coals, he promptly concluded that she lacked the vaguest notion of cooking. A series of maids-of-all-work were hired, but stayed only until they got a taste of Madame's temper. Rather than complicated meals, Helena required large quantities of fried foods, endless cups of coffee, and of course her cigarettes, but her eating habits were extremely capricious. One day she would ignore lunch altogether, the next day she would demand to be served an hour ahead of time, then complain over the half-boiled vegetables and underdone meat.

Her habits horrified Olcott. Not only did she overeat relentlessly, but she poured melted butter on her fried eggs and devoured the boxes of caviar, sweet cakes and other Russian delicacies that Nadyezhda thoughtfully provided. "Her only exercise," Henry recalled, "was to go to the dining room or bathroom and back again to her table."[158]

When the maid had either gone home or quit, Henry cooked while Helena sat at her desk writing and smoking; if she did come into the kitchen, it was only to pester him. When guests were present, she would grandly offer tea, ignoring Henry's desperate signals that the pantry was empty. Often at 1 A.M. he would set out to scour the neighborhood for milk and sugar. If his foray was successful, he would rush back to prepare the tea. In disgust he finally solved the problem by posting a sign:

* * *

TEA

Guests will find boiling water and tea
in the kitchen, perhaps milk and sugar,
and will kindly help themselves.[159]

Since self-service fit the bohemian atmosphere of the apartment, nobody seemed to object, and a procession of learned professors and elegantly dressed women could be seen quietly slipping into the kitchen to put on the kettle.

After initially rebelling against shared domestic responsibilities with the maid, Henry eventually surrendered. By his own admission, he and Helena were pupil and teacher, although some of their friends saw them as slave and master. Olcott took Helena's merciless bullying for granted, but it shocked others. Albert Rawson felt sincerely sorry for Henry who, despite his total devotion to Madame, was the object of her most vicious abuse.

"Those scenes," Rawson recalled, "were highly amusing, although somewhat hair-raising at the time."[160] R. B. Westbrook, an attorney friend of Henry's, did not find it amusing that Helena called Henry a liar before a room full of company. Westbrook decided the colonel was so deeply influenced "as to be utterly incapable of judging correctly anything she might say or do. He was as crazy as a loon on anything relating to Blavatskyism, though perfectly sane on every other subject." Nevertheless, her "contemptuous treatment of him was humiliating to behold."[161]

Henry always forgave Helena, for the truth was he had grown to love her. He adored her vitality, her cerebral playfulness, her brilliant conversation and epigrammatic wit, and he never failed to be enchanted by the clear, rollicking laugh that seemed to him the very essence of laughter.

What did it matter if she "swore like the army in Flanders?" She meant no harm. Was it really important if she "put on her night-dress, went to bed, and received a mixed company of ladies and gentlemen"[162] in her bedroom? Secretly he applauded her pranks to shock the prudish.

Of course she knew nothing about fashion or grooming, and he had to admit that her general appearance was outrageously untidy. Around the house she wore a dressing gown or a baggy shift that looked like a potato sack; when they went out she would make a stab at elegance and get herself up in a plumed hat, satin dress dripping with trimmings, heavy gold chain attached to a blue-enameled watch with a monogram of cheap diamonds, and a dozen or fifteen rings on her nicotine-stained fingers. He learned not to cringe when people laughed at her, but still recalled that "I have gone to the theatre with her when I expected the house to rise at us."[163] Her indifference to feminine concerns merely reflected, he thought, both her high birth and her subsequent revolt against the commonplace conventions. He had never known, could not have even imagined, a woman like Helena Petrovna. "Wouldn't it be nice," he mused one winter evening about 1 A.M., "to have some hothouse grapes?"

"So it would," she agreed blandly, and asked him to dim the gaslight. A moment later, hanging from a nearby bookshelf, he saw two large bunches of ripe black grapes "which we proceeded to eat."[164]

What other woman, or man for that matter, could create fruit out of season, or a red clay Turkish pipe with a purple velvet stem, or sugar tongs that resembled a pickle fork? Who else could fling out her hand and "*ping! ping!* would come the silvery tones of a bell?" Of course some people might think she concealed the bell under her dress, but Henry sincerely believed that the range of notes precluded any such trickery. Still, that did not prevent him from pestering her for explanations. How did she do it? It was hard to explain, she told him, just as difficult as for him to describe how he produced a whistle. Only when he persisted did she reluctantly speak of working "the astral currents by my trained will."[165]

Those who said, like Westbrook, that Henry tolerated Madame Blavatsky only to achieve adeptship were wrong. To be sure, he was excited by her phenomena, but he genuinely loved her. She may have abused him in public, but alone with him she could be whimsical and utterly lovable, drawing comic caricatures of him and calling him "Maloney" in her funny Russian accent. They were not merely a couple, but a family, because Henry bought a mate for her canary; Jenny and Pip, Henry remembered, "came to be almost like children as it were."[166] Later they added a cat named Charles.

Throughout the summer of 1876, work on *Isis* went steadily forward and in less than four months Helena had completed a second draft. The trouble with the earlier draft had been not merely a need for focus, but the utter lack of any structure. The ideas had come pouring out higgledy-piggledy, each paragraph complete in itself but bearing no relation to its neighbors. In desperation she had finally begun cutting apart the pages and trying to paste them back together into a coherent narrative. When this too proved a failure, Henry suggested dividing the material into two volumes, the first devoted only to science, the second to theology, then further subdividing each volume into chapters. To do this entailed the disheartening business of excising repetitions, transposing nearly every passage, and then interposing the transitions. As Helena's English was still far from perfect, Henry would read aloud her nearly indecipherable handwriting and translate the sentences into proper English while Helena copied them down. Without him, it is safe to say there would have been no book.

As poor as she knew the actual writing to be, H.P.B. felt lucky in one respect: no matter what the subject, whether it be philosophy, metaphysics or ancient religion, the words came easily. Writing was so simple, "the greatest pleasure,"[167] she wrote Vera, that it did almost seem as if someone were dictating to her.

It is interesting to note that the principles of what would later become Theosophy emerged in *Isis* only occasionally and in seminal form. She made no attempt to organize the whole field of human and divine knowledge, as she would a decade later when writing *The Secret Doctrine*. In 1876 she could only point to evidence for the existence of that knowledge, could only dimly suggest the outlines of a grand cosmic scheme. But if all she could manage was a panoramic survey of the literature from which she would eventually fashion the system of Theosophy, she would have done a great deal. To resuscitate archaic wisdom was an immense undertaking, even for one with extraordinary speed in absorbing material.

From where did Madame Blavatsky draw the self-confidence for such a project? She was not really a scholar, her research sources were limited to New York City, and her command of English was imperfect. Little wonder that she felt compelled to toss in first-person narratives with beginnings such as: "A fearful fever contracted by the writer near Rangoon after a flood of the Irrawaddy River. . . ."[168] But why did she pretend access to uncommon sources by writing "we have at hand a treatise by a pious Catholic, Jilbert de Nogen, on the relics of saints,"[169] when actually she copied Nogen's text from J. S. Forsyth's *Demonologia*. According to H.P.B., she had in her possession the single extant copies of many old manuscripts, photographs, drawings, and ancient tomes. Everything had been carefully skimmed from available sources in the course of careful research. Hence, there was no logical reason for not simply citing her real source. But she, who was not a scholar, had to make herself a super-scholar, and once again she went too far.

In trying to appear more knowledgeable than she actually was, Helena left herself open to charges of plagiarism. It cannot be denied that she was extremely careless about quotation marks, and, having once given a source, she would continue to quote it elsewhere without citing it. Moreover, either from laziness or ignorance, she fell into the habit of lifting from contemporary books the words of ancient authors while giving the impression that she had actually read the originals. For example, when she quoted from Plato's *Timaeus* and *The Laws*, she cited page numbers and even the original footnotes, but everything quoted can be found in Benjamin F. Cocker's *Christianity and Greek Philosophy* and Edward Zeller's *Plato and the Older Academy*. Strangely, H.P.B. failed to find anything wrong with this peculiar ethical procedure. Olcott, who might have set her straight, was not privy to her editorial shortcuts and believed in any case that she had read Plato in the astral light or received it from the Master's dictation. It would take another twenty years before he could admit that she "has sinned an hundred times against the canons of literary usage" by using "other men's writings as though they were her own."[170]

As the writing of *Isis* progressed, two central themes began to emerge: a venomous hatred of Christianity, which, Helena asserted, has copied most of its rites and dogmas from paganism; and her belief that the one source of all past wisdom was, not Egypt with its Isises and Brotherhoods of Luxor, but India. "When years ago, we first travelled to the East, exploring the penetralia of deserted sanctuaries, two [*sic*] saddening and ever-recurring questions oppressed our thoughts: Where, Who, What is GOD?"[171] But now she knew the answers were to be found in Hinduism and Buddhism. This she felt sincerely to be the truth, although she may have been less positive about the following statement:

> It was while most anxious to solve these perplexing problems that we came into contact with certain men, endowed with such mysterious powers and such profound knowledge that we may truly designate them as sages of the Orient. To their instructions we lent a ready ear. They showed us that by combining science with religion, the existence of God and immortality of man's spirit may be demonstrated like a problem of Euclid.[172]

Thus did revelation appear in a nutshell. The mysteries were not mysteries after all; miracles did not exist. The caretakers of the secret doctrine, members of the Indian Brotherhood incarnated at intervals in history to reveal mysteries of the divine wisdom, understood the secrets of atomic energy, gravitation, transmutation of metals, extraterrestrial communication and travel, in fact had more scientific knowledge than all modern physics, chemistry and metallurgy combined. Their books were written in an alphabet known only to themselves; and not only did they comprehend the principles of evolution and the decline of societies, but also possessed the most exhaustive cosmogony ever known to humanity. Undeniably, the idea was exhilarating. But it was hardly original to H.P.B., for as mentioned earlier, the concept of a secret brotherhood has always permeated occult tradition.

This is the place to emphasize the two main influences on Madame Blavatsky's philosophical vision. The first was Edward Bulwer-Lytton, who in his 1842 Rosicrucian novel *Zanoni* had written of a secret fraternity concealing themselves behind "the veil that hides the Isis of their wisdom from the world," and of the mysterious Indian Zanoni, who is rich, handsome, ageless, and a member of the Brotherhood. As we shall see, Helena's Mahatmas, Morya and Koot Hoomi, are fleshed out copies of Zanoni. H.P.B. herself is in several important respects reminiscent of Lytton's heroine Viola, who has seen her invisible protector in dreams since childhood but meets Zanoni in fleshly manifestation only as an adult. Bulwer-Lytton was of course writing fiction, but Helena believed quite seriously that he purveyed fact without knowing it.

Her second inspiration was Louis Jacolliot, a contemporary who had been French consul at Calcutta before writing works such as *The Bible in India* and *Occult Science in India*. Jacolliot stated categorically that the legendary society of unknown men actually existed. Deliberately concealed from public view, these ideal men scanned the world from their watchtower somewhere in

India, forever observing civilizations born, destroyed, reborn, always prepared to come to the rescue of the race.

Reality or magnificent legend? Like Jacolliot, Helena believed it all to be reality. Making Jacolliot's concepts her own, she began to quote extensively from his works, all the while resenting having to share these unknown Indians with Jacolliot. By the time she neared the end of *Isis*, she was calling his books "a curious conglomeration of truth and fiction," and Jacolliot little more than "a sensual French romancer"[173] who had worn out his spiritual welcome.

Slowly, the men who dictated to Helena had been transmogrified into Indians. To Vera she confided,

> I see this Hindu every day, just as I might see any other living person, with the only difference that he looks to me more ethereal and transparent. Formerly I kept silent about these appearances, thinking they were hallucinations. But now they have become visible to other people as well.[174]

One evening when work on *Isis* had been finished for the day, Henry said goodnight to H.P.B., went to his room, and sat down in a chair to smoke and read; he remembered, later, that it was not a ghost story he had opened but a travel book about Yucatán. Suddenly, from the corner of his right eye, he noticed towering above him a tall Indian dressed in white robes and a turban of amber stripes embroidered with yellow silk. Dropping his book, Henry stared in astonishment at the man's black beard, which was parted on the chin and twisted up over the ears in Rajput fashion, and at his unusual eyes. They were alive with soul-fire, he thought, piercing yet benign, the eyes of a loving father gazing on a son. Without thinking, Henry fell to his knees "as one does before a god or a god-like personage."

Bading Henry to rise, the visitor sat down beside him and began to talk: a great work could be done for humanity and Henry had the right to share in it, if he wished. He and Helena were bound by a mysterious tie which might be strained but could never be broken.

Would he see his visitor again?

Often, if he became a co-worker for the good of mankind.

As the Indian rose to leave, Olcott recalled thinking, "What if this be hallucination; what if H.P.B. has cast a hypnotic glamour over me?"[175] and he wished for some tangible object to prove that the Indian had really been there. Looking up, he saw the Indian smile as he saluted him farewell; then the room was empty and Henry was alone once more.

But not quite alone. On the table lay the man's embroidered turban. Clutching it, Henry ran to Helena's door and pounded.

* * *

Several possible explanations of the phenomenon present themselves, the most obvious being that Helena hired a man to dress up like an Indian. There is sufficient reason to believe she was capable of such a trick.

Secondly, Olcott's initial suspicion, that H.P.B. had hypnotized him, may have been essentially correct, in which case it would have been simple for her to have left the turban on his table.

More intriguing is a third possibility, that Henry had somehow been tuned into Helena's thought-form, in which case, he did actually see the Indian character she had created. While this may sound impossible, it is far from unheard of. For instance, "Seth," the famous trance personality of the Elmira, New York, medium Jane Roberts, has been seen and talked to by sensitives other than Ms. Roberts. And such a concept would not seem remarkable in Tibet, where the word *tulpas* connotes a magic formation generated by powerful concentration of thought.

Alexandra David-Neel, in *Magic and Mystery in Tibet*, tells how the *tulpa*, once endowed with enough vitality to be capable of impersonating a real being, tends to free itself from its maker's control and appear to others; and she goes on to recount how she herself decided to try to visualize, then animate, a *tulpa*. Choosing for experiment a short, fat, jolly monk, "I shut myself in *tsams* [seclusion] and proceeded to perform the prescribed concentration of thought and other rites. After a few months the phantom monk was formed. His form grew gradually *fixed* and life-like looking. He became a kind of guest, living in my apartment." Accompanying her on her travels, the monk walked, stopped and looked around him without speaking. Sometimes his hand actually seemed to touch her shoulder. "Once," she recalled, "a herdsman who brought me a present of butter saw the *tulpa* in my tent and took it for a live lama."

Before long, however, David-Neel would have cause to regret having created the monk, for he escaped her control and became bold and troublesome. To dissolve her mind-creature required six months of difficult struggle. In retrospect, the most interesting aspect of the experience was that others shared her own hallucination. "Tibetans disagree in their explanations of such phenomena"; she went on to add: "some think a material form is really brought into being, others consider the apparition as a mere case of suggestion, the creator's thought impressing others and causing them to see what he himself sees."[176]

In Madame Blavatsky's case, still another explanation suggests itself, which should be mentioned only because some people believed it to be the true one: that the Indian who Olcott met was a member of a secret brotherhood for which Madame Blavatsky was the visible agent. Certainly Henry had no trouble in accepting him as such. Little by little, Helena had been weaning him first from John King and then from the Egyptian Brotherhood of Luxor. Now, Olcott reports, "I was transferred to the Indian section and a different group of Masters."[177] It was all very neat and made a good deal of sense.

* * *

In August, Henry decided to scout a publisher for Helena's book, and he approached J. W. Bouton, who had published other works of an esoteric nature. Once Bouton saw the size of the manuscript, his interest quickly faded; he was about to sail for England, he told Henry, and had no time for reading. Refusing to accept rejection, Olcott continued to rave about Helena until Bouton, to get rid of him, told him to see Alexander Wilder, the scholar and editor who occasionally served as a first-reader of manuscripts. If Wilder judged the manuscript worthy of publication, Bouton might consider it.

Wilder, then fifty-three, was a tall, Lincolnesque man with a massive head of gray hair and speech full of quaint Saxon-Americanisms. Almost entirely self-educated, he was knowledgeable in medicine, mathematics and the classics, and his area of special interest was Plato and metaphysics. Although he had a definite taste for esotericism, he disliked individuals who pretended to possess superior powers, and he lacked the slightest impulse to join organizations such as the Theosophical Society. So when Henry Olcott arrived unannounced one afternoon at Wilder's home in Newark, New Jersey, and began to babble exuberantly about some manuscript by a crank, the editor reacted with extreme annoyance. He had never laid eyes on Olcott before, although they did have mutual acquaintances; and "I had barely heard of Madame Blavatsky," but what he had heard had not attracted him.

More than that, Wilder failed to understand why Bouton had sent Olcott to him, because he had talked to the publisher several times that week and Bouton had mentioned neither Madame Blavatsky nor her manuscript. Did Bouton seriously expect him to read the thousand pages? Suspecting that Bouton had foisted the pesky Olcott on him in order to avoid saying no himself, Wilder grumbled over the publisher's inefficiency but consented to look at the work.

Wilder read the manuscript with greater severity than he might have under other circumstances, and when he had finished there was no doubt in his mind that the book should be rejected. In his reader's report, he admitted that extensive research had gone into the project and "that so far as related to current thinking, there was a revolution in it," but in his opinion it was "too long for remunerative publishing." To his amazement, Bouton ignored his advice, accepted the manuscript and returned it to Wilder "with instructions to shorten it as much as it would bear."

Without much enthusiasm, Wilder sped through it and hacked out everything he judged superfluous. In a tactful letter to H.P.B., he explained his cuts and pointed out her faults of style; he also emphasized the importance of explaining her sources of information. Far from offended, Helena replied that "there are many parts in my Book that *I do not like* either, but the trouble is I do not know how to get rid of them without touching facts which are important, as arguments." Wilder of course was reading it objectively while her own "overworked brains and memory are all in a sad muddle." Still, she was "*very*, very thankful" for his suggestions and wished he had made more. As for his complaint about her lack of documentation, she passed over that quickly and merely commented that she could not, unfortunately, oblige. "I am a Thibetan Buddhist, you know, and pledged myself to keep certain things secret."

During this period, Olcott persisted in agitating for a meeting between Wilder and Madame, and although the editor hesitated, eventually he succumbed.

Having heard about the Madame's habit of receiving guests in her nightclothes, Wilder was disappointed to find her fully dressed. "In no respect was she coarse, awkward or ill-bred," and in fact he was obliged to admit that he found her courteous, cultured and extremely intelligent. "She expressed her opinions with boldness and decision, but not obtrusively." As for the miracles over which Olcott had raved, Wilder recalled quite vividly that she "never made any such claim to me." Of course she did mention her communications with mysterious persons whom she called "the Brothers," but Wilder, who assumed she was talking about telepathy, was inclined to attach little significance to these claims. From what he knew of such matters, an important condition for telepathy was absence from artificial stimulants such as meat, alcohol and narcotics of any kind, "but Madame Blavatsky displayed no such asceticism." It was obvious that she ate well and drugged herself with tobacco. Still, with Helena's talent for instant intimacy, she put him at ease so that afterward it seemed they had "become acquainted at once." She praised his abridgments, declared that what he had excised was "flapdoodle," and set about assiduously cultivating his friendship.[178]

By fall, 1876, the Theosophical Society had slowly withered and died, and after November even Henry no longer bothered to keep up the pretense. He canceled further meetings, suspended dues, and gave up the room in Mott Memorial Hall. Actually, the Society, despite its lofty objectives, had accomplished nothing, and its meetings had grown tiresome and silly. At one session, for example, Helena had announced that she now understood the process by which it was possible to rise from the earth and fly, and she was prepared to demonstrate. "With an electrical battery and powerful current we first ascertained by a well-known process what sort of magnetism there was in the carpet of the room; we electrified a cat, and it rose up several inches." Unfortunately, someone turned up the power "and of course the poor cat suddenly expired."[179]

This sort of experiment had been instrumental in driving away members. For R. B. Westbrook, one of the founders, the final straw turned out to be even more embarrassing. One evening he and his wife invited to their home a small party including Helena, Olcott, Emma Britten, and Reverend W. R. Alger, an eminent Unitarian minister from Boston, who was visiting New York and wanted to meet H.P.B. The evening began well, even though Helena was not on her absolutely best behavior and insisted upon making sniping remarks about Emma's mediumship. Toward the Reverend Alger, however, she was all charm. By 9 P.M. Emma's patience had exhausted itself and she excused herself, saying that she had to look after her aging mother. After her departure, Helena could not have been more bewitching as a conversationalist, to Alger's delight and the Westbrooks' inward rejoicing "that we had been successful in engineering this wonderful meeting of these wonderful people."

Not an hour later, however, the evening's amiability was abruptly shattered by the frantic ringing of the doorbell. Into the parlor dashed an outlandish figure draped from head to foot in rags and lengths of cloth and so disguised that Westbrook could not be certain whether a male or female lurked underneath; Alger likened the apparition to "the man in the iron mask." Mrs. Westbrook, alarmed that some mad laundress had wandered into the house by mistake, tried to shove the figure toward the door but, like a whirling dervish, it bounded over to Madame Blavatsky, saluted, and delivered a letter. Mission evidently accomplished, he, she or it stalked from the room and slammed the street door, leaving the assembled company gaping.

In the silence that followed, Olcott whispered gravely, "An elementary."

Helena, having torn open the envelope, expressed mild indignation that the Brothers should have troubled to send a special messenger on what she considered unimportant business; when Olcott asked what it all meant, she announced melodramatically that Dr. Seth Pancoast had just been refused admission to the Secret Brotherhood in India.

Throughout the commotion, Dr. Alger had managed to preserve his clerical dignity but now, understandably offended, he hurried to take his leave. At the door, he was heard to mumble contemptuously, "A put up job!"[180] Afterwards, Westbrook said, Madame Blavatsky professed to be hurt that Alger should have regarded her as a fraud.

Investigating this mortifying incident, Westbrook learned that Dr. Pancoast knew nothing about any application to the Brotherhood and, more damning, that Madame had promised an Irish servantwoman five dollars if she would impersonate an "elementary," but had failed to pay her. Furious over "this disgraceful attempt to impose upon the confidence of my distinguished clerical friend," Westbrook disaffiliated himself from the Theosophical Society.

What Helena hoped to accomplish by this absurd charade is impossible to determine. At this stage in her career she was lucky only with the phenomena she staged for Olcott; either she misjudged the credulity of her audience or she lacked the money to hire experienced actors.

Still bristling over the failure of her "elementary" production, H.P.B. continued to work almost compulsively on her book, turning most frequently to Alexander Wilder for editorial advice. Wilder was in the habit of commuting into New York from Newark several times a week to deliver lectures at a medical college, so Helena encouraged him to drop by. One day in early

December, having rung her bell in vain, he left a note and went away. H.P.B. wrote at once to say that he must have rung the wrong bell. "I do not go out of the house for the last two months, and the servant is always in the kitchen until half-past nine or ten." Why hadn't he pulled all the bells? "Well, you must come Monday—as you have to come to town and stop over till Tuesday. You can attend your College and sleep here the same, can't you?"[181]

Olcott, having finally arranged to cremate Baron de Palm, had gone to Washington, Pennsylvania. As this first cremation in the United States was thought to be an historic event, he had had no trouble inducing a large party of friends and journalists to accompany him, but Helena made excuses to remain behind. "I could *not* go," she confessed to Wilder. "To tell you the truth, I do not see the fun of spending $40.00 or $50.00 for the pleasure of seeing a man burnt"; the reason, she insisted, had nothing to do with squeamishness but rather "I have seen burnings of dead and living bodies in India sufficiently."

In all honesty, Palm's corpse had ceased to interest her, and what is more to the point, she had better things to do. She may have applauded Wilder's abridgments, but she wrote faster than he could cut. Throughout the winter and into the spring of 1877, even after the book had been set in type, she continued to make additions on the galleys and page proofs. Bouton complained to Henry that "the alterations have already cost $280.80, and at that rate, by the time the book appears it will be handicapped with such fearful expense"[183] that he would make no profit.

H.P.B. took no notice of Bouton. By the time *Isis* appeared on September 29, 1877, he would spend over six hundred dollars for corrections and the two volumes would mushroom to some twelve hundred and seventy pages. Still happily unaware of this, his correspondence with Madame centered on an appropriate title. The original title, probably Helena's choice although Wilder later attributed it to Bouton, was *The Veil of Isis*. However, when Bouton learned of an English book with the same title, he suggested changing to *Isis Unveiled* and Helena readily consented. Actually, both titles were misleading in that they gave the unmistakable impression the book dealt with Egypt, when in fact a large part of her material was devoted to India. But to Bouton, who had probably not read the book and who, in any case, had once published a treatise on ancient Greek art and added illustrations from Hindu mythology, the main consideration was a catchy title that might recoup his pyramiding investment. Helena, who favored the Isis concept, must have believed that the subtitle, "A Master-Key to the Mysteries of Ancient and Modern Science and Theology," would sufficiently indicate the scope of its contents.

As *Isis* neared publication, Helena began to turn her attention back to old, unpleasant matters. For the past two years, Michael Betanelly had lurked in the background of her life as a potential threat, not only because of the bigamous marriage but also because the existence of any husband would have publicly embarrassed Helena. She must have been hoping he would divorce her, but this had not happened, and now she was obliged to bring up the subject. Her feelings about Michael had been intensely exacerbated by a report that, on a recent visit to Russia, Betanelly had contacted her relatives with the expressed purpose of slandering her. In fact, everywhere she turned, she heard nightmarish gossip about herself and her relationship with Olcott, and once again she suspected Michael to be the source. To her further embarrassment, Olcott told her that Michael had never bothered to repay the loan that he had arranged from Everman.

At the beginning of May, H.P.B. wrote to Michael about these troublesome matters and brought up the subject of divorce. Several days later she received a bitter reply in which he complained of being almost destitute and revealed that "unless I pay Everman at least part of the money, he will take his revenge and have me arrested soon." If this happened, it would be her fault and Olcott's. He denied having gossiped about her by stating, "In the Caucasus I merely listened silently when you were scolded by your relatives and all who knew you."[184] He had never mentioned her name to Everman or to anyone else in America, and if people were talking about her, she had only herself to blame:

> You created for yourself scandal and notoriety. First you practised Spiritualism—you did not succeed. Now you have turned to Buddhism—you will succeed still less. Here you cannot play with the public as easily as you think. And by these experiments you are ruining other people, just as you ruined me by your Spiritualistic operations. If you had only kept quiet in your old age—nobody would have said anything.

After several pages of recriminations and threats, he declared that he had no intention of contesting a divorce, which he wanted "by any means." But that she must bear the expense because "I cannot pay; I have not money enough even to live. The cheaper you can arrange it the better. Only get it."[185] Finally, for unknown reasons, she dropped the idea. Scarcely an evening passed now that Helena and Henry did not entertain. Among the most frequent visitors to the "Lamasery," as she now called the apartment, were William Quan Judge and his seventeen-year-old brother John, the latter having offered to copy *Isis* in a neat hand for the printer. Now that William Judge was sharing office space with Henry, he returned to H.P.B.'s life as abruptly as he had departed, spending more time at the Lamasery than at his own home. When Helena told him that she had been experimenting with astral travel and could leave her body at will, Judge, fascinated, kept pestering for her secrets. If he wanted to become a holy arhat, H.P.B. finally told him, he must fast and give up alcohol. This advice must have gone to Judge's head, because a few days later he was experiencing visions and claimed that he left his body every night to roam in space. Helena, amused, wrote Aksakov on

June 15 that she would ring a bell in her apartment and Judge, eight miles away in Brooklyn, "starts off at once and in two hours appears at my call." Her last comment was: "See what fools they are, and how I lead them by the nose!"[186]

Her sister, however, proved less of a fool. When Helena offered to visit her in Tiflis "in the flash of an eye," Vera told her to cancel the flight—it might be dangerous. There was nothing to fear, Helena replied. Her physical body would be lying in bed at New York "in the state of a harmless idiot," while her astral body, attached by a thread, would be with Vera in Tiflis. Naturally, if Vera began to "shriek like mad," the thread would probably tear and then of course "I should die instantly."[187] Vera, now with three daughters by her second husband, had named her youngest Helena but that was as far as family loyalty went. There was not much about Helena Petrovna that she really liked, less that she took seriously.

In August, Helena and Henry had a letter from Emily Kislingbury, the secretary of the British National Association of Spiritualists, who was spending her holiday in the United States and wanted to meet them. Her routine request is of less interest than the letter itself. Addressed to Olcott from Niagara Falls, it contained a brief postscript obviously not penned by Miss Kislingbury: "She is a sweet, truthful, sincere nature. Would the heavenly powers there were a few more like her in London. Teach her and take care of her." The signature was written in a queer script Henry could not decipher until Helena explained that the message had been added phenomenally in transit by an adept whom she identified as "the old gentleman Narayan."[188] Narayan, she added, was one of the entities who had taken over her body during the writing of *Isis*. Olcott nodded solemnly, never suspecting that Helena herself might have intercepted the postman and steamed open the envelope.

Emily, as sweet and gentle as Narayan had promised, took to H.P.B. with a ferocity that amounted to worship and must obviously have hungered for a miracle. One day when the two of them were alone reading in the parlor, Helena obliged by causing the reflection in a wall mirror to move up and down.

"That's an atmosphere effect," H.P.B. yawned, and went back to reading her Russian newspaper.

Emily, however, continued staring intently at the mirror. Before her very eyes unrolled scenes of a port or harbor and a crowd of men dressed as Hindus. When she described these pictures, Madame seemed unimpressed.

"That is right," she acknowledged. "That is what I wished you to see,"[189] and she changed the subject.

The autumn of 1877 was particularly glorious, the rich colors of the foliage so remarkable that several excursions were made to the woods to collect leaves. Someone, perhaps Emily Kislingbury, thought it would be novel to decorate the dining room, and the project grew increasingly elaborate until finally one entire wall was covered by a mural of dried leaves showing an elephant, tiger, monkey, and at the side a serpent coiled around the trunk of a palm tree. Pleased by the startling jungle effect, Helena immediately began embellishing the mural with dried grasses and stuffed animals. Olcott was dispatched to purchase a lion's head, its jaws open and teeth menacing. Soon they added a few monkeys, an owl, several snakes and lizards, and finally a huge stuffed baboon which they dressed in white cravat and spectacles. To visitors, the Lamasery's dining room had to be the most original room in all of New York City, but to Helena it was an unconscious attempt to re-create the happy part of her childhood when she had wandered through her grandmother's museum and talked to the stuffed seals and flamingos.

On September 29, *Isis Unveiled* was published at last. "My darling," she announced joyfully to Aksakov, "was born last Saturday."[190] One of the first reviews, in the New York *Herald*, called *Isis* "one of the most remarkable productions of the century," which almost made her swoon since "I was prepared for abuse of every sort." Again to her surprise and enormous pleasure, the first edition of one thousand copies sold out within ten days of publication, even though Bouton had priced it at a steep $7.50. On the whole, the critics treated her kindly, although the New York *Sun* dismissed *Isis* as "discarded rubbish" and the Springfield *Republican* gleefully termed it "a large dish of hash." Bouton tried to persuade the New York *Times* to review it, but the editor told him that they had "a holy horror of Mme. Blavatsky."[191]

Just as Helena thought she had made her reputation as a scholar, she was stung to learn that Daniel Dunglas Home had published an autobiography, *Lights and Shadows of Spiritualism*, in which he devoted an entire chapter to insulting Henry Steel Olcott and his book *People from the Other World*. Still apparently smarting over Henry's unkind remarks about his mediumship, Home took it upon himself to destroy Henry's credibility as a rational person. Never mentioning Helena by name, he waspishly remarked that when he first began to read Olcott's book, he was sure it must have been written by a gushy woman of fifty under a nom de plume. *People from the Other World*, Home declared, was "beneath criticism," and "as a display of reasoning, it is altogether beneath contempt." The author of "this most worthless and dishonest book"[192] was a pompous fool who had been bamboozled at the Eddy séances by a nameless person who had foisted junk jewelry upon him. Referring to Peter von Hahn's buckle, he pointed out that in Russia "decorations are never buried with the dead. Until very recently, they were, without exception, returned to the government."[193] Of course the object that had "materialized" at Chittenden had been the buckle from her father's decoration, but with characteristic exaggeration Helena had taken to calling it the decoration itself.

Home, who did not believe for a minute that she received either a buckle or a decoration, could not let this opportunity for denunciation slip by. That he did not mention her name made no difference, for everyone knew who he was talking about.

Sickened, Helena began to think of him as a serpent endlessly spurting "venomous slime." It was his malignity that had ruined her in Russia, where people still remembered her as a harlot. In fact, a recent editorial in a Tiflis paper had called her a physically deformed, shifty-eyed charlatan, the embodiment of all vices. It was Home, she thought, who continued to poison her life in America, all because he could not forgive her for sleeping with Nicholas Meyendorff twenty years earlier and for having given birth to crippled Yuri. She moaned to Aksakov, "I want to go where no one will know my name,"[194] but she meant a place where Home's name was unknown. That place, she was convinced, was India.

During the writing of *Isis*, the idea of relocating in India had become increasingly attractive, and by this time Helena considered it imperative. It had begun as a lovely but impossible fantasy, but now H.P.B. determined to find a way, for in India waited the Secret Brotherhood and her Masters who would protect her from villains like Home.

The Brothers were real to her, and to Henry as well, but not to the world, particularly not to her family. "You do not believe that I tell you God's truth about my Masters," she chided Vera. "You consider them to be mythical."[195] Actually Vera regarded them as deliberate lies, but was too polite to say so. Nadyezhda, more sympathetic, thought it strange that a male Hindu would have the audacity to inhabit Helena's body, and she wanted to know if he wandered inside other people as well. "I'm sure I don't know," Helena replied stoutly. Perhaps it was not the man himself who possessed her, but only his power. "Through him alone I am strong; without him I am a mere nothing."[196] This answer had not satisfied Nadyezhda who could not conceive of her denying Christ for Buddhism or anything else. That was a sin. "Friend of my soul, Nadejinka," Helena replied in great agitation.

> I have at last decided to write you the whole truth, such as it is. I shall lay before you my soul, my heart, my brain . . . I am but the reflection of an unknown bright light. However this may be, this light has gradually been incorporated into me, it has been filtered into me, it has, as it were, pierced through me; and therefore, I cannot help myself that all these ideas have come into my brain, into the depth of my soul; I am sincere although perhaps I am wrong.[197]

Although Nadyezhda was not to know it, Helena no longer believed either in Christianity or a personal God. Hedging, she wrote, "I am not a Buddhist, but I am afraid also not a Christian in the ordinary church sense."

Then what *did* she believe? Nadyezhda demanded angrily.

She answered, "I believe in an indivisible and universal God, in the abstract spirit of God and not in an anthropomorphical Divinity." In letter after letter she flayed Nadyezhda with ideas, pausing now and then to wail, "I am so afraid Nadejda Andreevna, to upset you, for I love you so much, but still, I write the truth." It was a truth that Nadyezhda refused to hear and she asked Helena never to mention religion to her again.[198]

Throughout the fall of 1877 her obsession with India and a dark-skinned man she had begun to call Master M. continued to flourish. M., she told people, had a merry personality—he made jokes. "Sometimes he looks as if he were a living man . . . He will soon take us all to India, and there we shall see him in his body just like an ordinary person."[199] Precisely how this might come to pass she did not know, being forced to agree with Olcott that "our chances of getting to the Holy Land seemed very slight."[200]

The odds, however, climbed sharply one evening when James Peebles, recently returned from India, called at the Lamasery and noticed on the wall a photograph of two Indians, shipboard passengers with whom Henry had traveled to England in 1870. Coincidentally, Peebles had happened to meet one of them—Moolji Thackersey—while visiting Bombay. Taking Thackersey's address, Olcott wrote him the next day describing the Theosophical Society and its founders' interest in reviving the ancient knowledge of India. Thackersey, in turn, replied enthusiastically, raving to the colonel about his current interest in a reformer named Swami Dayananda Sarasvati who agitated for the abolition of the caste system and other Hindu abuses. Dayananda seemed to have been a Hindu version of the Reformation's Martin Luther. Through his organization, the Arya Samaj, Dayananda was exhorting his countrymen to give up Western ideas and return to pure Vedic religion.

This first contact with India excited Helena and Henry immensely and before long, letters were flying between New York and Bombay. Initially Henry dealt with the president of the Bombay Arya Samaj Hurrychund Chintamon, then with the Swami himself, who read Henry's letters in translation. When Chintamon pointed out that the purposes of the Arya Samaj and the Theosophical Society seemed identical and proposed amalgamation of the two groups, Henry did not wait for a second invitation. To form this union, he vowed dramatically, he was willing to sit at the Swami's feet and "be his servant."[201] That would not be necessary, Helena happily assured him, because the reason all of this had come about was that an adept of the Brotherhood occupied the Swami's body. As she had told him many times, the Masters were watching over them, drawing them closer to the land where they would do a great work for humanity. In her runaway enthusiasm, she wrote Chintamon a number of somewhat reckless letters in which she thoughtlessly described Olcott as a "psychologized baby" whom she led around by the nose.

Even before the communication with India, the moribund Theosophical Society had shown signs of reviving. To Helena's surprise, she had recently received overtures from the English Spiritualists Charles Massey, Stainton Moses, and her friend Emily Kislingbury about the forming of a London branch. Even though there had been disagreements over the T.S.'s opposition to Christianity, which seemed excessive to Massey, the kinks had been ironed out. By spring of 1878, the Society was a going concern, both in New York, where membership applications had been received from such well-known men as Thomas Edison and General Abner Doubleday, and abroad. In addition to the English group, Moolji Thackersey had founded a branch in Bombay, and now Olcott was preparing a circular for Lydia Paschkoff to take to Japan. By May, when the T.S. officially changed its name to "The Theosophical Society of the Arya Samaj," he was happily envisioning a worldwide organization.

While the union with the Arya Samaj seemed to bring India a step closer, practically it did nothing of the kind. Helena talked incessantly of the imminent departure, while to Henry the adventure remained, for the foreseeable future, a pipedream. He had responsibilities, he reminded her; as it was, his law practice barely provided for them and his ex-wife and sons. In India, where he would have no income whatsoever, they would all starve. Helena reproached him for his lack of faith in the Brotherhood; clearly, once they reached India, the Masters would take care of them. Henry was not persuaded.

Desperate for money, H.P.B. began barraging Russian papers and magazines with articles on divorce, suicide, feminism, epidemics, the phonograph, indeed on any American subject she believed of interest to Russians. When *Pravda*, who had bought two of her ideas, proved slow in paying, Helena wrote to Nadyezhda that the editor was "a pig! I shall not write anymore for him."[202] She begged her aunt to find her other markets and, possibly through Nadyezhda's efforts, she received a commission to write a series. It would be called "From the Land on the Other Side of the Blue Ocean," and would deal largely with such lurid American topics as abortion, sex crimes, grave-robbing and child abuse. When she chose to, Helena could churn out dozens of pages a day. Presumably she was doing it now because suddenly she had money. Lots of it. Once, when Henry took her shopping and grumbled about the cost of the dresses, she thrust fifty dollars into his hand; on another occasion he discovered that five hundred dollars had anonymously been deposited in his bank account. Obviously not privy to how much Helena had been writing, he could not understand where the money was coming from. Helena would explain that she had "materialized" it, or that Master M. had sent it. Knowing that the Brotherhood could provide hard cash reassured and enchanted Olcott, who made jokes about the Astral Bank for Savings.

However, it took tremendous effort for Helena to keep afloat the Astral Bank for Savings, and by the first week of April, she had worked herself into a state of emotional and physical exhaustion. She kept to her bedroom and allowed Olcott and his sister Belle Mitchell, "both of them pale, sour, wrinkled, as if they had been boiled in a sauce-pan,"[203] to fuss over her. Afterward she informed her sister that she had been unconscious for five days, but that "Master telegraphed from Bombay to Olcott: 'Don't be afraid. She is not ill but resting. She has overworked herself.' "[204] That Olcott, in his memoirs, failed to mention either the illness or the receipt of what would have been his first message from a Mahatma, suggests that Helena's version was grossly exaggerated.

Henry was baffled by certain changes in Helena's personality. The jolliness that he had loved was gone, and now, he wrote to Charles Massey, "she is all sobriety, dignity, stern self-repression."[205] Even though Henry felt that Helena could read his thoughts, he had yet to figure her out. He had even written to Nadyezhda for information about her childhood, but received only enough clues to mystify him further. Sometimes he thought that she was no more a *she* than he was, but "a very old man and most learned and wonderful man,"[206] a Hindu man. It was a totally fanciful description, but Helena was inclined to like it.

During May and June legal matters preoccupied her. First, Michael finally divorced her on grounds of desertion, and the decree was granted on May 25. Secondly, despite her growing antipathy toward America, she made the inconsistent move of applying for citizenship. Having filed for naturalization in September, 1874, she had recently abandoned any intention of following through, but Henry wisely pointed out that, given the tension between Russia and Britain, it would be far safer to arrive in British India with an American passport.

On July 8, he accompanied her to Superior Court to be sworn in. An hour after returning home, she was railing in a letter to Nadyezhda that "to my utter astonishment and disgust, I was compelled to repeat publicly after the judge, like a mere parrot," that she renounced her loyalty to Russia. "I was awfully scared when pronouncing this blackguardly recantation of Russia and the emperor,"[207] because while she managed to choke out the words, they were a lie.

Since H.P.B. had the distinction of being the first Russian woman to be naturalized, the press, true to form, descended on the Lamasery. Was it true, asked the *Daily Graphic* reporter, that Madame had become a citizen in order to take a leading role in the woman suffrage movement? Or, rather, to make extensive real estate purchases?

Madame, staring him down, solemnly intoned that she had been naturalized "because I love liberty. There is little liberty in Russia today." She was "glad" and "proud" to call herself an American.[208]

To the New York *Star* man, who wondered if she were married, she glowered, "I am a widow, a blessed widow and I thank God! I wouldn't be a slave to God Himself, let alone man."[209] She knew from Nadyezhda that Nikifor was still alive at Poltava, but that was no business of the reporter.[210] Her marriage to Michael seemed so unreal, she had no compunction in denying it had ever happened; even to friends such as Caroline Corson she wrote that anything she might have once confided about marrying Betanelly had been in jest. In any case, "that poor fellow who was twenty years younger than myself"[211] had actually married a Miss Allen.

Public personality that she was, she still avoided any comment to the press about her departure for India. Clearly, such an announcement would have been inappropriate at that time, but H.P.B. was never one to demure from unconventional behavior. She had another, more complicated reason to keep quiet. Only in principle Henry had agreed that the move was inevitable; in fact, he had procrastinated endlessly, refusing even to set a departure date. His lack of enthusiasm drove Helena wild, although she understood that raising the passage money would be far from easy. Throughout the summer, Olcott worked on various business ventures that he might undertake once they arrived in their new home, specifically trading American clocks for tiger skins and curios. In Albany and Philadelphia he managed to interest several companies in retaining him as their agent and also applied to President Hayes for a diplomatic passport, a letter of recommendation to all U.S. ministers and consuls abroad, and a commission to investigate the practicality of extending American commercial interests in Asia, all of which were granted in due time.

For Helena, the summer dragged on. When Henry went to Albany on business in mid-June, she did not care to remain at the Lamasery alone and made several excursions to New Jersey with Belle Mitchell and also with Edward Wimbridge, a tall English architect and artist who had grown so chummy with H.P.B. and Olcott that he practically lived with them. At the end of the month, still restless, Helena took the night boat to Troy, New York, and from there journeyed to Albany, where she joined Henry. Back in New York, she complained of finding the city's ninety-degree heat unbearably tropical and suggested a seaside vacation. On the thirteenth of July, she and Henry, accompanied by Wimbridge, left for a three-week vacation at East Hampton, Long Island, where they stayed at Captain Gardiner's Hotel. "A superb day," Henry wrote in his diary the next day,

> bright sun, cool, pleasant air, everything charming. We three took a carriage, drove to the beach and all bathed. H.P.B. presented a most amusing appearance; paddling about in the surf, with her bare legs, and showing an almost infantile glee to be in such a 'splendid magnetism.' [212]

When people stared at her, because women ordinarily did not bare their legs at the beach, nor did they smoke, she lit up another cigarette and dismissed them as "pious Xtians."[213] No doubt part of her friskiness can be attributed to having recently shed nearly ninety pounds.

During the writing of *Isis*, she was fond of describing her appetite as being like "three hogs"[214] and she had taken no exercise. By the book's completion, she was huge, and although she laughed about her obesity, her body disgusted her. When Belle Mitchell took her to a shop that owned a scale, and Helena found that she weighed 245 pounds, she resolved to reduce to an appropriate weight for traveling—156 pounds, she told Belle.

According to Olcott, her diet plan was simple. Ten minutes before each meal, she held her palm over a glass of plain water, stared hypnotically for a few seconds, and then downed the water in a single gulp. It was not more than a few weeks later, he maintained, that she went back to the shop with the scale and weighed in at 156 pounds.

That H.P.B. lived in a fever of nervous excitement during the autumn of 1878 is documented by her own pen. While she herself kept no diary, Olcott did, and since they had begun living together Helena fell into the habit of making entries in his daybook.[215] With Henry now frequently away hustling business deals, it was Helena who jotted down the minutiae of her daily life: an attack of neuralgia, the lack of hot water in the apartment, the grocer's dunning over an unpaid bill in the amount of a hundred dollars,[216] articles written, letters sent and received—many of them to and from Hurrychund Chintamon—and names of people, sometimes a dozen or more daily who drifted up to the Lamasery to wile away the afternoon or evening and sometimes spend the night. That Helena incessantly praised India at America's expense and even solicited contributions for the Arya Samaj deterred no one; indeed, it gave the visits exoticism. Not unexpectedly, word of her departure soon filtered down to the press and on Sunday, October 13, a gossipy editorial in the New York *Sun* announced that the colonel and the Madame were "packing up their trunks."[217]

The one overriding obstacle to the pilgrimage Helena felt might well come from Henry's ex-wife, whom she had mockingly nicknamed "Kali" after the malevolent Hindu goddess of death and destruction. That somehow she would prevent Henry from leaving, perhaps by having him arrested, tortured H.P.B. How strongly Mary protested the departure of her former husband is not known, but it stands to reason that the idea displeased her, since he was the sole support of herself and their two sons. Later William Judge would claim that by this time one of Henry's sons was working and the other was about to graduate from college; neither required his support. But the truth was quite a bit different, for Morgan and William were seventeen and sixteen respectively, and very much in need of their father's financial and emotional support. Henry's absconding to India with Madame Blavatsky must at best have been regarded as scandalous abandonment by both the boys and their mother. To mislead Mary Olcott and take some of the pressure off Henry, Helena dispatched a sarcastic reply to the *Sun*, protesting against "the chronic habit the papers have of constantly hitching our two names together like a runaway team bound on a race of destruction." As for the rumors about the two of them leaving town, "I wish sincerely we were; but we are not. America, my adopted country, will have to bear with me a little longer." She doubted very much that the colonel intended spending the rest of his life as an Indian mystic seated cross-legged in meditation or perched upon a pillar "with his gaze concentrated upon the tip of his nose."[218]

It was not only Mary Olcott who could throw a wrench into her plans; until the very last moment Helena would fear that Henry himself would find an excuse for backing out. Uprooting him from his native soil became almost a full-time occupation for not only H.P.B. but also for masters Serapis and M., whose bombardment of supernatural messages are regular entries in his diary: "*Orders* from Serapis to complete all by the first days of December"; "Furniture and rest must be sold and disposed of before the 12th. ORDERS"; "Definite orders from Serapis. *Have to go*; the latest from 15 to 20th Dec."[219]

Henry had to deal with their departure as a reality when he returned from Philadelphia in early November to find that H.P.B. had sold their carpets and that the Theosophical traveling party had become a quartet. It was at Helena's urging that they would be joined by Edward Wimbridge and Rosa "Taffy" Bates. Rosa, who was a temporarily unemployed English governess in her late thirties, had no more money than Wimbridge, so, at Helena's insistence, Henry assumed the cost of their steamship fares. It was definitely not the sort of plan Olcott would greet enthusiastically, especially since he was having enough difficulty rounding up the cash for two passages to India, but Helena convinced him that arriving in the company of two English people would give them an entrée they might not have as an American and Russian. In principle, Henry had no objection to Wimbridge, who was an agreeable fellow, but he insisted that Rosa Bates, whom he disliked, would only cause trouble. Behind her back, H.P.B. denigrated her as "Spinster Bates"—but felt she could be useful. Helena continued to insist to Henry that she knew best about Rosa and in the end he relented.

On the second of November, still edgy after her struggle on behalf of Wimbridge and Bates, she visited a friend on East Sixtieth Street and afterwards decided to return through Central Park on foot, a form of locomotion she ordinarily eschewed. It was an especially beautiful day, however, and she even sat down quietly under the trees for a while. Once she got home, she regretted the exercise because she began to feel chilled and that evening, tired and draggy, she was not her usual volatile self. When Gus Petri, who was a friend of Wimbridge's and an amateur fortune-teller, brought out a pack of cards and offered to prophesy their futures, his suggestion was taken up eagerly by everyone except Helena, who viewed the proceedings with barely veiled disdain. Once her turn came, however, she was appalled to hear him blithely predict that she would probably never reach Bombay. Unaware of her experiences on the S.S. *Eumonia*, he went on to venture that she would die at sea. Petri, according to Olcott's diary, "hinted shipwreck for us all, in which Wim and I would be saved and H.P.B. lost! Goak!"[220]

Although Helena pretended to brush off Petri's predictions as "flapdoodle," they threw her into a genuine fright. To make matters worse, she began to sniffle the next day, and for the next two weeks suffered from a running nose, coughing, and "fearful sleepless nights."[221] "O God," she wrote in Henry's diary, "O Indra of the golden face! Is this really the beginning and the end!"[222] It was not until the day after Thanksgiving, when Henry was off visiting his brother Emmet, that Helena's anxiety began to subside. Petri showed up for dinner and again read the cards. This time, to H.P.B.'s enormous relief, he "prognosticated delay for departure but safe arrival to Bombay." His next prediction was "death through murder for H.P.B. in 8 years at the age of 90(!!)," which made her howl with laughter. "Nothing like clairvoyance,"[223] she observed dryly. Nonetheless, she could not entirely forget Petri's ominous predictions.

In early December her life began to pick up speed. "Taffy" Bates, already gone ahead to England, had taken with her two of H.P.B.'s trunks, while others containing books were shipped by freighter directly to Bombay. Alexander Wilder took down the famous jungle mural from the dining room and carefully transported it to Newark where it continued to hang in his hallway for at least a dozen years. The remainder of the Lamasery's furnishings were to be disposed of by an auctioneer, but the night before the auction, Helena still seemed to have no clear certainty about her future. She wrote in a melancholy tone, "Tomorrow good-bye, all. But—will H.S.O. be ready? That's the question. One, only *one* week more! God help him if he fails." That night she stayed up talking until 4 A.M. and after two hours' sleep, woke to a gray rainy day. Gloomy and anxious, she could not bear the idea of watching strangers handle her things, so once the auctioneer had hung his red flag outside the building's street door, she fled into the rain, telling Olcott that she had an appointment to meet an adept at the Battery.

When she returned at 2 P.M., the red flag was drooping soggily and nearly all the furniture remained exactly where she had left it, the bad weather having kept away many potential customers. Although one of her friends, Mortimer Marble, had gleefully sold the landlord's window shades for fifty cents, Helena had to face the distressing fact that the auction had failed; in the end, she sold virtually the entire contents of the apartment to the auctioneer, who said he would dispose of them to a dealer. "All went for a song,"[224] she moaned.

The next morning, after breakfasting on a board, for lack of any other table, she was annoyed to find at the door a reporter from the *Daily Graphic*, whom she "respectfully begged to go to the devil"[225] and then reluctantly agreed to see.

When the reporter noted mildly that she appeared to be leaving America after all, she interrupted defensively, "You have liberty but that is all, and of that you have too much, too much!" Still in her nightgown, she rolled a cigarette and began an angry discourse on Americans in general and their press in particular:

Do you wonder I am anxious to leave when you know how I was received and the treatment I have met?

They said I was a Spiritualist, a heathen, a believer in all manner of impossible things; that I was an adventuress and had neither title nor family; that I was a felon and forger; that I had been married seven times and murdered six of my husbands; that I was a free lover and had never been married . . . Think of it all! Then the reporters came and asked me how much I was worth and wanted to see inside my mouth to count my teeth and see whether they were genuine or not.[226]

Dazed, the reporter tried to change the subject. "When shall you leave?" he faltered.

Although it seemed like an innocuous question, Madame had no intention of cooperating. She gazed at him haughtily and said, "I never know. I do not know what I shall do an hour beforehand."

Could she please furnish some information about her sailing plans? She could not. "I know neither the time nor the vessel, but it will be very soon and very secretly." On the receipt of a telegram, she would be gone in three hours.

By this point the *Graphic* man was reduced to pleading for scraps. Helena relented slightly by admitting that she planned to visit London, Paris and Bombay before "going to Northeastern India, where the head of the order is and where I shall obey whatever orders they may give and go where I am told." She sighed impatiently, "Oh! how glad I shall be to see my dear Indian home again."[227] Not once did she mention that the colonel was accompanying her.

Those final days in the now empty Lamasery passed in a blur of visitors, scarcely any sleep, food snatched on the run, and last-minute errands. On the twelfth, apparently fearful that India lacked dentists, H.P.B. took the precaution of having several teeth extracted, and the next day noted in the diary that she felt ill, perhaps with a swollen mouth. In any case, she did not feel well enough to accompany Henry to Menlo Park, New Jersey, where he borrowed a phonograph from Thomas Edison so that they could make tinfoil recordings of their voices. Even though the machine weighed nearly a hundred pounds, it was worth hauling back to the city. That night at the farewell party, tea was served in rotation as there were only three cups left in the apartment. Edison's phonograph was placed on a barrel, and a cluster of friends, including the Theosophical cat Charles, took turns shouting and purring into the "voice-receiver.[228] Despite the conviviality of the evening, there were some New Yorkers who felt, sadly, that an era was ending. One of them was David Curtis, a New York *Times* writer and the only journalist H.P.B. regarded as a real friend. "Her apartment," he wrote, "was a meeting ground for as strange a group of original thinkers as New York had seen, individuals who affirmed little and denied nothing."[229] After knowing the Madame two years, Curtis did not believe her either a charlatan or a self-deluded crackpot, as many said, but simply an enigma whom he would never forget nor figure out.

On the morning of December 17, H.P.B.'s last day on American soil, she exclaimed in Henry's diary, "Great day! Olcott packed up," and then she added fretfully, "What next? All dark—but tranquil." It was not until seven in the evening that Henry returned with three tickets for the British steamer *Canada* and then she triumphantly scrawled in large letters across the page: "CONSUMMATUM EST."[230] At midnight she took a last look at the brass chandelier with its flickering gas jets, closed the door on the Lamasery and drove to the steamer with Olcott. They spent a tormented night on the *Canada* because the ship's heating apparatus was not working and the weather had turned bitterly cold. "Got frozen, sleeping in wet blankets," Helena wrote, "and passed a sleepless night." In the morning, exhausted, she continued to suffer "trances of fear"[231] that Mary Olcott would suddenly appear at the dock to snatch back her ex-husband from the quest for truth.

India

1878–1884

I

Bombay

The voyage to India was a nightmare. It had taken the *Canada* two days just to leave American waters because it lost the tide. "Fits of fear lasted till 11," she wrote in Olcott's diary on December 19. "The body is difficult to manage." They had three days of good weather before being struck by rain and gale winds that tracked them all the way to the entrance of the English Channel. Excruciating seasickness afflicted all ten passengers, with the exception of Helena who, thinking of the *Eumonia* and Petri's prophecies, was merely terrified, although she dared not reveal it. Occasionally Henry would stagger from his bunk and try to cheer her up with a comic song, and one evening the captain regaled them with "fearful stories of shipwreck and drowning," to which Helena listened deadpan. "Oh for India and HOME!" she wrote, but she could not shake the feeling that she would never reach England, much less India. She proceeded to feed her anxiety by eating "like three hogs" and baring her teeth toward an Anglican clergyman whose profession she reviled, Olcott recalled, "with expressions fit to curdle the blood."[1] But apparently the clergyman took her ranting good-naturedly, because when the *Canada* finally docked at Gravesend on the morning of January 3, 1879, he begged her for a photograph.

H.P.B. and Henry were guests of the American medium Mary Hollis Billing and her physician husband in suburban Norwood. From almost the moment Madame stepped into the Billing home, she started performing phenomena in a fevered way that suggests extreme nervousness. Fearful that Henry might still develop cold feet and slink back to New York, desperate to impress Charles Massey and the other London Spiritualists, she felt compelled to attempt a few miracles. Convincing Mary Billing of the reality of the Indian Brothers did not prove difficult, and the flattering suggestion that her spirit guide "Ski" was probably one of their messengers was readily accepted; indeed both Mary and "Ski" were all too eager to believe and render services. Thus one foggy evening, when Henry, Massey and Dr. Billing returned to the house, Mary told them that a tall, handsome Hindu had been there conferring with Madame on occult business and that he had happened to mention passing the three men earlier on the street. That was true, Henry exclaimed at once, because he recalled glimpsing over his shoulder a man with the unmistakably transcendent face of an adept. His companions, more cautious, allowed that it might have happened but in the dense fog they certainly could not swear to it. After dinner, at Mary's instigation, Helena fished around under the table and "materialized" a Japanese teapot and later, as Massey was preparing to depart, she told him to reach into his overcoat pocket. To his amazed delight, he withdrew an inlaid Indian cardcase containing a slip of paper that bore Hurrychund Chintamon's autograph.

There was more to come. During a séance on the evening of January 6, "Ski" directed Olcott to Madame Tussaud's wax museum where he would find a note from a Brother under the left foot of Figure 158. The next morning, accompanied by Billing and Wimbridge, Olcott hurried around to Tussaud's, where of course he found the note. Even he had to admit there was no hard evidence for this phenomenon because Helena and Mary had visited the British Museum on the morning of the sixth and could easily have ducked into Madame Tussaud's to plant the note; still, in his opinion, it was genuine. All told, these miraculous events had their desired effect on Massey too because, by his moral code, no woman as high-born and frank as Madame Blavatsky could be capable of willfully stooping to trickery.

On January 14, Helena mailed her sister a packet of photographs of herself, and judging by the brief enclosure it is clear that she continued to be frightened. "I start for India. Providence alone knows what the future has in store for us." The pictures might be the last sight Vera would have of her; if she should perish, she hoped that her family would not forget her. "I shall write from Bombay *if I ever reach it.*" Four days later she went up to Liverpool with Olcott, Wimbridge and Bates, spent the day killing time at the Great Western Hotel, and at 5 P.M., in a driving rainstorm, boarded the *Speke Hall.* Helena's heart sank at her first sight of the decrepit ship with its filthy cabins and carpets stinking of mold and dampness, and even Henry thought it "a wretched omen."[2] No food was served during the first twenty-four hours on-board and had it not been for the bread and butter they unearthed from a bon voyage basket, they would have gone hungry.

One of the first things Helena noticed was that the vessel had been loaded almost to the water's edge with what she learned was railway iron. She expressed her displeasure so vituperatively that, according to Olcott, she was "unanimously voted . . . a nuisance."[3] Two days out she badly bruised her knee when rough seas flung her against a table leg in the dining salon, and after that she remained in her cabin bellowing at the stewardess, a Mrs. Yates. Olcott remembered that her cries of "Meeses Yetz" could be heard over half the ship.

By the time they anchored at Malta on January 28 to fill the coal bunkers, H.P.B.'s gloom had begun to lift and she went ashore with the others to tour the picturesque town and fortress. Five days later, reaching Port Said, the ship began to puff its way through the Suez Canal, at which time passengers discarded their heavy winter clothing and donned tropical outfits and pith hats. Henry, who did not own a pith hat, strutted on deck wearing the turban that Master M. had given him in New York, a bit of irreverent clowning that H.P.B. did not particularly appreciate. She was not amused when Henry played the fool. That night the *Speke Hall* tied up opposite the village of Khandara and the Theosophical party visited an Arab coffee house where they sipped black coffee and sampled the local tobacco. Helena was beginning to relax, but just as she teetered on the brink of belief that they would reach their destination, a flue in the boiler burst and this necessitated two more stops for repairs.

Helena remained on edge for the rest of the trip. Her terror of death at sea might seem a bit paranoid but, in fact, it was not entirely so. Perhaps she was picking up some kind of premonitory vibration, because six years later the *Speke Hall* would go down in the Indian Ocean without a single survivor.

The sun was shining gloriously in Bombay when they arrived in the early morning of the sixteenth of February, after having risen before dawn to glimpse the Elephanta Caves. Olcott's friend Moolji Thackersey and two companions came out to the ship in a bunder boat but, contrary to expectations, there was no sign of Hurrychund Chintamon or of a group even vaguely resembling a welcoming party from the Arya Samaj. The glow of anticipation having slightly dimmed, the newcomers collected their baggage and clambered aboard a boat to head for land. Henry solemnly knelt and kissed the granite quay before stepping ashore, but Helena did not permit herself such extravagant gestures. Her disappointment palpable, she kept scanning the dock in hopes that a welcoming committee would materialize. The scene she visualized, in vain, she described in a letter to Vera:

> We were met by a band of local, half-naked dancing girls, who surrounded us chanting their *mantra* and led us in state—all the time bombarding us with flowers—to a—maybe you think to a carriage? Not at all, to a white elephant! Good Lord, the effort it cost me to climb over the hands and backs of naked coolies to the top of this huge animal . . . The others were placed in palanquins, and lo! to the accompaniment of acclamations, tamborines, horns, with all sorts of theatrical pomp, singing and a general row, they carried us—humble slaves of God—to the house of the Arya Samaj.[4]

In lieu of that, she stood uncertainly on the quay with Olcott, Wimbridge and Rosa Bates in the burning noonday sun, all four looking lost and wilted. After a while, they saw running toward them a breathless, moon-faced Hindu who introduced himself as Chintamon and offered a number of implausible excuses for his tardiness. Although everyone smiled and insisted it did not matter, Helena felt it was a poor omen. Clearly Chintamon had thought so little of their coming that he had not bothered to inform the Arya Samaj.

Driving through the vast commercial bustle of downtown Bombay, she felt her dismay receding, for spread before her was the world she had dreamed of. Staring out of the carriage, she was confronted by Arabs from Muscat jostling Malays and Chinese, Parsi in their sloping hats, Rajputs, Afghans from the Northern frontier, and many that she could not identify. Carts drawn by sleepy-eyed oxen threaded their creaking way between tram cars, buggies, victorias, palanquins and handsome English carriages. People were doing a thousand things in the streets and sidewalks, gutters and open shops: barbers shaved their customers, sitar players twanged their wires, worshipers stood with clasped palms before images of Rama, beggars squatted in the blinding sunlight and rocked themselves to and fro, bare-limbed Indian women glided along with baskets of chuppattis or cow dung on their heads and with naked babies astride their hips. And overhead, in every open space, the feathered date trees waved, the sacred fig sheltered squirrels and parrots, and the air was literally peopled with the wheeling and screaming of gray-necked crows.

Olcott wrote in his memoirs that he would never forget the intoxication of his first sight of Bombay; Helena did not record her feelings, could not even honestly express them because she had told everyone that she had seen the sights of India many times. Before leaving New York, Henry had asked Chintamon to rent them a modest house in the Hindu quarter and hire the minimum amount of necessary servants "as we did not wish to waste a penny on luxuries."[5] For the second time that day, Chintamon proved his unreliability because they learned that he had not rented a house, but instead was taking them to his own hastily vacated bungalow. The small house on Girgaum Back Road had practically no furniture and of course no such Western conveniences as indoor plumbing, but they assured Chintamon that it was charming. With the perfume of the flowers and the fronds of cocoa palms nodding over the roof, it truly did seem like paradise after their dismal weeks on the *Speke Hall*. That afternoon, several Hindu women, friends of Chintamon's, called on H.P.B. and Rosa, and later in the day Ross Scott, a fellow passenger on the ship, who was coming out for a civil-service job, also paid a call. Helena had taken a fancy to the coarse-humored Irishman and when Scott begged for proof of her powers, she took from her pocket a handkerchief embroidered with "Heliona" and swiftly changed the name to "Hurrychund." Violently impressed, as were the dozen Hindus watching, Scott gave her a five-pound contribution for the Arya Samaj.

By the next morning, word of their presence spread through the native community and precipitated a rush of visitors. For two days they floated along blissfully: Chintamon invited three hundred people to a reception at which Helena and Henry were welcomed with garlands, limes and rose water, and Henry felt so touched that he began to cry. They took the six-mile boat ride across the harbor to the Elephanta Caves, inspected the sculptures of Shiva as half-man, half-woman, and enjoyed themselves thoroughly at a picnic luncheon. That evening, their necks wreathed with jasmine garlands, they sat in the box of honor at the Elephinstone Theatre for a special performance of a Hindu drama. During the intermission they listened to complimentary welcoming speeches from the stage. When the play had not yet ended at three in the morning, they excused themselves and departed, eyes barely open. It was, as Olcott called it, "unalloyed happiness."[6]

The next morning their bubble exploded when Chintamon presented them with an exorbitant bill for rent, food, repairs to his house and, appallingly enough, even the hire of the three hundred chairs for their reception and the cost of a welcoming telegram he had sent them en route. With a gasp, Henry stared shakily at the itemized bill and thought that at that rate they would soon be penniless. Helena protested furiously that Chintamon had given them the impression they were to be his guests. The session grew stormy and when Helena asked what had become of the six hundred rupees she had forwarded to him for the Arya Samaj, he confessed that he had failed to report its receipt and had, in fact, pocketed the money. Cruelly disillusioned, she and Henry resolved to have no further dealings with Chintamon and decided that the first order of business was to look for a house of their own. Nearby they found a small bungalow at 108 Girgaum Back Road for less than half the rent Chintamon had charged them and bought a few pieces of furniture. Through Moolji Thackersey they acquired a servant, a fifteen-year-old Gujarati boy named Vallah Bulla, which H.P.B. shortened to Babula. There were some who would say, later, that Babula once had been a conjurer's assistant and had been selected by H.P.B. to function as an accomplice. According to Olcott, he had previously worked for a Frenchman who was a former steward at Bombay's Byculla Club, and he had a gift for languages, speaking five of them including English and French.

Anglo-India in the 1870s was a country in which European visitors deposited their calling cards at Government House and socialized exclusively with other whites who unthinkingly referred to the natives as "niggers" and complained of their deceit and laziness. That Madame Blavatsky and Colonel Olcott chose to make their residence in a native section of Bombay and fraternized exclusively with Indians was enough to raise eyebrows. Loathing official life, Helena did not go near Government House and she was revolted by the Anglo-Indians' barbaric and righteous attitudes toward Hindus. If she and Olcott had been anonymous travelers, little note would have been taken of their choice of company, but there was no ignoring Madame. Less than a week after the Theosophists' arrival, they came under the contemptuous scrutiny of the Bombay *Review*. It quoted Rosa Bates as having said that she was "not a Christian," and went on to blast the Theosophists for "wanton aggressiveness"[7] in insulting the Christians in India. Helena could not resist shooting back a huffy retort calling the paper "a bigoted, sectarian organ of the Christians" and pointing out that among the two-hundred-and-forty million population, Christians "count but as a drop in the ocean."[8] Not content to leave it at that, she recklessly sprayed insults about the Bible, the British government, and the Sepoy Mutiny, which she blamed on the missionaries.

Basically a non-political person, Helena's pugnaciousness made her seem political, and the suspicious government immediately pricked up its ears, less because of her anti-Christian remarks than because she was Russian. For seventy years, England had been at odds with Russia over Afghanistan and in 1873 it obtained promises that the country would remain outside the sphere of Russian influence. However, a few months before Helena's arrival, Amir Sher Ali Khan had ostentatiously received a Russian delegation at Kabul while refusing a British delegation permission to cross his frontier. A few weeks after Helena's arrival in Bombay, the British would invade Afghanistan. British officials were consequently in no mood to take lightly any Russian visitor, especially so obvious a troublemaker. Concluding that Madame Blavatsky must be a spy, they placed her under police surveillance; fortunately, having followed Olcott's advice, she had been carrying an American passport, otherwise, sterner measures would probably have been taken.

All this publicity would reap undeniable benefits, for it enabled H.P.B. and Olcott to proselytize among Bombay's intellectual Hindus, many of whom seemed eager to join the Theosophical Society. Even more encouraging, Helena received an unusually warm note from Alfred P. Sinnett, editor of the *Pioneer,* a powerful, ultra conservative English daily that was virtually the mouthpiece of the British government. To her surprise, Sinnett hoped very much to meet her if she ever visited Allahabad and, moreover, would be interested in publishing an article about the Theosophical Society.

Helena was too happy to be unduly annoyed by either espionage charges or hostile newspaper articles, which insisted upon calling her a countess. Life on palm-shaded Girgaum Back Road had almost a dreamlike quality. Awaking at dawn to the cawing of crows, she dressed in light clothing and spent her days entertaining visitors on the veranda while Babula fanned her with a painted punkah. The balmy air was so fragrant with flowers that it made one forget the icy March winds sweeping through the streets of New York or Odessa. H.P.B. was so relaxed that she did not even feel much like writing letters, and in the end it was Henry who dutifully wrote William Judge, advising him to "keep the Society alive and active."[9] On April 2, a disappointed Judge responded with a complaint about the meagerness of Henry's letter. How in heaven's name was he to keep the Society alive when "we are entirely without money?"[10] And a week later he wrote again to wonder why H.P.B. had not written to him herself. Obviously he felt neglected and deprived: "Oh! how I wish I was with you at 108 Girgaum Back Road in your Bungalows. Have you been to any place where there are elephants in the grounds and a tame tiger?"[11] He could not understand Olcott's purposely vague condemnations of Chintamon, since Madame had assured him that Chintamon's leader, Swami Dayananda, was an adept. Had the Masters made a mistake? "What the deuce does it mean?"[12] he demanded.

Henry silently pondered the same question. Writing continually cheerful letters to Judge, his sister, and his sons, he mentioned that all of them were in good health and described how they had been feted by the Hindus, but he said nothing about his own abysmal depression. Not only had Chintamon's perfidy and the police surveillance thoroughly demoralized him, but he was also desperately worried about money. The trade arrangements he had made in the U.S. did not seem to be working out, and even though he made repeated visits to Bombay firms, he had little success peddling his alarm clocks. And in addition to this stressful pursuit, he was straining to establish the Theosophical Society as being of serious purpose. Hindus had begun to join the Society, but some of them were frightened by the surveillance rumors and at least one eminent physician hastily resigned. On March 23, Henry delivered a sober lecture at Framji Cowasji Institute on "The Theosophical Society and Its Aims," and a week later he wrote an article along similar lines for the Bombay *Gazette*.

Still, his low spirits began to chill Helena, who felt impelled to take steps to snap him out of it. She herself had begun to grow uneasy over the inauspicious start they had made in India; indeed, there must have been moments when she was more frightened than Henry. In New York, she had used her powerful evocative ability to persuade Olcott of the Brothers' reality and had promised these mighty sages would protect and look after them in their new home. It had been one thing to sit in her living room at the Lamasery spinning gorgeous hallucinations, but entirely another actually to arrive in her dreamland only to discover that holy men such as Chintamon were really liars and thieves.

A self-proclaimed non-believer in miracles, she had nonetheless counted on the presence of her supermen, never pausing to consider more realistic alternatives. Whatever else one might say about her delusions, she sincerely trusted in the wise men's existence. Since coming to Bombay, she believed it all the more firmly, for the Indians to whom she spoke affirmed the existence of those wise men they called mahatmas, the Great Souls. Helena continued to expect a mahatma to surface eventually. He would seek her out, and would make valid her visions. In the meantime, however, she was forced to improvise.

Her first target was Moolji Thackersey and, indirectly, Henry. On March 29, she asked Thackersey to lend her a buggy, which she needed for an errand. Mysteriously refusing to reveal the destination, she directed the driver up one street and down another, seemingly in circles. Eventually they arrived in Parel, a seaside suburb some ten miles from Girgaum Back Road, and pulled up at the gate of a magnificent private estate. Instructing Thackersey to remain in the carriage, H.P.B. walked up to the door, which was opened by a tall Hindu, then disappeared inside. Not long afterward, she reappeared carrying a bouquet of roses and climbed back into the buggy. To Thackersey's questions, she replied that she had been transacting a piece of business with an occultist; the roses were a gift for Henry.

Once they returned to the city Thackersey began to doubt what he had seen. For one thing, he was familiar with Parel because his mother had been cremated there, but he had never noticed this particular estate; secondly, the house, a rather spectacular structure, had not looked like any dwelling that might be found in India. When he announced his intention of going back for another look, to satisfy his curiosity if nothing else, Helena coolly bet him he would not be able to locate the house.

She was right. Even though Thackersey and Olcott prowled around Parel for more than an hour, they found nothing but sand and pine trees and returned home thoroughly mystified.[13] Pressed for explanations, Helena finally said that the estate was maintained by the Brotherhood as a resthouse for traveling gurus and chelas and "was always protected from the intrusion of strangers by a circle of illusion."[14] Naturally it would not be visible to curious passersby.

A day or so later, she asked Thackersey to engage a servant for her, making sure he was an intelligent Hindu of the better class and not a house menial. He found her a man named Baburao who must have passed inspection because after talking to him privately for a while and giving certain instructions, she sent him away. She warned Thackersey to say nothing about Baburao to Colonel Olcott, then announced to Henry that an adept of her acquaintance had invited them on a trip to the Karli Caves. When Henry cried poverty, as she knew he would, she assured him that most of their expenses would be taken care of by the Brotherhood.

H.P.B., Henry and Moolji, along with Babula, left Bombay by train on April 4. It was late in the day when they reached Narel station, but H.P.B.'s Hindu was waiting for them. With a snappy salute, Baburao rattled off a message in Marathi that Moolji, interpreting, said were the compliments of his master. Naturally Olcott assumed that Baburao's master must be one of *the* Masters. Would they prefer ponies or palanquins for their assent up the hill to the town of Matheran, Baburao inquired? Both were ready. Henry and Helena chose the litters, each with twelve bearers; Thackersey and Babula decided on using ponies. To Henry, the night trip up the mountain was "a poetical journey."[15] He would never forget the sky ablaze with stars, the rustling of the jungle leaves, the great bats sailing silently overhead. Ravenous by the time they reached the Alexandra Hotel, they ate a hearty supper at eleven and fell into bed.

The next morning Helena began to unfold a piece of absurdist theater conducted mainly with the help of hypnosis, and to a lesser degree, of Baburao and perhaps Thackersey. Before breakfast, Baburao announced that his masters wished to donate to the party a rent-free bungalow for as long as they desired it. Helena had not counted apparently on Olcott's accepting. When he did, she suddenly declared herself nauseated with "the aura of Anglo-Indian civilization" at Matheran and insisted they must depart immediately for Khandalla. Back down the hill to Narel they proceeded in heat that Henry likened to "that of the stoke-room on a steamer,"[16] and got a train to Khandalla. There they were greeted once again by the mercurial Baburao and escorted to one of the cheap wayside hostels the government maintained for travelers. Now miracles began to occur at a dizzying pace: unknown men appeared with messages, only to disappear as if by magic; letters were dispatched into thin air and answers received just as mysteriously; a bouquet of roses and a small lacquer box, both presumably gifts from the adept acting as their host, were ceremoniously delivered to Olcott.

Meanwhile there were the Karli Caves. The trek up was generally exhausting, since H.P.B., too winded to climb, had to be carried the last half of the way. At last they entered the largest of the caves, spread blankets on the rocky floor, and ate a picnic lunch. H.P.B. told Henry and Thackersey that in one of the smaller caves there was a secret door opening into a chamber in the heart of the mountain where a school of adepts made their home; Olcott promptly went around knocking on walls and trying vainly to locate the entrance. That evening, camping out in the hills near the caves, H.P.B. abruptly disappeared. Olcott, who had been puffing on his pipe and watching the scenery, heard the sound of a door slamming and then a burst of laughter, and when he searched for Helena, she could not be found. She returned a half hour later to explain casually that she had visited an adept in the secret chamber. The next day Helena passed on to Henry an order, telepathically received from her Masters, which summoned them to Rajputana in the Punjab. Olcott chose to ignore the summons, for he was too busy trying to make sense of the white-robed men who approached him and vanished, while he simultaneously calmed an hysterical Moolji, who had just watched Madame Blavatsky disappear before his eyes. Henry told him to "sit down and keep quiet, and not make such a fool of himself "[17] over hypnotism.

After four days of hallucination, they caught the mail train back to Bombay. Moolji stretched out on a bench and fell asleep. "I do wish," Helena said wistfully to Henry, "that ——— [she named an adept] had not made me pass on verbally to you his message about Rajputana."

"Why?" he asked.

"Because Wimbridge and Miss Bates will think it all humbug, a trick to make you take me on a pleasant journey and leave them moping at home."[18]

Henry hastened to assure her that her word was enough for him, but Helena insisted that Wimbridge and Bates would object. Finally Henry agreed that it would have been better if the message had arrived more formally, in a letter.

Perking up, Helena smiled and said that perhaps it was not too late after all; she would ask her Masters for a note. From a small pocket notebook she tore out a sheet and wrote: "Ask Goolab Singh to telegraph to Olcott the orders given through me at the cave yesterday; let it be a test to others as well as to himself."[19] After Olcott had inspected the note, she flung it from the train window. The time, Henry took care to note, was 12:45 P.M.

Back home that afternoon, Olcott ran out to do errands and when he returned an hour later, Rosa Bates handed him a telegram: "Letter received. Answer Rajputana. Start immediately. Goolab Singh."[20] The telegram had been sent at 2 P.M. from Kurjeet, the station they had passed shortly after H.P.B.'s note had been tossed from the train. Since neither Helena nor Thackersey had left their seats at Kurjeet, Henry concluded that she could not possibly have sent the telegram herself; it had to be genuine. It did not occur to him that Helena might have planned the whole thing in advance by asking Babula, who was in a third-class coach, to send the message, or even that her confederate Baburao might have been on the same train.

Helena's insistence on the Rajputana trip was far from a whim. Ever since the *Speke Hall* had steamed into Bombay harbor, she had been expecting to meet Swami Dayananda. By now she was forced to realize that he had no intention of making a special trip to Bombay to welcome her, so when she learned that he would be at Saharanpur in late April, she decided to go to him. Obviously she could have explained the situation to Olcott without bothering to drop notes from train windows, but such was not her way.

On Good Friday, April 11, again with Thackersey and Babula, she began a two-day train ride north to Allahabad. Indian railway stations were notoriously chaotic; whole families camped on the platform, cooking, sleeping and performing their ablutions until the train appeared. The cars themselves were filthy and primitive, offering no amenities such as food or bedding, and the lavatories and washbasins were appalling. Travelers carried their bedding with them; at the stations en route to their destinations they would get off to have a meal or, more often, open a picnic basket or have their servants cook in the carriage over a spirit lamp. Aside from these exotic inconveniences, Olcott remembered the trip to Allahabad as insufferably hot and dusty. When they finally chugged into Allahabad and secured rooms at the dâk-bungalow in the railway station, "the heat was so terrific as to make even the Hindu Mooljee catch his breath when we ventured outside the house."[21]

Ignoring the heat, Madame spent the next two weeks hunting for holy men to teach her their secrets and, she hoped, lead her to her Masters. At Allahabad, she happened upon a blind Sikh ascetic, who had been squatting in meditation for fifty-two years, leaving his station only at midnight to bathe in the Jumna. When Helena, through an interpreter, asked him to show her phenomena, she was horrified to hear him call them "playthings of the ignorant."[22] The truth, the Sunyāsi warned her, could only be perceived by keeping a calm mind and an unperturbed soul, two possessions that would always elude Madame Blavatsky. Moving on to Cawnpore, where they visited Ross Scott, they tracked down another Sunyāsi, this one a nude, emaciated man who had been living outdoors for over a year and whose stomach had collapsed. When Helena asked him for phenomena, he responded with contemptuous disdain. At Jajmow, which they reached by elephant, she was denied her wish for wonders for the third time in three days, and by now was growing irritable. During the four-mile ride between Cawnpore and Jajmow, she had behaved unforgivably, hogging the entire elephant seat for herself while her companions clung to other sections of the animal's back. It had not been a pleasant journey. "She rolled about wildly," Olcott recalled, "getting her fat shaken up and her breath squeezed out of her, until she grew furious."[23] On the return trip, disappointed over her lack of success with the Sunyāsi, she chose to ride in a cart.

But she was having a grand time. Writing to Alexander Wilder, Helena exclaimed that his soul "would jump out in fits of rapture"[24] if he were with her. Because of the heat, it seemed sensible to do their traveling early in the day, so they arose at 4 A.M. and went to bed at nine in the evening. For once, Helena did not object; she was, after all, seeing "*subterranean* India, not the upper one,"[25] as she proudly informed Wilder, and it was only a small exaggeration. Like everyone else, she trudged around tourist attractions such as the ruined temples of Amber, the rose-red city of Jeypore enclosed within its seven-gated walls, and the ghats of Benares, where a monkey snatched Olcott's spectacles. At Agra, a dirty town of half-ruined huts made of dried cow dung, she gaped at the Taj Mahal, which looked to her like "a magnificent pea on a heap of manure."[26] She omitted mentioning to Wilder that the Maharajah of Jeypore had invited them to stay at his palace, but hearing they were Russian spies, refused to provide food or beds and ejected them rather unceremoniously the next morning. Nor did she report the policeman who had been dogging their footsteps, or Olcott's complaints to the British resident who expressed regrets in the most courteous and ineffectual manner.

On their arrival at Saharanpur, still accompanied by their police escort, they were greeted warmly by the Arya Samajists who brought them gifts of fruit and sweetmeats and arranged a formal reception and banquet. The next morning the Swami was to arrive. Although this was the moment Helena had been awaiting, she grew suddenly apprehensive about his possible reaction to a woman, and delegated Olcott and Thackersey to pay their respects. An hour later, Henry appeared with the Swami at their dâk-bungalow. Fifty five years old, over six feet tall and stout, the Swami may have had the lofty, dreamy-eyed look of a mystic, but was actually an extremely practical person with a violent temper. Helena's fears were not ill-founded, for his views on women were virulently sexist. After greeting her with restrained cordiality, he proceeded to ignore her in favor of Olcott. Helena listened to him expounding on Nirvana and God and his seven years in the jungle, but she learned nothing about magic and phenomenal powers. Moreover, dialogue was difficult since he spoke no English, but she suspected it mattered little since he had no intention of taking her seriously. Having told Henry that Dayananda was a member of the Brotherhood, she must have been chagrined by his obvious disregard. She must also have been intimidated for she did not even bring up the subject of her Masters, as she did with everyone else she met.

On the seventh of May, they began the trip back to Bombay. Olcott professed not to find their experience with the Swami so disappointing as Helena; in any case, the high point of his trip had come at Bhurtpore, where one evening, while sitting on the veranda of their dâk-bungalow, an old Hindu had appeared, salaamed, and handed him a letter from Goolab Singh. "It was beautifully worded," he noted, "and, to me, a most important letter as it pointed out the fact that the surest way to seek the Masters was through the channel of faithful work in the Theosophical Society."[27] Helena would have done well to take this consoling advice herself. By the time the train pulled into Bombay early on the tenth, frustration and the torrid heat had sparked a temper tantrum. On the platform she marched up to their police escort and, according to Henry, "gave him a piece of her mind."[28] Flinching under this unexpected tongue-lashing, the man stammered and blushed. Instead of going to their house for a much-needed bath and breakfast, she then insisted upon driving to the U.S. Consulate, where she demanded that the Consul protest their treatment.

In the excitement of the past month, there had been much to see and little time to brood about their problems. Now, once more back in Girgaum Back Road, the despondence and tension in the household had increased. Wimbridge grouched a great deal, as did Rosa, who had taken over the housekeeping and now kept chickens and ducks in the yard behind the kitchen. Rosa's whining was grating intensely on H.P.B.'s nerves; once so insistent on bringing her to India, Madame now regretted it and called her, behind her back, "the maid," and she also fussed about Rosa's "malevolent magnetism." The police continued to spy and the money to dwindle. Henry began to send weekly articles about conditions in India to the New York *Sun,* while Helena tried to persuade Bouton to publish a pamphlet about curious religious sects. When all that failed, she succeeded in obtaining an assignment for a series of articles on occult India from Michael Katkov, a leading newspaper editor and publisher of the Moscow *Chronicle.* Under the pseudonym Radda Bai, these reports, actually highly skilled fiction, would eventually be published as *From the Caves and Jungles of Hindostan* and bring her literary praise in her native country.

In June, the monsoon began and Bombay turned into a passable imitation of Venice. The unconcerned Hindus, naked to the waist, paddled around on their daily business, but the four Theosophists suffered miserably. When the roof began to leak, they had to sit under umbrellas in the sopping drawing room; before long, clothing and furniture turned damp and began to mold, then rot. Every few days H.P.B. dried her books over a brazier. Soon the house was inundated with scorpions, centipedes, lizards, snakes and cockroaches. Making the rounds of the bungalow every night, "I became a bloodthirsty Nimrod and killed cockroaches as big as small mice, spiders which could be mistaken for moderate-sized crabs,"[29] Helena wrote. The rains did nothing to improve tempers, and Olcott, bitterly depressed and homesick, could be found weeping over his sons' pictures. He grimly told Helena that it had been "an act of lunatics"[30] to leave New York and they would surely all starve. This outburst brought a biting reprimand from Master Morya, who pointed out that nobody forced him to leave home and expressed regret that Henry did not fight like a man. "If you are unfit to pass your first probation and assert your rights of a future Adept by forcing circumstances to bow before you—you are as totally unfit for any further trials."[31]

If Helena hoped to shame the colonel into rallying, she was relatively successful. Soon, he stopped talking about home. A few weeks later, when informed that he had been cheated out of a ten-thousand-dollar fee owed him for a insurance case and that a silver mining investment would bring no return, he took the news fairly calmly. About this time, Helena herself received a letter more ominous than any prospect of starvation. Emma Cutting, her old friend in Cairo, was now living in Ceylon with her French husband, Alexis Coulomb. Seemingly friendly on the surface, Emma had nothing but woes to relate. Shortly after H.P.B. had left Cairo, Emma had married a man she believed to be rich, but "almost immediately we lost our fortune." Impoverished, the couple had found their way to India, where Alexis could find no employment and Emma was forced to support both of them as a teacher and tutor of rich young ladies; subsequently Emma had become ill and they moved to Ceylon and bought an old hotel that went bankrupt shortly. They moved again, this time to a rural area "hoping to be able to grow some European vegetables" but the soil was so stony, nothing would grow. Having exhausted all means of earning a living, Emma had been immensely pleased to read in the Ceylon *Times* about the arrival of Madame Blavatsky, which "I really considered a God-send."

Helena was petrified. There were a half-dozen people who knew enough about her to really ruin her and Emma Coulomb was one of them. Steeling herself, she took her cue from Emma and composed a newsy reply bringing her life up to date since they last had met: Paris, New York, the Theosophical Society, *Isis Unveiled*. She mentioned that in 1872 she had spend eight months in India. "My lodge in India, of which I may have spoken to you, had decided that as the Society established by myself and old Sebire was a failure, I had to go to America and establish one on a larger scale."

Emma had never heard Helena speak of any lodge, nor of India for that matter. Madame's letter "was all very fine, but did not open my way to get out of trouble. So sometime after I wrote to her again, and explained to her clearly our situation, and asked her to send us some money."

Although Helena had been expecting this all along, she was probably unsure whether Emma actually wanted back the money loaned in Cairo, or whether she was making a veiled blackmail threat. Was it better to ignore Emma and run the risk of her blabbing about Metrovitch and Yuri? Or would pacification be safer? In the end, H.P.B. amicably wrote to Emma that she herself, as poor as a church rat, had no money of her own and lived in a commune. From the last of her father's legacy, she received about a hundred rupees a month "but this belongs to the community, money which none of us can touch, for it is for the expenses of the house, and it is not much, I can assure you." However, if Emma and her husband should ever come to Bombay and join the Theosophical Society, employment might be found for them. It all depended on Colonel Olcott who would "take off his skin for a Fellow, but do nothing for an outsider."[32]

Mentioning jobs to the Coulombs was rash, but Helena felt that she would never be called upon to make good the offer. From Emma's doleful descriptions of their poverty, she doubted if they could raise the passage money for the journey from Galle to Bombay. At least, she prayed they could not.

In the summer of 1879, as the rains came, India slowly became aware that within it were two white foreigners who believed its culture to be supremely admirable. Indian patriotism in the 1870s was virtually comatose. The British had come here pledging to respect the native traditions, but at the same time had quickly admitted the Christian missionaries to convert the "heathen." Whatever social reforms British rule had brought were offset by the very presence of the white "sahib," and educated Hindus generally felt that Asian India was doomed to inferiority at the hands of the "Raj." Only a few Hindus, such as Swami Dayananda, were attempting to revive national pride in India's ancient heritage. It would take many years of bitter struggle before India fully awoke, but a tiny beginning had been made and Madame Blavatsky and Henry Olcott would be contributors to the awakening. As would one Annie Besant, although she did not yet know it. Helena had come to India in search of her Masters, but once there, found that mastering Hindi was no overnight project. Prohibited by language from the knowledge she sought, she was nonetheless a hopeful presence to Hindu intellectuals: if a foreign woman of importance, a countess it was rumored, came all the way to their poor country to seek the truth, Indians must be more than mere slaves of the British Empire; perhaps, in fact, East Indians actually were heirs to an esoteric body of learning.

Both H.P.B. and Olcott were aware that summer of some small spark of interest they had struck. Memberships in the Society continued to climb, as did the inquiries, and some nights Henry labored over the piles of mail until 2 or 3 A.M. Their friends now included several rich, influential Hindus, including Shishir Babu, editor of Calcutta's *Amrita Bazaar Patrika* and Prince Harisinghji Rupsinghji of Bhavnagar; while Helena would vehemently deny that the Society profited materially from these connections, the undeniable fact was that it did. True, H.P.B. never asked for gifts or favors from the wealthy; on the contrary, it sometimes seemed that she went out of her way to offend them. Once, when the aged Sardar of Dekhan introduced her to his ten-year-old wife, H.P.B. tactlessly shouted at him, "Your WIFE? You old beast! You ought to be ashamed of yourself!"[33] That child marriage was customary Helena saw as an invalid reason for disguising her disgust of it. On the other hand, the abominable position of Indian women did not appear to disturb her, nor was she visibly concerned that no native women had joined the Theosophical Society.[34]

Among the sensitive young Hindus drawn to Girgaum Back Road was Damodar K. Mavalankar, the twenty-one-year-old son of a wealthy Brahmin who, unknown to his parents, was full of notions about becoming an adept, perhaps even in some future life a mahatma. "It was the rainy season," Henry recalled in his memoirs, "and the dear boy used to come to see us of evenings, clad in a white rubber waterproof and leggings, a cap with flaps to match, a lantern in his hand, and the water streaming from the end of his long nose. He was as thin as Sarah Bernhardt, with lantern jaws, and legs—as H.P.B. used to say—like two lead pencils."[35] A serious, religious-minded young man with considerable intellectual gifts and an excellent English education, he had suffered two near-fatal illnesses during childhood and during each had seen visions of "a certain personage—whom I then considered to be a Deva, i.e., God—who gave me a peculiar medicine."[36] According to the dramatic account given by Damodar's biographer, the frail youth walked into 108 Girgaum Back Road to be greeted by a picture of his childhood savior whose name was Master Koot Hoomi and whose agent was none other than Madame Blavatsky. That Master Koot Hoomi would not even be born until September, 1880, over a year later, did little to diminish Damodar's immediate regard for H.P.B.

"About a month after I joined the Society," he recalled, "I felt as it were a voice within myself whispering to me that Madame Blavatsky is not what she represented herself to be." Rather, he intuited that she must be "some great Indian Adept,"[37] and so he confessed to her his dream of retiring from the world into some lonely jungle and giving himself up to God. That was a foolish idea, H.P.B. told him: if he really wanted to become an adept, he must struggle for the Theosophical Society and, someday, would be rewarded when the adepts summoned him to their sides. When Damodar implored her for the Brothers' names and addresses, Helena put him off by solemnly announcing she was sworn to secrecy. Apparently Damodar bowed to her wisdom and stopped nagging.

"No child was ever more obedient to a parent, than he to H.P.B.," Olcott wrote. "Her slightest word was to him law; her most fanciful wish an imperative command, to obey which he was ready to sacrifice life itself."[38] This fanatical devotion to Madame, which included fanning her to sleep on the hot nights when she suffered from insomnia, was scarcely an exaggeration on Henry's part; indeed, as will be seen, he was understating the situation.

On the Fourth of July, distressed by the stacks of unopened mail, all of which had to be answered, Helena and Henry hit on a solution to their communications lag: a Theosophist magazine. Any publishing venture required capital or credit, neither of which they had, but this problem could be circumvented by selling advance subscriptions. Two days later Henry wrote a prospectus for the periodical, which he distributed to the newspapers, while members of the Society were drumming up subscriptions. On July 16, Helena wrote to General Abner Doubleday, urging him to find New York subscribers for her "child, our sweet and holy virgin." That she had largely ignored her New York friends since coming to India seemed an irrelevancy to Madame. "Look here, dear General," she went on, "our paper is not to be an organ of Spiritualists and such flapdoodle, but a serious philosophical organ. . . ."[39] There was no reason why even a New York Brahmin like William Whitney should not be happy to subscribe.

During the next three months, Helena found herself as busy as she had been during the writing of *Isis Unveiled*. Night after night she worked on articles for the magazine's flagship issue; according to Olcott, Master Morya himself visited one evening in his physical body to talk over the journal and give editorial suggestions. As the Theosophists advertised widely and wrote to every potential reader they knew or knew of, the subscriptions began to trickle in. Wimbridge contributed a handsome cover design for the journal, which they were now calling the *Theosophist,* and Damodar became business manager and staff writer. Sometimes the young man sat up so late working that Olcott, concerned about the health of the frail disciple, took it upon himself to drive him home to bed. By now, they had overgrown the bungalow and were forced to rent the house next door as office space.

On Monday, September 29, Helena and Henry rose at 5:30 A.M. and rushed to the printer to make the last-minute corrections suggested by the Mahatma; two days later, they received the first run of four hundred copies and spent the entire morning addressing the mailing wrappers. There was nothing shoddy or amateurish about the thirty-two-page journal whose masthead read: "OM, THE THEOSOPHIST, a Monthly Journal devoted to Oriental Philosophy, Art, Literature and Occultism. Conducted by H. P. BLAVATSKY under the auspices of the Theosophical Society." The contents included extremely well-written articles on Buddhism, ancient China, trigonometry, a laudatory piece about Swami Dayananda, and of course low-key propaganda for the Theosophical Society. The periodical was nothing short of tasteful, and highly literate. Clearly non-political, it should have reassured the Bombay police, who still kept Helena under observation. Her sole intention for the journal, as she wrote in her first editorial, was that it, "should be read with as much interest by those who are not deep philosophers as by those who are," adding that "our pages will be like the many viands at a feast, where each appetite may be satisfied and none are sent away hungry."[40]

The *Theosophist* was an immediate success and the print run for the November order climbed to seven hundred and fifty copies. The monsoon was over and the sun began to shine in more ways than one. In October, no less a personage than the viceroy of India, Lord Edward Lytton, ordered that the Theosophical Society was to be caused no further harassment, at which news H.P.B. bubbled happily in the *Theosophist* of her gratitude "to the son of the author of *Zanoni*." Quite content to be swamped by piles of work, Helena put in endless hours editing the magazine as well as grinding out her own Radda Bai articles for Michael Katkov. For the first time since her arrival, she felt confident that she and Henry would be able to remain in India and in this halcyon time of relaxation and expansion she celebrated by buying herself another canary. Understandably disposed to ignore unpleasantness, she only glanced at the letters from William Judge, complaining rather shrilly that he had never seen an adept, and threatening to submit his resignation to the Society. She turned over the letters to Damodar, who replied coolly, "My dear Mr. Judge: I am very sorry to hear you write so disparagingly to Madame Blavatsky . . . You must neither despair, nor think there are no adepts simply because you have as yet seen none. If you have not met with any, you should know it is because you have not properly performed your duties. . . ."[41] And with that rebuke, Judge was forced to be content.

That H.P.B.'s mood during this period seems to have been almost playful, is borne out in a letter Henry received from the usually somber Master Morya: "If you want to oblige me *personally*," he wrote, "then will you hurry as quick as you can and put H.P.B.'s room in order. I have pressing business in the room tomorrow early morning and I would smother there were it left in that state of chaos."[42] Had Helena's relationship with Rosa Bates not grown spectacularly strained, Madame would certainly have asked "the maid" to tidy her room.

During this hectic period, Helena had been in constant correspondence with Alfred and Patience Sinnett, and the couple repeatedly urged Helena and Henry to visit them in Allahabad. Now the time seemed ripe, and Madame was eager to travel. "Thank God," she wrote Nadyezhda Fadeyev, "I am going away at the beginning of December to Allahabad, with a deputation of Rao-Bahadurs, which means 'Great Warriors.' " The deputation consisted only of Olcott, Damodar and Babula but apparently Helena did not feel those three sufficiently colorful. She went on to speak of the "prospect of calls, dinners, and balls in 'high life.'

> My hair stands on end at the very thought of it, but it must be done. I have warned Mrs. Sinnett that I, though not a Russian spy but an American citizen, will not listen to a single word of disrespect to Russia or to our Emperor. Just let them try, and how I will abuse their England! So let them be warned.[43]

Unable to afford first-class railway tickets, they had to suffer sleepless nights on the hard wooden seats in second class, although this time H.P.B. had the foresight to bring along a camp bed for herself. In any case, the benches would not have held her bulk; ever since New York, her weight had been inching upward again. The traveling inconveniences were forgotten, however, when they reached Allahabad in the early morning of December 5 and were met by an elegant barouche with coachman and two splendidly liveried footmen. Sinnett would never forget his first encounter with Madame Blavatsky:

> The train from Bombay used to come into Allahabad in those days at an early hour in the morning, and it was still, but just, time for *chota hazree,* or early breakfast, when I brought our guests home. She had evidently been apprehensive, to judge from her latest letters, lest we might have formed some ideal conception of her that the reality would shatter, and had recklessly painted herself as a rough, old, 'hippopotamus' of a woman, unfit for civilized society; but she did this with so lively a humor that the betrayal of her bright intelligence this involved more than undid the effect of her warnings. Her rough manners, of which we had been told so much, did not prove very alarming, though I remember going into fits of laughter at the time when Colonel Olcott, after the visit had lasted a week or two, gravely informed us that Madame was under 'great self-restraint' so far. This had not been the impression my wife and I had formed about her, though we had learned already to find her conversation more than interesting.[44]

H.P.B.'s six-week visit, Sinnett wrote, meant "a great and momentous change in my life." He does not state if the change was for better or worse.

Alfred Percy Sinnett, a slender, balding man with a well-trimmed mustache, was an unlikely candidate for a counter-cultural religious movement. At thirty-nine, he was one of the most influential men in India by virtue of his editorship of the *Pioneer,* but for many years he had been a person of no visible achievements and small hope for such. Born in London, his entire childhood had been marked by an unbroken series of deprivations; his father had died penniless when Alfred was only five and his widowed mother provided for her six children by newspaper articles and translations. Alfred did poorly in school and left without finishing his studies. Taking up mechanical drawing, he became a skilled draftsman, which enabled him to support himself and contribute to the meager earnings of his mother. Eventually, however, he was able to move into the newspaper field when he got a job as assistant editor of the London *Globe*, but this was short-lived; he was fired for neglect of his duties after being rejected by a German woman.

Next, he moved around aimlessly from one London paper to another until, in 1865, he was offered the editorship of the Hong Kong *Daily Press.* After three successful years in Hong Kong, he returned to England with eight hundred pounds and an excellent poker game and got a good job as an editorial writer on the *Evening Standard.* By 1870 he had met and married Patience Edensor, a rather frail, soft-spoken young woman who was later described by her friend Isabelle de Steiger as a person "whose patience and unvarying kindness never failed." She was extremely intelligent, rather more intelligent in fact than her husband but "too loving and lovable a woman actively to oppose him, and her devotion was too intuitive ever to irritate him with opposition," which Isabelle regarded as "unfortunate."[45]

In 1872, Alfred was presented with his biggest opportunity, to date, when George Allen, owner of the *Pioneer,* offered him the chance to go out to India as editor. The years since then had been the happiest of Sinnett's life. At last, he had an excellent income, a luxurious home, social position, servants, and professional recognition. For him and Patience and their son, Denny, it was a life of incredible ease. There were winters in Allahabad, summers at Simla, the government's hot-weather capital in the cool foothills of the Himalayas, mint juleps on verandas, games of tennis to work off the rich meals, and periodic, all-expense-paid trips home to England.

Several years prior to meeting H.P.B., Sinnett had attended a séance at the London home of the well-known medium Mrs. Guppy and was immediately intrigued, declaring the phenomena he had witnessed to be "overwhelming and precluded any conceivable theory of imposture."[46] He had read *Isis Unveiled,* which impressed him tremendously despite his assumption that Madame Blavatsky was a Spiritualist, and when the author and Colonel Olcott appeared in Bombay, he did not hesitate to contact them. "We thought they would be interesting people,"[47] he wrote blandly in his unpublished memoirs.

The Sinnetts outdid themselves to entertain Helena and Henry with dinner parties and introductions to prominent persons, among them Allan Octavian Hume, who would become the first chairman of the Indian National Congress. Sinnett had to admit that Helena failed to make a favorable impression on all his friends. "Anglo-Indian society is strongly coloured with conventional views, and Mme. Blavatsky was too violent a departure from accepted standards in a great variety of ways to be assimilated in Anglo-Indian circles with readiness."[48] That, perhaps, was to be expected. At the same time, the guests who appreciated bright, intelligent dinner-table conversation "were loud in her praises and eager of her society,"[49] and forbore to overlook her militant teetotaling and her bullying attacks on people who were merely sipping table wine. Alfred, who jokingly called her "Old Lady,"[50] took her idiosyncrasies about alcohol with equanimity, but he was secretly shocked by the way she nagged and abused Colonel Olcott. Once, after Henry had delivered a lecture that had not met with her approval, she "opened fire on him with exceeding bitterness."[51] The savagery of her outburst made Sinnett wonder why Olcott bore it so mildly, and after that could never think of Henry as anything other than spineless.

On December 15, the Sinnetts joined H.P.B. and Henry on a trip to Benares where they stayed at a house provided by the Maharajah of Vizianagram and visited a learned yogi, Majji, who made her home in a cave along the banks of the Ganges. Majji whispered in Henry's ear that Madame's body was being occupied by an important yogi—she was really a man. Henry could readily accept the idea, for he himself had often commented on Helena's maleness, but he could not understand why the wise Majji kept saying that the man had been inside Madame for sixty-two years (Helena was forty-eight). They also met briefly with Swami Dayananda before returning to Allahabad for Christmas.

Alfred had been observing Helena, trying to decide "whether Madame Blavatsky really did, as I heard, possess the power of producing abnormal phenomena." Nothing, he admitted, should have been simpler to ascertain, but after six weeks "the harvest of satisfaction I was enabled to obtain during this time was exceedingly small."[52] Of course she talked incessantly about the Brotherhood and favored the Sinnetts with a few demonstrations of raps, all of which were decidedly unspectacular. When Sinnett urged her to perform phenomena for scientists under test conditions, H.P.B. disdainfully refused, suggesting that the Brothers would regard such a feat as mere showing off.

Still, when Sinnett made it clear that he felt shortchanged, H.P.B. decided to toss one small scrap his way. In Benares, at the maharajah's, they were sitting in the drawing room with Swami Dayananda and others after dinner and, Sinnett remembered, "suddenly three or four flowers— cut roses—fell in the midst of us."[53] Patience and Alfred were sufficiently impressed to become members of the Theosophical Society; the Swami, however, had only watched critically and next day, when Damodar asked him who had thrown the roses, Dayananda answered that it had not been Madame Blavatsky. Who? Damodar demanded. The Swami would say nothing more.

On December 30, learning of a train for Bombay whose second-class carriages were fitted with cushions, the Theosophists made their exit. At the station Helena realized she had left behind a shawl and angrily blamed it on Henry; her irrational anger, accompanied by a torrent of biting language, mortified the Sinnetts who were unaccustomed to public scenes and made their farewells with almost visible relief.

The first months of 1880 passed peacefully. Helena was busy editing the *Theosophist,* writing her series for Michael Katkov, for which she was being paid the elegant sum of fifty rubles, (five pounds in those days), per page, and translating Nikolay Grodekoff 's *Through Afghanistan,* which ran as a series in the *Pioneer.* Henry had more than enough to do lecturing and supervising the affairs of the burgeoning Society. It was again the hot season; sometimes after working all day and receiving visitors, they would stay up until 4 A.M to finish their tasks, having taken a midnight drive to get a breath of cool air. By this time Damodar was living with them. His family had made no objections, and, in fact, his father joined the Society and thought so highly of Madame that he would present her with a carriage and horse as a gift. Still, he did not take seriously his son's ambition to become an adept, believing that once Damodar got this religion out of his system he would return to his normal life.

The view was shared by Damodar's young wife, who had been married to him as a child but had seen little of him since he had encountered the Theosophists.

In March, H.P.B.'s peace was abruptly shattered by a severe, scornful letter from Swami Dayananda who enclosed his Theosophical Society diploma and ordered his name stricken from their membership rolls. Although the contents of his letter were never made public, the nature of his feelings were abundantly clear in subsequent public statements that referred to H.P.B. and Olcott as "atheists believing in spirits and witches."[54]

H.P.B.'s chagrin at being unceremoniously dismissed by a man she had called an adept of her very own Brotherhood was overshadowed ten days later by the arrival of Emma and Alexis Coulomb. In the long run, the visit was to prove far more calamitous than the Swami's animosity. The French consul at Galle, as well as other charitable persons, had taken up a collection for the Coulombs' passages, and they arrived in Bombay on March 28 virtually penniless. As Emma recalled, they took a room at a seamy downtown hotel and had dinner, then in the evening caught a tram car to Girgaum Back Road. "As soon as Madame Blavatsky saw me she gave a loud cry of joy, and instantly asked us to take up our abode at the headquarters,"[55] and she went on to report that they moved in the next day at noon. According to Henry, he agreed to let the couple stay at the house, but only until Alexis, a mechanic, could find work. In fact, Olcott went out of his way to secure for Alexis a machinist's job in a cotton mill. But Alexis soon squabbled with the owner and was precipitously dismissed. "I found him a man very quick-tempered and hard to please in the matter of employers," Henry said, "and as no other opening occurred, he and his wife just drifted along with us, without any definite plans as to the future."[56] Since Emma and Alexis were clearly trying to earn their keep, he did not fuss about two extra mouths to feed.

The Coulombs were a strange couple whose appearance and manner did not readily endear them to most people. After years of penury and ill health, Emma had become haggard and wrinkled, and she seems to have been habitually grim, undoubtedly as the result of worrying about their next meal. Alexis, with his glass eye, pasty complexion and black beard, was no more prepossessing and his propensity for surliness did little to lighten his nature. He assured H.P.B. that he was accomplished in carpentry, a rare skill in India, and could repair almost anything. Since Anglo-Indian residents were forever complaining about the shortage of European-trained handymen, it should have been easy for him to find work, but for some reason, he felt disinclined to look.

From the outset of their visit, Helena must have seen that Alexis was content to let his wife play the decision-making role. While treating Alexis with deference and kindness, she directed her amicable overtures toward Emma. After warning her not to talk about their lives in Cairo, she went out of her way to be hospitable and, in fact, seems actually to have enjoyed Emma's company. Now that she was rarely even speaking to Rosa Bates, it was a comforting change to have a woman with whom she could gossip. Moreover, it occurred to her that the Coulombs might turn out to be extremely useful. One evening, Emma remembered, H.P.B. took her arm and said, "Look here, run and tell the colonel that you have seen a figure in the garden."

"Where is the figure?" Emma asked.

"Never mind, run and tell him so. We shall have some fun."

Emma did as she was told, but to her amazement the colonel took her seriously and declared that she had probably seen one of the Brothers. Emma professed to be as mystified by Madame's contriving such a lie as by the colonel's taking it for the truth. Nevertheless, she continued to perform similar services, including the embroidering of names on handkerchiefs, simply from an "earnest desire to please her in everything."[57]

Temporarily reassured in the matter of Emma, Helena turned her attention to a trip that she and Henry had been considering for some time. Olcott had been corresponding with several Buddhist priests in Ceylon, who urged them to visit the island. There was much to do before their departure, including the readying of several advance issues of the *Theosophist,* and neither he nor H.P.B. had time to worry about the Coulombs. To save expenses, it was decided that H.P.B., Henry and Wimbridge would make the journey while Rosa and Emma remained behind to look after the house. "As Miss Bates was a spinster and Mme. Coulomb an experienced housewife,"[58] Henry decided to make Emma officially responsible, although it seems reasonable to assume that it was H.P.B. who urged Rosa's demotion in favor of Emma. Rosa, smoldering, said nothing. On May 7, when the travelers embarked on the SS *Ellora,* the party included not only Wimbridge but Babula, Damodar, and five other Hindu members of the Society.

The next months were among the most relaxed and gratifying that Madame would spend in the East. Everywhere they went, the Theosophists were greeted by enormous crowds and showered with gifts.

> For three months we went from triumph to triumph—processions headed by Buddhist high priests and elephants—I rode a coffee-coloured one!— garlands and triumphal arches every ten steps along the road from one side of Ceylon to the other; women from the central provinces decked or rather *clothed* with a diamond necklace for only garment; processions of great Cingalese ladies dressed in the fashion of Dutch ladies of the Middle Ages coming to prostrate themselves before me.[59]

To H.P.B., who was only truly satisfied when being adored on a grand scale, "it was like a dream!"[60] At a temple in Galle, on May 25, Helena and Olcott formally became Buddhists, a rather odd step for two people who had heretofore presented themselves as staunch Hindus. This formal and flamboyant rejection of Christianity by two Europeans received wide publicity, which may account for the enthusiastic reception they received from the flattered Cingalese. During their stay, seven branches of the Theosophical Society were organized, and Henry encouraged the Buddhists to establish their own denominational schools.

Their return to India was marked by a rough passage during which almost all of the party were miserably seasick. In his diary Olcott noted that during the trip Helena had gained eight pounds, bringing her to 237 pounds, while he shed 15 pounds and Damodar was down to 90. "It rained cats and dogs on the last day of our return voyage,"[61] Henry also recorded, but the downpour was mild compared to the storm waiting for them at home: "Arriving house found a hell of a row on the carpet between Dame Coulomb and Spin. Bates."[62] Dagger drawn, Rosa said that Emma had tried to poison her and truculently demanded that both Emma and Alexis be expelled from the house at once; Emma, of course, denied everything. Charges and counter-charges flew thickly back and forth as Olcott tried to arbitrate the quarrel and H.P.B., furiously chain-smoking, threw in an occasional incendiary remark that caused tempers to sputter and blaze. Wimbridge managed to help Henry negotiate a temporary cease-fire, and everyone went to bed exhausted.

The squabble could not have come as a surprise to Helena because she had been hearing snatches of it all summer. Rosa, furious that a newcomer should have been given charge of the household, as well as being made editor of the *Theosophist,* had called Emma a meddler. Emma had been the first to agree, but H.P.B. assured her that she was nothing of the kind. "You are one of my 'Assistant Secretaries,' " she had written on June 16. "You are my friend— and that is more."[63]

For two weeks the battle raged, with H.P.B. taking her friend's side, Wimbridge supporting Rosa, and Olcott teetering helplessly in the middle but growing angrier every day. He had begged Helena not to bring Rosa to India, but she had bullied him into it and in the end he had yielded to "her presumably superior occult foresight." Now, through no fault of his own, he "had to assume the disagreeable task of forcing Miss Bates out of the Society. This was always my lot: H.P.B. made the rows and I had to take the kicks and clear out the intruders."[64] He suggested that the Society purchase Rosa a steamship ticket to New York; at first she agreed and the booking was made, but she changed her mind. Within a few days H.P.B. and Henry had abandoned the dining room to Wimbridge and Bates and began eating their meals in H.P.B.'s room. "Hell of an explosion between Rosa and us," Henry told his diary on August 6. "This settles her hash; she must go."[65] The situation grew steadily worse until none of the household was on speaking terms; Wimbridge and Bates moved their belongings into a separate section of the bungalow and actually bricked up the connecting doorway. The tension grew so deadly that it began to affect Helena's health and Olcott recalled that she "fretted herself into a fever."[66]

It was not only the feud that agitated her. During Helena's and Henry's absence, many of their new members had either lost interest in the Society or resigned, and she had also been greatly shocked to learn of Moolji Thackersey's unexpected death. After their remarkable success in Ceylon, it did not seem possible that the Society could lose ground, but that was precisely what appeared to be happening. She had crossed off the Society in the United States; Judge had enough trouble supporting himself and Ella on his legal earnings and had sent Madame letters to this effect, but she had no encouragement to give him. A few months earlier, she had written to a French correspondent that "at Lhasa, in Tibet, another branch is being formed under the direction of initiated Lamas. Within a few years you will see how our Society will be honored and sought after."[67] Of course she had yet to meet a Tibetan lama. She had felt certain that the Society would continue to expand; now, she was suddenly plunged into a fit of doubt. She drew closer to Henry, for he had the knack of pretending cheerfulness he did not feel, and together they commiserated over this kitchen row. It was pitifully childish and not worth brooding over; it would pass like a summer cloud.

On August 12, Wimbridge and Rosa left the house at last. Sometime before the separation, Olcott had used his personal influence with a Parsi friend to obtain capital so that Wimbridge might establish a furniture and interior decoration business. It was not as if he and Rosa were going off to starve, but still, H.P.B. was shaken by this transformation of old friends into enemies. She also felt that her charity in "boarding, lodging, washing, and in many instances CLOTHING Mr. Wimbridge and Miss Bates for over 18 months"[68] was being ill repaid.

As it happened, on the very morning that the enemy decamped, she and Henry received an invitation to visit the Sinnetts at Simla. The letter, Olcott remembered, "was like a draught of sweet water,"[69] and Helena, too impatient to wait on the mails, rushed to telegraph their acceptance. Nervous depression suddenly gone, she rattled joyfully about the house, then dragged Olcott with her to purchase a new outfit for her "debut" in the British summer capital.

She would have set out for Simla the very next day, but there was still work to be done: upcoming issues of the magazine, which Damodar would supervise, had to be finalized, and Emma, who would be left in charge of the house, had to be given her instructions. As a result of the recent imbroglio, the balance of power between Helena and the Coulombs had shifted dramatically. Thanks to H.P.B.'s sacrifice of Wimbridge and Rosa, Emma had been saved from becoming a charity case; Emma and Alexis were more than aware of what they now owed Madame.

Around this time, Helena moved the couple into a bedroom directly above Henry's office. On the twenty-third of August, when she was expecting a visit from the distinguished Dewan Sankariah of Cochin, she came to Emma's room to ask her to saw a hole in the floor, pointing out exactly where it should be made. The task completed, it was now possible for Emma to slide the entire length of her arm through the hole until it touched the ceiling cloth (used in India to prevent spiders and insects from dropping down one's neck) in the colonel's office. On Madame's instructions, Emma cut a slit in the cloth that was wide enough to slip an envelope through. During the meeting with the Dewan, Henry was startled to see an envelope fall through the air and whack a tin box on his desk. Opening it, he found a portrait of a yogi; he had last owned it in New York and believed it lost. A few moments later, a portrait of Swami Dayananda sailed down. As Helena had hoped, the Dewan was wide-eyed with astonishment.

Later, Emma felt sheepish about her deception of Colonel Olcott; she justified her actions by saying that Madame

> told me that she did these things to divert the Colonel's mind from certain painful occurrences that he had experienced while in America, and that if she had not got over him by these means he certainly would have destroyed himself, and also she added that she had prevented him from doing so by climbing through a window into his room when she found him with a revolver in his hands, ready to commit suicide.[70]

If the thought of Madame Blavatsky hauling her 237 pounds through a window made Emma smile, she managed to suppress her amusement; for all she knew the seemingly amicable colonel might very well be secretly contemplating suicide. At that point, Emma's livelihood depended on the Madame, and pushing letters through ceiling clothes seemed a trivial price to pay. A few days later, when Helena brought her three handkerchiefs and some blue silk, Emma embroidered "A. P. Sinnett" on each of them and did not even bother to ask for explanations.

II

~~~~~~~~~~~~~~~

The Mahatmas

On August 27, H.P.B. left Bombay on the evening mail train with Henry and Babula. They stopped briefly in Allahabad and then took another train to Meerut, where they planned to try to patch up their differences with Swami Dayananda. The heat was almost unbearable, and Helena sweated as Henry debated with Dayananda, mainly about the powers of yogis, prodding the Swami about H.P.B., without mentioning her by name. Was it possible, he asked, for a person to possess occult powers and perform supernatural phenomena without having submitted to the disciplines of yoga? Only, the Swami answered carefully, if they had practiced Hatha Yoga in a previous lifetime. Satisfied, Henry changed the subject.

Once again, Helena felt shut out. On one occasion, she seems to have got close enough to the Swami for a brief conversation about Buddhist and Brahmanist literature. The knowledge that Western scholars had of Eastern religion, said the Swami, amounted to rejected snippets from the sacred books; the *mlecchas* (foreigners) knew nothing about it and, furthermore, would have a long wait for enlightenment. The true ancient literature was not lost to the world but hidden in secret crypts in the Himalayas. Storing away this interesting idea, Helena occupied herself writing letters to the *Times of India* and the *Indian Mirror* in an effort to counter-act the vicious gossip that the dismissed Wimbridge had been blabbing to the press. If Helena had counted on her former friend dropping quietly out of sight, she was very much mistaken, for he seemed to take pleasure in denigrating both the Society and Madame. "Brotherhood and justice," Wimbridge charged, "are mere *ideas* in the Theosophical Society."[71] In his opinion, it was this hypocrisy which accounted for the flood of recent resignations. Indeed, he went on, more members would have resigned if not for H.P.B.'s "hasty flight to Simla." Although the article was not without some validity, Helena, when she pasted the clipping in her scrapbook, sprinkled the margins with comments such as "three *lies* in six lines," "the biggest fib," and so forth. The Theosophical quarrel, she pointed out to the *Indian Mirror,* was "a purely personal and domestic variance having no bearing whatever upon the question of Theosophy and of no importance to the public."[72]

In Allahabad she bought an embroidered white cotton cap for Damodar but mailed it instead to Emma with a note: "Manage in such a way so that Damodar may find this white cap somewhere without knowing where it comes from."[73] The boy would think it from a Brother, which would please him much more than any gift from her. Although Emma found the deception childish she followed instructions "because by complying with Madame's wish in these trifles it kept her in good humour."[74]

After a week at Allahabad, H.P.B. could no longer tolerate the Swami or the weather. On the sixth of September, after a wretched sweltering night, she barged into Henry's room and insisted they start for Simla at once; then she marched off to wire Sinnett of their expected arrival time. Henry, who had scheduled a lecture that evening, for once refused her, and finally, she was obliged to send the Sinnetts a second telegram countermanding the first. That night her bed was placed out of doors and covered with a large mosquito net, and she slept soundly for the first time in a week. The next day, they finally managed to depart by carriage.

In the late afternoon they stopped to visit Indian friends at Umballa, but at eleven that evening decided to keep going. In a *dâk-gharry,* a wooden litter on wheels, they drove all night up the mountain road into the foothills of the Himalayas, and the next morning, sleepless but excited, stopped for a five-hour rest at Kalka, an exceedingly ugly mud and stone village perched on a lower spur of the mountains. From there, like everyone else heading up the fifty-mile incline to Simla, they settled in for a perilous ride in a *tonga,* a low, two-wheeled spring cart hung very low, with the footboards only a few inches above the road, certainly a most uncomfortable conveyance for a person of Helena's bulk. A *tonga* had the notable advantage of maintaining speed up steep gradients, but the passengers were frightfully jolted and sometimes had been known to capsize on the hairpin turns. Even the most phlegmatic of Britons accepted the *tonga* ride with dogged despair, but Helena went further, taking out her fears on the driver, and reeling off a stream of curses at him, at the ponies and at his earsplitting safety horn. Henry simply ignored her and enjoyed the breathtaking scenery.

Just before sunset, as they came in sight of Simla, they saw one of Sinnett's servants waiting with *jampans,* those sedan chairs suspended from long poles and carried on the shoulders of coolies. At a height of 7,000 feet, peak-encircled Simla was Anglo-India's summer capital, the seat of the government for five or six months of the year, and the gayest, most cosmopolitan town in the country during the season. Surrounded by solemn forests of deodar and keloo pine, Simla's hillsides were enameled with wild geraniums, hill anemones, and columbine that peeped out from among ferns and feathery mosses; towering above the town loomed Mount Jakko, which at night seemed to almost shoulder the stars. In September, when the weather was often moist and cloudy, the hills were enveloped in mist, but in clear weather amber-tinged clouds curled up in fleecy bundles and hung on the brow of the hills. Simla's lower bazaar was a crowded rabbit warren abounding in shops where everything conceivable could be bought or rented for the season. Farther up were the homes of the civil servants, wooden houses leased for half the year, veranda connecting with veranda. Later Rudyard Kipling, in *Kim,* would provide a memorable description of Simla with its "pretty ladies' rickshaws, curio vendors, priests, pickpockets and native employees to the Government— here are discussed by courtesans the things which are supposed to be the profoundest secrets of the India Council."[75]

Standing on the veranda of "Brightlands," the Sinnetts' home just over the Mall, H.P.B. gazed out at the twinkling lights scattered on every level of the hill to make a double firmament; despite her outward contempt for Anglo-Indian society, she was deeply moved and eager to be accepted. Here were, after all, the best people in India, the kind of people with whom she had grown up, and whom she still wanted to impress. Early the next morning Alfred Sinnett took her aside for a serious talk, urging her to consider the visit a total holiday for the next three weeks, not even to speak about the Theosophical

Society or the ridiculous Russian espionage charges. He advised her to concentrate on making friends among her own kind, and H.P.B. smiled and politely agreed.

Alfred and Patience had had misgivings about inviting into their summer home a woman who, in Alfred's opinion, had been guilty of blundering both in the management of the Society and in her own conduct. Finally, he had concluded that her faux pas were caused by two factors: unfamiliarity with Indian life and her recent residence in the United States, where she had clearly picked up democratic ideas as well as a prejudiced view of upper-class Anglo-Indians. That the Society had managed to acquire new members failed to impress him because to his way of thinking, all she had done was flatter the natives. Now, despite her past mistakes, Sinnett consented to take her under his protection and help put the Theosophical Society "on the dignified footing it ought to occupy."[76]

If Sinnett had ambivalent feelings, Helena had more. She was shrewd enough to realize that he had not invited her to Simla for a sociable holiday, and one fact was clear: Sinnett lusted after miracles with a passion that made Henry Olcott seem an indifferent schoolboy. But Henry redeemed himself by sincerely believing in the brotherhood of mankind and by his genuine desire to help others. Sinnett's motives, on the other hand, seemed totally selfish. Aware of his disappointment over the lack of phenomena during their previous visit in Allahabad, Helena knew what was expected at Simla, and she came prepared: if Alfred wanted miracles, he should have them.

Unfortunately, that very day she had news from Bombay about the latest Wimbridge-Bates attack: "The next morning, as usual," Henry reported, "she made me the scapegoat, stamping up and down the room"[77] and blaming him for her troubles. Sinnett, heart sinking, took Henry aside to groan about the Old Lady's lack of control; if she continued this way, she would destroy her chances to make friends with the people she needed. The English, he warned Henry, always associated merit with self-control, and, although Henry sympathized, there was little he could offer in the way of reassurance.

Helena was clearly suffering from a bad case of opening-night nerves, and would have controlled herself if she could. To "Brightlands," Alfred invited a succession of important government officials, among them Rudyard Kipling's father, for whom Helena was expected to perform. This time she obliged, and, according to Henry, "began doing phenomena at once."[78] Aside from her raps, now old stuff to Sinnett, she brought out a handkerchief bearing her name and "transformed" it before his eyes into one with his name. According to Emma Coulomb, this was nothing more than a standard magic trick facilitated by the voluminous sleeves on Madame's gowns. Henry described the handkerchief phenomenon as a simple substitution; Emma later revealed that it was originally conceived as a complicated maneuver with Madame cutting the cloth into two pieces and sending half back to Bombay by occult means, but apparently something went wrong. "I believe the handkerchief is a failure," H.P.B. wrote Emma. "Let it go. But let all the instructions remain *in statu quo* for the Maharajahs of Lahore or Benares. Everyone here is madly anxious to see something."[79]

Many of them were not terribly particular about what they saw either. Sinnett waxed enthusiastic over the botched hanky phenomenon and positively went into raptures when she produced the sound of a silvery bell, sometimes a chime or trill or three or four bells on different notes.[80] "From this time on," Henry recalled, "no dinner to which we were invited was considered complete without an exhibition of H.P.B.'s table-rapping and fairy-bell ringing."[81] Of course some people whispered that she made the raps by her thumb and the ringings with apparatus concealed in her clothing, but Sinnett dismissed both theories as idiotic. While he did not question the raps and bells, he did sense that she was holding back, and "it was mortifying to approach no nearer to absolute certitude concerning the question in which we were really interested—namely, whether there did indeed exist men with the wonderful powers ascribed to the adepts."[82] Helena, volunteering nothing, answered questions only when asked and Sinnett thought that "it was tantalizing to feel that she could, and yet could not, give us the final proofs we so much desired to have."[83]

No doubt her tantalizing him was deliberate; the more she gave Alfred, the greedier he became. He actually had the nerve to grumble that she tossed out phenomena suddenly when people were off-guard and had no chance to focus their complete attention. This was, of course, the crucial gambit known to every magician but not, evidently, to Sinnett. For H.P.B.'s own good, he urged her yet again to do a phenomenon under test conditions to prove her validity. "It was an uphill struggle,"[84] he groaned. According to Madame herself, she was too excitable to do proper experiments and since the Brothers frequently assisted her, how could she be expected to ask them to participate in some silly experiment? If the Brothers were going to involve themselves, Sinnett countered, they might just as well do something that would leave no room for the imputation of trickery. Since his point was well taken, Helena began groping for a phenomenon that would satisfy him without, at the same time, involving her in any formal test.

"Day after day," Henry recorded, "we continued receiving visitors, dining out and being lionised generally. H.P.B. kept on with her phenomena, some of them very trifling and undignified, I thought, but still such as to make half Simla believe that she was 'helped by the Devil.' "[85] The time for departure approached and passed, but the Sinnetts said nothing about their leaving. Alfred still hoped for some spectacular proof of the Brotherhood, while Helena herself also felt vaguely dissatisfied with her achievements. Toward the end of September, Patience took Helena and Henry for a drive to the top of Prospect Hill. Sinnett did not accompany them but he described the afternoon's events in *Occult World*:

* * *

Madame Blavatsky asked my wife, in a joking way, what was her heart's desire. She said at random and on the spur of the moment, "to get a note from one of the Brothers." Madame Blavatsky took from her pocket a piece of blank pink paper that had been torn off a note received that day. Folding this up into a small compass, she took it to the edge of the hill, held it up for a moment or two between her hands and returned saying that it was gone.[86]

Helena then assumed an expression of intense concentration, after which she told Patience that the Brother wished to know where she would like to receive the letter. She'd like it to flutter down into her lap, Patience answered, but apparently that did not suit the Brother, and it was finally agreed that she would find her note in a tree. The two women began scrambling among the trees, searching for the note, and Patience climbed up into one of them and began beating the branches. At first she saw nothing but then, stuck on a twig, she spotted a pink note. The message could not have been more brief, nor more prosaic: "I have been asked to leave a note here for you. What can I do for you?" There was no signature, only a few Tibetan characters. Patience could not have been more flabbergasted.

Back at "Brightlands," Helena was just beginning to congratulate herself and possibly Babula, who no doubt planted the note, when Sinnett came home. To her disgust, his excitement over the note was mixed with criticism. If she had managed the afternoon better, he said, if only she had warned him of what was about to take place, it "would have been a beautiful test; but Madame Blavatsky, left to herself in such matters, is always the worst devisor of tests imaginable." His constant fault-finding and searching for loopholes were beginning to annoy her, and she pronounced his distrust "tiresome and stupid."[87]

Several days later she impulsively informed him that one of the Brothers was actually present in Simla and staying at a Tibetan temple. Immediately Sinnett ordered the carriage brought around so that Madame could lead him to the temple. There ensued a wild chase over the hills as Helena followed what she described as occult currents, but of course they found neither temple nor Mahatma. "After a while," Sinnett wrote, "the expedition had to be abandoned, and we went home much disappointed." That evening he announced plans for a picnic the following day, "not with the hope of seeing the Brother, but on the general principle of hoping for something to turn up."[88] Later, Sinnett would claim that he had been careful to keep track of Madame's movements that night; he could swear that neither she nor Babula left the house. In fact, in the middle of the night when he called his valet to fasten a rattly door, Helena had sent Babula to inquire what was wrong.

Early the next morning, Sunday, October 3, the Sinnetts, Henry, and H.P.B., a woman friend of Patience's, and Chief of Police Philip Henderson set out for a nearby valley on horseback. Just as they were leaving the house, a judge rode up and joined the outing to make a party of seven. The servants went on ahead with the hampers while the picnickers followed leisurely in single file down a rocky path. Finally they settled themselves on the grassy edge of a ridge, and the servants opened the tiffin baskets and built a fire to boil water for tea; only then did they discover that they had brought six cups and saucers. Turning to her guests, Patience said with a smile, "Two of you good people must drink out of the same cup, it seems." Henry suggested giving the cup to one person and the saucer to another, and somebody jokingly remarked to H.P.B., "Now, Madame, here is a chance for you to do a bit of useful magic." Picking up her cue, Helena offered to produce a cup and saucer phenomenally, but claimed that she must have the help of Major Henderson. Boldly snatching a table knife, she requested the police chief to follow her and led him to the side of the hill where she pointed and commanded, "Please dig here." After some difficulty cutting through roots, the Major unearthed a cup and saucer of the identical pattern as Patience's china set.

The materialization was greeted with exclamations of surprise and immense excitement. Enormously pleased, Helena delayed her first encore until after luncheon when she carefully steered the conversation to the greatly impressed judge. Someone, perhaps H.P.B. herself, proposed that he might like to join the Theosophical Society then and there, and the judge agreed on the condition that he would be presented with a diploma. Could Madame produce one by magic? Undaunted, she gave a dramatic sweep of her hand and pointed to a bush. The judge bounded over and pulled from the shrubbery a diploma of membership, filled in with his name and the day's date, together with an official letter of welcome from Olcott, which Henry insisted, "I am quite sure I never wrote, but which was still in my handwriting!"

By this time the whole group, Helena included, was in hilarious spirits and everyone sat down on the grass for coffee. No more wonders were expected, nor even necessary, yet, when they ran out of filtered water, "Madame suddenly got up, went to the baskets, a dozen or twenty yards off, picked out a bottle . . . and came back to us holding it under the fold of her dress." The bottle was full, of course, and Sinnett, mind reeling, proclaimed that it was entirely different from the usual Simla water.

At the time and even later Alfred could find no loopholes in what came to be known as "the cup and saucer incident." He based his conviction mainly on the fact that Madame Blavatsky could not have known in advance that there would be seven guests in the party, as the judge had arrived only at the last minute. Obviously she did know, and so did Patience Sinnett because Olcott overheard her telling the butler: "It was very stupid of you not to put in another cup and saucer when you knew that the other gentleman would have to have tea." It seems reasonable to assume that H.P.B. had instructed Babula to bury the cup and saucer, then led the picnickers to the spot herself. In fact, this notion had already occurred to the judge and police chief who later in the afternoon examined the site. Their final conclusion was that it was theoretically possible for someone to have tunneled in from below and thrust the cup and saucer up into the place where they were discovered. Apparently Babula later confided to Emma Coulomb that this was exactly what he had done. In the experts' opinion, the phenomenon could not be accepted as scientifically perfect and, somewhat indelicately, they challenged her to repeat it under test conditions.

Helena, who had worked hard to stage the tableau, could not keep herself from exploding. Henry vividly remembered that "she seemed to take leave of her senses and poured out upon the two unfortunate skeptics the thunder of her wrath. And so our pleasant party ended in an angry tempest."[89] However, the day's miracles had not yet ended, for Helena, ham that she was, had saved the most sensational phenomenon for last. That evening they were to dine with the Allan Humes at Rothney Castle and it was for Hume that Helena had planned a marvel to set Simla on its well-bred ear.

While Alfred Sinnett was an important man in Anglo-India, Allan Octavian Hume was even more important. The son of the fearless Scottish reformer Joseph Hume, who had made a fortune with the East India Company and bought himself a seat in the House of Commons where he served as leader for thirty years, Allan had inherited his father's ambition and zeal. At the age of thirteen he went to sea as a junior midshipman, and having got that out of his system, began his education at Halleyburg College, later studying medicine at University College Hospital. When he was twenty, Hume followed in his father's footsteps by going to India, where he was posted to the Bengal Civil Service. Promotions came rapidly. First he was appointed district officer, which post he held with outstanding bravery during the Sepoy Mutiny. As a result, he was created a Companion of the Bath by Queen Victoria. In 1867 he had been appointed Commissioner of Customs for the Northwest Provinces, and three years later made Secretary to the government of India.

When Helena first met him in 1879, he was fifty-years-old, tall, exceptionally handsome and exceptionally arrogant in a charming way. Earlier that year he had suffered a humiliating setback that might have chastened a less confident man, but which apparently had little effect on Hume. He had been dismissed from his post for insubordination and failure to cooperate with his superiors, and demoted to ordinary membership in the Revenue Board at Allahabad. Hume, outspoken and belligerent, believed himself superior to almost everyone, which no doubt figured in his career problems. After the demotion, he devoted himself to his greatest interest, ornithology, deciding to become an expert on the game birds of India. With a vengeance, he began cataloguing and collecting specimens, wrote several books on the subject, and published a quarterly journal, *Stray Feathers*. At Rothney Castle, built on Mount Jakko at a reported cost of a quarter of a million dollars, Hume had created a museum to house his collection of sixty-three-thousand skins and nineteen-thousand eggs.

Something about Hume powerfully attracted H.P.B.; perhaps his museum filled with stuffed birds reminded her of her grandmother's. Maybe it was simply the obvious fact of his wealth and influence. Having met him briefly the previous year at Allahabad, she knew that he had studied Eastern religions, spoke several Indian languages, and unlike Sinnett and most of the British, had a genuine concern for the Indian people. Far from despising them as an inferior race, he believed that eventually they should win control over their own country. This was enough, in Helena's opinion, to make him supremely eligible for conversion to belief in the Brotherhood. Unknown to Hume, Helena was already acquainted with his daughter Maria Jane Burnby, nicknamed Minnie, from whom she had acquired an intimate knowledge of the target. In February, Ross Scott had brought Minnie, with whom he had fallen in love, to Girgaum Back Road where they were house guests for three days. H.P.B. had not much liked Minnie, probably because the snooty Miss Hume had told her flatly that while she had lived in India ten years she had yet to touch the hand of a native. Helena wrote Nadyezhda on February 21 that she felt "embittered and somewhat angry" because "my house is full of disorder." Blaming Minnie, Helena added, "I am bored with her to the utmost possibility."[90] According to the letter, Minnie already had joined the Theosophical Society and now had come to be initiated. As it turned out, Minnie's visit had an importance that H.P.B. could only vaguely have foreseen: in Bombay, Minnie had in her possession an old-fashioned brooch set with pearls that had been handed down from her grandmother to her mother, and finally to her. About to take passage to London, she presented the pin to Scott as a love token. Since the clasp was broken, he promised to have it repaired; but temporarily low on funds, he pawned it instead. Whether he actually gave H.P.B. the pawn ticket, or whether she acquired it in some other manner is unclear. Nonetheless, she redeemed the brooch, had it repaired by a Bombay jeweler, Hormusji Seevai, and locked it away for safekeeping. In case she should again run into Minnie's parents, it just might prove useful.

At Rothney Castle on the evening of the third, there were eleven guests at table, with Madame seated next to Allan Hume. During the early part of the meal, she seemed unusually quiet, so Hume directed his conversation to a woman on his other side. Someone noticed that Helena was absently rubbing her hands over her metal plate warmer and jokingly asked her why. She remarked flippantly that they could all warm their hands and see what good it did them. She meant it as a rebuff, but several of the guests began to imitate her.

Allan's wife, Mary Anne, known as Moggy, held up her hands with a laugh. "But I have warmed my hands, what next?"

As Sinnett recollected the sequence of events, Madame Blavatsky reached out for Moggy's hands and asked, "Well then, do you wish for anything in particular?" Olcott's version ran that Helena ran her eyes around the table and queried, "Well, who wants something?" and Moggy chirped, "I do."

Then there ensued a torrent of advice urging Moggy to think of some object that Helena might bring to her as an apport, nothing simple now. The conversation continued.

Moggy said, "If I could really get it, I should like to have an old family jewel that I have not seen for a long time, a brooch set round with pearls."

"Have you the image of it clear in your mind?" Helena asked.

"Yes, perfectly clear; it has just come to me like a flash."

Others present reported that Madame began staring fixedly at Moggy, although she actually must have had her eyes glued to the woman for some time prior. Helena, to her horror, had discovered that Moggy drank, but now she saw how this cardinal sin could be turned to her own advantage. It was not unreasonable to assume that by that point in the evening Moggy had consumed her share of brandy and sherry. H.P.B. told her, "It will not be brought into this house but into the garden—I am told by a Brother."[91] There was a rush for wraps and lanterns and everyone except Moggy, who dared not expose herself to the cold night air, dashed into the garden, and began to dig. Finally Patience and a Captain Maitland found a small white package in a nasturtium bed. When unwrapped, it was revealed to contain the brooch.

Back in the house, Sinnett immediately sat down and composed an account of the phenomenon for the *Pioneer*. Everyone present read it and added their signatures as eyewitnesses. This time, Helena seemed to have pulled off an unimpeachable miracle. Unfortunately, several weeks later the jeweler Hormusji Seevai read the *Pioneer* article and told his side of the story to the Bombay *Gazette*. But that still lay in the future.

In triumph, Helena moved through three more weeks of picnics and dinners, and reveled in every moment. "Here the society is mad after me," she wrote happily to Emma. "The people in the highest position in Government are at my feet," and she went on to mention "Major Henderson, who has become my greatest friend and who entreats me to accept him as a theosophist. And do you know who Major Henderson is? The supreme chief of all the police and of the political foreign department of India. The most dreaded and the most influential personage here, who can *do everything*."[92]

No more miracles were called for, but from sheer pleasure she "doubled" a yellow diamond of hers and presented the apport to Patience, who on another occasion, found one of her own brooches inside a pillow. Prepared to retire from Simla with her laurels intact, Helena laughed when Sinnett, still dissatisfied that none of her phenomena had been done under test conditions, pestered her for further wonders. Thinking like a newspaperman, he proposed that the Brothers deliver to him in Simla a copy of the London *Times* on the day of its publication. Helena merely shrugged. Then Sinnett, turning to Olcott for support, took him to his club for a private conversation in which he deplored the whole situation as ridiculous. How, he asked Henry, could the Brothers have selected a person like Madame Blavatsky as their sole representative? The Old Lady was conspicuously boorish, ill mannered, foul-tongued, and seemingly determined to wreck any good work that the Brotherhood wished to accomplish. Olcott listened, with sympathy, but could offer no explanation. However, he could not have missed Sinnett's implications that the Brothers would have done better to select someone solid, someone more like himself. Possibly Henry passed this along to Helena, although she already was aware of Sinnett's wish to bypass her. Therefore, when Sinnett worked up the nerve to ask if she might forward for him a letter he was writing to the Brothers, Helena coolly reminded him that they were unapproachable to outsiders; however, she promised to try.

Toward the end of the first week of October, Sinnett wrote his first letter to an "Unknown Brother," and soon afterward, without waiting for a reply, dashed off a second. Probably on the evening of October seventeenth, he found on his writing table a letter written in black ink on regular white paper, addressed to:

Esteemed Brother and Friend,
Precisely because the test of the London newspaper would close the mouths of the skeptics—it is unthinkable. See it in what light you will— the world is yet in its first *stage* of disenthralment if not development, hence—unprepared.[93]

The letter, which continued on both sides of the sheet, patiently explained the Brother's reasoning: the general populace of the planet was not yet ready to assimilate such a "miracle," would not even believe it and would surely vent its rage on Sinnett and Madame Blavatsky. "We know something of human nature"; the world's prejudices had to be conquered step by step, not by airmailing newspapers across the globe. He cut Sinnett down to size by reminding him that "phenomena such as you crave, have ever been reserved as a reward" for devotion and service, and besides, Sinnett and his friends had already witnessed more than most neophyte adepts see in several years. If Sinnett sincerely wished to know more about the Brotherhood, he should publicize H.P.B.'s work in the *Pioneer* and regard it as his "sacred duty to instruct the public and prepare them for future possibilities by gradually opening their eyes to the truth." In conclusion, borrowing one of Master Serapis Bey's favorite admonitions, he advised Alfred to "TRY."[94] The letter appeared to have been hastily written; there were ink smears, misspellings and crossed-out words. Penned in slightly darker ink, the signature, Koot' Hoomi Lal Singh, was in a different script from the text.

Two days later Sinnett received a second letter, this time from Koot' Hoomi Lal *Sing*, who does not seem to have decided how to spell his own name. Adopting a "get tough" policy, the Brother stonily rejected Sinnett's pleas to communicate without the use of Madame as an intermediary, and went on to question the Englishman's motives. Why did Sinnett have so much difficulty accepting the Brothers as "real entities—not fictions of a disordered hallucinated brain?"[95] If he was as eager for occult knowledge as he claimed, let him give up his luxurious life for the truth, as had Madame Blavatsky and Colonel Olcott. Finally, addressing himself to Sinnett's complaints about Helena, Koot Hoomi did his best to proffer man-to-man sympathy. Unquestionably she was "an enfeebled female" housing a raging cyclone. "But, imperfect as may be our visible agent—and often most unsatisfactory and imperfect she is—yet, she is the best available at present, and her phenomena have for about half a century astounded and baffled some of the cleverest minds of the age."[96] Koot Hoomi could always be depended upon to put in a good word for H.P.B.

Before the Theosophists finally departed on October 21, Sinnett received three additional brief notes, one of which he found in a pillow and the others next to his plate at the dining table. Trivial in content, the notes are chiefly interesting because once again Koot Hoomi seems dubious about the spelling of "Singh," twice writing "Sing." Sinnett was now torn between his compulsion to believe and the suspicion that the Old Lady was making a fool of him. If Koot Hoomi truly existed and Madame Blavatsky was really his messenger, he had the biggest news scoop since the advent of Jesus. But if he did not exist, Sinnett would wind up the laughingstock of India. In any case, he did not care what Koot Hoomi said about Madame Blavatsky and still believed the Brothers would have been wise to have selected a better agent.

After making their descent down the *tonga* road, Helena and Henry stopped overnight at Laurie's Hotel in Kalka, then went on to Umballa, where they boarded a train for Amritsar. At this busiest and holiest of Punjabi cities, site of the Sikhs' Golden Temple, Olcott scheduled two lectures for himself while Helena occupied herself with activities about which he knew nothing. Having established a truce with Swami Dayananda in Meerut, they were welcomed by the local Arya Samajists and given use of a virtually empty bungalow as well as the services of a cook. After six weeks of luxury at Simla, the spartan housekeeping took getting used to, but Helena, uncharacteristically, was uncomplaining.

The next day, however, the *Times of India* published an article under the title "One Day with Madame Blavatsky," which catapulted her into a tremendous rage against Henry and against newspapers in general. At Simla, the day after the cup-and-saucer phenomenon, Henry had written Damodar all about the event. It was a rapturous description typical of Henry's letters to intimates, unimportant except that, somehow, it had found its way from Damodar's desk to the office of the *Times,* who were happy to reprint the full text. How, she demanded of Henry, did the editor come into possession of the letter, which must have been stolen from Damodar? And having got it, what legal right had he to publish it without Olcott's or Damodar's consent? More to the point, why had Henry written such a stupid letter in the first place? She ranted about the unfairness and impoliteness of the public who treated her like "a paid juggler,"[97] for, she insisted, she was not a professional medium, and had never even received so much as a rupee for her experiments. The only benefit she had ever reaped was abuse, she keened.

Newspaper mistreatment was nothing new to her, but after the splash at Simla, expecting more respect from the world, she was bitterly disappointed to find it not forthcoming. With a good deal of effort, she finally calmed down enough to concentrate on giving Sinnett unassailable proof of Koot Hoomi's existence. She now worked out an ingenious scheme whereby the Mahatma would send Sinnett a telegram thanking him for his letter; the hook would be that the telegram was to be dispatched at Jhelum, a hundred thirty-five miles from Amritsar, and dated two hours after receipt of Sinnett's letter in Amritsar. On October 27, after receiving an expected letter from Sinnett to the Mahatma, she telegraphed a confederate previously dispatched to Jhelum with a message in Koot Hoomi's handwriting, to send it to Sinnett. To her annoyance Sinnett failed to understand what had been done and had to have the timetable explained to him. As the Mahatma told it, H.P.B. had forwarded Sinnett's letter by mental telepathy at 2:05 P.M. and he had answered at 4. Unless Madame had flown from Amritsar to Jhelum, Koot Hoomi pointed out, "how could she have written for me the dispatch in my own handwriting at Jhelum hardly two hours after your letter was received by her at Amritsar?"[98]

The preparation for this feat was taxing to say the least, as was the hiring of a man to impersonate a Mahatma and present Olcott with a rose as they toured the Golden Temple. By the time they reached Lahore on November 3, Helena announced she was not feeling well. Olcott, as usual, spent most of his time hobnobbing with local dignitaries and lecturing, which gave H.P.B. the privacy to compose further Mahatma letters to Sinnett and to Allan Hume, who had been writing to Koot Hoomi. To keep both men interested in her philosophy yet also at arm's distance, meant treading a fine line. No, the Brotherhood could not send a private tutor to Allahabad for Hume and Sinnett because the laws of the order would not permit it; and no, it was not true that the Brotherhood had left no mark upon the history of the world and was therefore a failure. Sinnett's questions were often childish, but Hume's were sharp and positively devastating, yet in formulating replies H.P.B. was obliged to exercise tact, at which she never excelled. "Give to your fellow creatures half the attention you have bestowed on your 'little birds,'" she had Koot Hoomi gently advise Hume, "and you will round off a useful life with a grand and noble work."[99]

Two weeks later she came down with Punjab fever. She did not want a doctor but Olcott insisted, and she was dosed with quinine and digitalis. Once recovered H.P.B. bought a hundred rupees' worth of shawls and embroidery from a door-to-door peddler, which Olcott thought excessive. Possibly she had not fully recovered her strength because a few days later she suffered a relapse. For the next six weeks they were on the road almost constantly in the Northwest Province: Umballa, and Benares, where the maharajah graciously allowed the Theosophical Society to borrow his family motto: "There is no religion higher than truth,"[100] and twice they visited the Sinnetts at Allahabad.

Helena was happy to be away from Bombay at this particular time because during their absence Emma had been instructed to look for a new house. From Simla, she had made clear to Madame Coulomb exactly what she expected of her: "I beg you to take care of everything in the removal. Choose a good house. *Let it be useful.*"[101] Primarily, she needed a place adaptable for phenomena; lesser factors, such as size and location, did not much interest her. House-hunting and moving were among the disagreeable chores she left to Emma, who had little else to do anyway.

Meanwhile Helena had her hands full writing Koot Hoomi's letters. One surmises she alternated between excitement over her Mahatmic invention and extreme weariness at the demands of the task she had undertaken. There were times when she ran out of ideas and, in a pinch, would grab the nearest book or magazine, sometimes copying an item word for word. Just such an instance occurred in early December at the Sinnetts when she transcribed a passage from a speech made at Lake Pleasant, Massachusetts, on August 15, and reported in the *Banner of Light.* The speaker, Henry A. Kiddle, was unknown to her, but some of his points seemed reasonable, and she copied them into her K. H. letter without thinking twice. About this time, an excruciating pain that had begun to develop in her left wrist was diagnosed as *dengue,* a type of rheumatic fever, and with lightning speed her arm swelled to the shoulder, despite the ministrations of Sinnett's physician. By Christmas, after a week of agony, she had recovered and Henry, to celebrate, took her to the biggest store in Allahabad where she went on a buying spree.

The "Crow's Nest" was pasted on a rocky slope of Breach Candy in the northwest section of Bombay. Normally the bungalow rented for two hundred rupees a month, but Emma had bargained the owner down to sixty-five because it had a reputation for being haunted. Helena was charmed with the spacious, high-ceilinged rooms, the wide verandas, but especially with its sea view and cool breezes. Better yet, the house was located a distance from the center of the city, which meant fewer unannounced visitors at odd hours. She could not have helped but recognize the effort that Emma and Alexis had made in getting the place ready; still, she did not bother to express her gratitude adequately to Emma, who understandably felt used. All day long she worked and cooked, she said, and sometimes was too exhausted to sleep, but Madame never seemed satisfied.

So she used to get cross, despise everything, and hate everybody; and as we could not understand what she really wanted, she vented her rage on us by forbidding that a sufficient quantity of bread be brought into the house, saying that if we wanted more we were to buy it with our own money—and this, after we had worked like slaves for her![102]

During the winter and spring of 1881, Helena could not truly enjoy her new home, or her existence, which now focused exclusively on her writing table. Her output at this period included articles and a translation of passages from *The Brothers Karamazov* for the *Theosophist,* unsigned articles for the *Pioneer,* and most often, pieces for Russian newspapers. In addition to these enterprises, she continued to toil over Koot Hoomi's lengthy letters. However strenuous her schedule, H.P.B. never missed an opportunity to counter the plentiful attacks from critics, not only from the general press but especially missionary publications. Despite her now professed indifference to journalistic condemnation, she was tremendously disturbed. Much of the criticism *was* personal, as well as malicious. The kinder slurs aimed at her included: "unscrupulous," "untruthful," "ridiculous," and "discreditable"; Her avowals of universal love and brotherhood were labeled pretentious and hypocritical. Helena always managed to get in a few licks of her own but was careful to take a lofty, even sardonic tone. "The Methodist organs are very fond of me," she wrote the Bombay *Gazette.* "So foolishly fond, I am afraid, that rarely a month passes away but my Scytho-Sarmatian heathen name appears on their columns like a fly in a communion cup."[103] She excoriated the papers either as small barking curs or "so many Indian sewers" filled with filth and "public literary garbage." By spring, she was reduced to falling back on her sex, branding the editors cowards who were "ever ready to attack defenceless women."[104]

H.P.B. was going through a bad time in her personal relationships. Although Damodar's father had presented her with a horse and carriage, the extent of her hold on his son was only now occurring to him. Damodar, still living at the "Crow's Nest," refused to go home to his wife and parents and even relinquished his share in the family estate. As a result of this unpleasant breach, Damodar's brother joined Wimbridge and Bates in issuing a circular saying that the Theosophical Society picked the pockets of its members. In the end, the Society had to get an auditor's verification of their receipts and disbursements, which showed, incidentally, that they were about twelve thousand rupees in the red.

Before this upheaval was over, Helena clashed furiously with Olcott. When the Ceylon Buddhists invited him to make a return visit, he happily consented, because he derived the most pleasure from lecturing and raising money for schools. Suddenly H.P.B. decided she could not edit the *Theosophist* alone and demanded that he cancel the trip. When Henry said no, she cloistered herself in her room for one solid week and refused to see him, occasionally using Damodar or Emma to deliver notes threatening that the Mahatmas would have nothing more to do with him if he insisted on going to Ceylon.

This time, uncharacteristically, Henry did not kowtow; his tour had been approved by the Brothers and if they were so vacillating, he preferred to work without them. Moreover, he was dead set on going to Ceylon "even though I never saw the face of a Master again."[105]

A few days later, her ire burned out, she made the conciliatory gesture of inviting him for a ride in her carriage. Henry made clear that he wanted to reconstruct the Society on a different basis, putting public service and universal brotherhood in the forefront and, he added, "keeping occultism in the background."[106] At Simla, he had suddenly begun to feel uncomfortable with the miracles. After all, they were H.P.B.'s show, and he now wanted no part of them, maintaining he could best serve the interests of the Society in an administrative capacity. Helena had no choice but to acquiesce.

H.P.B., nearing her fiftieth birthday, was probably going through menopause, which may account for some of her extreme emotional fluctuations at this time. After seven years Henry had grown accustomed to her choleric aspect; even on those days when she went off screaming that "there were no Mahatmas, no psychical powers, and that she had simply deceived us from first to last,"[107] his deep affection for her had enabled him to take it. Emma Coulomb, however, was less understanding of Madame's jags.

> Some times when awake in bed, I used to torture my brain to find out what I could do to please her—for, bad as the place was, yet it was better than none; and although she was unjust, yet at times she used to have a good fit for two or three days, at which times she was more tractable, which made up for the past, and we pushed on.[108]

Helena paid little attention to Emma's piddling grievances, and eventually that mistake would catch up with her. She felt ill again, this time with back pains, and her doctor recommended cauterization. "Oh God!" she wrote despondently to Vera, "what a misery it is to live and to feel. Oh, if it were only possible to plunge into Nirvana. What an irresistible fascination there is in the idea of eternal rest!"[109] Talk of suicide humiliated her, and she did not speak of it again to Vera; what she longed for was not death, but rest and release from pain. Even though she had written a scant twenty Mahatma letters between mid-October, 1880, and the end of February, 1881, the assignment was beginning to take its toll. She failed to link the letters to her physical maladies, and yet the corollary is unquestionably there.

By April, however, circumstances conspired to give her a few months' sabbatical. Olcott had left for Ceylon, not to reappear for seven months. Alfred Sinnett and his pregnant Patience had gone to England for a holiday and were not due back until July. At last, H.P.B. was suddenly liberated from the necessity of impersonating a Mahatma and had an opportunity to catch her second wind. From Koot Hoomi, Sinnett had requested and received permission to publish extracts from the letters in a book that he planned to title

Occult World. He completed the entire manuscript at sea, gave it to a publisher when he arrived, and the first edition was issued in June. If he had hoped for a respectful hearing, he must have been disappointed. While the English reviewers roasted not only him but Madame and the Theosophical Society, they reserved their most scathing jibes for Mahatma Koot Hoomi's letters. "They are written," the British publication *Saturday Review* announced scornfully, "in very choice American, and the Oriental lore which they contain is exclusively derived from a perusal of Lord Lytton's novels and of a mystical jumble entitled *Isis Unveiled,* published some years ago by Madame Blavatsky."[110] Madame's miracles at Simla, chronicled in detail in *Occult World,* were dismissed as dull, and Alfred Sinnett's "mental faculties are so obscured that he cannot perceive the tricks of which he is the victim."[111]

In late June, Sinnett returned to India alone; complications had arisen during Patience's pregnancy, and on July 14 she would give birth to a still-born child. Since his steamer had docked in Bombay, he spent a few days at the "Crow's Nest" before continuing up-country to Allahabad. Helena did not spare herself in providing an enthusiastic reception, and even before his arrival, had asked Alexis Coulomb to prepare a trap in the attic floorboards above the room Sinnett would occupy. Just after breakfast on the morning following his arrival, Sinnett was sitting in his room when a letter dropped among the china and cutlery. Koot Hoomi, seemingly unaware of the miserable reception given *Occult World,* could not have been more solicitous or supportive:

> Welcome good friend and brilliant author, welcome back! Your letter at hand, and I am happy to see your personal experiences with the "Elect" of London proved so successful.[112]

There followed thirteen pages that alternated between a scholarly metaphysical treatise and a ragbag of gossip about various London occultists such as Stainton Moses, Anna B. Kingsford, and Charles Massey, who was inaccurately described as "the hapless parent of about half a dozen illegitimate brats."[113] In passing, K.H. warned Sinnett not to expect too much from Madame Blavatsky for "our old lady is weak and her nerves worked to a fiddle string; so is her jaded brain."[114]

At a reception that evening hosted by the Bombay Theosophical Society, Sinnett talked about his book and positively affirmed his conviction that Madame Blavatsky could not be the author of the Mahatma letters. It was, he assured his audience, "physically impossible"[115] and as proof he cited the telegram he had received from Jhelum. He went on to point out that K.H.'s handwriting and literary style were completely different from Madame's and that, for the most part, she knew nothing about the contents of the letters. As if all this were not sufficiently reassuring, he had received proof positive that very morning when a letter had suddenly fallen out of nowhere onto the table before him. Since Madame had been with him at the time, the mere hypothesis of fraud was, in his opinion, "contemptibly absurd."[116] Helena, sitting in the audience, must have breathed an imperceptible sigh of relief.

III

The Astral Post Office

It is hardly surprising that Sinnett's verdict should have been accepted at the time by a number of intelligent people, since despite the extracts published in *Occult World* and later in *Esoteric Buddhism,* almost no one concerned, except Sinnett and his wife, ever saw the letters in their entirety. Reading them today, there can be no reasonable doubt that Helena was their author.

Toward the end of his life, Sinnett admitted that the letters "were not, in the beginning, what I imagined them to be—letters actually written by the Master and then forwarded by occult means either to Madame Blavatsky or deposited somewhere about the house where I should find them."[117] But even if they were not what he imagined, he by no means saw them as totally fraudulent; simply, he had invested too much in the Mahatmas to deny their existence. All the letters were inspired by Koot Hoomi, "but for the most part, if not always, were dictations to a competent amanuensis and Madame Blavatsky was generally the amanuensis in question."[118] After he was no longer on speaking terms with H.P.B., and had begun communicating with the Mahatma through mediums, it was explained to him that Madame had added her own views to the Master's, generally tampering with the messages until they became a travesty of his meaning. (See Appendix B.)

The one hundred twenty letters written between 1880 and 1884 are a remarkable achievement for which H.P.B. should be given the credit she was forced to deny herself. The correspondence became for her a vehicle by which she could disseminate an occult religious philosophy she dared not claim as her own and that, moreover, she felt impelled to filter to the world's attention through two men, one of them fictional. From a distance of one hundred years, it is easy to criticize her methods, but Helena, by 1880, had already become a prisoner of her hallucinations. Having become entrapped by her own invention, forced to share her vision of the Brotherhood by proclaiming herself its messenger, she placed herself in an untenable position. Of necessity she was compelled to give her mythical Mahatmas credit for her philosophy and, as we shall see, to fashion ever more complicated lies so that the whole flimsy structure did not crash down upon her.

Like every literary genius, Madame Blavatsky could beget characters so full-bodied and distinctive that they truly seemed to live. Perhaps this talent was inherited from her novelist mother. Perhaps her skill is due to the fact that she modeled her characters on certain living individuals, admittedly rare but nevertheless real. In her century, there did exist hermits in Tibet and northern India, most of them practicing Buddhist ascetics and Hindu yogis who were making serious efforts to tread the path to arhatship, or enlightenment, and in so doing were able to liberate themselves from ill will, desire, ignorance, lust and anger. In the 1920s, the distinguished Tibetan scholar W. Y. Evans-Wentz would pose an interesting question that is highly relevant to Madame Blavatsky's life: are there members of the human race who have reached the heights of such spiritual and physical evolution as this planet permits, "and who being a species apart from other human beings, are possessed of mastery over natural forces as yet undiscovered, but probably suspected, by Western Science?"[119]

Eveans-Wentz hazarded a qualified yes, saying that as a result of his studies he had good reason to believe that among the Himalayan hermits "there are possibly some—if perchance there be but two or three"[120] who have attained arhatship.

Still, there are mahatmas and Mahatmas.[121] Helena's Mahatmas had been incarnated in embryo in New York in 1875 and fully perfected by 1880 in India. They should have ceased to exist by 1891, but lingered on remarkably, the product of Helena Blavatsky's inward life during her previous fifty-nine years. Piecing together their biographies from the letters, one can summarize them as follows:

Somewhere in Tibet live the few men who have reached sainthood and become members of the hierarchy that govern the world. Although the exact address of The Brotherhood of the Snowy Range is not divulged, it might well be Shigatse, a village south of Lhasa on the river Tsangpo, where Helena said she stayed in 1870 in the house of Master Koot Hoomi's sister. The Mahatmas appear to live in a type of communal setting reminiscent of a lamasery. As masters and teachers, they supervise apprentices who have resolved to devote themselves to humanity, and K.H. speaks of the house as being "full of young and innocent *chelas*"[122] preparing for initiation. The masters are not cloistered, indeed some of them travel a good deal; Koot Hoomi journeys to Bhutan and to the mountains of "Kouenlun" (K'uenlun) for business consultations, he writes letters from Kashmir and Amritsar and sends a telegram from Jhelum in the Punjab. On one occasion he mentions that he has just spent nine days on horseback. The Brothers go to Lhasa at the beginning of every lunar year to take part in the festivals, but ordinarily keep busy at home performing duties which are referred to but never described. Possibly much of their time is spent in study, since they seem to be curators of the largest and most complete library on earth.

Why Helena chose to present so few details about the daily lives of the Brothers is unclear. Granted, she was usually writing in a hurry, and the requisite religious research was sufficiently taxing to discourage research into details like life-style and diet. While she knew nothing of Tibet from personal experience, she might have checked more carefully into the works of Abbé Huc, William Rockville and other travelers, who painted a fairly accurate picture. As it is, there is nothing in the letters to indicate the Mahatmas were living in Tibet; for that matter, they could have been settled in Madras or London, even New York.

Perhaps because of lack of this essential knowledge, the Brothers Koot Hoomi and Morya are not, as one might expect, Tibetans, but Indians. K.H. was born in the Punjab in the early nineteenth century and came from an old Kashmiri family of the Brahmin caste. In his youth he studied in Europe, probably in Germany because he makes playful references to Munich beer-hall beauties. He does not, however, speak or write German, Punjabi, Hindi or Tibetan; his Latin is faulty, his Sanskrit non-existent, his French impeccable, his English queer. He also has a habit of overlining his *m*'s, a mannerism of Russians writing in English or French. Although his letters are written in English, it is not the English of an educated Indian and they sometimes falter in the use of punctuation, spelling and grammar. For example, he inserted commas between subject and predicate. Worse yet, K.H. is fond of American slang and his awkward sentence constructions lead one to believe he is thinking in French but translating his thoughts into English. "S.M. passes the two thirds (les deux tiers) of his life in Trance." "I write but seldom letters."[123] (Je n'ecrit que rarement des lettres.)

K.H. is in semi-command of Western literature, science, and philosophy; he quotes Shakespeare correctly, and Swift incorrectly, has a passing acquaintance with Thackeray, Tennyson and Dickens, and keeps au courant by reading current English novels. "My knowledge of your Western Sciences is *very* limited,"[124] he insists, which does not prevent him from aiming barbs at Darwin, Edison, Tyndall, and some thirty others. In personality, he was alternately witty, stern, cheerful, spiteful, highly idealistic, petty, and downright bitchy. But he was always entertaining.

When Alfred Sinnett first asked to be put in touch with a Mahatma, Helena responded with Koot Hoomi, who would sign the majority of the letters. One wonders why she created a totally new personage when she might have used one already at hand, Master Morya (usually called M.), her childhood protector already known to Henry Olcott as the man who left his turban in New York. Obviously Helena did not wish to share her personal master with

Sinnett, although when Koot Hoomi wearied of the correspondence, Morya was brought in as a relief writer. A Rajput of the Kshatriya caste, he is flinty, humorless, brusque and in most respects a totally different personality from K.H. M. is not fond of traveling, although he does make astral visits. He claims to know very little English and hates writing, which may account for the fact that his letters are concise and his comments snappish. Morya's single sensual indulgence is pipe-smoking and once, writing to Sinnett from Lhasa, he thanks him for sending him a pipe to replace the one he had broken in an unmahatmic rage. The pipe was a nice touch, but a mistake on Helena's part, for it was strictly forbidden to smoke in Tibet; one wonders how Morya escaped detection, or even where he managed to obtain tobacco. Helena, a tobacco addict, could not resist giving her favorite creation one of her own bad habits.

In addition to K.H. and M., there are glimpses of several minor characters:

Djual Khool (D.K.) was called "the Disinherited" because he had been disowned by his family when he became a *chela.* At the outset of the letters, D.K. was only a *chela,* but eventually he became a Master himself and K.H. refers to him as his alter ego. One of the Mahatma letters was written by D.K.

Above the Masters is the *Chohan,* a venerable personage who does not write letters. When the Masters submit questions or plans to him, he passes judgment in short, emphatic sentences, seldom giving reasons for his decisions. Once, congratulating Sinnett for a book review, K.H. tells him that he is "beginning to attract the *Chohan's* attention."[125] Generally, however, the *Chohan* is contemptuous and patronizing to the Westerners whom he calls "*pelings.*"

Still higher than the *Chohan* towers the *Maha-Chohan,* or "Chief," as K.H. calls him, who corresponds more or less to the concept of God. It is the *Maha-Chohan* who gives K.H. permission to correspond with Sinnett.

There are, of course, no women in this organization; in fact, a sturdy strain of anti-feminism can be discerned throughout the letters: "*Women* do lack the power of concentration"; "Generally I never trust a woman any more than I would trust an echo"; and so forth. Referring to H.P.B., who was after all the Brotherhood's official representative, K.H. is affectionately sexist: "We have nothing against the old woman with the exception that she is one."[126] Koot Hoomi vacillated between defense of H.P.B. and criticism of her shortcomings so devastating that many believed Madame Blavatsky could not possibly have written the letters. The misogyny had a definite purpose: it helped throw Sinnett off the track, at the same time as it boosted Helena above all others of her sex, awarding her a position comparable to the Virgin Mary's. She had the Masters bestow on her a modest title, *Upasika*[127] (female disciple), but there is no missing the powerful position she handpicked for herself in the divine plan.

* * *

Helena Petrovna Blavatsky was a woman who used her inner myths in a most unorthodox manner. During her lifetime, she was ignored by psychologists and psychic researchers, who assumed she was a fraud; she was revered by many thousands who believed that she spoke the truth about her Mahatmas, and who thought her unique. Both evaluations now seem to be somewhat wide of the mark.

Although some of her methods for publicizing herself and her ideas were blatantly dishonest and inexcusable, she sincerely believed that she was serving the cause of some greater truth higher than herself. Certainly her objective, synthesizing all human knowledge into a universal religion and a universal social order, cannot be called ignoble. There must have been periods when her perception of the Brotherhood was sufficiently potent, so that no tricks were necessary to sustain them, but there were also times when the visions faded, the voices vanished, and she was marooned on a sinking island of subliminal romance.

If she does not fit the category of fraud, neither was she unique, and it is interesting to compare Madame Blavatsky with parallel recorded cases in which individuals, usually women, have created dramatic personages who transmit writing of various kinds. (See Appendix C.)

Psychoanalytical and parapsychological literature is rich in references to individuals with Blavatsky's supposedly distinctive characteristics; these are women who write letters in handwritings not their own, who people their hallucinations with exotic men, invent languages, give birth to cosmic philosophies, and compose charming accounts of life after death. Occasionally one encounters a man; take, for instance, William James' case history of Sidney Dean, journalist, author and Congressman from Connecticut (1855–1859) whose automatic writing came through in hieroglyphics and obsolete languages. "It is an intelligent ego who writes," Dean told James. "It is not myself, of that I am conscious at every step of the process."[128]

The most common explanation offered for such behavior is multiple or disintegrated personality. In the simplest cases, the secondary personalities manifest themselves through hypnotic phenomena such as automatic writing. In more developed cases, such as that of "Helene Smith" and other trance mediums, the secondary personality fails to take on a completely independent existence, exhibiting itself only under special conditions, *i.e.,* the trance. In fully developed cases of multiple personality, the various identities truly alternate with each other and are capable of leading an independent existence.

As Carl Jung pointed out, "mediums are as a rule slightly abnormal mentally,"[129] frequently exhibiting hysterical symptoms. In Madame Blavatsky's case, it seems fairly clear that she possessed an hysteric personality and throughout her life suffered periodic experiences of dissociation along with definite personality alterations. Presumably she experienced subliminal reveries while awake in which a "brother" guided her hand over the paper in handwritings wholly different from her own. Although most mediums' handwritings change while in trance, it is necessary to stress that more than half of the Mahatmic writings are pure Helena Petrovna. They are a vivacious potpourri of gossip, homey advice, backbiting, and desperate struggles to cover her past deceptions and ward off troubles she saw brewing. There is, in fact, nothing in any of her writings that could not have been derived from normal sources of information or her own extremely fertile intellect and imagination.

If Helena had been the ordinary impostor that many labeled her, she might have busily gone her dishonest way without particular psychic strain; if she had been an ordinary trance medium working cooperatively with her "control" and doing a bit of automatic writing when the mood struck her, she might have led a reasonably stress-free life. It was Madame Blavatsky's peculiar misfortune to have fallen somewhere between those two positions. With the birth of Master Koot Hoomi, she created for herself an acute psychological dilemma in which she was forced to establish two separate compartments in her mind: one for her normal self; one for Upasika, messenger of the Brotherhood. When danger threatened, Upasika would step in and prevent her from admitting that she wrote the Mahatma letters.

This self-induced schizophrenia and her titanic effort to control it would considerably shorten her life.

Sinnett went home to Allahabad on July 8, leaving H.P.B. with nothing to do but eat during the sweaty, rainy Bombay summer. For want of something better, she asked Emma to construct a life-size doll that would resemble a Mahatma and produce a magical effect by moonlight. Cutting out a paper pattern of the face, she observed and criticized while Emma sewed and stuffed, but, unfortunately, the Mahatma turned out looking drab and elderly and had to be spruced up with paint. By the time they had made a jacket, the dummy appeared fairly human, and on the evening of July 13 made its debut before three Hindu Theosophists who were visiting the "Crow's Nest." They immediately composed a testimonial for a London Spiritualist paper to which Emma and Alexis attached their signatures affirming they too had seen the Mahatma. In time, H.P.B. would become curiously attached to "Christofolo," as she called the doll. Later, during one of her absences from Bombay, Emma would burn it in a fit of disgust. "Oh my poor Christofolo!" Helena lamented after Emma wrote her the news. "He is dead then and you have killed him? Oh my dear friend if you only knew how much I would like to see him revive!"[130] Emma, penitent, constructed another.

Several days after Christofolo made his first appearance, Helena received an invitation to spend August and September at Rothney Castle in Simla. With Patience in England and Olcott in Ceylon, Allan Hume had invited her and Sinnett to establish a Simla branch of the Theosophical Society. Off in a flash, Helena collected Sinnett in Allahabad and together they made the nerve-wracking journey up the *tonga* road from Kalka to Simla. During the course of which ride Helena upbraided the driver in such picturesque terms that Sinnett thought it a pity "to have had their comicality wasted upon an audience of one."[131]

The first days passed pleasantly enough. The luxury of Rothney Castle and the bracing air on Mount Jakko rejuvenated her spiritually and physically. During the mornings, Hume and Sinnett were involved in business; in the afternoons they played lawn tennis, after which there was brandy and soda on the veranda. In the quiet time before dinner, Sinnett would play waltzes on the piano. Avoiding the inebriated Moggy Hume whenever possible, Helena had plenty of privacy to catch up on her correspondence. Writing to Captain Adelberth de Bourbon who proposed forming a Theosophical Society in Holland, she apologetically refused his request for her portrait "for two reasons: (1) I haven't got it. (2) The portrait may give you a nightmare."[132] She also wrote an encouraging letter to William Judge, whom she felt guilty for having neglected; to Mary Hollis Billing she insisted that "Ski" was not a disembodied spirit but an initiate of the Brotherhood, indeed a personal friend of Master Morya's. "Why for pity's sake do you not tell people the truth about our Brother *Ski* . . . ?"[133] Apparently even Mary balked at making such a cockeyed announcement.

H.P.B.'s main activity continued to be keeping the Astral Post Office humming while Babula delivered mail. Once, while dressing for dinner, Sinnett found a letter in his coat pocket and upon arising one morning found another under his pillow. Pleased with herself, Helena kept the household entertained with anecdotes about the Mahatmas and the tinkling of her astral bell. On August 12, she celebrated her fiftieth birthday.

Almost imperceptibly, the blissful atmosphere began to turn acidic, owing to their host. Hume's sharp sense of humor frequently took the form of hostile attacks on people, and some of his jokes discomfited Helena. Particularly grating was his facetious remark that she was an impostor but he loved her just the same. Not only did he doubt the brooch phenomenon of the previous summer, he confided, but he positively knew it had been a fraud; he supposed that she was one of those people who believed the means justify the end. Crushed, H.P.B. listened while he spilled out his benevolent disdain for her deceptions and reassured her he would always remain her friend. She had felt certain of Hume but now, despite her best efforts, he seemed to be slipping from her grasp. Obviously something extraordinary was called for. She wrote excitedly to Emma and Alexis in a rash of underlining and exclamation points.

My Dear Friends,
In the name of heaven, do not think that I have forgotten you. I have not even time to breathe—that is all!! We are in the *greatest crisis* and *I must not LOSE MY HEAD.*

I cannot and dare not write anything to you. But you must understand that it is *absolutely necessary* that something should happen in Bombay while I am here. The King and Dam, must see one of the Brothers and receive a visit from him, and, if possible, the first must receive a letter which I shall send . . . The letter must fall on his head . . . We must strike while the iron is hot. Act *independently* of me, but in the habits and customs of the Brothers. If something could happen in Bombay that would make all the world talk it would be grand. But what! The Brothers are inexorable. Oh dear M. Coulomb, save the situation and do what they ask you.

Imagine! Mr. Hume wants to see Koothoomi *in his astral form* at a distance, so that if he (K.H.) complies he may be able to say to the world that *he knows* he exists, and *to write it* in all the papers; for at present he can only say one thing, viz—that *he believes* firmly and positively, but not that *he knows it* because he has seen them *with his own eyes,* as Damodar, Padshah, &c., have. Now then, there is a problem!

Understand then that I am going mad and take pity on a poor widow. If something unheard of should take place in Bombay, there is nothing that Mr. Hume would not do for Koothoomi on his demand. But K.H. cannot come here, for the occult laws do not permit him to do so. Goodby. Write to me.[134]

Evidently Emma did not follow instructions, because Hume's scoffings continued.

Attempting to hide her hurt, Helena spent evenings in the billiard room listening to Hume and Sinnett gossip indiscreetly about various Theosophists. Their primary target was Henry Olcott, whose blunders and banalities amused them, and whose adoption of sandals and Indian-style robes they found an endlessly rich topic for discussion. When finally they turned to business matters, it was to inform her that they wanted their own branch of the Society at Simla. It was to be an exclusive club that would admit no natives and owe no allegiance to the parent Society or to President Olcott. Suddenly, Helena was overwhelmed by everything she saw as despicable about the British. She reviled their haughty chauvinism, their prejudice, and their revolting drinking habits. The brandy fumes at Rothney Castle sickened her, as they did K.H., who railed against them in a letter. When she strolled through Hume's museum of stuffed birds, it no longer recalled long buried memories of her grandmother's home, for Hume had, she decided, "a bird-killing and a faith-killing temperament."[135]

In the end, with K.H.'s help, she was able to arrange the vetoing of their exclusive club and even managed to cut down on the frivolous gossip, but nobody stopped drinking. Hume had the audacity to write Master Koot Hoomi that it was a mistake to share metaphysical instruction with the superstitious Hindus because "not one in ten thousand native minds is as well prepared to realize and assimilate transcendental truths as mine." Needless to say, if the Mahatmas wanted blind followers, they should cater to the Hindus or "stick to your Olcotts," but if they "want men of a HIGHER class, whose brains are to work effectually in your cause,"[136] then people like himself should be cultivated.

Helena as K.H. was able to reply with beautiful control: "In your letter you show plainly that you are the beginning, the middle and the end of the law to yourself. Then why trouble yourself to write to me at all?"[137] Helena as Helena bottled up her feelings and struggled to remain calm in her daily dealings with Hume, but inwardly she felt sick. "Oh dear, how unhappy I am," she confided to Emma. "On every side unpleasantness and horror."[138] Confronting the fact that Hume was a liar and a "skunk,"[139] she was still unwilling to give up on him. He and Sinnett had agreed to write a series of articles for the *Theosophist,* and he alone was preparing a book; they bombarded H.P.B. daily with questions that forced her to clarify some of her theories. Still, Hume especially delighted in picking apart everything she said. Finally, unknown to H.P.B., the two men decided to bypass her completely and drafted a letter to K.H. urging he dispense with Madame's services and deal with them directly.

As usual, the problem was to get the letter posted without H.P.B.'s knowledge, and of course there was no way. It was inconceivable to Sinnett that the Old Lady would read communications addressed to the Master, although Hume suspected she did, but in the end they had no alternative. Helena was playing the piano in the drawing room when Sinnett brought in the letter and asked her to forward it. Cramming it into her pocket without a glance she went on playing. A few minutes later, the door to the library crashed open and an enraged H.P.B. confronted Sinnett: "What is it? What have you been doing or saying to K.H.?"[140] Drowning out his demands to know if she had opened the letter, she screamed that he had ruined everything: he would never hear from the Masters again; she and Olcott would move to Ceylon, where people trusted and appreciated them.

Sinnett, shaken more by Helena's hysterics than her threats, listened in dazed horror. Managing to maintain his English calm until she had stormed off to her room, he stood trembling. From that time on, he and Hume seemed to recoil from her. Hume did not ask her to leave, but barely looked in her direction and stopped speaking. He did not need to; he had made his feelings perfectly clear to her.

Afterward, Helena was depressed, not merely by the mens' treachery but by her unfortunate outburst, which she regretted but regarded as justifiable. For weeks Hume had been provoking her with his insults; did he believe that she had no feelings to wound? Bruised but sobered, she set about trying to pick up the pieces; K.H. had to explain to Hume and Sinnett that the behavior and temper "which so revolt you" was no fault of Helena's. Having obtained special permission from his superiors, K.H. was now at liberty to reveal that "this state of hers is intimately connected with her occult training in Tibet, and due to her being sent out alone into the world to gradually prepare the way for others." Although they would doubtless not understand, he would make an attempt to explain: any initiate trained in Tibet had to leave behind a piece of him or herself, one of the seven principles in the complete human being, to form a transmitting link and to assure that no secrets would be divulged. Therefore, even though Helena might seem "highly eccentric" and a "psychological cripple," their "contemptuous smiles" were nevertheless "positively sinful" and "CRUELTY still."[141] Hume, scoffing, wanted to know which one of her principles she had left.

If K.H. was not persuasive enough, and evidently Helena sensed he was not, Master Morya pitched in: he informed Hume and Sinnett that he had been in the room when Madame received their letter, and he could assure them she had not read it; the scene had resulted from her "shattered nerves," and in his opinion their continuing hostility toward her was "almost cruel." They were inflicting "upon her supersensitive nature severe and unnecessary pain."[142]

Sinnett finally forgave her because he realized that "she is not capable of bearing the annoyance of a pinprick with equanimity,"[143] but he never forgot the episode. Gradually the tension ebbed a little, but K.H. expressed both his and H.P.B.'s moods when he wrote, "I really feel weary and disheartened."[144] H.P.B. decided to remain at Simla throughout most of October because she had been offered a two-hundred-rupee job translating Russian statistics for the Foreign Office. When Damodar wrote proposing they all move there permanently, she answered through Emma by saying that the idea was "absurd. If I change my headquarters—and we have to do it, for I hate Bombay—I will have headquarters at Calcutta and Ceylon."[145] At most she would spend some of the summers at Simla where a three-room house cost twelve hundred rupees and everything was overpriced. That the town was full of vultures she had known from the day of her arrival, because on August 28 she had written to her Uncle Rostislav requesting an affidavit stating that she was really Helena Petrovna von Hahn Blavatsky, granddaughter of the Princess Dolgorukova and not "an insignificant adventuress." As she had lost track of Rostislav's whereabouts, she sent the letter to Prince Alexander Dondoukoff-Korsakoff, now governor-general of Odessa, and asked him to forward it. She hoped that he would "excuse the informal behavior of an old acquaintance whom you knew well in the past, in the happy days of your youth in Tiflis and elsewhere and who at present finds herself perched on one of the peaks of the Himalayas, in the manner of Prometheus—vultures not lacking in Simla."[146]

Rostislav had immediately sent her the affidavit and the prince also responded warmly that he had recognized her handwriting. Both of these

letters she exhibited to Hume, who by now avoided the subject of the Mahatmas, "except to sneer at them once or twice,"[147] but it was humiliating to
know that at age fifty, she had to prove her identity.

Toward the end of October she took her leave, but whether out of disgust,
spite, or simple exhaustion she decided to withdraw Master Koot Hoomi from
the postal service. Announcing that he would be taking a "long, *very* long
journey," he thanked Sinnett for his past kindnesses and asked him to extend
Allan Hume "my most friendly regards."[148] In his absence, Master Morya
would take over the correspondence, a switch that would relieve Helena
because as Morya she could be ruder to Hume.

The thought of returning to Bombay had little appeal and there was actually no pressing reason to do so, since Olcott would remain in Ceylon until
December and Damodar was perfectly capable of handling the Society's business affairs. Informing Sinnett that she had business to conduct for the Brothers, and alerting Emma that several people had invited her to visit them, she
roamed around northern India accepting their hospitality. After a few days in
Lahore, she made her leisurely way to Saharanpur, where two English couples who had expressed interest in joining the Society were honored to entertain her. She stayed up talking her head off until 1 A.M. Joined by Ross Scott,
who was to marry Minnie Hume in a few weeks, she swept on to Dehra Dun
where she had a grand time with the local Anglo-Indians and was particularly
delighted to meet a Mrs. Church, whose vocabulary of off-color words
excelled her own. Merrily she wrote to Sinnett in Allahabad, "Speak of me,
occasionally uttering improper things owing to my natural innocence and
improper knowledge of English. She tells things that made the root of my hair
turn red and burn with shame!"[149] Judging by the tone of her letters at this
time, many of them gleefully signed "Yours in Jesus," she seemed to be in
high spirits; of course she was deliberately tantalizing Sinnett, who was dying
to meet a Mahatma, when she told him that she had met Master M. at
Lahore. "He is very cross,"[150] she cautioned, pointedly adding that M. "said
something about going to see Damodar."[151]

There were new members to initiate in Meerut and a branch to establish at
Bareilly. At last, Helena was in her element, which always bolstered her spirits, so it is curious that she should write to Vera of a serious illness. Without
going into details, she reeled off a fantastic tale of being carried unconscious
into the jungles of "Deo-Bund" where she was cured by a famous lama and
later revived in a room full of carved stone statues of Buddha. "Around me
were some kind of smoking chemicals, boiling in pots, and standing over me
the Lama Debodurgai was making magnetic passes."[152] Helena, as has been
said, was fond of hashish, which was far easier to obtain in India than in New
York City, and this experience may simply have been a hashish dream. Since
at this time there is no indication of her having suffered any special illness,
she was probably trying to elicit sympathy from Vera, with whom she was
justifiably annoyed: without asking permission, her sister had taken it upon

herself to write an article, "The Truth about H. P. Blavatsky," and published it in Russia's parapsychological journal, the *Rebus*. H.P.B. had a horror of anyone writing the truth about her, especially the sister who knew too much. The article, of course, had displeased her, and she was feeling slightly huffy about Vera.

Toward the end of November she spent ten days with Alfred Sinnett at Allahabad, and despite the myriad opportunities for slipping letters under pillows, the Mahatmas, to Sinnett's great disappointment, were conspicuous by their absence. By the first of December, H.P.B. was back at the "Crow's Nest" and by the nineteenth, when Olcott was to return from Ceylon, she was eager to see him. The Ceylon junket had been their longest separation since they had met, and she must have missed him. At pains to show her affection, she prepared a special homecoming gift, making sure the Mahatmas would leave him a congratulatory note for the good work he had accomplished in Ceylon. Apparently both she and the Masters had forgotten last winter's angry threats to cast him into outer darkness. To Henry, the message came as a shock. How, he wondered, could the Mahatmas have forgotten? Certainly he had not. After that, he no longer trusted Helena: "Thenceforward, I did not love or prize her less as a friend and a teacher, but the idea of her infallibility, if I had ever entertained it more than approximately, was gone forever."[153] Once he had entertained it more than approximately, but that was too painful to reflect upon.

Henry still received letters from his sister and also from Judge, the most recent from Venezuela where he was trying to develop a silver mine he hoped would make "a good deal of money. Whether the Brothers help me or not I cannot know but trust they now and then look my way."[154] Mary Olcott had remarried recently, and Henry's sons appeared to have forgotten him. Since there was no going back to his old life, he had no choice but to make the best of his present lot. After his return from Ceylon, he resolutely closed his eyes to those things he did not wish to see.

In 1882 H.P.B. was laboring over a synopsized history of the universe for Alfred Sinnett, compacted in sixty-nine Mahatma letters running to over one hundred thousand words. In a sense it was a repetition of what she had done during the writing of *Isis Unveiled*, but at the same time, it was a dry run for her great opus *The Secret Doctrine*. Much of the theoretical and philosophical teachings she was now passing along to Sinnett emerged as a result of his specific questions; however, since she did not always have ready answers, she frequently found herself in the position of a teacher only one page ahead of her pupils. The text in this case was Buddhist and Hindu scriptures, and H.P.B. had never been able to decide which of the two religions she preferred; this indecisiveness now led to serious problems.

Even though the Mahatmas described themselves as Buddhists, calling Gautama their "Lord" and acknowledging the Dalai Lama as their priestly king, they seemed to be teaching Buddhism in Vedantist terms. The confusion increased, even to Sinnett, who knew little about either religion, when Koot Hoomi began discussing the Hindu atman (individual soul) as being part of Brahman (universal oversoul), both of which Buddha had denied. On the other hand, Koot Hoomi told Sinnett that as philosophers and Buddhists, the Brotherhood denied there was any such thing as God, either personal or impersonal. God, "not an innate but an acquired notion," was a delusion based on ignorance. Then, Sinnett demanded, what *did* they believe in? "MATTER alone," replied K.H. The existence of matter was a fact, as was the existence of motion, but the idea of pure spirit as Being or Existence "is a chimera, a gigantic absurdity."[155] Sinnett, the ever-inquiring newspaperman, interrogated, dug, and whirled in bewildered circles at the hybrid philosophy being tossed his way in pamphlet-sized letters that became, as time went on, increasingly sloppy and sometimes very nearly illegible. When Patience remarked that the messiness made K.H. seem more human, H.P.B. paid even less attention to her penmanship.

Helena clearly developed her system as she went along, but, not being an omniscient Mahatma, she frequently stumbled into contradictions, then had to exercise great ingenuity to account for them. Even the name she devised for her system, Esoteric Buddhism, got her in trouble. Later she would claim that she had used the word *buddhist* as *buddhi,* wisdom or enlightenment, not in the generally accepted meaning of the word. Using English translations by scholars such as Rhys Davids, whom she professed to despise, she busily ransacked Buddhist scriptures and then went on to riffle the *Purānas* and the Upanishads with the wanton determination of a shopper hunting for unbruised fruit. No religion was truly sacred to her, certainly not Christianity with its heaven and hell, nor Hinduism, whose practitioners Mahatma M. once disparaged as "fools and babus, etc.," not even Buddhism, whose founder had disdained the supernatural, saying that "by this ye shall know that a man is *not* my disciple, that he tries to work a miracle" and who on his deathbed reputedly said, "I have not kept anything back."[156] Helena Blavatsky's emerging esoteric doctrines leaned heavily on knowledge she insisted the Buddha had kept back, and as for miracles, she had never been able to resist them.

To Henry, the opening weeks of 1882 were memorable for the number of phenomena that took place at the "Crow's Nest," but he preferred not to describe or even enumerate them in his memoirs, because he thought them obviously fraudulent and added touchingly, "I try to be honest."[157] But they were not done for his benefit. On December 28, Ross Scott and Minnie Hume had been married at Simla with the blessing of both H.P.B. and the Mahatmas, and had come to honeymoon at Theosophical headquarters. Helena had entertained great hopes for Scott, even promising that the Masters would repair his lame leg and perhaps take him on as an apprentice, and Koot Hoomi had endorsed the union in the hope of bringing Minnie's father into the Theosophic fold. Of course the Mahatmic matchmaking had taken place before H.P.B.'s less than pleasurable experiences with Allan at Simla. Now she discovered that Minnie was her father's daughter.

If Minnie had ever believed in Madame's phenomena, she certainly turned into a skeptic once she learned that the brooch she had given Scott found its way into her parents' flower beds. So when a Mahatma letter dropped on her husband's head in the dining room of the "Crow's Nest," neither of them took it seriously. They were not brash enough to call their hostess a fraud, but after their departure they apparently had no hesitation in telling all. H.P.B. professed to have not the slightest idea why the couple had turned against her and rationalized it by saying that Minnie was jealous of the hold she had over Scott. "She owes her husband *to the Brothers and me*," she too confidently declared to Sinnett. "What more natural than that she should traduce both the 'Brothers' and myself!"[158]

Her mood was not improved when she received a denigrating letter from Allan Hume in which he described the pamphlet he was preparing on Theosophy. His plan was first to denounce the Society as a sham and then, having demolished it, to answer all the objections he had raised in regard to the Brothers, adding slyly to H.P.B., "if there *are* Brothers."[159] She had no illusions about the form his answers would take, not when he could write caustic statements like the following:

> You, you dear old sinner (and wouldn't you have been a reprobate under normal conditions?) are the worst breach of all—your entire want of control of temper—your utterly un-Buddha and un-Christlike manner of speaking of all who offend you—your reckless statements form together an indictment that it is hard to meet—I have I think got round it. But though I may stop others' mouths, I personally am not satisfied.[160]

The more he investigated her theories, he went on, "the less they seem to hold water. The more they bear the look of contrivances thrown out on the spur of the moment to meet an immediate difficulty."[161] Nobody saw Helena more clearly than Hume, and it must have chilled her. Certainly, she did not want "friends" like Hume defending her. At the end of January she was temporarily diverted by a short journey with Olcott to Poona but on her return she again panicked over Hume and felt the need to exhume Master Koot Hoomi. "My Brother," he wrote Sinnett, "I have been on a long journey after supreme knowledge, I took a long time to rest."[162] However, he was pained to learn that fearful developments had taken place in his absence. "A cloud does lower over your path—it gathers about the hill of Jakko," in the person of none other than Allan Hume, who "is under a baleful influence and may become your enemy."[163]

Having covered herself for the coming storm with this prophetic warning, H.P.B. allowed herself to be sidetracked, this time into the antique furniture and art business. As a result of her Simla letter to Prince Alexander Dondou-koff-Korsakoff, the two of them had started a flirtatious correspondence, even exchanging photographs. Giving way to nostalgia that she usually managed to hide, possibly because she knew that she would never see Alexander again, Helena retraced for him the largely fictional story of her life since she had fled Russia. Then she went on to describe her present circumstances in terms that Olcott and the other residents of the "Crow's Nest" would not have recognized. She told Alexander that she lived in a Chinese pagoda equipped with "halls for meetings, libraries, laboratories for chemical and psychologi-cal experiments, etc." The reception hall of her personal quarters was usually thronged with "some fifty fools of all races"[164] waiting to speak with her. In spite of this hectic schedule, she was delighted to put herself at Alexander's service and when he asked for Indian furniture and curios, she promptly replied: "Write to me exactly what you want, what kind of furniture, and for what price,"[165] and proceeded to compose a two-page description of her own bookcases and tables, including the prices she had paid.

Filling Alexander's shopping list occupied some of Helena's spare time that year, but she soon came to regret her commitment, for he was exceedingly slow in reimbursing her. Still, the Prince was the tie to a lost past so precious, she would overlook even his scorn for the contact. When she came across a nasty item about herself in a St. Petersburg paper and realized the source had to be Alexander, she corrected him without rancor. She had not invented a new religion, as the paper claimed; on the contrary, she took credit for invent-ing nothing. "My belief is a complete lack of belief, even in myself . . . I believe ONLY in human stupidity."[166] But, in fact, human stupidity often failed her, witness Henry, whom she had come to regard as the most gullible of all. By now she must have intuited his changed feelings toward her because he was spending as little time as possible at the "Crow's Nest" and, when he was home, their relationship seemed strained. On February 17, he set out on a tour of North India and his fully-detailed memoirs describe lectures, meet-ings, and assorted dignitaries whom he had inducted into the Society. Helena had usually been content to leave this sort of tiresome barnstorming to him but now must have needed a change of scenery. At the end of March she temporarily assuaged her restlessness with a short excursion to Allahabad where she persuaded Djual Khool to "precipitate" a portrait of Master Koot Hoomi. Alfred Sinnett, marveling, had no way of knowing how closely K.H. physically resembled Madame's old spirit friend John King.

A week later she joined Olcott in Calcutta where Henry described them "busy as working bees, writing, receiving visitors, holding discussions with outsiders, and meetings of the new local Branch."[167] On the fourteenth of April he recorded in his diary the election of new officers for the Bengal Theosophical Society; at the bottom of the page, Mohini Mohun Chatterji is listed as Assistant Secretary. At the time, Mohini was a twenty-four-year-old Brahmin attorney and poet, a descendant of the Hindu reformer Raja Ram-mohun Roy and a relation of Debendra Nath Tagore, father of the celebrated poet. He was a slender youth with thick blue-black hair falling in waves to his shoulders and magnificent velvety eyes that normally held a gentle expression. There was no mistaking his intelligence, nor overlooking the almost perfect beauty that two years hence would set aflutter the smart young women of Paris and London.

H.P.B. had always collected promising young men as her disciples; some, like Ross Scott, failed her, but when she exercised her judgment carefully and selected more serious types like Damodar, she was amply rewarded. Nevertheless, at Calcutta she seems to have taken small note of Mohini Chatterji, no doubt because she was in hot pursuit of another young man whom she needed far more. For several months she had been eying a high-caste Telugu Brahmin, T. Subba Row, who had exhibited a lively initial interest in the Theosophical Society. In due course, they were corresponding regularly.

Although Subba Row belonged to a family of distinction, his uncle being prime minister to the Rajah of Pithapuram, he had showed no unusual intelligence or a bent for mysticism as a child. After studying law at Madras Presidency College, he joined the legal firm of Grant and Laing and became a pleader in the Baroda High Court. By the time he met H.P.B. his practice had grown lucrative and he was on the threshold of becoming a prominent attorney, perhaps, in time, a statesman. Slowly his interests were being diverted to philosophy, and he now began to feel that a storehouse of occult knowledge and Sanskrit literature were suddenly opening to him; he felt that his familiarity with the *Gita* and *Upanishads* was perhaps a karmic carryover from a previous life. Hence by twenty-five, Subba Row had become a brilliant classical scholar, but how this had happened was a mystery even to his own mother. To her questions, he only answered that he dare not discuss these secret matters with her.

Despite his reticence, H.P.B. managed to learn that he was a disciple of Shankaracharya, a south Indian sage. Subba Row was the perfect person to consult on the Mahatma letters, and she began to envision the youth as the gateway to deep secrets and genuine adepts she had not yet reached. Subba Row, however, was an extremely reserved young man and when she had pressed him for introductions, he backed off. "It is *almost impossible,* Madame, to induce any of these mystics to come before the public and clear the doubts which skeptics entertain as regards the reality of Yoga Vidya and the existence of Adepts."[168] H.P.B. rejoiced in finding someone to corroborate her stories of Indian adepts, and when Subba Row expressed a desire to meet her, she could hardly wait to take him on. For some time now, Henry had been intending to visit Madras Presidency and suddenly he found H.P.B., who had never shown much interest in organizing tours, most anxious to accompany him.

They were to embark on the nineteenth of April from Calcutta, but the SS *India,* Olcott wrote, "lay at the wharf all night taking in cargo and what with this awful din, the scorching heat of the cabins and the mosquitoes, one may imagine the kind of night we spent and the kind of temper H.P.B. was in the next morning!"[169] By this time Henry much preferred to travel without Helena, and for good reason.

Subba Row could not have been more gracious, delegating himself to bring out to the ship a party of Madras dignitaries and a large crowd of sightseers. Then they drove along the beach road to the suburb of Mylapore, where H.P.B. and Olcott were grandly installed in a private house. To Henry the visit seemed nothing less than a total success: some of the city's leading men rushed to join the Society on "a wave of enthusiasm,"[170] as he called it. Unfortunately H.P.B. had less success, even though she presented her most charming side to Subba Row, to the extent of having him initiated into membership in a private ceremony. Still, he did not reveal anything useful. Toward the end of the week, feeling more than a little exasperated, Helena invited him and sixteen other newly admitted members on a jaunt to the nearby holy city of Tiruvellum, the site of one of Southern India's oldest temples. It was said that great sages had once dwelled in the town and perhaps some still did, and possibly H.P.B. counted on meeting one of them lurking around. Her party was greeted at the station with music and flowers, but H.P.B. could barely restrain herself and rushed off to see the temple. She got as far as the inner sanctuary only to be stopped by Brahmin priests who demanded a surcharge of twenty-five rupees per head. "We felt so disgusted," said Olcott, "that we refused to go into the polluted shrine, and returned the same day to Madras."[171]

On May 3, Helena and Henry left Madras and embarked on an idyllic four-week journey by houseboat up the Buckingham Canal to Nellore and Guntur. For the first time in years they were alone together, with only Babula and the boat crew for company, and Henry remembered that they "had never been so closely drawn together." For Helena it was a time of comfortable seclusion, when the chaos of her ordinary existence could be put aside; K.H. did not pick up his pen, nor did Master M., and blessedly she was beyond the reach of her enemies. It did not matter that the boat was cramped or that in the tiny cabin there was barely room for their camp cots, two lockers, a lavatory, and a portable table that folded up and hung from the ceiling. At night as they glided along, the only sounds they heard were the occasional yelp of a jackal and the lapping of the water, and they smelled nothing but the wet rice fields. In the mornings when they scudded up to the bank, the coolies would build a fire to cook curry and rice, while Babula prepared "a capital breakfast" for Helena and Henry, after which Henry would go for a swim.

The days passed in euphoric quiet, with H.P.B. in a shabby wrapper sitting on the locker opposite Henry, smoking and daydreaming. "She was in good health and spirits," Olcott remembered, "and there was nothing to mar the charm of our companionship." At Nellore they disembarked to organize a branch society, climbed back on the boat, and went on to Padaganjam where they had to abandon their floating haven and take *jampan* chairs for the thirty-five-mile trip through dense forests to Guntur. The journey was tedious, the thermometer read a blazing-hot ninety-eight degrees in the shade, and the coolies kept up a staccato refrain that eventually jarred the nerves. Fording a river, their bearers stripped naked to their breech cloths; the water turned out to be so deep that the chairs had to be held over the bearers' heads. Henry recalled: "H.P.B. began shouting at me that these men would surely upset her. I shouted back that it didn't matter, as she was too fat to sink and I should fish her out."[172] To take her mind off her predicament, she continuously cursed Olcott and the coolies who could not understand a word she said. Reaching the opposite bank at last, she puffed furiously on a succession of cigarettes until she had recovered her amiability. Life was good then.

At Guntur, where the whole town population greeted them, they plunged into a roistering welcome. It was one of the few times in her life when reality matched Helena's fantasies. Writing to Prince Alexander, she could have described the scene unembroidered and it would have seemed extraordinary. But habit dies hard, and, with her customary exuberance, she transformed her *jampan* chair into "a golden palanquin," and added a few nautch girls and banners reading "Welcome revered Madame Blavatsky."[173] Everyone loved her, but in the midst of her exhilaration she suffered from an acute spasm of depression and wondered, "What is the good of all these triumphs?" Suddenly, for no obvious reason, she was engulfed by homesickness and shared it with the Prince. "Oh, my dear Prince," she lamented, "if I were 20 or 25 years younger . . . I would have made the conquest of India without spilling a drop of blood and I would have given it to the motherland." The torchlight parades and the crowds of cheering Hindus meant, after all, little to her; it was Russia she longed for but would never see again. "I will die here and my sinful flesh and bones will be burned on a funeral pyre and my ashes scattered to the breadth of the Aryavartas." Then, ashamed of her morbid self-pity, she added impishly, "Shall I send you a pinch?"[174]

For some time now, H.P.B. and Olcott had been talking about buying a permanent headquarters for the Theosophical Society at some place other than Bombay, whose heat and dampness Helena had come to dislike. Their Cingalese friends had made liberal offers of rent-free houses, but she agreed with Henry that Ceylon was too far removed from the mainstream and too backward for their purposes. Now, returning to Madras on May 30, she found several of their members urging her to come there. She could not have been more pleased, for it was of consummate importance to be within consulting distance of the elusive Subba Row. Still, she was guarded in her response and replied that she would only consider the idea if a suitable house could be found. Henry also reacted cautiously: they were low enough on money so that he was loathe to embark on the move without a financial commitment, by contribution or loan, from local members. Luckily, three members pledged two hundred and fifty rupees apiece.

Early the next day, in a whirlwind of enthusiasm, the two sons of Judge Muttuswamy Chetty began to scout available real estate and by afternoon had come up with a property that was going cheap in the suburb of Adyar. That very evening the brothers drove Helena and Henry out along the Bay of Bengal to Huddleston Gardens, a twenty-one-acre estate on the banks of the sluggish Adyar River. Entering the gate and starting up the long avenue of mango and banyan trees, H.P.B. was already enchanted. From a distance the graceful pillared mansion appeared to be made of white marble, and although it was really brick plastered white, its elegance could not be denied. In addition to the main house, the grounds also afforded two small riverside bungalows, a brick stable and coachhouse, storage buildings and a swimming pool. It was like a small village. Soobiah Chetty told her that the modest asking price of nine thousand rupees (about three thousand dollars at that time) was due to the recent opening of the railway between Madras and the foot of the Nilgiri Hills, which made the summer resort of Ootacamund only a day's ride away. Fashionable people who had once made their homes at Adyar were migrating to Ooty, as it was nicknamed, and were throwing their opulent estates on a bidderless market.

When the carriage pulled up to the house, H.P.B. clambered down and went straight inside, while the Chetty boys and Olcott inspected the riverside bungalows and the outbuildings. After tramping about the lower floor, she climbed up to a large tower-like room on the flat roof. From there she could see on the opposite bank of the river a little island connected to the mainland by a pink bridge. The air was alive with the beating wings of large flying foxes who swooped out from the city at sunset and sat feeding among the branches of the mango trees. Here she felt was a place she could be happy in, especially here in the roof room, which of course would be hers. Descending the stairs, she sent for the Chettys. "Soobiah," she smiled, "Master says buy this."[175]

Master did not show the way to find nine thousand rupees, however, and it was Olcott and the Madras Theosophical Society who had to mastermind the transaction. Not until November would the purchase be completed.

Back in Bombay just in time for monsoon season, Helena was greeted by a plethora of calamities. The least of them was a letter from Vera with the wholly unexpected news that their brother Leonid had been involved in a scandal and dismissed from his judgeship at Stavropol. Fortunately he had been acquitted at his trial but now could find no other position; according to Vera, he and his family were impoverished. In no way did Helena enjoy playing the supplicant, especially for the always distant Leonid, but she swallowed her pride and wrote immediately to Prince Alexander asking him for help. "Do this good deed and I will die in peace, blessing you and your family, and I will be ever your servant here and after death," a rash promise from one who did not believe in an afterlife. Three months later, horribly embarrassed when she learned that Vera had exaggerated the whole thing, she reported to Alexander that her brother was "a weathercock of the family of weathercocks! Don't bother about him."[176]

Of greater concern during the next three months were catastrophes affecting what she had come to regard as her family in India. Her biggest solace and promoter in the past two years had been Alfred Sinnett, not merely as her friend and Koot Hoomi's star pupil, but in his capacity as editor of the *Pioneer*. While every other English paper in India exhibited rabid hostility toward her, she could always count on the *Pioneer* for vindication. And if Sinnett sometimes balked, Koot Hoomi would step in to explain why such and such an article had to be published. However, Sinnett's zealous propagandizing on behalf of the Theosophical Society was growing offensive to the paper's owners, who warned him to exercise restraint; he was making the *Pioneer* look ridiculous, and consequently the circulation was beginning to drop. Against his own better judgment but on the advice of the Mahatmas, Sinnett ignored the warnings, and in August he was notified that when his contract expired in 1883, it would not be renewed.

Sinnett had not expected that his loyalty to the Masters would cost him his job and now, terribly distressed, rushed to H.P.B. demanding to know what the Mahatmas were going to do about his dismissal.

Momentarily taken back, Helena rattled off soothing answers similar to those she had spoonfed Olcott in New York: not to worry, the Mahatmas were not ungrateful people who abandoned their own in time of trouble. On the contrary, Sinnett could expect to be taken care of; perhaps a way might even be found for him to remain in India. And now she was faced with having to devise a solution.

After high-level decisions in Tibet and consultation with the generally inaccessible *Chohan* himself, Koot Hoomi advised Sinnett to found an English-language newspaper financed by Indian capital. Reminding him that he was no businessman, and the Brotherhood not a bank, he went on to conjecture that five lakhs of rupees (approximately $170,000) might be sufficient as a start. The money could be raised in no time from native princes and bankers, he suggested, then proceeded to tick off editorial suggestions.

Helena needed Sinnett in India more than he needed the Mahatmas, and after her initial scare, she calmed down and came up with what seemed the ideal solution. A Sinnett-run paper would be the media outlet she needed to get the Mahatmas the respect they deserved. "Their names have been suffi ciently dragged in the mud," she wrote Alfred. "They have been misused and blasphemed against by all the penny-a-liners in India. Nowadays people call their dogs and cats by the name of 'Koot-hoomi' . . ." That these sentences occurred in the middle of a letter *protesting* Alfred's publicity efforts on behalf of the Masters only indicates how H.P.B.'s manipulation of Sinnett really worked. Even her capitalized proclamation, "I DO NOT CARE

ABOUT PUBLIC OPINION,"[177] merely camouflaged her fear of ridicule. She cared nothing about herself, she insisted, only about the Masters whose names must not be desecrated. Since she was the Masters, this protestation was both true and false.

During that summer, rats ate her canary, and Helena was feeling particularly vulnerable, though one would not have suspected it from the restraint and lofty objectivity of the *Theosophist.* Any hope she had cherished of achieving respectability through the Arya Samaj was dead; Swami Dayananda had actually gone to the expense of printing handbills denouncing her and Henry as "atheists, liars and selfish persons"[178] who knew the art of clever conjuring but nothing of the Yoga Vidya. In an editorial comment she gently chided him as an "eccentric,"[179] but claimed she could take his brickbats philosophically for she had anticipated them.

She also appeared to take lightly Allan Hume's *Hints on Esoteric Theosophy,* in which her writings were termed crude, unenlightened, and beneath the criticism of real scholars; her Society was an excuse for talk instead of action; her personal motives amounted to "the love of notoriety—the desire to be known—to be *somebody* instead of *nobody.*"[180] In Hume's opinion, neither he nor any other Theosophist had learned one iota about psychic power or the hidden mysteries of nature as a result of his membership in the Society. Helena reserved her disgust for Sinnett's ears: "Oh Jesus son of the nun and uncle of Moses!"[181] she erupted. She had had enough of "the great Hume, the Mount Everest of intellect"[182] and if he wished to leave the Society, she wished him a speedy farewell. Koot Hoomi did not go quite so far, merely attributing Hume's barbs to jealousy. "Did I not warn you?" he reminded Alfred.[183]

Dayananda and Hume had been anticipated. What Helena had not glimpsed in her crystal ball was trouble from Charles Massey, president of the British Theosophical Society. There were a few people she had taken real pains to win, and Massey was one of them. How could she know that rascal Hurrychund Chintamon would go to London, strike up an acquaintanceship with Massey, and squeal that Madame and her Mahatmas were frauds? It was a piece of bad luck. Nonetheless back in the summer of 1879 she had taken precautions to counteract Chintamon by appealing to her old friends and helpers Mary Hollis Billing and her spirit guide "Ski":

My dear Good Friend:
Do you remember what Z [Ski] told or rather promised to me? That whenever there is need for it he will always be ready to carry any message, leave it either on Massey's table, his pocket, or some other mysterious place. Well now, there is the *most important need* for such a show of his powers. Please ask him to take the enclosed letter and put it into M.'s pocket, or in some other still more mysterious place. But he must not know it is Z.[184]

* * *

The enclosure was a Koot Hoomi letter that Massey eventually discovered tucked inside the pages of the Society's minute book. Since no one could conceive of how it got there, Massey concluded it must have traveled from Tibet to London supernaturally, and he was thrilled—for the moment. Before long local skeptics, in the persons of Hurrychund and Mary's husband, whispered that the Mahatma letter had arrived by steamer from India and had in fact been delivered by Mary herself. Pressed for the truth, she admitted her role and even showed Massey Madame's letter of instruction.

Apparently this experience had not totally disenchanted Massey, for he never confronted H.P.B. directly, but he was transformed from a believer into a needling critic. In the July 1882 issue of *Light*, a London Spiritualist weekly, he posed a question more embarrassing than anything Hume had come up with: Why did the Mahatmas teach the concept of reincarnation as one of the basic tenets of their philosophy when their messenger, Helena Petrovna Blavatsky, had contemptuously denied reincarnation five years earlier in *Isis Unveiled*? To jog Madame's memory, he quoted from page 351 of the first volume of *Isis*, in which she stated that reincarnation was not a natural rule but "an exception like the teratological phenomenon of a two-headed infant."[185] It happens, she had written, only in cases of abortion, infant death, or incurable idiocy, that is, when nature had not been able to produce a perfect human being. Massey mused whether Koot Hoomi was not, "as has been maliciously suggested, an alias for Madame Blavatsky."[186]

Until coming out to India Helena had displayed quite a vocal abhorrence of reincarnation, not only in *Isis* but in person and in letters to friends. But in India, where the idea was taken for granted and where no respectable Mahatma would have been caught denying it, she had quickly altered her opinion, suddenly finding reincarnation quite feasible. Unfortunately page 351 of *Isis* still had to be explained. In the first place, she replied to Massey in the *Theosophist*, *Isis* was not only incomplete and clumsy but teeming with errors; secondly, while writing *Isis*, she had not been permitted to teach reincarnation. Now she was. It was that simple.

To her annoyance, this reply to Massey brought a snide letter from Allan Hume suggesting it was a pity that the Masters had not copyedited *Isis* more carefully, and further that it was "a sin on their part" to have withheld important information. In any case, the Mahatmas cared nothing about accuracy and "in one week I could teach any ordinarily intelligent man, all, that in eighteen months, we all of us have succeeded in extracting from them."[187]

By September Helena felt drained. Weeks earlier her exhaustion had taken the form of boredom with her charade; she felt that "inner suffering is drying up the marrow of my spine" and merely longed for death. It seemed to her that she had been "a hundred times happier in the days when I was hungry and lived in a garret."[188] Suddenly everything that she had worked for seemed insignificant, all the important people she had won to her cause only "stupid little donkeys." Perhaps, she wrote Prince Alexander, "when I die and all the philosophy and miracles cease, then they will become more intelligent."[189]

Virtually all of the summer's crises she had faced alone; Henry was now back in Ceylon and the overworked Damodar had collapsed and been sent away to recuperate. By autumn Helena's psychic tensions were erupting in serious illness because when she consulted a physician she was given the unexpected news that she had Bright's disease. Horribly discouraged and frightened, she sat down to compose a deathbed farewell to Patience and Alfred (and mailed an almost verbatim copy of the letter to her sister):

> I am afraid you will have soon to bid me goodbye . . . This time I have it well and good—Bright's disease of the kidneys; and the whole blood turned into water with ulcers breaking out in the most unexpected and the less explored spots, blood or whatever it may be forming into bags *à la Kangaroo* and other pretty extras and *etceteras*.[190]

Bright's disease is a kidney disorder characterized by large amounts of fluid in the intercellular spaces of the body (edema) and by albumin in the urine. H.P.B.'s description of edemic kangaroo bags seems to suggest the hemorrhagic type of Bright's disease, which is essentially an inflammation of the capillary blood vessels in the filtering units of the kidney and is believed caused by poisons that have been formed by a bacterial infection elsewhere in the body. Or, possibly it was another variety of kidney disorder in which waste products accumulating in the blood cause swelling; but, without medical records, one can only speculate.

On top of this affliction, she told Sinnett, "I have become so stupidly nervous that the unexpected tread of Babula's naked foot near me makes me start with the most violent palpitations of the heart." Reading between the lines, it seems clear that Dr. Dudley recognized her anxiety and advised rest in less hectic surroundings. Perhaps he did say, as she wrote Sinnett, that she "can kick the bucket at any time in consequence of *an emotion*," as well as suggest she take a vacation, for that seems to be the point of the letter. "Boss [Master Morya] wants me to prepare and go somewhere for a month or so toward the end of September." He had sent a *chela* who would escort her somewhere, "where I don't know, but of course somewhere in the Himalayas."[191]

Toward the end of September H.P.B. left Bombay for north India. No special escort arrived to squire her to the Himalayas, but she was accompanied, or perhaps trailed, by a half-dozen Hindu Theosophists who had heard of *Upasika's* plans and tagged along in the hope of glimpsing a Mahatma.

For years she had dreamed of visiting Tibet, but even she was well aware of the impossibility of crossing the border. It is interesting to notice that now an element of reality creeps into her fantasies. She saw pictures of herself getting only as far north as Sikkim and being refused a visa by the British Foreign Office, then walking to the frontier between Bhutan and Sikkim, "a fast-flowing stream with a swinging bamboo bridge,"[192] where guards would turn her back. In her fantasy she waited until the lama from a Sikkim monastery arrived to salute her, offer buttered tea and gifts, and personally conduct her across the border to the monastery.

> I lived in a small house at the foot of the monastery walls . . . and I spent hours in their library where no woman is allowed to enter—a touching testimony to my beauty and my perfect innocence—and the Superior publicly recognized in me one of the feminine incarnations of the Bodhisattva, of which I am very proud.[193]

Three days later, she said, the monks carried her back to the border. This account is actually found in a letter to Prince Alexander, dated October 1, and written from Ghum, a town near Darjeeling, which she told him was in Sikkim.

In a letter written to Vera from Darjeeling, Helena makes no mention of lamas recognizing her as an incarnation of Buddha, but only relates that she was half dead when Master Morya carried her unconscious body to the mountains where he cured her in no time by means of mesmeric passes.[194]

Her romances took a slightly different twist in an October 9 letter to Alfred where she claimed that both M. and K.H. had met her in their physical bodies and whisked her away to a hideout in Sikkim:

> Oh the blessed two days! It was like the old times . . . The same kind of wooden hut, a box divided into three compartments for rooms, and standing in a jungle on four pelican's legs; the same yellow chelas gliding noiselessly; the same eternal 'gul-gul-gul' sound of my Boss's inextinguishable chelum pipe; the old familiar sweet voice of your K.H. (whose voice is still sweeter and face still thinner and more transparent), the same *entourage* for furniture—skins, and yak-tail stuffed pillows and dishes for salt, tea, etc.[195]

From available evidence, it seems that H.P.B. actually spent about six weeks in the vicinity of Darjeeling. The mountain town, seven thousand feet above sea level, was built in a series of steps hanging precariously on to the sides of the lower Himalayas, and on clear days it was possible to see Mount Everest, some a hundred fifty miles away. The bracing mountain air apparently had an invigorating effect on Madame's health, though her Indian entourage was not properly dressed for the mountains and most of them caught colds. She wrote eight or ten Koot Hoomi letters, some of them quite lengthy, but containing less occultism than personal gossip, warnings and ill-humored comments on Hume, Massey and other enemies. Constantly she was keeping one eye peeled for furniture, carpets and brocades for Prince Alexander. Passing through Allahabad, she had already sent on to him a box of bronze trinkets. Still, haggling over bargains was exasperating and she complained that "those pigs of Parsees, Banias, vendors, etc., have simply worn me out."[196]

She had followed her doctor's advice to get away, but it does not appear that she allowed herself much rest. On the contrary, in addition to the Mahatma letters, she was masterminding phenomena simultaneously in Darjeeling, Simla and Bombay, using several Hindus she had recently recruited as her assistants. For the miracles back home she had to depend on Emma, who apparently needed a good deal of encouragement.

My dear friend,
Be good enough, O sorceress of a thousand resources, to ask *Christofolo* when you see him to transmit the letter herewith enclosed by an aerial or astral way, or it makes no matter how. It is very important. My love to you my dear. I embrace you.

Yours faithfully,
LUNA MELANCONICA

I *beg you* DO IT WELL.[197]

Sometimes Emma did not do it well, and occasionally she did not do it at all. Although H.P.B. poured on the flattery, Emma had fallen into the distressing habit of making irreverent remarks about the Mahatmas to people around town, including a few Christian clergymen in the city. From Ceylon, Henry had to caution her politely against discussing religion with outsiders, no matter whom, "for it looks bad that one so intimately connected with us as yourself should be thought to be so totally at variance with the views and objects of the Society's founders. Pardon the plain-speaking of a friend."[198]

H.P.B. was contending with even more aggravation from the young men in her party, most of whom turned out to be totally undesirable as agents. But, in no position to be choosy, she was still obliged to use whoever came to hand. Usually her recruitment methods worked like this: the prospect would receive a letter from Koot Hoomi asking if he would like to serve the Brotherhood as a lay *chela*. Next would follow a description of the assignment: "The task is easy and there will not be much to do for either but *be silent*, and successfully play their parts. If the mission is accomplished, in return I will permit some of our secrets to be taught . . ."[199]

From Darjeeling, H.P.B. dispatched to Simla two particularly inept young men, Keshava Pillai, a police inspector whom she had enlisted while passing through Nellore the previous May, and Darbhagiri ("Babaji") Nath, a clerk in the Collector's office at Nellore. Babaji, whose real name was S. Krishnamachari or Krishnaswami, was a tiny man with a fondness for aliases. For a while he called himself Gwala K. Deb; apparently homeless, he attached himself to the "Crow's Nest" and called H.P.B. his guru, but also boasted that he had previously spent ten years with Master Koot Hoomi. As for Keshava Pillai, his ignorance made her laugh.

"What is your idea of the Masters?"[200] she had demanded of him.

They were, he replied, ancient *Rishis* who had never died and were now some seven-hundred-thousand years old; they had long green hair and lived in trees. On hearing this, Helena conscripted him at once.

Babaji and Pillai were to dress themselves in yellow robes and caps and hand-deliver letters from Master Morya to Sinnett, taking care to go nowhere near Allan Hume and Rothney Castle. That Sinnett did not see through this farce is truly remarkable. Babaji, having lost the money Helena gave him for traveling, had to borrow thirty rupees from Sinnett, and when an embarrassed K.H. returned the loan he lowered his Mahatmic dignity to call Babaji "a little wretch."[201] No doubt Helena called him a far stronger name. Of course Babaji and Pillai were hopelessly lost when Sinnett demanded they transmit an astral letter to K.H. in his presence. Having no talent for improvisation, they fled back to Darjeeling.

As compensation for these partly botched maneuvers, H.P.B. received the unexpected boon of a phenomenon she had not engineered. Traveling among her party was an unstable young clerk from Tinevelly who had taken a leave of absence after suffering a nervous breakdown; now S. Ramabadra Ramaswamier announced dramatically that he was going to "find the Mahatmas, or—DIE."[202] Thoroughly annoyed, Helena told him frankly she did not appreciate his following her and wished he would tend to his own business. On October 5, wearing a yellow pilgrim's robe and carrying an umbrella, Ramaswamier set off for Tibet. According to him, he managed to go farther than H.P.B. in her fantasy, ferrying across the Sikkim border by boat and continuing about twenty miles into the kingdom on foot.

Two days later, he returned to Darjeeling in a state of complete exhaustion, babbling a bizarre tale of having met Mahatma Morya, whom he had recognized at once, having seen him one evening in his astral body on the balcony of the "Crow's Nest." Helena knew it was really Christofolo, but Ramaswamier was convinced it was Morya in the flesh; after all, the encounter had taken place between nine and ten in the morning under a sky of bright sunshine. The Mahatma was wearing a fur-lined yellow robe, yellow Tibetan cap, short black beard and long black hair that flowed down over his shoulders; he spoke very little English and instead had addressed Ramaswamier in his native Tamil. The Master's advice was fairly sage: Ramaswamier must return to Darjeeling and serve *Upasika*.

According to Ramaswamier, Madame "scolded me for my rash and mad attempt"[203] to find the Mahatmas, but one can imagine how secretly pleased she must have been. Soon afterward, totally convinced, he wrote an account of his adventures ("How a Chela Found His Guru") for the *Theosophist*, adamantly proclaiming that "now that I have seen the Mahatma in the flesh, and heard his living voice, let no one dare say to me that the BROTHERS *do not* exist . . . I KNOW!"[204]

Little wonder that Helena often thought of people as donkeys.

IV

Adyar

Moving into the new headquarters at Adyar on December 19, 1882, Helena felt that she had reached the pinnacle of happiness and security. After the affluence of her childhood, circumstances had seen fit to plunge her into poverty and disgrace, but now, after some thirty-five years of wandering, she had clawed her way back up the heights. A few months earlier she had written to Prince Alexander, "I am now on the rise and *by God* I will remain there";[205] at the time it had not been true but now, unquestionably, it was. Like a maharanee she surveyed her little kingdom from the airy roof bedroom, sitting quietly, writing and gazing out at the sparkling Bay of Bengal. On rough days it roared and hurled itself about in wrath, "but when it is quiet and caressing there can be nothing in the world as fascinating as its beauty, especially on a moon lit night." She never tired of looking at the moon, which seemed twice as big and ten times as bright as European moons. Adyar, she told Nadyezhda, "is simply delightful. What air we have here; What nights! And what marvellous quiet! No more city noises and street yells."[206]

Henry, who had taken one of the riverside bungalows for himself, wrote in his diary that their beautiful new home "seemed like a fairy-place to us. Happy days are in store for us here."[207] Still, the remaining days of 1882 were filled with the usual petty annoyances of moving: unpacking, buying furniture, hiring servants, and making necessary repairs around the place, about all of which Helena refused to cope. It was Emma who attended to these matters, also supervising the servants, buying food and arranging for meals. In the midst of the bustle, on December 29, H.P.B. called Henry up to her room and "made me promise that if she should die, no one but myself should be allowed to see her face." He was instructed to sew her up in a cloth and have her cremated. Why she should suddenly have thought of death is a mystery; perhaps she was reacting to the past scare with Bright's disease recurring now that life was serene. In the evenings Helena and Damodar would wander with Olcott down to the shallows in the river where he would give them swimming lessons. Helena paddled about happily, while Damodar exhibited a terror of water, to which Henry replied that a would-be adept should be able to vanquish fear.

With the move into the new house, H.P.B. seems to have been on pleasant terms with everyone. When Babula asked permission to marry, Helena readily bestowed her blessing and added the girl to her household; she went out of her way to make the Coulombs feel content by giving them the other bungalow near the river. Realizing that she had been bad-tempered, even violent, toward Emma, she now felt a welling up of affection and went so far as to give her pocket money. About this time she also bought several small dogs, and Emma, who loved animals as much as Helena, was put in charge of them as well as of the stray curs that she collected and nursed.

Attempting to banish a past in which she had appeared ungrateful, Helena began calling Emma and Alexis by the pet names, Marquis and Marquise. She had indeed owed Emma a debt from the Cairo days and she now felt that she had repaid it a thousandfold: without her could her old friend have ever hoped to live in an Adyar mansion?

Another recent pleasure was the publication of *Mr. Isaacs*, an American novel in which one of the leading characters, Ram Lal, an adept Brother, had obviously been modeled after Master Koot Hoomi. Set in Simla, the story was a florid, romantic sketch of Anglo-Indian life blended with Oriental mystery, and in its pages could be found references to Madame Blavatsky and Colonel Olcott as mysterious but important figures in Simla society. The author, Francis Marion Crawford, was the stepson of the American painter Luther Terry and a nephew of Julia Ward Howe; once his family had been rich but had recently lost its fortune. In 1879 he came to India to study Sanskrit and ended by editing the Allahabad *Indian Herald* and writing his first novel. He had never met Madame Blavatsky, although he must have heard a great deal about her, especially from his uncle, Sam Ward, a member of the Theosophical Society and an intimate of H.P.B.'s. Ward told her that his nephew had miraculously written the book in less than four weeks, to which Helena replied that Koot Hoomi must have inspired him. Actually Crawford had deliberately turned to fiction as a means of supporting himself in his accustomed style; he would go on to write more than forty overstuffed romances that he produced at a breakneck rate of five thousand words a day.

Reviewing *Mr. Isaacs* in the *Theosophist*, Helena, having forgotten K.H.'s encouragement of Minnie Hume and Ross Scott, pointed out that adepts do not normally function as matchmakers. Nor, she continued, do brokenhearted lovers drown their grief by running off to Tibet and joining the Brotherhood. Still, she felt extremely flattered: "We should nevertheless thank Mr. Crawford for one favour—he helps to make our Brothers conceivable human beings, instead of impossible creatures of the imagination. *Ram Lal* walks, talks, eats, and—gracious heavens!—rolls and smokes cigarettes."[208]

At the end of January, 1883, headquarters was honored by a royal visitor, the Thakur of Wudhwan, whom Henry had requested to bring only a few servants. When he arrived with nineteen in tow, Henry, stuck with more people than space in which to sleep them, could not help chastising the Maharajah, who expressed surprise and said he *had* brought only a small retinue. Usually he traveled with a hundred. When H.P.B. had last accepted the Thakur's hospitality, the previous year, she had sustained a moment of real horror at the railway station at Wudhwan: one of her disciples, a blue-eyed Englishman who called himself Moorad Ali Beg, had snatched a sword from a Sepoy and tried to kill her, shrieking that she and her Mahatmas were devils. She realized that the incident was not the Thakur's fault, for Godolphin Midford, alias Moorad Ali Beg, was most probably insane, and now she outdid herself to repay her guest in grand style.

In February Henry left on a tour of Bengal, one of several long trips he had planned for the year. In his memoirs he would think back to 1883 with poignancy, recalling that he traveled more than seven thousand miles, established forty-three new branches, and became a vegetarian; he thought that it was probably the happiest and most successful twelve months of his life. Helena, for once, was content to remain in one spot, refusing to partake of Henry's new diet; she still loved her eggs swimming in grease.

At that time of the year the weather in Madras was sublime. At night, it was warm enough to sleep on the veranda or on the roof with only a thin covering, and during the day, the quality of the light made the compound inexpressibly beautiful. The dark green palms, the intense blue of sea and sky, the wide stretches of sandy beach where the Adyar flowed into the Bay of Bengal were a source of profound pleasure to H.P.B., while the house itself could not have been brighter or more cheerful. During the days the roof terrace rang with the sounds of hammering and sawing because a troop of masons and carpenters had been brought in to remodel H.P.B.'s quarters under Alexis Coulomb's supervision. One corner of her large room was curtained off as sleeping quarters, and the rest turned into a sitting room; outside, on the northwest corner of the terrace, a kitchen had been installed so that she might have her meals prepared whenever the mood struck her. Olcott, grumbling about extravagance, complained that her personal expenses outran the maintenance of the entire compound. Resentful of his imputations, Helena felt that through her writings she contributed to the upkeep of the establishment and should be allowed a few luxuries. And there were certain expenses involved in arranging the phenomena that she could not disclose to him.

Apart from the renovation of her suite, she was having Alexis build what she called an Occult Room. Ever since the first night at Huddleston Gardens, her disdain for the trappings of religion notwithstanding, she had envisioned a special chamber in which she might erect a shrine to the Mahatmas. The addition of the Occult Room, built against the west side of Helena's room, was no small task, as it involved removing the north window and transforming the south one into the only door to the room.

Helena dedicated herself to working with Alexis on the design of the shrine itself, a cedarwood cupboard lacquered black to look like ebony. About four feet in width and height and twelve to fifteen inches in depth, it was to be made with three sliding panels at the back, which would be invisible to the casual observer. Not until much later did Helena, under pressure, concede the existence of the panels and even then claimed that their sole purpose was to facilitate dismantling for traveling purposes. However, since the rest of the shrine was of solid construction, it is difficult to understand the advantages in merely removing portions of the back. In any event, once the drawing was completed, she gave it to the Madras cabinetmaking firm of Duchamps.

By late February or early March, the finished cabinet was delivered and hung against the former north window of Helena's bedroom. The window was no longer visible because part of it had been filled in with brick and plaster and the small opening that remained was hidden by the shrine on one side of the wall, and by a wardrobe on Helena's side. If anyone wondered about the window, they were supposed to assume it had been boarded up.

Later, up until as recently as 1963, interested parties would attempt to reconstruct the relative positions of the shrine and wardrobe. Floor plans would be drawn, secret passageways hypothesized, wall thicknesses estimated, theories and counter-theories advanced in such dizzying profusion that one quickly becomes mired in a quicksand of so-called evidence. The Theosophists' explanation that the hidden opening eventually discovered between the two rooms was made after Madame Blavatsky went to Europe is possible, of course, but unpersuasive, since it violates common sense by implying that the shrine apports were genuine. Granted, common sense is not always an appropriate yardstick in psychical matters but it is the preferred solution. "The common sense rule of presumption in scientific logic," William James once stated, "is never to assume an unknown agent where there is a known one, and never to choose a rarer cause for a phenomenon when a commoner one will account for it. The usual is always more probable."[209] There is no good reason for supposing that the sole purpose of the shrine was anything other than a means of facilitating H.P.B.'s phenomena, mainly as a mailbox for Mahatma letters, although other gifts from the Masters were also slipped in through the back door.

Once the shrine arrived from Duchamps, Alexis personally undertook its installation; it rested on a shelf, but its chief support consisted of two thick iron wires attached to hooks near the ceiling. The wall behind the shrine was covered with white glazed calico while the other three walls of the room were tacked with red-and-white striped calico; the space around the shrine was enclosed by muslin curtains that could be drawn aside when anyone came to worship. The decor, Helena's creation, seems to have been immensely charming, and the feeling in the room was one of gaiety instead of the usual religious sobriety.

As the winter wore on, Helena busied herself with the *Theosophist* and her Mahatma correspondence, which was changing almost imperceptibly in its character and tone. Rarely did Koot Hoomi bother with the metaphysical treatises that had reflected H.P.B.'s higher self. Now the letters were chiefly notable for their observations of persons and events, the commentary frequently malicious, especially so coming from a Buddhist supposedly following the noble eight-fold path and practicing right speech. Sinnett had plans to incorporate the Mahatma's more recent teachings into a book and call it *Esoteric Buddhism*, which K.H. thought an excellent idea; but when Alfred suggested going to Darjeeling or Sikkim and meeting the Master face to face, he was gently dissuaded and his plan rejected as being "simply impracticable. The time has not yet come."[210]

Alfred's request reflected the ups and downs in his life then. His position at the *Pioneer* had grown intolerable and his prospects for establishing a new paper, to be called the *Phoenix* were bleak, since not one rupee of capital had thus far been raised. In February, months before his contract with the *Pioneer* was due to expire, he suddenly resigned, notifying Helena that he and his family would be visiting England; he had every intention of returning and promised to take no other position for a year. En route to London, they stopped for several weeks at Adyar where Alfred began the writing of *Esoteric Buddhism*. It seemed to him the perfect situation, since whenever he had questions for the Mahatmas, he could easily drop a request into the shrine and receive a reply almost immediately.

By the time Colonel Olcott returned from Bengal on May 25, it appeared that the shrine was in good working order: already it had processed Alfred's letters, a gift for Patience, and a string of encouraging notes for the Hindus who came to prostrate themselves before the curtained cupboard. Eager to show off her contrivance, Helena decided to arrange a special event for Henry's homecoming and sent Emma into town to purchase four Chinese vases, two small and two large. M. Faciole and Co. did not, evidently, have the vases in stock but offered to obtain them from Assam and Co. The shop gave Emma a receipt, dated May 25, for thirteen rupees (seven rupees for the larger pair of vases, six for the smaller).

The next day Helena escorted Olcott up to the Occult Room and opened the door to the shrine. Inside, draped with yellow silk, lay framed portraits of Morya and Koot Hoomi, and a silver bowl. The pungent aroma of incense filled the room. She would not be surprised, she told him, if the Mahatmas had left a token of their affection for him, as well as a welcoming note. The shrine doors closed, then reopened, and of course Henry found his note with a Chinese vase.[211] According to Emma Coulomb, it was Henry who then wondered if the vase could be "doubled." "Madame asked 'mentally' the permission of the Mahatma on duty," Emma said, and after obtaining it, the colonel was allowed to make a few mesmeric passes. When the cupboard was opened, "Lo! another vase was there."[212] That night Henry wrote in his diary, "May 26th. Fine phenomenon. Got pair of tortoise-shell and lacquer vases with flowers in a cabinet a moment before empty."[213] It felt good to be appreciated.

Madras in the summer was not so pleasant as Madras in winter. Toward the end of June, when the thermometer in the compound read a hundred twenty-eight degrees in the shade, the west wind began to blow at sunrise and howled incessantly until late afternoon; Helena was told that it kept right on blowing until the end of August. Protective measures had to be taken: all the doors and windows facing the wind were covered with thick *tattis* or mats, the chinks stopped up and even the most minuscule openings stuffed with cotton wool. But still the wind managed to infiltrate the books and manuscripts until the papers on Helena's desk rolled themselves up into tiny tubes. If the sofas and chairs in her room were not beaten every hour, they were soon covered with a layer of dust three-quarters of an inch thick.

For this reason, fashionable people began leaving in March for Ootacamund, the hill station in the Nilgiri Mountains. "I also decided to leave," Helena wrote, "but not in the spring; it was already the middle of July and the West-wind had had enough time to dry me to the marrow of my bones." More to the point, it was not until early July that she received a welcome invitation from Maj.-Gen. and Mrs. Henry Rhodes Morgan and their eight children to summer at Ooty on their tea-and-coffee plantation. The Morgans had become Theosophists and Helena liked them very much, especially Mrs. Morgan, a cultivated and intelligent woman who ran the plantation and also had written a book, *Witchcraft on the Nilgiri*. On the seventh of July, "half dead with heat, I rapidly packed my bags." Keys to the Occult Room were entrusted to Emma, instructions for the magazine given to Damodar, farewells made to Babaji, Ananda Charloo and a dozen other Indians now making their home in the compound. Despite Babula's protestations that he wanted to stay behind with his wife, the two of them boarded a train at 6 P.M., arrived the next noon at Metopolam in the foothills of the Nilgiris, and from there began the trip up to Ooty in "an abominable box on two wheels covered with a linen roof." The *tongas* on the road to Simla, Helena thought, were like royal compartments compared to her carriage, which reminded her of "a kennel where the dogs are kept during a voyage," nor was she reassured at the sight of "two miserable worn-out nags" pulling the conveyance.

The journey was not without incident: a half hour after they departed, one of the horses fell and the carriage tumbled into a ditch, the single casualty being Helena's dress, which was ripped in the accident. To make matters worse it began to rain. "My cab was soon transformed into a bathtub with shower," she recalled, adding that the temperatures soon began to plunge and

"I was freezing in my fur coat." But she was not seriously grumbling, for the brisk air, impregnated with the perfume of violets and pine, was delicious after the swelter of Madras. She arrived in Ooty on a Sunday evening, just as people were returning from evening church service, emerging shaken and disheveled from her carriage with her trunks "half broken and soiled with mud." That night, "I trembled with cold under my blankets and had to have a fire during the whole night."[214]

But Ooty was worth the climb; it had all Simla's benefits with one special advantage: this time she was a bonafide celebrity. Although she was embarrassed by the Morgans' unrelenting concern for her comfort, she could not help wallowing in the plethora of invitations to receptions, dinner parties and balls, savoring the delight of being "lioness of the day." To Sinnett in London, she could not resist the urge to brag:

> My graceful, stately person, clad in half Tibetan half night-dress fashion, sitting in all the glory of her Calmuck beauty at the Governor's and Carmichael's dinner parties; H.P.B. positively courted by the aide-de-camps! Old 'Upasika' hanging like a gigantic nightmare on the gracefully rounded elbows of members of the Council, in pumps and swallow tail evening dress and silk stockings smelling brandy and soda enough to kill a Tibetan Yak!![215]

To Sinnett's rather forlorn but insistent queries about the status of the *Phoenix*, she showed her impatience by replying airily, "You ask me, dear, . . . And how can I know!"[216] Even Koot Hoomi, she added, had given up in disgust and despair. She knew that the paper would never become a reality and regretted ever mentioning the idea. In Ooty, she wanted to relax, banish cares and enjoy herself for a change.

It took Helena only a few days to settle into a routine. In the mornings, when puddles in the road were covered with thin ice, she wrapped herself in her fur coat, settled in near a blazing wood fire and began to write articles about the Blue Mountains and its native tribes. The series would appear in Russia first as a series of newspaper articles and later as the book *The People of the Blue Mountains*; it would be probably her finest descriptive writing. Later in the day, when it had warmed up, she would drive around the lake or up into the hills famous for their lilies, heliotrope, masses of forget-me-nots, and cabbage roses that climbed up to the roofs of the houses. "Lord, what flowers!" she wrote her family in Russia. "I have not seen anything like them in my life . . . And all the hills are covered with raspberries and strawberries, blackberries also, each as big as your cherries." Everything about Ooty enchanted her; the mushrooms were "delicious" and even the boa constrictors "also are beautiful."[217]

Each morning the European residents gathered at the post office for the daily ritual of mail distribution. "When the post has come in," observed one sharp-tongued Englishwoman, "the excitement of the day is over for most people in Ootacamund."[218] For Helena, the suspense was just beginning, since it was by mail that she kept tabs on Emma and made sure the shrine continued to produce phenomena while she was three hundred seventy miles away. "It's just post time my dear," she scribbled to Madame Coulomb, "I have only an instant . . . Yes, let Srinavas Rao prostrate himself before the *shrine* and whether he asks anything or not I beg you to send him this reply by K.H. for he expects something. *I know what he wants.*" Srinavas Rao was a judge of the Court of Small Causes in Madras.

When another gentleman was expected to call at Adyar bearing a letter for K.H., she made sure he would not leave without a suitable reply. "In case he should do so here is Christofolo's answer. For God's sake arrange this and we are triumphant. I embrace and salute you." It was Emma she had come to trust and depend upon, but, naturally, the woman could not be expected to think of everything. H.P.B. is constantly reminding her of details: tell Damodar not to skimp on incense for the shrine because "it is very damp and it ought to be well-incensed"; try to see that phenomena occur before a larger audience "than our domestic imbeciles only." Helena saw little point in wasting perfectly good phenomena on the already converted.

At the beginning of August, when General Morgan informed her he was going to Madras for a few days on business, H.P.B. urged him to stay at Adyar; he thought it too far from town but said he would certainly go out to see the famous shrine. There was not the slightest doubt in her mind that the General would expect a phenomenon, "for he told me so," she wrote Emma. Probably he would put a question in the shrine, although he might be content merely to look at it. Either way, she wanted to make sure he left satisfied and impressed upon Emma that he "is worth his weight in gold. For the love of God, or of any one you please, *do not miss* this opportunity for we shall never have another."[219] The opportunity was, of course, her absence from the scene of the phenomenon.

Arriving in Adyar on the thirteenth, General Morgan was ushered into the locked Occult Room by Madame Coulomb, who opened the double doors of the shrine so clumsily that a china saucer sitting inside crashed to the floor. He remembered Emma reacting with horror, murmuring that Madame would be angry, as it was one of her favorite pieces, then scooping up the shards into a cloth and placing them in the shrine in a silver bowl. When the general helpfully tried to suggest that the saucer might be glued back together, Alexis Coulomb went off to find mastic, and someone, probably Morgan himself, remarked that the Mahatma might be willing to repair the dish. "Hardly had I uttered this," he recalled, "when Damodar said, 'There is a message.' " Inside the shrine, they found a letter from Koot Hoomi, reading "the mischief is easily repaired,"[220] accompanied by the broken saucer miraculously made whole. According to General Morgan, the entire episode took less than five minutes.

Later that same day, a weary Emma made a full report to Madame Blavatsky on the success of the saucer phenomenon, but a note of disgust had crept into her letter: "My Dear Friend, I verily believe I shall go silly if I stay with you."[221] The Adyar Saucer Incident, as it came to be known in Theosophical history, is chiefly notable for two reasons: it marked a subtle turn in Emma's readiness to cooperate with H.P.B., and it is also the first indication that Damodar had crossed from Mahatmic dupe to confederate.

By late August, Henry Olcott had returned from a two-month visit in Ceylon sporting a newly grown beard "down to the seventh rib,"[222] H.P.B. noted, and flowing hair to match, and he joined her at Ootacamund for a short holiday. It was clear, however, that he did not take to Ooty social life so zestfully as did Helena, for he continually harped on the work to be done at Adyar; annoyed, she contemplated staying on without him and even warned Emma to bury the key for the Occult Room since she knew he would examine the shrine if he returned alone. At the last minute she decided to accompany him. The weather had turned chilly and she caught "a most fearful cold,"[223] necessitating hot water bottles for her feet at night and layers of shawls and blankets during the day. Probably she developed the infection as a result of the thirty-two-degree difference in temperature between Ooty and Coimbatore, their first stop on the way home, but it does not seem to have incapacitated her in any way. In a bubbly letter she announced that, unless she heard from Emma to the contrary, she was going to buy her a French silk dress at Pondicherry as well as a suit for Alexis. She also announced Alexis's appointment as the Society's Librarian. Emma was instructed to buy him a desk and bookcase at Faciole's and, while she was there, to pick out two or three new sofas for the veranda, plus several other pieces of furniture. Altogether H.P.B. grandly authorized Emma to spend up to three hundred rupees; it was secondhand shopping binges like this that were dismaying Olcott.

To be sure, Helena's idea of making Alexis librarian was absurd, although it was intended purely as a gesture. Always generous to her friends, she demonstrated her fondness by showering them with gifts and she ended the letter with a touching admission of her feelings for Emma: "Truly, I love you. You are a *true* friend."[224]

On Sunday, the twenty-third of September, she returned home to find Headquarters in a shambles. During her absence, Damodar had continued to put out the magazine but correspondence had gone unanswered and manuscripts submitted for publication lay unopened. Damodar, terribly overworked, was hardly to blame, but she felt disappointed that so little had been done. When Sinnett reproved her for poor management, she snapped self-righteously that, unlike some people she knew, Olcott and herself began their day "at *five* in the morning with candle light and end it sometimes at 2 A.M. We have no time for lawn tennis as you had, and clubs and theatres and social intercourse."[225] As she had just returned from three months of whirligig living, this was harshly unfair as well as inaccurate, but it no doubt reflected her general distress. On her return to Adyar she had been confronted by the annoying obligation to defend Master Koot Hoomi on a charge of plagiarism.

While H.P.B. was being lionized at Ootacamund, the retired New York school superintendent named Henry Kiddle was deciding to pursue a matter that had been puzzling him for more than a year. The previous summer, while reading Alfred Sinnett's *Occult World*, he had been greatly surprised to find in one of Koot Hoomi's letters a passage taken almost verbatim from a speech he himself had made. The address was first presented at a Spiritualist camp meeting at Lake Pleasant, Massachusetts, in August, 1880, and was published the same month in the *Banner of Light*. Kiddle immediately wrote to Sinnett through his publishers, but after receiving no response, he decided to tell all in a letter to the English Spiritualist paper, *Light*. While a fairly well-known Spiritualist and president of the American Spiritualist Alliance, Kiddle does not seem to have been in the least anti-Theosophist; he was merely bewildered: "As Mr. Sinnett's book did not appear till a considerable time afterwards (about a year, I think) it is certain that I did not quote, consciously or unconsciously, from its pages. How, then, did it get into Koot Hoomi's mysterious letter?"[226] How indeed.

For the convenience of its readers, *Light* published in parallel columns the two passages:[227]

KIDDLE'S LECTURE, August 15, 1880.
Ideas rule the world; and as man's minds receive new ideas, laying aside the old and the effete, the world advances. Society rests upon them; mighty revolutions crumble before their onward march. It is just as impossible to resist their influx as to stay the progress of the tide, etc.

MAHATMIC LETTER, December 10, 1880.
Ideas rule the world; and as man's minds receive new ideas, laying aside the old and effete, the world will advance, mighty revolutions will spring up from them, creeds and even powers will crumble before their irresistible force. It will be just as impossible to resist their influence when the time comes as to stay the progress of the tide, etc.

This time Sinnett answered promptly with a letter to *Light*, explaining that Kiddle's initial query had been lost during his move back to England. Aside from this flimsy excuse, he could contribute little to clarify the event except to promise to check back with Koot Hoomi. Of course, he remarked, "to obtain further explanation of this mystery from India will take time"[228] but he felt confident it could be straightened out.

H.P.B.'s first inclination was to ignore Kiddle, and in fact, she chose not to respond to *Light* personally, allowing Henry to write the paper that he did not think the accusation "of much consequence."[229] This time, Helena concurred, for she was confident that few people would seriously believe a Mahatma could plagiarize from a nobody like Kiddle. The episode would surely be forgotten in a few weeks, and, meanwhile, the less said about it the better.

Unfortunately, neither H.P.B. nor Henry realized the excitement that Kiddle's charge was causing in London occult circles. Arthur Lillie, a Buddhist scholar, recalled meeting the editor of *Light* in Jermyn Street one day.

"Have you heard the news?" Stainton Moses asked him excitedly. "The Blavatsky bubble has burst."[230]

The bubble had not actually burst, but it had received a pinprick. It would be another two months before H.P.B. accepted the fact that the Kiddle unpleasantness would not dissipate by itself; some explanation would be necessary. Writing to Sinnett on November 17, she sputtered, "K.H. *plagiarised* from Kiddle! Ye gods and little fishes." If those "fools" and "Sadducees" in London knew what it took to dictate a precipitation at a distance of three hundred miles, they would not be so idiotic as to hurl accusations at an adept. "Plagiarise from the *Banner of Light*!! that sweet spirits' slop-basin—the asses! K.H. blows me up for talking too much—says He needs no defence and that I need not trouble myself." Several lines were erased and a comment "precipitated" in Koot Hoomi's handwriting: "I WILL TELL YOU ALL MYSELF AS SOON AS I HAVE AN HOUR'S LEISURE."[231]

Not until December did the Mahatma find the hour's leisure, and then his explanation seemed remarkably glib. "The solution is so simple and the circumstances so amusing, that I confess I laughed when my attention was drawn to it . . ."[232] No doubt he had picked up the quotations from Mr. Kiddle's speech in the astral light currents and stored them in his mind. As for the letter in question, he went on to say that it had been dictated just as he had returned from a forty-eight-hour journey on horseback, and he recalled being half-asleep at the time; moreover, he had mentally dictated it to a novice *chela* inexperienced in "psychic chemistry" and when the young man asked if K.H. would like to check it for accuracy, he had answered, "Anyhow will do, my boy—it is of no great importance if you skip a few words."[233] Now, having investigated the matter thoroughly, Koot Hoomi was prepared to supply the true text of his dictation, which turned out to be precisely the opposite in meaning as Mr. Kiddle's speech and his own original letter to Sinnett.

Although this was the best H.P.B. could do, it did not prove satisfactory to such important English Theosophists as Charles Massey and Stainton Moses, who submitted their resignations to the Society more in amusement than indignation.

In spite of Koot Hoomi's studied indifference, Helena felt secretly shaken. To be sure, her friends had rallied during the crisis; even the long-neglected William Judge had written a supportive letter to the *Religio-Philosophical Journal*, and Henry of course had blithely dismissed the brouhaha as a tempest in a teapot. At least, he appeared to be undisturbed. Helena could not always be sure about Henry, who needed periodic injections of reassurance about the Masters and she feared that a few ungerminated seeds of doubt may have lodged in Henry's mind as a result of the Kiddle business. What she needed was some fresh demonstration of the Masters' reality, but at the moment she could think of nothing sufficiently startling.

At any rate, it was all she could do to cope with daily life at the compound. The house was constantly full of people and even though she enjoyed having company, it occasionally jangled her nerves. Soobiah Chetty, to name only one, insisted upon exploiting the Adyar facilities. Since he spent every night there, Helena felt justified in occasionally commandeering his services. She had once given him a twelve-page manuscript to copy, and, he recalled, she "looked at it, crumpled it, and threw it into the waste-basket. She was in a rage." Apparently it did not occur to her to tell Chetty what he had done wrong.

Not until the next day did he realize that he had written on both sides of the paper, at which time he redid it. Madame did not apologize for her rotten temper and although Chetty felt that she treated him harshly, he knew that she treated everyone badly when in one of her moods. "Madame," he asked one day when she seemed amiable, "you preach control of temper, but you go into outbursts now and then."

Helena brushed off the criticism. "Soobiah, that is my loss and your gain. If I didn't have that temper, I should have become an adept by this time."[234]

Aside from the Hindus who camped at Adyar, there were frequent European visitors to Madras who drove out to meet Madame Blavatsky. Now an international figure, she received them on the veranda, fed them dinner and witty conversation, and sent them on their way. The experience with William Tournay Brown, however, was different. Brown arrived in late September with letters of introduction from Alfred Sinnett, informing her that he had heard of the Christlike life she was leading for the benefit of her fellow men and had traveled to India solely to meet her.

A nervous twenty-seven-year-old Scotsman from Glasgow, Brown had graduated from law school but never practiced owing to delicate health.[235] To be more precise, he suffered from periods of severe mental illness, possibly dementia, and had spent most of his adult life traveling in the United States and Canada, where he had sought help for his problems. Earlier that year, in London to consult a homeopathic doctor, he had met Sinnett and joined the Theosophical Society, and then, later, suddenly in August, 1883, decided that he must meet Madame Blavatsky in person, hoping she might provide relief for his instability. He brought with him a middle-aged Irish woman, Sarah Parker, whose fare to India he had partially or fully paid, and who was a Theosophist and a friend of H.P.B.'s old friend Emily Kislingbury. Hospitable as always, Helena welcomed them both. Brown impressed her as "a fine young fellow" and Mrs. Parker as "a lunatic in many things but no better, sincere, truthly, honest woman ever breathed in an Irish carcase." A week later Helena changed her mind in a hurry about Sarah Parker, who drove her wild by hanging over Damodar and the other Indians in the *Theosophist* office and crooning, "Oh, I am enjoying their magnetism—it is so pure!!" When Brown received a Mahatma letter and she did not, Sarah informed H.P.B. that the Masters were "ungrateful curs." Outraged, Helena had a few choice names for her, writing Sinnett that she was "an ungrateful, vain, selfish, ridiculous old mare."[236]

What exasperated her most about Brown and Parker was that they seemed to despise each other. Every time they met, they quarreled, always bickering at the dining table, until H.P.B. finally stopped coming down to meals. When Brown asked permission to join the colonel who was then touring in the vicinity south of Bombay, Helena gladly "packed him off to Olcott." When Parker came down with jaundice and abruptly announced that she would be moving on to Calcutta, Madame could not have been more relieved, although at the last minute she felt sorry for her and wrote letters of introduction to several Calcutta Theosophists.

In late October, still trying to round up money for the *Phoenix*, H.P.B. spent several days in Bombay on a fishing expedition for Koot Hoomi's newspaper; she had received an invitation to visit Maharajah Holkar of Indore, but when practically on his doorstep, she was refused an audience, receiving instead two hundred rupees to cover the expense of trekking back across India. "Holkar—fiasco," she wrote tersely to Emma. "I dare say he was afraid . . . Damn him."[237] At Bombay, she gratefully accepted the hospitality of the Flynn family and settled down for a two-day stay with, as she put it, "nice people."[238] When Olcott and Brown came into the city for a reunion, Flynn, a government translator, gave a dinner party and invited fifty local Theosophists. One of the Flynn children, Mary, who was just recovering from smallpox, seemed to be generally unstable. According to her father, she had become so taken with Madame Blavatsky that she wanted to join her at Adyar. When Flynn had refused, she had talked about suicide and at night gone out walking barefoot in the mud. When Flynn begged Helena to take the girl back to Adyar, for a month or so, she shrugged and agreed. As she told Emma, "He gives her plenty of money for her pocket expenses and she eats hardly anything."[239] Helena was observant enough to spot a neurotic when she met one, and she could not have helped noticing that a certain percentage of her converts were undeniably high-strung in one respect or another. Although one supposes she preferred dealing with healthy people, she did not go so far as to reject the crazies; on the contrary, part of her genius was in realizing how they might be useful to her.

Olcott, Brown and Damodar headed for Jubbulpore; H.P.B. with Mary Flynn and Babula started toward Madras, but on the way stopped at Poona to see Judge N. D. Khandalavala, who had guaranteed Helena an introduction to a wealthy industrialist, Jacob Sassoon, a man whom Helena thought of as "the happy proprietor of a crore of rupees." Hopes high, she accepted dinner and breakfast invitations from Sassoon, who announced that not only was he anxious to join the Society, but also was prepared to pay off the Adyar mortgage. Of course, he wanted a return on his investment, and if only he might witness a miracle or two, he would be reassured about the Mahatmas' existence. H.P.B. gave it a try but Sassoon, unimpressed by the phenomena, kept his rupees. Nothing seemed to go right at Poona. When, for four days Babula cried and pleaded to be sent home to his wife, Helena finally gave in and let him go. Next, a dress for which she had paid twenty-six rupees literally fell apart and "I just escaped coming home quite naked."[240] Nevertheless, the trip was worthwhile because it provided her with an unexpected inspiration: at Bombay she had had a chance to observe William Brown more carefully. Ever since his arrival in India he had been begging her to suggest some way in which he might help the Mahatmas; now she saw exactly how William Brown could serve.

By the middle of November, Henry Olcott was toiling his way through the Punjab in a peculiar combination of Anglo-Indian pomp and American Yankee camping. His party of six included his secretary and bearer, William Brown and his bearer, and Damodar. They traveled by rail and at each stop would hire a dozen coolies to carry their beds, chairs, food and water, as well as Henry's desk and official papers, then set up their tents. It was a primitive way of touring, but Henry hated to waste the Society's money on hotels and, in any case, enjoyed outdoor life. Occasionally a local raja would insist on their accepting his hospitality, and then elephants would be sent to escort the Theosophists to a few days of free and unbridled luxury. Henry always counted his rupees.

On November 19, at Lahore, they were greeted by local Theosophists and escorted to a camp of six tents and four open pavilions that had already been prepared for them on a plain north of the city. Throughout the day, the camp was mobbed with visitors, and Henry addressed an immense crowd that had congregated despite the freezing weather. That night, asleep in the tent he was sharing with Brown, Henry felt someone clutch him. Lurching awake, fearing a thief or assassin, he tussled with the intruder and prepared to grapple for his life but then he heard a sweet voice whisper, "Do you not know me? Do you not remember me?"[241] Bowing his head reverently, Henry tried to climb out of bed but Mahatma Koot Hoomi laid his hand on his forehead and blessed him before walking around the canvas screen to Brown's bed, where he sat down to a chat. When the Master had finally gone, Henry and Brown found that each of them had been left letters wrapped in silk cloth. Brown had been singled out for further honors with a white silk handkerchief embroidered with the initials "K.H." Damodar seems to have been omitted from the Mahatmic visitation, although no one heard him express disappointment.

The next evening all three men sat in Olcott's tent waiting for Koot Hoomi's promised reappearance. There was a quarter moon and the camp was quiet. Finally around 10 P.M., they saw approaching a tall Hindu who beckoned Damodar to come with him and then led him away a short distance down the field to Master K.H. After a brief conversation, Damodar returned and Olcott was summoned to the Mahatma. Their conversation lasted half an hour, Henry recalled. Those two nights at Lahore seemed to him proof that he was "watched and helped; never deserted, never forgotten, howsoever dark may seem the outlook."[242]

For William Brown, the honored recipient of a visit from Koot Hoomi in his physical body, something that had been denied even to the likes of Alfred Sinnett, it seemed he would never need a doctor again. The Mahatma told him that he would always be protected but he must be sure to tell his countrymen "that you are from personal knowledge as sure of our existence as you are of your own."[243] Brown was not one hundred percent sure of his own existence, but nonetheless, took comfort from the Master's words. For the next three years, Brown would staunchly insist that Mahatma Koot Hoomi was a living person because he had seen him in the flesh and still possessed his hankie. Not until 1887 would he call Madame Blavatsky "an untruthful and unscrupulous deceiver" who, like Faust, had "sold herself, for a temporary consideration, to the devil,"[244] and he offered himself as living proof of her satanic flimflammery.

In the late afternoon of January 10, 1884, Moncure Daniel Conway arrived at the entrance of the Theosophical compound at Adyar and stopped for a moment to admire the view before driving through the leafy park and pulling up at the main house. A Virginian and Methodist by birth, Conway had graduated from Harvard and become a Unitarian clergyman; now he had made an international reputation as the fiery liberal occupant of the pulpit at South Place Chapel in London. He had met Madame Blavatsky briefly on her way to India and at the time felt that she was little more than an entertaining gossip; more recently, however, he had become acquainted with Alfred Sinnett, who talked of nothing but Madame and her wonderful Mahatmas. Meeting Sinnett at a reception one night, Conway mentioned he was planning a trip to India and asked for instructions as to how he might meet one of the Mahatmas. Sinnett asked, "Do you mean, can you see and talk with a Mahatma as you are talking with me now?"

"Yes," Conway answered, feeling it a perfectly reasonable request. Would it not be possible for a visiting clergyman to pay his respects to the holy man?

Sinnett replied with a single word—"No."

From Sinnett's description of Madame's self-sacrificing devotion to the Cause, Conway was expecting a female yogi in an ashram, all austerity and martyrdom with time only for meditation and plain boiled vegetables. He was hardly prepared for the handsome mansion with its long veranda dotted with cushioned easy chairs, or for the table on which were spread the latest English and American magazines and novels. Having sent in his card and learning that Madame would be happy to receive him, he sat down and watched several young Indian youths strolling in meditation among the palms. "Their faces were serenely solemn," he recalled, "they did not talk or smile; they impressed me out there as rare plants in a nursery, that must be severally kept under glass in cold weather." He soon found himself chatting with two Europeans, a dour Scotsman whose name he learned was William Tournay Brown, and a Dr. Franz Hartmann. The latter, a thin-faced, beak-nosed German wearing a fez, said he had come to Adyar from Colorado about a month earlier for the sole purpose of meeting Madame Blavatsky "to learn from her the secrets of life and death." Both men talked volubly about the Occult Room and the messages they had received from Koot Hoomi, but when Conway intimated that he would love to have some little marvel of his own to carry back to London, he was told that unfortunately the Mahatmas were not receiving correspondence at the moment. That was just his luck, Conway replied; whenever a miracle occurred he was always too soon or too late to see it and he likened himself to Alice in her looking-glass—"Jam tomorrow, and jam yesterday, but never jam today." His quip was not well received.

His visit with H.P.B. was relaxed and thoroughly enjoyable. Conway remembered her sitting "in her large decorated chair, in an airy white beltless gown much in the style of the midsummer dress of Russian ladies, endlessly smoking cigarettes, conversing in a free and easy way, and putting on no airs at all." When the others had drifted away, she rose and asked Conway to follow her, leading him up the stairs to the privacy of her boudoir where she lit still another cigarette. She asked him why he had come to Adyar.

He had heard, he said, stories of her pulling teapots from under her chair and brooches out of flower beds and he wanted to know if such things had truly occurred; and, if so, "What does it all mean?"

Leaning back in her chair, Helena smiled. "I will tell you," she said with deliberation, "because you are a public teacher and you ought to know the truth: it is all glamour—people think they see what they do not see—that is the whole of it."

At seven they trooped down to an excellent non-vegetarian meal. Conway thought it impossible not to admire the artistry of Madame Blavatsky's confession, in that she had made it without witnesses.[245]

Helena, immensely pleased with the way she had handled Conway, gave a glowing report of his visit in the next issue of the *Theosophist*: "A more charming, intellectual and pleasant afternoon we have rarely passed."[246] Two weeks later, replying to a letter of Alfred's in which he proposed that she write the story of her life, she replied sharply, "Do not speak nonsense. My *Memoirs* will NEVER appear."[247]

Since the summer H.P.B. had known that Henry was planning a visit to London. Far from a pleasure trip, its purpose was to present the religious and political grievances of the Ceylon Buddhists to the British Foreign Office.

While sacred Christian celebrations like Christmas and Easter were official government holidays, the chief festival of the Buddhists, the Full Moon Day of Wesak, was not recognized and riots had broken out over this inequity. The Cingalese had delegated Olcott, all expenses paid, to present their case to the colonial secretary, Lord Derby, and he planned to take as his secretary the young attorney Mohini Chatterji. He did not propose to take H.P.B., nor did she bother to bring it up, for he would simply have said they could not afford it.

It is not surprising that toward the end of 1883 Helena began to feel ill with a mysterious ailment; her physician seemed unable to diagnose any specific disease and apparently did not believe it connected with her previous kidney disorder. However, she complained of excruciating pain and was clearly much too weak to walk. Morphine was injected and crutches ordered, but when his patient told him she felt deathly sick, the doctor could only nod helplessly. In a letter to Judge Khandalavala on February 14, Helena described her affliction as "simply life ebbing away, complete nervous prostration, weakness daily increasing, etc. Played out!"[248] and added that her doctor had frightened Olcott by stating that without an immediate change of climate and several months complete rest, Helena had no more than three months to live.

Naturally Helena insisted that she hated the idea of dying in some secluded village on the Riviera or in the Alps. If she had to go, she wanted it to be at Adyar. In the end it was the Mahatmas who settled the argument by declaring they wanted her to stay alive. But, objected Helena, they had cured her two summers earlier in Sikkim; why couldn't they give her relief now without sending her all the way to southern France? As luck would have it, the Mahatmas happened to be on a particularly heavy schedule that allowed no time to bother with Helena. In any case, her body required a certain type of air unavailable in India, and so, reluctantly, she agreed.

Her plans, she told Sinnett, remained vague. She thought that she might stop at Marseilles for a fortnight, see some cousins of hers in Paris, then head for some secluded spot in the mountains where "if I die, I will be put out of the way without fuss or scandal . . ."[249] However vague her itinerary, she felt certain of one thing: "I *must not, shall not, and will not, go to London.* Do whatever you may. I will not approach it even. Had my Boss ordered it to me even—I think I would rather face his displeasure and— disobey him." The very idea of London was "loathsome" and filled her with "inexpressible magnetic disgust."[250]

In truth, her chief reason for accompanying Olcott to Europe was to visit London. It was hardly the city that attracted her, for she had seen it before and left without regrets, nor was it a desire to see Patience and Alfred and her other friends. Rather, she planned to meet and demolish a woman whom she regarded as her chief rival, although she never admitted having rivals. The only means of doing battle with Anna Kingsford was to meet her on her home ground. Even the inconvenience of spending three months pretending to be an invalid was a small price to pay for the pleasure.

* * *

Dr. Anna Bonus Kingsford, the "divine Anna"[251] as H.P.B. called her when she was not reviling her, was president of the London Theosophical Society and, incidentally, one of the most beautiful women in London. As the frustrated wife of a Shropshire vicar, she had become passionately involved in the spreading anti-vivisectionist movement and at the age of twenty-eight had gone to study medicine in Paris. Taking her M.D. degree six years later, she decided against a private practice in order to devote herself to the anti-vivisection cause. Since her husband could not, or would not, leave his parish, she traveled in the company of a man twenty-two years her senior, Edward Maitland, her step-uncle by marriage who had agreed to act as her guardian and chaperon. The triangular arrangement occasioned a good deal of unpleasant gossip, particularly as little was ever seen of Reverend Kingsford.

Over the next fifteen years Edward Maitland rarely left Anna's side, content to function as her partner, admirer, collaborator and amanuensis. During her student days in Paris, both of them had become preoccupied with mysticism; soon, Anna began to experience macabre doomsday visions, and to conceive of herself as having been given a divine mission. Her visions, probably not unlike Helena's hashish hallucinations, owed something to her addiction to ether, which she had begun taking to relieve her asthma.

Since Anna Kingsford was basically a Christian mystic, it seems odd that she should have become involved with the Theosophical Society; in fact Maitland openly admitted in his biography of Anna that both of them initially distrusted H.P.B.'s organization and disdained her Eastern doctrines. It was Anna's good friend Lady Marie Caithness who begged her to take over the foundering London branch, which would surely "fall to the ground"[252] without her patronage. Finally Anna agreed on the condition that the name of the society be changed to the London Lodge of the Theosophical Society. Pledging that she would do her utmost to make the group "a really influential and scientific body," she emphasized to Lady Caithness that from then on the London Lodge would not confine itself to Orientalism, "but to the study of all religions esoterically and especially to that of our Western Catholic Church."[253] Given H.P.B.'s aversion to Catholicism, she felt justified in regarding Anna with horror.

At once resenting the younger woman's takeover of the London branch and yet acknowledging the need for her, Helena had to admit that Anna was a real catch. A person of remarkable charm, both of mind and body, she always drew crowds who came to look as well as listen. Her friends liked to think of her as a reincarnation of a great sibyl, perhaps Egeria or Hypatia. Tall, graceful, pale, beautiful at thirty-seven, she had, in Isabelle de Steiger's memory, "a goddess-like effect" on the lecture platform, "and as she had also a real gift for oratory both in style, choice and flow of words, she seemed to me the living type of what a goddess should and does look like! I felt that Olympus was a real abode."[254]

For more than a year, H.P.B. had been getting first-hand reports on Dr.

Kingsford, mainly from Sinnett, who had danced with her and afterward could not restrain himself from describing the lush Anna's charms in too vivid detail. Her hair, he wrote Helena, was "like a flaming sunset, yellow gold."[255] H.P.B. was wild with jealousy. At first she merely harped on Anna's appearance, demanding why "the mystic of the century" insisted on appearing in public "so undressed"; why did she wear a gown that resembled a zebra's coat, long black gloves, and crescent-moon tinkling earrings? Even if she was, as Alfred claimed, a fascinating woman, how could she confabulate with the gods when she looked like a jeweler's front window? In Helena's opinion, Anna Kingsford had to be "a selfish, vain and"—the worst insult in H.P.B.'s vocabulary—"*mediumistic* creature, too fond of adulation and dress and tinkling jewelry to be of the right sort."[256] Even so, anyone who loved animals could not be all bad to H.P.B., who might have overlooked the jewelry if Anna had believed wholeheartedly in the Mahatmas.

Anna did not outrightly reject the concept of persons like the Mahatmas existing, but she saw no sufficient evidence that they did, and always placed Koot Hoomi's name in quotation marks. Calling these men *masters* was ridiculous, she wrote a friend. Madame Blavatsky and Alfred Sinnett could do as they liked, but for her part, she would not apply that term to any earthly being whomsoever. For that matter, she marveled that "K.H." or any "adepts" should have permitted a man like Sinnett to act as the bearer of their philosophy, since he was utterly wanting in the qualifications necessary for the study of God.

In October, 1883, Anna had seen fit to spell out her reservations to Helena by announcing her fear that the English branch was degenerating into idolatry "toward these good and kind Adepts instead of preserving towards them an attitude of reverence only"; surely, the Mahatmas themselves must be displeased. In any case, it was unwise of the Society to present itself to the world "in the guise of a Sect having chiefs accredited with super-human powers of greatness";[257] not only did it smack of Catholicism but it left the Society open to press jibes, the latest from the London *Standard*, which had called them "a society founded on the alleged feats of certain Indian jugglers."[258]

All this Anna felt obliged to share with Helena, as well as the fact that she had tried to communicate magnetically with the Mahatmas and had failed. She went on to ask Helena to "lay this letter before K.H. himself and ask his Counsel." Thinking that K.H. might better understand her if he could see her face, she enclosed a photograph to "help him to a right analysis of my present personality."[259]

Having already made her analysis of "the sweet, fascinating creature,"[260] Helena took out her best stationery and a new pen and dashed off an eight-page reply telling Anna what she thought of her. But, as she informed Sinnett, Master Morya tore it up and K.H. instructed her to humor Anna.

Nursing second thoughts, Helena decided that Anna could be exploited to her advantage. But how?

* * *

Helena's obsession with Dr. Kingsford left her oblivious to changes taking place in a woman closer to home, Emma Coulomb. Over the past three years, but especially in recent months, she had come to take for granted Emma's cooperation, and the days when she worried lest Emma betray her relationship with Agardi Metrovitch had dimmed into oblivion. Emma, she was now convinced, was her loving friend.

By the same token, she could hardly have believed that Emma was entirely content at Adyar. Long ago she had accustomed herself to ignoring Emma's fishing for sympathy and her constant lament that she had sunk from a life of luxury to a position of servitude as Madame's housekeeper; this position she meant to escape, she repeatedly announced, once she saved enough money to buy a small hotel or boardinghouse. With visitors, she did not hesitate to insinuate that the Theosophical Society was a humbug, the phenomena produced by fraud, and that Colonel Olcott was a fool whom Madame led around by the nose. And she could reveal many more secrets if only she wanted to. When asked to elaborate, she would retort, "My mouth is shut up; I cannot talk against the people whose bread I eat."[261]

Emma was wrestling with a severe moral dilemma. After all the troubles life had dealt her, there was no denying that the temptation to remain in comfort at Adyar was enormous. In addition to courage, leaving Adyar required money, which she lacked. She and Alexis were paid only token salaries, and Madame's generous gifts did little to compensate for that fact. Each month Emma was able to pocket some two hundred rupees from the household expense allotment and to obtain small "loans" from visitors to Headquarters, but none of this added up to the kind of nest egg she and Alexis would need to strike out on their own.

Lately Emma was just beginning to suffer from belated pangs of conscience. In Bombay, she had not objected at all to Madame's deceptions because, she said later, they were worked on Hindus who already believed in miracles. It was only when the frauds were imposed on Europeans that she began to get nervous. More accurately, she had viewed Helena's early phenomena as small-time tricks, but in less than four years Madame had parlayed this trickery into an international reputation that attracted admirers from all over the world.

Slowly Emma had come to view the operating of the astral postal service and the shrine with distaste. "I cannot express in words," she wrote,

how this way of going on displeased me—how very unhappy I was to be obliged to keep silent. Oh, heavens, what misery! Every day I grew more and more disgusted. I knew it to be a lying business and a deceit, and yet I could not speak out my mind.[262]

Revulsion notwithstanding, her chief reason for not speaking up was that if she publicly accused Madame Blavatsky of fraud, she would be confessing to complicity. In betraying H.P.B. she would destroy herself as well, and while admittedly she had far less to lose than Madame, she did not care to be branded as a criminal; for all she knew, she might even wind up in prison.

In a moment of childish remorse, Emma wished that she could "tear out of my life the page that concerns my life with Madame Blavatsky,"[263] but since that was impossible she decided to take more practical steps. In December, at the annual Theosophical convention, she approached Prince Harisinghji Rupsinghji for a loan of two hundred rupies. The Prince, although he had just received a K.H. letter and a Tibetan coin from the shrine, was taken back at Emma's request and answered evasively that perhaps he would help her someday. And with that vague promise Emma had to be content.

As the day of departure approached, the pace of H.P.B.'s life quickened. They had decided to expand their traveling party to include the Parsi poet Sorab J. Padshah and Helena's servant Babula. Since they would be absent for at least four months, Olcott, in order to be sure that Headquarters ran smoothly, appointed a management committee of seven Europeans and Hindus, among them Damodar, Dr. Franz Hartmann, and St. George Lane-Fox, a wealthy British electrical engineer and new recruit to the Theosophical ranks. Alexis Coulomb was included only at the last minute.

H.P.B. provided the Board of Control with a written list of instructions, concerned mainly with extensive alterations she wanted Alexis to make on the roof, including the construction of a new study and library, a new kitchen for the preparation of her meals, the addition of a servants' staircase to the roof, and a partition for the Occult Room so that Damodar might use a section of it as his office. In strong terms she made a special point of informing the committee "*that no one shall bother and annoy M. Coulomb with unasked advice and meddling*, for he alone is responsible for the new studio and the occult room together with Madame Coulomb."

Stuck casually in the middle of the list was the most important directive of all, the one that allowed her to close down the Adyar branch of the astral post office temporarily. Hence, her rooms could be safely unattended for several months: "I leave my rooms *entirely in the charge of Madame and M. Coulomb*, my dogs likewise; and want Madm. to take charge of the cleaning with my bearer under her orders."[264] Leaving the keys with Emma, she had impressed upon her the importance of allowing no one to enter either her room or the Occult Room. This injunction mystified and annoyed Hartmann and Lane-Fox, who could not understand why Madame Blavatsky would entrust her personal quarters and the precious shrine to, as Hartmann remarked, "a weird witch-like creature"[265] who seemed to have nothing but malice for her. Even Damodar, who fully understood her reasoning, felt miffed at the arrangements.

The SS *Chandernagore* was due to sail from Bombay on February 20, but en route to the port of embarkation H.P.B. planned to stop a few days at Varel to see Prince Harisinghji and his cousin, the Thakur of Wudhwan. When

Emma learned Helena would be seeing Harisinghji, she begged to come along, and knowing nothing of Emma's attempts to borrow money from the Prince, H.P.B. readily agreed. About to depart for the exciting cities of Europe, she did not want to deny Emma the more modest indulgence of a holiday. Once at Varel, Emma immediately reminded the Prince of his promise and must have pursued him with such persistence that he finally complained to Madame Blavatsky.

Mortified, Helena promptly put Emma in her place, ordering her never again to hustle the Prince. When Emma burst into angry tears, H.P.B. hastened to ease her bruised feelings by promising to bring her a European watch and some real French coffee beans. Emma blew her nose, and said no more.

The day before sailing, Helena received news of the death of her beloved Uncle Rostislav. Although she revealed the contents of the cable to Emma, she pointedly said nothing to Olcott and the others. Later that day, either because she could not deal with her emotions or because she could never pass up the opportunity for a good phenomenon, she wrote one of the strangest letters ever to come from her pen. She was beginning her journey, she wrote Nadyezhda, "depressed by a terrible foreboding. Either Uncle is dead or I am off my head." Five days earlier, in a railway carriage, Rostislav had appeared to her, first looking pale and thin, and had said, "Farewell to you, Helena Petrovna." Shortly afterward she had seen him again, this time looking like a young man, and when she asked him if he was alive, he replied that he was more alive than ever: he was shielded from suffering and had seen his father and all the family. "Then I knew for certain," Helena went on to Nadyezhda, "he was no more in the world . . . he chose to come personally and say good-bye to me. Not a single tear in my eyes, but a heavy stone in my heart. The worst of it is that I do not know anything for certain."[266]

Next morning, aboard the *Chandernagore*, goodbyes were said. Emma, after many tearful hugs, stepped into the boat going back to shore, waved somberly at Babula, and then said in a quite different tone: "I shall be revenged on your mistress for preventing me from getting my two thousand rupees."[267] If Babula reported the threat to his mistress, and he certainly must have, it did not penetrate her deep and silent grief for Rostislav Fadeyev.

Europe

1884

I

~·~·~·~·~·~·~·~·~·

Paris

The sea voyage seemed exceptionally calm and pleasant to Helena, even though the first day out Mohini and Babula "brought up their dinners for the whole year 1883,"[1] while she suffered not a single minute of seasickness. In fact, her health improved so drastically once they left Bombay that Henry remarked on her miraculous recovery. They had day after day of fine weather, but Helena sat cloistered in the captain's quarters, working on a French translation of *Isis Unveiled*. By the time they reached Suez, she had almost finished the first volume. She would have been completely relaxed if not for Olcott's angry nagging about her extravagance; specifically, one particular bill of which he had learned shortly before leaving Bombay: apparently she had taken seven hundred rupees from the communal account and spent it on her personal suite. At Suez, Henry wrote to Alexis Coulomb that he was "tired of this hap-hazard, unsystematic and compromising way in which our whole financial affairs have been conducted,"[2] and that Madame Blavatsky had promised to assume total financial responsibility for her own quarters in the future. His continued harping on money bored Helena, and when he told her of his reticence about accepting St. George Lane-Fox's offer to endow the Society "lest . . . in becoming rich . . . it . . . should become vicious and proud,"[3] she tossed her head in furious frustration.

Arriving at Marseilles on the twelfth of March, she was greatly exasperated at being quarantined for twenty-four hours because of, as Henry called it, "the sanitary sins of Bombay."[4] Not until the following day were they able to continue on to Nice where they were met by Lady Marie Caithness, Countess of Caithness, and Duchess de Pomar. A year older than H.P.B., Lady Marie was a Spaniard who had survived two husbands to become an extremely wealthy widow with palaces in Paris and Nice. Now she had begun to use her fortune to finance her interest in occultism. Both a Spiritualist and a Theosophist, she believed herself to be a medium for the spirit of Mary, Queen of Scotland, who "came through" in automatic writing and at the weekly séances Marie hosted at her Paris palace, appropriately called Holyrood. Lady Caithness was a singularly charming woman renowned for her kindness and boundless hospitality, and when H.P.B. arrived in France, Lady Caithness was so pleased to meet her that she insisted upon underwriting many of her expenses.

At Nice, Mohini and Padshah were sent on to Paris while Helena and Olcott got a taste of fashionable Riviera society at Lady Marie's Palais Tiranty. Marie did everything in her power to make them feel at home by arranging soirées for vaguely noble locals to meet Madame, but Helena found her energies sapped by a host of minor maladies. Upon landing at Marseilles, she had suffered an upset stomach and then, dragged to the theater one evening, she felt so exhausted that she slept through three acts and caught a cold that turned into bronchitis. As if that were not aggravating enough, she suddenly erupted with "gum boils, neuralgia, rheumatics and sciatica, with fever in my ears and diphtheria in my toes."[5]

Gum boils notwithstanding, she was immensely pleased to find a colony of Russian aristocrats wintering in Nice, among them a Dolgorukov cousin and a woman Helena had played with as a child at Saratov. "She knew me by name, having heard of my felicitous marriage with old father Blavatsky, and fell this morning into my arms weeping and wiping her nose on my sympathetic bosom," wrote H.P.B, but she was clearly delighted to be carried off to their palaces for dinners and luncheons, "accepting my dressing gowns and evening deshabilles, cigarettes and compliments with a Christ-like forbearance doing great honour to their patriotic feelings." Everyone invited her to visit them in Russia, to which she commented cynically in a letter to Alfred Sinnett, "I wish they may get it,"[6] and they gushed over the picturesque Babula whom H.P.B. had dressed in flaming yellow livery and earrings. Helena jokingly remarked that before going to Paris she would have an extra earring put in his nose.

In the meantime she was not surprised to see dribbling in a half-dozen invitations from London Theosophists: Francesca Arundale, Isabelle de Steiger, the Sinnetts, and others whom she had never met were all urging her to visit. Since the letters were obviously sincere, she devised a standard reply saying that although she was deeply touched, they nonetheless must not expect her. She was crumbling into pieces like an old sea biscuit, she quipped, and "all that I hope to be able to do is mend my weighty person with medicines and will-power and then drag this ruin overland to Paris." Besides, she was not fit to meet civilized people, for "in seven minutes and a quarter I should become perfectly unbearable to you English people if I were to transport to London my huge, ugly person. I assure you that distance adds to my beauty . . ."[7]

Nobody agreed more emphatically with those last words than Alfred Sinnett, who was privately bewailing the appearance in Europe of both H.P.B. and Olcott. After his departure from India, Sinnett had hurried back to London, where he had established a Theosophical Society to his own taste and proclaimed himself the only true bearer of the Mahatmic message. Having been hobnobbing with a fashionable circle of wealthy intellectuals whom he had drawn into the T.S., he regarded the arrival of the founders as a mammoth embarrassment. Still, he was left with no alternative but to make the best of it.

Helena, despite her protestations, had every intention of appearing in London, but it would happen in her own newsworthy way. On the other hand, she felt sick and cross in Nice, partly from her cold and from other ailments she herself recognized as psychosomatic. Now that she had made the long trip from India, she began to dread facing the English Theosophists whose members had such small compunction about publicly insulting her and the Mahatmas. For over six months, while writing civil replies to Anna Kingsford, she had "accumulated bile and secreted gall,"[8] and now she was about to explode like a bombshell. "I *cannot* keep calm,"[9] she warned Sinnett.

H.P.B.'s private turmoil remained well hidden from Lady Caithness and the Russian women, who continued to humor her extravagantly, urging her to remain in Nice until at least May. After two weeks, though, H.P.B. and Olcott moved on to Paris, where Lady Marie had put at their disposal, gratis, an apartment at 46 rue Notre Dame des Champs. With an eye to making an impressive arrival, H.P.B. had taken care to arrange a reception for herself; it was Koot Hoomi who had suggested the choreography in a letter to Mohini at Paris: "Appearances go a long way with the 'Pelings.' One has to impress them externally before a regular, lasting, interior impression is made. Remember, and try to understand why I expect you to do the following."[10] When *Upasika* arrived, Mohini was to salute her by throwing himself flat on the ground and bowing his head. As if anticipating that even Mohini might be reluctant to make a public fool of himself, K.H. advised him to ignore the stares of the French and of Olcott, who would surely want to know what was going on. This was a test, K.H. was at pains to warn; the *Maha-Chohan* himself would be watching.

When Helena's train pulled into Paris, she was greeted on the platform by Olcott, her old New York friend William Judge, and an embarrassed but obedient Mohini, who managed a stylish nosedive. At the age of thirty-two William Judge was finally burning his bridges. During the five-year radical separation from H.P.B. and Henry Olcott, Judge had continued to write plaintive letters to Olcott and then to Damodar, beefing that he was being left out and begging for crumbs of news about the Masters. Happiness had eluded him: he had few friends, a miserably unhappy relationship with his wife, and a seemingly small knack for earning a decent living, even though he had made several trips to Venezuela, where he had invested in a silver mine. In his letters to India, he constantly mentioned Ella Judge, whose antipathy toward the Theosophical Society had, if anything, grown with the years. He wanted desperately to leave her but, as she often reminded him, it was not fair for him "to run off leaving debts behind me unpaid and a woman unprovided for who through my solicitation left a good paying position as a teacher to marry me. She cannot recover it." Feeling "truly in hell,"[11] he thought of himself as living "in a little private hot-house of my own construction," in which he could see the world passing but "the fear of being cut prevents me running through the glass windows."[12]

After their two-year-old daughter had died of diphtheria, he resisted Ella's demands for another child. He studied Sanskrit and phantasized schemes in which he fled to India without actually committing the sin of marital abandonment. Convinced of Helena's Masters, he felt that "M ∴ and the other are watching me—and maybe helping too—*but they say nothing.*" What he was waiting for, of course, was some sign from the Mahatmas, preferably a command, that would release him from Ella. Finally, in June 1883, on the back of a letter from Damodar, he had found a message in red pencil: "Better come. M ∴."[13] But it was not until February of 1884 that he sailed for Europe. After the reunion with Helena and Olcott, he would go on to Adyar, where he intended to spend the rest of his life.

Killing time while he waited for the arrivals from India, in London, he admitted to feeling "awful. Such an outside pressure on me to go back to the U.S. . . . suicide, anything." The magnetic atmosphere of London, he decided, was causing him to suffer continual nightmares and waves of despair. From a tailor on Ludgate Hill, he ordered a pair of trousers for four dollars, at a saving of six dollars, and most evenings, he was invited to dine at Alfred Sinnett's house where he picked at badly prepared vegetarian meals. Alfred regaled him with inside stories of the Mahatmas and showed him a picture of Koot Hoomi. It was quickly clear to Judge that Sinnett had no great love of Hindus, for when Olcott wrote from Nice that he was sending Sorab Padshah on ahead to London, Sinnett remarked that he couldn't imagine what Olcott expected *him* to do with Padshah. Now he proposed that Judge be the one to look after the Indian and find him a place to stay. While Judge thought the idea of asking a stranger like himself to show Padshah around London was "ridiculous,"[14] he agreed, but immediately after began shunning Sinnett's dinner invitations.

Lady Caithness's free apartment turned out to be a disappointment. The rue Notre Dame des Champs was a long dreary street on the Left Bank; the building at No. 46 was far from imposing and, worst of all for someone as heavy-set as Helena, one had to climb a steep, dark staircase to get up to the apartment. A Frenchwoman came every day to cook and put the rooms in order, but Madame preferred her meals prepared by Babula. Knowing he slept on the floor outside her room made her feel more secure at night.

The first few days, the apartment was generally full of visitors, which provided Helena with the attention she adored. Judge, on the other hand, was depressed by the clutter of people coming and going, especially since he had hardly managed a private word with Helena since her arrival. Soon he had worked himself into "the most awful blues that ever were," accompanied by uncontrollable fits of weeping. Recognizing his melancholia and worried that he might do something foolish, Helena told him that he was being attacked by "elementals" and lent him a ring inscribed with the Sanskrit word for life. That helped, as did her assurance that Master K.H. had promised "to do something with and for me."[15]

The most well-known portrait of H.P.B., taken by Enrico Resta, January 8, 1889, in London. NEW YORK PUBLIC LIBRARY PICTURE COLLECTION.

Henry Steel Olcott, co-founder and first president of the Theosophical Society. An expatriate American, he lived his last three decades in India. NEW YORK PUBLIC LIBRARY PICTURE COLLECTION

William Quan Judge, New York attorney and leading figure in Theosophy from its inception to 1875. After H.P.B.'s death, he broke with the parent society and founded the independent Theosophical Society in America. NEW YORK PUBLIC LIBRARY PICTURE COLLECTION

Right: Daniel Douglas Home, one of the most notable nineteenth-century mediums. His intense aversion to Madame Blavatsky resulted in a twenty-year feud. NEW YORK PUBLIC LIBRARY PICTURE COLLECTION. *Below:* Artist's sketch of "Katie King," the spirit that supposedly materialized at a Philadelphia seance, August 1874. A few months later "Katie" was revealed to be a living woman. NEW YORK PUBLIC LIBRARY PICTURE COLLECTION

William Butler Yeats in 1903. After meeting Madame Blavatsky at the age of twenty-two, he became one of her students. AMERICAN WEEKLY MAGAZINE.

Irish revolutionary Maud Gonne, about 1898 when she was having an unconsummated "spiritual marriage" with William Butler Yeats. Her association with the Society, encouraged by Yeats, turned out to be brief. NEW YORK PUBLIC LIBRARY PICTURE COLLECTION

Irish poet George Russell, 1930. "A.E.'s" work was deeply influenced by H.P.B.'s philosophy, particularly by *The Secret Doctrine*. ROBERT H. DAVIS, PHOTOGRAPHER. NEW YORK PUBLIC LIBRARY PICTURE COLLECTION

Mohandas K. Gandhi as a young lawyer in East Africa. Earlier, while a student in London, the future Mahatma first read the *Bhagavad Gita* at the suggestion of two of H.P.B.'s disciples. NEW YORK PUBLIC LIBRARY PICTURE COLLECTION

Annie Besant in about 1897, age fifty. H.P.B.'s chosen successor, she became president of the Theosophical Society after Colonel Olcott's death. NEW YORK PUBLIC LIBRARY PICTURE COLLECTION

Jiddu Krishnamurti and Annie Besant in the 1920 s. Mrs. Besant hailed him as the avatar of the New Messiah. UPI

Garlanded Jiddu Krishnamurti and Annie Besant returning to India in 1927 after a long tour abroad. "I have seen Buddha, I have communed with Buddha, I am Buddha," he said then. Two years later he resigned from the Society. WIDE WORLD PHOTOS

H.P.B. in London, 1889. NEW YORK PUBLIC LIBRARY PICTURE COLLECTION

That Helena had the patience for soothing Judge is proof of the self-control she denied having: shortly after her arrival in Paris, the mail from Adyar caught up with her. H.P.B. was assaulted with a batch of frenzied letters from Damodar, Hartmann and Emma, all of which related similar stories adding up to impending disaster for Madame Blavatsky. It seemed she had hardly left Bombay when war had erupted between the Coulombs and the Board of Control. The incident that set off the battle was trivial indeed: Hartmann, Lane-Fox, William Brown and Damodar had wanted to hold a business meeting in H.P.B.'s room, but were annoyed to discover that Madame Coulomb was hewing to the letter of Madame's instructions and refused to unlock the staircase door leading to the roof. This led to insults, which in turn infuriated Emma to the point where she forgot to be cautious. Madame Blavatsky was a fraud, she spat at them recklessly; Madame had forced her husband to build a trapdoor to deliver Mahatma letters and trick apparatus in the Occult Room. For a while Hartmann and Lane-Fox listened to the accusations in disbelief, then they responded in what they believed appropriate fashion by demanding that the Coulombs leave, with Lane-Fox promising Emma two thousand rupees if she would quietly disappear.

To everyone's surprise, Emma adamantly refused to budge, insisting that she had a home for life at Adyar. She could never be turned out because she knew too much about Madame Blavatsky. Madame had borrowed money from her in Cairo and never repaid it; Madame had once had a husband named Agardi Metrovitch; all of the English were dupes and idiots who had been taken in by H.P.B.'s invented Mahatmas; the *real* purpose of the Theosophical Society was to overthrow British rule in India. Revelation followed ugly revelation, but the only hard facts Hartmann and Lane-Fox gathered from her tirades were that she hated H.P.B. and that she seemed to be waging some sort of vendetta. They decided that Emma and Alexis must be expelled from the compound.

Now it was Damodar who stepped in to save Emma and, he hoped, Madame as well. What, he must have asked himself in anguish, would Madame do if she were here? What would Master Koot Hoomi do? On March 11, Damodar arranged to receive a K.H. letter advising pacification of the rampaging Emma: the Board of Control, said Koot Hoomi, was to keep in mind that she was a sick medium who could not be held responsible for her behavior. All he could advise was charity and forgiveness. The Mahatmic peacemaking pleased no one, least of all Emma, and when Hartmann continued to call her a liar, she coolly informed him that she could substantiate every one of her accusations from Madame's confidential letters.

While Emma ranted in Adyar, Helena, in Paris, was demonstrating an uncanny ability to face calamity with the serenity of a Mahatma. The result was a strangely compassionate letter to Emma and Alexis, studded with clever double entendres and sincere expressions of sorrow for Emma's foolishness. She began by addressing herself to both the Coulombs because she wanted them to put their heads together and give her words serious thought. Still, as her pen raced over page after page, the savagery of her feelings conquered her epistolary style, leaving only a desperate Helena Petrovna to speak her piece.

Oh Madame Coulomb! what then have I done to you that you should try to ruin me in this way!

What purpose have you in going and vilifying me secretly to those who love me and who believe in me? What [cause of vengeance] have you against me? What you do will never *ruin the Society*, only me alone, at the most in the estimation of my friends. The public has always looked upon me as *a fraud and an imposter*. By talking and acting as you do you will only gain one end, that is, people will say that you also are "*a fraud*"; and worse than that, that you have done *for your own interests*, what I have not done for myself, since I give all that I have to the Society, for I spend my life for it. They will say that you and M. Coulomb have helped me *not for the sake of friendship* . . . but in the hopes of "*blackmailing*" . . . But that is dreadful! You are truly sick. You must be so to do as foolishly as you are doing! Understand then that you cannot at this hour of day injure anyone. That it is too late.

. . .

If you compromise me before Lane-Fox, Hartmann and the others— ah well. I shall never return to Adyar, but will remain here on in London where I will prove by phenomena more marvelous still that they are true and that our Mahatmas exist, *for there is one here at Paris and there will be also in London*. And when I have proved this, where will the *trap-doors* be then?

. . .

Ah my dear friend how miserable and foolish is all this! Come! I have no ill-will against you. I am so much accustomed to terror and suffering that nothing astonishes me. But what truly astonishes me is to see you who are such an intelligent woman doing evil for its own sake, and running the risk of being swallowed up in the pit which you have digged— yourself the first [victim]! Pshaw! Believe both of you that it is a friend who speaks . . . Undo then the evil which you have unwittingly done. I am sure of this—[you are] carried away by your nerves, your sickness, your sufferings and the anger which you have roused in the board of Trustees who annoy me more than they annoy you. But if you choose to go on disgracing me for no good to yourself— do it—*and may your Christ and God repay you!*

After all, I sign myself, with anguish of heart which you can never comprehend

Forever your friend, H. P. Blavatsky.[16]

* * *

Emma might scream her head off in Bombay but she would never take Koot Hoomi and Morya from Madame. The Mahatmas' existence did not depend on Alexis's sliding doors and Emma's sewing abilities. Emma, who always babbled about Christianity, would see that God, if he existed, would not reward her for repaying kindness with evil. In the long run, Emma would suffer.

Meanwhile, H.P.B. braced herself to contend with Henry. The news from Adyar caused the first of many stormy scenes between them and inflicted wounds that would never heal. Henry knew he could not be certain that Emma was lying, since he had always suspected collusion between Helena and her; now, more severe than sympathetic, he demanded that Madame obtain a satisfactory retraction from the Coulombs. Helena held firm to her claim that Emma was mad and exhibited battered feelings over Henry's lack of trust. By the next day Henry was reassessing the situation calmly and wrote to Emma, giving his view of the matter. Distressed to hear of the unpleasantness, he believed that he must speak his mind plainly: "The Theosophical movement *does not rest at all for its permanency upon phenomena, and that even if you could prove that every supposed phenomena ever witnessed by me or any one else were false it would not alter* my opinion one iota as to the benefit to be derived by the world from our society's work." As for Emma's stories about trickery and trapdoors, he refused to believe that she could utter such falsehoods until she repeated them to his face. No one on earth could harm the Society, "which rests upon the everlasting rock of truth," and he went on to tell her emphatically that while he lived and fought for the Cause, "it will be impossible to overthrow it."[17]

Through mutual but probably unspoken consent, Henry and Helena tried to put Adyar from their thoughts and go about their business, although H.P.B. must surely have been far more distressed than she let on. Three days later, anxious to proceed on his commission for the Cingalese Buddhists, Henry left for London with Mohini. Given Helena's overriding need to convince him that Emma lied, what happened next was not only probable but predictable. Somewhere between Paris and the Channel, as the two men sat alone in the railway carriage, an envelope suddenly dropped from the ceiling. After some advice on Henry's deportment in London, Koot Hoomi warned, "Do not be surprised at anything you may hear from Adyar. You have harbored a traitor and an enemy under your roof for years."[18] In this instance there can be no doubt that Mohini acted as special-delivery carrier, and one wonders what exquisite bait persuaded him to go along with the scheme.

That same evening, Helena and Judge sat together in the parlor of the Paris apartment and spoke nostalgically of the Lamasery and the friends they had once shared in New York. The room was cold because Judge could not get the fireplace to work properly and two-thirds of the heat was going up the chimney. Helena shivered uncomfortably. "Judge," she suddenly said, "the Master asks me to try and guess what would be the most extraordinary thing he could order now."

"That Mrs. Kingsford should be re-elected president of the London branch," Judge offered.

"Try again."

"That H.P.B. should be ordered to go to London."[19]

Correct, and furthermore she was ordered to go over on the next evening's 7:45 express, to remain in London only twenty-four hours, and then to return immediately to Paris. Judge recalled that she seemed to dislike the order "awfully" and fumed that she would look a fool: after all her refusals to come to London, Sinnett and the others would think it was done for effect and when Olcott saw her, he would certainly begin swearing. Still, the London situation was serious, and the Masters knew what they were about. The following evening Judge escorted her to the station and settled her in a coach with her overnight bag.

On the evening of April 7, the London Lodge of the Theosophical Society prepared to conduct its annual election of officers, an event that promised to be enlivened by acrimony; for that reason the benches at the Lincoln's Inn meeting hall were unusually crowded. Seated on the platform, Olcott and Mohini made such a remarkable contrast that the audience could not help murmuring over them—the older man with his balding head and long white beard, the younger with his long black hair and small Indian cap.

By midevening, Henry was still having little success adjudicating the differences between Alfred Sinnett (pro-Mahatma) and Anna Kingsford (anti-Mahatma). Finally, when he proposed giving Anna a charter for her own separate branch called the Hermetic Theosophical Society, she accepted; elections for the London Lodge proceeded. A barrister, Gerard B. Finch, was elected to succeed Anna as president, and Alfred Sinnett was chosen vice-president. Anna, however, continued to show her disgust for the proceedings by interrupting every few minutes. When Olcott showed himself unable to handle her, the members got bored with the bickering and began whispering among themselves. Suddenly Mohini Chatterji sprang from the platform and leapfrogged toward the back of the room.

Several persons present that night wrote accounts of the event, but no two agreed. According to a new member named Charles W. Leadbeater, a stout woman in black slipped into the rear of the room and seated herself next to him. After listening to the wrangling for a few minutes, she slowly rose, bellowing what Leadbeater likened to a military command, "Mohini!", at which signal Mohini hurtled headlong down the aisle and threw himself at her feet. Members began craning their necks, and some even climbed onto the benches to get a better view. A moment later Sinnett careened after Mohini and announced in a portentous voice: "Let me introduce to the London Lodge as a whole—Madame Blavatsky!"[20] and led her to the platform.

Leadbeater's eyes were popping. "The scene was indescribable," he reported. "The members, wildly delighted and yet half-awed at the same time, clustered around our great Founder, some kissing her hand, several kneeling before her, and two or three weeping hysterically."[21] Evidently everyone, even those who had not been rehearsed, played their parts with gusto, awarding Helena the supreme pleasure of upstaging the divine Anna. Afterward, when Anna and Edward Maitland came over to be introduced, Helena "preemptorily bade us to shake hands with Mr. Sinnett, and let bygones be bygones for the sake of universal brotherhood." Maitland wrote that he also remembered how "she fixed her great eyes on us, as if to compel us by their magnetism to obey her behest."[22] Anna, unimpressed, stared back at Helena in defiant amusement.

Archibald Keightley, who claimed to have been sitting next to Madame, remembered meeting her the next day at the Sinnetts; he had been told that she had arrived at Charing Cross Station without knowing the address of the meeting place, that she had set out by foot and "followed my occult nose."[23] What Keightley did not realize, however, was that Helena never walked anywhere, except, as Olcott remarked, to the dining table or the bathroom. And now, though her robe concealed her edemic legs, even that small amount of exercise had become too much for her.

A week later Helena was back in Paris, blind panic alternating with rage at the thought of Emma Coulomb and what she might do. Appraising the situation, H.P.B. convinced herself that she could handle Emma, if she only kept calm. In any case, it was Damodar on whose shoulders her fate mainly rested; there was nothing she herself could do from Paris except to send him frantic letters of instruction. She had already ordered him to take Emma up to Ootacamund, where she would be isolated from Hartmann and the others; perhaps at Ooty the deranged woman would come to her senses and realize she had nothing to gain by betraying Madame. And it would not hurt to give Emma a taste of the luxuries she might enjoy if she remained Madame's friend. Emma, in the last analysis, was a solid sort.

What weighed most heavily upon H.P.B. were the letters she had written to Emma, letters whose contents she feverishly tried to recall. She could not have been careless enough to have incriminated herself, could she? After her long, arduous struggle to success, after all the sweat and suffering and lies of the last ten years, it was simply not possible that a disturbed woman with a bundle of letters could ruin her life. If she had believed in God, she might have prayed; as it was, she stole off one day to a Russian Orthodox church and "stood there, with my mouth wide open" for in her mind's eye she saw, not an unseen deity, not even her invisible Mahatmas, but something far more unexpected. She had the sensation of "standing before my own dear mother," and she reflected on the number of years since Helena Andreyevna von Hahn had died, and how she would never have recognized her fat daughter now. Afterward, leaving the church, she laughed and told herself that "my brains lack their seventh stopper,"[24] that she was silly and inconsistent for allowing herself to be overcome by the sight of a Russian church.

But the church gave her no solace, nor did her Masters. In the end, she almost succeeded in convincing herself that the crisis would pass; Emma would somehow be pacified, and if not, well, it did not matter much. The letters had to be harmless, she felt certain. Consequently, when she heard from Subba Row advising her to tell him if she had ever written compromising letters and, if so, to buy them, she answered that she had never written anything she feared to see published. Emma lied, she stated firmly, and could do whatever she pleased with the letters. At this moment, Helena had only two choices: to instruct Subba Row to buy up the letters, thereby admitting her guilt, or to outface Emma. In the sobering days ahead, she sensed that whatever decision she made, she would regret enormously.

Spring had come to Paris, but Helena barely noticed. She rarely left the apartment except to attend meetings of the Paris Theosophical Society at Lady Caithness's luxurious apartment in the rue de Grammont, or at Emile de Morsier's home at 71 Claude Bernard. Even these evenings she found to be frivolous as well as tedious and was just as satisfied to remain at home, which was merely boring. Judge's gloomy presence did nothing to boost her morale: when the man was not mooning about the apartment, his conversation turned obsessively to a rich American medium, Laura Holloway, who was expected in Europe momentarily; Mrs. Holloway, he repeated, was a genuine seer, as well as the purest person he had ever known, and he bet his head to a lemon she would make a superb successor to H.P.B. Very soon, Helena reached the breaking point: "O my God, if I shall only find in her A SUCCESSOR, how glad I will PEG OUT!"[25] and she meant every word. In the hope of seeing somebody's face beside Judge's, she placed a notice in the *Matin* announcing that she would be pleased to receive at home anyone interested in the Theosophical movement.

But it was not strangers she wanted to see. Ever since she had arrived in Paris she had been writing almost daily to Odessa, imploring Vera and Nadyezhda to visit her. Perhaps it was the death of Rostislav that suddenly made her aware of mortality; she ached to see her family again; she would never return to Russia, probably would never come to Europe again, and this would be the last chance for a meeting before she died. To be sure, the journey would be expensive and neither Nadyezhda nor the again-widowed Vera were well off, but "my dear, my sweet one, don't you bother about money. What is money? Let it be switched!" Recently Michael Katkov had asked her to do more articles and, if that didn't work, she was sure that somehow she could get the money from Olcott. Since she would pay the two women's rail fares, they could not use money as an excuse for not coming: "If for no other reason, come for the sake of the fun and see how I am worshipped as a kind of idol; how in spite of my fearful protests all sorts of Duchesses, Countesses, and 'Miladis' of Albion kiss my hands, calling me their saviour . . . You will see for yourself how they carry on about me . . ."[26] The aunt and the sister would see that they now could be proud of the prodigal daughter.

In the very last days of April Helena finally had a letter from Vera saying that she and Nadyezhda would arrive on May 12. H.P.B. was too excited to think of work; when Sinnett wondered why he had ceased to hear from Koot Hoomi, she told Patience to inform her husband there would be no more Mahatma letters for a while: "I am strictly forbidden by both Masters to serve henceforth as a postman."[27] Instead of writing, she decided to take up the overly zealous invitation of Count Gaston and Countess Marguerite d'Adhemar to be their guest at Enghien. Now that plans for the family visit were firm, Helena left hurriedly for Villa Croisac, which turned out to be an easy fifteen-minute trip by train from Paris. The Countess, born in Cincinnati, Ohio, was different from many of H.P.B.'s new friends, in that she liked Helena for herself, rather than her phenomena; Madame spoke warmly of her as "so nice and unpretentious."[28] Relaxing at Enghien, she continued to plead with Vera, "For God's sake, do not always change your mind; do not kill me. Give me this greatest and only happiness in the end of my life. I am waiting and waiting and waiting for you, my own ones, with an impatience of which you can have no idea."[29]

It was at Enghien that another chicken was seen to be coming home to roost: Charles Massey sent Helena a copy of the Mahatma letter he had received from "Ski" in 1879 and risked her embarrassment by asking why she had asked Mary Hollis Billing to place it in the Society's minute book. H.P.B. was hard put to contrive a reasonable answer, and in fact failed to do so, probably because her mind was on her relatives. She told Massey that the harmless lines of the letter were genuine and that the remainder was an anonymous forgery. Incredibly enough, she credited Henry Olcott with the idea of having Mary deliver it via the minute book. Madame Blavatsky's method of dealing with the man was laughable, and Massey greeted it in kind. By this point, Helena had probably ceased to care what Massey did or said; compared to Emma he was as insignificant as a buzzing mosquito.

Shifting back to the rue Notre Dame des Champs in early May, H.P.B. continued to count the days until her family arrived, but now there was no restraining her impatience. It was this anticipation of Russia, of her past, that prompted her to strike up a friendship with a Russian man who appeared unexpectedly at her door one afternoon.

Vsevolod Solovyov was spending the spring of 1884 in Paris as a tonic for what he called "sick nerves." The eldest son of the eminent historian Serguey Solovyov, the brother of the celebrated philosopher Vladimir Solovyov, he had taken his law degree from the University of Moscow and then abruptly turned to journalism and historical novels. His books were respectable commercial successes but could scarcely be called great literature, and, in comparison with his brother and father, Solovyov must have felt crass. At the age of thirty-five, his life and career appeared to be at a standstill, and it was in this depressed state that he came to Paris. Now he spent lonely days in the Bibliothèque Nationale reading works on the occult and lackadaisically planning his next novel, which he vaguely envisioned as dealing with the supernatural. He had read, for example, *From the Caves and Jungles of Hindostan* in the newspaper *Russky Vyestnik* and greatly admired the stories of "Radda Bai," whom he knew to be H. P. Blavatsky.

Later Solovyov would claim that he called on H.P.B. one afternoon after reading her announcement in the *Matin*, but the truth was more complex, and not the sort of story he wished publicized. Since arriving in the city, he had been hearing about Madame and her famous Theosophical Society from Justine Glinka, a member of the Paris branch, who happened to be his sister-in-law and former mistress. "Quite electrified" at the prospect of meeting a Russian seeress, he arrived at 46 rue Notre Dame des Champs expecting to see a line of carriages outside the door and solemn visitors crowding the drawing room. Not only was there not a single carriage in sight, but he was admitted to an empty apartment by Babula, "a slovenly figure in an Oriental turban," and rudely told to wait.

Solovyov remembered his first impression of Helena as a woman whose "plain, old, earthy-coloured face struck me as repulsive; but she fixed on me the gaze of her great, rolling, pale blue eyes, and in these wonderful eyes, with their hidden power, all the rest was forgotten." She greeted him so affectionately that after fifteen minutes he was talking to her as if she were an old friend and "all her homely coarse appearance actually began to please me." It was not idle curiosity that had brought him, he confided; he had been studying occult literature and had come for serious answers to serious questions. At once H.P.B. snowed him with a breathless sales plug for the Theosophical Society and the Mahatmas and then called in Mohini. "Madame Blavatsky raised her hand, and Mohini bowed himself to the earth and almost crawled as though to receive her blessing." When Solovyov tried to shake Mohini's hand, he shrank back and said that he could not; H.P.B. explained that the ascetic Mohini was not permitted to shake hands with a man or look at a woman.

By this time, Solovyov was spellbound. "Suddenly I heard distinctly, quite distinctly, somewhere above our heads, near the ceiling, a very melodious sound like a little silver bell or an Aeolian harp," and when he asked the meaning of it, H.P.B. said that it signified the presence of her Master, who had just informed her she could trust Solovyov "and am to do for you whatever I can." The bell, she told him, was only a bare beginning. "You shall hear and see still more, if you only wish."

"Of course I wish, Helena Petrovna,"[30] Solovyov responded gravely. He would later insist he left Madame that first day feeling confused and suspicious, and continued so throughout their relationship, but he was being less than candid. On the contrary, he felt strongly drawn toward her and paid her visits nearly every day for the next six weeks. Without being urged, he joined the Theosophical Society and made a nuisance of himself by nagging her for occult secrets; he gobbled up every word she said and repeatedly pleaded for phenomena. To everyone he met, he lauded Madame, swearing his belief in her psychic power and the miracles she produced. He even wrote her a poem:

> To the wonderful world, to the abode of far-off dreams,
> I seek to soar in spirit, if only for a moment,
> And knock again at the forgotten door
> With trembling hand.[31]

If the poem was puerile, the emotion behind it was not. To the young Russian, H.P.B. seemed "the one fresh and living interest in this lonely life," and if she had been young and beautiful, he might have fallen in love with her; since she was not, he had to content himself with the pleasures of companionship. He grew to love her apartment, which reminded him of a Russian country house, and he thought of Helena as "an incarnation of the type of old-time Russian country lady of moderate means, grown stout in her farm-house." Sitting across the table from her in the drawing room, he observed the flowing, one-piece black robe she always wore and the nicotine-stained fingers sparkling with diamonds, emeralds and rubies. She smoked constantly, spraying her clothing and the carpets with ashes, and she talked. To Solovyov, she was exhilarating and utterly absorbing.

During the month of May, Helena saw a good deal of Solovyov and his woman friend Justine Glinka. The daughter of a former Russian ambassador to Brazil, Justine held the rank of a maid of honor at the Russian court and moved in high social and political circles. According to Solovyov, she was "continually surrounded by 'phenomena' and miracles of all sorts; her marvelous stories of what happened to her at every step were enough to make one's head swim. She did not live in Russia and had lodgings in Paris; but she was continually vanishing, no one knew where, and was absorbed in some very complicated and intricate affairs of her own."[32] Since Solovyov was intimately acquainted with Justine, having seduced her when she was only thirteen, he knew very well that she was an agent of the Russian secret police. At one time, she had collected and forwarded anti-Semitic documents to Russia, and in 1881 was assigned to report on the activities of Russian terrorists exiled in Paris. Apparently she was not very good at espionage because her cover was quickly blown by the left-wing press.

Aside from intelligence-gathering, Justine Glinka's chief interest was occultism, and, when the occasion presented itself, she liked to combine the two. As a member of the Theosophical Society and a sincere admirer of its foundress, she had been greatly distressed to hear another maid of honor, Olga Smirnoff, casually remark that the Tiflis Police Court had convicted Madame Blavatsky of "theft, cheating and deceit."[33]

An indignant Justine told Smirnoff she could not believe that the author of *Isis Unveiled*, a woman "at a very high rank in the order of genius,"[34] could be a criminal, but Smirnoff insisted it was so. Furious because she lacked the facts to refute Smirnoff, Justine wrote to Prince Dondoukoff-Korsakoff asking for official clarification from the Tiflis court. Since this apparently was not forthcoming, she decided to conduct her own investigation and requested Olga Smirnoff to prepare a dossier listing everything she knew of Madame Blavatsky. Smirnoff, only too happy to oblige, seems to have gathered a great deal of information on H.P.B. and her family, some of it accurate, some false, and some hearsay abundantly laced with malice. Rostislav Fadeyev she described as the owner of "a not very enviable reputation" and Vera "married Jelihovsky, a true gentleman who became mad because of her bad conduct. After his death she left for Odessa where she continued to live in a disorderly manner." As for Madame herself, she was known to have had numerous lovers, including Prince Dondoukoff-Korsakoff "who had also a good time with her," bore "many" illegitimate children, and

> went so far as to try and obtain money, not only from her lovers, but by all sorts of dishonest and ignoble and unlawful means and by swindling. The police in Tiflis wanted to arrest her for her misdeeds, but she fled to her sister in Odessa. The police in Tiflis informed the police in Odessa and she again fled. Then she . . . came secretly to Tiflis, where she mixed with the lowest society, living a dissolute life, drinking and demoralizing the young girls, inviting them to harems and acquiring money by all kinds of low means, in a most disgusting and dirty way. Complaints were made to the police by the people whom she had deceived and robbed.[35]

The report concluded with a crisp summary: "For more than 30 years she has not dared to show herself in the Caucasus, knowing that she would be immediately arrested, put into prison and deported to Siberia, for she is well known and her affair is a criminal case."[36] Justine Glinka refused to believe Smirnoff's revelations and since she considered Madame Blavatsky a friend felt it only proper to show her the Smirnoff letter.

H.P.B. was furious, of course, as well as dismayed; on the heels of the exuberant welcome from the Russians in Nice, she had begun to feel less like an outcast; she had almost persuaded herself that people at home had forgotten her youthful indiscretions. But apparently she still had plenty of enemies, among them Olga Smirnoff, whom she had never met. Many things had been written about Helena, most recently by Emma to Henry disclosing everything she knew about Agardi Metrovitch and Yuri. The disclosures had elicited an indignant response from H.P.B.: "For those who know me from my childhood I am the personification of chastity,"[37] but nobody had yet dared call her a thief and swindler.

Smirnoff, "a withered old maid subject to hysteria and hallucinations,"[38] could have taken out a patent on poison; H.P.B. called her an "old hag spitting venom," and had to admit that "La Smirnoff "[39] had gone too far. With Emma's potential blackmail hanging over her head, she would have preferred to ignore this latest peril, but Glinka and Solovyov must have insisted that she sue for defamation of character. In the end, Helena wearily filed a petition, asking the court of Tiflis to certify that no criminal or civil case had ever been brought against her.[40]

When Vera and Nadyezhda arrived on May 12, Helena begged Solovyov to come at once and meet them. He found her in a jubilant mood that was delightful to see, as well as a little sad: the awesome high priestess had been completely transfigured into merely "an affectionate woman, worn out by long and far-off sufferings, by adventures of every sort, by work and troubles," who was reunited with her relatives after many years of exile. It was clear to him that Helena Petrovna was most attached to Nadyezhda, "an old maid of nearly sixty"[41] in Solovyov's phrase, because she immediately made her an honorary member of the Theosophical Society and crowed that her aunt's membership proved the Theosophists had nothing against Christianity since Nadyezhda was a fiery Christian. As for Vera, Solovyov noticed she received only an ordinary membership diploma and it also struck him that Helena was patronizing with her sister. If she was, it was certainly inadvertent because H.P.B. felt immensely happy to see both women. They had brought with them black bread and caviar, and Helena dove into them like a starving child.

Most of their initial conversation centered on Rostislav's death, which had hit Nadyezhda particularly hard. Curiously enough, his passing struck her as a supreme injustice and roused her indignation, but her shock is surprising because Rostislav had been ill for some time. They talked, too, of their childhood and when they insisted upon calling her a medium, H.P.B. would roll her eyes in exasperation and declare it was untrue. She hastened to explain that all her childhood phenomena had been the work of the Masters, who had preordained her as their emissary and subsequently guided her life. Before long, Vera and Nadyezhda were quarreling over Helena's powers.

Her relatives' presence had a therapeutic effect on H.P.B. until news of the troubles at Adyar began to pour in by letter and cable. The timetable of events seems to have gone like this:

May 14: The General Council of the Theosophical Society meets formally to lay twelve charges of blackmail, extortion, slander, etc., against the Coulombs, after which they are expelled from membership and requested to vacate the premises. The Coulombs refuse to accept the decision, or as Emma put it, "Of all this we took very little notice."[42]

May 16: In his official capacity as Pleader of the Madras High Court, Subba Row threatens the Coulombs with criminal and civil proceedings, stating that they have committed punishable offenses under Section 500 of the Indian Penal Code. Lane-Fox bars them from the dining room and kitchen.

May 17: At the request of the Board, H.P.B. sends a telegram authorizing Franz Hartmann to take exclusive possession of her room as well as the Occult Room.

May 18: Alexis Coulomb hands over the keys to H.P.B.'s rooms . . . H.P.B. sends the Coulombs a cable: "SORRY YOU GO, PROSPER. . . ."[43] Damodar advises the Coulombs they will be charged five rupees per day rent as long as they remain on the premises.

May 19: In Paris, H.P.B. receives a letter from Emma threatening to make public the incriminating letters. She cables back: "WHAT CAN BE DONE. TELEGRAPH."[44] She receives no answer. Hartmann and William Brown root up the hedges shading the windows of the Coulombs' rooms and threaten to remove the windows and doors. After Emma goes for the police, Lane-Fox completely loses his head and assaults the inspector, for which he is fined two hundred and fifty rupees.

May 22: The Board of Control offers to pay for second-class passages to San Francisco. To this Emma replies that they "would not leave the country except we had our journey paid and 3000 Rs. in hand—this was not for the sake of money, but to have means to come back in case Madame Blavatsky accused us of having done the sliding panels, etc., in her absence."[45] Her counter-offer is rejected by the Council.

May 23: The Coulombs leave Adyar and take a room in Madras.

Throughout the high drama, Helena entertained her relatives, smiled, played patience, finished off the rest of the caviar her aunt and sister had brought from Odessa—and churned with fear for what could still happen in India. Hypocrisy was not among her many shortcomings and it is probable she sincerely meant the last telegram to the Coulombs, expressing sorrow at their departure and wishing them luck. Possibly she believed that the unpleasantness had finally ended; but, at the same time, she was composing a point-by-point defense of each of Emma's accusations. This document, entitled "My Justification by H.P.B.," is marked by a frightening incoherence: "If you or any of you verily believe that I was ever guilty consciously of any *trick* or that I used the Coulombs as confederates or any one else, and that I am not quite the victim of the most damnable conspiracy ever set on foot, a conspiracy which was being *prepared for five years*—then telegraph me where I am *Never show your face again in the Society*—and I will not. LET ME PER-

ISH BUT LET THE SOCIETY LIVE AND TRIUMPH." May she never see the Masters again, she moaned, if she had ever used sliding panels or trapdoors, because "They would never have permitted *me* to do such a thing."[46] For whom she meant this manuscript is unclear, because it was not published until 1931.

At the end of May, when Olcott returned for a two-week visit, Helena had assembled around her everyone she could call her family. When outsiders inquired about her health, she would declare that she was not well, but it was obviously untrue. She appeared to be in excellent health and, better yet, in the best of moods, and Solovyov remembered her as wearing "a happy and good-naturedly subtle smile."[47]

On June 11, around noon, Solovyov paid his daily call and as usual found in the drawing room H.P.B., Olcott, Judge, Vera, and Emile de Morsier. Nadyezhda was in her room. While Helena Petrovna appeared a bit more high-strung than usual, nothing particular seemed to be in the offing. Presently the door bell rang and since his chair was facing the front door, Solovyov had a clear view of Babula answering it and returning with a letter which he handed to his mistress. After glancing at the envelope, both H.P.B. and Vera remarked that it was for Nadyezhda, from a relative in Odessa. As Solovyov recalled the sequence of events, "Helena Petrovna, quite unexpectedly to us all, proposed to read this letter in its sealed envelope."

"No, that is nonsense," Vera said in disbelief. "It is impossible. You will never do it."

Pressing the letter against her forehead, Helena began to speak haltingly and with her free hand began writing on a sheet of paper; when she had finished, a still-skeptical Vera declared that it was unlikely such sentiments would be found in the letter. Helena seemed irritated at her sister's carping because she drew the Theosophical symbol on her paper with a red pencil, then scowled at Vera and said: "This sign must be at the end of the letter."[48]

When the message was delivered to Nadyezhda's room and torn open, the contents were revealed to be similar, although not identical, to Helena's version. At the bottom of the page was the Theosophical sign.

Only afterward did it occur to Solovyov that the letter could have been intercepted by Babula and doctored by Helena with a red pencil, or that Nadyezhda had had plenty of opportunity to switch letters or envelopes. At the time, however, he had no such qualms, and he wrote an enthusiastic account of the phenomenon for the *Rebus*.

While the ability to read the text of letters in sealed envelopes is rare, it is not unique; even in Russia at that time at least one psychologist was conducting experiments with a patient suffering from hystero-epilepsy who could do exactly what H.P.B. claimed she had done. Nevertheless, given the behind-the-scenes struggle taking place in H.P.B.'s household at the moment, it is improbable that the letter phenomenon was genuine.

* * *

The visit with her sister was proving a strain for Vera Zhelihovsky. Honesty compelled her to admit that she had little in common with Helena, but, after so many years, she was accustomed to her unusual behavior. Helena had sometimes shocked her so terribly that she had closed her eyes rather than acknowledge her sister's actions; and also there were times when she regarded H.P.B. with overwhelming pity. When Helena had asked her to write for Russian journals about the Theosophical Society and her unique paranormal powers, Vera had obliged whenever possible, but now Helena was asking the impossible. She would sacrifice a great deal for her sake, but she was not prepared to forfeit her conscience.

For many years, but especially in the past few weeks, Helena had been begging a favor, a trifle she called it, "but for me, if I fell in with her wishes, it would be a crime," Vera confessed. Yet her sister persisted. "So it seems," she told Vera, "that you do not love me, if you will not even do this for me. What will it cost you? Don't you see that this is simply childish simplicity?"

Nadyezhda, eagerly leaping to Helena's aid, declared that if Vera really loved her sister, she would do as Helena asked. "No one but me loves Helena,"[49] the aunt exclaimed.

One afternoon in June, Vera sat on a bench in the Parc Monceau with Solovyov and tried to explain away her anguish without revealing its cause. Nadyezhda, she blurted out, "has no bounds for her pity for Helena, but is that real love? Can it be that one should take to falsehood and crime to prove one's love?"[50] As Rostislav was dying, she said, he had begged her not to yield to Helena's demands; instead she must show her sister that she was doing herself irreparable harm.

"You are only talking in riddles," a confused Solovyov finally grumbled.

"I cannot talk in any other way," Vera answered, adding that she had already said too much. She had dotted most of the *i*'s, and he could do the rest for himself.

Did she mean to insinuate, Solovyov demanded, that the Mahatmas and the phenomena were nothing but deceit?

"I say nothing," replied Vera, and refused to utter another word.

After a few weeks of uneasy community, Olcott went back to London and Judge left for India. Helena announced she was too weak to do more phenomena, although occasionally she did treat Vera and her aunt and Solovyov to the sounds of her silver bell. The group amused themselves, Solovyov recalled, by questioning Babula about life at Adyar. When Vera would ask him if he had ever seen the Mahatmas, he would laugh: "I have often seen them."

"What are they like?" she persisted.

"They are fine!" And with another laugh, he added, "Muslin!"[51]

Calling him a dreadful rascal, Nadyezhda repeated the question but all she could get out of Babula was the word muslin and roars of laughter.

Toward the end of June the Russian women talked about going home, and

Helena professed herself eager to shake from her feet the dust of Paris, "which city I hate."[52] Since there was nothing more for her to do there, she would go to London and stay with Francesca Arundale. Three days before the departure, Nadyezhda agreed to grant the favor that Vera had refused her; it was to be an act that would be Helena's life insurance against Emma Coulomb. On June 26, Nadyezhda wrote to Henry Olcott that, fourteen years earlier, she had felt very anxious about Helena, from whom she had not heard for some time. "We were ready to believe her dead, when—I received a letter from Him Whom I believe you call 'Kouth Humi,' which was brought to me in the most incomprehensible and mysterious manner, in my house by a messenger of Asiatic appearance, who then disappeared before my very eyes."[53] Nadyezhda did not have the letter with her, but, true to her word, sent it to Henry when she returned to Odessa.

Referred to by Theosophists as the French letter, the document is written in French by Koot Hoomi, although it does not bear his signature. On the lower lefthand corner of the envelope, Nadyezhda wrote in Russian, "Received at Odessa November 7, about Lelinka—probably from Tibet—November 11, 1870," and the letter itself reads:

To the Honourable,
Most Honourable Lady—
Nadyejda Andreewna Fadeew
Odessa
The noble relations of Mad. H. Blavatsky have no cause whatsoever for grief. Their daughter and niece has not left this world at all. She is living, and desires to make known to those whom she loves that she is well and quite happy in the distant and unknown retreat which she has selected for herself. She has been very ill, but is so no longer; for under the protection of the Lord Sangyas (Buddha) she has found devoted friends who guard her physically and spiritually. The ladies of her house should therefore remain tranquil. Before 18 new moons shall have risen, she will return to her family.[54]

In 1870, it will be remembered, Helena was living in Odessa with Agardi Metrovitch.

It is difficult to follow Nadyezhda's rationale for participating in the con. She was, to begin with, a confirmed Christian, who looked askance at religions such as Buddhism and Hinduism; on more than one occasion, she had called Helena's Mahatmas devils, probably because she thought them to be hallucinations. And yet, in the end, she lied for them. During the six weeks in Paris, Helena must have convinced her aunt of the necessity for an authentic Koot Hoomi document predating her arrival in India. Such a piece of evidence would prove she spoke the truth and Emma Coulomb lied; and, indeed, for many Theosophists, even today, the French letter is considered proof positive of Helena's sincerity. Ironically, it failed to convince either Henry Olcott, who did not even mention the letter in his memoirs, or Alfred Sinnett, who wrote Madame Blavatsky's biography without a single reference to it.

II

London

When the time for parting came, H.P.B. could not bear to be left behind and decided to start for London two hours before her sister and aunt were due to depart for Russia. As a result, everyone came to the Gare du Nord to see her off. That day her feet were especially swollen, and by the time they reached the station, she could only manage wobbling down the platform on Vera's arm. Tension was making Vera crabby, and when she began an angry tirade against the all-powerful Mahatmas for not alleviating her sister's suffering, H.P.B. snapped that the Masters did not interfere with karma. When she could stand no more of Vera's needling, she drew herself up and glanced over her shoulder. "Who touched me on the shoulder?" she demanded of Vera. "Did you see a hand?"

No one, of course, had noticed a hand, but their attention was immediately captured by Helena who, brushing aside Vera's arm, zigzagged briskly ahead on her own. "So now this is an answer to you, Vera," she cried vehemently. "You have been abusing them for their lack of desire to help me, and this moment I saw the hand of the Master. Look how I walk now."[55] Striding all the way to the railway carriage and yanking herself unaided into the carriage, she loudly assured everyone that the pain had gone.

Only after the train left the station did she begin to sob in agony, but, luckily, some kind French people in the compartment saw to it that she was taken care of.

After spending that night in Boulogne, she continued to feel shaky. Annoyed that Olcott had not met her, desperately needing attention, she spent the rest of the trip fantasizing that a delegation of Theosophists would suddenly materialize and carry her off the steamer; she would be "triumphantly brought to London" where the crowds at Charing Cross would frighten her to death "by falling down before me as if I had been an idol."[56]

Helena had not really expected Henry to appear at Boulogne. When he had written that she should not bother coming to London but should directly go on to Germany for a rest, she had been obliged to make her own travel arrangements. Feeling unloved, she had wondered if she would be in the way at Francesca Arundale's and had offered to take a hotel room, but Francesca would not hear of it.

Francesca Arundale, a moon-faced woman with tightly coiled thin hair and tiny spectacles perched on the bridge of her nose, was typical of the upper-class Englishwomen whose vacant lives were satisfied by pursuing mystic causes. A former Spiritualist and friend of Charles Massey, Mary Hollis Billing and Emily Kislingbury, Arundale had drifted first to the Allan Kardec reincarnationists, then to Anna Kingsford's select coterie, and finally had anchored in the exciting harbor of Theosophy. Proselytizing for the Society became a full-time occupation, and her home at 77 Elgin Crescent, Notting Hill, like the Sinnetts' new home in Ladbroke Gardens, soon became a gathering place for London Theosophists. Francesca lived with her mother Mary and her six-year-old nephew, George, whom she had adopted after her sister died in childbirth. According to Isabelle de Steiger's gossipy memoirs, George was in frail health due to some inherited family ailment, and Francesca had resolved never to marry in order to devote her life to rearing him; after she was converted to Theosophy, she determined to dedicate his life as well to the service of the Mahatmas.

While the Arundale home was not overly large or luxurious, it was more than comfortable and provided Helena with a convenient base of operations. Francesca, having rashly promised to place the household at H.P.B.'s disposal, soon found her guest to be more than she had bargained for; swearing, for instance, took getting used to. So far as Helena was concerned, Francesca had no cause for complaint since she had been given ample warning of her guest's eccentricities. Unphased, Madame proceeded to unpack her silver samovar, dress Babula in fresh white turban and dress, and make herself thoroughly at home.

During those first days in London, H.P.B. found that the main topic of conversation among her friends was the Society for Psychical Research, a group that had genuinely excited her when its formation was announced two years earlier. At the time she had thought wonderful the idea of an organization devoted to scientific investigation of paranormal phenomena; in fact she had rashly called the S.P.R. "our sister association"[57] and offered her help in any future project. Among the founders and early members of the S.P.R. were men who happened to be Fellows of the British Theosophical Society, Stainton Moses, Charles Massey, and Frederic Myers, and to H.P.B. the psychics must have seemed like an offshoot of her own Society. "Let the London *savants* but tell us what they want done," she had editorialized in an 1882 issue of *Theosophist*, "and we will take care of the rest."[58] She had not then divined that Massey and Moses would turn against her, nor did it occur to her that someday the S.P.R. would investigate the Theosophical Society.

During its first two years, the Society for Psychical Research had drawn into its ranks scientists and scholars, had held staid meetings, and done relatively little in the way of actual experimentation. However, with the arrival of Henry Olcott and Mohini Chatterji in the spring of 1884, the group could not ignore the rumors regarding occult letters and astral appearances by the invisible Brothers who directed the Theosophical Society. Since a few of its members were still Theosophists, it was only natural for the S.P.R. to consider the possibilities. Accordingly, on May 2, 1884, the S.P.R. appointed a committee to take evidence from the visiting Theosophists and to delve into four areas: "astral appearances" of living men, transportation of physical substances by "occult" means, the "precipitation" of letters, and "occult" sounds and voices.

As for Madame Blavatsky, her nomadic life and Spiritualist background appeared subversive to the S.P.R. committee. One of its members, Frank Podmore, although he had not actually read *Isis Unveiled*, accepted the judgment of competent persons who had and who described it as "only a chaotic apocalypse of ignorance." Moreover, he had not been especially impressed with the Mahatmas' reputed ability to transport objects phenomenally or with Koot Hoomi. The Master, he thought, "if a saint and scholar, was something less than a gentleman."[59]

According to Podmore, the S.P.R. launched its inquiry "led away by no craving for mysticism, nor buoyed up by the hope of introducing into Europe the lost secrets of Oriental magic,"[60] nor of proving Madame Blavatsky a fraud. Rather, the claims of the Theosophists happened to be analogous to cases of telepathic communication and spontaneous apparitions that the S.P.R. had already been investigating in England. "It did, indeed, seem to some of us probable that the alleged physical marvels would prove to be fraudulent,"[61] Podmore admitted, but on the other hand it was not impossible that they might prove legitimate.

On May 11, a self-confident Henry Olcott had his first sitting with the Committee. There was, he wrote, "entire cordiality and unsuspicious friendliness on our part; an equally apparent sympathy on theirs."[62] When Frederic Myers and Herbert Stack asked him when he had first seen a Mahatma, Henry happily described the incident in New York when Master Morya had appeared for a chat and disappeared as if by magic; and as an attorney who appreciated the value of evidence, he had even brought with him the silk turban. Proudly displaying it to the committee, he was more than a little indignant to notice them smiling.

Myers asked mildly, "I wish to see on what grounds you think it impossible that this was a living Hindu who left the apartment by ordinary means."

"In the first place," Henry exclaimed, "I never saw a living Hindu before I arrived in London on my way to India." Rattled, he apparently forgot about Moolji Thackersey, whom he had met several years prior to the astral appearance of Morya, as well as his correspondence with Hurrychund Chintamon and Swami Dayananda; consequently, he proceeded to insist that "I had no correspondence with anyone until then, and no knowledge of any living Hindu who could have visited me in America!"[63]

Myers and Stack seemed to accept his word and stopped smiling, and the examination continued without further incident. When Mohini was questioned on June 10, Stack zeroed in on the alleged astral appearance of Koot Hoomi at Adyar, inquiring how Mohini managed to recognize the Mahatma. Could the figure not have been anyone?

"I had seen his portrait several times before," Mohini replied.

"Had you ever seen him in the flesh?"[64] Stack persisted.

Unwilling to admit that he had not, Mohini hemmed and hawed and announced he was not permitted to answer that question. When questioned about the purported Tibetan letters, he also had to confess that he had no idea what a real Tibetan letter looked like, never having received one for the simple reason that no postal service existed between India and Tibet.

Poor Mohini had been subjected to nothing but suffering since he had come to Europe: in Paris he had lost his way every time he left the apartment, then had to bear with gaping Parisians; in London, Sinnett had given him an unheated room where it was too cold to sleep. At one of the Sinnetts' receptions, a man in black velvet knee breeches and white stockings, whose name he later learned was Oscar Wilde, had come up to be introduced and then whispered audibly to Patience, "I never realized before what a mistake we make in being white."[65] Now Mohini had to face cross-examination by this panel of smirking Englishmen. Somehow, he managed to retain his dignity.

Olcott felt quite pleased with the way Mohini had conducted himself and was confident that he, too, had made a good impression on the Committee. Therefore, it was disillusioning, to say the least, when H.P.B. suddenly popped up in London and started to criticize him. According to her sources, Olcott had given some extremely silly information to the Committee and she strongly advised him to stop feeding the S.P.R. "cock and bull stories."[66] Henry promised to be more discreet and even offered to escort her to an S.P.R. meeting: to H.P.B.'s consternation and disgust, he brought the meeting to a standstill by launching into a trite, rambling narrative about his experiences with the Mahatmas and then, to demonstrate a point, pulled from his pocket a little tin Buddha on wheels. At the sight of the toy the S.P.R. broke into riotous laughter.

Helena blanched, struck dumb with rage. Francesca Arundale, ringside, retained a vivid memory of "our journey home in the cab, the tense stern quietude of H.P.B. holding herself in till she got into the house, and then the fury with which she lashed Colonel Olcott with her words, her reproaches for having brought the names of the Masters into ridicule."[67] Henry reluctantly admitted that he had made a mistake by showing the toy Buddha, but H.P.B. was not to be mollified.

"What do you want me to do?" he flared. "Do you want me to commit suicide?"[68]

At this, Helena grew even wilder. He should resign from the Society, she screamed; she refused to be associated with a fool like him.

Gathering up the remaining shreds of his dignity, Henry replied gravely, "I do not care what you say. I am in the Society and I shall remain and work for it until the Master turns me out."[69] The verbal bloodbath continued until 3 A.M., when Helena abruptly stomped off to bed.

One did not have to be a psychic to intuit that the S.P.R. investigation would end unpleasantly. Nevertheless, H.P.B. was obliged to assume an attitude of cooperation. When Frederic Myers paid her a social call one afternoon and asked to see proof of her occult powers, she gave him a benign grin: "What would be the good? Even if you saw and heard, you would not be convinced."

"Try me," Myers countered.

Finally H.P.B. asked Francesca to bring a finger bowl full of water and place it before Myers. After a few moments of silence, the astral bell tinkled four or five times. Myers, who had been told of the bell, complimented her and wondered how the sound was produced.

Again Helena smiled. "Nothing very wonderful, only a little knowledge of how to direct some of the forces of nature."[70] Myers left on a wave of praise, but when Helena predicted it would last no more than a day or two, she was quite correct.

On the surface, however, the Theosophical Society's relationship with the S.P.R. continued to be chummy, and a few weeks later, when Helena was invited to Cambridge to meet informally with Eleanor and Henry Sidgwick, Richard Hodgson, and other members, she readily accepted, hoping to eradicate from their minds Henry's toy Buddha. Accompanied by Mohini and Francesca, she stopped for several days at a small hotel near the Union Society. At her meetings with the S.P.R. she went out of her way to be helpful; declining to perform phenomena, she disarmed her interrogators by stating that the Society's purpose was to promulgate religious doctrines, not to prove she possessed supernormal powers. Eleanor Sidgwick found her "reassuring and pleasant, in spite of having cigarette ashes in the flounces of her skirt,"[71] a generous assessment considering that Mrs. Sidgwick had once written to her husband that she believed "the Mahatmas are ordinary magicians and know no more of the universe than we do."[72]

H.P.B. was surprised to find that Laura Holloway, the American medium praised by William Judge, was also a guest of the hotel. Out of courtesy and curiosity, Madame invited her to her room for a chat. Laura recalled that Madame Blavatsky looked depressed and when asked the reason, H.P.B. told her: "Ah! my child, you little know what is to follow this Cambridge trip."[73] This made no sense to Laura, who thought that the Madame's visit had been an overwhelming success. It seems clear that Helena was preparing her followers for the S.P.R. denunciation she saw coming. Ironically, she was wrong, at least in the short run: six months later, the Committee would issue a preliminary report on its findings, and would not pronounce her a fake. To her astonishment, the overall tone of the report was favorable and seemed to accept the Mahatmas and their letters as genuine. This endorsement was deceptive, however, for the S.P.R. verdict had been decided on the basis of Olcott's honesty and Mohini's social standing; since the Committee was stumped by what either of them had to gain by cooperating in fraud, it found them honest by default.

July progressed in an exhausting round of visitors, dinners, meetings, and conversaziones, the drawing-room discussions that were the latest rage among London's smart set. To the mercurial H.P.B., it seemed like "mad turmoil from morning till night." Sinnett had arranged a reception for Madame at Prince's Hall, to which nearly a thousand people showed up. The reception had occasioned her buying a "black velvet dress with tail three yards long (which I hate)" but she rather liked Sinnett's windy tribute to her. Basking in the glory that had always made her happy, she still wished to go home without subjecting herself to the rigors of the reception line. "Just fancy," she moaned happily to Vera, "smiling and shaking hands with three hundred ladies and gentlemen during two hours. Oof !!"[74]

Not a late sleeper, Helena spent her mornings in her room, generally at her desk. When Francesca came up to say good morning, H.P.B. ignored her clucking about the burnt matches littering the floor. Helena, possessed by a mystifying aversion to ash trays, habitually tossed matches away without bothering to extinguish them. Francesca, careful housekeeper that she was, worried less about cleanliness than about the house burning down. As a result, she kept a surreptitious watch on H.P.B. so she could snatch up the flaming matches before they hit her carpets. And there were more problems. Even though Madame had established 4 to 6 P.M. as visiting hours, she did not stick to it. Sometimes, for no reason palpable to Francesca, she would refuse to come down from her room, and the guests, often from considerable distances, had to be sent away with whatever lame excuses Francesca could invent; at other times, the open house lasted all day long. H.P.B.'s samovar would glisten on the table and Babula would bear cups of tea and sweet cakes to the guests while Helena sat smoking in a big arm chair. Without regard for Francesca's grocery bill, she would grandly invite a whole room of people to stay for dinner so that, Francesca recalled, "I never knew whether I should have one person or twenty."[75]

Among the visitors not invited to dinner were Anna Kingsford and Edward Maitland. They arrived one afternoon just as Helena was setting out for a drive with Mohini and were invited to join her. Although Maitland recalled her as "very cordial and cheerful even to jocularity,"[76] H.P.B. immediately laced into Anna for a critical article she had written about Sinnett's latest work, *Esoteric Buddhism*, even quoting one particularly offensive sentence. Anna denied having written any such thing, but Helena insisted she had, and the exchange ended with both of them repairing to a confectioner's shop for chocolate.

By this time Anna Kingsford had ceased to interest Helena, who encountered another woman far more threatening than Anna, the American psychic, Laura Holloway. Clairvoyant and clairaudient, as well as rich and very pretty, Laura had been instantly scooped up by Alfred Sinnett, who invited her to stay at his home. She had read *Occult World* and *Esoteric Buddhism* and conceived the notion of becoming a pupil of Koot Hoomi. Thinking for some reason that Sinnett could arrange an introduction, she had come to London expressly to meet him. For Sinnett's part, he became enthralled with Laura after a séance she held in his drawing room on July 6; to his astonishment, once she had passed into trance, Koot Hoomi took possession of her body and spoke in the first person to Sinnett. After all these years, Alfred had found what he had long been seeking: the Mahatma without going through the Old Lady.

Once H.P.B. heard of these unprecedented events, she moved fast. Koot Hoomi quickly dashed off a starchy note to Sinnett in which he informed him that he had never communicated with him or anyone else through Laura Holloway, who, while "an excellent but quite undeveloped clairvoyante,"[77] was the unfortunate victim of evil spirits, or *dugpas*. Next, H.P.B. herself approached Laura: did she wish to become a *chela*? Laura swore she was ready to go to Tibet, if necessary, in search of the Masters.

At the Master's order, Laura was promptly removed from the Sinnett home and installed at Francesca Arundale's, where, to her delight, she began receiving letters from the great Mahatma. Admittedly some of them chided her for being young, ignorant and childish about occultism, but Koot Hoomi forgave her. "So far, you are not even one year old—and you would be treated like an adult! Try to learn to stand firm on your legs, child, before you venture walking."[78] Best of all, Laura was settled into an upstairs room with Mohini, the *chela* too pure to associate with women, and told that the two of them were to collaborate on a book. Through her control, "The Student," Laura the medium was instructed to "bring through" sketches of ancient history, while Mohini, the genuine sage, would make his contribution with the aid of the Masters.

Laura Holloway, who seems to have been a sincere and pleasant person, tried her best to cooperate, but when she insisted on interjecting her own ideas into *Man, Fragments of a Forgotten History*, Helena bristled. Privately dismissing Laura's insights as "flapdoodle," she suspected the finished book would have as much meaning as "the jabbering of a schoolboy."[79] Later, when the book was duly published, most of Laura Holloway's contributions would be deleted, although her name would remain as co-author.

All too soon, Laura Holloway's refusal to take direction drove Helena to write two Mahatma letters, one of them from a disgusted Master Morya, ordering her to stop wasting K.H.'s time with trivia like the letters to Laura. "All of you women are 'Zin Zin' fools," he grumbled.[80]

Although she supervised Laura's literary efforts, H.P.B. seems to have been doing little writing herself. For more than a year she had been considering a major new work, a revision of *Isis Unveiled* called *The Secret Doctrine,* and had even announced it would be run serially in the *Theosophist.* But, although William Judge had helped her in Paris by making a few notes for the book, she had not yet sat down to write it. The descriptive pieces for Michael Katkov were still not finished, the manuscript needed major revisions, particularly in grammar, and she moaned to herself that she could no longer write good Russian. She now had no money of her own and was reduced to begging a pittance from the miserly Henry. She did not find it pleasant to be living at Miss Arundale's expense, but her mental turmoil made work impossible and the extent of her productivity was a long fuzzy letter to *Light,* commenting on a pamphlet making the rounds of occult London. Arthur Lillie, the Buddhist scholar, had written an essay entitled *Koot Hoomi Unveiled,* in which he gleefully drew a bead on many of Madame's myths and proceeded to shoot. Only H.P.B. had the ingenuity to explain away, for example, her attachment to Spiritualism and John King in New York and to deny Lillie's charges that John was nothing but an alias for Koot Hoomi. She felt no obligation, she declared, to unbosom her private life to Arthur Lillie; whether or not he believed her, "I care very little."[81]

Much of her energy that summer was channeled into her new avocation—art patronage. Among recent recruits to the Society was a fashionable German-born painter, Hermann Schmiechen, much in vogue for his head-and-shoulders portraits of London society beauties in *décolleté* evening dress. Hardly had the ink dried on Schmiechen's Theosophical diploma than H.P.B. hastened to proclaim him a great artist. Ignoring the fluff, lace, and bare shoulders that normally characterized his work, she decided that he should be the one to paint her beloved Koot Hoomi. At the same time, she apparently commissioned Isabelle de Steiger to paint Morya and, as Isabelle put it, the work was to be done "of course, gratis." One day H.P.B. visited Isabelle at her studio in Holland Park Road, and Isabelle recalled "how with great difficulty she got out of a hansom cab unhelped and laboured up my one flight of steep stairs." Stopping before a life-size male head, Madame asked, "What do you call that picture?"

"John the Baptist," Isabelle told her.

"Well, then, you should not have forgotten that he was *Nazar,* and you have made him with his hair short."[82]

She was right, of course, and Isabelle subsequently corrected the hair length, but she never felt so warm toward Helena afterward. Still, when Colonel Olcott brought her a photograph of Morya, taken from a black-and-white drawing "precipitated" by Madame, Isabelle settled at her easel and "finished a fairly good piece of work which I would not have hesitated to place before any hanging committee. I had it packed and sent to Adyar . . ."[83] That, she reported, was the last she knew of the painting because she never received an acknowledgment. In due course she heard, however, that Schmiechen had finished his assignment with the aid of Koot Hoomi, who had actually given him a sitting, and that Madame, evidently forgetting Isabelle's commission, declared it a perfect likeness and directed him to do one of Morya.

At an afternoon conversazione in his studio, Schmiechen unveiled the Koot Hoomi painting for the Theosophists. Isabelle, admittedly biased, shuddered at the sight of "the plum-box Oriental style with extra large, lambent eyes, and encircled with glowing 'auras,' like those of the early Christ pictures,"[84] but everyone else expressed admiration for Herr Schmiechen's spirituality and his special artistic genius. Helena, of course, was well aware of the evenings that she had spent in the studio calling out directions ("Be careful, Schmiechen, do not make the face too round—lengthen the outline—take note of the distance between the nose and ears!"),[85] but she remained silent and let Schmiechen take full credit.

III

~~~~~~~~~~~~~~~

Elberfeld

Alfred Sinnett had still not forgiven Madame Blavatsky for bleeping out his ultrahigh frequency channel to Tibet, and even though Helena had insisted that she was unconnected to Laura Holloway's moving into Miss Arundale's, he continued to view the Old Lady with suspicion. For that matter, it occurred to him that the quality of Koot Hoomi's recent communications had sounded more Blavatskian than Mahatmic, and when he mustered enough nerve to bring this to K.H.'s attention, his letter was not answered. Unknown to Sinnett, his days as chief recipient of the Mahatma's messages were numbered. Helena had decided to phase him out.

The first inkling of his fall from grace came in early August as he was about to leave on a continental holiday. Since returning from India, he had made a practice of spending August with his family touring Switzerland and Germany, then stopping at the home of Gustav and Mary Gebhard in Elberfeld. Gustav Gebhard was an extremely wealthy banker and silk manufacturer, who had once held the post of consul to the United States; his Canadian-born wife, Mary, had been one of the few pupils accepted by the renowned Cabbalist Eliphas Lévi, and she had furnished an "Occult Room" in her mansion that outclassed anything H.P.B. had at Adyar. Each summer the Gebhards enjoyed keeping open house for their friends and the Sinnetts looked forward to a week or two of pure luxury, especially this year since the Gebhards had invited a large group of London Theosophists including the Arundales, Madame Blavatsky, Mohini, Laura Holloway, Bertram Keightley and Henry Olcott, who had successfully completed his mission for the Cingalese Buddhists and was enjoying a tour of Germany. However, to Sinnett's chagrin, he was informed "that Madame Blavatsky had given orders that we were not to be invited that year."[86] More than a little annoyed, the Sinnetts made other plans.

Aside from being a piece of pure spite on Helena's part, this dodge had its practical side, for Madame had no intention of allowing Sinnett to lure back Laura Holloway. In any case, she intended to enjoy herself in Germany and even talked of settling there if the climate agreed with her health; it was probably for this reason that she had sent Babula back to India. On the journey to Elberfeld, H.P.B. had felt like a queen; Gebhard was paying not only for Helena's expenses, but also for those of the dozen or so people in her party, and he made sure that along the way they were served baskets of fruit, tea sandwiches and lemonade.

Installed in a luxurious two-room suite, Helena pronounced both Elberfeld and the Gebhard family "charming" but also admitted to feeling "dead beat."[87] Her legs were so swollen with dropsy that it was painful to get around, she had attacks of rheumatism, and sometimes her heart pounded so alarmingly that she had difficulty breathing. In letters to her family, however, she minimized her physical discomforts and talked about the "lords, counts, and princes, all of them very decent people,"[88] who came and went during the next three weeks: the Count and Countess von Spreti, Frederic Myers and his physician brother (who examined H.P.B. and found nothing physically wrong), the diplomat Dr. William Hubbe-Schleiden, and Dr. Elliott Coues of the Smithsonian Institution in Washington, D.C., among them.

Despite her physical discomfort, Helena felt that she must take center stage, and soon the astral post office was back in business. Mahatma letters began materializing in people's pockets, falling from behind gilt picture frames and even thumping onto Dr. Hubbe-Schleiden's head while the doctor was traveling in a railway carriage. The delivery of these missiles required careful planning and execution, but even though Helena could barely walk down the stairs, she intended to find the strength to use this new challenge. Clearly, she wished to impress the distinguished audience; equally obviously, she knew she owed the Gebhards, who had been sincerely generous, a miracle or two. But more than that she wanted to reinforce the idea that her marvels could be done anywhere, anytime, without Emma Coulomb.

Since leaving Adyar, Emma had been ominously silent, too silent, according to H.P.B., about her threats to publish the letters. Damodar wrote that the Coulombs were living quietly in the section of Madras called Saint-Thome with a missionary's family and William Judge had also assured her that he arrived in India to find "the Coulomb affair" forgotten. But conscious of the fact that it was Emma who controlled the situation, Helena was not reassured. The strain of waiting for a blow that might strike tomorrow, or might never come at all, was unbearable, and must account for Henry Olcott's comment on Madame's violent mood swings. "H.P.B. savage,"[89] he succinctly wrote in his diary on August 24.

Profoundly conscious of her isolation from the Gebhards and their guests, Helena convinced herself that she would feel better if only she could see a Russian face; from Paris she summoned Vsevolod Solovyov and Justine Glinka who had proven themselves truly loving friends. While in London she had received two pitiful letters from Solovyov pleading with her not to forget him and insisting "he has never loved anyone outside of his family as he loves poor old me."[90] And dear Justine had printed and distributed five hundred copies of Prince Dondoukoff-Korsakoff's document clearing Madame of Olga Smirnoff's charges. How could Helena fail to be deeply affected by their loyalty?

Immediately upon arriving, the Russians went directly from their hotel to the Gebhard mansion, where they found Helena sitting in an enormous arm chair, almost immobilized by dropsy. Brightening when she saw them, she gaily announced that they had arrived just in time for a surprise. "The curtains were suddenly drawn back," Solovyov remembered, "and two wonderful figures, illuminated with a brilliant, bluish light, concentrated and straightened by mirrors, rose before us. At the first moment I thought I was looking on two living men, so skillfully was the whole thing conceived. But it turned out they were two great draped portraits of Mahatmas Morya and Koot Hoomi, painted in oils by Schmiechen."[91] For more than an hour Madame kept them staring at the portraits until Solovyov's head began to ache. Bidding Madame goodnight, he returned to the hotel, only to be awakened after midnight by a tall figure in white. The vision, who looked exactly like Master Morya, confided to him that he possessed latent occult powers, which could be developed if he prepared carefully.

Meeting Justine in the hotel dining room the next morning, he described the encounter as an hallucination induced by staring too long at the portraits. Immediately Justine took issue with his conclusions and confided that Morya had visited her and said, in Russian, "We have need of a 'little beetle' like you."[92] After breakfast the two of them set off for the Gebhards where Helena greeted them by remarking nonchalantly that the Master had been to see them. When Solovyov insisted the appearances had been delusive, Helena replied that his skepticism would drive her mad. Justine, of course, believed everything.

Helena had hoped to extract pleasure, if not comfort, from Solovyov's visit, and now, suddenly, he appeared to be turning on her. He sulked and spoke of leaving, even though Mahatma Morya honored Justine with a note which read: "Certainly I was there; but who can open the eyes of him who will not see?"[93]

When he came to say goodbye a few days later, Solovyov was shocked at the sight of Madame's "perfectly grey face, which betrayed extreme suffering." He could barely recognize the woman who just yesterday had been, if not spry, at least energetic and cheerful. "My God!" he exclaimed. "What is the matter with you?"

She explained that she had almost died from a heart attack during the night. "With an effort," Solovyov wrote, "she got her hand from under the bed-clothes. It was no more a hand; it was but an inflexible thick log."[94]

When he suggested sending for a doctor, she brushed aside the idea stating that if she died, she died. Not until Solovyov announced his departure did she start to cry, begging him to take pity on her. She felt desperately lonely: "All these people are strangers, strangers; they nurse me and attend to me, but I am sick of seeing them. I should like to beat them, to spit at them." Solovyov must stay with her so that if she died among these "loathsome" strangers, there would be a Russian to close her eyes.[95]

And another thing: the *Blue Mountains* manuscript had to be sent immediately to Katkov. Would Solovyov please stay to correct it? For God's sake, she gasped, he must do her this one last kindness.

Greatly moved, Solovyov agreed to remain another week and edit the *Blue Mountains.*

The summer had been painfully frustrating for Emma Coulomb. She had tried threatening the Theosophists with legal action and when that failed, had voiced her intention of commencing a lecture tour to expose the Society. So far these tactics had brought no results. When attempting to find employment, she found doors slammed in her face; she naturally attributed her rejection to the powerful influence of the Society in Madras. For a while she had even considered moving to Bombay and was now regretting not having accepted Lane-Fox's offer of passage to the United States. Somehow she and Alexis had to live.

On August 9 Emma bundled up H.P.B.'s letters and paid a call on the Rev. George Patterson, editor of the Madras *Christian College Magazine*. The Reverend did not appear overly eager at the prospect of reading Madame Blavatsky's mail and cautioned her that publishing the letters was a serious matter. How could he be sure they were genuine?

Patterson must have been more intrigued than he let on. In fact, one suspects that having begun to read the correspondence, he deliberately held back his excitement, knowing he must proceed with caution. He did not publish a muckraking journal; his paper, on the contrary, was a rather stodgy organ of the Scots Kirk missionaries. He could foresee personal condemnation if he printed the letters in Madame Blavatsky's absence, especially since they contained embarrassing references to leading Anglo-Indians such as Alfred Sinnett, Allan Hume, and Maj.-Gen. Henry Rhodes Morgan, not to mention various prominent Indians. Membership in the Theosophical Society was not, after all, a crime, but he still believed that to perform fraudulent phenomena as Madame had apparently done was "distinctly criminal."[96]

Since there were no handwriting experts in Madras, Patterson submitted the letters to the bank manager, James D. B. Gribble, who pronounced them genuine on some mysterious basis. After careful study and much weighing of the moral pros and cons, Patterson decided to go ahead. To Emma's disappointment, he did not offer to purchase them, only to rent them for the paltry sum of a hundred fifty rupees, or about fifty-four dollars in 1884. That was his usual rate, she could take it or leave it. She took it.

Selecting extracts from nineteen of the letters, Patterson himself wrote a two-part article titled, "The Collapse of Koot Hoomi," and planned to publish it in the magazine's September and October issues.

At Elberfeld the first signal of the approaching tempest arrived quietly on the tenth of September with a letter from Damodar that impressed Olcott as strangely lugubrious; Damodar had nothing concrete to relate, only that he had caught rumors of Emma hatching a plot with the missionaries. Increasingly uneasy, H.P.B. passed the time quietly with her friends, trying to forget the future. The leaves were beginning to turn and the weather remained glorious. That week Hermann Schmiechen arrived from London to add a few final touches to the portraits and insisted on painting Helena as well. Henry thought the result "gorgeous" and quipped that she looked "as if she were just digesting a missionary's head!"[97] The reference to the missionary is a good indication of what was on both their minds.

On September 15, Helena received Damodar's "explosion" cable and within days the European papers were full of dispatches from Calcutta and Madras, announcing the publication of Madame Blavatsky's compromising letters to her confederate Emma Coulomb. The full text of the Patterson article would not arrive for several weeks but the summaries gave an excellent idea of its contents. The Theosophists at Elberfeld reacted with predictable consternation despite H.P.B.'s vehement protestations that she had never written two lines to Emma; the rest of the group went to pieces, frantically cabling Alfred Sinnett, then in Switzerland, to rush to Elberfeld.

Seated in an arm chair, Helena smoked even more than usual as she watched Olcott, Sinnett and the others trying to decide on the best course of action. Slowly it began to dawn on her that everyone must assume she had written the letters since no one had bothered to offer her sympathy. Olcott could only obsess on the wretched missionaries whom he began calling fools and swine. He hoped they did not "fancy they could break *me* and my work down with such balderdash!"[98] (Koot Hoomi commented, "The situation is furiously serious. O. is a blockhead, but there is no one else."[99]) When Helena volunteered her resignation from the Society, "they all clutched at the idea with such delight"[100] that it disgusted her. Did none of them have any consideration for her feelings?

As in earlier traumas, Helena's instinct was to run, but this time her anguish was worse than ever: she had counted on Olcott to protect and baby her only to find that his sole concern was his own reputation. In despair she wrote Solovyov, whom she believed a real friend: "I will go to China, to Tibet, to the devil, if I must, where nobody will find me, where nobody will see me or know where I am; I will be dead to everyone but two or three devoted friends like you."[101] The notion of being believed dead seemed to please her. In a year or two, when people had forgotten all about Emma Coulomb's forged letters, she could suddenly reappear to great acclaim. But where to sojourn? She wrote to Solovyov that the Masters had not yet decided that question. All she could tell him was that it was "essential for my plans to vanish without a trace for a time."

Her emotions flipflopped from self-pity to shame and back again before she realized that it would be impossible to run anywhere; she could not even walk unassisted. In any case, she wrote pathetically to Solovyov, "I have no money."[102]

Abruptly the Theosophical house party at Elberfeld broke up and everybody scattered. Instead of escorting H.P.B. to England, Olcott sped off alone, announcing he planned to take the next steamer to India. Mohini went to Paris. Helena stayed on a few days longer before straggling to London on October 5 with Laura Holloway and the Gebhards' son Rudolf. She next wrote to Solovyov from 9 Victoria Road, Kensington, but did not explain in whose home she was staying or why she had not returned to Francesca Arundale's house. "This is my new address, for a fortnight, not longer." She spoke of "they" deciding to send her to Egypt and then to Ceylon, "nearer home, but not home."[103] In fact, "they" did not know what to do with her. Olcott said flatly that he could not afford to keep her in Europe but neither could he have her at Adyar until the scandal had quieted down. She did not know whether to feel angry or pleased by the authoritarian pose he had assumed: "Oh, this is nonsense," he blustered, "I will go and put it all right." Just how he would proceed to put it right remained unclear to her for as she told Solovyov, everyone "thought and thought, but thought out nothing."[104]

As she began to feel more and more like a pariah, Helena's physical condition naturally worsened. The paralysis she was experiencing in all parts of her body, especially the shoulder, she called rheumatism; but she believed that if the pain reached her heart it would kill her. It is a matter of speculation whether H.P.B.'s chronic ill health was psychosomatic, or due entirely to her kidney disorder, or partially pretended. One can only suppose that, even though she sometimes used illness as a cover for her phenomena, her body was now beginning to deteriorate from an admixture of Bright's disease, hysterical anxiety and obesity.

Some of Henry's bluster must have rubbed off on her because she wrote a scrappy letter to *Light* (which they did not print) announcing her resignation from the Theosophical Society and stating that "no such correspondence between myself and the wicked treacherous woman just expelled from the Society, ever took place." If all the fiends of the netherworld allied themselves against her, it was her karma. She had thrown before an unappreciative world the mysteries of the kingdom of Heaven and now had "to bear my penalty."[105]

But at this point she seems to have been mainly concerned with reassuring her family and friends that they needn't be ashamed on her behalf. To her sister:

There are more than a thousand people who have arisen in my defence. Not letters alone, but telegrams costing thousands of rupees have been sent to the *Times* of London . . . with the exception of two or three government papers in India, everyone is on my side.[106]

To Vsevolod Solovyov:

It is war to the death with the missionaries. *They or we*! 220 students of Christian College, all Hindus, have refused to attend the courses and have left the college, after this dirty plot of the missionaries and the letters they have printed as mine. . . .[107]

The missionaries, she kept insisting, had given Emma ten thousand rupees to destroy the Society; she had also heard of them posting thousands of handbills on street corners to announce "The Fall of Madame Blavatsky." This was completely untrue but the idea gave her courage and she told herself "I am not fallen yet, and please God I will let them see it. My 'fall' shall be a triumph yet, if I do not die."[108]

Helena did not lack defenders in India, and one of the most vocal, surprisingly enough, was Allan Hume. In spite of his own suspicions of H.P.B.'s fraudulence, he could not believe, he wrote the Calcutta *Statesman,* that she had written the letters in the *Christian College Magazine:*

Madame Blavatsky is no fool; on the contrary, as all who know her, be they friends or foes, will admit, she is an exceptionally clever and far-sighted woman, with a remarkably keen perception of character. Would such a woman ever give a person like Madame Coulomb the entire power over her future? . . . Believe me, Madame Blavatsky is far too shrewd a woman to have ever written to anyone, anything that could convict her of fraud.[109]

* * *

It was a backhanded compliment to be sure, but a telling point in Helena's favor, one that she herself could later make use of.

Of course it had been reckless of her to write so openly to Emma, but everyone occasionally does something self-incriminating, never supposing that the evidence will be kept as a weapon for future use. What Hume and others failed to understand was that Emma had not only been Helena's confederate, she had also been one of the few people in whom she could confide. With Emma, Madame could let slip the mask she had worn all day, every day, for nearly ten years; she could be herself, could boast a little about her success. Since childhood she had recognized her power over people and turned that power into a test of the limits of human credulity. Vsevolod Solovyov would one day speculate that the secret of Helena's success lay in the extraordinary cynicism that she ordinarily concealed with great skill: once he remembered her telling him that the simpler and the sillier the phenomenon, the more likely it was to succeed.

"If you only knew," she remarked to him, "what lions and eagles in every part of the world have turned into asses at my whistle, and have obediently wagged their long ears in time as I piped the tune."[110]

It may be suggested that Solovyov, who would come to despise her as a "thief of souls,"[111] invented those words, but they sound amazingly like the sentiments Madame expressed in letters to Prince Dondoukoff-Korsakoff.

On rare occasions H.P.B. could be highly impulsive and indiscreet; even though she made a fetish of refusing credit for her phenomena, her philosophy and her Mahatma letters, she was, after all, human. What pleasure was there in fooling the world if nobody knew about it? Perhaps Madame Blavatsky's single fatal flaw was her need to be acknowledged as her true self—fat little Lelinka von Hahn who was too crazy to ever amount to much, whose mother's dying words had been relief that she would not be around to see what became of her. Only to Emma Coulomb did Helena reveal the child within.

If Allan Hume believed H.P.B. too shrewd to leave herself open to blackmail, the Theosophists in India certainly could not give credence to the theory that Madame had dispensed bogus letters through a trick cabinet. During the autumn of 1884, the three Europeans still at Adyar, Franz Hartmann, William Brown, and William Judge, remained staunchly loyal to Madame, although it appears some doubts must have existed. After the Coulombs' departure, Damodar had taken possession of the keys to the Occult Room as well as to Helena's bedroom, and he refused to relinquish them to anyone, including Hartmann. But then William Judge had come, and then the article in the *Christian College Magazine,* by which time both Judge and Hartmann had ganged up on Damodar and demanded an inspection of the shrine. Since he knew what they would find, it is curious that Damodar allowed himself to be talked out of the keys.

Whatever the reasons, about midday on September 20, Hartmann, Judge, and Ananda Charloo, a native Theosophist, entered the room. Having removed the shrine from the wall and set it on the floor, Ananda boldly began to bang on its back remarking, "You see, the back is quite solid,"[112] when a spring snapped free and sent a panel flying upward. There is no record of the men's faces at that moment. When they went on to examine the wall behind the shrine, they found that an aperture had definitely existed, but had recently been plastered over.

After a general period of stunned silence, suggestions for coping with this unexpected crisis were tendered. Hartmann saw no reason why the discoveries must serve to discredit Madame Blavatsky; obviously, the removable panels and the hole had been made by Alexis after H.P.B.'s departure. Nevertheless, it was equally plain that their discoveries, were they made public, would precipitate grave misunderstandings. Judge, although he detested Hartmann from the beginning, was forced to agree with this line of reasoning. So far as he was concerned, the shrine had been sufficiently desecrated by Coulomb to be of no further use, and he suggested destroying it.

That very afternoon, the cabinet was moved to Damodar's room; the following evening Judge and Hartmann hauled it to a deserted corner of the estate and hacked it to pieces with an ax; and over the course of the following week, they burned the fragments piece by piece. Hartmann, apparently a souvenir collector, slipped two chunks of cedar into his pocket and hid them in his room in a brown envelope. When visitors to Adyar inquired about the shrine, they were told that it had most probably been stolen by the missionaries or the Coulombs.

Sometime during the month of October, William Judge abruptly left Adyar, sailing first to Liverpool and then to New York, where he landed on November 26. According to his biographer, Sven Eek, there is no clue as to why he left before Olcott and H.P.B. returned; in the bibliographic sketch of Judge in volume one of H.P.B.'s *Collected Writings,* his precipitous departure is again presented as a mystery. Actually, the reason for Judge's hasty retreat could not be clearer. In order to serve Madame's Mahatmas, he had given up his wife, his career, indeed his whole life, but now the Theosophical Society seemed to be crumbling around him. The moment of truth had come with the dissolution of the shrine, but his concern lay more with saving the situation than with avenging his shattered life. Blinded by the light of reality, he overreacted by burning the shrine and fleeing, in search of some solitude, where he could find his bearings and figure out how to pick up the pieces of his previous existence. As Henry Olcott later would tell Francesca Arundale, Franz Hartmann "had confessed that he dropped upon Judge's head a bogus Mahatma letter ordering him back to America,"[113] but the letter could not have influenced Judge's decision to leave, since now he realized exactly how it was produced.

In the end, Judge decided to keep quiet about Helena's frauds, choosing instead to use his knowledge to carve out a Theosophic kingdom in the United States. Never would he even imply that the Mahatmas were no more real than Santa Claus. Franz Hartmann, on the other hand, while continuing to insist upon the reality of the Masters, conceded that Madame occasionally "helped the spirits"[114] by performing sleights of hand. Still, "I would not criticize her too severely for it," he advises in his autobiography, "because her only purpose was to induce people to study the higher laws of life. . . ." He regarded her phenomena as "sweets, with which one coaxes the children to come to school and learn."[115]

IV

Homeward Bound

It was Helena's "karma," as she would have called it, to win new converts at times when she herself craved anonymity. Earlier that summer in the drawing rooms of Theosophic London, she had been introduced to newlyweds Isabel and Alfred Cooper-Oakley. Recent additions to the Society, they regarded Theosophy as a revelation and Madame Blavatsky as its prophet. Thirty-year-old Isabel had been born at Amritsar, the daughter of Henry Cooper, commissioner of Lahore and a strong advocate of education for women. At the age of twenty-three, she had suffered a severe accident that prevented her from walking for two years, during which time she investigated Spiritualism and women's suffrage and read *Isis Unveiled*. Entering Girton when she was twenty-eight, she met her future husband, Alfred J. Oakley, as well as his friend Archibald Keightley, at Cambridge and the three of them joined the Theosophical Society when Olcott had first arrived in London. While Alfred apparently had no objection to the unusual step of amalgamating his name with Isabel's, they were already experiencing marital problems.

When Helena reappeared in London in the fall, Isabel and Alfred were quick to offer both sympathy and their house in Kensington. Although grateful for the hospitality, Helena found Isabel's somewhat masculine face unattractive and her dressing style—for instance, a silk polka-dot dress adorned with a gold swastika, a cameo brooch and a feather boa flung over one shoulder— excessive. "Alf," who attracted Madame even less, was a chronically gloomy insomniac, addicted to sleeping remedies, who emitted exclusively gray vibrations. H.P.B. thought of him as "a man whose soul is filled with the scum falling from other people's wicked souls, with the puss [*sic*] exuding from other people's wounds."[116] Nevertheless she resolved to ignore the couple's defects for reasons of expediency. Less than a week after H.P.B. had arrived in Kensington, the Cooper-Oakleys suddenly became her staunch defenders, even disciples, and vowed they were ready to set out for India. "They have even sold their house," Helena wrote Solovyov, "and are going with me either to conquer the foe together or to die. . . . Think what devotion! You see they have broken up their whole career."[117] Helena had always appreciated, if not respected, those people who broke up their lives for her sake.

"Things are getting dark and hazy,"[118] she warned Alfred Sinnett, but, in actuality, she was beginning to see the light for the first time in weeks. With the Cooper-Oakleys at her side, she no longer had to worry about making the long sea voyage alone, so she decided to stop in Cairo and do a little detective work on the Coulombs. Since Emma had seen fit to broadcast her secrets to the world, she would see what skeletons were rattling around the Coulomb closet. Why, she wondered, had they left Egypt so suddenly? If Alexis's father had left his children a respectable fortune as well as a prosperous business, the Hôtel d'Orient, why had his son become a penniless bum? H.P.B. determined to discover the reason and then to "show up these rascals."[119]

Having rallied her strength, H.P.B. re-examined her most immediate enemies, namely Alfred Sinnett, who had dissociated himself from Koot Hoomi's recent correspondence on the grounds of triteness. Annoyed beyond words, H.P.B. decided that the Master would have to cease corresponding with Sinnett, and it fell to K.H. himself gently to announce the cessation of their relationship. The reason given was that H.P.B. no longer had the psychic stamina to transmit letters. Sinnett responded by calling the letter absurd and claiming that H.P.B. had concocted it; this letter provoked another letter from Master Morya, assuring Alfred that while Koot Hoomi could no longer use H.P.B. as a channel, it might in time be possible to find another transmitter. Helena, totally disgusted with Alfred, had to admit she much preferred Olcott who generally "behaved like an ass, utterly devoid of tact,"[120] but who at least possessed a few redeeming qualities, chiefly obedience and humility.

During the weeks in London, while making arrangements for her steamer passage, Helena received a piece of news that displeased her intensely: the Society for Psychical Research had taken oral testimony from the Theosophists and was writing a mildly favorable report, even though some of its members had no great faith in Madame's miracles. However, wrote Frank Podmore, once her letters had appeared in the *Christian College Magazine,* "it seemed desirable to us that a fuller investigation should be made on the spot";[121] if the letters were genuine, the Theosophists must be viewed in an entirely different light. As the S.P.R. had no funds to undertake a large-scale inquiry, one of its wealthy founders, Henry Sidgwick, offered to underwrite personally the expense of sending an investigator to India.

Officially Helena took no note of the S.P.R.'s newly-enhanced investigation. However, she wrote Solovyov that, while the world seemed upside down to her, "the battle is beginning and it is for life and death,"[122] without mentioning a word about the psychists. With an eye to her public relations, she agreed to give an exclusive interview to the *Pall Mall Gazette,* in which she would reveal for the first time the true story behind the Coulomb scandal. "The whole story," she began, "is very simple. Madame Coulomb was a woman whom I had befriended, and whose avarice I had checked."[123] Helena, in the *Gazette* version, reported she had foreborne Emma's unpleasant habits out of deference to Colonel Olcott, who believed utterly in her sincerity. The shrine, about which the reporter seemed most curious, was "nothing but a box in which we place our letters to our Masters,"[124] but it was far from essential to the Mahatma letters, which were received by persons all over the world. The letters themselves? Forgeries, with the exception of one, written from Suez in March, "and it contains absolutely nothing in which the most suspicious could detect fraud."[125]

It was in this interview that H.P.B. first took the position from which she would never deviate, that Emma had mixed genuine passages with forged excerpts describing fraudulent activities, and had either recopied them in H.P.B.'s handwriting or had somehow spliced them together. While her supporters professed to see the logic in this, others came away puzzled at exactly how it had been done. Arthur Lillie wondered, "How could a piece of paper be found with watermarks, etc., corresponding exactly with those of the letter altered, and how could two pieces of paper be spliced together so as to avoid detection?"[126] And why had Emma spent years as a low-paid housekeeper at Adyar when she possessed this remarkable talent? The *Pall Mall Gazette* reporter apparently neglected to press Helena on this point, merely inquiring what effect the alleged revelations were having on the Theosophical Society. She replied with an understated informality that one has to admire: "At first it created some uneasiness among those who did not know the Coulombs and whose faith was weak; as soon, however, as the full details of the so-called revelation reached us we exploded with laughter; the fraud was too silly to deceive anyone . . ."[127] She was returning to India, she declared, to prosecute the Coulombs.

In the last week of October, a few days before her departure, Helena's attention was drawn to a man who seemed to keep popping up in various Theosophical homes and meetings, never opening his mouth but never taking his eyes off her. She learned his name was Charles W. Leadbeater, which seemed familiar, and that he was a member of the Society as well as an Anglican clergyman. Almost at once, Helena remembered where she had heard his name: months earlier, her medium friend William Eglinton had forwarded to her a letter that Leadbeater had written to Master Koot Hoomi; at the time, embroiled in the daily dispatches from Adyar, she had not gotten around to answering Koot Hoomi's fan mail. Now she recalled Leadbeater's earnest wish to become a pupil of K.H.'s and his fervent hope that it would be possible to waive the seven-year Indian probationary period. Could it perhaps be done in Bramshott parish, England, he had asked, where he happened to be employed as a curate? In closing, he had begged the Mahatma's pardon for requesting shortcuts.

Helena could not know then that Leadbeater would become a power in the Theosophical Society. What she saw was an awe-struck clergyman who impressed her as an ass; nonetheless he might just be a useful ass. What a blow it would be to the Madras missionaries if she railroaded an ordained priest of the Church of England into giving up his religion and his career for the Society. Then too, she felt far from secure about traveling with the Cooper-Oakleys who might not care to cater to her whims. Leadbeater appeared to be a strong, healthy fellow, tiresome but dependable, and could be relied upon to take charge of the most bothersome of traveling details. It was time for Koot Hoomi to catch up on his unanswered correspondence.

Thirty-seven-year-old Charles Webster Leadbeater, "a village curate out on a bust,"[128] as Henry Olcott would describe him, had been fascinated by the occult since childhood. Little is known of his early life except that as a boy he accompanied his father, a railway contractor, to Brazil and led a life of hair-raising adventure. According to Leadbeater, his father "was killed by rebels, refusing to trample on the Cross, and he himself endured horrible torture and was tied to a tree at night; he felt arms come around him, his father's arms, and his bonds were cut and he was carried away by him and a Negro servant, who loved him."[129]

After returning to England, Leadbeater entered Oxford, left when the family's fortune failed, and finally succeeded in taking holy orders in 1878, after which he became a curate of St. Mary's, Bramshott, Hampshire, where his uncle was rector. It was in his seminary days that his homosexual tendencies first emerged; he learned to masturbate and probably became a practicing homosexual, although it was not until later, at St. Mary's, that his interest in young boys became obvious.

A tall, large-boned man, Leadbeater is said to have had a peculiar walk and a drawling parsonic voice. "His only unpleasant feature," an observer commented, "was a pair of very long yellow eye-teeth that invariably brought vampires to mind."[130] His contempt for women was noticeable, as was his charming manner with children, who invariably adored him. He lived at Hartford cottage first with his mother and then, after her death, with the parish's other curate and a tabby named Peter. Leadbeater played tennis, watched the stars through a twelve-inch telescope, and organized a club for parish boys over ten. As one of the boys, James Matley, would remember, "it was a club in which you promised not to be cruel to any creature";[131] they sang, told stories and Leadbeater provided refreshments in the form of cake, fruit and nuts.

On occasion he liked to travel to London, to take in a show, but the city's main attraction was its mediums. He was strongly drawn to Spiritualism and séances, and through them, to Theosophy. After reading Alfred Sinnett's two books, he applied for admission to the Society in 1883. At first Sinnett seemed reluctant to have him and Leadbeater recalled him saying "that would hardly do seeing that I was a clergyman."[132] After that, when Leadbeater made the fifty-mile trip to London every week for meetings, Sinnett issued a standing invitation to dine and spend the night.

When Leadbeater first glimpsed Madame Blavatsky during her surprise entrance, he said nothing about his letter to Koot Hoomi; indeed, he had been too awed to speak at all. Besides, it had never occurred to him that H.P.B. might know the contents of a letter addressed to Tibet. That summer he took James Matley and his brother Frank for a month's holiday at Ramsgate, then in the fall resumed his regular routines at St. Mary's. He had not forgotten his letter to Koot Hoomi, but by this time he had stopped looking for a reply.

On the morning of October 31, having come up to London for Madame Blavatsky's farewell party and stayed overnight at the Sinnetts, he took the 11:35 train from Waterloo Station and arrived at Bramshott about 1 P.M. Koot Hoomi's answer was waiting for him. Posted October 30 from H.P.B.'s own neighborhood, Kensington, the envelope appeared to have been hastily addressed. The stamp was misplaced and glued on upside down: the Mahatma had started to write *England* but had crossed out the capital E and wrote below it the word *Hants*, a postal contraction for Hampshire. Koot Hoomi told Leadbeater that it was not necessary to spend seven years in India, for a *chela* could pass them anywhere, but it would be worthwhile for him to spend a few months at Adyar. "Our cause needs missionaries, devotees, agents, even martyrs perhaps."[133] With that last phrase, H.P.B. had unerringly hit upon exactly the right words, for Leadbeater had a secret passion for martyrdom. Hurrying to the station, he caught the 3:56 train back to London.

That evening Helena was preparing to attend her final farewell gathering. The next morning she would depart for Liverpool to board the SS *Clan Drummond*, and she was ready to go. In the midst of her preparations, a delirious Charles Leadbeater rapped at her door. He had just received a letter from Master Koot Hoomi, he told her, but unfortunately had no idea of how to send a reply. Reading the letter, she asked him what he wished to tell Koot Hoomi. That it would be impossible for him to spend three months at Adyar and then return to St. Mary's, he said, "but that I was perfectly ready to throw up that work altogether and to devote my life absolutely to His Service."

Madame Blavatsky greeted Leadbeater's announcement with indifference. She did, however, make a point of not allowing him out of her sight, "even making me accompany her into the bedroom when she went to put on her hat," he recalled, and standing with him at the curb while he whistled for a hansom cab. During the ride he felt horribly self-conscious, both from the honor of riding with her and also because "I was crushed sideways into a tiny corner of the seat, while her huge bulk weighted down her side of the vehicle, so that the springs were grinding all through the journey."

Late that night, H.P.B. was seated in an easy chair near the fireplace, rolling a cigarette, when her hand suddenly jerked toward the fire; less than a second later a square of folded paper materialized in her palm. Matter-of-factly she handed it to Leadbeater: "There is your answer." Koot Hoomi did not bother to beat about the bush:

> The sooner you go the better. Do not lose one more day than you can help. Sail on the 5th, if possible. Join Upasika at Alexandria. Let no one know that you are going, and may the blessing of our Lord and my poor blessing shield you from every evil in your new life.
>   Greeting to you, *my new chela.*
>
>   K.H.

Leadbeater failed to question how the Mahatma, who lived in Tibet, could be familiar with the steamship routes to India. Neither did he hesitate to obey the Master's troublesome command that he leave England in the next four days.

As she left for Liverpool, Helena delivered her last words to Leadbeater, and they emerged a chilly "See that you do not fail me," rather than a warm farewell. Koot Hoomi's new chela spent the day "bustling around to steamer offices trying to obtain a passage for myself,"[134] but he discovered that the November fifth boat K.H. had recommended was already filled up. More disconcertingly, he learned that the only vessel sailing to Alexandria that arrived by the fifth of November was the SS *Erymanthe,* embarking from Marseilles the night of the fourth.

For the next four days, Leadbeater rushed madly around packing his telescope and books and buying tropical clothing. On the evening of November 3, he put on a promised fireworks display for his church before quietly stealing away, having not been to bed for four days and also having failed to notify his superiors that he was leaving his position. Only to his boys did he make a whispered farewell before boarding the train to Marseilles.

A breathless Leadbeater finally caught up with Madame Blavatsky at Port Said, having lost five days due to a cholera quarantine at Alexandria. When he arrived at the hotel, he found her sitting on the veranda with Isabel Cooper-Oakley. "Well, Leadbeater," she offered quietly, "so you have really come in spite of all difficulties." When he answered that of course he had because he always kept his promises, she gruffly remarked, "Good for you,"[135] and immediately turned her attention back to Isabel.

As the Cooper-Oakleys were already beginning to discover, traveling with H.P.B. was a unique experience, and those two weeks aboard the *Clan Drummond* had been enough to deflate anybody. With customary irascibility, H.P.B. had declared the steamer to be a rolling washtub, the steward "an infamy,"[136] and the galley hands part of a conspiracy to starve her. Considering that she weighed-in at two hundred forty-five pounds, such a conspiracy could only work in her best interests.

The party that gathered at Port Said on November 17 expected to spend a quiet few days until they boarded a steamer for Ceylon. Some years earlier the town had a well-deserved reputation for international crime, and travelers walked its streets after dark at their own risk. Now that gendarmes patrolled regularly, there were few serious disturbances lying in wait for tourists. Neither the Cooper-Oakleys nor Leadbeater had ever visited the Middle East, and all were anxious to tour the Arab bazaars and dine on the rock fish and salmon for which Port Said was famous. Most of all Leadbeater wanted a good night's sleep in a proper bed; he engaged a room, but would not have long to use it, for "Madame Blavatsky had one of those sudden flashes of inspiration which so frequently came to her from the inner side of things."[137] Instead of waiting for the Ceylon steamer, they were to leave immediately for Cairo. It was not her idea, indeed she felt somewhat annoyed about it, but the Masters had ordered her there to obtain information about the Coulombs. This was flagrant nonsense; she had been planning to stop at Cairo all along, had even pulled a few strings to get letters of introduction to the Egyptian prime minister, Nubar Pasha, and to the Russian consul. For inexplicable reasons, she chose not to share this information with her traveling companions.

They must leave at once, she declared, that very evening, in fact. As there was no railroad between Port Said and Cairo, they would be forced to take a tugboat down the Suez Canal as far as Ismailia, where then they would transfer to a train bound for the capital. The khedive's packet-boat, departing Port Said at midnight each evening and arriving at Ismailia in early morning, was the dirtiest and least convenient craft to which Leadbeater had ever been exposed. A ten-foot-square hutch in the stern passed for a cabin, inside of which was a windowless cupboard labeled *ladies room*. Actually, it was hardly a room at all, since, once the door was closed, it was totally dark. H.P.B. requisitioned the "ladies room" for herself and shut the door; a grumbling Alfred Cooper-Oakley, who had not yet adjusted to the sudden change in plans, threw himself down on a wooden bench and fell asleep. When Isabel and Charles noticed "the army of enormous cockroaches which was already in full possession of both cabins" and which instantly swarmed over the sleeping Alfred, they promptly retreated outside to the deck. Looking back on that night, Leadbeater recalled that Mrs. Cooper-Oakley, "who was a particularly fastidious person in ordinary life, was somewhat depressed," but he did his best to comfort her with glowing pictures of the beauty awaiting them at Adyar.

Suddenly the night stillness was shattered by "pitiable cries from Madame Blavatsky in her cupboard. Mrs. Oakley at once dashed in bravely, facing the insect plague with only a momentary shudder," and as Leadbeater put it delicately, found Madame "vehemently demanding conveniences which on that squalid little tug-boat simply did not exist." Fortunately the captain agreed to stop at the next village so that Madame could find a toilet, but it turned out that there was no gangway or wharf, only a plank about a foot wide. Oakley and Leadbeater carried Helena down the plank and afterward back up again, an experience that Leadbeater described as "nervous work" because "Madame Blavatsky's language on that occasion was more conspicuous for strength than suavity." Finally, with H.P.B. stowed in her cubbyhole once more, the tug continued on its way.

Next morning, after stopping for breakfast at a hotel, they moved on to Cairo by rail. By now, nerves were beginning to fray, and the travelers sat in the four corners of the compartment glowering at one another. H.P.B. kept up a steady stream of insults about enfeebled European occultists who fell apart at the first bit of inconvenience. Obviously she wanted to provoke a reaction but nobody responded; Alfred merely stared at her with the resigned expression of an early Christian martyr while Isabel, "with a face of ever-increasing horror," wept profusely. Finally Helena brought out a book and began to read, no easy task owing to the clouds of desert dust pouring through the open window and coating the pages. When Alfred made a motion as if to close the window, Helena pinned him to his seat with a scornful look.

"You don't mind a little dust, do you?" she barked.

He shrank back against the seat like a snail retreating into its shell.

Leadbeater found the dust "rather trying, but after that one remark we thought it best to suffer in silence." For the rest of the journey he watched with fascinated horror as Isabel's feather boa slowly turned into "a solid rope of sand, the feathers being indistinguishable."[138]

At Cairo, Alfred and Charles saw the mounds of luggage safely piled into a carriage and set off for Shepheard's, the great hotel at which English visitors invariably stopped; Helena herself had stayed there in 1851 on her previous visit to Cairo. In the lobby, however, thirty or forty other Britons were milling about trying to get accommodations. "Our luggage," wrote Leadbeater, "of which we had a considerable amount, had been piled upon the floor in the middle of the hall; and Madame Blavatsky sat upon it, while Mr. Oakley was trying to fight his way through the crowd to the clerk's desk in order to engage rooms for us." But the minute Helena saw him fighting his way back, she sprang up and shouted to him that they could not stay at Shepheard's after all, but were to move over to the Hôtel d'Orient, once owned by Alexis Coulomb's family. "Poor Mr. Oakley had to go back and countermand the rooms which he had engaged,"[139] Leadbeater wrote, and one can imagine that by this time Oakley was wishing he had never laid eyes on Madame.

During her ten days in Cairo, H.P.B. enjoyed herself enormously, playing to the hilt the role of the visiting empress. The Hôtel d'Orient on Ezbekieh Square, if not so fashionable as Shepheard's, proved more than comfortable, and she had a pleasant room overlooking the garden. To her delight, the Russian consul, M. Hitrovo, sent her a bouquet of flowers every morning and treated her as a true descendant of the Dolgorukov princes. "You cannot imagine," she raved to Vera, "how much was made of me. As soon as Hitrovo learned that I had arrived, he invited us to his house and immediately began all sorts of dinners, lunches, picnics, till the sky was very hot." For several pages she went on name-dropping and gossiping in the inimitable style she employed for letters to her family: the prime minister's wife was "a real *grand dame*," the viceroy's wife "positively a beauty, a most charming face, but it is a pity she is too stout."[140]

From the owner of the d'Orient, M. Fortune, she learned a great deal of interesting gossip about the Coulombs, nearly all of it hearsay from a man who had been at odds with them for some time before their departure for India. Apparently Coulomb, Senior, had left the hotel and a respectable fortune to his children, who had promptly run the business into bankruptcy; Fortune also told H.P.B. that Emma Cutting, whom he recalled as "more mischievous than mischief itself,"[141] had wormed her way into the affections both of Alexis's mother and of Alexis himself. No doubt Fortune's recollections of Emma were colored by the fact that as an employee of the hotel in the 1870s, he had been dismissed at her instigation. Leaping on these few scraps, H.P.B. immediately enhanced them: Now the Coulombs were "fraudulent bankrupts who had decamped on the sly by night and had several times been in prison for slander."[142] As she wrote Vsevolod Solovyov, Emma "is a well-known charlatan and 'sorceress' who revealed buried treasure for money, and was caught red-handed . . . The French consul gave me official authority to hang them (!) and entrusted me with power of attorney to get 22,000 francs from them."[143]

The French consul had done no such thing, but Helena must have reasoned that it would reassure Olcott, to whom she cabled: "Success complete. Outlaws. Legal proofs. Sail Colombo. Navarino."[144] Her legal proofs consisted of nothing more than written statements from Fortune and several other disgruntled ex-employees of the Coulombs, which, as Olcott subsequently pointed out, would scarcely stand up in court. Still optimistic, H.P.B. believed herself fortified for whatever ordeals awaited her at home. When Henry cabled back that Helena was to return to India at once, she wound up her visit with a sightseeing trip to the Boulak Museum. She introduced herself to the curator, and spent two pounds on a tiny bottle of attar of roses, minimizing her extravagance by saying that she planned to use it to perfume the shrine at Adyar. She was not aware that Judge and Hartmann had destroyed the shrine, nor that Henry had subsequently gutted the Occult Room.

At Suez she waited two days for the SS *Navarino*. Once aboard, she found to her annoyance that her sailing companions included "a party of eight disgusting missionaries,"[145] who happened to have with them copies of the *Christian College Magazine*, and who would spend the next two weeks baiting her. Isabel recalled that "every insulting remark that could be made about H.P.B. was heard," adding that she had found the voyage "very unpleasant."[146] More accustomed to abuse, H.P.B. dismissed the missionaries' jibes as mere cackling. "I looked at them as an elephant looks at a pug-dog," she said, "and got my own restlessness calmed down."[147]

If Isabel found the voyage unpleasant, Leadbeater thought it excruciating: Madame was making a point of testing his loyalty. A bashful person, he had the average Englishman's horror of appearing conspicuous or ridiculous. One of the first tasks Helena set him was to carry her full chamber pot along the main passenger deck in broad daylight. By the time they dropped anchor in Colombo, Ceylon, he could say that "I had reached a stage in which I was absolutely hardened to ridicule and did not care in the slightest degree what anybody thought of me."[148]

Olcott and a party of Theosophists were on hand to greet the arrivals. During the two-day wait before the *Navarino* continued on to Madras, Helena provided Charles Leadbeater with a challenge considerably more serious than making him parade her excrement on the ship's deck. Reminding him that on their first trip to Ceylon, she and Olcott had formally professed themselves Buddhists, she asked him if he would be willing to follow their example. She warned that the decision was his, but felt that his openly accepting Buddhism might make him far more useful in his work for the Mahatmas. When Leadbeater agreed on the condition that he need not abjure the Christian faith, she assured him that there was no incompatibility between Buddhism and *true* Christianity, only the counterfeit being preached by the missionaries, whereupon Leadbeater was presented to High Priest Sumangala and given *pansil*.

Arriving in Madras on the twenty-first of December with her confidence high and her psyche in fighting strength, H.P.B. found waiting on the pier a student delegation from Pachiappa's College and the Indian approximation of a brass band, "weird Indian musical instruments,"[149] as Leadbeater called them. Along the pier ran a tramway-line with a single primitive car to which a dozen of the more enthusiastic students had harnessed themselves, insisting that they be allowed to tow H.P.B. and her party to shore. Isabel retained the "quaint" impression of "masses of smiling dark faces"[150] and paper roses festooning the tramcar. Leadbeater recalled that

> quite a number of Europeans had also come down to see the fun, and were seated in their carriages at the end of the pier. I think that the Oakleys felt distinctly conspicuous and uncomfortable, and I must admit that I was a little embarrassed myself, as the whole proceeding was, to say the least of it, unconventional, but Madame Blavatsky accepted all

this homage with great dignity as a matter of course, and indeed seemed rather to enjoy it.[151]

H.P.B. had found the demonstration mildly disappointing, for the crowd was comprised mainly of gawking Anglo-Indians and college students out on a romp; she looked in vain for members of the Theosophical Society. Describing the homecoming to Solovyov, with her usual pathological exaggeration, she said that the anchor had hardly been dropped before a crowd of Theosophists swarmed over the sides of the ship. "They threw themselves down and kissed my feet," before escorting her ashore where she was "almost deafened by the furious cries of triumph and delight. We were drawn, not by horses, but by Theosophists, in a chariot preceded by a band walking backwards." And she added, "Lord, if you had only been there; how proud you would have been of your countrywoman!"[152]

One does not have to read between the lines to catch glimpses of her fantasies: three hundred students from Madras Christian College, the very school whose missionary administrators published her letters, rushed her off to Town Hall where a cheering crowd of five thousand was waiting to reassure her of their belief in her innocence. Actually the students were from Pachiappa, a rival of Madras Christian, and they took her to their campus auditorium where, undeniably, they did applaud her with enthusiasm and ask her to make a few remarks. While a brilliant conversationalist, H.P.B. had an aversion to public speaking: now, for the first and last time in her life, she consented to give an address. She began well enough, saying that she was touched by their affection, that it demonstrated what she had always known, that the people of India would not accept these "vile, cowardly, loathsome and utterly abominable slanders, circulated by these unspeakable missionaries . . ."[153] Olcott, suddenly realizing the hysterical turn her remarks were taking, hurriedly broke in and, as Leadbeater said, "somehow persuaded her to resume her seat."[154]

Back at Adyar, standing on her terrace and looking out over the mango trees at the Bay of Bengal, she found herself just as restless and anxiety-ridden as ever. From the moment of her arrival, she had exhorted Olcott to take her to a judge or a solicitor so she might begin legal action against the Coulombs and Madras Christian College. After reading the written statements she had collected in Cairo, he told her that "she had made a mess of the affair," that while the declarations might suggest "a line of inquiry that should be followed in case the matter should come to trial,"[155] they could not, in their present form, be introduced in court. He positively forbade her to go off half-cocked to file a libel suit. When the Society's annual convention opened, he would lay her case before the delegates and appoint a special committee of their ablest lawyers to decide what, if any, steps should be taken. Olcott wrote in his memoirs,

* * *

She fretted and stormed and insisted, but I would not stir from my position, and, when she threatened to go off by herself and "wipe this stain off her character," I said that I should, in that case, resign my office and let the Convention decide between us: I knew too much about legal practice to do any such foolish thing. She then yielded.[156]

Helena never forgave him, still reviling him several years later as a faint-hearted coward who had prevented her from clearing her name. The truth was too unpleasant to admit: not only Henry but Subba Row and the other attorneys in the Society realized the unfavorable impression she would create in a witness box. They shuddered to imagine what she might say in the hands of a cross-examiner, or what she might not say, for her refusal to answer questions about the Mahatmas could cause her to be cited for contempt of court. Furthermore, word had it that some of the English judges were hoping to get Madame Blavatsky into court so that "this damned fraud may be shown up,"[157] and its perpetrator shipped to a penal colony in the Andaman Islands.

More than one of the delegates to her ninth annual convention suspected Madame Blavatsky of perpetrating the Coulomb letters, and the convention-eers as a body voted unanimously that she "should not prosecute her defamers in a Court of Law."[158] Lacerated by their lack of faith in her and in the Mahatmas, she wrote to Solovyov, "You are my one friend, for God's sake, my angel . . . Answer me soon; I don't believe that you have turned my enemy, too."[159] In India, the adopted homeland she had envisioned as her haven of peace, she now found herself forsaken and friendless. Marooned in her rooftop bedroom, there must have been moments when she mourned the loss of her closest friend, Emma Coulomb.

THE SECRET DOCTRINE

1884–1887

I

~~~~~~~~~~~~~

The Investigation

The Society for Psychical Research, in the person of Richard Hodgson, was waiting for Helena in Madras. On December 18, Hodgson had presented himself at Theosophical Headquarters and asked Damodar if he might have a look at the Occult Room and also inspect samples of Madame Blavatsky's handwriting. Damodar replied that, in the absence of both Madame and the colonel, he had no authority to grant either request, but that he expected them back any day. Hodgson said that he would return.

Chief among the Theosophists' complaints about Richard Hodgson was his lack of experience as a psychical researcher. However, it must be kept in mind that in 1884 virtually no researchers existed, experienced or otherwise. Ironically, Hodgson would make his reputation as a result of the Theosophical investigation and go on to become widely recognized as possibly *the* greatest psychical researcher of the Victorian era. At the time he met H.P.B. he was a twenty-nine-year-old university lecturer of little apparent brilliance.

An Australian by birth, Hodgson had taken a doctorate in law at Melbourne University before going to England in 1878 and entering Cambridge, where he studied moral sciences. One of his professors was Henry Sidgwick, a professor of moral philosophy and a founder of the S.P.R. It was as a result of his friendship with Sidgwick that Hodgson joined an undergraduate group called the Cambridge Society for Psychical Research. The society conducted a few unsatisfactory experiments with mediums, but since its members were students with presumably more pressing concerns, it remained a dilettante avocation and soon expired. After completing his course, Hodgson became a lecturer with the University's Extension Service, mainly in the north of England, teaching the philosophy of Herbert Spencer. In 1882, he joined the newly organized Society for Psychical Research.

In the highly rarefied atmosphere of Cambridge, Hodgson had stood out as a man of quirky, if not eccentric, sensibilities. For example, he had refused to accept his degree because the graduation ceremony required him to kneel before the vice-chancellor; although he did not kneel to any man, his friends persuaded him to make an exception in this case. Hodgson's stubborn individualism carried over to his dress—he wore a brown evening suit instead of the customary black—and his breezy manners and booming voice put off more than a few people. However, those who knew him well came to cherish his absolute sincerity as compensation for his lack of humor, and to appreciate that, whether it was a game of handball or the investigation of a medium, he was always in deadly earnest and hated losing a game or being defeated in an argument. William James, who later would bring him to the United States as head of the American Society for Psychical Research, called him "a real man,"[1] and added that while Hodgson believed in the reality of many Spiritualistic phenomena, "he also had uncommon keenness in detecting error; and it is impossible to say in advance whether it will give him more satisfaction to confirm or to smash a given case offered to his examination."[2]

Later Hodgson would insist that when he took up his assignment in India, he felt favorably disposed toward H.P.B., although he never specified whether it was toward her personality, her phenomena or her philosophy. Certainly he was not at all offended by her earthy language or candid manner, as he himself could not be bothered with social niceties. As for her teachings, he did not propose to analyze them because the S.P.R. considered philosophy beyond the range of its inquiry; its sole concern was with the phenomenal aspect of Theosophy. Personally, Hodgson's chief area of interest was personal survival: is the human personality obliterated at death—can consciousness continue to function in the absence of nerve tissue? To Hodgson, all other considerations were purely secondary. Hodgson approached H.P.B. with the attitude of a first-rate detective: all he sought were facts, which, once and for all, would prove or disprove her phenomena.

When Hodgson reappeared at Adyar on December 22, Helena's mood could not have been more downcast. She and Olcott were constantly at each other's throats, but she was careful to conceal the bickering from Hodgson. There was no reason why she should have liked the man, yet her own statements give the impression that she did. That she judged him a friendly, pleasant young man, unlike those haughty, detestable English types, only demonstrates what a poor judge of persons she could be. She seems not to have totally glossed over his potential danger, but rather to have minimized it, perhaps because his attitude was cordial and he was a friend of the Cooper-Oakleys. In a flurry of hospitality, she invited him to come out to Adyar as her house guest, assuring him of her utmost cooperation in whatever inquiries he wished to make.

Encouraged by this amicable beginning, Helena must still have realized she was treading a treacherous path. Hodgson's first request could not have been unexpected: he wanted permission to examine the shrine and Occult Room. Helena replied innocently that the shrine seemed to have disappeared during her absence, and so far she had been unable to discover its whereabouts. When Damodar and Hartmann were asked for information, both of them denied any knowledge of the cupboard. The matter should have ended there, but to Helena's dismay, Hodgson refused to give up. As he later wrote,

> It was only after repeated and urgent requests to be told what had happened that I learnt from the halting account given by Mr. Damodar and Dr. Hartmann that the Shrine had been removed from the Occult Room into Mr. Damodar's room at about mid-day of September 20th, that on the following morning, at 9 o'clock, they found the Shrine had been taken away, and they had not seen it since.[3]

Since all of them knew perfectly well the shrine's ultimate fate, Helena must have been particularly relieved to see Hartmann and Damodar lying for her. As for the famous Occult Room, all Hodgson could perceive was an ordinary room with freshly plastered walls.

By the time he requested a sample of her handwriting to compare with the Coulomb documents, Helena began growing uneasy. When she offered to write him a letter as a test specimen, he replied that he needed script dating from before the appearance of the *Christian College Magazine* articles, inferring that she might have altered her script in the aftermath. Coming to her aid, Olcott fended off Hodgson, stressing the fact that the request could only be granted with the approval of the Theosophical Society as a whole. Undaunted, Hodgson asked to see a Mahatma letter, which he intended to submit to a calligraphic expert, but again Olcott put him off. By this juncture Helena must have been utterly frantic.

Over the next ten days, Hodgson stayed at Adyar, cross-examining every Theosophist on the premises and a few who did not live there. He would ask them to describe the occasions when they had seen the Mahatmas, either in their physical or astral bodies; when had they received Mahatmic letters and in what manner; how the shrine worked and what the Occult Room looked like. No one, including Babula, was excused from his interrogation, which could be both tough and tenacious. Objectively, it appeared that H.P.B. had little cause for concern, since no one had said anything incriminating; indeed, when Hodgson bore in too dangerously close on some point, she had watched people, unconsciously or deliberately, falsifying their stories.

While Hodgson seemed to be making little progress with his interviews, he did however manage to obtain some Mahatma letters from Damodar and from Hartmann, who also gave him one of H.P.B.'s letters written to him from Elberfeld. In the meantime, he had been in touch with George Patterson, who offered to loan him several of the Coulomb letters with the proviso that Hodgson keep them away from Adyar lest Madame tamper with them.

H.P.B. appeared to be following this line of investigation with little interest: while Hodgson recalled that she occasionally asked him if he had seen the letters, she expressed no desire to inspect them herself. He found it odd that she should display such indifference to what she called forgeries, since, had she wanted to see them, Patterson would certainly have permitted a viewing before witnesses. Afterwards Helena often referred to the unfairness of the investigation, claiming she had asked repeatedly to see the letters, but had been refused. According to Patterson, however, "no Theosophist has ever asked to see any other letter, or his request would have been, under proper precautions, at once complied with."[4] Hodgson, interestingly enough, was not convinced that the letters were H.P.B.'s work, or at least did not accept the sole opinion of the Madras bank manager, James Gribble, who had attributed them to her; instead he sent three or four of the disputed letters, along with one of Helena's own notes, to Frederick George Netherclift, one of the leading handwriting experts in the world and a consultant for the British Museum.[5]

By the end of the first week of January, Hodgson, having little more to do at Headquarters, moved back to Madras and on the ninth he paid a call on Emma and Alexis who were living at Saint-Thomé with a missionary family, the Dyers. In the course of a general conversation, about premonitions, Hodgson was just admitting he had no theory to account for them, when

something white appeared, touching my hair, and fell on the floor. It was a letter. I picked it up. It was addressed to myself. M. and Madame Coulomb were sitting near me and in front of me. I had observed no motion on their part which could account for the appearance of the letter. Examining the ceiling as I stood I could detect no flaw; it appeared intact. On opening the letter, I found it referred to the conversation which had just taken place.[6]

There is no doubt that the Coulombs' demonstration of a Mahatmic mail delivery was more impressive than any verbal description they might have supplied. The ceiling, Alexis explained to Hodgson, was supported by main beams and cross beams, the spaces filled in by blocks of wood and mortar. He had scraped out the mortar from one of the interstices, inserted the letter with a piece of thread wrapped around it, and given the end of the thread to an accomplice who, upon hearing him call the dog, caused the letter to take a nose dive. Their discussion of premonitions had been adroitly led up to without Hodgson's realizing it. While Hodgson would assert that he did not regard as evidence any unsupported statement of the Coulombs because he regarded them as unscrupulous persons, one must assume that the demonstration had an effect on the investigation. It would be almost unimaginable had it not.

Throughout this period Helena was keeping a careful watch on Hodgson's movements. He appeared frequently at Adyar for dinner and talked freely about his work; and there was little that he did or said elsewhere that did not find its way back to her. Once she realized that he was interviewing people she regarded as her enemies, she grew uneasy. On January 3 she had written almost gaily to Solovyov that unquestionably she was the victim of a conspiracy and that Hodgson "too finds that it is a huge plot."[7] As for herself, "I am worn out and harassed, but still living, like an old cat with nine lives."[8] By the end of the month it was a different story. Olcott had gone off again, this time to Burma with Leadbeater, but even though they had nothing but angry words for each other now, she felt intensely alone without him.

Evenings were the worst. Insisting that everyone who worked at Adyar come to her room, she would gather them around her for what she called a family party. One or two of the Hindus would be requested to sit on her bed and massage her aching legs. "My child," she would say, "mesmerize my legs."[9] Later, when sleep refused to come to her, one of the Indians would remain all night on the sofa in her room but she would gruffly warn that snoring was not tolerated.

By the end of January, her formal black company gown sat in her wardrobe, for she almost never left her bed. Within the space of three days she instructed Damodar to cable Henry at Rangoon, "Return at once. Upasika dangerously ill";[10] and then summoned Maj.-Gen. Henry Rhodes Morgan, Subba Row, and two other Hindus to witness the signing of her will. Her books and furniture she left to Henry, as well as two pairs of candlesticks that Nadyezhda had given her. Candlesticks were also bequeathed to Dr. Hartmann; silver mugs to Damodar, Ananda and Babaji; and her clothing to Vera's daughters in Russia. She instructed that her body was to be burned and the ashes buried at Adyar, "and that none who are not Theosophists shall be present at the burning." And finally, "I desire that yearly, on the anniversary of my death, some of my friends should assemble at the Headquarters of the Theosophical Society and read a chapter of Edwin Arnold's *Light of Asia* and *Bhagavad Gītā*."[11]

Having put her affairs in order, she lay down and prepared herself for death, only to discover that her body refused to cooperate.

During the previous four years, Helena had been afflicted from time to time with a number of mysterious ailments. Generally she did not go into details when describing her symptoms to correspondents, but merely tossed out vague hints that she had been unconscious or at the point of death when the Mahatmas intervened to save her life. There is no question that many of her illnesses were psychosomatic; the insomnia, pounding of the heart, and sensations of suffocation were all symptoms of severe anxiety complicated by depression. As for the symptoms diagnosed as Bright's disease in 1882, these may have gone into remission because the several doctors who subsequently examined her in 1884 and '85 failed to mention it. At no time, however, did she seem to have been totally incapacitated: at those very moments when she claimed to be bedridden, she was generally rushing about to arrange some phenomenon. However, during her nine months in Europe a second identifiable disease began to emerge and from that time forward she speaks frequently of rheumatism and gout. Many who knew her corroborated the fact that she had trouble walking on her painfully swollen legs.

While no medical records are available, it seems safe to conclude that from 1884 to the time of her death she did in fact suffer from gout, a serious and potentially crippling form of arthritis. The disease, known from antiquity as an affliction of the upper classes, was commonly attributed to gluttony. We know today that most cases of gout are caused by an inherited metabolic defect resulting from an overaccumulation of uric acid in the blood. The onset of an attack is generally related to a particular event: infection, overindulgence in food or alcohol, ill-fitting shoes, fatigue or emotional stress. At least two of these precipitating factors seem to be present in H.P.B.'s case, overeating and prolonged stress.

Despite its reputation as a status symbol, gout is an extraordinarily painful inflammation that can flare up suddenly, often in the night. The affected joint becomes swollen and tender, the surrounding skin tightens and turns red or purplish. Other symptoms include fever, rapid heartbeats, chills and malaise, and some sufferers develop deposits of tophi, a chalky white derivative of uric acid. It is not known what, if any, treatment H.P.B.'s doctors advised since gout symptoms dissipate without treatment in a week or two. There is no cure for gout, but today anti-inflammatory drugs are used to treat acute attacks and prevent future incidents. In the nineteenth century, attacks of gout tended to become more severe and frequent, often leading to eventual kidney damage from deposits of urate, to the formation of kidney stones, and finally to permanent damage to the joints.

If Helena had lived a hundred years later, she would have been advised to prevent recurrent attacks by avoiding stress and losing weight. But even had she known about rest cures, she could not at this time afford the luxury of quiet. On the contrary, Hodgson's investigation had pushed her to the point of nervous collapse, which in turn aggravated her arthritic condition. Even if she had understood the ways in which her illnesses were interrelated, she would have been incapable of dealing with the situation. To her, the only relief was death.

Although in no danger of dying, she felt as if she were, and these feelings must be viewed against a backdrop of the events taking place at Adyar aside from Hodgson's activities. As she now realized, it had been a mistake to bring the Cooper-Oakleys to India because their marital difficulties had apparently come to a head and their domestic rows reverberated throughout the compound. Furthermore, Isabel was unable to handle the responsibility of caring for a woman she believed to be mortally ill. Night after night she sat beside Helena's bed or paced the roof trying to get a breath of cool air. Later it would be said that the Indian climate did not agree with her, but since she had grown up in India this seems unlikely. Most probably it was the strain of round-the-clock nursing duty that caused her to break down. By the end of

February her own strength would be gone, and by March she would not be able to stand without crutches.

If H.P.B. could derive no comfort from Isabel, neither did she find solace in Franz Hartmann or in St. George Lane-Fox, who had recently returned from London. While she remained cloistered in her rooftop suite, the two men put their heads together and decided to reorganize the management of the Society; Olcott would be relieved of his position as president and the executive authority transferred to a committee, composed mainly of themselves. A document to this effect was drawn up and brought upstairs for H.P.B.'s signature. Even allowing for her hostility toward Henry at that time, it seems incredible that she agreed to sign it, but she did, although immediately afterward she panicked.

On February 5, the mail brought a copy of the S.P.R.'s preliminary report, which sent her into a towering rage. As has been noted, the report was really a private and confidential memorandum to members, based on evidence taken from Olcott and Mohini months before Hodgson had reached India. On the whole, it treated Madame Blavatsky rather gently, but Helena could not avoid detecting the sly contempt for Olcott, revealed for all the world to see as a childish purveyor of fairy tales. All Helena could think of while reading his testimony was the absurd toy Buddha, and her fury at him and the S.P.R. mounted. In the margin of the report, she scrawled in blue pencil:

Madame Blavatsky, who will soon be dead and gone, for she is doomed, says this to her friends of the P.R.S.: 'After my death these phenomena, which are the direct cause of my premature death, will take place better than ever . . . Never, throughout my long and sad life, never was there so much of uncalled for, contemptuous suspicion and contempt lavished upon an innocent woman as I find here in these few pages published by so-called friends.[12]

In a pitiful postscript she added, "On my death-bed."

Later that day, when Henry arrived at Adyar, Hartmann and Lane-Fox served him with papers divesting him of his presidency. Dazed, he lumbered up to Helena's room with the dismissal notice in his hand. Was it fair, he asked mildly, that a person who had built up the Society from nothing "should be turned out on the road to go hang" without so much as a thank you or a character reference? Helena moaned that she had signed something Hartmann and Lane-Fox brought to her without reading carefully. She begged him to tear it up.

As much as she often disliked Olcott, she realized that she could not do without him; accordingly Hartmann and Lane-Fox were put in their places by a timely message from Mahatma Morya, who said that Olcott was doing a fine job and that the Masters would not agree to the Hartmann-Lane-Fox reorganization scheme. Henry's reappearance seems to have strengthened

H.P.B. because he noted in his diary that she was "about again and so much better."[13] When he received a telegram from Leadbeater on February 10 asking when he planned to return to Burma, Henry saw no reason for not going back and Helena consented. When they said goodbye, she cried and called him her old chum.

Perhaps Henry was relieved to flee Adyar, heavy with intrigue and sickness. If so, he was not the only one, because ten days later Damodar Mavalankar also made his exit. Having broken with his family, deserted his wife and sacrificed his fortune to follow the Mahatmas, he must have found it hard to admit it was not a Brotherhood for whom he had sacrificed himself, but a middle-aged Russian woman who wished to use him as a confederate. There is no doubt of Helena's fondness for Damodar, or of her well-placed confidence in his loyalty. By the winter of 1885, however, he had grown too disillusioned to function productively. The months of strain during which he had fought a losing battle against Emma and Alexis, struggled to shore up the front-line defenses while Madame roamed about Europe, and lied hand over fist to Hodgson, all these must have taken their toll, emotionally and physically, because he began to experience a return of his previously arrested tuberculosis.

Even with the Society crumbling and Madame dying, Damodar could not completely let go of his belief in the Mahatmas. For nearly six years he had served as their *chela*, but now, weary and frightened, he wished to retreat from the pain of this world; like Ramaswamier, who had taken his umbrella and walked north to find the Masters or die, Damodar decided that he too would journey into the unknown. Leaving Adyar on February 23, he traveled in slow stages toward the Tibetan border by way of Calcutta and Benares and finally reached Darjeeling, his last stop before crossing the border into Sikkim.

Sometime in July, Henry Olcott would receive word that Damodar's naked corpse, frozen stiff, had been found in the snow near Chumboi, Sikkim, with his clothing scattered a little distance away. Henry refused to believe that the body was Damodar's. It was not until a year later that the Society officially acknowledged Damodar's departure in its magazine, stating that he "has safely reached his destination, is alive, and under the guardianship of the friends whom he sought."[14] For several years, Henry kept a bag packed so that in case he heard from Damodar, he would be ready to entrain immediately for Darjeeling.

At the time of Damodar's going, Helena must have been too embroiled in her own troubles to object or even to warn him that his health made such a strenuous journey ill-advised. Certainly she sympathized with his need to escape from Adyar for a while, and she gave him her blessing. "Happy Damodar!" she wrote. "He went to the land of Bliss, to Tibet and must now be far away in the regions of our Masters." But perhaps she did realize the dangers because she added a realistic postscript, "No one will ever see him now, I expect."[15]

Damodar had fled through the looking glass into Madame Blavatsky's fantasy world, but for Helena there could be no such convenient escape. Her fears continued to build when Richard Hodgson returned to Adyar in the company of Allan Hume, who had been rendering him assistance as a kind of deputy-detective. By this time, Hodgson had taken a completely different view of Madame Blavatsky. He had visited Bombay, where he took pains to crawl around the dusty attic of the "Crow's Nest" checking to see if letters could be slipped through the rafter cracks; he had visited Hormusji Seevai, the jeweler who had repaired Minnie Hume's brooch; he had talked to Edward Wimbridge about his experiences at Girgaum Back Road; and he also chanced to meet Hurrychund Chintamon, recently returned from England and eager to testify against the Theosophists. Apparently Chintamon had saved the 1878 letters Madame had written him from New York, those in which she had characterized Olcott as a "psychologized baby."[16] The Yankees, she had written, thought themselves very smart; Colonel Olcott believed himself smart even for a Yankee, but he would have to get up much earlier in the morning to be as smart as she.

Back in Madras, with his dossier on Madame growing daily, Hodgson had inspected the receipt ledgers at M. Faciole and Co. and found entries for the saucers and vases that had subsequently appeared in the shrine as apports from Tibet; and he had finally wormed a confession from Franz Hartmann who told him the entire story of the shrine's dismantling. After two-and-a-half months of painstaking legwork, Hodgson had arrived at five main conclusions: that no Brotherhood of Mahatmas existed, with or without occult powers; that Morya and Koot Hoomi were fictitious personages whose correspondence had been written by Madame Blavatsky, assisted on occasion by Damodar; that Madame had written letters to Emma Coulomb giving instructions for fraudulent phenomena; that no single phenomenon of the Madame's could be regarded as genuine; and finally that the shrine had been nothing but a conjurer's box designed to produce spurious miracles. The chief witnesses to the existence of the Brotherhood had been the Hindus at Adyar, but Hodgson felt convinced they had made false statements. The other witness of course was Henry Olcott, and while Hodgson suspected his testimony was often at variance with the facts, he did not think him guilty of willful dishonesty, only of stupidity and absurd credulity.

As for Madame Blavatsky's teachings, Hodgson would later write:

Of those streams of superhuman knowledge I will only say I prefer to tap them at least one stage nearer the fountainhead. I lay claim to no vast erudition, but the sources which were good enough for Mme. Blavatsky were good enough for me and, so long as Bohn's *Classical Library* and Trubner's *Oriental Library* are within reach of a modest purse I prefer to draw on these useful repositories for my ideas of Platonic and Buddhist thought, even though I should be thus obliged to receive these ideas in bald, old-fashioned shape, unspiced with fraudulent marvels and uncorroborated by the forged correspondence of fictitious teachers of Truth.[17]

While Hodgson had absolutely no doubt he had reached the proper conclusions, he continued to be baffled by Madame's motives. It was true that the Theosophical Society had supported her for the past six years, but it had certainly not provided her with any great wealth. What satisfaction could she have gained from her chicanery? At a dinner party one evening, in the presence of Allan Hume and the Cooper-Oakleys, he reeled out a tentative theory that Madame must be a Russian spy. Even Hume burst out laughing at the idea of Helena, whose cover would be blown in five minutes, spying for anyone, but Hodgson was not so sure. Madame, he had come to believe, was a woman capable of every and any crime.

When this dinner table diatribe was reported to Helena, presumably through the Cooper-Oakleys, she responded with an indignant letter to Hodgson: she cared very little whether or not he thought her a fraud, but he had no right to make public slanderous statements that she was an agent of the Russian government. She ought to have him arrested, she wrote, and would have but for the fact that he was a friend of the Cooper-Oakleys and a person for whom she herself had once had "affectionate regard."[18] Not only did she fail to take out a warrant for his arrest, she neglected even to mail the letter.

Helena's inability to handle large-scale catastrophe was never more evident than during the next weeks. On March 13, Hodgson and Hume strode boldly into the Adyar compound and made themselves at home while Helena foolishly hid upstairs. At a series of conferences with the leading Theosophists, Hodgson discussed the results of his investigation while Subba Row, Hartmann and the others sat around looking glum. The next day Hume chaired a meeting in which he candidly admitted having changed his mind about the authorship of the Coulomb letters. In the light of Hodgson's findings, he now believed them genuine and of course had always assumed the phenomena to be fraudulent. However, since he believed the Society worth saving, he proposed that H.P.B., Olcott and a few others resign and the organization be reconstituted along scientific-philosophical lines; phenomena were to be prohibited. While his resolutions were thought far too radical to be carried out, the compound remained in a state of extreme tension. Helena, holed up in her bedroom, had been invited to the meetings but sent word that she was too ill to attend.

On the nineteenth, Henry Olcott arrived to put things right, but it seemed too late. "Black care was enthroned at Adyar when I got back from Rangoon," he wrote, "the very moral atmosphere was dark and heavy; H.P.B. was struggling for life and as vehement as an enmeshed lioness."[19] Despite his picture of Helena as a lioness in its death throes, she finally summoned sufficient strength to descend the stairs to meet with Hodgson, who was about to return to England. He frankly told her that he had no choice but to find her phenomena false and went on to explain his reasons. Helena listened stoically, and when Hodgson had finished, she told him that the Brotherhood did not want the world to believe in its existence, that he had in fact been guided by the Mahatmas during his investigation to the verdict of fraud. She acknowledged freely that he had done the best he could. "With me personally, face to face," Hodgson would later recall, "she was courageous unto the last."[20]

Olcott, still trying to get his bearings, paid a last-minute call on Hodgson in Madras. Henry had always respected Hodgson, he had even gone out of his way to be helpful by donating to him half-a-dozen undershirts and insisting he not bother with reimbursement until he reached England. How could a man to whom he had given his underwear suddenly turn on him? It was, to Henry, as inconceivable as Hodgson's condemnation of H.P.B. In Olcott's view the case against Helena was not proved because, as he would write Francesca Arundale, "no one, at least no credible witness, *saw* her write to [*sic*] C. letters . . ."[21] Whether he offered this feeble defense to Hodgson is unknown; probably not, since he suspected that H.P.B. had been guilty of bogus phenomena in moments of mental instability. However, the conversation took a brutal turn when Hodgson told him about Chintamon's letters and Helena's flippant boasting of her ability to control Olcott by merely looking into his face.

Henry crumpled. "In my whole experience in the movement," he wrote, "nothing ever affected me so much as this. It made me desperate, and for twenty-four hours almost ready to go down to the beach and drown myself in the sea."[22] When he was finally able to confront Helena, she replied only that she must have been joking.

Feeling that all was lost, Henry lived in hourly dread of fresh revelations. "If you had had the hell to pass through that I have had," he wrote Francesca, "I think you would be nearly crazy."[23] As it happened, he had no time to dwell on his sorrows because on March 28 the Theosophists were thwacked by still another blow. For six months Emma Coulomb and her missionary advisers had been awaiting H.P.B.'s lawsuit, not merely in response to the articles but also to a pamphlet Emma had published in December, "Some Account of My Intercourse with Madame Blavatsky," in which she had supplied further details on H.P.B.'s activities and additional extracts from their correspondence. As time passed and H.P.B. made no move, Emma looked for other means of luring her into court. Thus when Maj.-Gen. Henry Rhodes Morgan issued a fiery defense of H.P.B. and called Madame Coulomb a forger, Emma shifted gears at once and merrily sued Morgan for libel.

At Adyar an already volatile atmosphere was about to explode. Helena, "saying wild things,"[24] tramped up and down her room as she denounced Emma, the missionaries and Colonel Olcott. Henry recalled that "it was awful to see her, with her face empurpled by the blood that rushed to her head, her eyes almost standing out from their orbits and dead-looking."[25] An all-night conference ensued, in which it was agreed that the Society would certainly go under if Helena were called as a witness in the Morgan case. Girding himself for action, Henry insisted she be kept out of sight either until the trouble died down or Emma withdrew her suit. Personally, he thought that Helena had got all of them in serious trouble. Still, he had to extricate them if he could, but this time, Madame would obey him. First she must resign her office as Corresponding Secretary, and second, leave the country without delay.[26]

Helena listened to his ultimatums without sacrificing her equilibrium. She was willing to resign her office, but leaving India was quite another matter. Did he expect a seriously ill person to run away? Had he forgotten she could barely walk without assistance?

Henry refused to listen. It was not, as she claimed, his testimony to the S.P.R. or his Buddha on wheels that had brought this misery on them; it was she who had insisted on going to Europe and stirring up trouble with phenomena he had suspected all along of being phony. It was she, he cried, who suffered from "mental aberrations" and behaved like an "insane lunatic."[27] Now it had fallen to him "to get the ship through the breakers,"[28] and he had not the smallest doubt that if Helena remained in India, she would end in prison. She must leave quietly and swiftly, for if the missionaries heard of her departure they might take legal action to detain her. As for her inability to travel, he suggested that she take with her Mary Flynn, the suicidal girl from Bombay who had spent a year at Headquarters.

Helena watched Henry strut and sputter. He was, she thought to herself, "a perfect bag of conceit and silliness. *Il pose pour le martyr!* The—poor man."[29] He had been her devoted friend for ten years, her "chum," but she pitied him for failing to comprehend "that if we were *theosophical twins* during our days of glory, in such times of universal persecution, of false charges and public accusations, the 'twins' have to fall together as they have risen together, and that if I am called . . . a fraud by him, then must he be one also?"[30] When he had finished railing, she ordered Babula to begin packing her bags.

The next day Olcott went into Madras and bought second-class tickets on the next ship scheduled to sail whose destination happened to be Naples. At the last moment, Franz Hartmann offered to accompany Madame because he felt she should be traveling with a physician, then Helena insisted on bringing Babaji.

On the morning of March 31, virtually unable to stand, "I was carried from my sickbed in an invalid chair, lowered into the boat, and then transferred to the steamer, like a bale of goods, hardly conscious of what was going on."[31]

Madame Blavatsky's life in the land of the Mahatmas had come to an end.

* * *

By the time the SS *Pehio* docked at Naples on the twenty-third of April, 1885, Helena had almost completely shifted her rage from the Coulombs and Hodgson to Henry Olcott. Olcott was the ogre who knew that "I have not a brass farthing in my pocket" but who had nonetheless "sent off this servant of God, with three others, and 700 rupees in our pocket,"[32] apparently expecting them to live on it. Equally infuriatingly, he had entrusted the money to Hartmann, whom she had grown to despise, and to Babaji who had never been out of India, had no business sense in the first place and was slow-witted in the second. Choosing to ignore the fact that Olcott had struggled to scrape up the seven hundred rupees, Helena could only remember bitterly his admonitions that she find cheap lodgings in Italy and settle down to wait out her exile as best she could. In trivial matters, he had offended her too; for example, he had canceled the fifteen pounds' worth of books she had ordered from London through Francesca Arundale, writing himself to Francesca that he could not afford books that Helena might not live to read, and more to the point, that he did not have fifteen pounds in his London bank account.

Once in Naples, it took Hartmann and Babaji days to find a sufficiently inexpensive pension for them; it was not in the city or in any of the pretty little resort towns along the coast, but in a wretched village some ten miles south of Naples, at the foot of Mount Vesuvius. Today Torre del Greco is an industrial suburb boasting a few coral factories, where guided tour buses to Pompeii stop so that passengers may purchase coral and cameo knickknacks. In 1885 Torre del Greco offered even smaller interest to the average tourist, which explains its bargain rates. The Hotel del Vesuvio agreed to let the party occupy four furnished rooms for ninety francs a week, board included, but demanded three months' rent in advance. When H.P.B., who had taken no part in these negotiations, learned that Babaji had parted with a considerable portion of their funds, she could only splutter helplessly. Now she must stay there whether she liked it or not.

Initially she found Torre del Greco perversely suited to her mood and felt that "here in loneliness and quiet on the slopes of Vesuvius I must either recover—or die."[33] On the day of her arrival, she sent a dramatic letter to Vsevolod Solovyov in Paris urging him to come quickly as she was sure to die any day and she had many things to tell him "before I go off." Besides, he would like the town for "the view is marvellous, the air healthy, and the living 'cheaper than stewed turnips.' "[34]

At the same time, she sent a report of her new home to Henry, whom she addressed icily as "My dear Colonel Olcott": she was sitting in a damp room on the side of Vesuvius with her feet resting on an uncarpeted stone floor, in a country where stoves were apparently unknown and arctic air whistled under doors and through windows. While she understood perfectly that he had sent her away to die and that he had no money for better accommodations or for frivolities such as carpets, would he please ship her the old carpet from Bombay so that she might cut it into two pieces. Otherwise she could see no way of avoiding another attack of gout.

It was unseasonably chilly for April, and she proved accurate in predicting a worsening of the gout; by the end of May, when the weather was still freezing, her right hand had swollen until she had trouble holding a pen. Not only was she physically uncomfortable but she shivered from the chill of a crushing emotional abandonment. Increasingly obsessed with Henry's treachery, she knew she could never forgive his cruel taunts at Adyar; as for the rest of them, the Cooper-Oakleys and Subba Row and Hartmann, they made her churn with disgust. "My heart is broken—physically and morally," not by her enemies whose persecutions she could have borne, but by selfish, weakhearted friends who believed in her guilt yet were eager to lie on her behalf "since I was a convenient step to rise upon." Human nature, for which she had no high regard anyway, had never seemed so obscene. Nevertheless, "with most of them, I shall remain on good terms to my dying day. Nor shall I allow them to suspect I read through them from the first."[35] She would not give them the pleasure of revealing how much she hated them, but asked only "to be left to die like a mangy dog, quietly and alone in my corner."[36]

She continued to shoot off a stream of angry letters to Henry, accusing him of cowardice and demanding that he remove her name from the *Theosophist*. When he replied that her letters hurt him, she responded with a half-hearted apology. Looking back only a year to the days when Theosophy had become almost fashionable, she mourned for lost fame and absent friends. Even Solovyov, her "little father,"[37] had written that, although he would like to see her again, his liver had been acting up, and he simply was in no shape for a journey. Hartmann had gone, but that had been a relief, because she knew him for a cunning, vindictive liar; suddenly, she felt cut off and surrounded by tiresome people. Babaji, simply an extra mouth to feed, was of no use to her whatsoever. Mary Flynn meant well but was also "an arrant fool, spoilt at home, and does not even know how to boil water in a coffee pot. One cannot talk to her about anything but dress."[38] Besides, she longed for "something to eat besides the eternal macaroni."[39]

Having no one to talk to and no energy for writing, Helena, suddenly seeing Torre del Greco as more isolated than Siberia, decided on a change of scene. In April, Michael Katkov had published the final installment of the *Blue Mountains* and, while she did not know exactly how much he owed her, she was sure it could not be less than several thousand francs, enough to leave Italy. Dead set against settling in London, Paris or any other large European city, she considered Würzburg, Germany; at least the Germans had warm stoves and double windows and knew the meaning of comfort. She liked Würzburg because "it is near Heidelberg and Nuremberg and all the centres one of the Masters lived in."[40] It is reasonable to assume that she was familiar with this section of Germany, probably from the days when she lived with Agardi Metrovitch, and that she retained fond memories of it. Another consideration was that Würzburg seemed closer to Odessa than did France or England, and the likelihood of Nadyezhda's visiting her was greatest there. The prospect of a cozy German apartment, where she could set up her samovar and feel comfortable, brightened her mood a little. Upon her arrival at Torre del Greco, she had felt like hiding, had in fact warned Solovyov not to reveal her whereabouts; now, however, she began to reestablish contact with people. Neither she nor Koot Hoomi had written to Alfred Sinnett in months, and she had not heard from him; she must make an immediate effort to win him back. From Mohini, who was now living in London, she learned that Alfred had lost nearly all his life savings in an unfortunate business venture. Hard pressed to support his family, he had recently written an occult novel, *Karma*. Even Patience had turned out a manual called "The Purpose of Theosophy." Helena had deliberately neglected to read *Karma*, in which she appeared as a main character, since she could well imagine what Sinnett had done to her; she had read Rosa Praed's *Affinities*, in which Mohini figured prominently. She had thought it simply dreadful, and it had made her wonder about Mohini, who had become fashionable as London's resident Indian mystic.

Deciding to approach Sinnett in a roundabout fashion, she wrote Mohini and asked him to show her letter to Alfred; but if this was an attempt to recapture the old friendship, she had set about it in the worst possible way. In a typical counter-attack, she flung the blame for the Coulomb charges onto Sinnett. Were it not for his greediness for phenomena and his hotheaded rush to thrust two books of the Masters' teachings before the unenlightened public, none of this would have happened. She had "never *deceived him*, never tried to *mislead*, never *lied* to him"[41] but now she was dying; it was she who suffered the karmic results of his ill-timed and selfish zeal. For her part, she could no longer act as intermediary between him and the Masters. "Let him drop me out of his life like a bad penny,"[42] and, if Sinnett wished, he should feel free to find other channels to Tibet. The latter was a realistic concession because after Laura Holloway had returned to the United States, Sinnett had tried reaching the Mahatmas through other mediums; H.P.B. knew there was no way to stop him. And at that point, she hardly cared.

Sinnett did not reply to her, doubtless because of the Mahatmas' letters, encouraging him to write *Occult World* and *Esoteric Buddhism* and expressing their utmost confidence in his judgment as to how the teachings should be presented. But Patience must have intuited the pain behind H.P.B.'s words and wrote gently that "[I] cannot imagine how anyone knowing you can believe you guilty."[43] Even were she convinced that Madame "had written those wretched letters, I should love you still."[44]

How Helena must have groaned to realize that even the saintly Patience seemed less than totally convinced of her innocence. Soothing reassurances of affection were not what she needed; nothing would do but to make everyone believe wholeheartedly in her innocence.

All of Helena's correspondence from this period fiercely proclaims that she had never deceived anyone and never written Emma incriminating letters; one almost senses she was hiding from herself the full extent of her guilt, or, even more incredibly, that she could not bear to face reality and had actually convinced herself that she had done nothing to warrant blame. Still, in her reply to Patience written on July 23, she peels away an important layer of her psyche to reveal complete awareness of her situation and the terrible price she was paying for a career built on deception.

Had I written *even one* of those idiotic and at bottom *infamous* interpolations now made to appear in the said letters; had I been guilty *only once*—of a deliberate, purposely concocted fraud, especially when those deceived were my best, my *truest* friends—no "love" for such a one as I! At best—pity, or eternal contempt. Pity, if proved that I was an irresponsible lunatic, a hallucinated *medium* made to trick by my "guides" whom I was representing as *Mahatmas*; contempt—*if* a conscious fraud—but then where would be the *Masters*? Ah, dear child of my old heart, I was, I *really was* guilty, of but one crime . . .[45]

That single crime was concealment of certain secrets she was not permitted to divulge without betraying the Masters. "Never, never shall you, or even could you, realize . . . all I had to suffer for the last ten years!"[46] Then she insisted on enumerating the crimes with which she had been charged: "ambition," "love of cheap fame," "fraud and deceit," "cunning and unscrupulousness," "lying and cheating," and "deliberately bogus phenomena." These, she said, were part of the exterior carcass that the world perceived as Madame Blavatsky; they did not see "the interior wretched prisoner,"[47] nor was she able to explain herself due to the pledge of secrecy she had made to the Brotherhood. Only in some future existence did she hope for justice.

Clearly, this wishful thinking was an attempt to twist truth into a defense for defenseless actions, but it had a more serious purpose than merely assuaging her personal agony: if she were to salvage anything from the wreckage she had left behind in India, she firmly believed her one hope lay with the European Theosophists. Thus, during the summer at Torre del Greco, she made an important decision: to break secretly with Henry Olcott, to undermine his power quietly without jeopardizing her monthly allowance and to transfer the heart and soul of the Society from India to Europe. In Helena's opinion, the Society, like herself, had outgrown Henry Olcott. The first clue to her thinking crops up in a letter to Francesca Arundale and her mother, Mary, odd confidantes considering that they were Henry's closest friends in London.

"Listen: *try to disconnect the L.L.* [London Lodge] *as much as you can* from H.Q. You may be at heart—*one*. Try to become *two* in the management."[48] Adyar was full of traitors and Judases who hated Europeans. Even Subba Row, she said, had called her "a shell deserted and abandoned by the Masters" because she had committed the most terrible of crimes by revealing occult secrets to whites. Henry, "a wind-bag full of vanity,"[49] had fallen under Subba Row's influence.

Thus she planted the seeds of schism, suspecting that the Londoners would not be so quick to abandon her if they believed she still had tantalizing tidbits to solve the riddle of the universe. The public could never get enough of two things: phenomena and occult secrets. With the first she could no longer oblige them, but if they liked, they should have secrets such as they had never dreamed of. Long ago she had learned that human nature could be repulsive; now she vowed to use that insight for her own ends. And it might just be possible to save herself.

At the end of July, accompanied by Babaji and Mary Flynn, Madame Blavatsky bid farewell to Vesuvius, taking with her as a momento a cold she had caught in their last hours before departing. After a week's stopover in Rome, she started north to join Vsevolod Solovyov and Emile de Morsier at the fashionable Swiss resort of St. Cergues. One afternoon at about 3 P.M. she arrived on the Geneva diligence that stopped at the front door of Solovyov's hotel, the Pension Delaigue. The journey had exhausted Helena; worse, she had grown so maddened by the ineptness of her two companions that she wanted to throttle them. Solovyov, standing outside the pension, found himself mortified at the sight of H.P.B. and her entourage, which must have presented a bizarre spectacle in the provincial town. Nevertheless, his description of her arrival, more vicious than amusing, is best described as racist, sexist, and generally insensitive:

Suddenly there sprang from the diligence a strange creature, something half way between a great ape and a tiny black man. Its leanness was amazing. A poor half-European sort of dress dangled on it, as though there were nothing but bones beneath, a face the size of a fist, of a dark cinnamon colour and without any signs of vegetation; on the head a dense cap of long black curling hair; huge eyes, also perfectly black, of course, with a frightened and suspicious expression.[50]

Babaji repelled the Russian. Mary Flynn merely embarrassed him. She was "a clumsy young person, with a red, disconcerted and not particularly intelligent face . . ."

The public gazed open-mouthed at the black man. But the most interesting was yet to come. The black man and the clumsy young woman, and then I and Madame de Morsier, succeeded with great difficulty in extracting from the diligence something that was shut up in it. This something was "Madame" herself, all swollen, tired out with travelling, grumbling; with a huge dark-grey face, and wide open eyes, like two round discoloured turquoises. On her head was set a very high grey felt fireman's helmet with ventilators and a veil. Her globular figure seemed yet more globular from an incredible sort of sacque in which she was draped.[51]

After embracing her friends, Helena aimed a stream of invective at Mary, "Mashka" she called her, and at Babaji, until the two of them stood distraught in the road. "This idiot of a girl," Helena declared, was so stupid that she disbelieved a bigger fool had ever appeared on earth, and she cursed the day she had agreed to bring her along. Babaji, she fumed, "spins like a top and never stirs from his place."[52] Having got that out of her system, H.P.B. was further annoyed to learn that the pension had not given her three adjoining rooms as she had requested, and she stormed off to another hostel down the road.

By evening she had not yet calmed down. At dinner Solovyov and Madame de Morsier listened while Helena picked at her food and continued to grumble that Mashka was driving her to madness. And yet it was amazing that even a fool like her could see the Masters every day.

"Mary," she called. "Come here. Tell the truth. Do you see the Master?"

"Oh yes," Mary agreed. "I see him."

Turning to Solovyov and de Morsier, Helena crowed, "There now, you see! Why should she lie. And she is such a fool that she could not even make up a lie. She does see, and there is an end of it."[53]

When she switched the subject abruptly to the Coulombs and Hodgson, Solovyov reported, "there poured from her lips such contradictory assertions, and such choice abuse, that Madame de Morsier and I quite lost heart, and almost stopped her mouth and quieted her by force."[54]

Helena spent eight days at St. Cergues. The pleasant weather turned cold and rainy, and her gout grew worse. When Mary Flynn dressed up and wandered off without permission to a nearby country fair where she sang, danced, and delivered an impromptu sermon on Buddhism, Helena reached the end of her patience. Posthaste, she packed Mary off to an uncle in England, having first made other arrangements for a servant. In the pension she found a Swiss maid, Louise, who spoke French and German, and was willing to go to Würzburg, and who did not appear to be a fool.

II

Würzburg

By August 12 Helena was installed in a suite of spacious rooms at No. 6 Ludwigstrasse, one of the best addresses in town. Despite her comfortable new apartment, or perhaps *because* of it, her finances were perilous. Two weeks later she wrote Francesca that the colonel had left her to starve; in Italy she had been obliged to wipe her face "with towels made out of an old chemise of mine and I ate only one meal a day." It was the little money she had received from her Russian articles that had made possible the move to Würzburg, but now even that was nearly gone, and she expected to be penniless in no time. On Henry's allowance of 400 francs a month "it is next to impossible for me to live decently."[55] Her complaint to Francesca, forwarded to Adyar, produced a sarcastic reply from Henry; if anyone was starving, he snapped, it was the people left at Headquarters, all of whom were subsisting on less than he sent her each month. However, her similar complaint to the Gebhards at Elberfeld brought in response a large, comfortable arm chair, which Helena installed at her writing table.

Würzburg, on the Main River, was a picturesque town of cafés, medieval towers and baroque palaces surrounded by vineyards and rolling farmland. Helena saw none of it. Still suffering severely from gout, she was able to hobble about a little in her rooms but did not feel up to venturing out of doors. She spent the days at her desk, finishing an article for *Russky Vyestnik* and contemplating the new book, *The Secret Doctrine*.

For more than two years she had been talking about her rewriting *Isis Unveiled*. She was no longer proud of it; in fact, it had embarrassed her as far back as August, 1882, when Master Koot Hoomi had casually remarked to Sinnett that *Isis* "really ought to be rewritten for the sake of the family honour."[56] In January, 1884, just before H.P.B. left for Europe, the *Theosophist* had carried an announcement of *The Secret Doctrine*, "A New Version of 'Isis Unveiled,' "[57] which would be written in collaboration with Subba Row and issued in monthly installments over a period of two years. Subscriptions were invited. From time to time, Helena had declared that she was at work on the book, or that she had "received" an outline from Master Morya, but if the Mahatma gave her editorial suggestions, they must have been of little use. The truth of the matter was that ever since the trouble at Adyar and the S.P.R. investigation, Helena had been unable to concentrate on anything but her personal problems. The *Theosophist* had been obliged to announce several postponements and assure subscribers that their remittances were being kept untouched in a special bank account.

In recent months, however, it occurred to Helena that *The Secret Doctrine* might offer an ideal means of vindicating herself. Instead of rewriting *Isis*, she could use the fragmentary teachings in the Mahatma letters as a foundation on which to build a system. With the help of her Masters, she would produce a masterwork twenty times more learned that either *Isis* or Sinnett's *Esoteric Buddhism*. It would be a magnum opus unveiling to the nineteenth century certain portions of the hidden knowledge and proving that occult doctrine is the foundation of all religions, including Christianity. "I will show what a Russian spy can do, an alleged forger-plagiarist."[58] Hodgson, she thought, was a clever man but not "clever enough for *truth, and it shall triumph*, after which I can die peacefully."[59] But before she could produce truth, she needed comfortable surroundings where, undistracted, she might settle down to the same intense routine she had developed at the Lamasery while writing *Isis*.

Unfortunately, Würzburg was not New York, and she could no longer avail herself of the emotional support and editorial assistance of Olcott and Alexander Wilder. She did not even have the help of Subba Row, who aside from the fact of his being in Madras, had recently exhibited signs of hostility. During those first floundering weeks at Würzburg, she must have been overwhelmed by the dimensions of the task she had set for herself. Her forte had always been short pieces, such as essays, fiction and letters; longer works required careful organization and precise conception, two properties which were not native to her character. When an idea struck her, she would grab her pen and reel off twenty or thirty pages at a sitting, but, since she peregrinated from one idea to another, she consistently wound up with unrelated short essays that did not add up to a book.

Aside from her literary frustration, she discovered that the isolation she had sought in Würzburg was depressing her, and almost immediately she began inviting friends up for a visit. The first two guests to arrive were Vsevolod Solovyov and Justine Glinka, who stayed nearby at Rugmer's Hotel. Solovyov seems to have spent most of his time with Helena; she could not do without him a single day and would send Babaji to the hotel to say that Madame was feeling very bad, that her doctor was alarmed and that Solovyov must come at once. From behind these transparent ruses, there emerges the picture of a sick, lonely woman desperate for company. To keep Solovyov in constant attendance, she would attempt to reward him with some minor phenomenon: on one such occasion, she rehearsed Babaji to write in Russian "Blessed are they that believe," then tried to persuade Solovyov that the Hindu had received the words in a paranormal manner. Solovyov shook with laughter when he saw that Babaji had mistakenly written, "Blessed are they that *lie*,"[60] but Helena did not find it amusing. Clearly her heart was not in performing; her swollen limbs made the slightest movement difficult, and because of her clumsiness, she even dropped her "astral bell" machine. When Solovyov hurried to pick it up, she snatched it from his hands while he politely changed the subject. On another occasion, after Solovyov had asked for some Indian attar of roses, she produced "phenomenally" a flask of oil of orange, no doubt supposing that he would not notice the difference. When he pointed out that her Master had made a mistake, Helena exclaimed, "Eh, devil take it!"[61]

Writing to Vera at this time, she claimed to be beleaguered by invitations. The Hindus were demanding that she return to India while her faithful London Theosophists simply "won't leave me alone." She was ignoring them, preferring to sit quietly in Würzburg, "waiting for Nadya's promised visit and won't stir from here. I am writing a new book which will be worth two such as Isis."[62] Around the first of September, the guests whom she had begged to visit finally began to trickle in: Francesca and Mohini from London, her aunt from Odessa, Patience and Alfred who were vacationing in Belgium, and a little later, the Hermann Schmiechens, Franz Hartmann, and Dr. William Hubbe-Schleiden. During the next weeks she could not complain of loneliness since visitors were constantly in and out of her flat. During the Sinnetts' stay there, they began to discuss his idea of writing her biography. He had broached the subject several years earlier but, understandably, she had laughed it off as ridiculous; never, she had told him, would she consider such a project. Now, Alfred strongly urged her to reconsider. Since Emma Coulomb and others on all sides seemed to be making false accusations about her, it might be good public relations for the Society if she published the true story of her life. Of course the last thing H.P.B. wished to do was publish the truth about herself, but she could appreciate the wisdom of Alfred's plan and vaguely promised to cooperate.

Now Helena breakfasted, lunched, dined, and talked non-stop all day long. At night she stayed up with the treasured Nadyezhda, because her aunt was in the habit of sleeping during the day. By the time the last of her guests went home in early October, Helena was completely exhausted, and on the night of the ninth she had to send for the doctor at 11 P.M. to administer morphine and digitalis. "Such palpitations and cramps in the heart that I thought they were the last!" she reported to Sinnett. "I am now ordered to hold my tongue, hence I have more time to hold my pen . . ."[63]

Alone again, it was easy to hold her tongue; holding her pen proved more difficult. Even though she wrote Olcott that she was in the middle of Part One, *The Secret Doctrine* still remained little more than a nebulous idea in her head. According to Sinnett, the book was untouched when he saw her in September; Dr. Hubbe-Schleiden said that "when I visited her in October, 1885, she had just begun to write it, and in January, 1886, she had finished about a dozen chapters . . ."[64] In November, to Henry again, she offered a clue to her problems when she boasted:

* * *

Ah, you think I cannot write the S.D. without *you* or anyone sitting near me and helping? Well you shall soon find out your mistake. I have three Chap. ready, the *fourth* nearly finished and the S.D. shall be another, quite another kind of a hair-pin than *Isis*. It is a song from quite another opera, dear.[65]

From these various statements one gathers she had made a start of some kind, and that she was sufficiently satisfied to brag about functioning without a collaborator.

The actuality was somewhat different: she may have been capable of writing without a collaborator, but she could do little without a person to function as her companion-caretaker-nurse-editorial assistant. But where was such a miracle worker to be found?

During the month of October, all Helena could manage was stumbling to her desk in the mornings. The midnight summonses to Dr. Leon Oppenheim became more frequent. It was on one of these visits that H.P.B. first conceived of the idea that Vera would later call her single largest folly. Given Helena's fifty-year "folly" record, that estimate may sound excessive, but nonetheless it does seem rash for a twice-married woman of fifty-four suddenly to proclaim herself a virgin.

It happened in this way: apparently Helena was having problems with her bladder and Dr. Oppenheim, advising a gynecological examination, brought "his instruments, looking-glass or mirror to look *inside* and other horrors," Helena wrote.

"Were you ever married?" he asked her.

"Yes," she replied briefly, not wanting to go into details. Then she added, "But never had any children."

"No, surely," Dr. Oppenheim allegedly declared. "How could you since for all I can see, you must have never had connection with your husband."[66]

Gasping at this unsolicited medical opinion, H.P.B. quickly relayed the news to Sinnett, who had heard Emma's vague rumors about Agardi and Yuri; now he saw this odd new occurrence as a solution to one of Helena's problems. "Have a certificate, Old Lady, have one!"[67] he urged.

Dr. Oppenheim told her, as Helena revealed to Olcott, that "I have from birth the uterus crooked or hooked inside out, and that I could not, not only *never have children*, but that it is now the cause of my suffering with the bladder . . . and that if I had ever tried (thanks!) to be *immoral* with anyone, I would have had each time an inflammation and great suffering. There! So much for the Coulombs' three children, my marriage with Mitra, etc., etc."[68] She went on to say that once she had explained to the doctor about her enemies' accusations of immorality, he had readily agreed to sign a certificate.

The certificate said:

* * *

The undersigned testifies as requested, that Mme Blavatsky of Bombay–New York, corresponding secretary of the Theosophical Society, is at the present time under the medical treatment of the undersigned. She suffers from *Anteflexio Uteri*, most probably from the day of her birth, as proved by minute examination; she has never borne a child, nor has she had any gynecological illness.

(Signed) Dr. Leon Oppenheim

WÜRZBURG, 3 November, 1885.

The signature of Doctor Leon Oppenheim is hereby officially attested. WÜRZBURG, 3rd November, 1885.

The Royal Medical Officer of the District

(Signed) Dr. Med. Roeder.[69]

Unfortunately Dr. Oppenheim's certificate turned out to be less than satisfactory since it did not state that H.P.B. had never been pregnant, only that she had never borne a child and it did not mention virginity. At Helena's request, he wrote a second certificate slightly more to the point: "I hereby certify that Mme. Blavatsky has never been pregnant with child and so consequently can never have had a child. Oppenheim."[70] Once again, however, there was missing even an implication of virginity. When H.P.B. forwarded a copy of the document to Sinnett, she was forced to enclose a note explaining that "gynecological illness" really meant intactness: "it is a *delicate* and *scientific* way of putting it, and *very clear*."[71] Actually it was far from clear; Dr. Oppenheim was not so foolish as to state in writing that Madame Blavatsky had never experienced intercourse, although later, probably under pressure, he did tell Constance Wachtmeister that while no doctor could positively certify virginity, to the best of his knowledge Madame had not had sexual relations.

Several of Madame Blavatsky's biographers have advanced the theory that she herself forged the certificate. This seems unlikely because she circulated the document in Würzburg while under Oppenheim's regular care; surely he would have protested a forgery. Moreover, the fact that the certificate is worthless seems to indicate that it is genuine. As it happens, though, the paper was also worthless as proof that she never bore a child.

In the first place, from everything known about the professional relationships between women and their physicians in the 1880s, it seems unlikely that H.P.B. ever had a gynecological examination, certainly not a proper one. In that prudish period women customarily described their symptoms and then were escorted to the bedroom where a superficial examination took place. Even in cases where a diagnosis was urgently needed, there were widespread objections to being examined by male physicians.

Secondly, and more significant, the term *anteflexio uteri* means only that the uterus is tipped forward, a condition common to about twenty-five percent of all women; and it does not prevent a woman from bearing children. Finally, in a fifty-four-year-old, post-menopausal woman, the uterus that once could accommodate a fetus has already begun shrinking to the size of a womb that has never experienced pregnancy. Therefore, given Helena's age at the time of Dr. Oppenheim's examination, it would have been virtually impossible to determine whether or not she had ever been pregnant.[72] Nevertheless, to this day Helena's supporters continue to cite the Oppenheim certificate as unassailable evidence that she had never consummated the sexual act nor borne an illegitimate child.

Although Helena proclaimed Dr. Oppenheim's proof as "a great triumph,"[73] and spoke about her supposedly deformed uterus in detail to Sinnett and Olcott and other trusted friends, there were times when she thought the whole thing shameful. In her elder years she had grown particularly prudish, even for a Victorian, and the necessity of mentioning unmentionable organs distressed her. Mailing the certificate to Sinnett, she enclosed a pathetic note saying that "I had always had a dim conception that 'uterus' was the same thing as 'bladder,'" and signing herself, "Yours dishonoured in my old age."[74]

In November a tinge of unexpected tragedy entered her life when she learned that her brother Leonid had died at the age of forty-five. They had never been close, and she could not truly mourn for him, but the news of his passing saddened and depressed her. Writing to Mary Gebhard, she did not mention Leonid, but asked how one could help being lonely with only Babaji and Louise for company. Most probably she was hinting that she would appreciate a visit from Mary, since their residences were less than a day apart, but Madame Gebhard could not spare time from her family. However, she did show the letter to her friend and house guest Countess Constance Wachtmeister and suggest that she might visit H.P.B. for a few weeks. "She needs sympathy," Mary told the countess, "and you can cheer her up."[75]

The countess was stopping at Elberfeld on her way to Rome, where she planned to join friends for the winter. However, thinking over Mary's suggestion, she decided her friends could wait a few weeks while she paid a sympathy call on a needy, sick woman, and wrote to Würzburg indicating her wish to visit H.P.B., if it met with her approval. To the countess's consternation, it did not. Madame was sorry, but she had no room for the countess and, besides, was so preoccupied with her *Secret Doctrine* that she had no time to entertain; still, she hoped they might meet on the countess's return from Italy.

This was not Constance's first contact with Helena. In the spring of 1884, they had been introduced at one of Alfred Sinnett's receptions, and she had been arrested by Madame's eyes "which seemed to penetrate and unveil the secrets of the heart." She had been repulsed by the coterie of sycophants sitting at H.P.B.'s feet and hanging on every word she said, so she had not joined the group, who were gazing up at Madame "with an expression of homage and adoration."[76] A few weeks later, she had been astonished to receive a letter from H.P.B., inviting her to Paris for a private talk. Even though she was on her way back to Sweden at the time, Constance was sufficiently curious to make the detour to Paris.

Catching up with H.P.B. at Enghien, where she was visiting the Count and Countess d'Adhemar, she sent in her card only to be told that Madame was busy and could not see her. "I replied that I was perfectly willing to wait," Wachtmeister recalled, "because having come from England at Madame Blavatsky's behest, I declined to go away until my errand was accomplished."[77] Apparently that was the correct answer, because she was immediately ushered into a crowded salon and led up to the main celebrity, Madame Blavatsky, who paid her scarcely any attention.

For several days Constance trailed after H.P.B., both at Enghien and then in Paris, waiting to learn the reason for Madame's summons, but the information was not forthcoming. When at last she informed Madame that she was leaving, Helena condescended to take her aside. Within two years, she said, Constance would be devoting her life wholly to Theosophy. That was impossible, the countess replied, for she had a son and family ties in Sweden.

H.P.B. smiled and said, "Master says so, and therefore I know it to be true."[78]

Now, at Elberfeld, Constance read her letter of rejection to Mary Gebhard, who found it incomprehensible. Putting Helena from her mind, she prepared to set out for Italy. It was at the last moment, when her luggage was piled at the door and a cab waiting, that a telegram from H.P.B. arrived: "Come to Würzburg at once, wanted immediately—Blavatsky." Continuing to the station, Constance exchanged her Rome ticket "and was soon travelling onwards to work out my karma."[79]

Constance Georgina Louise Wachtmeister, née de Bourbel de Montjuncon, was the daughter of the Marquis de Bourbel, a French diplomat, and Constance Buckley, an Englishwoman. Born in Florence in 1838 and orphaned while a child, she was raised by an aunt in England and when she was twenty-five made an excellent marriage with her cousin, Count Karl Wachtmeister, then Swedish and Norwegian Minister to the Court of St. James. After three years in England, the count was assigned to the Danish court at Copenhagen and then brought home to be Sweden's Minister of Foreign Affairs. When Constance was thirty-three, her husband died and left her a sizable estate and a six-year-old son to raise. As befitted a woman of independent means, she kept a stately home in Sweden, spent her winters in Italy, and traveled in England, France and Germany as the mood struck her. Apparently disinclined to remarry, she devoted herself to her son and to the fashionable hobby of mysticism, becoming first a Spiritualist and finally a Theosophist. One observer described her as "a lovely woman of *blonde-cendrée* hair and 'Lost Lenore' expression," who always reminded him of "Bulwer's violet-velvet heroines."[80] No doubt her ruffled gowns and beribboned hats helped contribute to this misimpression, for, in reality, Constance was far from helpless.

Arriving at Würzburg in December, 1885, remembering the Paris summons, when she had cooled her heels waiting for Madame to notice her, she half expected to be back on the train for Rome within hours. At forty-seven she was, as H.P.B. called her, "no woman of gush or impulse."[81] Worse yet, she did not in the least resemble a prospective invalid's attendant, a fact of which H.P.B. was well aware. Her curt note to Constance at Elberfeld had simply been the reflection of her understandable fear that the Countess would not want to put up with a sick person in a cramped apartment. Confessing her embarrassment, she apologized to Constance for having "only one bedroom here and I thought you might be a fine lady and not care to share it with me."[82] But when the Master had assured her that Countess Wachtmeister would not mind, she had sent the telegram and spent the day fixing up the bedroom. She had bought a large screen to divide the room and hoped it would not be too uncomfortable.

Constance replied graciously that whatever the surroundings to which she had been accustomed, she would willingly relinquish them for the pleasure of Madame's company. Then they sat down in the dining room to take tea.

The next day Constance "began to realize what the course of H.P.B.'s life was, and what mine was likely to be while I stayed with her."[83] If the rhythm of Helena's daily routine was undeniably dull, Constance must have felt that it would be endurable for a few weeks until she could politely make her departure for sunny Italy. It would be many weeks, perhaps months, before she realized she had been entrapped.

The two women's day soon fell into an unvarying pattern. Louise wakened them at six o'clock with coffee, after which Madame rose and dressed, and by seven was seated at her desk in the study. After a pause for breakfast at eight, H.P.B. returned to her desk and began the day's work in earnest. At one o'clock Constance would stand outside Madame's door and ring a small bell to announce dinner. Sometimes H.P.B. came at once, but at other times her door would remain closed all afternoon until finally Louise would come crying to the countess, desperate over Madame's dinner, which was getting cold, burnt, or dried up. When Helena eventually emerged, a fresh dinner would have to be cooked, or Louise would be sent to Rugmer's Hotel for a hot meal. At seven, the writing was put aside for the day and tea would be served. H.P.B. would lay out her cards for a game of patience to relax her mind, while the countess read aloud from newspapers, books and magazines. Once a week Dr. Oppenheim came by to inquire after H.P.B.'s health and usually stayed to gossip for an hour; occasionally the landlord would stop in. At 9 P.M. Helena got into bed with her Russian newspapers and read until midnight.

If Constance found the days monotonous she could say the same of the nights. Beginning at ten each evening, the raps would begin, continuing at intervals of ten minutes until six the following morning. When Constance asked for an explanation, Madame said that it was only the psychic telegraph that linked her to the Masters in Tibet, who watched over her body while she slept. Even though a screen divided the bedroom, there was no way to shut out the sound, or the lamp that Helena kept burning. Understandably, Constance had difficulty sleeping and one night, when the clock had struck one and the light still burned, she tiptoed around the screen, found Madame asleep, and extinguished the lamp. Back in bed, she was annoyed to see the room brightly illuminated as before. Three times she got up to turn off the light; three times if flamed up again, until finally she could take no more and woke H.P.B. by yelling her name. Then came an agonized gasp, "Oh, my heart! my heart! Countess, you have nearly killed me." Constance flew across the floor.

"I was with Master," H.P.B. whispered. "Why did you call me back?"[84] It was dangerous to shout at her when her astral form was absent from her physical body, she explained.

Thoroughly frightened, Constance gave her a dose of digitalis and promised she would never do it again.

Obviously possessed of a genuinely gentle nature, the countess quickly accustomed herself to the nightly sound-and-light shows, growing used even to a defective cuckoo clock that emitted strange sighs and groans. What she could not bear was being boxed in twenty-four hours a day. Eventually, she made it a daily practice to escape for a half-hour's walk, look in shop windows, and breathe the fresh air unavailable in the apartment where the windows were never opened and the stove roared full blast day and night. Only three times during her months at Würzburg, did Constance recall Helena leaving the apartment to go for a drive, and that was at Constance's insistence. Helena admitted that she enjoyed the outings but also thought them an outrageous waste of time.

By early December the two women had settled into tedious tranquillity. Babaji had been sent to Elberfeld, probably at Constance's suggestion, because his bright, beady eyes made her uncomfortable. H.P.B., deep into her writing, worked with iron-willed concentration; Constance shielded her from annoyances and made herself useful by making fair copies of the completed pages. What she described as a "quiet studious life"[85] continued until New Year's Eve when a Society member, Professor Sellin, brought Helena a copy of the Society for Psychical Research's final report on Theosophy. After Sellin left, she crumpled over her desk and when Constance came in, she attacked her savagely. "Why don't you leave me?" she snarled. "Go before you are defiled by my shame."[86]

"You may imagine," Constance wrote in agitation to Sinnett the next morning, "what a lively time we had of it. Palpitations of the heart, digitalis, etc."[87] First Helena began to write letters of protest, then she announced that she was leaving for London to annihilate the S.P.R. in person. Not until evening did Constance manage to pacify her. Writing her second letter to Sinnett that day, the countess acknowledged her weariness and summed up the newest traumas by saying, "We have had a terrible day."

H.P.B.'s outrage was to be expected, but in all honesty she had to admit there was nothing surprising about Hodgson's report. His general conclusions had been known to her since March, when he had personally explained them at Adyar and, in June, they had been read aloud in London at a meeting of the S.P.R. What did astound her was that he had not abandoned his theory that she was a Russian spy. "I should consider this Report incomplete," he wrote, "unless I suggest what I myself believe to be an adequate explanation of her ten years' toil on behalf of the Theosophical Society." What could have induced her to labor over a fantastic imposture? Was it egotism? Such a supposition he dismissed as "quite untenable." Was she a plain fraud? "She is, indeed, a rare psychological study, almost as rare as a 'Mahatma!' " Religious mania then? "Even this hypothesis I was unable to adopt." Then what *was* her motive for a career of deception? "Her real object has been the furtherance of Russian interests . . . I suggest it here only as a supposition which appears to best cover the known incidents of her career during the past 13 or 14 years."[88]

Helena was quick to understand that the blatant absurdity of the spying charge weakened Hodgson's case. He had tripped himself up a second time when he used the testimony of the handwriting expert to prove she forged the Mahatma letters. "He calls me a forger!" she exclaimed in a letter to Olcott. "Funny and stupid. *If* I invented the *two Masters*, then they do not exist, and *if they do not* exist, how could I forge *their* handwritings which did not equally exist *before I invented them*?"[89] Both the spy and forgery charges were so silly that Helena could, and would, pounce on them as a pretext for declaring the rest of the S.P.R. Report equally inaccurate. Nevertheless, it must have been mortifying to read the conclusions that the S.P.R.'s committee had attached to Hodgson's work:

> For our own part, we regard her neither as the mouthpiece of hidden seers, nor as a mere vulgar adventuress; we think that she has achieved a title to permanent remembrance as one of the most accomplished, ingenious, and interesting imposters in history.[90]

And it was similarly disconcerting to see that Hodgson had let Henry Olcott off scot-free. The "Theosophical twins" no longer stood or fell together; she had toppled, but Henry remained upright. He was a fool in Hodgson's opinion, but an honest fool. How bitterly she must have smiled as she wrote Henry, "Now you see *you* are SAVED not dishonoured by my referring to you as a 'psychological baby' and saying I am smarter than you to H. Chintamon. This said in fun has saved you." And she added, "Your Karma, dear."[91]

Needless to say, work on *The Secret Doctrine* ground to a halt. The S.P.R. Report had done both H.P.B. and the Society untold damage, as evidenced by the growing number of resignations, and the countess recalled that "every post only increased her anger and despair."[92] Professor Sellin called the Society "a humbug";[93] Hubbe-Schleiden wanted either to resign or to drop the word Theosophical from the German branch. Sinnett, while shaken, "*can-*

not leave, too far deep in it,"[94] H.P.B. assured Olcott. She wrote a letter of explanation to the London *Times*, who did not have the courtesy to publish it, and she scratched out private explanations to friends, encouraging *them* to write protests to the papers.

Sometimes Constance did not know where she would find the physical strength to bear up under Madame's problems. On the fourth of January, she thought H.P.B. would have an apoplectic fit after Professor Sellin brutally accused her of plagiarizing *Isis Unveiled* from other books. "A violent attack of diarrhea saved her," Constance wrote Sinnett, "but I do weary of it all so much."[95]

For two solid weeks Helena's energies were thrown into a futile counterattack. She admitted to feeling like "an old, squeezed-out lemon, physically and morally, good only for cleaning old Nick's nails with, and perhaps to be made to write 12 or 13 hours a day the Secret Doctrine under dictation . . ."[96] However, she was not destined to return to work for many weeks because the S.P.R. Report was shortly followed by a series of alarming attacks. At Elberfeld, where Babaji had been keeping the Gebhards entertained with stories of his forest-dwelling days, the little man suddenly went berserk and began foaming at the mouth, smashing mirrors, and screaming terrible accusations at Madame Blavatsky: she had desecrated the Masters by sharing their secrets with Europeans and by mixing up Their names with "phenomena, women and common worldly matters";[97] she used trickery to perform her marvels and hypnosis to turn her followers into sheep who then believed they saw things that did not exist; she wrote the Mahatma letters herself. Madame, he howled, should be thrown out of the Theosophical Society, which itself was rotten to the roots.

Babaji's revolt terrified Helena. Determined to quiet him, she sent Constance back to Elberfeld but Babaji continued to rave. During the years when he had submitted meekly to Madame's bullying, he had stored up an abundance of animosity and, unluckily for H.P.B., he had also kept his eyes open. His charges may have sounded like gratuitous insults, but they certainly supplied interesting details. Madame, he told the Gebhards, had extorted money from Prince Harisinghji Rupsinghji; she had almost caused Olcott's suicide; she had recently written two Mahatma letters to Hubbe-Schleiden. Constance thought that Babaji was "really a lunatic," but nevertheless her faith in H.P.B. began to waver. Since coming to Würzburg, she had shut her eyes to "little irregularities"[98] in Madame's household by telling herself that she did not understand occult laws, but Babaji was talking of extortion, a crime that was punishable by law. If H.P.B. had really extorted money from Prince Harisinghji, Constance felt that "I cannot remain in a Society where the Founders lie under the imputation of criminal fraud." From Olcott she demanded that the prince sign a statement exonerating Madame of the charge: "I must see my way clearly and honestly before me and not blush to be called a Theosophist."[99]

Henry refused to bother the prince with a trifling matter. Everyone knew that Babaji was a "half-crazy"[100] epileptic. Did Constance actually expect him to repeat Babaji's deranged assertions and ask for a written document that the prince had *not* been swindled? Put yourself in my place, Olcott begged. The countess did not press him.

Helena asked her friends at Elberfeld to hustle Babaji off to London but, she moaned to Sinnett, "Babaji has unsettled the Gebhards entirely. If he is permitted to return—say good-bye to the German branch and our mutual friends. Let *this be a prophecy*."[101] The Gebhards did not resign but they began asking embarrassing questions about certain Mahatma letters received by them and their friends. H.P.B. was obliged to account for the general crudenesses of the series with a complicated and incomprehensible dissertation on the hazards of "precipitation" by inexperienced *chelas*. The Gebhards, still suspicious, remained in the Society, but Dr. Hubbe-Schleiden finally lost faith and submitted his resignation, taking with him his two personal Mahatma letters.

Babaji's dramatic defection, which H.P.B. called "the basest ingratitude from one I have loved as my son,"[102] gave her pause for reflection. Vacillating between sorrow and "ice-cold indifference and callousness," she opted for the tougher stance. She had been "a big, stupid, trusting fool," who had allowed herself to be harassed by "a thick crowd of circling traitors, fiends and tigers in human shape."[103] Therefore, when Mary and Gustav Gebhard's twenty-year-old son Walther shot and killed himself three months later, it was on Babaji that Helena laid the blame for the tragedy.[104]

Neither of the two Hindu *chelas* she had transported to Europe, Babaji Nath and Mohini Chatterji, had turned out according to Helena's expectations. Despite Babaji's stupidity, she had felt affection for him, but now, since the betrayal, her feelings had turned to sadness. Mohini was another, more crucial matter. At some point in the past year when her attention had been directed on herself, Mohini had escaped Madame's domination and aggressively carved out an independent career for himself as a Mahatmic messenger. This did not seem quite fair to Helena, who had snatched him from a boring lawyer's job in Calcutta and, exercising to the hilt her flair for the dramatic, costumed him in a black-velvet tunic bordered with glossy black fur and high Russian boots. It was she who had arranged his debut on the glittering stage of Paris and London high-society drawing rooms, having heralded him as a *chela* of the superhuman Brotherhood and therefore one of the most privileged human beings in the world. Could she have forecast that Mohini's remarkable beauty, his silent dignity, and his refusal to touch the hands of men or raise his eyes to women would make him an international sex object?

"He pleased us all," wrote Isabelle de Steiger, speaking for the London women. "He pleased me extremely."[105] Not until much later did Isabelle learn that Mohini Chatterji could not have been so chaste as everyone supposed because he had a wife in Madras, but at the time nobody could have imagined such a thing. Isabelle, an artist who appreciated beauty for its own sake, was content to view Mohini from a distance. Other English and French female Theosophists were bolder: a Miss Leonard, an Englishwoman living in Paris, made it her business to get acquainted with Mohini and found her interest very much reciprocated.

It seems clear that Mohini and Leonard became lovers. Parisian Theosophists such as Emile de Morsier were usually tolerant of such affairs, but in this case, they raised their brows and passed the news along to Madame Blavatsky, who responded with a mixture of repugnance and jealousy. That Mohini might be a willing participant, even the aggressor, never occurred to her. "Cold marble with horror,"[106] she immediately began conjuring historical panoramas of ancient Rome and Egypt in which Mohini was engulfed by bare-bosomed Messalinas and Potiphars. As Paris gossips continued to report further details, she learned that there was a whole covey of Anglo-French rapists "who burn with a scandalous ferocious passion for Mohini—with that craving of old *gourmands* for *unnatural* food, for rotten Limbourg cheese with worms in it to tickle their satiated palates—or of the 'Pall Mall' iniquitous old men for *forbidden* fruit—ten year old virgins! Oh, the filthy beasts!! the sacrilegious, hypocritical harlots!"[107] Noticeable in this passage, aside from the startling comparison of Mohini to wormy Limburger, is Helena's own thrill at imagining "a nut-meg Hindu" in the arms of a fair-skinned "too erotic spinster."[108] Her sexuality, rigidly repressed for a decade, could not help but reveal itself.

According to H.P.B.'s informants, the erotic Miss Leonard had sworn to seduce Mohini; she pursued him into his bedroom and when that failed, she finally stripped to the waist one afternoon in a public park. It was plain to Helena that poor Mohini had not understood at all what Miss Leonard wanted. "To show to her that I know all,"[109] H.P.B. wrote Miss Leonard a long letter full of reprimands for tampering with the chastity of a holy man and bristling, one can only suppose, with Messalinas, Potiphars and other such epithets. In response, Leonard turned Helena's letter over to her London lawyers along with the hundred-odd love letters Mohini had written her and instructed them to prosecute for defamation of character. Miss Leonard, no doubt in order to show Madame that she too *knew all*, ordered her lawyers to address the notice of legal action to "Mme. Metrovitch otherwise Mad. Blavatsky."[110]

Having fled India to avoid prosecution, Helena took this new threat with a surprisingly lighthearted attitude. "The Countess and I," she wrote Alfred, "are sitting looking at each other and feel convulsed with laughter." Trying to be helpful, Constance told her that if she did not appear in the London court on the date specified, she probably would be extradited. This information sobered H.P.B. "Is that so?" she demanded of Alfred. "Can they force me to go to London? . . . Please consult a lawyer and I will pay, it's only a trifle."[111] By this time Sinnett was receiving several panicky letters a day from both Constance and Helena and must have dreaded the postman's ring; he had no intention of allowing H.P.B. to get near a courtroom and in the end, due to the combined efforts of himself, the countess and Olcott, the case was settled out of court and H.P.B. wrote Miss Leonard an apology.

Attributing the recent succession of unexpected blows to karma, Helena felt as if she were sitting "at the foot of a karmic Vesuvius covering me with uninterrupted eruptions of *mud*."[112] But by the beginning of February, 1886, just as she had convinced herself that nothing more could possibly happen, she was buffeted once again by a treachery more painful than anything she had yet faced. Attacks from outsiders and even disloyalty from her supporters and co-workers were no longer surprising. What did startle her was betrayal by her own relatives and by the people she regarded as her second family. Among those whom she genuinely cherished was Vsevolod Solovyov, her "little father." From the day he had unexpectedly wandered into her life two years earlier, she had felt that he might almost be a younger brother, one who loved her as her own brother had not. After his last visit in September, Solovyov had gone to St. Petersburg, where Vera was now living, and Helena had been pleased to learn that they had become close friends. As a frequent visitor at Vera's home, he had grown to know her daughters and now seemed virtually a part of the family.

Throughout the fall Helena had continued to write him but eventually realized that there would be no reply. Hurt and bewildered, she temporarily stopped writing, and it was not until February that friends in Paris informed her of the stories about her past life which were making the rounds of the Theosophical salons. The source of the gossip was none other than Solovyov. Suddenly fifteen years of painful personal history that she had carried with her and so carefully suppressed seemed to be a subject of idle chitchat of people she had never laid eyes on. Now Helena understood how Miss Leonard had known of Agardi Metrovitch: all at once, family secrets twenty and thirty years old were no longer secrets, and it did not take her long to understand where Solovyov had got his information.

Recently Vera's letters had been "as cold and haughty as ice on Mont Blanc." Helena's initial reaction was anger. "She may go to grass,"[113] she thought, and wrote Vera that she was murdering her. But it was difficult for Helena to remain furious with her sister and she wrote again to ask mildly where Solovyov could have heard about Metrovitch and Meyendorff. "I suppose there are people in St. Petersburg who know it; they might have told him, but not in such detail, Vera."[114] She was not angry with her, only hurt.

All these nightmares of my youth, which have worn me out, are now the property of Madame M[orsier]'s *salon*, and were written down by Solovyoff in your house. It is useless to hide the truth; neither the Coulombs nor the psychists, no one, has ever done me so much damage as this gossip of Solovyoff's. For fifteen years I have worked unweariedly for the good of men; I have helped whom I could; I have tried by my actions to expiate my sins . . . and now I myself stand bespattered—nay, covered with a thick layer of filth, and by whom?[115]

By Solovyov who had seduced Justine Glinka, his wife's younger sister, when she had been thirteen years old. "He—with his own heavy sin on his soul—he is the first to cast a stone at me!"

In no time, rancorous letters were flying between Solovyov in Paris, Nadyezhda Fadeyev in Odessa, and Vera in St. Petersburg. Both women urged Solovyov to keep quiet lest Helena spread vicious stories about the skeletons in his own closet. If he valued his reputation, he would have nothing more to do with "unhappy, crazy Helena," Vera warned. "Helena is dead; what has she to lose? She has long ago burnt her boats."[116] Ignoring Vera's advice, he sent H.P.B. a venomous letter, railing at her to leave him alone before he blabbed still more of her secrets: not only was "old Blavatsky whom you have prematurely buried"[117] still alive but Nicholas Meyendorff had personally told him all about their affair, as well as the birth of Yuri and about her other lover, Agardi. If she created trouble for him, he would not hesitate to smear her with a scandal so dirty that even her devilish Mahatmas would not be able to save her.

A half-dozen years later, Solovyov would write a series of eight articles, published first in *Russky Vyestnik* and afterward as the book *Modern Priestess of Isis*, in which he represented himself as skeptical of Madame Blavatsky almost from their first meeting in 1884. However, judging from the letters he wrote, this assertion seems to have been far from true. While visiting Würzburg, his faith in Madame's powers began to wane, but it was not until he became intimate with Vera and learned about Helena's earlier secret life, that he turned against her. His subsequent vilification of Helena seems to have been directly proportionate to the intensity of his disillusionment.

Sickened that Solovyov had turned on her "like a mad dog,"[118] Madame spilled out her pain in letter after letter to Alfred Sinnett, whom she had now come to regard as "my *last*, real *male* friend in Europe. If you were to despise me—I would commit suicide I think."[119] It is curious to note that in the midst of her present troubles, she made no mention of her Mahatmas, who, despite the psychic telegraph and the cuckoo clock, were hiding silently behind the Himalayas while their messenger was being crucified. It was to Sinnett, not to them, that she looked for help.

During the first weeks of February, H.P.B. worked herself into a suicidal depression. She described herself to Sinnett as an innocent, harmless boar who asks only to be left quietly in her forest, when suddenly "a pack of hounds is let loose to get him out of that wood and tear him to pieces."[120] In this self-destructive mood she made up her mind no longer to permit the past to torture her; at last, she would reveal to the world exactly what Helena Petrovna Blavatsky really was. Accordingly, she wrote Solovyov a letter titled "My

Confession." By this time Countess Wachtmeister understood Madame's maniacal compulsion for writing self-damaging letters and routinely censored all outgoing mail, but somehow the letter to Solovyov slipped through.

As in her letter to Sinnett, she began with the allegorical allusion of a boar, a wild, ugly creature who grunts to himself while eating roots with his bestial friends. Hounds appear, followed by men who threaten to kill him and burn the forest. The boar begins to run but soon realizes the forest is on fire. "What is there for the boar to do? Why this; he stops, he turns his face to the furious pack of hounds and beasts, and shows himself wholly as he is, from top to bottom, and then falls upon his enemies in his turn and kills as many of them as his strength serves till he falls dead."

Like the boar, Helena resolved to "fly no more." Instead, she vowed to write down the true history of her life for the world to read. Unsparing of herself, "I myself will set fire to the four quarters of my native wood . . . and I will perish, but I will perish with a huge following." It was for the sake of the Theosophical Society that she had protected her reputation these past ten years. Having tortured herself with fear, "I was ready to go on my knees to those who helped me cast a veil over my past," but now she was determined to torture herself no more. She would snatch the weapons from her enemies' hands and write a book "which will make a noise through all Europe and Asia." What had she to fear from Blavatsky, alive or dead? Or Meyendorff? "I do not care a straw about that egoist and hypocrite! He betrayed me, destroyed me by telling *lies* to the medium Home, who has been disgracing me for ten years already, so much the worse for him." Her autobiography, she assured Solovyov, would be "a Saturnalia of the moral depravity of mankind," a worthy epilogue for her stormy life. "I shall conceal nothing."

In her confession to Solovyov, however, she blotted out almost everything: she had hated Nikifor Blavatsky and left him, but she had not slept with him; she had loved one man deeply and "wandered with him here and there"; there had been only an adopted child; from the time she was eighteen, there had always been gossip about her "hundreds" of lovers, but she had encouraged people to talk about her. Suddenly her eyes had been opened and she had gone to America to expiate her sins. She would tell, too, "a great deal of which no one ever dreamed, and *I will prove it.*"

Face to face with herself at last, she tried not to lower her eyes, but ended by turning away in shame. She could admit to deserting Nikifor but was careful not to admit knowing he was alive; she could even own up to having had relationships with other men but could not tell the truth about her son. Nor could she repudiate the Mahatmas, though it is clear that she was tempted. She told Solovyov:

I will say and publish it in the Times and in all the papers, that the "master" and "Mahatma K.H." are only the product of my imagination;

that I *invented* them, that the phenomenon were all more or less *spiritualistic* apparitions, and I shall have twenty million *spiritists* at my back. I will say that in certain instances I *fooled* people; I will expose dozens of *fools, des hallucinés*; I will say that I was making trial for my own satisfaction, for the sake of experiment.

It would be easy to make these admissions, but she would not do it because it would be "the greatest of lies." All she wanted now was "that the world may know all the reality, all the *truth*, and learn the lesson. And then *death*, kindest of all."[121] Solovyov, she concluded, was free to reveal the contents of her confession, even to publish it in Russia if he liked, because she no longer cared.

Solovyov did not publish the letter until after Helena's death, but he did show it to members of the Paris Theosophical Society and before long its contents had crossed the Channel to Alfred Sinnett, who had been spending the past six months trying to extract autobiographical nuggets from Madame. Greatly agitated, he demanded to know what was going on. Why was she announcing that she would write the story of her life? Had she forgotten his project? His whole purpose was to vindicate her, but from what he had heard of her letter to Solovyov, it sounded as though she were hellbent on destroying both herself and the Society.

Sinnett's task as the biographer of H. P. Blavatsky was far from a snap: first, he had submitted a long list of questions and had also written Vera for a copy of her 1881 *Rebus* article, "The Truth about H. P. Blavatsky." Unfortunately it was written in Russian and he had to ask H.P.B. for a translation, which gave her the opportunity to make whatever changes she pleased. By March, Helena's continued reticence to speak about the past was making him frantic.

Her years in the United States? "Why goodness me I may as well try to tell you about a series of dreams I had in my childhood."[122]

Her experiences with Garibaldi? "Please do not speak of Mentana."[123]

The Agardi Metrovitch incident? "I WILL NOT WRITE ANYTHING about 'the Metrovitch incident' . . ."[124]

The adoption of a child? "Impossible even to touch upon the child. There's the Baron Meyendorffs and all Russian aristocracy that would rise against me if . . . the Baron's name should be mentioned."[125] And besides, if D. D. Home should see the book, he would cause trouble.

By April a frustrated Sinnett began to complain. He had Helena's version of Vera's article, as well as some of Helena's correspondence in which she explained that Metrovitch, her best friend's husband, had met an untimely death at the hands of Papal agents and that Yuri was the illegitimate son of Nicholas Meyendorff and an unnamed woman. However, she would permit him to use none of this material as it was designated off-the-record information. When Sinnett pressed her for more details, warning her that the book was shaping up into an extremely dull work, she nodded sympathetically and promised to help enliven it "however disagreeable it may be for me personally."[126]

Reduced to pleading for her cooperation, Sinnett reminded her that her memoirs must be unexpurgated if she wished to refute Hodgson's Report. Nothing of the kind, H.P.B. snapped; if she were to give him the whole truth, no doubt "all Europe would jump from its seat"[127] but he knew quite well that the Masters would not permit such revelations. Therefore, she sighed, "What shall we, what can we, do?"[128]

In Sinnett's opinion, she was a public personality who had stimulated interest in herself and now she had an obligation to satisfy public curiosity; H.P.B. warily had to agree he had a point. If she were one of those women who had pursued her feminine duties, she replied, "sleeping with her husband, breeding children, wiping their noses, minding her kitchen, and consoling herself with matrimonial assistants on the sly and behind her husband's back,"[129] no one would care about her private life. Since she had chosen a career, she had to expect people poking their noses into her secrets. At the same time, she felt strongly that her life should be a matter of public record only since the founding of the Theosophical Society in 1875; anything that had happened prior to that date was nobody's business. Sinnett may have been inexperienced as a biographer, but realized that eleven years out of fifty-five was not enough to make up a proper biography. Accepting the fact that he would never be able to coax a coherent narrative out of her, Sinnett looked at the hodgepodge of unrelated stories and decided to account for the fragments by titling the book *Incidents in the Life of Madame Blavatsky*. He ignored both the Mahatma letter supposedly received by Nadyezhda Fadeyev in 1870 as well as Dr. Leon Oppenheim's "virginity" certificate.

But, above all, Sinnett hoped that no one would notice the obvious: that his subject had made a fool of him.

III

Ostend

Despite three months of almost unrelieved trauma, Helena had been working intermittently on *The Secret Doctrine* and had now accumulated about three hundred pages of foolscap. That she had been able to accomplish that much was entirely because of the presence of the capable Constance Wachtmeister who protected her from petty annoyances and battled valiantly against the major crises. H.P.B. had grown to rely enormously on the countess, who, by early March would have to begin planning her return to Sweden: her son's twenty-first birthday was approaching, and her own affairs had been neglected all winter. While Helena insisted that she would get along on her own, Constance must have felt guilty about deserting her, especially since it was unsafe to leave Madame alone to vent her feelings in those letters: "*I have saved* her again and again from these indiscretions."[130] Her proposal that H.P.B. accompany her to Sweden was firmly rejected, ostensibly because the country was cold, but more likely because it was dull.

In desperation, Constance appealed to Alfred: did he know of any woman in London who would come and spend a few weeks with Madame, all expenses paid, someone trustworthy who would not worm her way into Madame's confidence and then betray her later? He did not, nor did he react favorably to the Old Lady's proposal that he sublet his home and take a house on the French coast at Boulogne, Calais or Dieppe, so she might live with him. By sharing expenses it would be cheap and "we could settle lovely, I think."[131] Sinnett adroitly wriggled out of that tight corner without hurting H.P.B.'s feelings.

As the weeks passed with no replacement for the countess, Helena began thinking seriously about her future. When she had left India, it had been assumed that she would return once the furor had died down; in fact Henry Olcott was still proceeding on that assumption. In recent letters he had advised her to begin hoarding her spare shillings, francs and thalers toward her passage home by October or November. Think twice, he said, before buying perfume and other gim-racks. At first his letters annoyed her, then made her furious, and finally convinced her that she would not return to Adyar. Extravagance, Henry sermonized, would not be permitted. "So when you come home just make up your mind that the days of full swing and the gratification of the least whim are gone forever, and that you must live quietly like the rest of us," and furthermore, he would not permit her to keep the Society "in hot water" by performing phenomena and getting into fights with individuals. "Now, mark my words, dear chum. Adyar is your only home, the only refuge you have upon earth. The proverb says, 'It's an ill bird that fouls its own nest.' Don't make yours uninhabitable."[132] She marked his words with some blistering words of her own, perhaps the mildest being "Balaam's she-ass,"[133] as she called him in a letter written about this time.

If Henry wanted to go on imagining she would return under those humiliating restrictions, he was free to do so. In the meantime, determined to make plans of her own, she had to face the fact that she had no idea of where she wanted to go. Of course, she could remain in Würzburg, but recently the city had been making her uncomfortable. At the university there was a Sanskrit professor with friends in India who received all the gossip about Madame

Blavatsky. Even though she rarely poked her head out of the apartment, she suspected that people were promenading outside her window, whispering and pointing fingers, and it made her nervous. With Miss Leonard's libel suit pending, she dared not go to England or France, even under an assumed name. Finally she decided that the safest place to go would be Belgium. "O lovely, peaceful old age!" she moaned. "To have to play at the Wandering Jew, to hide like a culprit, a felon . . ."[134]

By the end of March it was all settled: the countess would "pack up for me my goods and chattels, books and frying pans before she goes."[135] On April 15, when her rent ran out, she would proceed to the Belgian seaside resort of Ostend where she hoped to find comfortable warm lodgings. Her selection of Ostend, a fairly expensive place, was predicated on an unexpected hundred twenty-five dollars she had just received from J. W. Bouton, probably a belated royalty payment from *Isis*. When Bouton promised there might be more, she began doing as Henry had directed and tallied her small change. With the four hundred francs a month she received from Adyar, augmented by Bouton's dollars, she calculated she could afford the move. At Ostend, she could patch up her quarrel with Vera by inviting her for a visit; Ostend was an impressive enough lure. To make the offer doubly tempting, she invited Vera to bring along one of her daughters and concluded by remarking that Vera must come to say goodbye because she would be dying shortly.

Vera hesitated. She suspected that the visit might be unpleasant and when Vsevolod Solovyov warned that it was a trick, she was secretly inclined to agree. On the other hand, she felt that a reconciliation would only be possible if they met. Perhaps Helena truly was ill, in which case Vera would never forgive herself for having refused her last request. She wrote her acceptance, promising to meet Helena in Ostend and help get her settled in a new apartment.

It was not until the eighth of May that H.P.B. finally left Würzburg, for the departure had proved a bigger headache than she supposed. The countess had packed her belongings and had also wrapped in oilcloth and shipped to Adyar a copy of *The Secret Doctrine* manuscript completed to date, so that Subba Row could make corrections. However, that left the problem of how H.P.B. was to get to Ostend. Constance had accepted an invitation to visit Austria with Mary Gebhard, who could not recover from the suicide of her son, so she could not assume this task herself. Providentially, there turned up at the last minute H.P.B.'s old friend Emily Kislingbury, who had been vacationing in Germany and stopped off to see Helena. Since she would be passing through Ostend on her way back to London, she said it would be no trouble to shepherd Madame and Louise to their destination. Emily was no longer a Theosophist, in fact she had converted to Catholicism, but H.P.B. was happy to see her and grateful for her help.

On the last morning at Würzburg, Constance looked in dismay at the nine pieces of luggage and thought that just getting H.P.B. and her bundles into the train would be a formidable task; she suggested they start early for the station. "Poor H.P.B. who had not been out of her room in weeks, had to walk all along the platform, and this was performed with difficulty,"[136] Constance recalled. By the time she and Emily had bribed the conductor to give H.P.B. a compartment to herself, got Madame comfortably seated, and stowed around her coverlets, pillows, luggage and the precious box containing *The Secret Doctrine*, all three women were exhausted. Just as Constance was congratulating herself on having managed things so well, a railway official began objecting sternly to the use of a passenger compartment for baggage. All the luggage must be removed at once, the official yelled in German, but Madame shouted back in French, and Constance and Emily winced from the sidelines. Luckily the whistle blew and the train began moving out of the station, leaving the irate rail man behind. As Constance watched it go, "a feeling of pity came over me for Miss Kislingbury"[137] who would be responsible for unloading and reloading H.P.B. and her luggage at the train change in Cologne, getting her through customs, and finally settling her at Ostend.

At Cologne, however, Emily won an unexpected reprieve when they were greeted at the station by Gustav Gebhard, who happened to be in the city visiting his daughter. Three months earlier Gebhard had teetered on the brink of bolting the Society; in February he had even submitted samples of H.P.B.'s writing and a few Mahatma letters to Ernst Schutze, the imperial calligrapher; in Schutze's opinion, they were not written by the same person. Satisfied with Madame's honesty, Gebhard had once again become a loyal supporter and now prevailed upon her to break the journey by spending a day or two at Elberfeld.

The day after H.P.B.'s arrival at the Gebhards, she slipped on the parquet floor of her bedroom and sprained her ankle. At first inclined to dismiss the injury as trifling, she changed her mind when it began to throb; once again, she would be confined to her bed and her armchair. The immobility actually turned out to be more pleasant than she had expected: Mary Gebhard hurried back from Austria to nurse her personally, and the entire household fussed over her extravagantly. Vera was notified of the accident and invited to Elberfeld with her daughter for the recuperation.

By mid-May Helena was enjoying herself as much as could be expected under the circumstances. "The old leg goes a little better," she reported to Constance, "pain gone, but it is entirely helpless, and heaven alone knows *when* I will be able to walk with it even as superficially as I did before."[138] With the arrival of her sister and twenty-two-year-old niece Vera, whom she was meeting for the first time, H.P.B.'s contentment was almost complete. The three of them sat on the terrace or in the garden talking in Russian; suddenly, the quarrels of the past winter no longer were important. It seems likely that during those tearful conversations the sisters came to a mutual understanding of sorts, because never again would Vera express open criticism of Helena's follies or speak of being asked to perform actions against her conscience. From her later declarations that Theosophy was a pure and lofty doctrine and from her panegyrics on behalf of H.P.B., one can presume that Helena somehow won her promise of public support, regardless of her private reservations about the reality of the Mahatmas.

The one-day stopover at Elberfeld lengthened, eventually, into two months. At first the sprain prevented Helena from working, but as soon as she began to feel better she went back to *The Secret Doctrine*; she would work in the evenings, arise early the next morning to revise the previous night's copy, and read it aloud to her sister in the afternoons. During these readings, Vera was struck by the picturesqueness of the language and the complex scientific explanations, but she also found it puzzling that Helena was unable to read the algebraic and geometric calculations she had written down. Why not? she asked her.

The reason was obvious, Helena laughed. She knew nothing of higher mathematics.

Still perplexed, Vera persisted. "Then how is it that you have written all this without knowing anything about it?"

It was not she who wrote, Helena answered with some impatience; she only copied material that the Master presented to her. "I know that you have always disbelieved me, but in this case you see one more proof that I am only the tool and not the master."[139]

Vera still doubted.

Helena, for the moment, was happy to linger at Elberfeld, where life was pleasant and everything was free. In the first days of June, however, a black cloud in the form of Babaji Nath appeared on her horizon. Since January Babaji had been living in London with Francesca Arundale and had already become a burden to everyone concerned. Unaccustomed to European winters, he had suffered from fevers and colds for months and now, terribly homesick, he wanted only to return to India. Since he had no money for the return passage, he was forced to wait until Henry Olcott could send him funds. When Francesca arrived at Elberfeld for her annual visit, she brought Babaji with her.

Helena must have made it clear to the Gebhards that she would not stay in the same house as Babaji because he was sent to stay with their elder son, Franz, who lived nearby. From that vantage point, Babaji churned out a steady stream of character defamation against his former guru. Madame, he told Franz Gebhard, had never heard of a mahatma before she came to Bombay and furthermore knew nothing of esoteric teaching; indeed her "esoteric Buddhism" was sheer nonsense and hallucination. As for himself, he still believed in the existence of mahatmas, but he knew positively they would never write what he termed "spook" letters; in fact they did not write letters at all. Helena was dismayed to find Franz taking Babaji's side. No doubt

Babaji's constant needling and his threats to write a pamphlet denouncing her frauds had something to do with her swift departure from Elberfeld the first week in July.

Nothing had gone according to plan. She had wanted to reach Ostend in April, find an inexpensive place to live before the season began, and spend a few weeks taking the saltwater cure. Instead she arrived at the height of the season when the town was jammed with tourists and could find no accommodations that were not outlandishly expensive. There was no time left for a proper holiday with her relatives because once Helena was settled, Vera had to be getting back to St. Petersburg.

Ostend, once an ancient fishing village, was now the major Belgian port for mail boats and steamers coming from England, as well as a terminal for trains departing to all areas of Europe. At the same time it was a fashionable resort and the summer residence of the Belgian royal family. The Promenade, flanked by deluxe hotels and villas, overlooked a sandy Lido where visitors sat under umbrellas and dined in the evenings on the luscious oysters for which Ostend was famous. It was an engrossing scene if one had the money to participate. Helena, sadly disenchanted, could not believe the hotel prices. "Ye gods of Avitchi!" she wrote Constance. "For one night at the Continental I had to pay 117 francs for our rooms."[140] Next day they switched to the Villa Nova at 10 Boulevard Isaghem (Iseghemlaan) while a desperate Vera spent most of her time walking the streets looking for more suitable lodgings. More or less by chance she stumbled upon a five-room apartment in the rue d'Ouest. For H.P.B. there was a lovely three-room suite including a bedroom separated from a large study by satin hangings and a drawing room with a piano; across the hall was a parlor and another bedroom.

The apartment covered the entire ground floor of the building. This was considerably more space than Helena needed and the price of a thousand francs for the remainder of the season and a hundred francs a month thereafter was obviously too expensive. "But what can I do?"[141] she sighed. A little elegance was certainly a welcome change especially since Madame rarely went out of her quarters.

By mid-July Vera and her daughter had gone. When Helena tried to get back to writing, she found it difficult to concentrate, and when Alfred Sinnett came for a few days she found it convenient to blame her lack of progress on him. All he wanted to talk about were the memoirs, which H.P.B. now sorely regretted having agreed to. To have to dredge up from her imagination plausible explanations for Agardi Metrovitch and Michael Betanelly, whom Sinnett had somehow learned of and coyly referred to as "the Philadelphia marriage incident,"[142] required a major expenditure of time and energy. The more she reflected on the memoirs, the more she felt they should not be labeled as such. What Sinnett had managed to pluck out of her was "neither an autobiography nor a biography, but simply stray facts collected and strung together" and she did not need the gift of prophecy to foresee that she would be "publicly whipped for it by kind and merciful readers and critics."[143]

Once Sinnett left, there was no one for company but Louise and the landlady. Madame had found a doctor who seemed intelligent and agreed to visit her once a week; otherwise, she did not know a soul in Ostend, "not one solitary Russian here this season except myself, who would rather be a Turk and go back to India."[144] If only she had the use of her legs, she brooded; it was terrible to be alone, ill, and immobile.

On top of all this, she suddenly discovered that she had lost her passport and left her naturalization papers at Adyar; without either of these documents she did not even have the protection of the American consul. Writing to William Judge in great agitation, she asked him to please go at once to City Hall and have copies made, and to see why J. W. Bouton had not sent a check in June as promised. If Bouton had sent the money to Olcott, she planned to cause trouble, because the royalties from *Isis* belonged solely to her. These days she had little good to say for Henry who was "fast turning the Society into a Salvation Army business"[145] ever since he had been left to his own devices in India. There was nothing she could do about that except dissociate herself from him; at this point, she had no intention of permitting him to profit from her work.

In order to finish *The Secret Doctrine* she felt the need of Countess Wacht-meister. In letter after letter she urged her return: "I am very weak, dear, I feel so poorly and legless as I never did when you were there to care for me."[146] As a result of these lamentations, Constance hastened to her side before the end of August, installed herself in the suite across the hall, and once again they settled down together. Throughout the late summer and into the autumn, Helena was content. Occasionally Constance would coerce her into a sunbath on the esplanade, but, once the weather grew chilly, Helena refused to go outdoors. In her own suite the windows were never opened and the rooms kept heated to well over seventy degrees; and she would not venture into the dining room until Louise assured her that the windows had been closed and the room heated. Any temperature under seventy would be fatal, Madame declared.

On the rare occasions when visitors sought them out, Helena found the audiences provided her with small pleasure. Mohini Chatterji's two-week stay, for instance, left her coiled with rage; she had been slow to recognize and even slower to admit that Mohini had sprouted into another Babaji, but now she could not help noticing the transformation. The real mahatmas, he had come to believe, were unreachable beings who neither communicated by writing letters nor concerned themselves with worldly matters; therefore it followed that Madame's Masters could not be mahatmas. Of course "Mr. Mohini Babu," as she now scornfully referred to him, did not have the courage to announce these heresies to her face, but she knew that elsewhere he spoke of them openly and that he had persuaded Francesca Arundale and others. With Helena, his manner was dignified and reserved, as no doubt befitted "a Jesus on wheels & a *Saint*,"[147] and for a moment he made her appreciate Olcott who "*is* a conceited ass, but there is no one more faithful and true than he is to the Masters."[148] When Mohini told her of his plans to visit America, she trembled at the thought of the trouble he would cause there and suspected it could mean the end of the Society in the United States.

H.P.B. invited other guests that fall: Dr. Anna Kingsford and Edward Maitland. It occurred to Madame that Anna might like to return to the Theosophic fold, perhaps even as president of the London Lodge now that Sinnett had allowed the group to wither. So when Anna and Edward arrived in Ostend on the third of October and registered at a nearby hotel, Helena overwhelmed them with reproaches and insisted they check out and move at once into her apartment. Recently Anna had been suffering from severe asthma as well as facial neuralgia, and Maitland, who was currently taking her to southern Italy for the winter, hesitated to leave the privacy of the hotel, where Anna could quietly take her whiffs of chloroform as she needed them. Maitland also objected to the move on the grounds that Anna required a vegetarian diet and that she might be molested by Madame's powerful and hostile "occult influences." He did not, of course, mention that final reservation to H.P.B.

In the end, however, Helena prevailed by assuring Anna that the diet was no problem because, while she herself required meat, Countess Wachtmeister was a vegetarian; and besides, she would introduce her to Mahatma Koot Hoomi. This promise Anna found irresistible, and she packed her belongings immediately. In his biography of Anna, Maitland recalled their three-day stay as enjoyable because "the hospitality and geniality of our hostesses was unbounded." Eager to show herself in the most favorable light, Helena laid out her patience in the evenings and disarmed them with her usual candor, admitting, for example, that her troubles with the Society for Psychical Research had partially resulted from her own foolishness and lack of discretion. If only she had had someone to coddle her, as Anna had Maitland, she would never have done the things that had landed her in trouble; of course there was Henry Olcott, but he had never been of the slightest use as a protector. Now she could not take a step without opposition, and the public prejudice had spilled over onto the Theosophical Society. But if Anna would consider assuming the presidency of the London branch, they would be able to disarm the opposition and create a movement that would be universally accepted. Maitland vetoed the idea on the grounds that their missions were totally different: he and Anna sought to restore the true esoteric Christianity to mankind while Madame's goal was the total subversion of the Christian ideal.

Helena took the rejection quietly, perhaps because she realized that Anna was an extremely sick woman who had not much longer to live. In fact, on their second evening with Helena, Anna was stricken with a particularly severe asthma attack and begged Maitland for chloroform. Immediately she began to hallucinate, first complaining that the ceiling was too low, then shifting to her favorite subject, anti-vivisection. H.P.B. must have listened in horror while Anna described how she used her psychic ability to "project" killing thoughts against certain doctors and scientists who used animals in their experiments. One of the men against whom she had directed her projections was Claude Bernard, and he had obliged her by dying. If she lived long enough, Anna planned to kill several others, including Louis Pasteur. She suggested that H.P.B. join forces with her.

Declining gently, Helena pointed out that Anna would do better to attack the principle of vivisection rather than personalities, because she did injury to herself and her victims "without much benefitting the poor animals."[149]

After experiencing Anna's psychic mad song, H.P.B. was content to spend her time with the countess. During the remainder of the year and through the first months of 1887, the world heard little of Madame Blavatsky; there were no furious letters to magazine and newspaper editors, no disputes with her enemies; what few personal letters she did write were mainly progress reports on *The Secret Doctrine*. By this time she had completed what she believed to be a first volume and was starting on a second in which she planned to deal with Hindu esoteric doctrines; so far she felt enormously pleased with her results. About a year earlier, in a moment of inspiration, she had taken a giant leap forward by devising a unifying theme for the work, and after that everything seemed to have fallen into place.

The device was not only both ingenious and simple but extremely provocative as well: somewhere in this wide, wide world, as she would explain in the introduction to *The Secret Doctrine*, there exists an archaic manuscript known as the *Stanzas of Dzyan*. These fragments of Tibetan sacred writings comprise the oldest book in the world; in fact, an ancient Hebrew document on occultism, the *Siphra Dzeniuta*, had been compiled from them. "A collection of palm leaves made impermeable to water, fire and air, by some specific unknown process,"[150] the *Stanzas* were written in "Senzar," a language unknown to philology, and were buried along with similar priceless manuscripts in the secret crypts that formed the library system of the Brotherhood. At one time, according to H.P.B., the human race had been granted a primeval revelation in which the principles of civilization were set forth; and even though this root knowledge basic to all religion, science and philosophy had gradually disappeared from view, it had not been lost. H.P.B.'s stated intention in *The Secret Doctrine* was to translate and reveal that portion of the revelation contained in the *Stanzas of Dzyan*, "that can be given out to the world in this century."[151]

In an obvious effort to forestall objections, she warned in advance that her book would doubtless be regarded by a large section of the public as the wildest sort of romance, "for who has ever even heard of the book of

Dzyan";[152] still, she was prepared to face the charge of having invented it. To her judges, she had nothing to say, nor would she condescend to notice "those crack-brained slanderers"[153] who maintained she had invented the Mahatmas and plagiarized her previous writings from Eliphas Lévi and Paracelsus. To open-minded readers, she repeated the words of Montaigne: "I have here made only a nosegay of culled flowers, and have brought nothing of my own but the string that ties them," to which she added, "Pull the 'string' to pieces, if you will. As for the nosegay of FACTS—you will never be able to make away with these. You can only ignore them, and no more."[154]

It would be charged, subsequently, that Madame Blavatsky had plagiarized the *Stanzas of Dzyan* from a combination of sources. According to William Emmette Coleman, the sources were mainly from H. H. Wilson's *Vishnu Purana* and Alexander Winchell's *World Life*. Other plagiarized works included: Donnelly's *Atlantis*, Dowson's *Hindu Classical Dictionary*, Oliver's *Pythagorean Triangle*, Decharme's *Mythologie de la Grèce Antique*, and Myer's *Qabbala*, plus some sixteen other works. Reported Coleman, "I find in this 'oldest book in the world' statements copied from nineteenth century books and in the usual blundering manner of Madame Blavatsky."[155]

In comparing *The Secret Doctrine* with the works mentioned by Coleman, it is immediately clear that H.P.B. did in fact use them as references and in many cases lifted sizable chunks of material, with or without accreditation, just as she did in *Isis Unveiled*. But Coleman may have erred in limiting her source material to nineteenth-century writers. As pointed out by Gershom Scholem, today's greatest living scholar of Jewish mysticism, the *Stanzas* "owe something, both in title and content, to the pompous pages of the Zoharic writing called *Sifra Di-Tseniutha.*" Madame Blavatsky, he goes on to add, "has drawn heavily upon Knorr von Rosenroth's Kabbala Denudata (1677–1684), which contains (vol. II, pp. 347–385) a Latin translation of the *Sifra Di-Tseniutha.* The solemn and magniloquent style of these pages may well have impressed her susceptible mind."[156]

Whether Helena actually did gain access to this obscure seventeenth century translation is impossible to know for certain; she herself is the last person to consult for enlightenment because from the outset she surrounded the writing of *The Secret Doctrine* with the kind of mystery she adored. She announced in almost every letter she wrote that she would use no reference material whatsoever. To Alfred Sinnett: "Now I am here alone with the Countess for witness. I have no books, no one to help me. And I tell you that the *Secret Doctrine* will be 20 times as learned, philosophical, and better than *Isis* . . ."[157] To Henry Olcott: ". . . I am here quite alone with no books around me . . ."[158]

These statements had definite purpose, indeed were essential "to show whether Masters are or *are not.* If not—then *I am* the Mahatma . . ."[159] Conversely, if she could write the book without references, she was not the

Mahatma, and Richard Hodgson was a liar. It will be remembered that she made similar claims for the writing of *Isis*, but it will also be recalled that she was working with a library of perhaps a hundred books in New York. Olcott, her only witness, did not believe that she could possibly have written *Isis* from her own library, and he felt sure that she did no outside library research because she never left the house. No matter what Henry believed, the fact remains that it was entirely possible, virtually certain, that she did compose *Isis* from those books plus a few others borrowed from friends, and it is also probable that she left the apartment. There was no reason why she could not have, for she was in good health.

At Würzburg and Ostend, however, immobilized as she was, it is unlikely that she went cavorting through book shops. That was one reason her friends believed she had no books; the other was that she brainwashed them so consistently on this point that even those closest to her, Countess Wachtmeister for one, would continue to insist that Madame spoke the truth. In fact, every person involved with Madame Blavatsky during the writing of *The Secret Doctrine* seems to have gone out of their way to mention the curious lack of reference works, until it sounds as if they were patterning their accounts on a central press release.

The truth is, H.P.B. did own an unspecified number of books and did use them as source material. No one understood this better than the countess, who had packed those nine bulky pieces of luggage upon leaving Würzburg and probably knew the exact number of books in Madame's traveling library. At the beginning of her association with H.P.B., she must have entertained suspicions about Helena's work methods because once, when a page had to be rewritten twelve times, she asked why the Mahatmas made mistakes. It was not their error, H.P.B. explained; pictures and astral counter-parts of books were passed before her eyes but reading them correctly required concentration on her part. If she was upset or distracted, she naturally made mistakes. After that, Constance asked no further questions and accepted the role of witness to Madame's lack of reference material, while at the same time assuming the responsibility for ordering the volumes H.P.B. needed. On December 13, 1885, for instance, Constance asked Sinnett to get them a copy of Hargrave Jennings' *Phallicism*, also to "beg Mohini to write out the esoteric meaning of some of Shakespeare's *plays*. Madame wants it for the S.D. and will put it in Mohini's name."[160] On October 13, 1886, she reminded Sinnett that H.P.B. wanted H. H. Wilson's *Vishnu Purana*, the very work that William Coleman would find to be Helena's chief source, but to make sure he bought the ten-shilling edition. As for the other book on Odin and Scandinavian mythology, he was to please cancel it because H.P.B. could not afford it. This particular letter is doubly interesting because it supplies a glimpse of the financial priorities in Helena's life; instead of the mythology book, Sinnett was asked to stop at Mr. Wallace's in Oxford Circus and purchase four bottles of No. 3 medicine.

Unfortunately for H.P.B. there was no one in whom she could confide her fears and frustrations. Naturally nobody expected her to need books, not even Constance, who may have convinced herself by this time that Madame used them only to verify quotations she had received in the astral light. So H.P.B. had to keep her problems to herself. The fact was, in October of 1886, she was stuck. With little difficulty she had completed a first volume, mainly her interpretation of the *Stanzas of Dzyan*. Now that she was set to tear into a second volume dealing with Hindu cosmogony and theogony, the source, to her, of the true archaic doctrine, she was compelled to admit to herself that her knowledge in this area was sketchy. All along she had been counting on the help of Subba Row, to whom she had already sent the first volume for reading and revision; but to her enormous distress, she learned from Henry that Subba Row wanted nothing to do with *The Secret Doctrine*. After reading the material, he commented that it was so full of mistakes that if he touched it, he should have to rewrite it altogether, and he did not even want to look at a second volume.

Forgetting that she was supposedly receiving help from the Mahatmas, she sent Henry an anguished reply. There were Sanskrit words and sentences she needed, not to mention the esoteric meanings of Hindu allegories. "Can you ask Srinavas Row and Bhavani Row to help me? Then I could send you the 2nd Vol. consisting of Books 1. 2. and 3. Unless someone helps me I do not know what to do. And who will make the glossary? I can't and have no time, and Mohini hardly will. Please answer immediately."[161]

But Henry had no help to offer from his end.

Helena spent New Year's, 1887, by herself. It was the first time in her life that she had awoken on the first day of a new year and found herself alone, "as if in my tomb."[162] Shortly before Christmas the countess had gone to London on business and Helena missed her terribly. "Ever since you went away," she wrote her, "I have felt as though either paralysis or a split in the heart would occur. I am as cold as ice and four doses of digitalis in one day could not quiet the heart."[163] She spent the first weeks of January scratching out passages of the manuscript, rewriting, and adding new material. With the exception of Louise, she did not talk to a single person for weeks, not even to her doctor, who was ill and could not pay his regular weekly calls.

Toward the middle of the month she had a letter from one of the few remaining members of the London Theosophical Society, a journalist and subassistant editor of the *Daily Telegraph* named Edward Douglass Fawcett. Born in Brighton, educated at the Westminster School where he was Queen's Scholar, a student of philosophy and metaphysics, and a passionate sportsman, Fawcett was not yet twenty-two years old. He wondered if Madame needed editorial assistance on her book; if so, he would be happy to come over to Ostend and lend a hand. At the moment H.P.B. needed all the help she could get and besides, she felt "nearly half crazy with solitude."[164] When he arrived, however, she decided to play the grandam and kept him at arm's length by locking her door during the days and granting him brief audiences in the evening. Shortly afterward, Fawcett was joined by two more loyal London Theosophists, Bertram and Archibald Keightley, who also tendered their services. The three young men were handed stacks of manuscript three feet high, asked to correct the English and punctuation, and urged to give their opinion of the contents. There was no doubt in their minds that *The Secret Doctrine* was destined to become the most important contribution of the century to the literature of occultism, but they also must have realized that the manuscript in its present form was a confused muddle. What Archibald saw was a mass of materials with no definite form; to Bertram, it was "another *Isis Unveiled,* only far worse, so far as absence of plan and consecutiveness were concerned."[165] Topics were started, dropped capriciously, taken up again, and dropped a second time. It was clear to both Keightleys that the manuscript needed drastic revision before it could be shaped into a publishable book.

Probably it was just as well they kept these feelings to themselves because it would have been a devastating blow to Madame's ego. Instead, they spent the evenings sitting with both her and the countess, who had returned from London. Helena played patience while the Keightleys talked about the real reason for their visit: they hoped to persuade her to move to England.

Since Dr. Archibald Keightley and Bertram Keightley would soon undertake the responsibility of more or less supporting H.P.B., these two young men, who appeared almost as magically as Mahatmas from Tibet, are of special interest. Mohandas K. Gandhi, meeting them two years later, would take them for brothers. This was an easy mistake as they were about the same age and shared a physical resemblance. Archibald, a doctor, had a grave round face with full beard and glasses; Bertram, a lawyer who was more grave-looking, sported a mustache and wispy beard, and he too wore glasses. Actually, twenty-eight-year-old Archibald was the nephew of Bertram, his father's youngest brother. To make the situation even more confusing, Bertram, while Archibald's uncle, was a year younger than Archibald. They came from a wealthy Liverpool family in which the teachings of Emanuel Swedenborg were greatly admired; both boys had their early education at Charterhouse and then went on to Cambridge where Bertram studied medieval mysticism and Archibald natural science before entering the Royal College of Surgeons in London. Attracted by Spiritualism and mystical philosophy in general, they saw an advertisement for Alfred Sinnett's *Esoteric Buddhism* and, after reading it, obtained an introduction to the author. In early 1884, when H.P.B. was visiting Europe, the Keightleys joined the Theosophical Society around the same time as the Cooper-Oakleys, and during the remainder of Helena's visit were among the entourage that Constance Wachtmeister mentioned as idolatrous flatterers. In the spring and summer, Bertram trailed Helena to Paris and Enghien, and later to Elberfeld; Archibald, busy with his medical studies, had no time for long trips but when H.P.B. returned to England in October, 1884, just prior to sailing for India, he accompanied her and the Cooper-Oakleys as far as Liverpool.

Helena had taken no more notice of the men than she did of many other young people who, initially thrilled to be part of her court, had quickly drifted away, especially after the release of the S.P.R. Report. Interestingly enough, the names of neither Bertram nor Archibald occur in any of her voluminous letters, ordinarily crammed with personality stories, until the spring of 1887 when she mentioned Archibald rather blandly to Vera.

For several months prior to their visit to Ostend, the Keightleys had been writing Madame about the sorry state of London Theosophy; there were few active members left, maybe five or six, who met once a week for discussion, but could do little else since Sinnett refused to activate the Society. It was only out of desperation that they were turning to Madame herself to ask how they might work for the Masters and revive Theosophy. Would it be possible, they wondered, for her to move to London to teach occultism?

As Helena later explained to a correspondent, she had little to say about their proposal. "Be off with you! I thought to myself, let me alone to write my book quietly."[166] What she did not tell the Keightleys was that she had been secretly contemplating just such a move since the previous fall when the trouble with Miss Leonard had been settled. As always, money held her back; because of her incapacity, she needed a flat on the ground floor, but could pay no more than seven pounds a month. Since a furnished flat could not be had for that price, it would be necessary to buy furniture on a monthly installment plan. At the time, the very thought of undertaking such a move wearied her.

The Keightleys' plan, however, had appealed to Helena, for it would guarantee her financial independence from the miserly Henry Olcott. If she would agree to come, a beautiful house with a garden was hers, free of charge. Everything would be arranged for her personal convenience, and furthermore they would personally transport her and her belongings across the Channel in their arms if need be, they insisted. Hiding a purr beneath the famous grumble, Helena finally consented but refused to set a definite date for the move.

At the end of March, despite the fact that she had not been out of the house or opened a window since November, Madame caught a cold that quickly turned into bronchitis. When the Old Lady began falling asleep in the middle of the day, Constance first suspected something more serious than a cold was bothering her and summoned the doctor. He diagnosed a kidney infection, but his prescriptions did little good, and H.P.B. continued to get worse. Seriously alarmed, the countess cabled Mary Gebhard to come at once, but, meanwhile, exhausted herself with round-the-clock nursing duties. The only person she could find to relieve her was a Catholic *soeur de charité* "whom I soon discovered was worse than useless; for whenever my back was turned she would hold up her crucifix before H.P.B. and entreat her to come into the fold of the only church before it was too late. This nearly drove H.P.B. wild."

Meanwhile Helena lay in a state of lethargy bordering on coma, from which she could not be roused. Since the Belgian doctor's treatment had failed, Constance took the liberty of cabling an eminent London doctor who was also a Theosophist, Ashton Ellis. At 3 A.M. one morning, Ellis arrived at their door. After listening to Mary Gebhard and Constance describe H.P.B.'s symptoms and examining the prescriptions ordered by the local physician, Ellis dosed Madame with his special medicine, then caught a few hours' rest. The next morning he consulted with Helena's regular doctor, who held out little hope for their patient's recovery. Although Ellis did not disagree, he decided to try stimulating the kidneys by massage.

For the next two days he sat at Helena's bedside, administering hourly massages until he himself was exhausted. Still she continued to fail. On March 31, Mary suggested that H.P.B. make a will, for, if she died intestate in a foreign country, the confusion over her property would never end. Helena had no property to speak of, but she feared that if she failed to make a will, Constance would not be permitted to have her cremated. She was "struck with horror at the thought of being buried, of lying here with catholics, and not in Adyar," and told Mary to go ahead and contact a lawyer. Taking the watch that night, Constance "began to detect the peculiar faint odor of death which sometimes precedes dissolution." Once Helena opened her eyes and said she was glad to die; finally they both fell asleep. When Constance shook herself awake the next morning, terrified that Madame had died in the night, she saw H.P.B. sitting up in bed watching her. The Master had been there, she said, and when he had offered her the choice either of ending her life or of finishing *The Secret Doctrine*, she had accepted the extension. The countess would please fetch her coffee and breakfast, and bring her tobacco box since she was dying for a cigarette.

The parties concerned with preparing the will arrived to find H.P.B. dressed and seated in the dining room. A lawyer and the American consul entered with long serious faces, expecting to encounter a dead or dying woman, and instead found the corpse offering them a smoke. The countess remembered animated and amusing conversation before the meeting was called to order and the lawyer began asking questions. Did Madame have any relations? Did she have a husband?

By this time H.P.B. was in fine fettle and snapped that for all she knew, old Blavatsky was dead long ago, and if they wanted to know more, they could go to Russia to find out; she had summoned them to write *her* will, not Blavatsky's. Once this hurdle had been passed, it took only a few minutes to complete the transaction. There was no mention in the will about her possessions or cremation, only that she wished the countess to take her body to London and to make all necessary arrangements. Coffee was served and the men lingered three hours talking. Finally the American consul rose and said,

"Well, I think this is enough fatigue for a dying woman,"[167] and the will-signing broke up amidst peals of laughter. When Constance and Mary tried to put Madame to bed, she objected vigorously and sat up late playing cards.

Although Madame recovered rapidly, the brush with death had frightened her more than she cared to admit. Still, it proved a boost to her psychic well-being, since it had shown her that people still cherished her. Why, she asked herself, should the countess be so devoted if she did not love her? Why did Mary remain with her, nursing her like a baby, instead of spending Easter with her family? And Ashton Ellis, a stranger, had left his job at Westminster Dispensary without permission and been dismissed as a result; moreover, he refused to accept any money from her. "I really do not know what to think!" she wrote Vera. "What am I to them?"

What struck her as curious was that, apart from gratitude, she could muster no real feeling for the people who had made personal sacrifices to save her. As she confessed to her sister, "I cannot love anyone personally, but you of my own blood."[168] Perhaps, thought Helena, it was her karma to inspire devotion she could not reciprocate; perhaps it had become impossible for her to love anyone who was not Russian. On Easter Sunday, still brooding about this puzzle, she turned as she always did when overcome with bittersweet nostalgia, to Nadyezhda.

My old comrade and friend, You ask whether you should send me something, whether I want something? I do not want anything, darling, except yourself. Send me yourself. We have not seen each other for a year and a half, and when shall we meet again? Maybe, never.[169]

The household at Ostend began to disperse: the frazzled countess, for once acknowledging her physical and mental exhaustion, longed for a complete rest and, after promising to join H.P.B. in London in the fall, departed for Sweden. Mary Gebhard agreed to remain with H.P.B. When the Keightleys arrived in the last week of April, some of the packing had already been completed under Mary's supervision, but the bulk of it, H.P.B.'s books and papers, still remained to be done. This job was, Bertram recalled, "a truly terrible undertaking, for she went on writing until the very last moment, and as sure as any book, paper or portion of manuscript had been carefully packed away at the bottom of some box, so surely would she need it, and insist upon its being disinterred at all costs."[170] Nevertheless, the Keightleys were full of enthusiasm as they told Madame about "Maycot," her future home, a little cottage in Norwood, and about its owner, Mabel Collins, a ferociously dedicated Theosophist, who felt honored to be sharing her home with H.P.B. If Helena had doubts about the paradisiacal aspects of the new arrangement, she kept them to herself.

The morning of May 1 dawned cold and foggy. The forty-degree temperature worried Helena, who had not been outside for the past six months, and she fussed so furiously, Archibald began to worry that she would never survive the Channel crossing. But somehow, between the two men and Louise, the boxes and trunks were toted down to the steamer and H.P.B. was carried aboard. Despite everyone's apprehensions, not to mention a rough crossing and a slippery pier at Dover, the move proceeded largely without incident: they finally reached "Maycot" where, Bertram noted with amazement, "before we had been two hours in the house, H.P.B. had her writing materials out and was hard at work again."[171]

LONDON

1887–1891

I

Priestess of Lansdowne Road

In the spring of 1887 London was at its grimy best. Under a canopy of pale green leaves, the squares and gardens of Norwood were scented with grape-clusters of lilac and the yellow tendrils of laburnum. Towering above the labyrinth of cottages and villas, each with its smoke wreath trailing away to the east, loomed the twin towers of the Crystal Palace, which had been dismantled after the Great Exhibition of 1851 and transplanted in this quiet south London suburb. If the sight of the glass palace stirred up three-decade-old memories, Helena did not acknowledge them to anyone, nor did she comment on the fact that living in Norwood was Allan Octavian Hume, who was said to have decorated the walls of his Kingswood Road villa with heads and horns of Indian big game. These painful reminders of her past did little to endear Norwood to Helena.

"Maycot," on Crown Hill in Upper Norwood, was invariably described as small, pretty and charming, which is not surprising because Mabel Collins was a woman with a taste for the precious; she liked tiny, old-fashioned houses, rustic verandas shaded by roses and canary creepers, and elaborate interior decoration. One of her later homes in the fashionable West End would be described in a newspaper article as "a perfect cage, delightfully appointed for the little bird it holds."[1] Unfortunately there was nothing bird-like about H.P.B., who expressed her opinion of "Maycot" with characteristic bluntness: "This house is a hole."[2] Since walking up and down stairs had become so excruciatingly painful that she no longer even attempted it, she was given two rooms on the ground floor but, she reported to Countess Wachtmeister, they were so tiny that when three people came in, "we tread uninterruptedly on each other's corns; when there are four, we sit on each other's heads." She used one of the rooms for her office and the other as a bedroom, although the room was too small for a bed, and could only accommodate a sofa. Equally annoying, "there is no quiet here, for the slightest noise is heard all over the house."[3]

There was still another difficulty with "Maycot," and that was Mabel Collins. H.P.B. had disliked her on sight when they had first met in 1884. At that time, Mabel had written a charming mystical story, *The Idyll of the White Lotus,* which she showed in manuscript to Colonel Olcott, claiming it had been dictated to her while in trance by some mysterious person. When H.P.B. had remarked matter-of-factly that the person sounded like an old friend of hers, a Greek adept named Hilarion, the suggestible Mabel had pounced on this and dedicated her book "To the *True Author, the Inspirer* of this work." Evidently encouraged, she immediately plunged into a similar treatise on Eastern wisdom, *Light on the Path,* this one carrying the by-line "Sri Hilarion, written down by MC." When H.P.B. finally got around to reading *Light on the Path* with its forty-two axioms for spiritual enlightenment that Mabel claimed she had found splashed on the walls of "a certain place to which I obtained admission," some of it struck her as grossly unacceptable. Especially disturbing was the rule advising students to yield to their senses by "plunging into the mysterious and glorious depths of your own being."[4] To the puritanical Helena, this was dangerous advice smacking of Tantric black magic and what she called "occult venom."[5]

Mabel Collins was tall and willowy, a Titian beauty, with an exquisite oval face, ivory complexion, and gleaming auburn hair. Daughter of the well-known novelist Mortimer Collins, she was born in 1851 and educated at home, and at the age of twenty married Dr. Kenningale Robert Cook, scholar, poet and editor of the *Dublin University Magazine.* Isabelle de Steiger, who lived opposite them in Bedford Gardens when they were first married, remembered the newlyweds as a beautiful young couple living in an old-fashioned villa with a square garden full of apple and pear trees; Mabel, she said, was a "much-admired private medium and by no means regarded as an ordinary one,"[6] who also contributed short stories to various magazines under her maiden name. By the time she met H.P.B. Mabel had published no less than nine novels and had also taken a brief fling at acting. Her most notable role had been a portrayal of Madame Helena Modjeska. Personally she had not fared so well since her childless marriage to Dr. Cook had gradually soured and she had already left him when he died in 1886.

There is a photograph of Mabel in ultrafashionable fur-trimmed hat and suit; it gives unmistakable proof of her glamour. What it fails to provide is the slightest indication of a woman willing to sit at the feet of a guru, especially one as irascible as Madame Blavatsky. Still, that seems to have been just what Mabel had in mind when she rashly offered H.P.B. her home. Never did she dream that a spiritual teacher would be capable of expressing her displeasure by screaming abuse that could be heard over half the neighborhood; and never *never* had she imagined that the abuse would be directed at her. Speedily disillusioned, Mabel would later remind herself that whatever else H.P.B. had done, she had taught her a valuable lesson. "I learned from her how foolish, how 'gullible,' how easily flattered human beings are, taken *en masse.*"[7] She decided that Madame's contempt for people was on the same gigantic scale as everything else about her. Except for her delicately-tapered fingers, Helena impressed her as excessive.

* * *

She had a greater power over the weak and credulous, a greater capacity for making black appear white, a larger waist, a more voracious appetite, a more confirmed passion for tobacco, a more ceaseless and insatiable hatred of those whom she thought to be her enemies, a greater disrespect for *les convenances,* a worse temper, a greater command of bad language, and a greater contempt for the intelligence of her fellow-beings than I had ever supposed possible to be contained in one person. These I suppose, must be reckoned as her vices, though whether a creature so indifferent to all ordinary standards of right and wrong can be held to have virtues or vices I know not.[8]

To be sure, these aggravations built over the course of time; in May of 1887, Mabel was still smiling and playing the hospitable hostess.

It could not have been more distressing to both Mabel and the Keightleys that Madame was in a vile temper most of the time; Helena herself admitted as much in a letter to her sister: "I grumble at them, I drive them away, I shut myself off from all these *mystical vampires,* who suck all the moral strength out of me—no! all the same they rush to me like flies to honey."[9] A few days after her arrival, she demanded to know what they wanted of her; to revive the Theosophical movement and work for the Masters, they told her, as well as to teach them occultism. H.P.B. responded that she must disappoint them in the matter of lessons, at least for the present; her job now was to finish *The Secret Doctrine,* but in order to do it she required their help. Those present—Mabel, the two Keightleys, Ashton Ellis and Thomas Harbottle—assured her of their willingness to work.

"All right then," she replied. "Here you are—get to work right away."[10] She scooped up every scrap of paper she had written so far and handed the piles to Arch Keightley. As a first step, he and the rest of them were to read through the pages, then comment on what they each felt needed to be done.

Over the following days, Arch, Bert and Mabel read every line; after comparing notes, they screwed up their courage to face Madame with the news that it was "a confused muddle and jumble,"[11] which needed to be rearranged according to some workable structure. Helena sat as stiff as a board and listened without interruption, but when they had finished she burst forth with a fireworks display of profanity. Then she turned to Mabel and asked if she agreed with the Keightleys' analysis. Entirely, Mabel replied; they were quite right.

"Go to hell,"[12] H.P.B. roared. So far as she was concerned, she was sick of *The Secret Doctrine*; she washed her hands of it and they could do with it as they liked.

Her anger camouflaged despair and the discouraging realization that the Keightleys were telling the truth. She could not produce a coherent manuscript by herself, any more than she had been able to write *Isis Unveiled* alone; she especially smarted at their criticism of her awkward, amateurish English. That these people had willingly dropped their own activities to devote themselves to rescuing her produced no gratitude in Helena, only smoldering resentment that she vented in sarcasm, indifference and unadorned nastiness.

When a young Theosophist named Alice Cleather asked Bert to arrange an introduction to Madame, he warned that it might be a trying encounter. Undeterred, Alice replied that she was facing an inner crisis and simply had to see Madame, and so an appointment was made. At that time Alice was living in Eastbourne with her husband and two children and, as they were not well-off, she had to scrimp to put money aside. Now she decided to use her savings for the pilgrimage to H.P.B. Met by Bert at the West Norwood station, she was told that Madame frequently argued with Mabel Collins and sometimes when the windows were open could be heard halfway down the road. This revelation turned out to be prophetic. "Sure enough," Alice recalled, "when we got within a hundred yards of Maycot, I heard loud and apparently angry voices floating—or rather ricochetting—towards us down the road." Already aghast, she was further distressed when Bert murmured that if the Old Lady was in "one of her tempers,"[13] she would probably refuse to see Alice at all.

Left quaking outside on the doorstep, Alice could hear Madame dressing down Bert for bringing a total stranger to call at such an inopportune moment. She would not see anyone, she barked. When he reminded her that she herself had made the appointment and added that Alice had made a long journey up from the country to keep it, H.P.B. refused to listen. A greatly disappointed Alice returned to Eastbourne without her savings, blaming herself for her unworthiness to meet H.P.B.

Another visitor during those first weeks in London was twenty-year-old Charles Johnston, the son of a Protestant member of Parliament from Ulster, who had planned to become a missionary until he read Sinnett's *Esoteric Buddhism*. Converted instantly, he rounded up a few of his school friends who were also interested in Eastern religion and, with William Butler Yeats and Claude Wright, founded the Dublin Hermetic Society in 1885. Yeats, the chairman, had read a paper on whether or not the Mahatmas really existed, but apparently had offered no definite conclusion because Johnston had come to "Maycot" to get the answer from H.P.B.'s own lips.

Arriving at twilight one evening, he was advised that Madame had not yet finished her day's work and was sent upstairs to wait. When finally ushered into her presence, he received an initial impression of rippled hair, a dark blue dressing gown, and "marvellously potent eyes." All graciousness, she gave him a hearty handshake and quickly invited him to stay for tea. After bellowing for Louise, she snuggled in her armchair, rolled him a cigarette made of Turkish tobacco and proceeded to interrogate him. Had he read the S.P.R. Report, or as she called the psychists, The Spookical Research Society? Did he know that she was a Russian spy and champion impostor of the century? What impression had Richard Hodgson, "the frisky lambkin from Australia," made upon him?

Perhaps intuiting exactly how to please her, Johnston answered that if he had not already been a member of the Theosophical Society, he should have joined merely on the strength of Hodgson's report. In his opinion, there was not a shred of real evidence in it.

Helena beamed. "I am so glad you think so, my dear, for now I can offer you tea with a good conscience."

After Louise had spread a white cloth and lit the lamp, she brought in a tray of tea, toast and eggs. When Bert joined them, Helena began to criticize the S.P.R. and then turned on Bert, whom she branded as "greedy, idle, untidy, unmethodical and generally worthless." When he ventured a mild defense, she flared up anew, declaring he was "born a flapdoodle, lived a flapdoodle, and would die a flapdoodle." Johnston recalled that Bert got so rattled he lost his grip on the cutlery, which left a wake of egg yolk in its path across the white tablecloth. A few minutes later he bolted the room.

For several hours Helena regaled Johnston with stories of the Mahatmas, answered his questions with the patience of a true guru, and finally dismissed him smoothly by saying that it was late and she felt sleepy. As Johnston stepped out into the spring night, he ruminated that Madame, "the most perfect aristocrat I have ever known," had not performed a single miracle for him but nevertheless "conveyed the sense of the miraculous." Something in her personality suggested a bigger world, deeper powers, unseen might. "Her mere presence testified to the vigour of the soul,"[14] he decided.

Back in Ireland, Charley founded the Dublin Lodge of the Theosophical Society and continued his studies at the university, planning after graduation to relocate in India.

Johnston and Cleather were not the only ones attracted to "Maycot"; indeed, once Helena's presence in London became known, there were others who hastened to beat a path to her door. Of course her neighbor Allan Hume was not among them and curiously enough neither was Alfred Sinnett, whose London Lodge was by now largely defunct. Barely three weeks after her arrival those who assembled one evening in her rooms were all young, eager, and quick to dismiss Sinnett and his Lodge as "altogether hopelessly asleep, if not dead";[15] they, on the other hand, wanted to do something active to publicize Theosophy and proposed as a first step the forming of their own group. Out of respect for H.P.B. they wanted to call it "The Blavatsky Lodge of the Theosophical Society." Helena offered no objections but pointed out that although the rules of the Society demanded the signatures of seven members when applying for a charter, there were only six of them. When Mabel suggested that Madame herself sign the application, she roared with laughter and finally agreed. Secretly terribly flattered, she dashed off a note to Vera the next morning: "Just fancy that—they unanimously called it 'The Blavatsky Lodge of the T.S.!' This I call hitting the Psychical Research Society straight in the face; let them learn of what stuff we are made!"[16]

Sinnett, by the way, greeted this rival group with a notable lack of enthusiasm; in fact, he immediately issued an announcement that any Theosophist who wished to join the Old Lady's Lodge would no longer be welcome at his. According to Alice Cleather, "quite half the members, including myself, promptly left. How could we hesitate for a moment between H.P.B. and Mr. Sinnett?"[17]

Alfred and Patience must surely have called on H.P.B. in Norwood, but the relationship had nonetheless disintegrated into icy politeness. Around the tenth of May, H.P.B. sent what appears to be her last letter to the Sinnetts, informing Patience of an unexpected and disagreeable visit from Isabel Cooper-Oakley, whom Madame now loathed. Apparently she had expressly forbidden Patience to give Isabel her address, and even though Isabel had told a wild tale of having taken the train to Norwood in a trance and been led to "Maycot" by a mysterious power, Helena believed that Patience had supplied the address and wanted her to know that she was aware of her disloyalty.

All the old friends were slowly falling away from her: Subba Row made no secret of his loss of faith and was on the verge of resigning;[18] had she read the New York papers she would have known that Mohini Chatterji, while still calling himself a member of the Society, did not like to call himself a Theosophist. But Mohini had begun his subtle denigration of her long ago. What did take her back, although she should have expected it, was the attitude of Alfred and Patience, both of whom had ceased to believe in her and who displayed no compunction about saying so.

H.P.B. made it her business to keep abreast of what transpired at Patience's Tuesday afternoon receptions; and she knew that Alfred disliked her being in London and thought the Blavatsky Lodge a mistake. He also had the audacity to insist that everything the Old Lady knew about Theosophical teachings had been picked up from the letters the Mahatmas had sent him. Of course she had been able to expand the information, but nevertheless he felt convinced that she herself received no teachings from the Masters.

H.P.B. could afford to smile at Sinnett's egomania. It had been two years since she had discontinued his Mahatmic mail service and she had no intention of resuming it. Let him continue his pathetic attempts to communicate with the Mahatmas by hypnotizing Laura Holloway and later Alice Cleather and even his own wife. Madame alone could state with absolutely no fear of contradiction that Sinnett would never reach the Masters.

Henry Olcott had recently informed Helena that his budget could no longer cover her allowance and that unless she returned to Adyar and "shared my crusts,"[19] as he put it, she would have to find another means of support. While it was true that H.P.B. did not have to pay for room and board, she nevertheless refused to accept so much as a shilling in cash from either the Keightleys or Mabel, supplying herself with pocket money for tobacco and small personal items by writing for Russian papers. Aside from the annoying hours spent producing these articles, she devoted her time to *The Secret Doctrine* on which she was again working. Arch and Bert had gone to the expense of having the manuscript professionally typed; then, reading it through a second time, they devised a plan for dividing the material into two volumes, cosmogenesis and anthropogenesis. Each of these was to be based on the *Stanzas of Dzyan* and would consist of three parts: first the *Stanzas* with H.P.B.'s commentary; second symbolism; and finally various appendixes and addenda. This still left some material that seemed to fit nowhere; Helena set it aside for an intended third and fourth volumes.

As soon as the Keightleys had arranged the material for Volume One, they gave it back to H.P.B. with detailed notes pointing out gaps and omissions. Next, she went to work on the typescript with scissors, paste and pen, after which it had to be retyped once more. Apparently it was not until the retyping that they realized Madame's commentary on the *Stanzas* amounted to a measly twenty pages; this brevity would not do for what, in her preface, she promised to be a full explanation.

"What on earth am I to say?" H.P.B. wailed. "What *do* you want to know? Why, it's all as plain as the nose on your face!"[20]

Bruised, the Keightleys retired for a consultation, finally deciding that if they were not smart enough to understand Madame, neither were potential readers. It was many months, however, before they came up with a solution: each sloka of the *Stanzas* was slashed from the typescript and pasted at the head of a sheet of paper; below, the Keightleys and others listed all the questions they could think of upon that particular sloka. All Helena had to do was answer the queries.

On June 21, Queen Victoria celebrated her Golden Jubilee commemorating the fiftieth anniversary of her reign; a massive pageant winding its way from Buckingham Palace to Westminister Abbey included the heads of Europe's royal families riding in fifteen closed carriages. All over London people decorated their houses, hung out garlands, and slung their streets with banners reading "God Bless Our Queen." For two days crowds thronged the streets until late at night, shouting, drinking and singing "Rule Britannia." In suburban Norwood, where the hijinks were a good deal more sedate, H.P.B. did not permit the patriotic frenzy to interfere with her daily regimen. She was at her desk by seven but allowed no one to enter the room until she called for her midday meal. As always, this repast might be called for any time between noon and four, a disconcerting development to Mabel Collins' cook. The rest of the afternoon Arch and Bert rushed in and out of her office, asking questions, sorting papers and consulting her on the manuscript. In the late afternoon, depending on her whim, she might or might not see the many callers who appeared, often with appointments. "But Maycot was a long way out of London," Archibald Keightley would recall, "and *we* had to face the disappointed pilgrims!"[21]

Finally at 6:30, Helena would join the rest of the household for the evening meal and later, when the table had been cleared, she would relax with tobacco and talk. Dipping into the Ceylon grass basket that held fine-cut Egyptian and Turkish tobacco, she would roll cigarettes and pass them around the table, then lay out her game of patience. At one of these nightly get-togethers, Helena had decided to lay her cards on the table in another sense because she stated politely, but emphatically, that she could not remain at "Maycot." Not only was it too far from the center of London but, more important, it was obviously too small to use either as an office or a meeting place for the new Lodge. Sympathetic, the Keightleys agreed to look for a suitable house in London.

A second source of her discontent, she told them, was Henry Olcott. For the past two years he had been editing the *Theosophist* and running the Society as he saw fit; lately Helena had been having difficulty getting her views expressed in the magazine, particularly when speaking of the Mahatmas. Henry's attitude could not have been clearer: his sole concerns now were the Society and himself, or rather, for the Society as personified in himself. He credited the organization's troubles not to his mistakes but solely to H.P.B.'s obsession with her Masters and occult phenomena. What he had been doing was publicly trying to unhitch Theosophy from supermen by avoiding references to the Masters in the magazine.

Helena was furious, but could not afford to smear Olcott, since he was one of the founders. Luckily, she had to do little more than hint at this dreadful state of affairs before the Keightleys jumped to her support. Knowing little about Olcott's untiring labor on behalf of the Society, they saw the colonel as an old fussbudget out in India who was trying to obstruct H.P.B.'s Cause; needless to say, Helena did not disabuse them of these notions. When they urged public propaganda for the Masters and talked about publishing their own magazine so that Madame might express her views, she smiled benignly. As it turned out, they were also talking about starting a Theosophical Publishing House[22] that would issue not only the magazine, but *The Secret Doctrine* as well. Initially, the fourteen members of the Blavatsky Lodge contributed seven hundred pounds toward the publishing house, probably the bulk of which was furnished by the Keightleys.

After much discussion of names for the magazine, they decided on *Lucifer,* or Light-Bringer. One or two members vehemently opposed the name as diabolical and unconventional, which naturally won the more avant-garde to its side. "Don't allow yourself to be frightened," H.P.B. assured Vera, "it is not the devil," but merely the name of the Morning Star or "bringer of light"[23] sacred to the ancient world.

With the advent of *Lucifer,* to be co-edited by H.P.B. and Mabel Collins, Helena began feeling pressured. How was she to find time for a magazine, the book, and Thursday evening meetings of the Blavatsky Lodge? "I do not know myself!"[24] Somehow she managed not only to find time, but also to feel healthier than she had in years. By summer's end, the Keightleys had located a house at 17 Lansdowne Road in the Notting Hill section of London. This was a convenient location for the brothers because Arch owned a house nearby and Bert lived with his mother at the top of Notting Hill, at 30 Linden Gardens. While Helena had not gone personally to inspect her new quarters, she felt reassured by the Keightleys' description of its good-sized dining room wth folding doors opening into a large airy drawing room. It was decided that the expenses would be shared by herself, the Keightleys, and Countess Wachtmeister, who was returning to London shortly, and that it would be used both as a residence and Society Headquarters.

In September all the pieces of H.P.B.'s new life fell into place. On the fifteenth, the first issue of *Lucifer* was premiered, and the countess arrived at "Maycot" with two Swedish servants. For unknown reasons, H.P.B. at once dubbed them "the Swedish virgins," although a more accurate term would have been "the Swedish saints" because they proved patience personified in ministering to her wants and whims. "After three days of packing, planning and arranging everything," Constance recalled, "we one morning got into a carriage and drove up to London, to 17, Lansdowne Road."[25] According to Arch, the move was not so horrific as the transfer from Ostend "for the books and papers could be arranged, packed and unpacked, and rearranged the same day."[26] And Helena had only lost one day's work.

This time even Madame was hard put to complain. The house itself was a pleasant one in a quiet neighborhood: It backed a small private park and fronted on Holland Park. Helena's ground-floor rooms, which consisted of a small bedroom leading into a large office plus a lavatory, could not have been more comfortable. Her desk faced a large bay window overlooking the luxuriant green of Holland Park; at her right and left were tables and book racks filled with the reference works she claimed not to need, and all around had been set out the Indian souvenirs she had been carting about for the past two-and-a-half years: Benares bronzes, Palghat mats, Adoni carpets, Moradabad platters, Kashmiri plaques, and Cingalese statues. On the wall she hung her Swiss cuckoo clock, still broken except on those unpredictable occasions when its little door would fly open and the bird would momentarily pop out. Visitors who witnessed this performance were dumbfounded, but H.P.B. would sternly glance up, utter a firm Damn you, and then go on with her conversation.

Everything about the Lansdowne Road establishment was designed to accommodate Madame Blavatsky: Mabel Collins was no longer the consummate annoyance that she had been when they shared a roof; in Mabel's place was the saintly Countess Wachtmeister, who ran with efficiency a household that now included Bert and Arch. While the cuisine was not so strictly vegetarian as to prohibit fish and eggs, meat as a rule was not served. One wonders how Helena greeted this innovation, since only the previous year she had insisted that flesh food was necessary to her health, but apparently she went along with the new diet. She also instituted a rule of her own: everybody had to be in bed by twelve because she said, "Master goes His 'rounds' at midnight."[27] And if that were not sufficient reason for the curfew, she added that one hour's sleep before midnight was worth four after, owing to magnetic changes that took place in the earth at that time. To carry the asceticism still further, she would soon recommend the even more controversial injunction: celibacy. While repression of the sexual urge would remain an option for Lodge members, it was nonetheless an ideal practiced by many, certainly by those who aspired to become one of Madame's *chelas*. Celibacy, she told them, was merely basic training in the "occult hygiene of mind and body."[28]

Now that Madame was more accessible, the Thursday evening meetings rapidly increased in popularity: admission for non-members was strictly by invitation and these cards of entry were always in hot demand. Alice Cleather, for whom Thursday was the most important day of the week, recalled that "some crank" once obtained admission, asked permission to speak, and immediately launched on a windy exposition of some philosophical theory. "H.P.B. stood it for a few minutes, and then, to the consternation of the chairman—a very conventional person—raised her voice in a stinging and sarcastic rebuke to the effect that people were invited to the meetings of the Blavatsky Lodge to listen to *her* views—i.e., to Theosophical teaching—not to air their own."[29] The man slunk out of the room.

H.P.B.'s testiness did not fade as her confidence grew: some of her disciples had to remind themselves that Madame was in constant pain and on these grounds should be forgiven her outbursts. In the countess's opinion, Helena's abuse was calculated as a trial through which she deliberately put people to test their devotion to the Cause. Madame herself may have flogged her naturally mercurial nature in order to set herself outside the realm of civility and courtesy: after Alice Cleather had once spent weeks helping prepare the index for *The Secret Doctrine,* she brought her work to Madame who "flicked it contemptuously with her beautiful forefinger saying, 'This is not in the least what I wanted, my dear; it won't do at all,' thereupon she tore the sheets across and flung them into the waste paper basket." Alice burst into tears, but Helena paid no attention. To Alice, Madame's response was perfectly justified; she had known nothing about indexing and must have completely botched the job. And Alice felt that spiritually H.P.B.'s rebuff was "extremely good for me at that early stage."[30]

Most people lacked the nerve to talk back to Helena, but Bert, after months of abuse, was growing angry. So one day when Helena viciously attacked him, "hitting just every one of my weakest and tenderest spots," he rebelled and "suddenly felt a surge of red-hot anger rise within me." One moment Madame had been squawking furiously, he recalled; the next she stopped dead and stared at him. Looking him up and down, she remarked coldly, "And you want to be an occultist."

It was then, he said, that he "saw and knew, and went off deeply ashamed, having learnt no small lesson."[31] It seems remarkable that he failed to question how Madame had managed to become an occultist if she could not restrain herself; in the end, the fact that he and the other disciples took her mistreatment says more about them than about H.P.B. The only person exempt from her "training" was Archibald, and when Bert once asked her why she never scolded Arch, she replied that it was because he had a blue liver, and would not explain what that meant.

In 1887, the fantastics began to take over London. The century was gearing up for the "Yellow Nineties" with its *fin de siècle* daring, its tolerance of novelty in ideas and art, its Wildes and Beardsleys with their refined perversities. It was also working up to economic depression. Essentially, however, 1887 was the curtain-raiser to a decade of hope and action, when people believed anything might happen; for the young, anything that did happen had to be good so long as it was new. With the most cherished principles of the Victorian Age about to be dumped overboard, experiment became the watchword and people set about testing life for themselves. People of all ages convinced themselves that they were passing into a new social and moral system; still it was mainly the young men and women who especially felt they were stepping out of the caged past into a freedom full of limitless possibilities. There was so much to think about, so much to discuss, so much to see: aesthetics in art and literature; celebrity breakfast parties; anything Oriental from Gilbert and Sullivan's *Mikado* to mystics like Mohini Chatterji; Buffalo Bill; bright new restaurants and "tea shops"; and the only just invented safety bicycle that became a symbol of the new freedom.

Soon after Helena's arrival in London, she had rather shyly told Vera that "it appears that your sister is getting to be the fashion in Europe,"[32] and even though it had been an exaggeration at the time, by early 1888 it would be a fact. Séances were still a stylish pastime for fashionable London society, and the city's clairvoyants continued doing a brisk business, but none of them had the foresight to predict the 1890s, nor did they divine that Madame Blavatsky and her Theosophy would soon become a fashionable cult. As a matter of fact, H.P.B. herself did not foresee it.

From the time she moved to Lansdowne Road, more and more people were drawn into her orbit, not only the Thursday attendees at the Blavatsky Lodge, but visitors who just wanted to meet the famous Madame. "We were hardly settled in the house," recalled the countess, "when people began to call on H.P.B. The visitors grew so numerous, and she was so constantly interrupted in her work, that it was considered advisable for her to have a day for reception."[33] Accordingly, H.P.B. had a calling card printed:

* * *

MADAME BLAVATSKY
AT HOME,
SATURDAY, 4 TO 10 O'CLOCK.

17 Lansdowne Road
Notting Hill, W.

The four to ten hours were totally ignored because, as Constance admitted, "from 2 P.M. till 11 or 12 at night there would be a succession of visitors and H.P.B. would frequently have a group around her asking questions, to which she would answer with unvarying patience."[34] At the same time Helena did not hesitate to ask questions of her guests, the most frequent to newcomers being, "Do you believe in a P.G.?"[35] (Personal God).

Aside from the Saturday At-Homes, she welcomed a stream of guests every night of the week. Looking back, the artist Edmund Russell thought that he had never seen such hospitality. "With five or six in the family, the table was spread for twenty. Once-invited-always-invited. One took a vacant seat without ceremony, came in at any time, left in the middle of a meal, sat by some poor student for one course, moved over beside a princess for another, or, as special privilege finished the repast with 'The Old Lady' herself." The food was vegetarian but "no one would ever have known it, so rich and varied the magical dishes."[36] A platter of chicken fricassee, prepared for the compulsively carnivorous, was usually carried away untouched.

Corpulent, unhealthy, and habitually untidy, Helena nevertheless struck most of her guests as captivating. To *Pall Mall Gazette* editor W. T. Stead, who was simultaneously delighted and repelled, Helena presented her portrait and declared that he might call himself what he liked but she knew he was a good Theosophist. Stead thought that she had the manners of a very unconventional man, but he liked her. Her repartee was marvelous of course: when someone called her the worst-dressed woman in the world, she retorted that was impossible, since she didn't dress at all. When asked if the stories about her were apocryphal, she never bothered to affirm or deny. "Mud," she would say, "has rained down on me for so long I no longer attempt to open an umbrella."[37]

There was not a would-be mystic in London who sooner or later did not beat the path to Lansdowne Road. Among the first was William Butler Yeats, a tall, pale, angular youth of twenty-two, "all dreams and all gentleness,"[38] as one of his friends described him. Despite his maiden speech at the Dublin Hermetic Society, it was neither Madame Blavatsky nor her Mahatmas who had initially drawn Yeats to Theosophy but Mohini Chatterji, whom he had met in Dublin in 1885.[39] "He sat there beautiful," Yeats recalled, "as only an Eastern is beautiful, making little gestures with his delicate hands, and to him alone among all the talks I have heard, oratory, and even the delight of ordered words, seemed nothing, and all thought a flight into the heart of truth."[40] In London, Yeats talked incessantly about Indian mysticism and the wonderful seer Mohini, and in Bedford Park, where he lived with his family, he painted the signs of the zodiac on the ceiling of his bedroom.

Soon after his friend Charley Johnston met H.P.B., Yeats armed himself with a letter of introduction from him and called upon Madame at Maycot, where he found "an old woman in a plain loose dark dress: a sort of old Irish peasant woman with an air of humor and audacious power."[41] She also seemed to him "a sort of female Dr. Johnson, impressive I think to every man or woman who had themselves any richness."[42] Playing patience at a small table, she kept scribbling on the green baize with a stick of white chalk while she talked to Yeats, who saw at once that she had "more human nature than anybody else."[43] Unlike many of her other visitors, he had carefully read the S.P.R. Report and he was plagued by whether or not to believe Hodgson. His poet friend William Ernest Henley had shrugged off that question as irrelevant by saying that "she is a person of genius, but a person of genius must do something—Sarah Bernhardt sleeps in her coffin."[44] Yeats could not accept that explanation, nor could he reconcile the weight of Hodgson's evidence with what he saw and heard of H.P.B. and so he kept waiting "with impatience for the explanation that never came."[45]

When Helena moved into London, Yeats was still waiting, but by then had joined the Theosophical Society where he got an earful of dogma from her disciples. It must have been either Bert or Arch who told him "how he heard often her Master's mystic ring in the middle of the night, and though the sound was faint and sweet the whole house was shaken,"[46] and someone else whispered to him that "she is not a living woman at all, the body of the real Madame Blavatsky was discovered thirty years ago on the battlefield of ―――."[47] Yeats could not remember the name, something Russian he thought, but doubtless he had encountered the most recent version of the Mentana story.

Helena herself had enough weird adventures to keep him intrigued and sometimes, when she was feeling tired or low, she would ramble on dreamily. "I go on writing as the Wandering Jew walks," she sighed. "I once used to blame and pity the people who sell their souls to the Devil; I now only pity them—they do it to have somebody on their side."[48] And then she would switch to Alfred de Musset, whom she said that she had known and disliked, and Balzac whom she had met only once, and George Sand with whom she had dabbled in magic even though "neither of us knew anything about it."[49] That was fascinating to Yeats and thoroughly believable, but he had to lift his eyebrows at some of her more grisly stories. "Once my knee was very bad," she confided to him, "and the doctor said I would be lame for life. But in the middle of the night the Master came in with a live dog split open in his hands, and he put the dog over my knee so that the entrails covered it, and in the morning I was well."[50]

Yeats decided that Madame "dreamed awake," which not only was a nice way of putting it but as good a theory as anyone's. Never present at a temper tantrum, Yeats thought Madame extremely kind and ventured to remark upon "how careful she was that the young men about her should not over-work." Actually she worked them like galley slaves, but perhaps Yeats's impression is based on an incident involving him: when someone reproved the poet for talking too much and wearying Madame, she clucked gravely, "No, no, he is very sensitive."[51]

After a while Yeats seems to have given up trying to figure out Madame, and decided simply to enjoy her and to tell his friends about her. To the Irish poet Katharine Tynan, he was obviously trying to make Lansdowne Road sound entertaining:

A sad accident happened at Madame Blavatsky's lately, I hear. A big materialist sat on the astral double of a poor young Indian. He was sit-ting on the sofa and he was too material to be able to see it. Certainly a sad accident![52]

He wanted to bring all his friends into the high priestess's circle, most of all Maud Gonne, a Junoesque Irishwoman famous both as a beauty and a revo-lutionary, and, to Yeats, "the trouble of my life."[53] The bedazzled, lovesick young man was delighted to learn of Maud's interest in the occult, even of her experimentation with hashish, which, in large doses, produced an out-of-body experience.

"When I was experimenting with the occult," she said in her autobiogra-phy, "always in the hope of gaining power to use for the great object of my life, I joined the Theosophical Society and went with Willie Yeats to visit that strange old woman, Madame Blavatsky, its founder." Motioned to sit next to Madame, who was playing patience, she would best remember H.P.B.'s "big pale luminous eyes" and recall that she had glanced around the room at the Theosophists who "looked a nondescript gathering, though Willie told me there were interesting people among them." The great-limbed Maud, no shrinking Alice Cleather, demanded of Madame whether politics were com-patible with Theosophy; Maud, who had been criticized for her political views by the Dublin branch, sought absolution from no less than Madame her-self.

"My dear child," H.P.B. murmured, "of course you can do what you like in politics. That has nothing to do with Theosophy. They must be flapdoodles in that Dublin branch. I will tell them so."

Maud noticed that the gas chandelier was flickering, no doubt because of air in the pipes. "Spooks in the room," announced Helena loudly, then whis-pered to Maud, "They are all looking for a miracle."

When the gas finally went out completely, she declared in an even louder tone, "Spooks!" while keeping up a low commentary to Maud. "Now they think they have seen one. They also are flapdoodles."[54]

Others of Yeats' friends found H.P.B. less to their taste: the Welshman

Ernest Rhys, best known today as editor of the Everyman Library classics series, had apparently expected 17 Lansdowne Road to be a sort of Oriental temple of mysticism transplanted to London. Hence, he was disappointed to find a Victorian villa "with an air of prosperity suggesting the well-to-do bourgeois class." He first met H.P.B. one twilight evening in the winter of 1888 when the fog was so thick that one could not see across the river and indoors heavy curtains shut out the fading daylight. Seated under a shaded gas lamp, Madame was playing cards with three pale young men "whose faces looked as if the diet and discipline they were subjected to were affecting their health." H.P.B., dressed in a plain black gown girdled with a black rope, paused to glance up at Rhys and after holding out her hand briefly, went on with the game; her partners did not look up at all. Rhys and Yeats sat down to watch. Suddenly one of the players cried out in a shrill voice, "H.P.B., you're cheating!"

"Did you only find that out now?" She laughed and threw down her cards. "I have been cheating all through the game."

Listening and observing, Rhys was conscious of a powerful force radiating from H.P.B., "a something almost hypnotic, not accountable to ordinary human laws,"[55] but finally she failed to convince him, and he did not become a convert. Afterward, when Yeats asked him what he thought of Madame, Rhys hesitantly confessed he had seen nothing to make him feel Theosophy offered great spiritual regeneration to mankind. Yeats countered that it was not fair to judge H.P.B. by a single meeting and urged him to return when Madame was giving instruction to her disciples.

Helena was to exercise a peculiar fascination on the young Irish literary set who were searching for a fresh and comprehensive cosmology. To Yeats, Charles Johnston, Claude Falls Wright, George Moore, and George W. Russell ("Æ"), Madame seemed to be trying to hold the world in the palm of her hand, whatever else might be said of her. Some of them, like Moore, who had encountered Mohini by chance and "fled before him,"[56] continued to observe with interest from the sidelines. "Æ," however, despite an initial attraction to Mohini "instinctively as to a destiny," drew the line at actually joining the Dublin Theosophical Society. By the fall of 1888, he was just beginning to waver when he wrote H.P.B.: "I am not a proclaimed Theosophist. I do not belong to the Society. For some reasons I am sorry; for many reasons I am glad." One reason, he said, was that the T.S. was not representative of Theosophy, "only of itself—a gathering of many earnest seekers after truth, many powerful intellects, many saints and many sinners and lovers of curiosity." Speaking for himself, he confessed that he would not mind witnessing phenomena or calling spirits from the "vasty deep," but if that was Theosophy, he wanted none of it. "My ideal is to worship the One God in spirit and truth."[57]

Printing "Æ's" letter in *Lucifer*, Helena added an editorial footnote to his comment about phenomena: "It is not in the Theosophical Society that our

correspondent can ever hope to evoke spirits or see any physical phenomena,"[58] a rather remarkable statement considering her penchant for burying
cups and saucers. Quickly "Æ" replied that he had not meant he really
wanted to see spooks; it had been his lower self speaking. "I earnestly trust no
Member of the Society will ever indulge in the evocation of phenomena,
whether for curiosity or for the gratification of the intellect." He did, however, honestly believe that "the formation of the Society was a mistake," not so
much in motive but in leadership; since the speed of the slowest ship measures
a fleet's rate of progress, "the weak ones of the Society marks its position in
the world."[59]

By the end of the year, however, "Æ" would begin to read *The Secret
Doctrine*, which he believed to be the faith of the future, and then would join
the Dublin Society. Soon after his induction, he moved out of his parents'
home and went to live at the Society's Headquarters at 3 Upper Ely Place. He
survived his twelve-hour day as a clerk at the Guiness Brewery only by the
prospect of returning to Ely Place and immersing himself in the pages of *The
Secret Doctrine*. "Æ" was twenty-one at the time, and his literary career still
lay before him. Critics have commented that his poetry suffered from the
limitation of a Theosophical world view, but to "Æ" Theosophy was the only
world. Forty-five years later, writing to Sean O'Faolain a month before his
death, he would say, "You dismiss H. P. Blavatsky rather too easily as 'hocus
pocus.' Nobody ever affected the thought of so many able men and women by
'hocus pocus.' "[60]

It would be poets such as "Æ" and Yeats who would continue to celebrate
H.P.B.'s visions long after she had departed the scene. To "Æ," it did not
matter if *The Secret Doctrine* was merely a romantic compilation; it still
contained the grandest cosmogony ever conceived and would always remain
to him one of the most provocative books ever written. To Yeats, who realized
that Helena's phenomena might well have been fraudulent, her philosophy
had independent, inherent value and her Tibetan Mahatmas remained in-
finitely fascinating:

Anashuya. Swear by the parents of the gods,
Dread oath, who dwell on sacred Himalay,
On the far Golden Peak; enormous shapes,
Who were still old when the great sea was young,
In their vast faces mystery and dreams . . .[61]

H.P.B. loved being adored by sensitive young men of artistic temperament,
but of all of them who descended on Lansdowne Road, only one would achieve
for Madame a special significance. His worth would come not from his poetic
vision because he was not literary, but from his willingness to sacrifice his
personal concerns in order to serve her. His name was George R. S. Mead, the
son of a colonel in the Ordnance, and he had taken honors at Cambridge after

shifting from mathematics to the classics. For a while he taught school but after reading *Esoteric Buddhism* and meeting Mohini and Bertram Keightley, he began to study Hindu philosophy, later entering Oxford to take up philosophy in general, then moving on to the University of Clermont-Ferrand. However, it was not until meeting H.P.B. in 1887 that he made a complete conversion to Theosophy and joined the Lansdowne Road household as her private secretary. His clipped beard, narrow nose, and long curved mustache gave his face a sharp intellectual look, but to Willie Yeats, who took an instant dislike to him, Mead's intellect was "that of a good size whelk,"[62] and his manner overrighteous. Annie Besant, describing him several years later, would find Mead an "earnest disciple, a man of strong brain and strong character, a fine scholar and untiring worker."[63]

Such were the major figures who drifted in and out of Helena's world, but there were others: the Wilde family would be mildly impressed, especially Oscar's older brother, Willie, a journalist on the *Telegraph*, who did his best to see that nothing derogatory about H.P.B. appeared in that paper's columns; their mother Lady Wilde, who dabbled in Spiritualism and seemed to think that Madame's At-Homes were séances; and finally Oscar's wife, Constance, who had spent the early years of her marriage arranging receptions for literary figures. Of late, however, since Oscar had become rich and famous and had mysterious new companions of whom his wife knew nothing—young men whom Oscar entertained in hotel rooms and explained his frequent absences by saying he had taken up golf—the shy Constance had little to do. She decided to write a book because everyone wrote books; she joined ladies' committees, promoted missions to the heathen, and had herself initiated into what purported itself to be an occult Egyptian order; and she also joined the Theosophical Society, where she became acquainted with H.P.B. Just being around Madame gave her a second-hand importance, and besides, it always provided an interesting talking point for those dreary receptions Constance was obliged to attend.

Everyone who wanted to appear au courant went to see H.P.B., or at least talked as if they had; and even thirty-five years later the fabulous Lady Margot Asquith would recall in her memoirs that she had attended one of H.P.B.'s séances. She had met Madame, "a Russian Jewess," at a private home in Brook Street to hear her views on God. But once Lady Asquith got a glimpse of Madame's "heavy white face, as deeply pitted with smallpox as a solitaire board," and of the "palpitating ladies" who surrounded her, she took a seat near the window, as far from H.P.B. as she could get without actually leaving the room. According to Asquith, the Madame gave a conclusive shudder, heaved her bosom, and whispered, "A murderer has passed below our windows." Swiveling around to peer out, Lady Margot wrote that "I strained my eyes up and down Brook Street to see the murderer, but there was not a creature in sight." Of course, she remarked in her autobiography, the Madame had been "an audacious swindler."[64]

Obviously it was not H.P.B. whom Lady Asquith met, for she rarely left Lansdowne Road and certainly not to conduct a séance, nor had she ever had smallpox. But it made for a story.

It is surprising that in this hectic period H.P.B. got any work done at all but she did. Keeping sacrosanct the hours between 6 A.M. and 6 P.M. she spent the first half of 1888 on *The Secret Doctrine*. Most of Volume One and part of Volume Two was being retyped by the Keightleys, with Bert working at a small table near the end of her desk. Between them sat a large ash tray that always served as an excellent barometer of the day's progress; if things were going well, the ash tray would hold a few half-smoked stubs; if she were encountering blocks, the dish would be heaped with butts and matches by six o'clock. Sometimes she made Bert rummage through every drawer and piece of paper in search of some obscure note, and accompanied the request by "a stream of scolding, stinging comments on my work, laziness and general incompetence."[65] One of Bert's biggest headaches was that of verifying Madame's countless quotations, a difficult task because she claimed the books were not in the house and also because the page numbers were always wrong. After hours at the British Museum, Bert finally figured out that Madame reversed the page numbers, writing p. 321 for p. 123; once he made this discovery, his job went somewhat more smoothly.[66]

During this period Helena also had the editorial assistance of Edward Douglass Fawcett, who had briefly given her a hand at Ostend the previous year. How much Fawcett actually helped is a matter of controversy: both the Keightleys would later single him out as a source of immense assistance, claiming he supplied many quotations from scientific works and also did some of the writing; Fawcett himself went much further, implying that much of the second volume was his.

Throughout the summer H.P.B. read two sets of galley proofs and then a set of page proofs, all the while correcting, adding and altering up to the very last moment. The printer's bill for corrections amounted to a staggering three hundred pounds.

Doubtless no one knew better than H.P.B. that the dream she had sought all her life was finally becoming a reality. It pleased her to know that her teachings were spreading and that she was surrounded by devotees whose only wish was to broadcast throughout the world her personal vision of the cosmos. Still, there were times when she could not help screaming in pain to Vera: "I feel so sad, oh so sad! Oh, if I only could see you."[67] Her constant cry was for something Russian, something familiar, somebody or something from her childhood: to please her, Vera offered to ask the minister of the Russian Embassy Church in London, Reverend E. Smirnoff, to call on her. "But will he not refuse?" she countered. "Maybe he also takes me for the Antichrist."[68]

She professed to feel astonishment that she, a detractor of Protestantism and Catholicism alike, should suddenly find herself drawn toward the Russian Church. "I am a renegade, a cosmopolitan unbeliever—everyone thinks so, and I also think so, and yet I would give the last drop of my blood for the triumph of the Russian Church and everything Russian." Calling herself a silly old fool, she had a secret interview with Reverend Smirnoff, after which she concluded that Russia must be in her blood and "I can't help it."[69]

Around this time, the Bright's disease began recurring. Madame's physician frightened her by saying that the microscope revealed enormous crystals of uric acid in her blood, that in his opinion the fact that she was still alive must be judged a miracle. It was not only her own approaching end that made her turn back to her Russian past and her family, but the fact that suddenly she sensed death on all sides; in February, 1888, Anna Kingsford had died at the age of forty-one. All the hostility Helena had once harbored for Anna had long since evaporated and the previous August, when she learned that Anna was spitting blood, she had advised Edward Maitland to have her drink the oil of cactus leaves. With characteristic honesty, she admitted to Maitland that even though she had admired Anna, she had never really liked her until the Ostend visit. Now, she said, "I love her as a woman."[70]

Four months later, when she received word that one of Vera's sons from her first marriage had died,[71] she felt her sister's sorrow as acutely as if it had been her own and begged Vera to bring her daughters to England, where perhaps "in a country new to you all, you, maybe, will find some relief. Come all of you, my dears." Her house had a nice shady garden with singing birds, just as if it were in the country, and Vera would have a separate room. "You shall be comfortable, and the poor girls will have what little distraction is possible for them." Because she could not discuss her intense grief even with the countess, she sent for Reverend Smirnoff, the only person with whom she could share these feelings. When Vera replied that she would bring her daughter Vera to England in July, H.P.B. hailed the news as a "ray of light in the darkness"[72] and emptied her savings account to finance their trip.

The darkness she felt enveloping her is partially traceable to her life-and-death struggle with Henry Olcott over ownership of the Theosophical Society. Ever since her relocation in London had won her fame as well as new converts, she had been gradually cutting herself off from Adyar; by this time, she felt strong enough to capitalize on her popularity by demoting Olcott to figurehead position. Her general discontent, as well as the chronic displeasure with Henry that had been festering ever since he hustled her out of India, were summed up in one of the rare Mahatma letters she addressed to herself. Olcott, K.H. told her, "says he has saved it [the Society]. He saved its body, but he allowed through sheer fear, to [*sic*] its soul to escape, and it is now a soulless corpse, a machine run so far well enough, but which will fall to pieces when he is gone."[73] What she meant of course was that the Society was bound to crumble when she died, and she intended taking positive steps to prevent that. If it was necessary to emasculate Henry in the process, she counted this a trifling price to pay.

The formation of Madame's own Blavatsky Lodge stunned Henry, but he managed to accept it; her second blast, the founding of *Lucifer* as a rival to the *Theosophist*, had impressed him as unbusinesslike, but once again he had given in. It was her third innovation that hurled him into an uproar: her intention, as she announced it, was to establish a secret organization within the Blavatsky Lodge to be known as the Esoteric Section—the E.S. The hand-picked candidates, admitted only after a rigorous perusal of their former lives, were obliged to sign a pledge of absolute obedience, affirming their belief in both H.P.B. and in the Mahatmas, and vowing to defend them all, subject to their consciences. Probationers would be expected to practice abstinence and asceticism, to give up meat, alcohol and sex, and to spend several hours a day meditating before a photograph of the Masters, who ruled the E.S. As the Mahatmas' representative, Helena would give individual instruction in occultism.[74]

Olcott was alarmed by the news: he feared this secret society would be nothing more than a device for continuing her fraudulent marvels; that the same gimmickry as her shrine and Occult Room would once again appear to wreck Theosophy. When he opposed the idea as unconstitutional, she countered with a volley of letters that were characterized, he thought, by "language violent, passion raging, scorn and satire poorly covered by a skin of soft talk."[75] He replied that he refused to have the whole machinery of the Society upset to gratify her whims and, incidentally, she should remember that the more she threatened him, the more stubborn he would become. Helena expressed herself even more bluntly:

Now look here, Olcott. It is very painful, most painful, for me to have to put to you what the French call marché en main, and to have you choose . . . But this [the E.S.] is no threat at all, but a *fait accompli*. It remains with you to either ratify it or to go against it, and declare war to me and my Esotericists. If, recognizing the utmost necessity of the step, you submit to the inexorable evolution of things, nothing will be changed. Adyar and Europe will remain allies, and, *to all appearances*, the latter will seem to be subject to the former. If you do not ratify—well, then there will be two Theosophical Societies, the old Indian and the new European, *entirely independent of each other*.[76]

Clearly the altercation was snowballing into a battle for supremacy, and Olcott knew it. For his part, he had little taste for such a struggle; in recent months he had been suffering from rheumatism, boils and carbuncles. At the age of fifty-five, his hair and beard had already turned white; he looked ten years older than his age and, even worse, felt it. In March, while spending several weeks at Ootacamund as the guests of Maj.-Gen. and Mrs. Henry Rhodes Morgan, he had bought a plot of land on which he planned to build a retirement cottage. The last thing he wanted, or had expected, was an ugly confrontation with his old chum, but at the same time could not permit her to destroy everything he had worked for. At last, the colonel had decided to stand up to the Old Lady.

What Henry did not anticipate was H.P.B.'s having the cunning to enlist allies. On July 6, she cabled William Judge that American support was necessary to save the Cause and ordered him to have the U.S. branches adopt the following resolution: "In event of the President in India declining to recognize Madame Blavatsky's authority in the West, we undertake to support her in any course she may consider necessary to adopt."[77]

Although head of the American Theosophical Society, Judge was in an extremely precarious position: for the past year, persistent attempts to oust him had been made by Dr. Elliott Coues, the well-known Washington, D.C., scientist and ornithologist. Not six weeks earlier, Judge had assured Henry of his loyalty: "I am always striving to keep your name at the top, for until your death you must be at the head," but when it came to a showdown between the founders, he preferred to place his bets on Madame. Only H.P.B. was crafty enough to put Dr. Coues in his place and clamp down on the fake Mahatma letters Coues manufactured to enhance his position. In asking the American branches to adopt her resolution, Judge was careful to add that in his own case, "what she orders me I do as she says without reasons,"[78] a phrase designed to warm Madame's heart. Not surprisingly, all but three branches passed the resolution.

By mid-summer the Olcott/Blavatsky situation had deteriorated to the point where Henry felt obliged to travel to London personally to stay Helena's hand. H.P.B., in turn, felt the necessity for a timely miracle. Leaving Bombay on August 4 aboard the SS *Shannon*, Olcott reached the Italian port of Brindisi on the morning of the twenty-third. According to him the day before the ship docked, a letter from Master Koot Hoomi dropped from nowhere into his cabin. "Your revolt, my good friend, against her infallibility—as you once thought it—has gone too far and you have been unjust to her, for which I am sorry to say, you will have to suffer hereafter along with others." K.H. went on to say that when Henry arrived in London he must keep in mind that there were two sides to the Society, its external administrative and its internal esoteric one. "Keep the former under your control . . . *leave the latter to her*."[79]

How Helena managed to have this letter delivered is impossible to say; it is perhaps the only one of her drops that cannot be easily explained. Later, in London, Olcott would show it to Sinnett, who apparently had trouble suppressing his temptation to laugh. Olcott, he wrote Charles Leadbeater, "in his simple guileless way takes the letter as genuine without a thought of questioning it . . . and I have not thought it of the least use to tell Olcott that I do not believe in the authenticity of the letter."[80]

Once again, Helena's reliance on higher authorities had paid off: by the time Henry reached London in late August he accepted defeat as meekly as Helena could have wished. Once he learned that she had lined up not only the

Mahatmas but the American branches as well, Henry had no choice but to agree to a division of the Society; she could have her Esoteric Section and be queen in Europe, while he continued as king at Adyar. After months of wrangling, their bitterness was not easily mended, and a photograph from this time shows them sitting in the garden at Lansdowne Road, Helena clutching her Ceylon basket of tobacco and Henry fiddling with a hat and cane. Both are staring tight-lipped into the camera. No doubt Henry would have looked even more unhappy had he known the mocking nickname that some of her E.S. students had given him: "the Fairies' Friend,"[81] although in the photograph he might be taken for a silvery-bearded, bespectacled leprechaun. In another shot the two of them are joined by Vera Zhelihovsky, her daughter, and Charles Johnston, and in this case there is a similar downcast expression on all the faces except the two young people's.

That summer Johnston had graduated with honors from Dublin University, passed the notoriously stiff examination for the Indian Civil Service, and came to London to while away a few months before leaving for Bengal in the fall. Naturally he went straight to Lansdowne Road. "Charley Johnston," remarked Yeats to Katharine Tynan, "was at Mme. Blavatski's the other day with that air of clever insolence and elaborate efficiency he has ripened to such perfection . . . If you only saw him talking French and smoking cigarettes with Madame's niece. He looked a veritable peacock. Such an air of world-worn man of society about him, as if he also were one of the penitent frivolous instead of a crusading undergraduate."[82]

At twenty-four, the young Vera Zhelihovsky was a merry-eyed blonde, with a Kewpie-doll face. Yeats thought her "very nice, decidedly pretty, and has a laugh like bells of silver,"[83] as did Johnston who began by asking her to teach him Russian and proceeded to fall in love with her. How he and Vera managed to conduct a serious romance is impossible to say, for the atmosphere was not conducive to love: Helena could not broach the subject of marriage without expostulating bitterly on the institution, after which she would follow up with a disparaging discourse on the weaknesses of the female sex. As it happened, there was usually at least one woman present with the temerity to offer a mild contradiction: "My dear," H.P.B. would growl, "I am a woman, and so I know."[84]

On joining the Society, Johnston had adopted the rule of celibacy and also had actively inculcated the ideal in other male members. Now, when he and Vera announced their intention to marry, a hurricane of consternation ripped through the T.S. in England and Ireland. "Theosophy despairs," Yeats remarked jokingly. "Johnston *was* in the running for Mahatmaship and now look how the mighty have fallen![85] "Æ," an admirer of Johnston's asceticism and one of those who had been struggling to emulate him, expressed his shock to Yeats by swearing that he would never again make anyone his ideal. Later he would say of Johnston, "I always wonder whether there is any real C. J. under that smiling, handsome exterior, or only a bundle of mental attributes."[86]

Those most unconcerned were Johnston himself, who announced his apostasy with easy assurance—"She is my excuse. They have only to see her"—and H.P.B., who must have felt in an expansive mood; even though she called the couple flapdoodles, she undertook arrangements for the wedding at the Russian Church. The elder Vera could not contain her weeping and, according to Henry, took herself back to Russia before the ceremony. Young Vera's wedding was one of the very rare occasions when H.P.B. set foot out over the threshold of 17 Lansdowne Road.

It was not until the first week of October that Henry signed the order officially sanctioning the Esoteric Section, but he could not help showing his hostility in the wording of the document. The E.S. was to be the sole property of H.P.B. and "has no official or corporate connection with the Exoteric Society."[87] Persons wishing to apply for membership should communicate directly with Madame. Because both of them realized that their feud looked bad to outsiders, they issued an announcement of a truce:

> To dispel a misconception that has been engendered by mischief makers, we the undersigned Founders of the Theosophical Society, declare that there is no enmity, rivalry, strife, or even coldness between us, nor ever was . . . As we have been from the first, so are we now united in purpose and zeal, and ready to sacrifice all, even life, for the promotion of Theosophical knowledge, to the saving of mankind from the miseries which spring from ignorance.[88]

That this communiqué fooled no one is obvious from an article in which the *Religio-Philosophical Journal* felt obliged to provide an interpretation for its readers:

> Since I, the President-Founder, was such an idiot as to pit Blavatsky's skill as a trickster against the investigation of the Psychical Research Society, and since Hodgson exploded our psychic and mahatmic fakes; and moreover, since the old Bourbon, Blavatsky, is not amenable to reason any more, it is useless longer to work the phenomena branch of our business. Hence I will turn it over to Madame as her share of the assets; then I will depreciate her stock and belittle her occultism, for thereby I shall get even with her and at the same time tickle the public and gain favour for my scheme which is no less a fake, but not so easily detected.[89]

The *Journal*'s reasoning may have been nastily phrased but it was not entirely inaccurate.

Twenty years later, in a character sketch of H.P.B. for his memoirs, a still bitter Henry would say that she could slather people with charm when she chose "and she chose it when she wanted to draw persons to her public work." When it came to himself and Helena's intimate colleagues, "I should not say she was either loyal or staunch. We were to her, I believe, nothing more than pawns in a game of chess, for whom she had no heart-deep love."[90] The only human beings who won her love and loyalty, he said, were her Russian family and the Mahatmas.

This was very nearly true: even to those whom she owed a great deal, like Countess Wachtmeister, she generally presented her worst possible side: when Edmund Russell persuaded her to be photographed at the studio of Vander Weyde in Regent Street, she carried on like Queen Elizabeth about to set off on a royal progress, and it was the countess who had to bear the brunt of it. When the day of the appointment dawned rainy and windy with scurries of autumn leaves, Helena refused to go, claiming that the awful weather would cause her death. Besides, since she never went outside, she did not even own a cloak. For five hours a cab was kept waiting while the countess cajoled and pleaded and improvised a makeshift outfit by bundling H.P.B. in furs and shawls, some of them borrowed from the servants. Outfitted against the weather, Helena refused to leave after all, remaining stolidly in her chair like a stubborn Buddha.

"I will not go," she muttered. "I cannot step on the wet stones."

At her wit's end, Constance ordered carpets laid from the door of the house to the carriage, but even then the wind was gusting so heavily that they threatened to blow away; in the end Constance had to hold them down. Afterward she told Russell that when she had first lived in London as an ambassadress, "in Hyde Park two powdered footmen followed me. If my poor husband could know the day had come when I held down carpets for another woman to tread on he would turn over in his grave." She spoke with a smile, however, because as Russell pointed out, "she would have lain herself down for Madame to walk on."[91]

More than the weather, H.P.B. was held back by the prospect of having her image preserved on film. Every reference that she now made to her physical appearance suggests self-loathing: "This loathsome, old ruined body," and "an old, rotten, sick, worn-out body."[92] Her face had grown increasingly unattractive: due to her illness, her complexion yellowed almost to a coffee color; the formerly lovely eyes were also marred by jaundice, and the face scored by a thousand wrinkles. The crinkly hair, now iron-gray, was gathered into an untidy knot at the nape of her neck and stuck through with a broad comb. Only her hands, with their lithe, tapering fingers, remained remarkably beautiful; she always made sure they were visible in her portraits by propping her double chin on one hand.

On October 20, she said goodbye to Henry, who was returning to India in the company of Charles and Vera Johnston and Richard Harte, a New York newspaperman they had known in their Lamasery days. Harte, the new editor of the *Theosophist*, was a replacement for Alfred Cooper-Oakley, who had won H.P.B.'s enmity by subtly denigrating her in print. That she had been able to persuade Olcott both to dismiss him from the staff and to expel him from the Society was a small but significant victory.

On the very morning of their departure, the first volume of *The Secret Doctrine* came off the press at Allen Scott and Company, with the second volume to follow in December. An eager Richard Harte sent a courier to 30 Bouverie Street, thus winning for himself the distinction of getting a copy before H.P.B. herself, and wrote in blue pencil on the flyleaf, "This is the first copy ever issued. I got it from Printer by special Messenger on the morning of 20 Oct. '88 as I was leaving the house 17 Lansdowne Road."[93] Presumably Helena and the rest of the household got their copies within hours. Constance Wachtmeister recalled that "H.P.B. was happy that day. It was the one gleam of sunshine amid the darkness and dreariness of her life."[94] In a prophesying mood, Madame told Constance that the book would be studied by only a few during her lifetime but would be fully appreciated in the twentieth century.

The two-volume, fifteen-hundred-page *Secret Doctrine* is an epic search for the beginnings of civilization, written at a time when everything on the subject was thought to have been said. Momentous in length, weight, complexity, and subject, it is an account of how the universe is created, where it came from and where it is going, what force fashioned it, and what it all means. In supplying these answers H.P.B. would re-zone heaven in so compelling a manner that today, ninety-two years later, the work is still selling in complete and abridged editions and is still being read and analyzed by students of the occult.[95]

The work rests on the premise that life is eternal, without beginning or end. Its one absolute attribute is eternal, ceaseless motion, which esoterists call the "Great Breath." Eternal life exhales and inhales periodically, producing universes and withdrawing them. The terms "Days" and "Nights" of Brahm describe this swinging back and forth of the Life Force between periods of activity (Manvantara) and periods of rest (Pralaya). The Eternal Parent (God), that which was, is, and will be whether or not there is a universe, is Space and it is space from which the universe emerges and into which it disappears.

The Secret Doctrine is based on three fundamental principles:

1. The omnipresent and eternal reality on which all speculation is impossible since it transcends the power of human conception and can only be dwarfed by any human expression. It is the unthinkable and unspeakable, the infinite cause, the rootless root.

2. The absolute law of periodicity, of flux and reflux, ebb and flow, that governs the universe and all its creatures.

3. The fundamental identity of every individual soul with the universal oversoul, the microcosm within the macrocosm, and its obligatory pilgrimage through the cycle of incarnations in accordance with the law of cause and effect (karma).

* * *

Forming the skeleton of Volume One (cosmogenesis) are seven stanzas from the secret *Book of Dzyan*, the original of which is written in Senzar, the sacred language of the Initiates. Stanza One describes the Night of Brahm when the worlds were not, time was not, mind was not, matter was not; and Stanza Two continues this account to the point of reawakening when the Cosmic Egg is fertilized.

In Stanza Three, the vibrations of eternity begin to thrill through boundless space, sounding the cockcrow of a new Manvantaric daybreak as the universe reawakens to life after Pralaya.

Stanza Four shows this primordial essence splitting itself into seven "Sons" or Rays, who frame, shape and ultimately create the universe. They are the intelligent beings, generically known as the *Dhyan Chohans*, who employ the universal agent *Fohat* (electricity) to create and evolve our world.

Stanzas Five and Six describe the creative process of world-formation: first diffused cosmic matter, next the fiery whirlwind, and finally the formation of a nebula that condenses before passing through various transformations to form a solar universe, a planetary chain or a single planet. The progress of life is measured by Rounds, Root Races, and Sub-Races, and also by the number seven (seven rounds, seven races, et al.). The earth must pass through seven rounds, the first three taking it through the process of materialization, the fourth crystallizing and hardening it, the last three taking it gradually out of the physical, back to ethereal and finally spiritual form.

By Stanza Seven the descent of life has been traced down to the appearance of humans at the beginning of the Fourth Round.

The second volume (anthropogenesis)[96] chronicles the evolution of the human race from its advent on this globe several hundred million years ago to the year 1888: there have been four races on earth before the present one, and there will be two more after ours disappears. The first of the seven races inhabited the "Imperishable Sacred Land," an unnamed continent lying in a undesignated sector of the globe where the climate was suitable. These first entities would not be recognizable as human, for they were boneless, formless spiritual essences without physical bodies. The Imperishable Sacred Land finally sank into the ocean after some great cataclysm.

The Second Race, called Hyperboreans, were also bodiless. They lived near what is now the North Pole but, owing to the position of the earth's axis, the climate at that period was mild, even tropical.

Lacking dense physical bodies such as exist today, these first two races were obviously sexless. First Race entities possessed only astral shells, and reproduction, if it can be called that, was merely a matter of periodic spiritual rejuvenation when an entity simply revivified itself by its own will. Among the Hyperboreans, reproduction continued to be spiritual, but of a form that might accurately be described as asexual; the process, H.P.B. explained, approximated what biologists would call "budding." However, during the latter Second and continuing into the early Third races, procreation evolved further with entities becoming first oviparous and hermaphroditic and finally androgynous. In the first stage of androgynous development, reproduction took place by a modified budding process; extruded spores separated from and then grew into a copy of the parent. Later, instead of mere miniature copies, these extruded spores would develop into an egg or embryo. However, these beings were not fully androgynous because procreation did not require fertilization by a specialized male organ. After further evolution, the entity would contain within itself both the ovum and the male organs necessary to fertilize it.

It was not until the middle of the Third Root Race, some eighteen million years ago, that human life as we know it can properly be said to have begun. At that time, during the Fourth Round, certain *Kumaras* or "princes"— beings living on spiritual planes who yearned to taste physical experience— made their descent and stepped down (the "Fall") into earthly encasement. True physical beings with bony structures, they were still somewhat un- evolved physically, emotionally and mentally, possessing, for example, only three senses: hearing, touch and sight. Taste would not appear until the Fourth Root Race, smell not until the Fifth. For the first time separation of the sexes occurred, and gradually our present method of reproduction was developed. The cradle of the Third Race, the vast continent of Lemuria, is said to have been in the Pacific Ocean and to have stretched through what is now Central Africa. Remnants of Lemuria still remained, one being Austra- lia and another Easter Island. The continent was destroyed mainly by fire and what remained was sucked into the ocean.

With the sinking of Lemuria, its successor rose in the Atlantic Ocean and became the dwelling place of the Fourth Race some eight hundred and fifty thousand years ago. This was the fabled Atlantis alluded to by Plato and other ancient writers and affirmed by Madame Blavatsky. Like the last of the Lemurians, the Atlanteans were a compound of mind, body and spirit, and as such its men and women would be easily recognizable as human today. In psychic and technological respects, the Atlanteans were more highly develop- ed than are we; they invented airplanes and understood how to tap electric and super-electric forces. In the early centuries of the Fourth Race civiliza- tion, human beings were gigantic in stature, a fact that accounts for certain colossal forms of architecture such as Druid temples and the pyramids. Because the Atlanteans misused their knowledge, the race began to degener- ate and portions of the continent gradually began to submerge; the surviving remnants of the race, living in the land called Poseidon, met their watery doom only eleven thousand years ago. This final cataclysm was the basis for the deluge myth.

Our present Aryan Race, the Fifth, began to develop in northern Asia and then spread south and west. The fifth Sub-Race of the Fifth Race is our own Anglo-Saxon, and the germ of the sixth Sub-Race was already beginning to take form in the United States at the time that *The Secret Doctrine* was being written. Eventually the Aryan Race will be swept away; as Lemuria succumbed to fire and Atlantis to water, the Aryans will be undone by subterranean convulsions of the earth's crust. According to H.P.B., two more races are due to appear before the end of the Fourth Round, after which present humanity will have reached the end of its alloted cycle of evolution. Then the life impulse will withdraw and our globe will be left in a condition of Pralaya. When will this happen? "Who knows save the great Masters of Wisdom, perchance, and they are as silent upon the subject as the snow-capped peaks that tower above them."[97]

It was to be expected that *The Secret Doctrine* would meet with a mixed reception. For Theosophists, it was a new revelation; those with a mystical inclination, like "Æ," hailed it as the most stimulating work they had ever read. Reviewers in the secular press treated it as they had *Isis Unveiled*, that is, patronizingly or humorously; the U.S. periodical *Science* went so far as to call it one of the finest contributions to contemporary humorous literature. The New York *Times* rendered its verdict with a review titled "Ten Pounds of Occultism" and declared that Madame Blavatsky could not expect serious consideration of her work because it was unreadable, incomprehensible, and literally choked to death by "vast quantities of indigestible materials . . . So esoteric is her method, if not her matter, we rarely understand Madame Blavatsky for a whole chapter, and sometimes not for a whole page." The review went on to suggest that she "is one of those whom much reading of weird, wild books has made mad."[98]

If the general press could not be bothered with *The Secret Doctrine*, H.P.B. knew by now that she could count on serious critical attention from William Emmette Coleman, who gave her a five-part, pamphlet-length review in the *Religio -Philosophical Journal*. The book infuriated Coleman, who was a member of the Pali Text Society and the Royal Asiatic Society and considered himself an authority on Eastern religion. *The Secret Doctrine* is, he wrote, "a remarkable work of a remarkable person," but what made it so was its gigantic pretensions. While he could not truthfully question its author's intellectual vigor and untiring zeal, he thought it a pity that her "masculine intellect" should not have been used for the advancement of humanity instead of this propagation of delusion and untruth. As soon as he glanced at the *Stanzas of Dzyan*, he knew there was no such book in existence, that it was only an invention of the ingenious Madame herself. "Of course Madame Blavatsky does not believe any of the nonsense she compiles and fabricates. It is only her credulous followers who are foolish enough to seriously accept as eternal verities the extravagant absurdities with which she regales their infantile minds."[99]

Madame, he charged, was grossly ignorant of Eastern philosophy. Not only did she misspell certain Sanskrit words—although he admitted her spelling had improved since *Isis* when she misspelled *Bhagavad-Gītā*, but she also made some six hundred false statements relating to Hinduism, Judaism, Chinese literature, Egyptology, Assyriology, and Christianity. These appalling errors about the most simple matters, such as the date of the Trojan War, demonstrated that her "mahatmas are as mythical and their vast libraries and their god-instructed wisdom as mythical as their own existence." Coleman's most damaging criticism, however, was devoted to contradictions between *Isis* and *Secret Doctrine* on such basic theories as:

1. Reincarnation, which in *Isis* (Vol. 1, p. 351) she denied, except in the cases of infants and idiots, was presented as fact throughout *The Secret Doctrine*.

2. The nature of elemental spirits, which in *Isis* (Vol. 1, xxix) never evolved into humans, were described in *The Secret Doctrine* (Vol. 1, p. 277) as disembodied or future humans.

3. The septenary constitution of human beings. In *Isis* (Vol. 2, p. 367) she stated that they had six principles, but after going to India she learned they had seven. Actually, Coleman theorized, she got the idea of a seven-fold human from neither Buddhism nor Brahmanism, but from Paracelsus.

Even more devastating than Coleman was Oxford professor Max Müller, a distinguished Orientalist and translator of the forty-eight volume *Sacred Books of the East*. H.P.B., Müller believed, should be given credit for good intentions but

when we come to examine what these depositories of primeval wisdom, the Mahatmas of Tibet and of the sacred Ganges, are supposed to have taught her, we find no mysteries, nothing very new, nothing very old, but simply a medley of well-known though generally misunderstood Brahmanic or Buddhistic doctrines. There is nothing that cannot be traced back to generally accessible Brahmanic or Buddhist sources, only everything is muddled or misunderstood. If I were asked what Madame Blavatsky's Esoteric Buddhism really is, I should say it was Buddhism misunderstood, distorted, caricatured. There is nothing in it beyond what was known already, chiefly from books that are now antiquated. The most ordinary terms are misspelt and misinterpreted.[100]

Between the Theosophists and the Coleman–Müllers, there were many who would agree with Maurice Maeterlinck when he wrote some years later that *The Secret Doctrine* was a "stupendous and ill-balanced monument" that combined "speculations which must rank with the most impressive ever conceived" with a colossal junkyard

into which the highest wisdom, the widest and most exceptional scholarship, the most dubious odds and ends of science, legend and history, the most impressive and most unfounded hypotheses, the most precise and most improbable statements of fact, the most plausible and most chimerical ideas, the noblest dreams and the most incoherent fancies are poured pell-mell by inexhaustible truck-loads.[101]

If only, Maeterlinck mused sadly, Madame Blavatsky had seen fit to give the world more information about the *Book of Dzyan*; if it were truly an authentic prehistoric document, her explanation of the evolution of the world and of human life would be "truly sensational."

II

Sweet Mango

With *The Secret Doctrine* out of the way, H.P.B. continued to maintain the same work schedule as before. Even if she had wished to slow down it seemed impossible, and at times she felt like "a poor weak donkey full of sores made to drag up hill a cart of heavy rocks."[102]

During the winter of 1888–1889, life was frequently so hectic that she could not find time to write Vera or Nadyezhda. When Vera demanded to know why she could not spare a minute to write, Helena answered with exasperation: "Friend and sister: Your thoughtless question, 'What am I so busy with?' has fallen amongst us like a bomb loaded with naive ignorance of the active life of a Theosophist . . . 'What am I busy with?' I, is it? I tell you, if there ever was in the world an overworked victim it is your long-suffering sister."[103] To begin with, the entire burden of editing *Lucifer* rested on her shoulders now that she had dismissed Mabel Collins, explaining away her absence as "a continuing severe illness."[104] Moreover, H.P.B. was helping to edit a new French Theosophical magazine, *La Revue Theosophique*, to be published by the Countess d'Adhemar; she was working sporadically on a third volume of *The Secret Doctrine* that would deal with the great occultists of all ages; preparing forty or fifty pages of monthly instructions for her Esoteric Section students; composing a question-and-answer-style manual, *The Key to Theosophy*, that would describe the fundamental principles of Theosophy; and "then I must also eat, like anyone else, which means supplying some other bread-winning articles"[105] for her Russian newspapers.

At the same time she was doing a prodigious amount of research for her presentations at the Thursday meetings of the Blavatsky Lodge. "The people who come here," she told Vera, "are no ignoramuses from the street," but intelligent people who demanded intelligent answers. She was particularly careful in what she said because the Lodge had hired a stenographer to record her words and was planning to publish them in a pamphlet, "Transactions of the Blavatsky Lodge." So far as H.P.B. was concerned, they were spending "such a lot of money that my hair stands on end."[106] She felt secretly flattered, but it meant long hours at her desk wearing holes in the elbows of her sleeves and "sweating for everybody." To maintain this taxing schedule, she drove herself mercilessly. Even for a healthy person, it would have been an immense strain, and to H.P.B. it was excruciating. As her renal disorder continued to worsen, Dr. Z. Mennell had been giving her six grains of strychnia daily, which provided some measure of relief.

Longing for emotional tranquillity, she wrote William Judge that "I am with perhaps a few years or a few months only (Master knoweth) to remain on this earth," and went on to add that she was disgusted with almost everyone she knew. When she looked around at the London Theosophists, she felt sick at heart because all she saw was selfishness, personal vanity, and petty ambitions. Since it was against the Society's rules "to live like cats and dogs," was it any wonder that the Masters had retired into the background where they observed across "an ocean deep of sad disgust, contempt and sorrow?"[107]

As a matter of fact, much of the infighting and enmity was Helena's own fault. After Henry had returned to Adyar, her letters to him were so hostile that he began finding them tiresome and wrote back vowing that if he received more "I should neither read nor answer them."[108] Their battle for control had broadened into a three-way struggle between Adyar, London and New York, and by now Olcott had wised up to William Judge's two-faced politicking: Judge had sent the *Theosophist* a laudatory article about H.P.B., in which he declared that the Society's real center of authority was wherever Madame Blavatsky might be; an irate Henry refused to print it in its entirety, but did hasten to set Judge straight by saying that, begging his pardon, the center of power was wherever *he* happened to be domiciled. Judge, he snapped, was suffering from "mayavic delusions."[109]

As Judge was well aware, he had nothing to gain by supporting Olcott in his duel with H.P.B., while he could gain considerably from sticking with Helena. Indeed, she had made quite clear that the reward he might expect was to be named her successor when she died. Addressing him as "my *only friend*," she assured him that "you *are* going to replace me, or take my place in America."[110] Actually she had promised the succession to a number of people, always in order to achieve some immediate end, and had no intention of naming anyone to take her place, but Judge was happily unaware of this. On the other hand, she probably did feel more kindly disposed toward Judge than anyone else, and it is possible that he truly may have headed her list.

During the past five years she had slowly come to appreciate Judge for the qualities that had once drawn her to Henry, obedience and willingness to work hard. She knew that when he had returned to New York after Adyar, he had thrown himself into reviving interest in the defunct Society by holding regular meetings to study the *Bhagavad-Gītā*. He had founded a magazine, *The Path*, and had also published pseudo-translations of the *Gītā* and of Patanjali's *Yoga Philosophy*. By 1889, the American Section of the Society had thriving branches in half-a-dozen major cities and enough members to hold an annual convention. In December, when Judge visited Madame and she issued a special order appointing him her only American representative, some cynics at Adyar and in the U.S. began referring to him as "a sucking dove."[111] Judge did not care what people called him so long as he remained Helena's favorite, and he continued to follow her instructions to the letter.

Despite Helena's apparent support, Judge had a rival for leadership in America, and it made him nervous: after lurking in the background for several years, Dr. Elliott Coues had suddenly thrust himself forward as a contender for Judge's position. When they had first met in 1884 at Elberfeld, both she and Olcott had been impressed. An extreme radical and free thinker in religious matters and an eloquent champion of women's rights, Coues was the sort of highly educated, articulate professional that the Society liked. Like Allan Hume, Coues was a respected ornithologist, best known for his *Key to North American Birds* and his association with the Smithsonian Institution. Interested in psychic research for many years, he was a member of the British Society for Psychical Research and later would be active in the formation of the American Society for Psychical Research. A tall man of distinguished bearing and engaging urbane manner, Coues had a jolly sense of humor that appealed to Helena. He was enough of an amateur psychologist to recognize the route to Madame's goodwill and, while a normally aggressive man, he had perfected the techniques of dove-sucking as well as Judge. "I think," he once wrote her, "you are the greatest woman in the world, controlling today more *destiny* than any queen upon her throne."[112]

As a result of this flattery, and because H.P.B. and Olcott liked him, Coues found himself appointed Chairman of the American Board of Control. By 1889, both of the founders were writing him chummy, conspiratorial letters in which they used him as a convenient outlet for releasing their grievances against each other. Olcott warned Coues to ignore any order H.P.B. might issue outside the perimeters of the Esoteric Section; he would "stand no nonsense, nor shall I ratify a single order or promise of hers made independently of me . . . She seems a Bourbon as to memory and receptivity and fancies the old halcyon days are not gone."[113] For her part, Helena contented herself with sniping references to Olcott as a "psychologized baby."[114]

Apparently Coues could not resist taking advantage of the strained relations: he began sending H.P.B. mocking letters jeering at "Your 'first-born,'

LONDON *1887–1891* **421**

the meek Hibernian Judge" and at "your psychologized baby Olcott," at the same time patronizing her as "the greatest woman of the age, who is born to redeem her times."[115] The point of this fulsome message was an almost threatening request, that she cable the American convention gathering shortly in Chicago and order the delegates to elect him president. H.P.B. did no such thing.

Seeking a way to retaliate, Coues hit upon the idea of joining forces with another dissatisfied Theosophist, Mabel Collins, and the two of them attacked in a way that H.P.B. could not have anticipated. Coues had never met Collins, although in 1885 he had written her after the publication of *Light on the Path* to inquire who might be the real author, and she had explained that he was an adept of Madame's acquaintance. In the spring of 1889, however, he suddenly received another letter from Mabel confessing that Madame's friends had nothing to do with *Light on the Path*; she was the sole author and the reason she had lied four years earlier was that H.P.B. "begged and implored me to"[116] and that she had dutifully written the letter at her dictation. The fact of the matter was that Helena could not have begged Mabel because at that time she scarcely knew the woman and, moreover, was not even in England in 1885, when her book was published. Now, neither Collins nor Coues, bound by their mutual hatred for Madame Blavatsky, were paying strict attention to truthful details, and Coues made sure that Mabel's letter was published in the *Religio-Philosophical Journal.*

Mabel was feeling particularly resentful; not only had she been unceremoniously ousted from *Lucifer,* but H.P.B. had told people she was suffering from a mental breakdown. Then in April Madame expelled Mabel from the Society, an event which proved unnerving for Mabel, but entertaining for the rest of the Blavatsky Lodge. "There has been a great row," Yeats wrote Katharine Tynan,

> Madame Blavatsky expelled Mrs. Cook (Miss Mabel Collins) and the president of the Lodge for flirtation, and Mrs. Alicia Cremers, an American, for gossiping about it. As a result, Madame Blavatsky is in high spirits. The society is like the "happy family" that used to be exhibited round Charing Cross Station—a cat in a cage full of canaries. The Russian cat is beginning to purr now and smoothen its fur again—the canary birds are less by three—the faithful will be more obedient than ever.[117]

From Yeats' sardonic description, it sounds like a Theosophical version of *The Mikado,* in which the punishment for flirting is decapitation; Madame merely exacted her most deadly penalty on the pretty Mabel, but to some in the Lodge, expulsion was on a par with beheading. Later Yeats would supplement this gossip with another tidbit and claim that Mable, who impressed him as a "handsome clever woman of the world," had actually been involved with two of H.P.B.'s young ascetics; when Helena got wind of the double affair, she allegedly lectured Mabel on the beauty of chastity and concluded with unexpected tolerance: "I cannot permit you more than one."[118] The story is probably apocryphal since H.P.B. was as adamantly anti-sex as she was anti-Mabel; she had been looking for an excuse to banish her, and flirtation seemed as good a pretext as any, but she had no illusions that the unrepentant Mabel would silently disappear. As Koot Hoomi warned her, "you have deprived her of a toy" and must now expect Mabel to retaliate because "she will not repent as you hope and death alone can save her from herself."[119] Once again Koot Hoomi proved a shrewd observer, for soon Mabel learned of uncomplimentary comments about her in Madame's private correspondence and speared her with a libel suit. However, since Helena had somehow come into possession of even more unpleasant, indeed positively hateful, letters Mabel had written about her, she could afford to smile, sit back, and wait until the case came to trial.[120]

Next, she decreed her standard penalty for Elliott Coues and ordered his expulsion from the Society in June, hoping vainly that he would not be heard from again.

But by the time she got around to chastizing the combative bird-lover, there had come riding into her life a shining knight on a white horse to perform the classic last-minute rescue. Her name was Annie Besant, and it was she who would make it possible for Helena to die content.

By the time she was forty, Annie Besant was known over half the world as one of the most remarkable women of her day. She was an agitator in radical political circles, a strike leader and union organizer, a champion of science and materialism working in partnership with the radical free thinker Charles Bradlaugh, an atheist, a feminist, a social and educational reformer, an early convert to Fabian Socialism by her friend Bernard Shaw, a prolific author as well as editor and publisher, the first prominent woman to wage open battle on behalf of birth control, and, not least, an orator of such power that her contemporaries unanimously acclaimed her as the greatest woman speaker of the nineteenth century.

Born Annie Wood on October 1, 1847, in London, she was three-quarters Irish, a fact which she frequently mentioned with pride. Her mother's Irish family, the Morrises, were said to have had royal blood in their veins, while her father's people were a prosperous, highly respected clan who had done well for themselves in commerce and public life, one of them having even served as lord mayor of London and as a member of Parliament. However, William Wood, Annie's father, was much too volatile to settle down and, despite a medical degree from Trinity College, Dublin, decided to accept a position with a London commercial firm rather than practice medicine. Annie and her two brothers grew up in the middle-class neighborhood of St. John's Wood, and her recollections were of an uneventful but happy childhood.

When she was five, her father died unexpectedly and left the family almost destitute; Emily Wood moved them to Harrow, where she enrolled her son Harry in the school and opened a sort of dormitory-boardinghouse catering to Harrow boys. When Annie was eight, she caught the notice of a local Lady Bountiful, the wealthy, unmarried Ellen Marryat who satisfied her maternal needs by taking on bright but genteelly impoverished children whom she reared and educated. Annie had spent most of her adolescence at Miss Marryat's estate on the Devon border.

A rather precocious bluestocking, Annie was also a pious girl whose adolescent daydreams centered, not on romance, but on the apostles and martyrs of the early Christian Church. She read St. Augustine, went to weekly communion, fasted herself into ecstatic meditations, and dreamed of the days when girls could become martyrs. In this mood of religious preoccupation, she met and married in 1867 the Rev. Frank Besant, a cold, domineering martinet of an Anglican minister. As her friend W. T. Stead put it in later years, "She could not be the bride of Heaven, and therefore became the bride of Mr. Frank Besant. He was hardly an adequate substitute."[121] The marriage was troubled from the beginning because Annie could not be so submissive as Frank thought proper and they quarreled fiercely, sometimes physically. Once, she asserted, he threw her bodily over a fence and later, threatened to shoot her with the loaded gun in his study. After a miserable six years in the provinces, and having had two children, Mabel and Digby, Annie could no longer endure her husband and fled to London. Since divorce was out of the question, a separation agreement was drawn up by which four-year-old Digby would stay with his father and three-year-old Mabel would live with Annie, with summer visitation privilege.

Faced with respectable starvation on the hundred ten pounds a year Besant gave her from his modest salary, Annie began to look for work and finally found a position as a governess. Soon afterward she met forty-year-old Charles Bradlaugh and began her career as a militant atheist, exhorting, organizing, writing, speaking and leading thousands for whom she would come to symbolize the triumph of science over the decaying old faiths. At the same time, she spent four years at London University trying unsuccessfully to earn a B.Sc. degree, despite having failed chemistry three times.

In 1877 the crusading Besant and Bradlaugh published a forty-year-old American medical pamphlet advocating birth control and specifically describing several methods—*Fruits of Philosophy; or, The Private Companion of Young Married Couples*, by Charles Knowlton. Since distribution or advertisement of contraceptives was illegal, the police took swift action and Besant and Bradlaugh were prosecuted on the grounds that the pamphlet was "lewd, filthy, bawdy, and obscene." Both of them suffered violent public abuse and social ostracism; worse still, Frank Besant sued to remove Mabel from Annie's custody on the grounds that the child was in moral danger through association with an atheistic woman who published "indecent and obscene" writings. Despite Annie's vehement defense, she was deprived of the right to see either of her children until they attained their majority; in the opinion of the Lord Chief Justice, she had violated "morality, decency, and womanly propriety," both in her writings and in publication of a pamphlet "so repugnant, so abhorrent to the feelings of the majority of decent Englishmen and Englishwomen."[122]

During the early 1880s, Annie threw herself into work with a ferocity that astonished her contemporaries. Recalled Bernard Shaw:

> Her displays of personal courage and resolution, as when she would march into a police-court, make her way to the witness stand, and compel the magistrate to listen to her by sheer force of style and character, were trifles compared to the way in which she worked day and night to pull through the strike of the over-exploited matchgirls who had walked into her office one day and asked her to help them somehow, anyhow. An attempt to keep pace with her on the part of a mere man generally wrecked the man.[123]

By 1889, however, despite her enviable reputation and excellent income from writing and speaking, Annie was forced to admit that she still had not found happiness. She had seen neither of her children for more than ten years, although she hoped that someday they would return to her of their own free will. In spite of her intimate association with Bradlaugh, a stormy romance with Shaw, and close friendships with a number of men, some of whom she had been in love with, she seems to have successfully repressed her need for physical love. Hypatia Bradlaugh once commented that had her father and Annie Besant both been single, they would have wed; still she believed their love unconsummated because Annie "was the one person who was capable of the deepest affection without any thought of sex."[124] In the opinion of one of her biographers, Arthur Nethercot, "it is very unlikely that she ever took a lover,"[125] a supposition that is probably correct because if she had, it would have come to the attention of the detectives Frank Besant hired to shadow her movements for evidence of immorality.

Generally disillusioned with life, Annie slowly came to feel that "my philosophy was not sufficient; that life and mind were other than, more than, I had dreamed." A professional atheist, she suddenly began to interest herself in psychology, hypnotism and Spiritualism. "Fact after fact came hurtling in upon me, demanding explanation I was incompetent to give."[126] In February, 1889, she undertook a private course in psychic training, probably in telepathy, from a Rev. J. Williams Ashman, an Anglican clergyman who was interested in the occult and, coincidentally, acquainted with H.P.B. though not a member of the Theosophical Society. On February 14, she wrote Ashman, "I have *studied* nothing in 'occult' science, only read anything that came in my way—two books of Sinnett's, some stray pamphlets. I have not been able to get anything. But I am quite ready to study carefully any works throwing light on the matter. Thank you very much for giving me the possible chance of knowing more."[127]

She was ripe for change of some sort, but no one, including Annie herself, would have predicted that the answers she sought could be found in Theosophy.

In early March, a copy of *The Secret Doctrine* reached the editorial offices of the *Pall Mall Gazette*. As W. T. Stead had met Madame Blavatsky, he felt an obligation to take review notice of her, although the two thick volumes made him "shrink in dismay" from mastering their contents himself. Aware that Annie Besant had been quietly pursuing a study of other-worldly subjects and had even attended a few séances, he took the books to her.

"Can you review these?" he asked. "My young men all fight shy of them, but you are quite mad enough on these subjects to make something of them."[128]

There is, however, an alternate version of how *The Secret Doctrine* found its way to Mrs. Besant. According to Shaw, it was he who had been given the assignment, no doubt because he had previously reviewed the S.P.R. Report and also Sinnett's biography of H.P.B.; he had passed on the job to Annie who had recently asked him to get her reviewing work from the *Gazette*. Why she would have needed Shaw as an intermediary is puzzling, since she and Stead were close friends, but in any case, she took home "my burden" and sat down to read. From the outset she was totally absorbed, in fact, she later admitted, "I was dazzled, blinded by the light in which disjointed facts were seen as parts of a mighty whole, and all my puzzles, riddles, problems, seemed to disappear."[129]

Acknowledging that the book did not offer easy reading, she penned a facetious little note to Stead: "I am immersed in Madame B! If I perish in the attempt to review her, you must write on my tomb, 'She has gone to investigate the Secret Doctrine at first hand.' "[130] If reading H.P.B. seemed an arduous proposition, reviewing her was worse, and Annie started out by declaring that to ninety-nine out of every hundred readers, "the study of the book will begin in bewilderment and end in despair." The average person might just as well skip it; all who did decide to attempt it "must have an intense desire to *know*."[131]

After handing in the review, she asked Stead for a letter of introduction to Madame Blavatsky, which she proceeded to forward along with a note asking permission to call. On March 15, Helena wrote back,

Dear Mrs. Besant,

I too have been long wishing to make your acquaintance, and there is nothing in the world I admire more than pluck and the rare courage to come out and state one's opinion of the face of all the world—including Mrs. Grundy.

I am at home every evening from tea time at seven till eleven o'clock;

and I shall be delighted to see you whenever you come. On Thursdays I have a meeting here, so on that night you would not find me alone; but all the rest of the week you would find me quite free.

Hoping that I shall soon have the pleasure of seeing you, believe me.

Yours very sincerely,
H. P. Blavatsky

P.S. This invitation includes of course Mr. Burrows or anyone whom you may choose to bring with you.[132]

Seemingly Helena and Mrs. Besant had nothing in common, except a mild awareness of each other's careers over the past six years; on June 18, 1882, for example, Annie had devoted part of her "Daybreak" column in Bradlaugh's *National Reformer* to the attention being given the Theosophical Society in India, mentioning Henry Olcott, whom Bradlaugh had once met during a visit to the U.S. Unacquainted with the Society, Annie limited herself to criticizing its vague doctrines and belief in apparitions. Two months later, H.P.B. replied gently in the *Theosophist* that Mrs. Besant was laboring under a complete misconception about the Society's objectives; for one so highly intellectual as she to utter dogmatic statements, especially after she herself had suffered so cruelly from bigotry in her struggle for freedom of thought, seemed absurdly inconsistent. Mrs. Besant chose not to respond.

Over the next few years, as H.P.B. continued to send the *Reformer* copies of her magazine, relations between the two publications grew strained. Bradlaugh had a habit of making snide remarks about Theosophical "miracle working, even to the extent of restoring a broken china plate to its perfect state without cement or patching," and he suggested it would be nice to have a Theosophical maid in households where there were frequent breakages. He also said that some of H.P.B.'s and Olcott's statements were so loony that he could not regard the *Theosophist* as a serious publication, nor could he treat Theosophists as serious persons. "Many of them are very respectable, very good, and very mad. Some of them are less mad and less good." In respect to Emma Coulomb's revelations, he acquitted H.P.B. as an enthusiastic semi-Spiritualist "who has managed to get fairly crazed in dabbling with the wonderful in company with many simpletons."[133] In these scornful opinions he was supported by Annie.

It is curious to note that Annie's name appears twice in the Mahatma letters to Alfred Sinnett. In January, 1884, Koot Hoomi mentioned his respect for Bradlaugh and Besant and his belief that they were not immoral, but he firmly regarded *Fruits of Philosophy* as "infamous and *highly pernicious.*" He had not read the book, nor did he intend to, but its "unclean spirit, its brutal aura" offended him and he thought the advice it contained was "abominable."[134] Both K.H. and H.P.B. strongly opposed birth control, even though in 1883 she had carried ads for *Fruits of Philosophy* in the *Theoso-*

phist. Apparently she had no idea of the book's contents, because when Anna Kingsford complained, she hastily removed them.

There is another Koot Hoomi letter, undated but probably received in the summer of 1883 after Sinnett had returned to England, in which K.H. advised him to "use every effort to develop such relations with A. Besant that your work may run on parallel lines and in full sympathy . . . You may, if you see fit—show this note to her only."[135] According to Sinnett's notation, he did show her the letter, but it is inconceivable that she would have felt her work running along Theosophical paths. Even as late as the autumn of 1887 she had no sympathy whatever with Theosophy and in her monthly literary magazine, *Our Corner*, she expressed a bemused opinion of the new publication *Lucifer*: "What is to be said of such a magazine as *Lucifer*, 'a theosophical monthly'? It has a very effective cover, but the contents are mere ravings; it may suffice to say that during the perusal of one story the reader is requested to accept 'the theory of the reincarnation of souls' as a living fact."[136] Little did she realize that in less than two years she would become the editor of *Lucifer* and accept reincarnation as "a living fact."

It was a soft spring evening in late March when Annie Besant and Herbert Burrows, a Socialist friend who was interested in Theosophy, walked from Notting Hill Station to the door of 17 Lansdowne Road. When they were ushered in, Helena saw a petite, slightly stooped woman with a gently rounded face and close-cropped hair that showed streaks of silver. A few years earlier Annie had been slimmer, prettier; she had worn tightly buttoned gowns that showed off her slender figure and cameo brooches at her throat, and she had curled her hair into short bangs over the forehead with the rest wound in plaits at the back of her head. Now, no longer so slim, she had taken to wearing a sort of working-class uniform—short skirt that skimmed the top of her thick, laced boots (usually muddy) and a red neckerchief or Tam O'Shanter. But the sweet face remained.

Helena reached out for her hand and gave it a firm shake. "My dear Mrs. Besant," she said, "I have so long wished to see you."

Annie was conscious of a sudden leaping of her heart—"was it recognition?" she asked herself later—followed immediately by "a fierce rebellion, a fierce withdrawal, as of some wild animal when it feels a mastering hand."

The rest of the visit proved anticlimactic. When Annie explained that she was interested in Madame's work and would like to know more about it, Helena, "her eyes veiled, her exquisitely moulded fingers rolling cigarettes incessantly," talked about Egypt and India and then turned the conversation to more general topics. Nothing was said about occultism, no mysteries were subtly conveyed. Slightly disappointed, Annie and Burrows rose to leave but at that last moment, Annie would recall, "the veil lifted, and two brilliant, piercing eyes met mine, and with a yearning throb in the voice: 'Oh, my dear Mrs. Besant, if you would only come among us!' " The younger woman, struggling against an almost uncontrollable desire to bend down and kiss Helena, steeled herself and turned away "with some inanely courteous and evasive remark."

During the next weeks Annie Besant struggled against the temptation to go back and drown herself in "that yearning voice, those compelling eyes,"[137] but she could see what throwing herself at Madame's feet entailed. She had finally overcome many years of public ostracism and now saw a smooth road stretching before her. Was she to begin a fresh fight for an unpopular cause and make herself an object of ridicule again? Must she turn against materialism and face the humiliation of publicly confessing that she had been wrong? "What would be the look in Charles Bradlaugh's eyes when I told him that I had become a Theosophist?"[138] she wondered. Aside from these agonizing questions, she also felt perplexed as well as repulsed by H.P.B. Madame Blavatsky was obviously wasting away and Annie repeatedly asked herself how this was consistent with her occult training: if the Mahatmas existed, why did they permit their representative to suffer? "And does it not seem rather cruel," she wrote Reverend Ashman, "if they have used her, worn her out, & thrown her away? They remain vigorous and strong. If they trained her, why does she not share their higher vitality, instead of being exhausted. I am puzzled altogether."[139]

When Annie's review appeared on April 25, she sent Helena a copy and was invited to call again. By this time it must have been obvious to H.P.B. that while Annie wanted to join the Society, pride was holding her back. She was, H.P.B. decided and later told her, "as proud as Lucifer himself." When Annie returned yet a third time and continued to ask questions about Theosophy and made it clear she was close to a decision, Helena took an immense gamble. Looking at her piercingly, she asked, "Have you read the report about me of the Society for Psychical Research?"

No, Annie replied, she had not even heard of it although the statement is hard to believe.

"Go and read it," Helena suggested. "And if, after reading it, you come back—well." And she changed the subject.

For two days Mrs. Besant read and re-read Richard Hodgson's findings. Everything, she thought, turned on the veracity of the Coulombs who admitted themselves partners in the alleged frauds. Could she believe their word as against "the proud fiery truthfulness" that shone from Madame's blue eyes? Was the author of *The Secret Doctrine* "this miserable impostor, this accomplice of tricksters, this foul and loathsome deceiver, this conjuror with trapdoors and sliding panels?" She could not believe it.

On the tenth of May she visited the office of the Theosophical Publishing Company in Duke Street and asked Countess Wachtmeister for an application. Filling it in then and there, she left and hurried straight to Lansdowne Road where she found H.P.B. alone. Without a word, she went up to her chair and bent to kiss her.

Deeply moved, Helena nevertheless set her face in a stern expression and asked. "You have joined the Society?"

"Yes."

"You have read the report?"

"Yes."

"Well?"

Kneeling beside her, Annie clasped both of her hands and looked deep into her eyes. "My answer is, will you accept me as your pupil, and give me the honour of proclaiming you my teacher in the face of the world?"

With tears gleaming in her eyes, Helena rested her hand on Annie's head. When she could trust herself to speak, she murmured, "You are a noble woman. May Master bless you."[140]

No one knew better than H.P.B. what this decision would cost Annie Besant and what it would mean to the Theosophical Society. For her, it was literally a dream come true and it provoked joyous tears; it was one of the rare instances in her life when anybody saw her cry.

Due to the fact that Annie's *Pall Mall Gazette* review had been unsigned, news of her conversion took several weeks to become public. There was a personal item in the *Sun* on June 16 announcing briefly that she had turned Theosophist and had been admitted to "the Esoteric Section of the famous Blavatsky Lodge," and a few days later Annie wrote a piece for the *Star*, "*Sic Itur ad Astra*": or, Why I Became a Theosophist. Bernard Shaw, while paying a call on the editor, happened to glance at a set of proofs littering the table and saw Annie's by-line. Staggered, he galloped over to her office in Fleet Street and "asked her whether she was quite mad." Did she know that Madame Blavatsky had been exposed as a fraud by the Society for Psychical Research? If Annie sincerely felt in need of a mahatma, he teased, he would be her mahatma. After playing all his usual tricks to stir her indignation or her wit, he could see that "it was no use." She listened patiently with a half smile and then remarked only that she had become a vegetarian, as he was; perhaps the new diet had enfeebled her mind. "In short," Shaw concluded, "she was for the first time able to play with me; she was no longer in the grip of her pride; she had after many explorations found her path and come to see the universe and herself in their real perspective."[141]

Charles Bradlaugh was aghast. Viewing Annie's conversion with "the very gravest misgiving," he deeply regretted that his colleague and co-worker had accepted as fact "matters which seem to me as unreal as it is possible for any fiction to be." The Theosophists' Tibetan Masters "are to me as the 'inhabitants' of the planet Mars, and equally fall into the category of Romance, whether vouched for by Mme. Blavatsky or by M. Jules Verne."[142]

If Annie's transformation stupefied her friends, it convulsed the public and touched off a flurry of debate in the press: had Mrs. Besant's mind suddenly become unhinged, or had Madame Blavatsky unfairly snared her by some supernatural means? The *Daily News* assured its readers that hypnotism had been a factor in the conversion, and some of Annie's later biographers, while not going quite that far, would suggest that she was an extremely suggestible person who could be influenced by strong personalities. In the past, she had been influenced by men, but Madame, they wrote, was sufficiently masculine as to be included in that category. Annie's about-face may have seemed sudden to most people but, as we have seen, it followed a long period of incubation extending back to the religious ecstasy of her girlhood when she had yearned to be a martyr; it continued through her adult career, in which she devoted herself to good works that might be expected to bring grievous but pleasurable suffering. Shaw believed her shift to H.P.B.'s ranks reflected the fact that "she was a born actress. She was successively a Pusyite Evangelical, an Atheist Bible-smasher, a Darwinian secularist, a Fabian Socialist, a Strike Leader, and finally a Theosophist, exactly as Mrs. Siddons was a Lady Macbeth, Lady Randolph, Beatrice, Rosalind, and Volumnia. She 'saw herself' as a priestess above all. That was how Theosophy held her to the end."[143]

Helena, who had been observing the furor with interest, quickly moved to set people straight by emphatically insisting that she had nothing to do with Annie's joining the Society. She also denied that "I ever put any pressure upon her—whether hypnotical or *magical*." Had she bestowed such a valuable acquisition on the Society, she remarked self-deprecatingly, "it would have been a matter of pride, but it was not so." Pointing out that "Mrs. Besant yields to no pressure, except that of her own reasoning power,"[144] she asked mildly whether it might not be possible for there to be value in a philosophy that attracted such individuals.

As a matter of fact, no one could have been more surprised over Annie Besant's conversion than Madame Blavatsky. After all the "miracles" she had staged on behalf of her own cause, this was a genuine miracle, and she had played no part in it.

During the summer of 1889 Helena experienced a renascence of psychic, physical and emotional well-being. One sign of it was an immediate improvement in her health, another was the budding of emotions frozen so long ago that she concluded they were sealed forever. Annie stirred up feelings that she had experienced only for Yuri, Nadyezhda and a very few others. Judging by her letters from this period, one cannot avoid the impression that she had fallen in love and the fact that the object of her passion happened to be an individual of her own sex, a sex which incidentally neither she nor Annie liked very much, had no bearing on the matter. That there were, as Annie's most recent biographer, Arthur Nethercot, pointed out, definite lesbian overtones in their relationship is a fact too obvious to overlook. This is not to imply that they were lovers in the physical meaning of the word; rather, theirs was a union of mind and emotions that supplied the missing piece both had been needing in their lives. Helena, overflowing with happiness, spilled out endearments with characteristic candor: "Dearly Beloved One, I *am proud of you*, I love you, I honour you. You are and will be yet before all men—the star of salvation." Annie was her "sweet mango"; "my darling Penelope" to her "female Ulysses"; "My dove-eyed one"; her "dearest" whom she longed to kiss "on both your big lotus-like eyes peeping into mine."[145]

To her Russian family, she raved about Annie and even a rash of exclamation points could not adequately convey her bliss: "What a kind, noble and wonderful woman she is! And what an orator she is! One cannot have enough of her. Demosthenes in petticoats! It is such an achievement [getting her, I guess] and gives me endless joy."[146]

Annie expressed her devotion by calling H.P.B. her "saviour," and by vowing that she would forsake neither her nor the Theosophical cause. Her letters to Helena have not survived, but from descriptions of her behavior recorded by those who knew them, one can readily guess that she shared Helena's satisfaction with the relationship. Edmund Russell recalled that Annie would sit on the floor beside H.P.B. during a card game and reverently press one of Madame's hands to her cheek. All evening she would clutch H.P.B. like some shipwrecked mariner clinging to the tentacle of a giant octopus. Helena treated her with a tenderness that her other friends and pupils rarely glimpsed, a calculated move in the opinion of Alfred Sinnett, who cynically observed that Madame "took care to keep her loftiest characteristics in evidence."[147] Annie Besant, he added, never knew the Old Lady during the stormy period of her life when temper tantrums were the rule rather than the exception.

But after only a short time in H.P.B.'s company, Annie was well aware of her temper and noted that she treated people variously, depending on their natures: patient at times, she lashed out scornfully when she detected vanity, conceit or hypocrisy. She believed that her sole purpose was to get across her points as a teacher, "careless what they or anyone else thought of her." As for herself, immune to Helena's barbed tongue, Madame was a "noble and heroic Soul" who had brought her "through storm to peace."[148]

In mid-June, bubbling with new-found energy, Helena took the uncharacteristic step of actually leaving her house to make a public appearance. On Monday, June 17, the day after Annie first announced her conversion in the *Sun*, she accompanied her to the grand opening of Isabel Cooper-Oakley's Dorothy Restaurant for working women in the West End. Isabel was making a reputation for herself as an entrepreneur: in addition to this restaurant, she was also the proprietor of another Dorothy tea shop for "ladies" and a Bond Street boutique, "Madame Isabel," agent for Felix, Pasquier, Virot and Reboux and carrying "the Latest Models in Dresses, Mantles, Bonnets, & c . . . . First-Rate Fit Guaranteed."

H.P.B., of course, had no particular affection for Isabel, never went to restaurants, and under other circumstances would not have been caught near such a flamboyantly commercial event. Still, Annie planned to attend and probably Helena could not resist appearing in public with her dearest pupil.

As it turned out, H.P.B. wandered straight into one of the season's most sensational social affairs. While the restaurant may have been designed to cater to working-class women, the first day it was difficult, if not impossible, to find any among the gaggle of ladies crowding the shop: Lady Colin Campbell, Lady Mary Hope, the Baroness de Pallandt, Mrs. Oscar Wilde, and so forth. But the two women around whom the reporters most eagerly clustered were Madame Blavatsky, who puffed cigarettes and declared that she certainly did not approve of mesmerism, and Annie Besant, who merely listened to Madame and played the role of devoted disciple.

According to the *Sun*, all the women were charmingly attired, although one wonders if this blanket description included Helena in her dowdy bag and Annie whose equally tacky uniform made her look like one of the working women to whom the Dorothy would be catering. After luncheon, which was reported to be excellent, Madame drank coffee, smoked more cigarettes and engaged in a spirited debate with Oscar Wilde on the relative merits of aestheticism and Theosophy; both debaters ignored the crowds who had gathered outside, pressing their noses against the window to get a peek at the reclusive, cigarette-smoking Madame and the elegant Wilde.

Two weeks later, still in exuberant spirits, Helena set off on a Continental holiday with a rich American Theosophist, Ida Candler, who had appeared in London with her daughter, scooped up H.P.B. and insisted on taking her to Fontainebleau for a few weeks' rest. Ida was not what H.P.B. called a deep Theosophist but rather a kindhearted woman who wanted to do something nice for Madame. The fact that H.P.B. so readily acceded was undoubtedly owing to the fact that Annie along with Herbert Burrows would be nearby in Paris attending the International Labour Congress and promised to join her afterward. While Annie was sitting through long days of speech-making and brushing off jibes from her trade-unionist friends about her recent spiritual transformation, Helena went sightseeing with a gusto that astounded Mrs. Candler who considered her an invalid and had rented a bath chair to wheel her about in. Madame refused to ride. "Out of the fifty-eight state rooms of the palace," she reported happily to Nadyezhda, "I have done forty-five with my *own, unborrowed legs*!! It is more than five years since I have walked so much!" She insisted on examining Marie Antoinette's bedroom and inspecting the dance hall where Diane de Poitiers had once cavorted; she raved over the Gobelins, the Sèvres china, and a table on which Napoleon had signed his resignation. Merely strolling under the great oaks and Scotch firs and inhaling air impregnated with the resin of pine "has revived me, has given me back my long lost strength."[149]

It was in the restful glades at Fontainebleau that a relaxed H.P.B. felt inspired to begin a new book, her last, and by the time Annie and Burrows arrived from Paris she had already composed many passages. *The Voice of the Silence*[150] is a slender volume of poetic maxims meant to serve as an inspirational guide for those students attempting the path of true occultism.

She told Annie that the aphorisms were not her invention but merely translations of fragments from a mysterious book she called *The Book of the Golden Precepts*. Annie recalled that "she wrote it swiftly, without any material copy before her, and in the evening made me read it aloud to see if the 'English was decent.' " It was in perfectly beautiful English and Annie could find only a few words that needed to be changed. Helena, she said, "looked at us like a startled child, wondering at our praises."[151]

In her preface to the work, H.P.B. noted that she had done her best to preserve the poetic imagery of the original, a companion piece to the *Stanzas of Dzyan*, but the question of her success she would leave to the reader's judgment. Whatever her reservations, there is no doubt that she produced an exquisite prose poem:

Before the Soul can see, the harmony within must be attained, and fleshly eyes be rendered blind to all illusions.

Before the Soul can hear, the image (man) has to become as deaf to roaring as to whispers, to cries of bellowing elephants as to the silvery buzzing of the golden firefly.

Before the Soul can comprehend and may remember, she must unto the Silent Speaker be united, just as the form to which the clay is modeled is first united with the potter's mind.

For then the Soul will hear, and will remember.

And then to the inner ear will speak—

THE VOICE OF THE SILENCE[152]

If *The Voice of the Silence* is any indication, Helena was in a highly creative state at Fontainebleau. Feeling better physically than she had in years, she even undertook to perform a few phenomena for Annie and offered to show her how the raps at Spiritualist séances were made.

"You don't use spirits to produce taps," she told her. "See here." Placing her hands slightly above Annie's head, careful not to touch her, she sent gentle taps pinging down on the bone of her skull, each one thrilling a tiny electric shiver down Annie's spine. For several decades Helena had matter-of-factly been rapping for audiences on various continents but it was startling and extremely impressive to Annie. Later that evening, still keyed up from Madame's demonstrations, she retired for the night in a small room adjoining H.P.B.'s. After she had been sleeping for some time, she suddenly woke "to find the air of the room thrown into pulsating waves, and then appeared the radiant astral Figure of the Master, visible to my physical eyes."[153] In this, her first psychic experience, she not only saw, but heard and touched Mahatma Morya and smelled the odors of sandalwood and other Oriental spices.

In late July Annie headed back to London where she had promised H.P.B. help on getting out the next issue of *Lucifer*. Helena trundled along in the wake of Ida Candler, who dragged her back to Paris to view the Eiffel Tow-

er—"one of the latest fungi of modern commercial enterprise,"[154] Helena
sniffed—and from there to the Exposition Universelle where Mrs. Candler
spent two hours searching for a Parsi who sold paper knives "whom we only
found at the last moment when there was a great rush of spilt porte-monnaies,
lost pocket-handkerchiefs, umbrellas, above all (Karma.)"[155] Ida had a habit
of losing her belongings: at Fontainebleau she had accused Helena of having
stolen a silver-headed umbrella that she had actually left on the train, and at
Paris, Helena joked, she had nearly lost the train. Disorganized, Mrs. Candler
left her daughter and H.P.B. at the Gare St. Lazare while she flapped back to
their lodgings for the luggage and did not return until the train was about to
pull out. The trip to Granville on the coast, normally a four-hour ride on the
express, lasted seven-and-a-half hours, and when they finally arrived after
midnight, there were no vacant rooms at the first hotel they tried. Helena,
"unwilling to submit my unfortunate knees to further tortures by climbing
back in the omnibus," walked two blocks in a rainstorm to another hotel,
checked in, and fell into bed at 3 A.M.

The next day they sailed "in an old wash-tub called a steamer" to St.
Heliers on the Channel island of Jersey. Its yellow sand and camellias and
roses had an Italianate air that enchanted Helena; she was amused by the
inhabitants, who got terribly offended if anyone called them English, French,
or anything but *Jerseymen*. She wrote Annie that she did not much care for
the Eagle House hotel, which was run by "a mother and daughter who have
seen better days" and one servant "incapable of discerning a stinking chop
from a fresh one."[156] Amazed that her system had withstood the recent dousing at Granville, she told herself that she must be stronger than she imagined
if it had not resulted in a cold; still, her knees were beginning to ache slightly
and she took the precaution of spending a day in bed. Perhaps because the
Eagle House cuisine proved inedible, Ida decided to transfer to the town of St.
Aubins where the Theosophical party took a honeysuckle-twined cottage, Bel-
grave Villa. "Dearest," H.P.B. wrote Annie on August 2,

> We had to move these last two days and were like Marius on the ruins of
> Carthage, sitting disconsolate on our trunks. Now we are within reach of
> pen and ink once more. Thousand thanks for your dear ash-tray and your
> thought of me, you, sweet *mango*, among women. I will not dirty and use
> it, but look at it standing before me. It is lovely for it comes from
> you . . . [157]

And a few days later, bemoaning Bertram Keightley's inefficiency (or so she
regarded it) in handling the editing of *Lucifer*,

> Now my trust and only hope is in you—Bert is positively losing his mem-
> ory. It is impossible to rely upon him in anything as far as memory and

recollection go. It is simply awful. Oh Lord how I do wish to see you.[158]

At St. Aubins she worked simultaneously on *The Voice of the Silence* and *Lucifer*, the latter's proofs sent over by mail. When she saw that this procedure was not working, she cabled George Mead to join her. "No sooner had I arrived," Mead recalled, "than she gave me the run of all her papers, and set me to work on a pile of correspondence that would otherwise have remained unanswered till doomsday, for if she detested anything, it was answering letters." One day she came into his room and handed him *The Voice of the Silence.* "Read that, old man," she said, "and tell me what you think of it."[159]

Smoking and tapping her foot restlessly against the floor, she finally interrupted with a sharp "Well?"

When Mead told her that it was the grandest piece of Theosophical literature he had read, she appeared unconvinced and replied that, in her opinion, the translation failed to do justice to the original.

Around the end of August, when Mead and the Candler women accompanied her back to London, Helena continued to sparkle with vitality and good humor. During the trip home on the Channel steamer, H.P.B. fell into conversation with a young man from Birmingham in the course of which the subject of Theosophy arose.

"They are a rum lot, them theosophists," he snorted.

"Yes, a rum lot," Helena agreed.

"And that rum old woman at the head of them—"

She cut in smoothly, "That rum old woman, H. P. Blavatsky, has now the honor of speaking to you."

"Ah! I do not mean that old woman," he stammered, "but another old woman."[160]

During Helena's six-week absence, the Theosophical Society, commanded by its newest convert, continued to be the center of lively controversy; not a week went by that some newspaper or journal did not throw fresh branches on the fire. Since many of the statements made about the situation were absurd and some decidedly malicious, Annie scheduled two lectures on August 4 and 11 in the Hall of Science to explain "Why I Became a Theosophist." To packed houses, she bravely charged into such subjects as reincarnation, hypnotism, the Hodgson Report, the Coulombs, and of course the mentorship of Madame Blavatsky. In a stouthearted defense of H.P.B., Annie lashed out at those who declared that if Madame had truly been the victim of slander, she should have prosecuted the Coulombs and the S.P.R. To this Annie replied that "I have been accused of the vilest life a woman could lead. Have I prosecuted? No. A strong woman and a good woman knows that her life is enough to live down slander."[161] When news of these remarks reached Helena's ears, she must have known for a surety that in Annie Besant she had found a jewel beyond value.

All the publicity had its down side. Many had been stimulated to investigate Theosophy; memberships in the Society began to climb until the Thursday meetings of the Blavatsky Lodge were so packed the house could not contain the crowd; however, H.P.B. found the press taking advantage of the occasion to exhume incidents from her past she would have preferred to forget. Her impulse was to ignore the exposés as befit a sage engaged in matters more important than answering every nit-picker with access to a printing press. But, Helena being in a feisty mood could not resist defending herself. Clearly at her instigation, the Society established a Press Bureau, headed by Alice Cleather, whose function was, one, to answer attacks on H.P.B., and, two, to collect press clippings.

Helena could not resist shooting off a personal response which struck an attitude halfway between disdain and sarcasm. If the public wanted the true facts of her life, she said huffily, they could go whistle for it. She had no intention of gratifying anyone's curiosity, least of all her enemies who were "quite welcome to believe in and spread as many cock-and-bull stories about me as they choose." As for various statements published about her by her own Theosophists, she could not hold herself responsible for their "blunders, inaccuracies and contradictions,"[162] including those written by Alfred Sinnett in her biography, a book she claimed not to have read because she suspected it was full of errors. In replying to a New York *Sun* editorial that had both characterized Olcott and H.P.B. as clever impostors who had gotten rich on swindling dupes, and had gone on to call Helena "a snuffy old woman," she took issue with the adjective "snuffy." "Surely this is an incorrect epithet, a mistake proceeding from a confusion of snuff and tobacco," and she suggested that the correct description would be "a *smoky* old woman."[163]

Obviously there was plenty of fight left in her, which was a good thing, because in the first week of September Henry Olcott arrived in London to do battle. On his way he disembarked at Marseilles and stopped at Paris to tour the same exposition H.P.B. had visited a month earlier. But Henry had not made the long and expensive voyage to stare at exhibits: all year, he had suspected that Helena considered him an unimportant old man sitting beneath his banyan tree at Adyar, a suspicion only too strongly and unpleasantly confirmed by one of her Esoteric Section clauses demanding total obedience to herself and nobody else. Naturally this made him speculate about her loyalty to him as president. Was it possible that she was trying to control Adyar? When he had presented these ruminations in a letter, she had replied that he missed the point entirely. It was neither to him nor Adyar that she owed loyalty, but only to the Cause. Should he deviate in any way in *his* loyalty to the Cause, she would lop him off like a rotten branch. An irate Henry focused his revulsion for her highhandedness on the Esoteric Section, whose obedience clause must have symbolized her reborn autocracy. His back against the wall, he declared that he would resign unless she emended the clause, a threat Helena preferred to ignore.

This time there was no miraculous Mahatma letter at sea to pacify Olcott, but waiting for him at Lansdowne Road was Helena's newest weapon, Annie Besant. By the time he arrived, Annie had temporarily vacated her house in St. John's Wood and moved bag and baggage into 17 Lansdowne Road, but on the evening of his arrival, she was nowhere in sight. According to Henry, Helena greeted him warmly and as if nothing were amiss, kept him up talking, Lamasery-fashion, until 2 A.M. It was not until the following evening that he finally met Annie, who immediately impressed him as "a natural Theosophist," even though he was a bit taken back by her appearance and thought her costume made her look like an "Annie Militant." Finally, he liked her very much and as president of the Society had to admit that "she is the most important gain to us since Sinnett." As they parted that evening, he took her hand and said solemnly, "I think you will find yourself happier than you have ever been in your life before, for I see you are a mystic and have been frozen into your brain by your environment. You come now into a family of thinkers who will know you as you are and love you dearly."[164]

Helena watched with satisfaction as their friendship quickly ripened: the next day he accompanied Annie to pay a call on Charles Bradlaugh, whom he had known in New York and had nominated for membership in the Lotos Club, and on Sunday he attended one of her lectures at the Hall of Science; after that he saw her frequently at the house and attended her lectures whenever possible, sometimes sharing the platform with her. To keep Henry gainfully occupied, Helena set up a table beside her desk and put him to work writing letters and articles for *Lucifer* and also helping her prepare teaching papers for her Esoteric students. Olcott enjoyed this for a while, then balked at being tied to her desk and began to schedule appointments and lectures. "She called me a 'mule' and all sorts of pet names of the kind,"[165] he recalled, but he held firm to his independence.

In time, both of them softened slightly. Seeing Henry again did have an effect on Helena because she began to confide in him her feelings about various members of the London group and solicited his advice about the best way to handle certain problems. Needless to say, the advice was not followed. By the time Henry left in December she must have mellowed considerably because she agreed to a slight amendment of the E.S. obedience clause: she did not even protest when he made doubly clear that the Esoteric Section had no official connection with the Society by changing its name to the "Eastern School of Theosophy," nor did she object noticeably when he avoided giving her decision-making powers by appointing a special four-person Board of Control for Britain that could decide on his behalf. Of course Helena was chairman but he hoped to staunch her tendency toward autocracy by adding to the committee Annie, Herbert Burrows and William Kingsland, all of whom he respected. The formal order was drawn up on December 25, 1889, but, as Henry noted in his memoirs, it looked to Helena "a larger Xmas present than it really was,"[166] because it forbade her making any decision alone. Privately he believed that his mission to London had been successful, since "H.P.B.'s angry feelings were subsiding, and all danger of a disruption was swiftly passing away."[167] In reality, she was merely making a tactical withdrawal, the better to fight again another day, and within six months would once more push Olcott to the point of resignation.

Unknown to Henry, Helena was busy sinking the foundations of a kingdom that would survive both of them, by unobtrusively grooming her successor. For the remainder of that year and all through the next, Annie would break most of her ties with her own past life, resigning her membership in the Fabian and other Socialist societies, participating less actively in strikes and labor demonstrations and making fewer speeches to factory workers. In some aspects, this was both predictable and natural but in others, H.P.B. can be seen aiding an historical process by gradually handing over authority to her personal heir. In September she made Annie co-editor of *Lucifer*, and four months later, after the president of the Blavatsky Lodge, William Kingsland, had "resigned," Annie was elected to the position.

By now, the personal intimacy between the two women had deepened until Annie felt unhappy being separated from her friend and teacher. Perhaps as a result of the weeks she spent with Helena during Olcott's visit, she realized that the house had outgrown its adequacy as a headquarters, but still she wanted to be near H.P.B. When Annie proposed making her house at 19 Avenue Road into both the Society's Headquarters and H.P.B.'s residence, Helena at first refused, perhaps for decorum's sake, and then seeing the younger woman's disappointment, submitted to the idea. To her surprise, this unilateral decision was greeted with indignation by the other members of the household. Bert, Arch, Mead, and the countess all protested that Madame had not only failed to consult them but now was "authoritatively and *autocratically*"[168] trying to force her decision upon them. Mrs. Besant's generosity was all very well, and of course they had no objection to her intrusion per se, but what would happen if H.P.B. died, or if Annie suddenly decided to turn them out, or if, as somebody suggested, Annie died in a railway accident? The Society would be out in the cold; verbal agreement between Madame and Mrs. Besant was clearly unsuitable. The transfer must be done legally.

For ten days Helena could not bring herself to mention the contretemps to Annie, but finally she explained the situation in a letter. Her worries proved groundless for Annie understood at once, and before the end of 1889, she formally deeded her house to the Theosophists for the remainder of her eighteen-year mortgage. About this time she issued an appeal for a "Theosophical Building Fund" both to remodel her house and build a new structure that could be used as a meeting hall and as living quarters for the T.S. staff. Since one anonymous donor provided almost the entire cost of this work, the necessary renovations and construction got under way immediately and Annie was predicting the transfer could be made in June, 1890.

During the winter of 1889–1890, the explosion of energy Helena had experienced in the summer gradually evaporated, and, while she was probably allowing herself to relax a bit now that Annie could shoulder the burdens, she was clearly slowing down: instead of presiding over E.S. meetings herself, she let Annie run them. Hence, she was not present on December 20 when Willie Yeats proposed that the group undertake a few occult experiments. Suspecting that Madame would disapprove "on the ground of danger by opening up means of black magic,"[169] he was pleased when Annie promised to refer his idea to H.P.B. and more than a little shocked when Madame actually gave them a go-ahead and appointed Yeats to head a paranormal research committee.

Whether H.P.B. kept track of Yeats' work is doubtful since most of it was conducted at the Duke Street office, which she never visited. One moonlit night the researchers burned a flower and then tried to reincarnate it with an air pump, but the ashes refused to cooperate. In another experiment, they suspended a needle by a silk thread under a glass case, then tried to move it by psychokinesis; next they brought in a medium named Monsey to mesmerize Yeats. None of these experiments could be termed successful; in fact, as time went on they grew increasingly silly, and nine months later Madame would put an end to Yeats' career as a psychic researcher. His final appearance at the Blavatsky Lodge was a lecture on "Theosophy and Modern Culture"; shortly afterward Mead called him into his office and said that his presence and conduct were causing disturbances; quite honestly, one female member had complained about him. Feeling that the poet was not in full agreement with the Society's methods or philosophy, Mead asked Yeats to resign. Yeats complied regretfully, but not unhappily, because he had recently been initiated into the Order of the Golden Dawn, another secret society in communication with unknown supermen.

While Yeats was trying to raise the ghosts of flowers, another young man found himself attracted to the Theosophical Society through his admiration for Annie Besant. Mohandas K. Gandhi was a twenty-one-year-old Indian law student, nondescript, and frail, with a tiny mustache and bow tie. During his year's stay in London, he had made a number of acquaintances at vegetarian restaurants, among them Bert and Arch Keightley who were reading the *Bhagavad-Gītā* in Sir Edwin Arnold's popular translation called *The Song Celestial*, and they invited him to join them. Ashamed that he had never read the *Gītā* either in Sanskrit or Gujarati, Gandhi went through it and Arnold's *Light of Asia* with their help. The Keightleys invited him to a meeting of the Blavatsky Lodge and introduced him to Madame Blavatsky and Annie Besant, whose recent conversion he had followed in the papers with great interest. The shy Gandhi felt out of place, and when the Keightleys asked him if he would care to join the Society, he declined politely by saying,

"With my meagre knowledge of my own religion I do not want to belong to any religious body."[170] He did, however, follow their suggestion that he read Madame's recently published *Key to Theosophy*, which "stimulated in me the desire to read books on Hinduism and disabused me of the notion fostered by the missionaries that Hinduism was rife with superstition."[171]

Though Gandhi would later deride both Theosophy and its unseen Mahatmas as humbugs, he would nevertheless credit the Society as the means by which he began to discover his own heritage. With Annie Besant, who some twenty-five years later would become a brilliant advocate of Indian freedom and President of the Indian National Congress, Gandhi may have had political differences, but his veneration would never diminish.

On Gandhi's sole visit to Lansdowne Road, Helena took no more notice of him than she did of hundreds of others who entered her rooms and were led up to her chair for a brief introduction, nor did she intuit nor infer from her Mahatmas the fact that she had encountered, for a few minutes, a genuine mahatma, or at least one who would be regarded so not only by his own countrymen but the world. Such were the ironies of Madame Blavatsky's life.

As the year 1890 opened, H.P.B. began to suffer attacks of extreme fatigue. Seated in her armchair behind her desk, rolling the ubiquitous cigarettes and occasionally handing one to Mead, she would be busy writing when her head would start to nod. Sometimes there would be palpitations of the heart and a ringing in her ears that made her feel almost deaf, and spasms of weakness so intense that she had difficulty lifting her head. When Dr. Mennell diagnosed exhaustion and nervous prostration due to overwork, and ordered a complete rest, Helena responded with annoyance and said she had too much work to do. Mennell did not bother to argue but merely alerted the rest of the household, who promptly determined that Madame must be parted from her papers and books, if necessary by force. One way to limit her activities, perhaps the only way, was to remove her from London. Word traveled quickly around the city and even to the United States that Madame was extremely ill; in no time contributions came pouring in so that she could take a vacation. "America especially," she remarked in some amazement, "is so generous that, upon my word, I feel ashamed."[172]

In early February she was taken to Brighton so that she might, in her phrase, "inhale the oceanic evaporations of the Gulf Stream." Shifts of two or three of her students would come to stay with her, but keeping her quiet was no easy matter. "I am forbidden to write or read or even to think," she wrote Vera, "but must spend whole days in the open air . . ."[173] In her opinion, Brighton was a frightfully expensive place and, initially, she worried about the money she was spending; after a while, however, she decided to enjoy herself for the weather was splendid. "The sun is simply Italian, the air is rich; the sea is like a looking-glass, and during whole days I am pushed to and fro on the esplanade in an invalid chair. It is lovely."[174]

After several weeks, she began to rally and felt well enough to write Vera. This slight exertion immediately brought a concerned protest from one of her caretakers who poked his nose in the door and asked her to please stop. She had to let her family know she was still alive, she retorted, and went on writing.

III

Twilight

The sea air seemed to have done Helena good, and she returned to London thinking that she might resume her old schedule. This proved far too optimistic an expectation, for tiring easily, she had to voluntarily curtail her twelve-hour workday, insisting she intended to resume it once she had regained her health. By April Dr. Mennell had to call another halt to work and put Helena to bed with orders to do absolutely nothing; this caused her real torture because, in spite of her failing physical strength, her mind remained as active as ever, if not more so. In her idleness she fretted about matters that under ordinary circumstances would not have held her attention for more than a few minutes: Ida Candler was already planning another summer junket and writing to ask where Madame felt inclined to spend the season this year; there was also an invitation from Theosophists in Sweden suggesting that she visit their country, and one of them offered to put at her disposal a villa and yacht. These invitations merely distressed her as she did not feel up to traveling and was obliged to compose polite refusals. What she really wanted was a visit from Vera, and wrote to tell her so.

But mostly she occupied herself with second-hand reports on the progress taking place at 19 Avenue Road. Of course the most exciting feature of the new headquarters would be the lecture hall that was now half completed, but H.P.B.'s main concern seems to have been her personal quarters. Annie had decided Madame must have two connecting rooms on the ground floor just off the main hall. One of these, formerly Annie's study, would make a perfect office and there was also a small adjoining room that could be Madame's bedroom. These rooms required little alteration but, to accommodate Madame, a short passageway was to be built from the bedroom to a spacious addition designed specifically for the Esoteric Section; even more secret was a windowless octagonal room about eight feet in diameter, which she called her Occult Room. Few people saw this room, and those who did were reluctant to say much about it; apparently, it had a dark blue glass roof and concave mirrors that were supposed to concentrate light and occult influences on those seated in the room. It also had a special ventilating system that never worked properly. Finally, there was to be a small observation window in Helena's bedroom through which she could look into the Occult Room.

Although she knew exactly what she wanted and had given detailed instructions for the builders, Helena suspected the job was being botched: the ventilators to be installed near the ceiling had been entirely omitted, which would cause her to suffocate after ten minutes; she feared that fifty additional mistakes had also been made. In a black mood she urged Annie to remove the workmen from the Occult Room and give them something else to do. "Put the keys in your pocket and give it to no one, please. When I am on the spot I can direct myself . . . Please darling, do so." Feeling "most *profoundly miserable*," she told Annie that she could not begin to explain the reasons for her depression. Growing somber, she cautioned her to remember that "I believe but in *one* person in England and this is YOU."[175] Nevertheless, she constantly changed her mind about the placement of her desk and clothespress, fussing over doors opening into or out from her room, fretting that her bed might be in the direct line of some stray draft. All of this vexation could have been avoided if only she might visit Avenue Road and show people what she wanted. As it was, she was reduced to making apologetic suggestions and drawing floor plans to be passed along to Annie.

By the beginning of July, when the new headquarters was finally ready for occupancy, it had been transformed into the office complex of the British and European Sections of the Society, as well as a communal residence of Madame's most trusted workers and students. Two blocks from Regent's Park, 19 Avenue Road was a large square house covered with stucco and painted the same coffee color as many London homes; the grounds contained flower beds, lawns and several tall trees, all enclosed within a high brick wall. The ground floor was set aside for Helena's apartments, offices and for the dining room that had been refurbished as a reception room; upstairs were bedrooms, one of which Annie reserved as her own bedroom–study.

In what had once been a large garden stood the new meeting hall. It had not turned out exactly as H.P.B. had envisioned; she had wanted an Oriental-style building made of brick "to keep out the cold,"[176] with wood-lined interior, and what she got was a rather ugly, hundred-foot-long shell made of corrugated iron and sheathed inside with unpainted wood. The sloping ceiling, designed by Theosophist R. A. Machel had been painted with intricate blue designs symbolizing the six great religions of the world and the twelve signs of the zodiac. At the south end of the hall was a low platform for speakers, behind which flashed a large mirror bearing the six-pointed Theosophical star and other occult emblems. On the second floor were sixteen bedrooms for the staff, eight large and eight small. If it was not so beautiful as H.P.B. had hoped, at least the new hall was functional.

As the time approached to vacate the old house, Madame began to feel increasingly morose, and this mood rubbed off on those around her. Speaking for herself, Countess Wachtmeister remembered the move as "a sore upset," and the amount of papers and books Madame had accumulated over the past three years as "quite appalling."[177] Beyond that, both she and H.P.B. sadly realized that the new place was Annie's house rather than Madame's, and they were profoundly conscious that a happy phase of their lives was drawing to a close. On the day before the transfer, a lovely warm afternoon, Constance insisted on taking Helena for an outing in Hyde Park. Throughout the carriage ride, H.P.B. grew more and more upset and when she returned to the house seemed to be in a highly excitable state. Alice Cleather, who was sitting in the drawing room with Isabel Cooper-Oakley, sensed that what first appeared to be anger was actually "a passion of grief."[178] Helena paced the room with tears sliding down her cheeks, muttering in a sing-song voice, "Not a Soul among them—not *one!*" which Alice interpreted as compassion and pity for the thousands of park-goers who had been born too soon in human form.

The next day when Helena arrived at her new home, her mood continued to be gloomy, because as she entered the house she was heard to remark, "I shall not live long in this house—it does not bear my lucky number seven." And she added very quietly, "I shall leave here only to be cremated."[179]

On July 3 when the new headquarters was officially opened to the public, H.P.B. attended the dedication ceremony. She was still clinging to her depression. An armchair had been set up for her near the platform "and I sat as if enthroned." Still, she was "hardly able to keep myself together, so ill was I," and Dr. Mennell hovered nearby in case she should feel faint. An estimated 250 people jammed the hall, fifty over capacity, while many more watched the proceedings through the windows; others had to be turned away. The press had various comments to make on the event; the *Vanity Fair* reporter described the audience as mainly "human curiosities" and the *Star* provided more specific details on stern-faced young women with short hair and the suspicion of a mustache, and haggard young men with abundant locks and colorful neckties. While none of the reporters noticed Mrs. Edward Benson, wife of the Archbishop of Canterbury sitting in the front row, Helena spotted her at once. "Imagine my astonishment,"[180] she later reported to Vera. "What are we coming to!"

Perhaps the startling sight of Mrs. Benson aroused her, for during the rest of the dedication, H.P.B. pepped up and listened to the speeches with great pleasure. As president of the Blavatsky Lodge, Annie delivered one of her eloquent speeches, after which she turned over the podium to Alfred Sinnett, president of the London Lodge, who gave an enthusiastic address on the future of Theosophy. Next came short speeches by Bertram Keightley and a Mrs. Woolf, who represented the American Section, then Mrs. Besant officially threw open the hall and the ceremony ended. H.P.B., as always, did not speak, but no doubt every eye in the hall was on her at one time or another.

This was the first time Helena had seen Sinnett in nearly two years for there had been, in his words, "a complete extinction of our former intimate relations."[181] Occasionally when a member of the rival group would stray into H.P.B.'s camp, she did not give the person a welcome that would encourage a second visit. The previous year, after five years in Ceylon, Charles W. Leadbeater had returned to London and came to pay his respects to the Madame— once. Helena had almost forgotten the existence of the bearded curate whom she had carried off to India and left there in 1884. Not only had he done anything he was told, from sweeping floors to clerical work, but he had offered no protest when Olcott had shuffled him off to Ceylon for Theosophical field work and supervision of the Society-sponsored schools for Buddhist children. Indeed not a meow had been heard from him until 1889 when, understandably, he grew restless and began to write Sinnett that he had developed psychic powers by which he communicated regularly with the Mahatmas.

Even though Sinnett professed to be in close touch with Koot Hoomi through various mediums, the truth was that none of them had proved entirely satisfactory. Cautiously perking up his ears at this news, he suggested that C.W. might like to return to England as tutor to his son Denny, and Francesca Arundale's nephew George. Leadbeater must have realized he had captured Sinnett's interest because he felt confident enough to demand a condition for his return; he wanted to bring with him a fourteen-year-old Cingalese boy, C. Jinarājadāsa, whom he described as his protégé, but who, as he would later confide to Annie, was actually his reincarnated younger brother Gerald, who had been murdered by bandits in South America in 1862. It was rumored that Leadbeater practically kidnapped the boy, whose father had pursued him to the steamer, took him home at gun point, then relented and allowed him to sail. Although Jinarājadāsa himself described the story as ridiculous and implausible, the rumor persisted.

In London, Leadbeater stayed at the Sinnetts', which was only a ten-minute walk from 17 Lansdowne Road, and one day he took Jinarājadāsa to call on Madame Blavatsky. Looking back forty years later, Jinarājadāsa would retain a vague impression of her as "a large lady in a large chair"[182] who ignored him. After that visit, Leadbeater associated exclusively with the London Lodge where Sinnett praised his "wonderful clairvoyant faculties"[183] and appointed him secretary. Later, after Miss Arundale learned of his reputation with young boys and removed George from his care, Sinnett found him a position in the London office of the *Pioneer*. No doubt this last scandal, as

office. Propping herself against her desk, she asked that the armchair be swiveled around and a card table set up so that she could "make a patience." It was, Mead thought, "a last and supreme effort of will, for she was so weak that she could hardly speak or hold up her head."[213] When Mennell arrived at five, he was surprised to find her sitting up and praised her courage.

H.P.B. whispered, "I do my best, Doctor,"[214] but to utter even those few words was a strain. She handed him a cigarette that she had managed, with difficulty, to roll for him.

That evening, Mennell brought in his partner, a Dr. Miller, for consultation, and afterward the two physicians told Laura and Isabel that Madame's condition was very serious; they advised a tablespoonful of brandy every two hours, the quantity to be increased if necessary. In spite of Helena's aversion to alcohol, she began sipping the brandy at once and found that it seemed to alleviate her congestion, at least for a while. That night Laura and a professional nurse watched over Helena, who was unable to sleep. There was no position in which she could find comfort and finally, seated in a chair and propped with pillows, she managed to doze off about 4 A.M. By then the cough had almost stopped, due to her exhaustion.

On the morning of Friday, May 8, Dr. Mennell came by about nine and appeared pleased with Madame's progress; the brandy seemed to be having a good effect and her pulse was stronger. Believing there was no cause for immediate alarm, he advised Laura to get a few hours' rest and told Isabel that she could leave to attend to her businesses. Two hours later, though, Claude Wright woke Laura to tell her there had been a turn for the worse and that H.P.B. could not live much longer. "She was sitting in her chair," Laura said, "and I knelt in front of her and asked her to try and take the stimulant; though too weak to hold the glass herself she allowed me to hold it to her lips, and she managed to swallow the contents, but after that we could only give a little nourishment in a spoon."

Very soon after, when Laura tried to moisten Helena's lips, she realized that Madame's eyes were growing dim. H.P.B. used to tap one foot when she was thinking intently "and she continued that movement almost to the moment she ceased to breathe," Laura recalled.

Claude Wright and Walter Old knelt before Helena's chair, each holding one of her hands, while Laura supported her head. Shortly after noon, her heart stopped beating. "We remained motionless for many minutes," Laura said, "and so quietly did H.P.B. pass away that we hardly knew the second she ceased to breathe; a great sense of peace filled the room, and we knelt quietly there until, first my sister, then the countess arrived."[215]

Shortly before 10 A.M. on the morning of May 11, the hearse moved quietly away from 19 Avenue Road with only three of the staff in attendance, H.P.B. having expressly forbade a cortege, and drove to Waterloo Station. Some twenty-five miles outside of London, at Woking, the coffin was transferred to another hearse for the trip to the Necropolis, where Madame would be cremated. Three months earlier the crematorium apparatus had been out of order and those who had wished to be burned, like Charles Bradlaugh, who had died in January, had to settle for burial instead. But now there was no problem.

It was a fine May day with blue skies and birds chirping, a chilling contrast to the red-brick crematorium that blended the worst features of a chapel, factory and tile-kiln. The hundred or so persons who gathered to pay their last respects to Helena Petrovna Blavatsky congregated in the mortuary chapel; beyond, through heavy oak folding doors, they could see an inner chamber, where an immense iron object resembling a locomotive boiler stood embedded in masonry. When some of the more curious mourners crowded into the furnace chamber, an attendant opened a door at one end and everyone took turns peeping in, but most gave no more than a quick glance before turning away with a shudder.

At the sound of the hearse on the gravel outside, people uncovered their heads and watched as the flower-laden coffin was borne into the chapel and laid on an oak trestle; then George Mead stepped forward to read a brief address that had been composed by the Headquarters staff. Finally the door to the cremation room creaked open and four men, who looked like stokers or butchers to eyewitnesses, advanced toward the coffin in a businesslike manner, lifted both coffin and trestle, and carried them inside. Four Theosophists followed this procession to the furnace but returned a moment later. Then the oak doors slammed and were bolted with a final thud like the fall of some macabre portcullis.

H.P.B.'s ashes were placed in an urn and brought back to her bedroom. Later they were divided into three portions: that destined for India was carried to Adyar by Henry Olcott and buried under a statue that he erected to her memory in the Hall. A second portion was taken to New York by William Judge and today is in the keeping of the Theosophical Society at Pasadena, California. The third, kept in London for a time, was eventually removed to India by Annie Besant and dropped into the Ganges.

Epitaph

Madame Blavatsky's death was front-page news in England and the United States. The *Pall Mall Gazette,* for instance, headed its rather satirical obituary "The Prophetess of the Buried Tea-Cup," but nevertheless admitted that she had been "one of the most remarkable women of our generation," a person sincerely "possessed" by the ideas she had successfully inculcated in her not unintelligent followers.

Although most New York papers took the sensational angle and rehashed the fraud charges, the *Tribune* said that while few women of the nineteenth century had been more persistently maligned, "there are abundant indications that her lifework will vindicate itself, that it will endure and that it will operate for good." No one in the present generation, it thought, "has done more toward opening the long sealed treasures of Eastern thought, wisdom and philosophy." The *Religio -Philosophical Journal* found it hard to believe that the announcement of H.P.B.'s death was not one of her schemes for attracting attention. "As a moral monstrosity she stands without peer among her sex in this century. The specious fake which she originated to gratify her love of deception and ambition, and to cover her real sins, has ended with her death."

That was wishful thinking. There was no question of the Society folding at H.P.B.'s death because she had taken care to ensure its continuation with Annie Besant. What was expected to end, however, were the messages from the Mahatmas. Both they and Madame had announced that when she was gone, there would be no more communications. These statements had been interpreted in two ways: by Theosophists to mean that when the Masters' messenger died, they intended using no other to receive their messages; and by non-Theosophists to reflect the opinion that since Madame herself had written the letters, they would automatically cease.

So it was a matter of some wonder when, four months after Helena's death, Annie Besant electrified a sold-out lecture audience at the Hall of Science by casually remarking that if Madame Blavatsky had been a fraud, so was she herself. "I tell you," she went on, "that since Mdme. Blavatsky left I have had letters in the same handwriting as the letters which she received. Unless you think dead persons can write, surely that is a remarkable feat. You are surprised; I do not ask you to believe me, but I tell you it is so."

The news reverberated around the world. Mostly the reaction consisted of jeers, satires, and speculation that Annie was deliberately trying to trigger a posthumous Blavatsky boom. More open-minded people raised the question of whether the Society for Psychical Research had possibly done Madame an injustice; and in any case they thought that Mrs. Besant should be given a chance to explain herself. Newspaper reporters descended on Avenue Road to quiz her for details on the controversial letters. Was this a case of postal communication from the world beyond, or had they arrived by ordinary mail? No, Annie replied, they had come by paranormal means, either falling from the ceiling or appearing suddenly in unexpected places when no other person was in sight. She refused to exhibit the letters to reporters nor, as she was urged, would she submit them to handwriting experts because, she said sharply, the purpose of Theosophy was not to play up the supernatural but to inaugurate a movement of international brotherhood. However, Isabel Cooper-Oakley was not quite so righteous because she wrote to several newspapers swearing that she had examined the letters; they were written in red or blue crayon on rice paper and the handwriting corresponded exactly with that in the communications H.P.B. had received from the Masters.

The furor went on for several months: scores of letters were printed daily in the papers; attendance at the Blavatsky Lodge skyrocketed, as did that at Annie's public lectures; the Theosophical Press Bureau was deluged with hundreds of letters a day and could barely keep up with the avalanche of clippings waiting to be filed; Mabel Collins' most current novel, *Morial the Mahatma,* was being serialized in the magazine *Short Cuts*; a stylish hatter announced its new Mahatma hat for only three shillings, eleven pence. Among smart society people, the new trendy greeting was to ask one's friends, "How's your karma today?"

Once again, however, the Theosophical miracles proved nothing of the kind; in this case, they were only part of a bitter struggle for power. Before H.P.B.'s death she had verbally invested Mrs. Besant with control of the Esoteric Section and had also informed William Judge that Annie would be "my successor when I shall be called to leave you." As soon as news of her passing reached Judge, he cabled Annie: "Do nothing till I arrive" and took the next steamer for England; he proposed that the two of them share the Esoteric leadership, he in America and she in Europe. It was Judge who discovered Madame's supply of rice paper and crayons, as well as the brass seal of the Mahatmas, and it was he who slipped a note into Annie's drawer with the words, "Judge's plan is right." She accepted the message as genuine and the division of jurisdiction was made: the Mahatma messages continued.

Two years later, a number of Theosophists, Mrs. Besant included, were beginning to question the genuineness of the letters and some went so far as to speculate that they did not come from Tibet at all but had been written by Judge. Admitted Annie: "When I publicly said that I had received, after H.P.B.'s death, letters in the writing H. P. Blavatsky had been accused of forging, I referred to letters given to me by Mr. Judge, and, as they were in the well-known script, I never dreamed of challenging their source. I know now that they were not written or precipitated by the Master, and also that they were done by Mr. Judge."

When his accusers asked for proof that the Mahatma letters were genuine, Judge refused to cooperate but, writing to a friend, he sniffed: "Proofs. Proofs be damned. What proof did they ever get from H.P.B.? None." In 1894, a Judicial Committee was appointed to look into the alleged fraud, but Judge claimed that the Committee had no right to make an inquiry because it involved the question of whether or not the Masters existed. In the end, the Committee upheld him on that point and matters reached an impasse. In November of that year, Judge announced that he had received orders from the Masters insisting Mrs. Besant be removed as European head of the Esoteric Section because she was under the influence of "Dark Powers of evil"; instead the Masters had appointed him as the sole head. Most European Theosophists laughed at Judge, while most of the Americans supported him. The situation was resolved on April 28, 1895, when three-quarters of the American branches seceded from the parent Society and formed a new organization called "The Theosophical Society in America," electing Judge as its lifetime president. Over the next several years, there was further splintering of the American Society.

William Judge died in 1896, Henry Olcott in 1907. During the last months of Olcott's life, his thinking became increasingly muddled; in his final illness he would leap out of bed and fall to his knees, claiming that K.H. and M. were in the room. His death left Annie Besant as the acknowledged head of the Society. Soon after, she made her permanent home at Adyar and became part of the destiny of India.

It seemed the Society's karma to suffer periodic scandals. After H.P.B.'s death, Annie Besant came to depend greatly on Charles Leadbeater and made him assistant secretary of the European Section, after which he achieved a solid reputation as a clairvoyant, writer, speaker and teacher. In the early years of the twentieth century, he made long lecture tours of the United States, Canada and Australia, always accompanied by several young boys. The growing gossip about him was indignantly denied by Annie Besant, until, in 1906, two of his protégés told their shocked parents that Leadbeater had encouraged them to masturbate. A type-written note in cipher was found on the floor of a Toronto apartment where he had stayed with one of the boys and was said to have been written by Leadbeater. Decoded, it read: "Glad sensation is so pleasant. Thousand kisses, darling."

Leadbeater denied having written the incriminating note, but he did not deny having advocated masturbation. He maintained that when celibacy was impossible and marriage out of the question, masturbation was a lesser evil than consorting with prostitutes. This view was fiercely condemned by most Theosophists, and, when the Society put him on trial, he accounted for his sexual philosophy by saying that in a former incarnation he had been an ancient Greek. He was asked to resign. When made public, this scandal shook the Society to its foundations; three years later, however, Annie Besant took him back into her advisory circle and he was invited to rejoin the Society by a nearly unanimous vote of the general secretaries.

None of this dimmed Annie's personal prestige; indeed it increased with the years, particularly in India, where she attracted some of the country's most outstanding minds. Thirteen-year-old Jawaharlal Nehru joined the Society after hearing her lecture at Allahabad and was initiated by Annie herself. He would always retain warm admiration for her and call her "the most magnificent lady" he had ever met, but the ideas of Indian nationalism soon drove Theosophy from his head. Politically oriented herself, she became president of the Indian National Congress and was once imprisoned briefly by her own countrymen for her activities on behalf of Indian independence. With the rise of Mohandas Gandhi, her influence in the Indian Home Rule movement began to wane and it was then she confined herself to Theosophy. Becoming more mystical, she instituted rites and rituals and adopted flowing white robes as her everyday dress.

In 1909 Annie took as her protégé a young Hindu boy, Jiddu Krishnamurti, and before long she was hailing him as the avatar of the New Messiah who would regenerate the world. It was the Mahatmas themselves, she said, who had warned her of the coming of the World Teacher and now she believed that she had found him. The care and education of both Jiddu and his brother Nitya were entrusted to Charles Leadbeater, despite the fact that the boys' father brought an unsuccessful suit for the custody of his sons. Mrs. Besant, convinced that the voice of Jesus spoke through Krishnamurti, announced to the Associated Press that "the Divine Spirit has descended once more on a man, Krishnamurti, one who in his life is literally perfect . . . The World Teacher is here."

In the 1920s, Mahatmas Koot Hoomi and Morya were still very much alive in the minds of Theosophists; their messages were received by Leadbeater, Francesca Arundale's nephew George and a few others who claimed to be communicating clairvoyantly on the astral plane. Many of these messages contained directives for Krishnamurti, and once Master K.H. was said to have appeared in astral form to Nitya, with the message that Krishnaji was to develop a larger vocabulary.

As Annie grew older, she offered her protégé reverence and humility in such an ostentatious manner that she would insist upon sitting on the floor at his feet during public events. Nevertheless, by 1926, it was clear that the Coming was going wrong. Krishnamurti seemed to be moving away from the role written for him; there were occasions when he was heard to speak as if he did not believe in the Masters. Three years later he severed himself from the Theosophical Society and repudiated all claims to Messiahship, although he has continued his career as a spiritual teacher. It had never occurred to Annie that the World Teacher might disown the organization that had proclaimed him, or that the Masters could have been wrong.

In her eighties, she was visibly weary and there were rumors among her intimates of her senility, but to the world at large she remained one of the most remarkable women of the age. The New York *Times* placed her in the company of Madame Curie, Jane Addams and Anna Pavlova; a London paper called her one of the most unique women of all time, to be ranked with the Duchess of Marlborough and Elizabeth Barrett Browning. She died at Adyar on September 20, 1933, age eighty-six, after five days of semi-consciousness in which she refused to eat or drink water. Her body, clad in white silk, was cremated on a pyre of sandalwood.

To the last she believed that she had kept faith with H.P.B.'s message, but the fact was that she had not; along with Leadbeater, Arundale and others, she gradually betrayed the original vision by enveloping Theosophy in a religious atmosphere that its founder would have considered odious. Helena's sublime aims of brotherhood were neglected in expectation of the Messiah, her Esoteric Buddhism watered down and relegated to the background in favor of an Esoteric Christianity. Finally a full circle was made when Leadbeater and Arundale declared themselves bishops and, under the name of the Liberal Catholic Church, instituted candles, High Mass and vestments, and labored to build up exactly that which H.P.B. had tried to destroy.

The Theosophical Society today continues to thrive in sixty countries. There are approximately forty thousand members worldwide, with some fifty-five hundred in the United States. The international headquarters, still at Adyar, is now a beautiful estate of two hundred sixty-six acres along the banks of the Adyar River, and the Adyar Library is world famous for its unique collection of Oriental literature.

Each year, Theosophists commemorate the anniversary of H.P.B.'s death on May 8, which they call White Lotus Day.

Appendix A: The Question of H.P.B.'s Psi Faculties

H.P.B. is associated with a wide range of paranormal phenomena, some of which was confirmed by witnesses. Physical phenomena she is said to have produced include spirit photography, levitation of objects, raps, apports, poltergeists, materializations called "ectoplasm," and out-of-body experiences. In the category of mental phenomena, Madame Blavatsky claims to have had psi faculties for telepathy, clairvoyance, clairaudience, clairsentience (the sensing of unseen presences), and mediumistic communications.

Whether or not H.P.B. possessed all or some of these capabilities, it is necessary to examine the evidence of such phenomena because they are as controversial today as they were during the past century. Few parapsychologists are convinced about the reality of most of the physical phenomena that flourished in H.P.B.'s time. Such things as ectoplasm, apports, levitation and psychic photography are regarded as doubtful, firstly because almost every physical medium of the nineteenth century is known to have cheated on occasion, thus casting doubt on the genuineness of all the other phenomena. Secondly, very few agreed to scientific testing under controlled conditions. It is ironic, and perhaps to be expected, that today when the techniques for detecting fraud have advanced enormously, physical mediums have become extremely rare. Just about the only physical phenomena for which there is some evidence would be "poltergeists," now termed Recurrent Spontaneous Psychokinesis, or RSPK.

In recent years the paranormal phenomena receiving the most attention from both parapsychologists and the general public are those falling into the category of mental phenomena. The widely held assumption is that certain persons do have the psi faculty (General Extrasensory Perception). Recently, complicated machinery and procedures have been devised to determine the existence of telepathy, clairvoyance, precognition and retrocognition. A type of mental phenomena currently under investigation, one which directly relates to H. P. Blavatsky, involves mediumistic data. The term medium, first used in a religious context by Spiritualists to denote a person who could communicate with the surviving spirits of the dead, is no longer in vogue. Parapsychologists prefer "sensitive" or "psychic," terms that do not imply acceptance of survival after death.

One kind of sensitive is the "trance medium," who is able to put herself (the majority of psychics are women) into a self-induced hypnotic state that may range from a very light dissociation to an extremely deep one. While in this altered state of consciousness, another personality appears to control the psychic's body and voice, either by involuntary ("automatic") writing or by "direct voice," that is, directly controlling the sensitive's entire body. It is a matter of debate whether a psychic's controlling personality is in fact the discarnate it often claims to be, or merely a secondary personality, or a dream-creation existing only when the psychic is entranced. The dream-creation is consolidated by repetition into personalities consistent enough to play their assigned roles.

More common today is a second type of sensitive, the "clairvoyant medium," who claims to psychically see, hear and sense unseen presences while in her normal state of consciousness.

From a distance of one hundred years, the evidence for H.P.B.'s psi faculty for physical phenomena appears to be extremely shaky and in some instances completely non-existent. For that matter, much of the evidence points to fraud. On at least two occasions she seems to have hired individuals to impersonate her Mahatmic entities. The most that can be said for her in these instances is that if she was not cheating, she had the bad luck to look as though she were.

On the other hand, I do not believe there can be much doubt that she was a genuine sensitive. Members of her family attested to the fact that since early childhood she claimed to see and hear invisible entities, and later as an adult H.P.B. herself supplied detailed accounts of hypnotic states in which other personalities seemed to be colonizing her body. Apparently it was not until her forties that she began attaching names to these unseen personages, whom she called Masters or Mahatmas, feeling that they were supplying her with information. Unlike other sensitives, she rejected the idea that they might be spirits of the dead, nor would she have accepted the more recent theory that they might be secondary personalities of hers. Developing her own interpretation of these experiences, she preferred to believe that the communicating entities were living men who had chosen her as a channel through which they could feed messages to the world. She believed that they spoke to her telepathically or visited her in their astral and physical bodies. Theoretically, it is possible that she was tapping some cosmic reservoir of memories or tuning into the minds and/or memories of living persons, but whether these people were, as she thought, supermen living in Tibet or simply symbolic forms of dramatization is an unanswerable question.

In psychical research, the principal test for mediumistic data is whether or not it can be verified. Is the knowledge being presented available in the sensitive's own memory or the memory of some other persons, or can it be found in publications, extant documents or objects? In the case of H.P.B., virtually all her data was available in Eastern scripture or from occult writings. Even though she synthesized the material in a fresh, provocative way, the fact remains that it predated her psychic experience. At the same time, it should be kept in mind that, while she was not a formal scholar, she did happen to be a voracious reader with a remarkably retentive memory. Analyses of her two major works, supposedly written with the aid of her Mahatmas, reveal nothing that was not already known—there are no unexpected discoveries, no startling revelations, and in fact the data could be found in books readily available to anyone willing to take the time and effort to seek it.

In spite of the fact that the first full-scale investigation conducted by the Society for Psychical Research was an inquiry into Theosophical phenomena, Madame Blavatsky's psi faculties were never tested. It is unclear whether the S.P.R. ever requested her to undergo testing, but it appears that they did not. If they had suggested the idea, she would not have cooperated because she refused to submit to even the simplest test when repeatedly urged to do so by some of her followers. The fact that her phenomena occurred spontaneously and unexpectedly lends some validity to the charge that they were consciously prearranged to achieve certain effects. Without exception, the psychical researchers of the past century have given H.P.B. short shrift, either ignoring her completely or dismissing her as did Frederic Myers when he called her an imposter, or William James, who in personal letters rather uncomplimentarily termed her a "jade."

On balance, there is Madame Blavatsky's own word for the genuineness of her psi feats, and the testimony of many individuals who swore they had witnessed them, opposed by the conclusions of the Society for Psychical Research, which investigated the Theosophical Society but did not test H.P.B. (nor did its investigator personally witness a single phenomenon of hers). My own guess is that unusually strong hypnotic powers may account for some of her phenomena, that she did indeed possess genuine psi powers to a degree but they fell far short of the miraculous productions with which some have credited her.

Appendix B: The Mahatma Papers

The question arises as to just how Alfred Sinnett, and later others, managed to carry on a correspondence with individuals they had never seen and whose precise whereabouts remained unknown. Supposedly the letters from Koot Hoomi and Morya were not written by hand, in fact were not written at all, but were produced by a paranormal process called "precipitation." It is interesting to note that Sinnett failed to notice anything unusual about them until K.H. pointed out, "Bear in mind that these my letters are not written but *impressed* or precipitated, and then mistakes corrected"; and then of course Sinnett asked how this particular process worked. K.H.'s explanation did not provide a great deal of enlightenment:

> I have to *think* it over, to photograph every word and sentence carefully in my brain, before it can be repeated by "precipitation." As the fixing on chemically prepared surfaces of the images formed by the camera requires a previous arrangement within the focus of the object to be represented, for otherwise—as often found in bad photographs—the legs of the sitter might appear out of all proportion with the head, and so on; so we have to arrange our sentences, and impress every letter to appear on paper, in our minds before it becomes fit to be read. For the present, that is *all* I can tell you. When science will have learned more about the mystery of the *lithophyl* (or lithobiblion) and how the impress of leaves comes originally to take place on stones, then I will be able to make you better understand the process. But you must know and remember one thing: we but follow and *servilely copy nature* in her works . . .

Presumably K.H. was describing telepathy; nevertheless, the fact remains that his messages did materialize as letters, and someone would have had to pick the words from his mind and transfer them to paper. These amanuenses, who served as psychic centers for the transmission of letters through space, were, K.H. explained, agents of the Brotherhood (*chelas*), of whom H.P.B. was one. According to Koot Hoomi, "Very often our letters—unless something important and secret—are written in our handwritings by our chelas." The messages would then be delivered to their destinations paranormally, as when an envelope dropped on someone's head or was found in the Adyar shrine. Or, as often happened, they would arrive by regular post.

So much for messages *from* the Mahatmas; it was also necessary for *chelas* to send letters *to* them. The general procedure was described as follows: Sinnett would write his letters by hand, place them in envelopes and either give or mail them to Madame Blavatsky, who would forward them to Tibet. One method of transmission, she said, was "to put the envelope sealed on my forehead; and then, warning the Master to be ready for the communication, have the contents reflected by my brain carried off to His perception by the *current formed by Him*." In an alternate process, she supposedly unsealed the letter,

> read it *physically* with my eyes, without understanding even the words, and *that which my eyes see* is carried off to the Master's perception and reflected in it in His own language, after which to be sure no mistake is made, I have to burn the letter with a stone I have (matches and common fire would never do), and the ashes caught by the current become more minute than atoms would be, and are *rematerialized* at any distance where the Masters may be.

Theosophical writers who have undertaken the unenviable task of making sense of the Mahatmas' methods of composition argue that the letters were not written with ordinary pen and ink: the calligraphy is actually imbedded in the paper. To non-Theosophists who have examined that portion of the correspondence in the British Library, there is not the least sign of mystery about them; they do not appear to differ from any collection of letters written a century ago. The instruments used were steel pens, red and blue pencils, and various color inks, mainly black and red, but also brown and yellow. The paper used in the early letters was glossy rice paper, commonly available in India, and later a variety of stationery in pink, yellow and blue tints.

One curious aspect of the letters is that the calligraphy varies greatly. Although much publicity was given to "the familiar K.H. hand," in truth there was no standard Koot Hoomi script. For example, in the first letter he sent to Sinnett, there were three different scripts within the text and a fourth for the signature. The first letter from Master Morya also contains several different kinds of calligraphy. For a while both K.H. and M. developed a more or less recognizable script, although in 1886 William Hubbe-Schleiden received a letter from Koot Hoomi in a totally different hand from any of his previous communications. Theosophists account for this by explaining that many *chelas* were employed to actually pen the messages. In addition to the several handwritings of K.H. and M., it should be remembered that there were other Masters who corresponded: Serapis Bey, Tuitit Bey, Hilarion, Djual Khool, and "the old Gentleman."

Superficially, none of these Mahatmic scripts seem to resemble each other, or for that matter, Madame Blavatsky's handwriting. During her lifetime two professional handwriting experts compared Mahatma letters with her admitted letters. Richard Hodgson submitted several samples to F. G. Nethercliff of the British Museum who first decided they could not have been written by Madame Blavatsky, but after being given some earlier Mahatma letters changed his mind and finally concluded that the entire bundle was her work. Two years later, suspicious Theosophists submitted specimens of Mahatmic writing to Ernst Schutze, calligraphist to the German emperor, who reported they could not have been produced by H.P.B.

Since no satisfactory conclusion can be reached on the basis of either expert's testimony, it is necessary to look elsewhere for answers. That H.P.B. was capable of writing in a variety of scripts is known from Henry Olcott's recollections that the manuscript of *Isis Unveiled* contained "three or four" calligraphies, very often two of them on one page.

Moreover, it is also a fact that she was able to reproduce the handwritings of other people, apparently quite successfully:

1. At Simla, on October 3, 1880, the day of the cup and saucer phenomenon, a judge received a membership diploma bearing Henry Olcott's signature, along with a letter in Henry's handwriting, neither of which Olcott had written.

2. In August, 1883, while H.P.B. was vacationing at Ootacamund, Forster Webster, a secretary to the British government, received a letter written in handwriting that he swore was his own.

3. On October 24, 1885, in a letter to Sinnett from Würzburg, H.P.B. penned a bit of doggerel in what she claimed was Richard Hodgson's handwriting: "In India I was a *fool*—in the West I have become a *donkey*. Theosophy alone is true—and S.P.R. is an old monkey." If she wanted to, she told Sinnett, she could forge a letter that would so closely resemble Hodgson's script that an expert could not detect the truth.

Putting together everything that is known of H.P.B.'s life, it would be illogical to assume that she did *not* write the letters from the various Masters.

Appendix C: Parallel Cases

• Catherine Elise Muller ("Helene Smith") was an unmarried woman who held a responsible job with a Geneva business firm. In 1891, after becoming interested in Spiritualism, she joined a séance circle where her mediumistic talent quickly surfaced and while in trance she unfolded memories of three previous incarnations. Claiming to have once been Marie Antoinette, she wrote in what she said was the queen's handwriting. To be sure, the script was different from her own, but it was later determined that it was not Marie Antoinette's either. Going back to the fifteenth century when she had been the Arab wife of a South Indian prince, Catherine was able to write rudimentary, ungrammatical fragments of Sanskrit and also showed considerable familiarity with the history of that period. Finally, as a former inhabitant of Mars, she described the planet's flora, fauna and intelligent beings, and wrote what she claimed was the Martian language. It was subsequently determined that her "Martian" was mainly derived from French.

Many features of the "Helene Smith" case, as studied by Swiss psychologist Theodore Flournoy, seem to parallel Madame Blavatsky's: Catherine's mediumistic trances, her sense of actually becoming her control "Leopold," whom she said penetrated her body, the changes in handwriting while she was in trance, her various mixed states of consciousness. Flournoy, distrusting a single formula for describing mediumistic states, rejected the theory of multiple personality in Catherine's case and instead suggested an interplay of factors in which telepathy worked in alliance with cryptomnesia (hidden and disguised memories). Environment, he believed, was one of the keys to Catherine, who from her earliest years had felt superior to her surroundings. Flournoy explained her visions as escapes from, and compensation for, her commonplace daily life.

• In 1913, Pearl Lenore Curran, a thirty-one-year-old St. Louis housewife, suddenly began to "bring through" on the Ouija Board the spirit of "Patience Worth," who claimed to have lived in the seventeenth century. Through Mrs. Curran, "Patience" produced remarkable poems, novels, and parables and could switch at will from a style ninety percent Anglo-Saxon to one as modern as Jane Eyre; she also possessed extensive historical and Biblical knowledge, particularly of Palestine and Rome, that would have taken years of study to acquire. "Patience" seemed to be a genius, but Pearl Curran was neither scholar nor writer, not even much of a reader. More significantly, she was not a medium.

According to psychologist Walter Franklin Prince, who spent ten months studying Mrs. Curran, she was an intelligent, vivacious woman who had never manifested any talent for literature, philology, history or deep philosophical thinking prior to the emergence of "Patience Worth." Neither did she possess an extraordinary memory, so that he was forced to rule out the possibility of her having spent years in libraries indulging a passion for antiquities and philology before the accumulated knowledge suddenly burst forth when she was thirty-one. Because she failed to display the common symptoms of hysteria, such as childhood illnesses, somnambulism, nervousness, sensory hallucinations, Prince rejected the theory that a self-conscious secondary personality with "Patience's" knowledge and aptitudes had formed within Mrs. Curran's conscious mind.

Dr. Prince concluded: "Either our concept of what we call the subconscious must be radically altered, so as to include potencies of which we hitherto have had no knowledge, or else some cause operating through but not originating in the subconscious of Mrs. Curran must be acknowledged." The "Patience Worth" case remains as puzzling today as when Dr. Prince studied it in 1927.

• Alice Bailey was born into an upper-class English family in 1880; her mother died when she was six, her father two years later, and she was raised by her grandparents. An ill-adjusted and headstrong child whose heroine was Joan of Arc, she suffered a miserable adolescence ("nobody loved me and I knew I had a hateful disposition"). One Sunday morning when she was fifteen and sitting alone in the drawing room reading, the door opened and in walked a tall man wearing European clothes and a turban. He told her that if she could achieve self-control, he had an important work for her to do someday. In 1918, then living in Southern California, Alice joined the Theosophical Society and was admitted into the Esoteric Section. The first time she entered the Shrine Room at the Krotona center in Hollywood, she saw a portrait of her visitor and was told that he was Master Koot Hoomi. The following year, sitting on a hill near her home, she was startled to hear a strain of music, then a voice saying, "There are some books which it is desired should be written for the public. You can write them. Will you do so?" Alice called this entity "The Tibetan" (subsequently identified as Master Djual Khool).

As a result of her thirty-year collaboration with Djual Khool, Alice Bailey received clairaudiently, and later telepathically, a virtual library of metaphysical and spiritualistic writings. She insisted that she did not do automatic writing, which she believed dangerous. Rather, "I simply listen and take down the words that I hear and register the thoughts which are dropped one by one into my brain." She rejected, too, the idea that the writings came from her subconscious and when she learned that Carl Jung took the position that "The Tibetan" was her personified higher self and Alice the lower self, she replied: "Some of these days (if I ever have the pleasure of meeting him) I will ask him how my personified higher self can send me parcels all the way from India, for that is what He has done."

Alice Bailey did not long remain a Theosophist; in 1923 she established her own organization, the Arcane School.

Notes and Sources

Documentation is supplied for all quotations and for items that might be considered debatable or controversial. Otherwise, I have given references only when they seem important or useful to the reader, who may wish to further pursue the life of Madame Blavatsky.

CW   Collected Writings
HPBSP   H.P.B. Speaks
INC   Incidents in the Life of Madame Blavatsky
LBS   The Letters of H. P. Blavatsky to A. P. Sinnett
LMW   Letters from the Masters of Wisdom
ML   The Mahatma Letters to A. P. Sinnett
ODL   Old Diary Leaves

RUSSIA

1. CW, vol. 1, p. 401.
2. Ibid., p. xxvii–lxxii; HPBSP, vol. 2, p. 62.
3. CW, vol. 1, p. xxviii.
4. Haxthausen, *The Russian Empire,* p. 417.
5. Extracts from *The World's Judgment,* quoted in *Theosophical Forum,* August, 1948.
6. H.P.B. to A. N. Aksakov, December 13, 1874, Solovyov, p. 234.
7. CW, vol. 1, p. xxix.
8. Bergamini, p. 310.
9. Jerrmann, p. 116.
10. July 31, Old Style. According to the Gregorian calendar, in use almost everywhere in the world, the date would have been August 12. Russia used the Julian calendar until 1918. In the nineteenth century, it was twelve days behind the Gregorian calendar.
11. INC, p. 13.
12. Extracts from *The World's Judgment,* quoted in *Theosophical Forum,* August, 1948.
13. She was a cousin of Peter von Hahn's. INC, p. 75.
14. LBS, pp. 159–160.
15. INC, p. 19.
16. Ibid., p. 16.
17. Ibid.
18. Description of Astrakhan: Hommaire de Hell, pp. 165–185; Blavatsky, *Isis Unveiled,* vol. 2, p. 603 footnote.
19. H.P.B. to P. C. Mitra, April 10, 1878, *Theosophist,* August, 1931.
20. INC, p. 19.
21. LBS, p. 150.
22. H.P.B. to Henry Olcott, January 6, 1886, *Theosophist,* August, 1931.
23. Neff, p. 36, quoting Nadyezhda Fadeyev.

24. LBS, p. 150.
25. Billington, p. 352.
26. *Theosophical Forum,* August, 1948.
27. Extracts from *The Ideal,* quoted in *Theosophical Forum,* August, 1948.
28. Ibid.
29. Neff, p. 17.
30. ODL, vol. 3, p. 9.
31. INC. p. 29.
32. *Lucifer,* November, 1894.
33. INC, p. 22.
34. Medium Eileen Garrett, under hypnosis, was able to recall the names of her three invisible playmates; she also remembered that the two girls had died before she was born, but she had seen photographs of them in an album, and that the boy was a neighbor who had drowned.
35. INC, p. 23.
36. Vera Zhelihovsky to V. S. Solovyov, quoted in Solovyov, p. 193.
37. INC, p. 24.
38. INC, pp. 27–28.
39. Besant, *HPB and the Masters of Wisdom,* p. 7.
40. Witte, p. 8.
41. Besant, *HPB and the Masters of Wisdom,* p. 7.
42. Hume, pp. 86–92; Neff, pp. 18–22.
43. Garrett, *My Life as a Search,* p. 133, and *Many Voices,* p. 94.
44. INC, p. 34.
45. LBS, p. 150.
46. According to Boris de Zirkoff, editor of H.P.B.'s *Collected Writings* and her only known living relative, "There is no confirmation of any such trip at that time." CW, vol. 1, p. xxxiii.

47. ODL, vol. 2, p. 458.
48. INC, p. 71.
49. Neff, p. 19.
50. Ibid., p. 18. According to H.P.B., this took place in 1843, but her dating seems to be in error. The only time she lived in Katherine Witte's house was 1846–1847.
51. Description of Tiflis: Haxthausen, *Transcaucasia,* pp. 45, 94–95.
52. Neff, pp. 20–21.
53. INC, p. 23.
54. H.P.B. to Alexander Dondoukoff-Korsakoff, March 1, 1882, HPBSP, vol. 2, pp. 62–63.
55. Neff, p. 32.
56. Ibid.
57. H.P.B. to Alexander Dondoukoff-Korsakoff, December 5, 1881, HPBSP, vol. 2, p. 28.
58. H.P.B. to Alexander Dondoukoff-Korsakoff, March 1, 1882, ibid., p. 62.
59. Ibid., pp. 50, 102, 123, 128.
60. Ibid., p. 113.
61. General P. S. Nikolaeff, *Reminiscences of Prince A. T. Bariatinsky,* quoted in INC, p. 110.
62. H.P.B. to Alexander Dondoukoff-Korsakoff, March 1, 1882, HPBSP, vol. 2, p. 61.
63. Ibid., p. 60.
64. The alchemists' philosophers' stone was not a means of making gold, but a symbol of hidden knowledge—the secrets of nature and possession of perfect wisdom.
65. Ibid., p. 62.
66. *Theosophical Forum,* July, 1913.
67. New York *Daily Graphic,* November 27, 1874.
68. INC, p. 40.

69. Ibid.
70. H.P.B. to Alexander Dondou-koff-Korsakoff, March 1, 1882, HPBSP, vol. 2, p. 63.
71. *Lucifer,* November, 1894.
72. LBS, p. 157.
73. Ibid., p. 214.
74. *Lucifer,* November, 1894.
75. H.P.B. always insisted that the marriage took place in 1848, when she was sixteen. But according to Vera's diary, it happened immediately after their cousin Sergei Witte was born, and this date was June 17/29 1849.
76. INC, p. 40.
77. Ibid.
78. Ibid.
79. Ibid., p. 41.
80. H.P.B. to Alexander Dondou-koff-Korsakoff, March 1, 1882, HPBSP, vol. 2, p. 63.
81. Ibid., p. 64.
82. H.P.B. to V. S. Solovyov, circa February, 1886, Solovyov, p. 177.

THE VEILED YEARS

1. H.P.B. to Alexander Dondou-koff-Korsakoff, March 1, 1882, HPBSP, vol. 2, p. 64.
2. H.P.B. to Alexander Dondou-koff-Korsakoff, August 7, 1883, HPBSP, vol. 2, p. 116.
3. Ibid.
4. INC, p. 43.
5. Ibid., pp. 44–45.
6. H.P.B. to Alexander Dondou-koff-Korsakoff, March 1, 1882, HPBSP, vol. 2, p. 66.
7. LBS, p. 154.
8. Ibid., p. 151.
9. Rawson, *Frank Leslie's Popular Monthly,* February 1892.
10. LBS, p. 151.
11. Rawson, *Frank Leslie's Popular Monthly,* February, 1892.
12. Ibid.
13. Wolff, *The Two Worlds,* December 11, 1891.
14. Rawson, *Frank Leslie's Popular Monthly,* February 1892.
15. Ibid. Rawson mistakenly identifies the countess as "Kazenoff."
16. INC, p. 44.
17. H.P.B. to Alexander Dondou-koff-Korsakoff, March 1, 1882, HPBSP, vol. 2, p. 66.
18. Quoted in Hart, p. 111.
19. CW, vol. 1, p. 4. H.P.B. told Sinnett (INC, pp. 46–48) that in July, 1851, she went to Canada for the purpose of meeting Red Indians and learning the secrets of their medicine men, but that they stole her boots. From there she reported traveling to Missouri, Louisiana, Texas and Mexico. However, she told Countess Wachtmeister that the seaside sketch was made on August 12, 1851, "the day I saw my blessed Masters." (Wachtmeister, p. 45). In my opinion, the sketchbook definitely places her in London during the summer of 1851.
20. Bulwer-Lytton: Liljegren, p. 28. The author believes that H.P.B. had a schoolgirl crush on Bulwer-Lytton. It is known that the novelist visited Ramsgate in the summer of

1851. Liljegren theorizes that Helena saw him from a distance.
21. CW, vol. 1, p. 5.
22. Ibid.
23. H.P.B. to Alexander Dondou-koff-Korsakoff, March 1, 1882, HPBSP, vol. 2, p. 66.
24. Gauld, p. 67.
25. In 1874, H.P.B. told a reporter that the Princess willed her forty thousand dollars and would have left more "if I had been with her before her death" (New York Graphic, November 9, 1874).
26. INC, p. 44.
27. Ibid., pp. 46–55.
28. Ibid.
29. Three persons offered testimony that Theosophists accept as corroboration of H.P.B.'s claims:
1. In 1892, Anna Ballard told Henry Olcott that H.P.B. had mentioned a Tibetan trip during an interview Ballard had conducted with her in 1873 while a reporter for the New York Sun (ODL, vol. 1, p. 21).
2. On March 3, 1893, Olcott met Major-General C. Murray on a train between Calcutta and Nalhati. Murray, a former commander of the Frontier District between Nepal and Tibet, told Olcott that in 1854 or '55 a European woman had tried to cross the border but had been brought back by guards (ODL, vol. 1, p. 265).
3. In 1927, Major Cross, manager of a tea plantation belonging to the Dalai Lama, said that he had recently talked to people in northwest Tibet who remembered the visit of a white woman in 1867 (Canadian Theosophist, June, 1927).
In my opinion, none of these accounts can be accepted as reliable evidence.
30. CW, vol. 11, p. 263.
31. LBS, pp. 143–144.
32. Witte, p. 5.
33. H.P.B. to A. N. Aksakov, December 6, 1875, Solovyov, p. 268.
34. Witte, p. 6.
35. Theosophist, July, 1913.
36. De Zirkoff, p. 51.
37. H.P.B. to A. N. Aksakov, December 6, 1875, Solovyov, p. 228.
38. Witte, p. 6.
39. New York Daily Graphic, November 13, 1874.
40. Quoted in Maskelyne, p. 29.
41. Vera Zhelihovsky to Constance Wachtmeister, January 15/27, 1886, LBS, p. 274.
42. Nikifor Blavatsky to Nadyezhda Fadeyev, November 13 (O.S.), 1858, Theosophist, August, 1959.
43. Ibid.
44. INC, p. 101.
45. Lucifer, November, 1894.
46. INC, pp. 67–68.
47. Ibid., pp. 70–74.
48. Ibid., p. 75.
49. Ibid., pp. 91–102.
50. Ibid., p. 105.
51. Witte, p. 4.
52. INC, pp. 108–110.
53. Lucifer, November, 1894; INC, p. 107.
54. Witte, p. 6.
55. H.P.B. to Alexander Dondou-koff-Korsakoff, June 3, 1884,

HPBSP, vol. 2, pp. 152, 156. In her famous confession letter written to Solovyov in February, 1886, she says that she lived with Nikifor only three-and-a-half days, but that letter was composed in a state of emotional stress. In a legal petition to the General Commander-in-Chief of the Caucasus, she states the time as approximately one year, which I believe is correct.

56. Witte, p. 7.
57. General P. S. Nikolaeff, *Reminiscences of Prince A. T. Bariatinsky,* quoted in INC, p. 111.
58. Ibid., p. 112.
59. Quoted in Maskelyne, p. 29.
60. V. S. Solovyov to H.P.B., circa April, 1886, LBS, p. 207.
61. Witte, p. 7.
62. LBS, p. 144.
63. CW, vol. 1, p. 10.
64. LBS, p. 145.
65. Haxthausen, *Transcaucasia,* pp. 17–31.
66. INC, p. 114.
67. Ibid.
68. Quoted in Murphet, *When Daylight Comes,* p. 51.
69. LBS, p. 151; Bechhofer-Roberts, p. 51.
70. INC, p. 116.
71. Ibid.
72. Ibid., p. 115.
73. Ibid., p. 117.
74. *The Path,* May, 1895.
75. Passport for Yuri and H.P.B.: CW, vol. 1, p. xlvi.
76. LBS, p. 177.
77. While he denied paternity in 1862, he told Solovyov in 1886 that Yuri was his and H.P.B.'s child (LBS, p. 208).
78. Bechhofer-Roberts, pp. 51–

52.
79. H.P.B. to Alexander Dondoukoff-Korsakoff, December 5, 1881, HPBSP, vol. 2, pp. 19–20.
80. LBS, p. 151.
81. Ibid., p. 208.
82. Solovyov, p. 177.
83. INC, pp. 85, 119.
84. CW, vol. 1, pp. 11–25.
85. LBS, p. 144.
86. ODL, vol. 1, p. 9; Corson, p. 34; CW, vol. 6, p. 277.
87. Witte, p. 8.
88. H.P.B. to Alexander Dondoukoff-Korsakoff, December 5, 1881, HPBSP, vol. 2, pp. 19, 27.
89. H.P.B. to Nadyezhda Fadeyev, October 28, 1877, HPBSP, vol. 1, p. 210.
90. However, in a September 25, 1877, letter to the New York *World,* H.P.B. placed herself in Russia by saying that she had been an eyewitness to a riot that had taken place in Odessa during Easter Week, 1870 (CW, vol. 1, p. 263).
91. Witte, p. 9.
92. *London Forum,* December, 1934; Witte, p. 9.
93. Neff, p. 182.
94. LBS, pp. 189–190.
95. INC, p. 125.
96. Coulomb, pp. 3–4.
97. INC, p. 125.
98. Ibid.; Neff, p. 166.
99. Coulomb, p. 4.
100. INC, p. 125.
101. Peebles, p. 315.
102. ODL, vol. 1, pp. 20, 27–28.
103. H.P.B. to Alexander Dondoukoff-Korsakoff, December 5, 1881, HPBSP, vol. 2, p. 23.
104. Solovyov, p. 228.
105. ODL, vol. 1, pp. 28–29.

NEW YORK

1. New York *Sun*, July 28, 1873.
2. Holt, *Theosophist*, December, 1931.
3. H.P.B. to A. N. Aksakov, December 6, 1875, Solovyov, p. 267.
4. Holt, *Theosophist*, December, 1931.
5. McCabe, p. 830.
6. Wolff, *The Two Worlds*, December 11, 1891.
7. CW, vol. 1, p. 56.
8. ODL, vol. 1, p. 1.
9. Ibid., p. 2.
10. Hume, p. 132.
11. H.P.B. to Nadyezhda Fadeyev, July 19, 1877, HPBSP, vol. 1, p. 187.
12. Doyle, vol. 1, p. 254.
13. Olcott, *People from the Other World*, p. 17.
14. Ibid., p. 61.
15. ODL, vol. 1, p. 10.
16. In 1888, Margaret Fox stated publicly that she and her sister were responsible for making the rapping noises. Later, however, she repudiated her confession.

    Other individuals have revealed their methods of producing raps: beneath their skirts, women would suspend weights on elastic strings and it took only a slight movement to strike the weights against the floor. Popular methods by men involved use of fingernails, knees and shoes (Price, pp. 171–172).
17. In a letter to Caroline Corson, August 28, 1878, H.P.B. stated that he was twenty years her junior, although this may have been one of her typical exaggerations.
18. LMW, vol. 2, p. 21.
19. *Religio-Philosophical Journal*, June 13, 1874.
20. H.P.B. to Franz Hartmann, April 3, 1886, *The Path*, March, 1896.
21. ODL, vol. 1, pp. 1–7.
22. Ibid., p. 6.
23. New York *Sun*, October 29, 1874.
24. Olcott, *People from the Other World*, p. 298.
25. *Religio-Philosophical Journal*, December 12, 1874.
26. Olcott, *People from the Other World*, p. 298.
27. Neff, p. 199.
28. Olcott, *People from the Other World*, p. 303.
29. Ibid., p. 297.
30. New York *Sun*, October 29, 1874.
31. *Religio-Philosophical Journal*, December 12, 1874.
32. New York *Daily Graphic*, November 9, 1874.
33. Olcott, *People from the Other World*, p. 294.
34. Ibid., p. 360.
35. H.P.B. to Vera Zhelihovsky, circa 1874–1875, *The Path*, February, 1895. In 1886, H.P.B. rewrote this letter for inclusion in Sinnett's biography of herself. I am quoting from the original.
36. Olcott, *People from the Other World*, pp. 355–359.
37. H.P.B. to Nadyezhda Fadeyev, July 19, 1877, HPBSP, vol. 1, p. 187; H.P.B. to Franz Hartmann, April 3, 1886, *The Path*, March, 1896.

38. New York *Daily Graphic*, October 27, 1874.
39. New York *Daily Graphic*, October 30, 1874.
40. Ibid.
41. H.P.B. to A.N. Aksakov, October 28, 1874, Solovyov, pp. 225–226.
42. Michael Betanelly to Henry Olcott, October 29, 1874, Olcott, *People from the Other World*, pp. 305–306.
43. Ibid., p. 306.
44. New York *Daily Graphic*, November 9, 1874.
45. New York *Daily Graphic*, November 13, 1874.
46. ODL, vol. 1, p. 32.
47. H.P.B. to A. N. Aksakov, November 14, 1874, quoting Aksakov letter to A. J. Davis, Solovyov, pp. 227–228.
48. Ibid., pp. 228–230.
49. Ibid.
50. ODL, vol. 1, pp. 31–32.
51. Ibid., p. 55.
52. H.P.B. to A. N. Aksakov, December 13, 1874, Solovyov, p. 231.
53. *Religio-Philosophical Journal*, January 9, 1875.
54. H.P.B. to A. N. Aksakov, February 11, 1975, Solovyov, p. 239.
55. Ibid., p. 240.
56. Supreme Court, Hall of Records, New York County, Index Number GA 719-0-1.
57. Olcott, *People from the Other World*, p. 455.
58. *Religio-Philosophical Journal*, September 14, 1889.
59. H.P.B. to A. N. Aksakov, February 11, 1875, Solovyov, p. 243.
60. Ibid.
61. H.P.B. to F. J. Lippitt, June 12, 1875, HPBSP, vol. 1, p. 86.
62. H.P.B. to F. J. Lippitt, February 13, 1875, HPBSP, vol. 1, p. 6.
63. Andrew Jackson Davis's expense ledger, Archives of Edgar Cayce Foundation.
64. H.P.B. to F. J. Lippitt, March, 1875, HPBSP, vol. 1, p. 58.
65. H.P.B. to A. N. Aksakov, April 12, 1875, Solovyov, p. 250.
66. Betanelly to F. J. Lippitt, March 22, 1875, HPBSP, vol. 1, p. 59.
67. ODL, vol. 1, p. 56.
68. Ibid.
69. Ibid.
70. H.P.B. to F. J. Lippitt, April 3, 1875, HPBSP, vol. 1, p. 64.
71. Solovyov, pp. 164–165.
72. H.P.B. to A. N. Aksakov, April 12, 1875, Solovyov, p. 247.
73. HPBSP, vol. 1, p. 8.
74. H.P.B. to A.N. Aksakov, April 12, 1875, Solovyov, p. 247.
75. H.P.B. to F. J. Lippitt, June 12, 1875, HPBSP, vol. 1, p. 85.
76. ODL, vol. 1, pp. 44–45.
77. Ibid., p. 47.
78. H.P.B. to A. N. Aksakov, April 12, 1875, Solovyov, pp. 247–248.
79. H.P.B. to Olcott, May 21, 1875, HPBSP, vol. 1, p. 45.
80. ODL, vol. 1, p. 34.
81. H.P.B. to F. J. Lippitt, early April, 1875, HPBSP, vol. 1, p. 75.
82. Ibid., p. 71.
83. LMW, vol. 2, p. 11.

84. Ibid., p. 18.
85. Ibid., pp. 16–18.
86. CW, vol. 1, p. 88.
87. H.P.B. to A. N. Aksakov, May 24, 1875, Solovyov, p. 251.
88. Ibid., p. 252.
89. Ibid., p. 253.
90. H.P.B. to Henry Olcott, May 21, 1875, HPBSP, vol. 1, p. 37.
91. H.P.B. to F. J. Lippitt, June 12, 1875, HPBSP, vol. 1, pp. 80–82.
92. Ibid., p. 84.
93. Ibid., p. 91.
94. Michael Betanelly to F. J. Lippitt, June 18, 1875, HPBSP, vol. 1, p. 93.
95. LMW, vol. 2, pp. 24–25. Serapis had more to say about Helena and Michael, but the editor of the published letters saw fit to exercise censorship on the grounds that some remarks dealt with "incidents in H.P.B.'s inner life" and "none have a right to peer inquisitively into the workings of the soul."
96. Ibid., p. 26.
97. Ibid., pp. 27–29.
98. H.P.B. to Olcott, circa May–June, 1875, HPBSP, vol. 1, p. 3.
99. Ibid., pp. 3–5.
100. Louisa Andrews to Hiram Corson, December 1, 1875, Department of Manuscripts & University Archives, Cornell University Libraries.
101. LMW, vol. 2, pp. 30–33.
102. Ibid.
103. ODL, vol. 1, p. 114.
104. The Liberal Christian, September 4, 1875.
105. H.P.B. to A. N. Aksakov, July 18, 1875, Solovyov, p. 253.

106. INC, p. 146. According to Judge, the prophecy to his friend turned out exactly as predicted.
107. Lillie, p. 44–45.
108. ODL, vol. 1, p. 186.
109. Ibid., p. 202.
110. New York Tribune, August 30, 1875.
111. Ibid., September 17, 1875.
112. ODL, vol. 1, pp. 117–118.
113. Lucifer, April, 1895.
114. ODL, vol. 1, p. 132.
115. H.P.B. to A. N. Aksakov, September 20, 1875, Solovyov, p. 256.
116. Olcott to Hiram Corson, September 14, 1875, Corson, p. 24.
117. Hiram Corson to Eugene Corson, undated, Corson, p. 27.
118. H.P.B. to A. N. Aksakov, September 20, 1875, Solovyov, p. 257.
119. Hiram Corson to Eugene Corson, October 2, 1875, Corson, p. 118.
120. Corson, p. 37.
121. Olcott to H.P.B., September 25, 1875, Corson, p. 50.
122. H.P.B. to Hiram Corson, circa October–November, 1875, Corson, pp. 170–171.
123. James Robinson to Frederick W. Hinrichs, November 2, 1875, Flint, p. 128.
124. H.P.B. to A. N. Aksakov, December 6, 1875, Solovyov, p. 265.
125. Quoted in Ransom, p. 83.
126. ODL, vol. 1, p. 137.
127. Ibid., p. 138.
128. Louisa Andrews to Hiram Corson, December 1, 1875, Department of Manuscripts & University Archives, Cornell University libraries.
129. H.P.B. to Hiram Corson, cir-

ca October or early November, 1875, Corson, p. 170.

130. ODL, vol. 1, p. 203.

131. H.P.B. to Hiram Corson, January 8, 1876, Corson, p. 175.

132. CW, vol. 1, p. 160.

133. H.P.B. to Hiram Corson, January 8, 1876, pp. 173–174.

134. Rawson, *Frank Leslie's Popular Monthly*, February, 1892.

135. H.P.B. to Vera Zhelihovsky, circa 1876, *The Path*, December, 1894.

136. ODL, vol. 1, p. 203.

137. Solovyov, p. 354.

138. ODL, vol. 1, p. 207.

139. Ibid., p. 206.

140. Ibid., p. 208.

141. Ibid., p. 209.

142. Ibid., p. 211.

143. H.P.B. to Vera Zhelihovsky, undated, 1876, *The Path*, January, 1895.

144. Ibid.

145. H.P.B. to Vera Zhelihovsky, circa 1876, *The Path*, December, 1894. The medium, Mrs. Willett, who worked with the Society for Psychical Research, gave a similar description: "When all went well and I was deeply in trance, I became partly identified with the communicator. It seemed as if somebody else was me, as if a stranger was occupying my body, as if another's mind was in me . . . Lifted up on wings, I was in a state in which I understood all things."

146. Ibid.

147. H.P.B. to Nadyezhda Fadeyev, circa 1876, *The Path*, December, 1894.

148. Ibid.

149. Ibid.

150. Rawson, *Frank Leslie's Popular Monthly*, February, 1892.

151. The tests conducted by Eleanor Sidgwick with Gladys Osborne Leonard and her trance personality "Feda" were characterized by vagueness. For example, "Feda" might tell the sitter to go to a bookcase in his study, remove the seventh book from the left on the third shelf, open to page 48, and one third of the way down the page the sitter would find a meaningful passage. While "Feda" could give an accurate physical description of a book, he did not supply book titles nor did he quote from the works. (Society for Psychical Research, *Proceedings*, vol. 31, April, 1921, "An Examination of Book-Tests Obtained in Sittings with Mrs. Leonard.")

Others who possessed clairvoyance for printed matter were Stainton Moses, William Eglinton, and Eileen Garrett. Again, none of them actually quoted from books.

152. *Religio-Philosophical Journal*, April 29, 1876.

153. Boston *Herald*, March 5, 1876.

154. H.P.B. to A. N. Aksakov, Spring, 1876, Solovyov, p. 268.

155. ODL, vol. 1, pp. 151–158.

156. H.P.B. to A. N. Aksakov, July, 1876, Solovyov, p. 269.

157. ODL, vol. 1, p. 161.

158. Ibid., p. 452.

159. Ibid., p. 410.

160. Rawson, *Frank Leslie's Popular Monthly*, February, 1892.

161. *Religio-Philosophical Journal*, September 14, 1889.
162. ODL, vol. 1, p. 461.
163. Ibid., p. 459.
164. Ibid., pp. 16–17.
165. Ibid., pp. 425–426.
166. Ibid., p. 429.
167. H.P.B. to Vera Zhelihovsky, circa 1877, *The Path*, January, 1895.
168. Blavatsky, *Isis Unveiled*, vol. 2, p. 621.
169. Ibid., p. 71.
170. ODL, vol. 3, p. 316.
171. Blavatsky, *Isis Unveiled*, vol. 1, p. vi.
172. Ibid.
173. Ibid., vol. 2, p. 584 footnote.
174. H.P.B. to Vera Zhelihovsky, circa 1876–1877, *The Path*, January, 1895.
175. ODL, vol. 1, pp. 377–381. The turban is in the archives of the Theosophical Society at Adyar.
176. David-Neel, pp. 313–315.
177. ODL, vol. 1, p. 18.
178. *The Word*, May–June, 1908.
179. H.P.B. to A. N. Aksakov, circa September, 1876, Solovyov, p. 275.
180. *Religio-Philosophical Journal*, September 14, 1889.
181. H.P.B. to Alexander Wilder, December, 1876, *The Word*, June, 1908.
182. Ibid.
183. J. W. Bouton to Henry Olcott, May 17, 1877, ODL, vol. 1, p. 216.
184. Michael Betanelly to H.P.B., May 7, 1877, *The Theosophist*, August, 1959.
185. Ibid.
186. H.P.B. to A. N. Aksakov, June 15, 1877, Solovyov, p. 276.
187. H.P.B. to Vera Zhelihovsky, circa 1877, *The Path*, January, 1895. "Astral body" is also termed "etheric body." Spiritualists believe it to be the vehicle for the spirit in the first stages after death when it separates from the physical body. Supposedly it is the astral body that is sometimes faintly perceived as apparitions or ghosts.
188. LMW, vol. 1, p. 94.
189. *Religio-Philosophical Journal*, January 12, 1878.
190. H.P.B. to A. N. Aksakov, October 2, 1877, Solovyov, p. 276. As far as is known, the manuscript of *Isis Unveiled* was destroyed after publication.
191. ODL, vol. 1, p. 296.
192. Home, p. 308.
193. Ibid., p. 326.
194. H.P.B. to A. N. Aksakov, November 6, 1877, Solovyov, p. 278.
195. H.P.B. to Vera Zhelihovsky, fall, 1877, *The Path*, January, 1895.
196. H.P.B. to Nadyezhda Fadeyev, 1877, *The Path*, January, 1895.
197. H.P.B. to Nadyezhda Fadeyev, July 19, 1877, HPBSP, vol. 1, pp. 165–166.
198. Ibid., pp. 180, 188, 209.
199. H.P.B. to Vera Zhelihovsky, undated, *The Path*, January, 1895.
200. ODL, vol. 1, p. 395.
201. Ibid., p. 397.
202. H.P.B. to Nadyezhda Fadeyev, July 3, 1877, HPBSP, vol. 1, p. 202.
203. H.P.B. to Vera Zhelihovsky, May, 1878, *The Path*, March, 1895.
204. Ibid.

205. Henry Olcott to Charles Massey, 1878, Besterman, p. 149.
206. Ibid., p. 148.
207. H.P.B. to Nadyezhda Fadeyev, July 8, 1878, *The Path*, February, 1895.
208. New York *Daily Graphic*, July 9, 1878.
209. New York *Star*, June 28, 1878.
210. Nadyezhda Fadeyev to H.P.B., October 1/13, 1877, CW, vol. 1, p.xxxvi, note.
211. H.P.B. to Caroline Corson, August 28, 1878, Corson, p. 199.
212. ODL, vol. 1, p. 454.
213. CW, vol. 1, p. 409.
214. Ibid., p. 433.
215. He kept a diary at least from 1875 to the time of his death in 1907. The diaries for 1875–1877, however, mysteriously disappeared and the colonel had no idea what became of them.
216. The grocer refused to extend further credit, presumably because an unpaid account of one hundred dollars represented a sizable sum in 1878 (the equivalent of eight hundred to nine hundred dollars in today's terms). In view of Olcott's last-minute scramble for money, there is little likelihood that this bill was paid.
217. New York *Sun*, October 13, 1878.
218. New York *Sun*, October 18, 1878.
219. CW, vol. 1, pp. 415–420.
220. Ibid., p. 417.
221. Ibid., p. 419.
222. Ibid., p. 420.
223. Ibid., p. 423.
224. Ibid., p. 428.
225. Ibid., p. 429.
226. New York *Daily Graphic*, December 10, 1878.
227. Ibid.
228. These tinfoil recordings were kept at Adyar until 1895 when Olcott tried to have the sound transferred to more modern wax cylinders. By that time, however, the grooves had flattened out.
229. New York *Times*, January 2, 1885.
230. CW, vol. 1, p. 431.
231. Ibid.

INDIA

1. ODL, vol. 2, pp. 1–4.
2. Ibid., p. 1.
3. Ibid., p. 9.
4. H.P.B. to Vera Zhelihovsky, February, 1879, *The Path*, March, 1895. Describing her arrival in Bombay to Alexander Dondoukoff-Korsakoff in a letter of December 5, 1881, H.P.B. wrote that "after a deputation of 200 Hindus had gone on board to fetch us, we were received by a crowd of 50,000 people."
5. ODL, vol. 2, p. 16.
6. Ibid., p. 18
7. CW, vol. 2, p. 25.
8. Ibid., p. 26.
9. Henry Olcott to William Judge, February 24, 1879, *Theosophist*, January, 1931.
10. William Judge to Henry Ol-

cott, April 2, 1879, *Theosophist*, January, 1931.
11. William Judge to Henry Olcott, April 9, 1879, *Theosophist*, January, 1931.
12. Ibid.
13. The overwhelming probability is that H.P.B. induced an hallucination in Thackersey by means of post-hypnotic suggestion. Normally this consists of the hypnotizer making a statement to the hypnotized subject that at a given time the subject will have a specified experience. For example, the hypnotizer may say, "Next Friday morning at ten A.M., an Eskimo will enter your room, shake your hand and leap out the window." At the hour specified, the subject will in fact have precisely that experience. This type of induced hallucination, common in hypnotic practice, can be performed on any suitable subject.
14. ODL, vol. 2, p. 45.
15. Ibid., p. 47.
16. Ibid., p. 48.
17. Ibid., p. 57.
18. Ibid., p. 59.
19. Ibid., p. 60.
20. Ibid., p. 61
21. Ibid., p. 63.
22. Ibid., p. 65.
23. Ibid., p. 69.
24. H.P.B. to Alexander Wilder, April 28, 1879, *The Word*, July, 1908.
25. Ibid.
26. Ibid.
27. ODL, vol. 2, p. 71.
28. Ibid., p. 82.
29. CW, vol. 2, p. 82.
30. LMW, vol. 2, p. 68.
31. Ibid., p. 69.

32. Coulomb, pp. 4–7.
33. ODL, vol. 2, p. 91.
34. There were virtually none during H.P.B.'s lifetime. The exception was Mrs. Anandabay Joshi, who graduated an M.D. from Women's Medical College, Philadelphia, but died a year later of tuberculosis in Poona. Not until 1893, during Annie Besant's first tour of India, did women veiled in purdah attend her lectures.
35. ODL, vol. 2, pp. 95–96.
36. Barborka, *The Mahatmas and Their Letters*, p. 262.
37. Eek, *Damodar and the Pioneers of the Theosophical Movement*, p. 5.
38. ODL, vol. 2, p. 212.
39. H.P.B. to Abner Doubleday, July 16, 1879, *Theosophical Forum*, September, 1933.
40. *Theosophist*, October, 1879.
41. Damodar Mavalankar to William Judge, October 5, 1879, *Theosophical Forum*, November, 1934.
42. LMW, vol. 2, p. 71.
43. H.P.B. to Nadyezhda Fadeyev, November, 1879, *The Path*, March, 1895.
44. INC, p. 172.
45. De Steiger, pp. 157–158.
46. Linton and Hanson, p. 251.
47. Ibid., p. 252, quoting Sinnett's unpublished memoirs.
48. INC, p. 173.
49. Ibid.
50. LBS, p. 17.
51. ODL, vol. 2, p. 118.
52. Sinnett, *Occult World*, p. 42.
53. Ibid., p. 51.
54. Symonds, p. 11.
55. Coulomb, p. 8.
56. ODL, vol. 2, p. 145.
57. Coulomb, p. 8.

58. ODL, vol. 2, p. 151.
59. H.P.B. to Alexander Dondou-koff-Korsakoff, December 5, 1881, HPBSP, vol. 2, pp. 29–30.
60. Ibid.
61. ODL, vol. 2, p. 207.
62. CW, vol. 2, p. xxxii.
63. H.P.B. to Emma Coulomb, June 16, 1880, *Christian College Magazine*, September, 1884. H.P.B. disowned authorship of letters to Emma Coulomb but in my opinion they are genuine. Hereafter they are quoted as sources.
64. ODL, vol. 2, p. 110.
65. CW, vol. 2, p. xxxii.
66. ODL, vol. 2, p. 209.
67. CW, vol. 2, p. 208.
68. Ibid., p. 479.
69. ODL, vol. 2, p. 213.
70. Coulomb, p. 9.
71. CW, vol. 2, pp. 479–480.
72. Ibid.
73. Coulomb, p. 16.
74. Ibid., p. 15.
75. Kipling, p. 124.
76. Sinnett, *Occult World*, p. 38.
77. ODL, vol. 2, p. 226.
78. Ibid., p. 227.
79. Coulomb, p. 14.
80. According to Emma Coulomb, the sound was produced by a small music box that H.P.B. hid under her dress, slightly above the waist. A slight pressure of her arm against her side set the bell ringing. (S.P.R., *Proceedings*, p. 263.)
81. ODL, vol. 2, p. 227.
82. Sinnett, *Occult World*, p. 48.
83. Ibid., p. 49.
84. Ibid., p. 92.
85. ODL, vol. 2, p. 242.
86. Sinnett, *Occult World*, pp. 61–63. The "pink note," the first Mahatmic message received in India, can now be seen in the manuscripts department of the British Library. Puncture holes visible in the paper show that the note had been pierced when fastened to the twig. Interestingly, the calligraphy of the message is different from all other specimens of Mahatma Koot Hoomi's writing.

H.P.B. did this trick, said Emma Coulomb, with the aid of Babula, who had been sent ahead with instructions to plant the note in a particular tree. In Patience's presence, Helena took an identical slip of paper from her pocket, folded it into a triangle, and threw it over the edge of the hill. Then she directed Patience to the tree where Babula had pinned the message.
87. Ibid.
88. Ibid., pp. 65–66.
89. Sinnett, *Occult World*, pp. 66–74; ODL, vol. 2, pp. 233–236.
90. H.P.B. to Nadyezhda Fadeyev, February 21, 1880, HPBSP, vol. 1, p. 226.
91. Sinnett, *Occult World*, pp. 78–79; ODL, vol. 2, pp. 238–239. Even in H.P.B.'s time, it was known that people could be hypnotized at a distance without their being aware of it. In 1884, Dr. Pierre Janet, well-known French psychiatrist, was able to hypnotize Leonie, a peasant woman and clairvoyant, at a distance in the same room without saying or doing anything perceptible, but merely willing the entrancement.

92. Coulomb, pp. 18–19.
93. ML, 1–5. This first letter contains two glaring factual errors, one stating that Mary Magdalene had witnessed the resurrection of Christ, the other that Sir Francis Bacon helped found the Royal Society in 1662 (although he died in 1626). Sinnett did not, evidently, wonder why an omniscient Mahatma was so misinformed, or perhaps he simply did not catch the errors.
94. Ibid.
95. Ibid., p. 7.
96. Ibid., p. 9.
97. CW, vol. 2, p. 489.
98. ML, p. 19.
99. Conger, p. 38.
100. Ransom, p. 151.
101. Coulomb, p. 30.
102. Ibid.
103. CW, vol. 3, p. 120.
104. CW, vol. 2, p. 78.
105. ODL, vol. 2, p. 294.
106. Ibid.
107. Ibid., p. 135.
108. Coulomb, pp. 30–31.
109. H.P.B. to Vera Zhelihovsky, early 1881, The Path, April, 1895.
110. Saturday Review, June 25, 1881.
111. Ibid.
112. ML, pp. 38–39. In a volume of memoirs published posthumously, The Early Days of Theosophy in Europe, Sinnett acknowledged his belief that this letter was delivered by trickery: "On my return to India, after having published Occult World—after she knew that I was rooted in a personal conviction not only that she possessed magic powers, but that I was in touch with the Masters and devoted to the theosophical cause, she employed M. Coloumb to drop a letter from the Master . . . through a crack in the rafters above, trying to make me believe that it had been dropped by the Master himself—materialized then and there after transmission from Tibet."
113. Ibid., p. 39.
114. Ibid.
115. Theosophist, August, 1881.
116. Ibid.
117. Sinnett, The Early Days of Theosophy in Europe, p. 27.
118. Sinnett was by no means the only recipient of Mahatma letters. Masters Morya and Koot Hoomi wrote to countless other individuals, including Madame Blavatsky, who received three. The reason she got so few, according to C. Jinarajadasa, compiler of Letters from the Masters of Wisdom, was "because her consciousness was so linked to the minds of both the Masters M. and K.H. that she heard Their voices with occult hearing at once, and there was no need for written communications."
119. Evans-Wentz, Tibet's Great Yogi Milarepa, p. 20.
120. Ibid., p. 22.
121. Later, two European visitors to Tibet questioned lamas about H.P.B.'s Mahatmas. Alexandra David-Neel reported that "communications from mystic masters to their disciples through gross material means, such as letters falling from the ceiling or epistles one finds under one's

pillow, are unknown in lamaist mystic circles. When questions regarding such facts are put to contemplative hermits, erudite lamas or high lamaist dignitaries, they can hardly believe that the inquirer is in earnest and not an irreverent joker" (David-Neel, p. 234). A similar reaction was reported by William Rockville: "When told of our esoteric Buddhists, the Mahatmas, and of the wonderful doctrines they claimed to have obtained from Tibet, they (the lamas) were immensely amused." (Rockville, p. 102.)

Beginning in 1912, a young Californian named Edwin G. Schary made three attempts to find H.P.B.'s Masters in order to become their disciple. His account of these Tibetan travels, *In Search of the Mahatmas of Tibet*, amounts to a chronicle of nightmarish physical hardship: snow blindness, difficulty in breathing at high altitudes, thirst, hunger so intense that he ate field daisies, and general inhospitableness of the Tibetans who set their dogs on him. Schary's quest ended in failure.

122. ML, p. 243.
123. Ibid. pp. 43, 241.
124. Ibid. p. 166.
125. Ibid., p. 431.
126. Ibid., pp. 36, 302, 428.
127. The word is the feminine of the Pali word *Upasaka* (disciple). The nearest Western translation would be Lay Brother and Lay Sister. H.P.B. said that during her residence with the Masters in Tibet, she took the vows of a Lay Sister.
128. James, *Psychical Research*, p. 50.
129. Jung, p. 101.
130. *Christian College Magazine*, September, 1884.
131. INC, p. 189.
132. H.P.B. to Adelberth de Bourbon, September 4, 1881, HPBSP, vol. 2, p. 7.
133. H.P.B. to Mary Hollis Billing, October 2, 1881, *Theosophical Forum*, May, 1936.
134. *Christian College Magazine*, September, 1884.
135. ML, p. 260.
136. Ibid., pp. 213–214.
137. Ibid., p. 214.
138. Coulomb, p. 44.
139. LBS, p. 50.
140. ML, p. 220.
141. Ibid., pp. 203–204.
142. Ibid. p. 221.
143. INC, p. 193.
144. ML, p. 207.
145. Coulomb, p. 42.
146. H.P.B. to Alexander Dondoukoff-Korsakoff, August 28, 1881, HPBSP, vol. 2, p. 14.
147. H.P.B. to A. P. Sinnett, November 2, 1881, LBS, p. 10.
148. ML, pp. 440–441.
149. H.P.B. to A. P. Sinnett, received November 10, 1881, LBS, p. 11.
150. H.P.B. to A. P. Sinnett, November 2, 1881, LBS, p. 9.
151. Ibid., p. 10.
152. H.P.B. to Vera Zhelihovsky, November, 1881, *The Path*, April, 1895.
153. ODL, vol. 2, p. 236.
154. William Judge to Damodar Mavalankar, October 26, 1881, Eek, p. 73.
155. ML, pp. 52, 56.
156. Smith, pp. 93, 96.

157. ODL, vol. 2, p. 327.
158. H.P.B. to A. P. Sinnett, May 8, 1882, LBS, p. 15.
159. Allan Hume to H.P.B., January 4, 1882, LBS, p. 306.
160. Ibid.
161. Ibid., p. 307.
162. ML, p. 264.
163. Ibid., p. 268.
164. H.P.B. to Alexander Dondoukoff-Korsakoff, February 7, 1882, HPBSP, vol. 2, p. 43.
165. Ibid., p. 45.
166. H.P.B. to Alexander Dondoukoff-Korsakoff, March 1, 1882, HPBSP, vol. 2, p. 53.
167. ODL, vol. 2, p. 342.
168. Subba Row to H.P.B., February 3, 1882, LBS, p. 317.
169. ODL, vol. 2, p. 342.
170. Ibid., p. 343.
171. Ibid., p. 344.
172. Ibid., pp. 347–352.
173. H.P.B. to Alexander Dondoukoff-Korsakoff, May 17, 1882, HPBSP, vol. 2, p. 74.
174. Ibid., p. 75.
175. *Theosophist*, March, 1926.
176. H.P.B. to Alexander Dondoukoff-Korsakoff, June 25, 1882, HPBSP, vol. 2, p. 81; October 1, 1882, HPBSP, vol. 2, p. 95.
177. H.P.B. to A. P. Sinnett, June 20, 1882, LBS, p. 18.
178. Linton and Hanson, p. 268.
179. *Theosophist*, June, 1882.
180. Hume, p. 11.
181. H.P.B. to A. P. Sinnett, August 26, 1882, LBS, p. 34.
182. Ibid., p. 31.
183. ML, p. 288.
184. S.P.R., *Proceedings*, p. 397.
185. Blavatsky, *Isis Unveiled*, p. 351.
186. *Light*, July 8, 1882.
187. *Theosophist*, September, 1882.
188. H.P.B. to Alexander Dondou-koff-Korsakoff, June 25, 1882, HPBSP, vol. 2, p. 87.
189. H.P.B. to Alexander Dondoukoff-Korsakoff, September 1, 1882, HPBSP, vol. 2, p. 94.
190. H.P.B. to A. P. Sinnett, Received September 19, 1882, LBS, p. 37; H.P.B. to Vera Zhelihovsky, September, 1882, *The Path*, September, 1895.
191. H.P.B. to A. P. Sinnett, Received September 19, 1882, LBS, p. 37.
192. H.P.B. to Alexander Dondoukoff-Korsakoff, October 1, 1882, HPBSP, vol. 2, p. 98.
193. Ibid., pp. 99–100.
194. H.P.B. to Vera Zhelihovsky, circa October, 1882, *The Path*, September, 1895. In an undated letter to M. Biliere, Paris, Helena supplied further details on Master Morya's medical treatment. "He gave only a potion to drink seven times a day, from a plant of the Himalayas." (*Theosophist*, December, 1930.)
195. H.P.B. to A. P. Sinnett, October 9, 1882, LBS, p. 38.
196. H.P.B. to Alexander Dondoukoff-Korsakoff, December 15, 1882, HPBSP, vol. 2, p. 104.
197. *Christian College Magazine*, September, 1884.
198. Henry Olcott to Emma Coulomb, September 25, 1882, *Christian College Magazine*, October, 1884.
199. LMW, vol. 2, pp. 116–117.
200. H.P.B. to Franz Hartmann, April 3, 1886, *The Path*, March, 1896.
201. ML, p. 446.
202. Barborka, *The Mahatmas and Their Letters*, p. 323.

203. Ibid., p. 329.
204. Ibid.
205. H.P.B. to Alexander Dondou-koff-Korsakoff, December 5, 1881, HPBSP, vol. 2, p. 17.
206. H.P.B. to Nadyezhda Fad-eyev, circa January, 1883, *The Path*, September, 1895.
207. ODL, vol. 2, p. 392.
208. *Theosophist*, February, 1883.
209. James, *William James on Psychical Research*, p. 145.
210. ML, p. 201.
211. In a letter to Sinnett, dated January 9, 1886, H.P.B. made a general admission that the materialized vases and other "apports" pre-existed as objects and were purchased from a shop. The point of these phenomena, she asserted, did not rest on the vases themselves but on their having been made to pass through walls and doors before appearing in a closed cabinet.
212. Coulomb, p. 66.
213. S.P.R., *Proceedings*, p. 325.
214. Blavatsky, *The People of the Blue Mountains*, pp. 109–113.
215. H.P.B. to A. P. Sinnett, August 15, 1883, LBS, p. 45.
216. Ibid., p. 43.
217. H.P.B. to either Vera or Nadyezhda, July or August, 1883, *Theosophist*, May, 1959.
218. Marryat, p. 98.
219. *Christian College Magazine*, September 1884.
220. S.P.R., *Proceedings*, p. 322.
221. Ibid.
222. H.P.B. to A. P. Sinnett, July 15, 1883, LBS, p. 43.
223. Coulomb, p. 65.
224. Ibid.

225. H.P.B. to A. P. Sinnett, September 27, 1883, LBS, p. 57.
226. *Light*, September 1, 1883.
227. Ibid.
228. Ibid., September 22, 1883.
229. Ibid., November 17, 1883.
230. Lillie, *Modern Mystics*, p. 117.
231. H.P.B. to A. P. Sinnett, November 17, 1883, LBS, p. 66.
232. ML, pp. 421–422.
233. Ibid., p. 422.
234. *Theosophist*, October, 1931.
235. It is possible that H.P.B. recognized Brown's symptoms at once. In a letter of April 3, 1886, to Franz Hartmann, she wrote: "Brown was crazy before he came to us, unasked and unexpected." (*The Path*, March, 1896.)
236. H.P.B. to A. P. Sinnett, September 27 and November 17, 1883, LBS, pp. 55, 67–68.
237. Coulomb, p. 66.
238. Ibid., p. 69.
239. Ibid.
240. Ibid., pp. 68–69.
241. ODL, vol. 3, p. 36.
242. Ibid., p. 40.
243. Barborka, *The Mahatmas and Their Letters*, p. 243, quoting Brown's pamphlet, *My Life*.
244. *Religio-Philosophical Journal*, July 23, 1887.
245. Conway, pp. 195–205.
246. CW, vol. 6, p. 162.
247. H.P.B. to A. P. Sinnett, January 25, 1884, LBS, p. 75.
248. H.P.B. to N. D. Khandala-vala, February 5, 1884, *Theosophist*, August, 1931.
249. H.P.B. to A. P. Sinnett, January 25, 1884, LBS, p. 75.
250. Ibid., p. 74.
251. H.P.B. to A. P. Sinnett, No-

vember 17 and 26, 1883, LBS, pp. 66, 71.
252. Maitland, vol. 2, p. 81.
253. Anna Kingsford to Lady Caithness, June 8, 1883, Ibid., p. 120.
254. De Steiger, p. 167.
255. H.P.B. to A. P. Sinnett, August 23, 1883, LBS, p. 52, quoting Sinnett.
256. H.P.B. to A. P. Sinnett, November 26, 1883, LBS, p. 69.
257. H.P.B. to A. P. Sinnett, November 26, 1883, LBS, p. 70, quoting Anna Kingsford's letter to H.P.B., October 26, 1883.
258. Ibid.
259. Ibid., p. 71.

260. Ibid.
261. Besant, *H.P.B. and the Masters of Wisdom*, p. 26.
262. Coulomb, p. 74.
263. Conway, p. 213.
264. *Christian College Magazine*, October, 1884.
265. Besant, *H.P.B. and the Masters of Wisdom*, p. 26.
266. H.P.B. to Nadyezhda Fadeyev, circa February, 1884, *The Path*, May, 1895. H.P.B. mentioned learning of her uncle's death before leaving Bombay in a letter to Emma Coulomb, dated April 1, 1884.
267. Besant, *H.P.B. and the Masters of Wisdom*, p. 27.

EUROPE

1. H.P.B. to Emma Coulomb, circa March 4, 1884, *Christian College Magazine*, October, 1884.
2. Henry Olcott to Alexis Coulomb, March 4, 1884, *Christian College Magazine*, October, 1884.
3. H.P.B. to Emma Coulomb, circa March 4, 1884, *Christian College Magazine*, October, 1884.
4. ODL, vol. 3, p. 76.
5. H.P.B. to A. P. Sinnett, March 21, 1884, LBS, p. 83.
6. Ibid.
7. *The Path*, May, 1895.
8. H.P.B. to A. P. Sinnett, March 21, 1884, LBS, p. 81.
9. Ibid.
10. LMW, vol. 2, p. 111.
11. William Judge to Damodar Mavalankar, January 11,

1883, Eek and de Zirkoff, p. 76.
12. William Judge to Henry Olcott, August 1, 1882, *Theosophist*, September, 1931.
13. William Judge to Henry Olcott, January 16, 1882, *Theosophist*, May, 1931.
14. *The Word*, March, 1912.
15. Ibid., April, 1912.
16. H.P.B. to Emma and Alexis Coulomb, April 1, 1884, *Christian College Magazine*, October, 1884.
17. Henry Olcott to Emma Coulomb, April 2, 1884, *Christian College Magazine*, October, 1884.
18. LMW, vol. 1, p. 43.
19. *The Word*, April, 1912.
20. Leadbeater, p. 37.
21. Ibid.
22. Maitland, vol. 2, p. 166.

23. A. Keightley, *Theosophical Quarterly*, October, 1910.
24. *The Path*, November, 1895.
25. William Judge to Henry Olcott, April 30, 1884, *Theosophist*, November, 1931.
26. H.P.B. to Vera Zhelihovsky, circa March–April, 1884, *The Path*, May, 1895.
27. H.P.B. to A. P. Sinnett, April 27, 1884, LBS, p. 84.
28. H.P.B. to Vera Zhelihovsky, circa April, 1884, *The Path*, May, 1895.
29. Ibid.
30. Solovyov, pp. 11–24.
31. *Theosophist*, May, 1959.
32. Solovyov, p. 34.
33. Justine Glinka to Alexander Dondoukoff-Korsakoff, January 3, 1884, HPBSP, vol. 2, p.158.
34. Ibid., p. 157.
35. Ibid., pp. 149–151.
36. Ibid.
37. H.P.B. to Henry Olcott, spring, 1884, Neff, p. 182.
38. H.P.B. to Alexander Dondoukoff-Korsakoff, June 3, 1884, HPBSP, vol. 2, p. 151.
39. Ibid., p. 145.
40. Ibid., pp. 155–156. The petition, granted later in 1884, is chiefly interesting because she signs herself Nikifor Blavatsky's wife, not widow, the only public admission she had made of this fact in thirty-five years.
41. Solovyov, p. 39.
42. Coulomb, p. 109.
43. Ibid., p. 111.
44. Ibid.
45. Ibid., p. 112.
46. *Theosophist*, August, 1931.
47. Solovyov, p. 47.
48. Ibid., p. 43.
49. Ibid., p. 59.
50. Ibid.
51. Ibid., p. 65.
52. *Theosophist*, May, 1959.
53. CW, vol. 6, p. 274.
54. LMW, vol. 1, p. 84.
55. *The Path*, May, 1895.
56. *The Path*, June, 1895.
57. *Theosophist*, December, 1882.
58. *Theosophist*, July, 1882.
59. Podmore, p. 165.
60. Ibid., p. 186.
61. Ibid.
62. ODL, vol. 3, p. 99.
63. Hastings, *New Universe, Try*, no. 1.
64. S.P.R., *Proceedings*, p. 352.
65. Leadbeater, p. 24.
66. LBS, p. 102.
67. Arundale, p. 51.
68. Sinnett, *The Early Days of Theosophy in Europe*, p. 60.
69. Arundale, p. 52.
70. Ibid., p. 36. In 1960, when Theosophist Walter A. Carrithers petitioned the S.P.R. to examine unpublished documents pertaining to its examination of the Theosophical Society, he discovered that both Myers and Edmund Gurney had heard H.P.B.'s astral bell. While not ruling out trickery, Gurney thought it a free sound unlike that produced by mechanical objects concealed in clothing, and Myers mentioned that he could not discern any deadening of the clear tingling sound. Both men's comments were deleted from the final draft of the S.P.R.'s 1884 preliminary report on the Society.
71. Sidgwick, p. 105.

72. Ibid., p. 59.
73. Eek, *Damodar and the Pioneers of the Theosophical Movement*, p. 625.
74. H.P.B. to Vera Zhelihovsky, July, 1884, *The Path*, June, 1895.
75. Arundale, p. 30.
76. Maitland, vol. 2, p. 182.
77. ML, p. 355.
78. LMW, vol. 1, p. 147.
79. H.P.B. to A. P. Sinnett, Received November 4, 1884, LBS, p. 93.
80. LMW, vol. 1, p. 157.
81. CW, vol. 6, p. 271.
82. De Steiger, pp. 176–179.
83. Ibid.
84. Ibid.
85. *The Word*, July 1912.
86. Sinnett, *The Early Days of Theosophy in Europe*, p. 73.
87. Solovyov, p. 73.
88. *The Path*, June, 1895.
89. ODL, vol. 3, p. 175.
90. *The Path*, June, 1895.
91. Solovyov, p. 78.
92. Ibid., p. 81.
93. Ibid., p. 85.
94. Ibid., p. 87. According to Solovyov, the medical diagnosis for H.P.B.'s poor health at that time was "fatty heart, diabetes, and acute rheumatism" (Solovyov, p. 298).
95. Ibid., p. 88.
96. *Christian College Magazine*, October, 1884.
97. Henry Olcott to Francesca Arundale, September, 1884, *Theosophist*, August, 1932.
98. Henry Olcott to Francesca Arundale, November 25, 1884, *Theosophist*, August, 1932.
99. Solovyov, p. 96.
100. Ibid., p. 94.
101. Ibid.
102. Ibid., p. 99.
103. Ibid., p. 100.
104. Ibid., p. 104.
105. *Theosophist*, August, 1931.
106. H.P.B. to Vera Zhelihovsky, circa September–October, 1884, *The Path*, June, 1895.
107. Solovyov, p. 101.
108. Ibid., p. 102.
109. Besant, *H.P.B. and the Masters of Wisdom*, p. 36.
110. Solovyov, p. 72.
111. Ibid., p. 97.
112. S.P.R., *Proceedings*, p. 224.
113. Henry Olcott to Francesca Arundale, April 1, 1885, *Theosophist*, October, 1932.
114. *Occult Review*, January, 1908.
115. Ibid.
116. LMW, vol. 1, p. 102. Alfred Cooper-Oakley died of an overdose of barbiturates around 1890.
117. Solovyov, p. 104.
118. H.P.B. to A. P. Sinnett, October, 1884, ML, p. 461.
119. *The Path*, June, 1895.
120. H.P.B. to A. P. Sinnett, October, 1884, ML, p. 460.
121. Podmore, p. 170.
122. Solovyov, p. 104.
123. *Pall Mall Gazette*, October 23, 1884, Reprinted in CW, vol. 6, p. 308.
124. Ibid.
125. Ibid.
126. Lillie, p. 158.
127. *Pall Mall Gazette*, op. cit.
128. Henry Olcott to H.P.B., January 19, 1886, LBS, p. 327.
129. Nethercot, *The First Five Lives of Annie Besant*, p. 325, quoting Leadbeater's collection of stories, *The Perfume of Egypt and Other Weird Stories*.
130. M. Lutyens, p. 202.

131. Jinarājadāsa, *The "K.H."*
Letters to C. W. Leadbeater,
p. 106.
132. Leadbeater, p. 18.
133. LMW, vol. 1, p. 30.
134. Leadbeater, pp. 50–56.
135. Ibid., p. 57.
136. ML, p. 467.
137. Leadbeater, p. 58.
138. Ibid., p. 59–66.
139. Ibid., p. 67.
140. H.P.B. to Vera Zhelihovsky,
November, 1884, *The Path*,
July, 1895.
141. Eek, *Damodar and the Pio-*
neers of the Theosophical
Movement, p. 574.
142. Solovyov, p. 107.

143. Ibid.
144. ODL, vol. 3, p. 189.
145. Solovyov, p. 107.
146. *Lucifer*, June, 1891.
147. Solovyov, p. 107.
148. Leadbeater, p. 76.
149. Leadbeater, p. 95.
150. *Lucifer*, June, 1891.
151. Leadbeater, p. 96.
152. Solovyov, p. 109.
153. Leadbeater, p. 98.
154. Ibid.
155. ODL, vol. 3, p. 189.
156. Ibid., p. 190.
157. Ibid., p. 195.
158. Ibid., p. 192.
159. Solovyov, p. 112.

THE SECRET DOCTRINE

1. James, *William James on*
Psychical Research, p. 111.
2. Ibid., p. 32.
3. Society for Psychical Research, *Proceedings*, p. 220.
4. *Christian College Magazine*,
April, 1885.
5. While Gribble believed that
H.P.B. had written the Coulomb letters, he did not think
her the author of the Mahatma letters. Shown several letters while visiting Adyar on
October 3, 1884, he decided
that "Koot Hoomi's hand-
writing is very peculiar,
upright and somewhat
rounded," unlike Helena's
running hand.
6. Richard Hodgson to Frank
Podmore, January 9, 1885,
Podmore, p. 177.
7. Solovyov, p. 111.
8. Ibid., p. 105.
9. *Theosophist*, October, 1931.

10. ODL, vol. 3, p. 206.
11. CW, vol. 6, p. 322.
12. ODL, vol. 3, p. 101.
13. Ibid., p. 208.
14. Eek, *Damodar and the Pio-*
neers of the Theosophical
Movement, p. 17.
15. H.P.B. to A. P. Sinnett,
March 17, 1885, ML, p. 468.
In the fall of 1885 or early
winter of 1886, she wrote to
Franz Hartmann that if reports of Damodar's death
were true, "why I think I
would commit suicide; for it is
out of pure devotion for me
that he went. I would never
forgive myself for this, for letting him go." (H.P.B. to
Franz Hartmann, *The Path*,
February, 1896.)
16. S.P.R., *Proceedings*, p. 311.
17. S.P.R., *Proceedings*, vol. ix, p.
159.
18. LBS, p. 94.

19. ODL, vol. 3, p. 217.
20. S.P.R., *Proceedings*, vol. ix, p. 135.
21. Henry Olcott to Francesca Arundale, July 8, 1885, *Theosophist*, October, 1932.
22. ODL, vol. 3, p. 221.
23. Henry Olcott to Francesca Arundale, July 8, 1885, *Theosophist*, October, 1932.
24. ODL, vol. 3, p. 222.
25. Ibid.
26. Soon after H.P.B.'s departure, Emma withdrew her legal action against Maj.-Gen. Henry Rhodes Morgan. Little is known of her subsequent life, except that she and her husband soon separated and Alexis returned to Egypt. By 1886, she was said to be living in Bombay in poverty. According to Sven Eek *(Damodar and the Pioneers of the Theosophical Movement)*: "It has been presumed that she ended her days in some evangelical home for the aged."
27. H.P.B. quoting Olcott in a letter to A. P. Sinnett, August 19, 1885, LBS, p. 115.
28. Henry Olcott to Francesca Arundale, April 1, 1885, *Theosophist*, October, 1932.
29. H.P.B. to A. P. Sinnett, August 19, 1885, LBS, p. 111.
30. H.P.B. to A. P. Sinnett, September 2, 1885, LBS, p. 119.
31. CW, vol. 11, p. 388.
32. Solovyov, p. 123.
33. H.P.B. to V. Solovyov, April 29, 1885, Solovyov, p. 119.
34. Ibid.
35. H.P.B. to Patience Sinnett, July 23, 1885, LBS, p. 104.
36. H.P.B. to Mohini Chatterji, May 17, 1885, LBS, p. 97.
37. Solovyov, p. 18.

38. H.P.B. to V. Solovyov, May 23, 1885, Solovyov, p. 124.
39. Ibid., p. 122.
40. H.P.B. to Patience Sinnett, July 23, 1885, LBS, p. 105.
41. H.P.B. to Mohini Chatterji, May 17, 1885, LBS, p. 97.
42. Ibid.
43. Quoted in H.P.B. letter to Patience Sinnett, July 23, 1885, LBS, p. 102.
44. Ibid., p. 103.
45. Ibid.
46. Ibid.
47. Ibid.
48. H.P.B. to Mary and Francesca Arundale, June 16, 1885, LBS, p. 95.
49. Ibid.
50. Solovyov, p. 133.
51. Ibid., p. 134.
52. Ibid., p. 135.
53. Ibid., pp. 135–136.
54. Ibid., p. 136.
55. H.P.B. to Francesca Arundale, August 29, 1885, Arundale, p. 60.
56. ML, p. 130.
57. *Theosophist*, January, 1884.
58. H.P.B. to A. P. Sinnett, January 6, 1886, LBS, p. 480.
59. Ibid.
60. In *Modern Priestess of Isis*, Solovyov gives the impression that he was alone at Würzburg, but from other sources it is known that he was accompanied by Glinka.
61. Solovyov, p. 150.
62. H.P.B. to Vera Zhelihovsky, September, 1885, *The Path*, August, 1895.
63. H.P.B. to A. P. Sinnett, October 10, 1885, LBS, p. 134.
64. Wachtmeister, p. 98.
65. H.P.B. to Henry Olcott, November 25, 1885, De Zirkoff, *Rebirth of the Occult Tradi-*

tion, p. 10.
66. Neff, p. 187.
67. Ibid.
68. Ibid.
69. ODL, vol. 3, pp. 319–320.
70. Neff, p. 187.
71. H.P.B. to A. P. Sinnett, January 4– 6, 1886, LBS, p. 177.
72. Dr. Gideon G. Panter, New York Hospital—Cornell Medical Center. Interview with author.
73. Neff, p. 187.
74. H.P.B. to A. P. Sinnett, January 4– 6, 1886, LBS, p. 177.
75. Wachtmeister, p. 11.
76. Ibid., p. 4.
77. Ibid., p. 7.
78. Ibid., p. 9.
79. Ibid., p. 12.
80. Russell, *Herald of the Star*, May 11, 1916.
81. H.P.B. to Franz Hartmann, April 3, 1886, *The Path*, March, 1896.
82. Wachtmeister, p. 12.
83. Ibid., p. 14.
84. Ibid., p. 33.
85. Ibid., p. 18.
86. Ibid.
87. C. Wachtmeister to A. P. Sinnett, January 1, 1886, LBS, p. 270.
88. S.P.R., *Proceedings*, pp. 313–317.
89. H.P.B. to Henry Olcott, January 6, 1886, *Theosophist*, August, 1931.
90. S.P.R., *Proceedings*, p. 207.
91. H.P.B. to Henry Olcott, January 6, 1886, *Theosophist*, August, 1931.
92. Wachtmeister, p. 19.
93. H.P.B. to Henry Olcott, January 6, 1886, *Theosophist*, August, 1931.
94. Ibid.
95. C. Wachtmeister to A. P. Sinnett, January 4, 1886, LBS, p. 272.
96. H.P.B. to A. P. Sinnett, January 1, 1886, LBS, p. 135.
97. C. Wachtmeister to A. P. Sinnett, January 26, 1886, LBS, p. 279.
98. Ibid., p. 282.
99. Ibid., p. 281.
100. Henry Olcott to C. Wachtmeister, March 2, 1886, LBS, p. 331.
101. H.P.B. to A. P. Sinnett, April 6, 1886, LBS, p. 199.
102. H.P.B. to F. Hartmann, undated, 1886, *The Path*, February, 1896.
103. Ibid.
104. Five years earlier, Walther Gebhard's identical-twin brother had also taken his own life with a pistol.
105. De Steiger, p. 260.
106. H.P.B. to A. P. Sinnett, October 9, 1885, LBS, p. 123.
107. Ibid.
108. H.P.B. to A. P. Sinnett, March 3, 1886, LBS, p. 192.
109. H.P.B. to A. P. Sinnett, circa October 12, 1885, LBS, p. 127.
110. H.P.B. to A. P. Sinnett, March 13, 1886, LBS, p. 189.
111. H.P.B. to A. P. Sinnett, January 29, 1886, LBS, p. 178.
112. Ibid.
113. H.P.B. to A. P. Sinnett, February 7, 1886, LBS, p. 181.
114. H.P.B. to Vera Zhelihovsky, March 28, 1886, Solovyov, p. 315.
115. Ibid.
116. Ibid., p. 193.
117. H.P.B. to A. P. Sinnett, February 7, 1886, quoting V. Solovyov, LBS, p. 180.
118. H.P.B. to A. P. Sinnett, Feb-

ruary 2–7, 1886, LBS, p. 175.
119. Ibid.
120. H.P.B. to A. P. Sinnett, February 7, 1886, LBS, p. 179.
121. Solovyov, pp. 176–181.
122. H.P.B. to A. P. Sinnett, January 15, 1886, LBS, p. 150.
123. Ibid.
124. H.P.B. to A. P. Sinnett, April, 1886, LBS, p. 148.
125. H.P.B. to A. P. Sinnett, January 15, 1886, LBS, p. 154.
126. H.P.B. to A. P. Sinnett, April 3, 1886, LBS, p. 142.
127. Ibid.
128. Ibid., p. 145.
129. Ibid.
130. C. Wachtmeister to A. P. Sinnett, March 9, 1886, LBS, p. 293.
131. H.P.B. to A. P. Sinnett, March 3, 1886, LBS, p. 194.
132. Henry Olcott to H.P.B., March 17, 1886, LBS, p. 133.
133. H.P.B. to Franz Hartmann, April 3, 1886, The Path, February, 1896.
134. H.P.B. to A. P. Sinnett, March 17–18, 1886, LBS, p. 201.
135. Ibid., p. 200.
136. Wachtmeister, p. 48.
137. Ibid.
138. Ibid., p. 49.
139. Ibid., p. 93.
140. Ibid., p. 50.
141. Ibid.
142. H.P.B. to A. P. Sinnett, August 18, 1886, LBS, p. 216.
143. Ibid.
144. Wachtmeister, p. 51.
145. H.P.B. to William Judge, August 22, 1886, Theosophical Forum, November, 1933.
146. Wachtmeister, p. 50.
147. H.P.B. to William Judge, October 3, 1886, CW, vol. 7,
p. 136.
148. Ibid., p. 137.
149. Maitland, vol. 2, pp. 253, 274.
150. Blavatsky, The Secret Doctrine, 1928 edition, Theosophical Press, vol. 1, p. 31.
151. Ibid., p. 22.
152. Ibid., p. xxi.
153. Ibid., p. 28.
154. Ibid., p. 29.
155. Solovyov, p. 359.
156. Scholem, pp. 388–389.
157. H.P.B. to A. P. Sinnett, January 6, 1886, ML, p. 481.
158. H.P.B. to Henry Olcott, January 6, 1886, De Zirkoff, Rebirth of the Occult Tradition, p. 23.
159. Ibid.
160. C. Wachtmeister to A. P. Sinnett, December 13, 1885, LBS, p. 266.
161. H.P.B. to Henry Olcott, October 21, 1886, Theosophist, March, 1925.
162. H.P.B. to Henry Olcott, January 5, 1887, Theosophist, August, 1931.
163. Wachtmeister, p. 56.
164. H.P.B. to A. P. Sinnett, February 16, 1887, LBS, p. 205.
165. Wachtmeister, p. 78.
166. H.P.B. to Vera Zhelihovsky, undated 1887, The Path, September, 1895.
167. Wachtmeister, pp. 59–64, H.P.B. must have destroyed the will because it was not found among her papers at her death.
168. H.P.B. to Vera Zhelihovsky, April, 1887, The Path, October, 1895.
169. H.P.B. to Nadyezhda Fadeyev, Easter Sunday, 1887, The Path, September, 1895.
170. Wachtmeister, p. 78.
171. Ibid.

LONDON

1. *Religio -Philosophical Journal*, September 21, 1890.
2. Wachtmeister, p. 65.
3. Ibid.
4. CW, vol. 8, pp. 427–429.
5. Ibid., p. 430.
6. De Steiger, p. 241.
7. Maskelyne, p. 62.
8. Ibid., pp. 62–63.
9. H.P.B. to Vera Zhelihovsky, May, 1887, *The Path,* October, 1895.
10. B. Keightley, *Theosophist,* September, 1931.
11. Ibid.
12. Ibid.
13. Cleather, *As I Knew Her,* p. 3.
14. *Theosophical Forum,* April–July, 1900.
15. B. Keightley, *Theosophist,* September, 1931.
16. H.P.B. to Vera Zhelihovsky, May, 1887, *The Path,* October 1895.
17. Cleather, *As I Knew Her,* p. 9.
18. He left the Society in 1888 and died two years later of blood poisoning.
19. ODL, vol. 4, p. 22.
20. Wachtmeister, p. 79.
21. A. Keightley, *Theosophical Quarterly,* October, 1910.
22. According to an H.P.B. letter to Countess Wachtmeister, the company was formed specifically to publish *Lucifer* and *The Secret Doctrine.* However, Bertram Keightley stated that George Redway published the first issues of *Lucifer* and was due to do *Secret Doctrine* as well, but they dropped him after a dispute over financial terms. It was only later, probably in November, 1887, that the Theosophical Publishing Society took over the publication of both book and magazine and rented an office in Duke Street.
23. H.P.B. to Vera Zhelihovsky, May 1887, *The Path,* October, 1895.
24. Ibid.
25. Wachtmeister, p. 67.
26. Ibid., p. 85.
27. Cleather, *As I Knew Her,* p. 14.
28. *Lucifer,* January, 1889.
29. Cleather, *As I Knew Her,* p. 8.
30. Ibid., p. 13.
31. B. Keightley, *Theosophist,* September, 1931.
32. H.P.B. to Vera Zhelihovsky, May, 1887, *The Path,* October, 1895.
33. Wachtmeister, p. 72.
34. Ibid.
35. Maitland, vol. 2, p. 315.
36. Russell, *Herald of the Star,* May 11, 1916.
37. Ibid.
38. Ellmann, p. 40.
39. Yeats would remember that Mohini was asked if one should say prayers at bedtime, to which he replied, "No, one should say before sleeping: 'I have lived many lives, I have been a slave and prince. Many a beloved has sat upon my knees and I have sat upon the knees of many a beloved. Everything that has been shall be again.'" Forty years later, Yeats would turn those words into verse:

I asked if I should pray,
But the Brahmin said,

"Pray for nothing, say
Every night in bed,
'I have been a king,
I have been a slave,
Nor is there anything,
Fool, rascal, knave,
That I have not been,
And yet upon my breast
A myriad heads have lain."
"Mohini Chatterjee," *Collected Poems of W. B. Yeats,* p. 242.

Mohini, on a visit to London shortly before his death in 1936, had his daughter read the poem to him, since he was almost blind from cataracts.

40. Yeats, *Letters to the New Island,* p. 21.
41. Moore, p. 23.
42. Ibid.
43. Yeats, *Memoirs,* p. 24.
44. Ibid.
45. Ibid.
46. Ibid., p. 25.
47. Ibid.
48. Ibid., p. 26.
49. Ibid.
50. Ibid., p. 25.
51. Ibid., p. 26.
52. W. B. Yeats to Katharine Tynan, February 12, 1888, Yeats, *Letters of W. B. Yeats to Katharine Tynan,* p. 45.
53. V. Moore, p. 24.
54. MacBride, pp. 246–247.
55. Rhys, pp. 105–106.
56. G. Moore, p. 26.
57. "Æ" to H.P.B., November 6, 1888, Russell, *Letters from Æ,* p. 6.
58. Ibid., p. 8.
59. Æ to H.P.B., December, 1888, ibid., p. 9.
60. Eglinton, p. 164.
61. "Anashuya and Vijaya," Yeats, *The Collected Poems of W. B. Yeats,* p. 12.

62. Yeats, *Memoirs,* p. 282.
63. Besant, *Autobiography,* p. 362.
64. Asquith, vol. 1, p. 142.
65. B. Keightley, *Theosophist,* September, 1931.
66. It is not uncommon that those who receive mediumistic communications through automatic writing write backwards, transpose letters, or write mirror script. According to William James (*William James on Psychical Research,* p. 55), "All these are symptoms of agraphic disease."
67. H.P.B. to Vera Zhelihovsky, undated, 1887, *The Path,* October, 1895.
68. H.P.B. to Vera Zhelihovsky, undated, 1887 or 1888, *The Path,* November, 1895.
69. Ibid.
70. H.P.B. to Edward Maitland, August, 1887, Maitland, vol. 2, p. 316.
71. It is unclear which son died. According to the genealogical table in H.P.B.'s *Collected Writings,* vol. 1, Feodor Yahontov died in 1920, Rostislav in 1922. Obviously the table is in error.
72. H.P.B. to Vera Zhelihovsky, May, 1888, *The Path,* November, 1895.
73. LMW, vol. 1, p. 101.
74. According to H.P.B. (CW, vol. 11, p. 428), celibacy and vegetarianism were optional both for members of the Society as well as the Esoteric Section. "A large proportion of the members are married people, and some eat meat, and, when sick, drink wine *even in the inner circle.*" Technically, this may have

been true, but from writings of E.S. members, one cannot avoid the impression that these habits, while not expressly prohibited, were strongly disapproved of.

75. ODL, vol. 4, p. 53.
76. Ibid., p. 55.
77. *Religio-Philosophical Journal,* July 27, 1888.
78. William Judge to Henry Olcott, May 21, 1888, *The Theosophical Movement,* p. 231.
79. LMW, vol. 1, pp. 45–46.
80. A. P. Sinnett to C. W. Leadbeater, October 23, 1888, Jinarājadāsa, *The "K.H." Letters to C. W. Leadbeater,* p. 75.
81. Yeats, *Letters to the New Island,* p. 84.
82. Yeats, *Letters to Katharine Tynan,* p. 68.
83. Ibid., p. 70.
84. Rohmer, p. 183, quoting E. J. Dunn, *The Vahan.*
85. Yeats, *Letters to Katharine Tynan,* p. 70.
86. Russell, *Letters from Æ,* p. 48.
87. ODL, vol. 4, p. 65.
88. Ibid., p. 68.
89. *Religio-Philosophical Journal,* July 27, 1889.
90. ODL, vol. 1, p. 463.
91. Russell, *Herald of the Star,* May 11, 1916.
92. *The Path,* July–August, 1892.
93. CW, vol. 10, p. 157.
94. Wachtmeister, p. 72.
95. Most recently, *The Secret Doctrine* received publicity in 1968 when Sirhan Sirhan, convicted assassin of Robert Kennedy, asked for and received a copy of the work.
96. She was violently opposed to Darwin's ideas of evolution,

especially the hypothesis that humans descended from apes, and called them "wild theories."
97. Blavatsky, *The Secret Doctrine,* vol. 2, p. 464.
98. New York *Times,* July 8, 1889.
99. *Religio-Philosophical Journal,* August 10, 17, 24, 31, September 24, 1889.
100. Müller, *Nineteenth Century Magazine,* May, 1893.
101. Maeterlinck, pp. 201–203.
102. H.P.B. to William Judge, December 1, 1888, *The Path,* July, 1892.
103. H.P.B. to Vera Zhelihovsky, fall, 1888, *The Path,* November, 1895.
104. CW, vol. 10, p. 159.
105. H.P.B. to Vera Zhelihovsky, fall, 1888, *The Path,* November, 1895.
106. Ibid.
107. H.P.B. to William Judge, December 1, 1888, *The Path,* July 1892.
108. ODL, vol. 4, p. 73.
109. *Theosophist,* September, 1889.
110. *The Path,* July, 1892.
111. Richard Harte to H.P.B., August 26, 1889, *Theosophical Forum,* January, 1934.
112. Elliott Coues to H.P.B., March 20, 1886, LBS, p. 357.
113. Henry Olcott to Elliott Coues, undated, New York *Sun,* July 20, 1890.
114. *The Theosophical Movement,* p. 189.
115. Ibid.
116. *Religio-Philosophical Journal,* May 11, 1889.
117. Yeats, *Letters to Katharine Tynan,* p. 95.
118. Yeats, *Four Years,* p. 74.

119. LMW, vol. 1, pp. 96–97.
120. When the case came up for trial in July, 1890, H.P.B.'s counsel showed Mabel's counsel a letter that Mabel had written libeling Madame Blavatsky. Collins' attorney then asked the court to dismiss the case.
121. Quoted in Nethercot, *The First Five Lives of Annie Besant*, p. 30.
122. Tingley, p. 55.
123. Weintraub, p. 140.
124. Quoted in Nethercot, *The First Five Lives of Annie Besant*, p. 106.
125. Ibid.
126. Besant, *Autobiography*, p. 339.
127. Annie Besant to J. Williams Ashman, February 14, 1889, Nethercot, *The First Five Lives of Annie Besant*, p. 400.
128. Besant, *Autobiography*, p. 340.
129. Ibid.
130. Nethercot, *The First Five Lives of Annie Besant*, p. 285.
131. *Pall Mall Gazette*, April 25, 1889.
132. H.P.B. to Annie Besant, March 15, 1889, *Theosophist*, January, 1932.
133. Nethercot, *The First Five Lives of Annie Besant*, pp. 198, 288.
134. ML, p. 405.
135. Ibid., p. 245.
136. Nethercot, *The First Five Lives of Annie Besant*, pp. 288–289.
137. Besant, *Autobiography*, p. 341.
138. Ibid., p. 343.
139. Annie Besant to J. Williams Ashman, March 22, 1889, Nethercot, *The First Five Lives of Annie Besant*, p. 401.
140. Besant, *Autobiography*, pp. 342–343.
141. Weintraub, p. 142.
142. CW, vol. 11, p. 333; Nethercot, p. 298.
143. Weintraub, p. 142.
144. CW, vol. 11, p. 421.
145. H.P.B. to Annie Besant, August, 1889, *Theosophist*, February, 1932.
146. H.P.B. to Nadyezhda Fadeyev or Vera Zhelihovsky, fall, 1889, *London Forum*, July, 1935.
147. Sinnett, *The Early Days of Theosophy in Europe*, p. 108.
148. Besant, *Autobiography*, p. 363.
149. H.P.B. to Nadyezhda Fadeyev, July, 1889, *The Path*, November, 1895.
150. In the preface to the published work, H.P.B. stated that the aphorisms belonged to the same series as the *Stanzas of Dzyan*, supposedly written in Senzar, but in a letter to Vera she mentioned having translated them from Telugu, a South Indian dialect. According to William Coleman, *The Voice of the Silence* was compiled from Brahmanical books on yoga, southern Buddhistic works written in Pali and Cingalese, and northern Buddhistic writings in Chinese and Tibetan, all of which were available in convenient English translations. He mentioned the following works: Schlagintweit's *Buddhism in Tibet*, Edkin's

Chinese Buddhism, Hardy's *Eastern Monachism,* Rhys David's *Buddhism,* Dvivedi's *Raja Yoga* and *Raja Yoga Philosophy*; also an article, "The Dream of Ravan," published in the *Dublin University Magazine,* January, 1854, extracts from which appeared in the *Theosophist,* January, 1880.

151. Besant, *Autobiography,* p. 353.
152. Blavatsky, *The Voice of the Silence,* pp. 2–3.
153. In all, about nine or ten persons testified to having seen the Mahatmas: Annie Besant, Henry Olcott, Damodar Mavalankar, Isabel Cooper-Oakley, William Brown, Nadyezhda Fadeyev, S. R. Ramaswamier, Justine Glinka and Vsevolod Solovyov. Franz Hartmann said that while he never actually saw them, he felt their presence.
154. *Lucifer,* October, 1891. (Written in 1889.)
155. H.P.B. to Annie Besant, July 26, 1889, *Theosophist,* January, 1932.
156. Ibid.
157. H.P.B. to Annie Besant, August 2, 1889, *Theosophist,* February, 1932.
158. H.P.B. to Annie Besant, August, 1889, *Theosophist, February, 1932.*
159. *Lucifer,* June, 1891.
160. Yeats, *Letters to the New Island,* p. 84.
161. Nethercot, *The First Five Lives of Annie Besant,* p. 314.
162. *Light,* July 27, 1889.
163. *Lucifer,* August, 1889.
164. ODL, vol. 4, pp. 184–185.

165. Ibid., p. 193.
166. Ibid., p. 196.
167. Ibid., p. 193.
168. H.P.B. to Annie Besant, *Theosophist,* May, 1932.
169. Ellmann, p. 66.
170. Gandhi, p. 91.
171. Ibid.
172. H.P.B. to Vera Zhelihovsky, February, 1890, *The Path,* December, 1895.
173. Ibid.
174. Ibid.
175. H.P.B. to Annie Besant, circa April or May, 1890, *Theosophist,* April, 1932.
176. H.P.B. to Vera Zhelihovsky, July, 1890, *The Path,* December, 1895.
177. *The Path,* December, 1890.
178. Cleather, *As I Knew Her,* p. 19.
179. *London Forum,* July, 1935.
180. H.P.B. to Vera Zhelihovsky, July, 1890, *The Path,* December, 1895.
181. Sinnett, *The Early Days of Theosophy,* p. 110.
182. *Theosophist,* October, 1931.
183. Sinnett, *The Early Days of Theosophy,* p. 111.
184. She later married George Mead.
185. Cleather, *As I Knew Her,* pp. 23, 84.
186. *Lucifer,* April, 1895.
187. *Religio -Philosophical Journal,* July 13, 1889. Reprinted Washington *Evening Star.*
188. New York *Sun,* June 1, 1890.
189. *Religio -Philosophical Journal,* see issues, July 1889– July 1890.
190. Ibid., August 10, 1889.
191. New York *Sun,* July 20, 1890.
192. Ibid.

193. *The Path*, September, 1890. Postponements delayed the *Sun* libel case coming to court during H.P.B.'s lifetime. Her death automatically terminated the suit, but on September 26, 1892, the *Sun* voluntarily apologized for printing the Coues interview, which it said, "appears to have been without solid foundation" and "should not have been printed."

194. *Lucifer*, June, 1891.

195. Cleather, *As I Knew Her*, p. 22.

196. Bright, p. 20.

197. ODL, vol. 4, p. 262.

198. H.P.B. to Vera Zhelihovsky, July, 1890, *The Path*, December, 1895.

199. H.P.B. to Henry Olcott, fall, 1890, *Theosophist*, November 1907.

200. Koot Hoomi to Allan Hume, November 1, 1880, Conger, p. 38.

201. CW, vol. 11, p. 263.

202. H.P.B, probably to William Judge, undated, *The Path*, August, 1892.

203. LBS, p. 97.

204. ML, p. 299.

205. H.P.B. to K. Khandalavala, November 21, 1889, *Theosophist*, August, 1932.

206. The projected third and fourth volumes of *The Secret Doctrine* were never published and the manuscript, if there was one, mysteriously disappeared. As there is no record of the material having been destroyed by H.P.B., fanciful legends have circulated through the years about its whereabouts, including assertions that some of the manuscript was purposely hidden and will be released at an appropriate time.

The so-called third volume, published in 1897 by Annie Besant, is nothing more than a collection of unfinished articles found in H.P.B.'s desk at the time of her death, but certainly this was not what she intended as Volume Three. According to George Mead (*Lucifer*, July 16, 1897), H.P.B. labored under the misconception that she had enough unused material to fill two additional volumes, but that this was not actually the case.

207. *Lucifer*, June, 1891.

208. H.P.B. to Ursula Bright, quoted in Nethercot, *The First Five Lives of Annie Besant*, p. 355.

209. H.P.B. to William Judge, Ibid., p. 306.

210. *Lucifer*, May, 1891. In my opinion, the date of this article, April 27, 1891, is erroneous because on that date H.P.B. was mortally ill. Presumably it was written sometime before the twenty-sixth.

211. Ibid.

212. *Lucifer*, June, 1891.

213. Ibid.

214. Ibid.

215. Ibid.

Bibliography

Books and Pamphlets

ALLEN, J. A., "Biographical Memoir of Elliott Coues," Washington, D.C., National Academy of Sciences, Biographical Memoirs, Vol. VI, 1909.

ANRIAS, David, *Through the Eyes of the Masters*. London: G. Routledge & Sons, Ltd., 1932.

ARNOLD, Edwin, *India Revisited*. London: Trubner & Co., 1886.

ARUNDALE, Francesca, *My Guest—H. P. Blavatsky*. Madras: Theosophical Publishing House, 1932.

ASQUITH, Margot, *Margot Asquith: An Autobiography*. London: Thornton Butterworth, Ltd., 2 vols., 1920.

BACHCHAN, Harbans Rai, *William Butler Yeats and Occultism*. Delhi: Motilal Banarsidass, 1965.

BAILEY, Alice A., *The Unfinished Autobiography of Alice A. Bailey*. New York: Lucis Publishing Co., 1951.

BAIRD, Alexander T., *Richard Hodgson, The Story of a Psychical Researcher and His Times*. London: Psychic Press, Ltd., 1949.

BARBORKA, Geoffrey A., *H. P. Blavatsky, Tibet and Tulku*. Wheaton: Theosophical Publishing House, 1966.

———, *The Mahatmas and Their Letters*. Wheaton: Theosophical Publishing House, 1973.

BARKER, A. Trevor., comp., *The Letters of H. P. Blavatsky to A. P. Sinnett*. Pasadena: Theosophical University Press, 1973.

———, comp., *The Mahatma Letters to A. P. Sinnett*. Pasadena: Theosophical University Press, 1975.

BECHHOFER-ROBERTS, Carl Eric, *The Mysterious Madame*. New York: Brewer and Warren, Inc., 1931.

BERGAMINI, John D., *The Tragic Dynasty, A History of the Romanovs*. New York: G. P. Putnam's Sons, 1969.

BESANT, Annie, *Annie Besant: An Autobiography*. Philadelphia: Henry Altemus, 1893.

———, *H. P. Blavatsky and the Masters of Wisdom*. Madras: Theosophical Publishing Society, 1907.

———, *The Masters*. Los Angeles: Theosophical Publishing House, 1918.

———, *The Theosophical Society and H.P.B.* Three articles by Annie Besant and H. T. Patterson with notes by H.P.B. Madras: Theosophical Publishing House, 1932.

BESTERMAN, Theodore, *Mrs. Annie Besant: A Modern Prophet*. London: K. Paul, Trench, Trubner & Co., 1934.

BILLINGTON, James H., *The Icon and the Axe*. New York: Alfred A. Knopf, 1966.

BISHOP, Mrs. Isabella L. Bird, *Among the Tibetans*. London: Religious Tract Society, 1894.

BLAVATSKY, Helena P., *Collected Writings*. Compiled by Boris de Zirkoff, 11 vols. (1874 –1889). Wheaton: Theosophical Publishing House, in progress 1950 –1973.

————, *From the Caves and Jungles of Hindostan*. London: Theosophical Publishing Society, 1892.

————, *Isis Unveiled: A Master-Key to the Mysteries of Ancient and Modern Science and Theology*. New York: J. W. Bouton, 1877; Pasadena: Theosophical University Press, 2 vols., 1972.

————, *The Key to Theosophy*, being a clear exposition, in the form of question and answer, of the Ethics, Science, and Philosophy for the study of which the Theosophical Society has been founded. London: The Theosophical Publishing Co., Ltd., 1889; Pasadena: Theosophical University Press, 1972.

————, *H.P.B. Speaks*. C. Jinarājadāsa, ed., Madras: Theosophical Publishing House, 2 vols., 1950 –1951.

————, *Nightmare Tales*. London, New York, Madras: Theosophical Publishing Society, 1892.

————, *The People of the Blue Mountains*. Wheaton: Theosophical Press, 1930.

————, *The Secret Doctrine: The Synthesis of Science, Religion, and Philosophy*. London, New York, Madras: Theosophical Publishing Co., Ltd., 2 vols., 1888; Pasadena: Theosophical University Press, 1974.

————, *Studies in Occultism*. Pasadena: Theosophical University Press, 1973.

————, *The Theosophical Glossary*. G.R.S. Mead, ed. London: Theosophical Publishing Society, 1892.

————, *Transactions of the Blavatsky Lodge of the Theosophical Society*. London: Theosophical Publishing Society, 1890–1891.

————, *The Voice of the Silence, and Other Chosen Fragments from the Book of the Golden Precepts*. London: Theosophical Publishing Society, 1893.

BLAVATSKY Association, The, *H.P.B.—In Memory of Helena Petrovna Blavatsky, by some of her Pupils*. London: 1931.

BLINOFF, M., *Life and Thought in Old Russia*. University Park, Pennsylvania: Pennsylvania State University, 1961.

BLOOM, Ursula, *Victorian Vinaigrette*. London: Hutchison and Co., 1956.

BRAGDON, Claude, *Episodes from an Unwritten History*. Rochester, New York: The Manas Press, 1910.

BRIDGE, John Ransom, *"Helena Petrovna Blavatsky,"* New York, *The Arena*, April, 1895.

BRIGHT, Esther, *Old Memories and Letters of Annie Besant.* London: Theosophical Publishing House, 1936.

BRITTEN, Emma Hardinge, *Nineteenth Century Miracles.* London: William Britten, 1883.

BULWER-LYTTON, Edward, *Zanoni.* Philadelphia: J. B. Lippincott, 1882.

BURTIS, Mary Elizabeth, *Moncure Conway,* 1832–1907. New Brunswick, New Jersey: Rutgers University Press, 1952.

BUTT, G. Baseden, *Madame Blavatsky.* London: Rider & Co., 1925.

BYRNE, Patrick, *The Wildes of Merrion Square: The Family of Oscar Wilde.* New York: Staples Press, 1953.

CARDOZO, Nancy, *Lucky Eyes and a High Heart. The Life of Maud Gonne.* New York: Bobbs-Merrill Co., 1978.

CARRINGTON, Hereward, *The Physical Phenomena of Spiritualism.* New York: Dodd, Mead & Co., 1920.

CARRITHERS, Walter A., Jr., *"Madame Blavatsky: 'One of the World's Great Jokers,' "* Journal of the American Society for Psychical Research, Vol. LVI, July, 1962.

———, *The Truth about Madame Blavatsky. An Open Letter to the Author of* Priestess of Occult. Covina, California: Theosophical University Press, 1947.

———(pseudonym, Adlai E. Waterman), *Obituary: The "Hodgson Report" on Madame Blavatsky 1885–1960.* Madras: Theosophical Publishing House, 1963.

CLEATHER, Alice Leighton, *H. P. Blavatsky, As I Knew Her.* Calcutta: Thacker, Spink & Co., 1923.

———, *H. P. Blavatsky. A Great Betrayal.* Calcutta: Thacker, Spink & Co., 1922.

———, *H. P. Blavatsky. Her Life and Work for Humanity.* Calcutta: Thacker, Spink & Co., 1922.

COCKER, B. F., *Christianity and Greek Philosophy.* New York: Harper & Bros., 1870.

COHEN, Daniel, *Masters of the Occult.* New York: Dodd, Mead & Co., 1971.

———, *The New Believers.* New York: Ballantine Books, 1976.

COLEMAN, William Emmette, "The Sources of Madame Blavatsky's Writings," Appendix C, in Solovyov's *Modern Priestess of Isis.*

COLLINS, Mabel, *Light on the Path.* Wheaton: Theosophical Publishing House, 1970.

CONGER, Margaret, *Combined Chronology for Use with the Mahatma Letters to A. P. Sinnett and the Letters of H. P. Blavatsky to A. P. Sinnett.* Pasadena: Theosophical University Press, 1973.

CONWAY, Moncure Daniel, *My Pilgrimage to the Wise Men of the East.* London: Archibald Constable & Co., 1906.

CORSON, Eugene R., *Some Unpublished Letters of Helena Petrovna Blavatsky.* London: Rider & Co., 1929.

COULOMB, Emma, *Some Account of My Intercourse with Madame Blavatsky*. London: Elliot Stock, 1885.

CRAWFORD, F. Marion, *Mr. Isaacs. A Tale of Modern India*. New York and London: The Macmillan Co., 1882.

CROW, Duncan, *The Victorian Woman*. New York: Stein & Day, 1972.

CRUMP, Basil, *Evolution as Outlined in the Archaic Eastern Records*. London: Luzac and Co., 1930.

DAVID-NEEL, Alexandra, *Magic and Mystery in Tibet*. New Hyde Park, New York: University Books, 1956.

DE STEIGER, Isabelle, *Memorabilia. Reminiscences of a Woman Artist and Writer*. London: Rider & Co., 1927.

DEVANT, David, *Lessons in Conjuring*. London: G. Routledge & Sons, 1922.

DEVEREUX, George, ed., *Psychoanalysis and the Occult*. New York: International Universities Press, 1953.

DE ZIRKOFF, Boris, *Rebirth of the Occult Tradition: How the Secret Doctrine of H. P. Blavatsky Was Written*. Wheaton: Theosophical Publishing House, 1977.

DINGWALL, Eric J., ed., *Abnormal Hypnotic Phenomena: Survey of Nineteenth Century Cases*. London: J. & A. Churchill, Ltd., 4 vols. (Vol. IV edited by Allan Angoff), 1968.

DONNELLY, Ignatius, *Atlantis: The Antediluvian World*. New York: Harper & Bros., 1882.

DOYLE, Sir Arthur Conan, *The History of Spiritualism*. New York: Arno Press, 2 vols., 1975.

EDWARDS, Michael, *A History of India*, New York: Farrar, Straus and Cudahy, 1961.

EEK, Sven, *Damodar and the Pioneers of the Theosophical Movement*. Madras: Theosophical Publishing House, 1965.

———, and de Zirkoff, Boris, compilers, *William Quan Judge: 1851–1896, The Life of a Theosophical Pioneer and Some of His Outstanding Articles*. Wheaton: Theosophical Publishing House, 1969.

EGLINTON, John (pseudonym, William Kirkpatrick Magee), *A Memoir of Æ*. London: Macmillan & Co., Ltd., 1937.

ELLMANN, Richard, *Yeats: The Man and the Mask*. New York: E.P. Dutton, 1948.

ELLWOOD, Robert S., *Religious and Spiritual Groups in Modern America*. Englewood Cliffs, New Jersey: Prentice-Hall, Inc., 1973.

ENDERSBY, Victor A., *The Hall of Magic Mirrors. A Portrait of Madame Blavatsky*. New York: Carlton Press, 1969.

ERIKSON, E. H., *Gandhi's Truth*. New York: W. W. Norton Co., 1969.

ERNST, Robert, *Immigrant Life in New York City, 1825–1863*. New York: King's Crown Press, 1949.

EVANS, Henry Ridgely, *Hours with the Ghosts*. Chicago: Laird & Lee, 1897.

EVANS-WENTZ, W. Y., *The Tibetan Book of the Dead*. London: Oxford University Press, 1927.

————, *Tibet's Great Yogi Milarepa*. London: Oxford University Press, 1928.

FARQUHAR, J. N., *Modern Religious Movements in India*. New York: The Macmillan Co., 1915.

FLEW, Antony, *A New Approach to Psychical Research*. London: Watts & Co., 1953.

FLINT, Charles R., *Memories of an Active Life*. New York and London: G. P. Putnam's Sons, 1923.

FLOURNOY, Theodore, *From India to the Planet Mars. A Study of a Case of Somnambulism with Glossolalia*. New Hyde Park, New York: University Books, 1963.

FORSYTH, J. S., *Demonologia*. London: A. K. Newman and Co., 1831.

FRANCIS, T. M. (pseudonym), *Blavatsky, Besant and Co. The Story of a Great Christian Fraud*. St. Paul, Minnesota: Library Service Guild, 1939.

FREEDLAND, Nat, *The Occult Explosion*. New York: G. P. Putnam's Sons, 1972.

FREUD, Sigmund, *Studies in Parapsychology*. New York: Collier Books, 1963.

————, *Dora: An Analysis of a Case of Hysteria*. New York: Collier Books, 1963.

GALBREATH, Robert, ed., *The Occult: Studies and Evaluation*. Bowling Green, Ohio: Bowling Green University Popular Press, 1972.

GANDHI, Mohandas K., *Autobiography*. Washington, D.C.: Public Affairs Press, 1948.

GARRETT, Edmund, *Isis Very Much Unveiled*. London: Westminster Gazette, 1894.

GARRETT, Eileen J., *My Life as a Search for the Meaning of Mediumship*. New York: Oquaga Press, 1939.

————, *Many Voices: The Autobiography of a Medium*. New York: G. P. Putnam's Sons, 1968.

GASKELL, George A., *Exeunt Mahatmas*. London: Watts & Co., 1907.

GAULD, Alan, *The Founders of Psychical Research*. New York: Schocken Books, 1968.

GODWIN, John, *Occult America*. New York: Doubleday and Co., 1972.

GOODWIN, Nathaniel (revised ed. by Henry S. Olcott), *The Descendants of Thomas Olcott*. Albany, New York: J. Munsell, 1874.

GURNEY, Edmund, Frederic W. H. Myers, and Frank Podmore, *Phantasms of the Living*. Gainesville, Florida: Scholars' Facsimiles & Reprints, 2 vols., 1970 (original ed. 1886).

HANSEL, C. E. M., *ESP. A Scientific Evaluation*. New York: Charles Scribner's Sons, 1966.

HANSON, Virginia, ed., *H. P. Blavatsky and The Secret Doctrine: Commen-*

taries on Her Contributions to World Thought. Wheaton: Theosophical Publishing House, 1971.

HARE, Harold E. and William L. Hare, *Who Wrote the Mahatma Letters?* London: Williams & Norgate, Ltd., 1936.

HART, Roger, *English Life in the Nineteenth Century.* New York: G. P. Putnam's Sons, 1971.

HARTMANN, Franz, *Report of Observations, Made During a Nine Months' Stay at the Head-quarters of the Theosophical Society at Adyar [Madras], India.* Madras: Scottish Press, 1884.

HASTINGS, Beatrice, *Defence of Madame Blavatsky.* Worthing, Sussex: The Hastings Press, 2 vols., 1937.

————, *New Universe—"Try." A Review Devoted to the Defence of Madame Blavatsky.* Worthing, Sussex: The Hastings Press, July 1937–July 1938.

HAXTHAUSEN, Baron August Von, *Transcaucasia.* London: Chapman and Hall, 1854.

————, *The Russian Empire.* London: Chapman and Hall, 1856.

HAYES, Carlton J. H., *A Generation of Materialism, 1871–1900.* New York: Harper & Row, 1963.

HERVEY, Mrs. *The Adventures of a Lady in Tartary, Thibet, China and Kashmir.* London: Hope and Co., 3 vols., 1853.

HINKSON, Katharine Tynan, *Memories.* London: Nash, 1924.

HOLLOWAY, Laura C. Langford, "Helena Petrovna Blavatsky: A Reminiscence," New York: *The Word,* Vol. XXII, December, 1915.

HOLT, Elizabeth G. K, "A Reminiscence of H. P. Blavatsky in 1873," Bombay, Madras, *The Theosophist,* Vol. LIII, December, 1931.

HOME, Daniel Dunglas, *Lights and Shadows of Spiritualism.* New York: G. W. Carleton, 1879.

HOMMAIRE DE HELL, Xavier, *Travels in the Steppes of the Caspian Sea, the Crimea, the Caucasus, etc.* London: Chapman and Hall, 1847.

HONE, Joseph, *W. B. Yeats.* New York: Macmillan Company, 1943.

HOWELL, Basil P., ed., *The Theosophical Society: The First 50 Years.* London: Theosophical Publishing House, 1925.

HUC, Abbé Evariste Regis. *High Road in Tartary. An Abridged Revision of Abbé Huc's Travels in Tartary, Tibet and China During the Years 1844–1846,* Julie Bedier, ed., New York: Charles Scribner's Sons, 1948.

HUME, Allan O., *Hints on Esoteric Theosophy.* Calcutta: The Theosophical Society, 1882.

JACKSON, Holbrook, *The Eighteen Nineties.* New York: Capricorn Books, 1966.

JACOLLIOT, Louis, *The Bible in India: Hindoo Origin of Hebrew and Christian Revelation.* New York: Carleton Publisher, 1870.

————, *Occult Science in India and Among the Ancients.* London: William Rider & Son, Ltd., 1919.

JAMES, William, *The Varieties of Religious Experience*. London: Longmans, Green, and Co., 1902.

———, *William James on Psychical Research*. Gardner Murphy and Robert O. Ballou, eds., New York: Viking Press, 1960.

JENKINS, Lady Catherine M., *Sport and Travel in Both Tibets*. London: Blades, East and Blades, 1909.

JERRMANN, Edward, *St. Petersburg. Its People, Their Character and Institutions*. New York: A. S. Barnes & Co., 1855.

JINARĀJADĀSA, C., *Did Madame Blavatsky Forge the Mahatma Letters?* Madras: Theosophical Publishing House, 1934.

———, comp., *The Early Teachings of the Masters*. Chicago: The Theosophical Press, 1923.

———, ed., *The Golden Book of the Theosophical Society, A Brief History of the Society's Growth from 1875–1925*. Madras: Theosophical Publishing House, 1925.

———, comp., *The "K.H." Letters to C. W. Leadbeater*. Madras: Theosophical Publishing House, 1941.

———, comp., *Letters from the Masters of Wisdom*. Madras: Theosophical Publishing House, 2 vols., 1948.

JOHNSON, Raynor C., *Psychical Research*. New York: Funk & Wagnalls, 1968.

JUNG, C. G., *Psychology and the Occult*. Princeton, New Jersey: Princeton University Press, 1977.

KARDEC, Allan (Hippolyte Léon Denizard Rivail), *Experimental Spiritism: Book on Mediums*. Emma A. Wood, tr., New York: Samuel Weiser, 1970.

KEIGHTLEY, Archibald, "Reminiscences of H. P. Blavatsky," New York: *The Theosophical Quarterly*, Vol. VII, October, 1910.

KEIGHTLEY, Bertram, "Reminiscences of H. P. Blavatsky," Bombay, Madras: *The Theosophist*, September, 1931.

KEYSERLING, Count Hermann von, *The Travel Diary of a Philosopher*. J. H. Reece, tr. , New York: Harcourt, Brace & Co., 1925.

KING, Francis, *Ritual Magic in England*. London: Neville Spearman, Ltd., 1970.

KINGSFORD, Anna, and Edward Maitland, *The Perfect Way, or the Finding of Christ*. London: Field & Tuer, 1882.

KINGSLAND, William, *The Real H. P. Blavatsky: A Study in Theosophy and a Memoir of a Great Soul*. London: John M. Watkins, 1928.

KIPLING, Rudyard, *Kim*. New York: Dodd, Mead & Co., 1962.

KUHN, Alvin Boyd, *Theosophy: A Modern Revival of Ancient Wisdom*. New York: Henry Holt and Co., 1930.

LEADBEATER, Charles W., *How Theosophy Came to Me*. Madras: Theosophical Publishing House, 1930.

LEONARD, Gladys Osborne, *My Life in Two Worlds*. London: Cassell & Co., Ltd., 1931.

LEONARD, Maurice, *Madame Blavatsky: Medium, Mystic, and Magician.* London and New York: Regency Press Ltd., 1976.

LEUBA, James H., *The Psychology of Religious Mysticism.* London: Kegan Paul, Trench, Trubner & Co., 1925.

LÉVI, Eliphas (Alphonse Louis Constant), *The History of Magic.* Los Angeles: Borden Publishing Co., undated.

LILJEGREN, Sten B., *Bulwer-Lytton's Novels and Isis Unveiled.* Cambridge, Massachusetts: Harvard University Press, 1957.

LILLIE, Arthur H., *Madame Blavatsky and Her "Theosophy."* London: Swan Sonnenschein & Co., 1895.

————, *Modern Mystics and Modern Magic.* London: Swan Sonnenschein & Co., 1894.

LINTON, George E., and Virginia Hanson, eds., *Reader's Guide to the Mahatma Letters to A. P. Sinnett.* Wheaton: Theosophical Publishing House, 1972.

LIPPITT, Francis James, *Reminiscences.* Providence, Rhode Island: Preston & Rounds Co., 1902.

LUTYENS, Lady Emily, *Candles in the Sun.* Philadelphia and New York: J. B. Lippincott Co., 1957.

LUTYENS, Mary, *Krishnamurti. The Years of Awakening.* New York: Farrar, Straus and Giroux, Inc., 1975.

MACBRIDE, Maud Gonne, *A Servant of the Queen: Her Own Story.* Dublin: Golden Eagle Books, Ltd., 1950.

MCCABE, James D., *Lights and Shadows of New York Life.* Philadelphia: National Publishing Co., 1872.

MACKENZIE, Norman, ed., *Secret Societies.* New York: Collier Books, 1967.

MAETERLINCK, Maurice, *The Great Secret.* Bernard Miall, tr., London: Methuen, 1922.

MAGRE, Maurice, *Return of the Magi.* London: Philip Allan, 1931.

MAITLAND, Edward, *Anna Kingsford. Her Life, Letters, Diary and Work.* London: George Redway, 2 vols., 1896.

MARRYAT, Florence, *"Gup": Sketches of Anglo -Indian Life and Character.* London: Richard Bentley, 1868.

MASKELYNE, J.N., *The Fraud of Modern "Theosophy" Exposed.* London: G. Routledge & Sons, Ltd., 1913.

MAVALANKAR, Damodar, *Damodar, The Writings of a Hindu Chela.* Sven Eek, comp. Point Loma, California: Theosophical University Press, 1940.

MEHTA, Ved, *Gandhi and His Apostles.* New York: Viking Press, 1977.

MENOTTI, Gian-Carlo, *The Medium.* New York: G. Schirmer, 1947.

MOON, Penderel, *Gandhi and Modern India.* New York: W.W. Norton Co., 1969.

MOORE, Clark D. and David Eldridge, eds., *India Yesterday and Today.* New York: Praeger Publishers, 1970.

MOORE, George, *Salve*. New York: Boni and Liveright, 1923.

MOORE, Virginia, *The Unicorn: William Butler Yeats' Search for Reality*. New York: The Macmillan Co., 1954.

MORGAN, Henry Rhodes, *Reply to a Report of an Examination by J. D. B. Gribble*. Ootacamund: Observer Press, 1884.

MORRIS, Isabel, *A Summer in Kieff*. London: Ward and Downey, 1891.

MORTON, Eleanor, *The Women in Gandhi's Life*. New York: Dodd, Mead and Co., 1953.

MOSCHELES, Charlotte, *The Life of Moscheles*. A. D. Coleridge, tr. London: Hurst and Blackett, 2 vols., 1873.

MOWAT, Robert B., *The Victorian Age*. London: George G. Harrap & Co., 1939.

MÜLLER, Max, *Theosophy or Psychological Religion*. London and New York: Longmans, Green and Co., 1893.

MUNDY, Talbot, *The Nine Unknown*. Indianapolis: Bobbs-Merrill Co., 1923.

MURPHET, Howard, *Hammer on the Mountain: Life of Henry Steel Olcott (1832–1907)*. Wheaton: Theosophical Publishing House, 1972.

———, *When Daylight Comes, A Biography of Helena Petrovna Blavatsky*. Wheaton: Theosophical Publishing House, 1975.

MYERS, Frederic W.H., *Human Personality*. London: Longmans, Green and Co., 2 vols., 1904.

NEFF, Mary K., *The "Brothers" of Madame Blavatsky*. Madras: Theosophical Publishing House, 1932.

———, comp., *Personal Memoirs of H. P. Blavatsky*. Wheaton: Theosophical Publishing House, 1971.

NETHERCOT, Arthur E., *The First Five Lives of Annie Besant*. Chicago: University of Chicago Press, 1960.

———, *The Last Four Lives of Annie Besant*. Chicago: University of Chicago Press, 1963.

OLCOTT, Henry Steel, *Old Diary Leaves: The True Story of the Theosophical Society*. New York and London: G. P. Putnam's Sons, 4 vols., 1895.

———, *People from the Other World*. Hartford, Connecticut: American Publishing Co., 1875.

OLCOTT, Mary Louisa Beatrice, *The Olcotts and Their Kindred from Anglo - Saxon Times*. New York: National Americana Publications, 1956.

OSTRANDER, Sheila and Lynn Schroeder, *Psychic Discoveries Behind the Iron Curtain*. Englewood Cliffs, New Jersey: Prentice-Hall, Inc., 1970.

PATTERSON, George, "The Collapse of Koot Hoomi," Madras, *Christian College Magazine*, September, October, 1884.

PAUWELS, Louis, and Jacques Bergier, *The Morning of the Magicians*. New York: Stein & Day, 1963.

PAYNE, Robert, *Life and Death of Gandhi*. New York: E. P. Dutton Co., 1969.

PEARSON, Hesketh, *Oscar Wilde. His Life and Wit*. New York: Harper & Bros., 1946.

PEEBLES, James M., *Around the World*. Boston: Colby and Rich Publishers, 1875.

PODMORE, Frank., *Studies in Psychical Research*. London: Kegan Paul, Trench, Trubner & Co., Ltd., 1897.

POORTMAN, J. J., *Philosophy-Theosophy-Parapsychology*. Leyden, Netherlands: A. W. Sythoff, 1965.

Posthumous Memoirs of Helena Petrovna Blavatsky Dictated from the Spirit World. Boston: J. M. Wade, 1896.

PRAED, Mrs. Campbell, *The Soul of Countess Adrian*. New York: United States Book Co., 1891.

PRICE, Harry, *Fifty Years of Psychical Research*. London: Longmans, Green and Co., 1939.

PRIESTLEY, J. B., *Victoria's Heyday*. New York: Harper & Row, 1972.

PRINCE, Morton, *The Dissociation of a Personality*. London: Longmans, Green and Co., 1906.

PRINCE, Walter Franklin, *The Case of Patience Worth*. Boston: Boston Society for Psychic Research, 1927.

RACOWITZA, Princess Helene von, *An Autobiography*. Cecil Mar, tr. New York: The Macmillan Co., 1910.

RAHULA, Walpola, *What the Buddha Taught*. New York: Grove Press, Inc., 1959.

RANSOM, Josephine, *A Short History of the Theosophical Society*. Madras: Theosophical Publishing House, 1938.

RAWSON, Albert L., "Mme. Blavatsky. A Theosophical Occult Apology," New York: *Frank Leslie's Popular Monthly*, February, 1892.

RHYS, Ernest, *Wales England Wed*. London: J. M. Dent, Ltd., 1940.

RIASANOVSKY, Nicholas V., *A History of Russia*. New York: Oxford University Press, 1977.

RICHARDSON, H. E., *A Short History of Tibet*. New York: E. P. Dutton & Co., 1962.

RICHARDSON-GARDNER, R. *A Trip to St. Petersburg*. London: T. Brettell & Co., 1873.

RICHET, Charles, *Thirty Years of Psychical Research*. New York: The Macmillan Co., 1923.

RIJNHART, Dr. Susie Carson, *With the Tibetans in Tent and Temple: Narrative of Four Year's Residence on the Tibetan Border and of a Journey into the Interior*. Edinburgh: Oliphant, Anderson & Ferrier, 1902.

ROBERTS, Jane, *The Seth Material*. New York: Bantam Books, 1976.

ROCKHILL, William Woodville, *The Land of the Lamas*. New York: The Century Co., 1891.

RODERICK, Colin, *In Mortal Bondage—The Strange Life of Rosa Praed*. Sidney: Angus and Robertson, 1948.

ROHMER, Sax, *The Romance of Sorcery*. London: Methuen & Co., Ltd., 1915.

ROLLAND, Romain, *Prophets of the New India*. New York A. & C. Boni, 1930.

Row, T. Subba, *A Collection of Esoteric Writings of T. Subba Row.* Bombay: The Tatva-Vivechaka Press, 1910.

Rudhyar, Dane, *Occult Preparations for a New Age.* Wheaton: Theosophical Publishing House, 1975.

Russell, Edmund, "As I Knew Her." London: *Herald of the Star,* Vol. V, May 11, 1916.

Russell, George, *The Candle of Vision.* London: Macmillan and Co., Ltd., 1919.

————,*Letters from Æ.* London: Abelard-Schuman, 1961.

Ryan, Charles, *H. P. Blavatsky and the Theosophical Movement.* Pasadena, California: Theosophical University Press, 1937.

Sarasvati, Swami Dayananda, *An English Translation of the Satyarth Prakash,* V. Shashtri, J. Vidyarthi, and B. Bath, eds. New Delhi: Jan Gyan Prakashan, 1970.

Saurat, Denis, *Literature and Occult Tradition.* Port Washington, New York: Kennikat Press, 1930.

Schary, Edwin G., *In Search of the Mahatmas of Tibet.* London: Seeley, Service & Co., 1937.

Scholem, Gershom G., *Major Trends in Jewish Mysticism.* Jerusalem: Schocken Publishing House, 1941.

Sheehan, Vincent, *Lead Kindly Light.* New York and Toronto: Random House, 1949.

Shepard, Leslie, ed., *Encyclopedia of Occultism and Parapsychology.* Detroit: Gale Research Co., 1978.

Sidgwick, Ethel, *Mrs. Henry Sidgwick, a Memoir by Her Niece.* London: Sidgwick & Jackson, Ltd., 1938.

Sinnett, Alfred Percy, *The Early Days of Theosophy in Europe.* London: Theosophical Publishing House, 1922.

————, *Esoteric Buddhism.* London: Trubner & Co., 1884.

————, *The Occult World.* Boston: Colby & Rich, 1882.

————, ed., *Incidents in the Life of Madame Blavatsky.* London: George Redway, 1886.

Smith, Huston, *The Religions of Man.* New York: Harper & Bros., 1958.

Smith, Warren S., *The London Heretics, 1870–1914.* New York: Dodd, Mead & Co., 1968.

Society for psychical research, "Report on Phenomena connected with Theosophy," *Proceedings of the Society for Psychical Research,* Vol. III, December 1885.

Solovyov, Vsevolod S., *A Modern Priestess of Isis.* Walter Leaf, tr. London: Longmans, Green & Co., 1895.

Somerlott, Robert, *Here, Mr. Splitfoot.* New York: Viking Press, 1971.

Spear, Thomas G. Percival, *A Modern History* [India]. Ann Arbor, Michigan: University of Michigan Press, 1961.

Strachey, Rachel Conn, *Religious Fanaticism.* London: Faber & Gwyer, Ltd., 1928.

SYMONDS, John, *Madame Blavatsky—Medium and Magic*. London: Odhams Press, 1959.

The Theosophical Movement, 1875—1925. A History and Survey. New York: E. P. Dutton & Co., 1925.

THOMPSON, Oscar, ed., *International Cyclopedia of Music and Musicians*. New York: Dodd, Mead & Co., 1975.

TINGLEY, Katherine, and De Purucker, G., *Helena Petrovna Blavatsky*. Point Loma, California: The Women's International Theosophical League, 1921.

TINGSTEN, Herbert, *Victoria and the Victorians*. New York: Delacorte Press, 1965.

TIRYAKIAN, Edward A., ed., *On the Margin of the Visible*. New York: John Wiley & Sons, 1974.

TYRRELL, G. N., *Apparitions*. New York: Collier Books, 1953.

VONNEGUT, Kurt Jr., "The Mysterious Madame Blavatsky," New York: *McCall's*, March, 1970.

WACHTMEISTER, Constance, *Reminiscences of H. P. Blavatsky and The Secret Doctrine*. Wheaton: Theosophical Publishing House, 1976.

WALLACE, Alfred Russell, *Miracles and Modern Spiritualism*. London: Nichols and Co., 1901.

WEBB, James, *The Occult Underground*. La Salle, Illinois: Open Court Publishing Co., 1974.

———, *The Occult Establishment*. La Salle, Illinois: Open Court Publishing Co., 1976.

WEBSTER, Nesta H., *Secret Societies and Subversive Movements*. London: Britons Publishing Co., 1964.

WEDDERBURN, Sir William, *Allan Octavian Hume, C.B.* London: T. Fisher Unwin, 1913.

WEINTRAUB, Stanley, ed., *Shaw. An Autobiography, 1856–1898*. New York: Weybright and Talley, Inc., 1969.

WHYTE, Frederic, *The Life of W. T. Stead*. London: Capp, 2 vols., 1925.

WILLIAMS, Gertrude L., *The Passionate Pilgrim: A Life of Annie Besant*. New York: Coward-McCann, 1931.

———, *Priestess of the Occult*. New York: Alfred A. Knopf, 1946.

WILLIAMS, Montagu S., *Leaves of a Life*. London and New York: The Macmillan Co., 1890.

WILSON, Colin, *The Occult: A History*. New York: Random House, 1971.

———, ed., *Dark Dimensions*. New York: Everest House, 1978.

WILSON, H. H., tr., *The Vishnu Purana*. London: Trubner & Co., 5 vols., 1864 –1877.

WINCHELL, Alexander, *World Life*. Chicago: S. C. Griggs & Co., 1883.

WITTE, Count Sergei, *The Memoirs of Count Witte*. Garden City, New York and Toronto: Doubleday, Page & Co., 1921.

WOLFF, Hannah M., "Madame Blavatsky," London: *The Two Worlds*, Dec. 11, 1891, reprinted from *The Better Way*.

YEATS, William Butler, *The Collected Poems of W. B. Yeats*. New York: Macmillan, 1956.

————, *Four Years*. Churchtown, Dundrum: Cuala Press, 1921.

————, *Letters to the New Island*. Cambridge, Massachusetts: Harvard University Press, 1934.

————, *Letters to Katharine Tynan*. New York: McMullen Books, 1953.

————, *Memoirs*. Denis Donoghue, ed. New York: Macmillan, 1973.

YOUNG, Samuel, *Psychic Children*. Garden City, New York: Doubleday & Co., 1977.

ZELLER, Edward, *Plato and the Older Academy*. London: Longmans, Green and Co., 1888.

ZIFF, Larzer, *The American 1890's*. New York: Viking Press, 1966.

Periodicals

The Arena, New York
Banner of Light, Boston
Christian College Magazine, Madras
Frank Leslie's Popular Monthly, New York
Herald of the Star, London
International Journal of Parapsychology, New York
The Liberal Christian, New York
Light, London
Lucifer, London
Nineteenth Century Magazine, London
Occult Review, London
The Path, New York
Religio -Philosophical Journal, Chicago
The Saturday Review of Politics, Literature, Science and Art, London
The Theosophical Forum, New York
Theosophical Quarterly, New York
Theosophical Review, London
The Theosophist, Bombay, Madras
The Word, New York
The Two Worlds, London

Index

Addams, Jane, 460
Adhemar, Count Gaston d', 295
Adhemar, Countess Marguerite d',
    295, 418
Affinities (Praed), 349
"Agardi, Endreinek," 157
Aksakov, Alexander Nikolayevitch,
    116, 130–36, 142–43, 152,
    153, 155, 164-65, 177, 179,
    180
Albert, Prince, 68
Alcock, John, 111
Alexander I, Czar, 20, 52
Alexander II, Czar, 75, 82, 102,
    129
Alexandra, Empress, 19
Alger, W. R., 174–75
Allen, George, 211
Allen Scott and Company, 413
American Bibliopolist (periodical),
    150
American Publishing Company, 132
American Society for Psychical Re-
    search, 336, 420
American Spiritualist Alliance, 269
Amrita Bazaar Patrika (periodi-
    cal), 206
Ancient Wisdom, 72
Andrews, Em, 146
Andrews, Louisa, 133, 146, 156
Anthony, Susan B., 107
Arcane School, 468
Arnold, Sir Edwin, 339, 439
Art Magic (Britten), 149, 164
Arundale, Francesca, 286, 313, 317,
    355, 374, 377, 444, 460

H.P.B. as houseguest of, 305,
    307–12
Olcott and, 320, 345, 347, 350,
    353
Arundale, George, 305, 444, 460,
    461
Arundale, Mary, 305, 350
Arya Samaj, 181–82, 185, 195–97,
    203, 228, 254
Aryan Race, 415–16
Ashman, J. Williams, 424, 428
Asquith, Lady Margot, 405-6
Assyriology, 417
Atlantis, 415, 416
Atlantis (Donnelly), 379
Atwood, I. G., 130
Augustine, St., 423

Babu, Shashir, 306
Babula, 197–98, 200, 202, 209, 250,
    256, 272, 280–81, 285, 313,
    337, 346
    in Ceylon, 214
    as H.P.B.'s accomplice, 222–24,
        240
    in London, 305, 309
    marriage of, 261, 265
    in Paris, 288, 296, 302
Babuna, Maria Solomonovna, 51
Baburao, 200–2
Bagration, Princess, 129
Bai, Radda, 204, 209, 296
Bailey, Alice, 468
Ballard, Anna, 102
Banner of Light (periodical), 110,

140, 142, 156, 164, 230, 269–70
Baroda High Court, 249
Bates, Rosa ("Taffy"), 186, 187, 194–97, 201, 204, 209, 214–16, 220, 231
Beard, George, 126–27, 129
Beecher, Henry Ward, 111
Beg, Moorad Ali, 262
Bel Ibrahim Bek Ogli, Safar Ali, 56–57
Belinsky, Vissarion, 33
Ben Makerzi, Sheik Yusaf, 65
Bengal Civil Service, 224
Benson, Mrs. Edward, 443
Benzenger, Vassily, 34
Bernard, Claude, 378
Bernhardt, Sarah, 401
Besant, Annie, 151, 206, 405, 422–47, 450, 452–53, 456–61
Besant, Digby, 423
Besant, Frank, 423, 424
Besant, Mabel, 423
Betanelly, Michael, 116–19, 127–28, 131, 157, 375, 449
    marriage of H.P.B. and, 136–39, 143–45, 156, 176–77, 183
Bey, Serapis, 139, 142, 144–45, 186, 227, 466
Bey, Tuitit, 139, 142, 466
Bhagavad-Gītā, 249, 339, 416, 420, 439
Bible in India, The (Jacolliot), 170
Bible Society, 52
Bibliothèque Nationale, 296
Billing, Mary Hollis, 193–94, 240, 254–55, 295, 305
Blavatsky, Helena Petrovna (H.P.B.)
    adolescence of, 41–52
    in America, 101–89
        Boston, 145–46
        immigration, 101–4
        Ithaca, 152–54
        Long Island farm, 109–10, 141
        naturalized citizenship, 15, 183
        in New York, 101–10, 126–32, 147–89
    obsession with India, 180–89
    Philadelphia, 133–40, 142–45
    Annie Besant and, 422, 425–47, 450, 452–53
    Beard and, 126–29
    Betanelly and, 116–19, 127–28, 136
    divorce, 183
    marriage, 133, 137–39, 143–45, 176–77
    birth of, 21
    birth of son Yuri to, 86–92
    break with Olcott, 350–51, 407–12, 419–20, 437–38, 450–51
    in Brotherhood of Luxor, 138–42, 150
    childhood of, 24–27, 29–40
    in Constantinople, 62–64
    death of, 454–56
    departure from Russia, 61–62
    in Egypt, 64–66, 93–96, 326–29
    at Elberfield, 312–17, 373–75
    Emma Coulomb's denunciation of, 289–91, 293–95, 299, 303, 313–19, 322–23, 355, 356, 426, 428, 448
    family background of, 15–21
    first meeting of Olcott and, 118–26
    at founding of Theosophical Society, 151–52, 154–56
    Hannah Wolff and, 106–9
    Home and, 73–74, 179–80
    in India, 195–279
        Bombay, 195–200, 204–9, 212–17, 231, 245–48, 252–56
        Calcutta, 248–49
        Darjeeling, 256–59
        Karli Caves, 200–1
        Madras, 250–52, 260–65, 268–72, 274–76, 330–32, 335–46
        Punjab trip, 202–4
        Sinnett and, 209–12, 216–30, 239–48, 253
    John King and, 135–39, 141, 144
    Kingsford and, 276–78
    in London, 66–68, 193–94, 292–93, 305–12, 321–26

during final years, 389–456
marriage of Nikifor Blavatsky
and, 52–57, 75–76, 82, 83,
85–86
newspaper articles by, 156–57
for Russian papers, 182, 204,
231, 266, 395, 418
obituaries of, 456–57
at Ostend, 375–86
Palm and, 164–66
in Paris, 96–97, 287–304
psi faculties of, discussion of,
461–64
return to Europe from India,
285–87
return to Russia, 74–86
Society for Psychical Research
and, 305–9, 322–23
Hodgson investigation, 335–45
Spiritualism and, 115–16, 126–
28, 140, 150
Holmes scandal, 134–35
in Switzerland, 351–52
in Torre del Greco, 347–51
Wilder and, 173–75
writing of Isis Unveiled by, 152–
53, 156–64, 168–74, 184
in Würtzburg, 353–73
Yeats and, 400–4
Blavatsky, Nikifor, 61, 64, 123,
127,141, 367, 368, 384, 452
marriage of H.P.B. and, 36, 52–
57, 75–76, 82, 83, 85–86
Yuri's birth and, 86–90
Blavatsky, Yuri, 87–92, 96, 121,
127, 135, 162, 180, 205, 299,
356, 367, 369, 430, 449
Blavatsky Lodge of Theosophical
Society, 393–94, 396, 398,
399, 408, 419, 421, 436, 438,
439, 443, 450, 453
Bohn (author), 343
Bombay Gazette, 199, 226, 231
Bombay Review, 197
Bonaparte, Napoleon, 20
Book M, 72
Book of Dzyan, see Stanzas of
Dzyan
Book of the Golden Precepts, The,
433
Boston Herald, 164
Boudreau, Zephrin, 120–21
Boulak Museum, 329
Bourbel, Marquis de, 359
Bourbon, Captain Adelberth de,
240
Bouton, J. W., 173, 176, 179, 204,
372, 376, 453
Bouyrak, Baranig, 37
Bradlaugh, Charles, 422–24, 426,
428, 429, 437, 456
Bradlaugh, Hypatia, 424
Brahm, Days and Nights of, 413,
414
Bright, Esther, 450
Bright, Ursula, 450, 453
Bright's disease, 256, 260, 317, 339,
407, 454
British Library, 465
British Museum, 406, 466
British National Association of
Spiritualists, 178
Britten, Emma Hardinge, 149–51,
154, 163–65, 174–75
Britten, William, 149
Brotherhood of Luxor, 138–42, 150,
172
Brotherhood of the Snowy Range,
235
Brothers Karamazov, The (Dos-
toyevsky), 231
Brown, Gerry, 129, 140, 142, 144,
150, 157
Brown, John, 111
Brown, William Tournay, 271–75,
319
Browning, Elizabeth Barrett, 74,
460
Browning, Robert, 74
Buckley, Constance, 359
Buddhism, 29, 30, 73, 170, 177,
180, 208, 214–15, 218, 330
in Ceylon, 275–76, 291
Mahatma letters and, 245–46

Bulla, Vallah, *see* Babula
Bulwer–Lytton, Edward, 28, 163, 170
Burnside, General, 112
Burrows, Herbert, 426, 427, 432, 437, 445, 447

Cabalistic literature, 72
Cabbala, the, 141, 151
Caithness, Countess de, 285
Caithness, Lady Marie, 277, 285–88, 294
Calcutta *Statesman*, 318
Cambridge Society for Psychical Research, 335
Cambridge University, 335
Campbell, Lady Colin, 432
Candler, Ida, 432–35, 441
Carey, Mrs. M. B., 120, 122
Catherine the Great, Czarina, 17, 51
Cayce, Edgar, 159
Ceylon *Times* 205
Charles X, King of France, 20
Charloo, Ananda, 265, 319–20, 339
Chatterji, Mohini Mohun, 248–49, 285, 313, 364, 380, 394
    in Leonard affair, 365
    in London, 292, 349, 355, 399–401, 405
    Olcott and, 276, 291
    in Paris, 286–87, 296, 317
    Society for Psychical Research investigation and, 335–39, 341
    Würzburg visit of, 376–77
Chekhov, Anton, 22
Chetty, Judge Muttuswamy, 252
Chetty, Soobiah, 252, 271
Child, Henry, 135, 142
Chinese literature, 416–17
Chintamon, Hurrychund, 181, 185, 194, 195–99, 254–55, 306, 343, 345, 362
Chohan, 237, 253
Christian College Magazine, 315,

318, 319, 322, 329, 337
Christianity, 417
    H.P.B.'s rejection of, 169, 180, 181, 215, 246
Christianity and Greek Philosophy (Cocker), 169
Church, Mrs., 244
Civil War, 111–12
Classical Library (Bohn), 343
Cleather, Alice, 392–94, 398, 436, 443, 446, 450
Clermont–Ferrand, University of, 405
Cochrane, Elizabeth ("Nellie Bly"), 69
Cocker, Benjamin F., 169
Cody, Buffalo Bill, 399
Coleman, William Emmette, 158, 159, 379, 380, 416–17, 448, 453
"Collapse of Koot Hoomi, The" (Patterson), 316
Collins, Mabel, 385, 389–97, 418, 420–22, 458
Collins, Mortimer, 390
Conan Doyle, Sir Arthur, 113
Constantine, Grand Duke, 20
Conway, Moncure Daniel, 274–75
Cook, Kenningale Robert, 390
Cooper, Henry, 321
Cooper, Laura, 445–47, 454–55
Cooper-Oakley, Alfred, 321–22, 327–28, 336, 340, 344, 348, 382, 412
Cooper-Oakley, Isabel, 321–22, 348, 382, 394, 443, 445, 458
    business ventures of, 431
    in Egypt, 326–28
    at H.P.B.'s death, 454, 455
    in India, 330, 336, 340–41, 344
    in Inner Group, 446
Cornell University, 152–53
Corson, Caroline, 152–54, 183
Corson, Eugene, 152, 153
Corson, Hiram, 133, 144, 152–54, 156, 164

Coryn, Herbert, 446
Cosmic Egg, 414
Coues, Elliott, 313, 409, 420–22, 447–49
Coulomb, Alexis, 205–6, 213–16, 285, 320, 331, 347, 352, 435
  at Adyar, 261, 268, 279
  in Egypt, 328–29
  and Emma's denunciation of H. P. B., 289, 313, 315, 322, 428
  as H.P.B.'s accomplice, 233, 239, 240, 263–64, 267, 280
  Hodgson investigation and, 338
Coulomb, Emma (née Cutting), 205–6, 213–18, 224, 226, 232, 243, 244, 258, 272, 272, 347, 350, 352, 435
  at Adyar, 260, 261, 279
  denunciation of H.P.B. by, 289–91, 293–95, 299, 303, 313–19, 322–23, 355, 356, 426, 428, 448
  in Egypt, 95–96, 327, 329
  as H.P.B.'s accomplice, 214, 216–18, 220–21, 230, 239–41, 264–65, 267, 279–81
  Hodgson investigation and, 337, 338, 343–44
  lawsuit threatened against, 331, 332
Crawford, Francis Marion, 261
Cremers, Alice, 421
Crimean War, 69
Crookes, Sir William, 74
Curie, Marie, 460
Curran, Paul Lenore, 367–68
Curtis, David, 188
Cutting, Emma, see Coulomb, Emma

Dalai Lama, 245
Dana, Charles, 140
Dana, David, 140–41, 143, 144
Darwin, Charles, 129, 236
David–Neel, Alexandra, 172

Davids, Rhys, 246
Davis, Andrew Jackson, 115, 130, 131, 136, 142, 156, 158, 163
Dayananda, Swami, 181, 198, 202–3, 206, 208, 212–13, 217–18, 228, 254, 306
Days of Brahm, 413
Dean, Sidney, 238
Deb, Gwala K., 258
Debodurgai, Lama, 244
Decharme (author), 379
Dekhan, Sardar of, 206
Demonologia (Forsyth), 158, 169
Derby, Lord, 276
Descendants of Thomas Olcott, The, 111
Dhyan Chohans, 414
Diaki, 105
Dickens, Charles, 236
Djelaleddin (Hahn), 33
Djul Khool, Mahatma, 237, 248, 466, 468
Dolgorukov, Prince Gregory, 15
Dolgorukov, Princess Helena, see Fadeyev, Princess Helena Pavlovna
Dolgorukov, Henrietta, 16
Dolgorukov, Prince Ivan, 15
Dolgorukov, Princess Katherine, 15
Dolgorukov, Prince Paul, 16, 48
Dolgorukov, Prince Serguey, 15
Dolgorukov family, 15–16, 145, 329
Domovoy, 25
Dondoukoff-Korsakoff, Prince Alexander, 48, 50, 51, 55, 91–92, 258, 298, 314
  H.P.B.'s letters to, 243, 248, 251–53, 256, 257, 260, 319
Donnelly (author), 379
Dorothy Restaurant, 431–32
Doubleday, General Abner, 181, 208
Dowson (author), 379
Druid temples, 415
Dublin Hermetic Society, 392, 400
Dublin University, 410
Dublin University Magazine, 390

Duchamps (cabinet maker), 263
Dudley, Dr., 256
Dunbar, Mrs., 121
Dunlap, S.F., 158
Dyer family, 338

Eastern School of Theosophy, 437
Eddy, Horatio, 110, 111, 113–14,
    118, 120–29, 179
Eddy, William, 110, 111, 113–14,
    118, 120–29, 179
Eddy, Zephaniah, 114
Edensor, Patience, see Sinnett,
    Patience
Edison, Thomas Alva, 181, 188,
    236
Eek, Sven, 320
Eglinton, William, 323
Egyptology, 417
Ellis, Ashton, 384, 385, 391
Ennemoser, Joseph, 158
Esoteric Buddhism (Sinnett), 235,
    246, 264, 310, 349, 354, 382,
    392, 405
Esoteric Section, 408, 410–11, 418,
    420, 429, 436, 437, 439, 442,
    458–59, 468
    Inner Group of, 446
Eternal Parent, 413
Evans–Wentz, W. Y., 235
Everyman Library, 403
Exposition Universelle, 434

Fabian Socialism, 422, 438
Fadeyev, Andrey Mihailovich, 38,
    39, 45, 54, 61, 76, 129
    bureaucratic career of, 26, 28,
        33, 35, 46, 83–84
    death of, 92
    marriage of Helena Dolgorukov
        and, 16–17
    at time of wife's death, 81, 82
Fadeyev, Princess Helena Pavlovna
    (née Dolgorukov), 16–19, 21,
    23–24, 27, 47–49, 162, 243

    death of, 81, 82
    declining health of, 51, 54, 61
    during H.P.B.'s childhood, 35–39,
        45
Fadeyev, Nadyezhda, 25, 36, 43,
    46, 51, 76, 83–84, 92, 294–
    95, 339, 370, 430
    birth of, 17
    childhood of, 21, 28, 31, 39, 40
    H.P.B.'s letters to, 95–96, 125,
        162, 180, 182, 209, 225, 281,
        385, 418
    and marriage of H.P.B. and Niki-
        for Blavatsky, 53–54, 75,
        183
    Paris visit of, 294, 295, 299–303
    Würzburg visit of, 349, 355
    Yuri's birth and, 88, 90
Fadeyev, Rostislav, 88, 90, 243, 298
    childhood of, 17, 30–31
    death of, 281, 294, 299, 302
    military career of, 37, 84
Fales, William, 141, 154
Fawcett, Edward Douglass, 381–82,
    406
Felt, George H., 150–51, 155, 165
Fifth Root Race, 415
Finch, Gerard B., 292
First Root Race, 414
Flournoy, Theodore, 467
Flowergirl, The (Hahn), 34
Flynn, Mary, 272, 346, 348, 351–52
Fohat, 414
Forsyth, J. S., 158, 169
Fortune, M., 329
Fourier, Charles, 163
Fourth Root Race, 415
Fourth Round, 414–16
Fox, Kate, 114–15
Fox, Margaret, 114–15
Framji Cowasji Institute, 199
French letter, 303–4
From the Caves and Jungles of
    Hindostan (Blavatsky), 204,
    296
"From the Land on the Other Side
    of the Blue Ocean" (Blavat-

sky), 182
Fruits of Philosophy; or, The Private Companion of Young Married Couples (Knowlton), 423, 426–27
Furness, William H., 137

Gagarin, Princess Lydia, 55
Gandhi, Mohandas K., 380, 439–40, 460
Garibaldi, Giuseppe, 91, 107, 118, 123
Garrett, Eileen, 42
Gebhard, Franz, 374
Gebhard, Gustav, 313–14, 363, 364, 373
Gebhard, Mary, 313–14, 358, 359, 363, 364, 372–73, 383–85
Gebhard, Rudolf, 317
Gebhard, Walter, 364
General Extrasensory Perception, 462
Gerebko, Clementine, 109, 141, 145
Gilbert, William S., 399
Glinka, Justine, 296–99, 314, 354, 367
Goddard, Arabella, 44
Godolphin (Bulwer-Lytton), 28
God's Judgment (Hahn), 33
Golitsyn, Prince Alexander, 51–54, 61
Gonne, Maud, 402
Gougenot Des Mousseauc, Henry Roger, 158
Grant and Laing (legal firm), 249
"Great Breath," 412
"Great Mare's Nest of the Psychical Research Society, The" (Besant), 453
Gribble, James D. B., 316, 338
Grodekoff, Nikolay, 212
Guegidze, Michalko, 121–22, 128
Guinness Brewery, 404
Guppy, Mrs. (medium), 211

Hahn, Alexander (Sasha) von, 21, 23

Hahn, Alexis Gustavovich, 19
Hahn, Gustave von, 124, 127
Hahn, Helena Andreyevna von, 17–24, 26–29, 31–35, 50–51, 294
Hahn, Leonid von, 33, 35, 36, 39, 75, 77–78, 97, 252–53, 358
Hahn, Liza von, 75, 77, 78, 105–6
Hahn, Nicholas von, 97
Hahn, Peter Alexeyeivich von, 35, 41, 43–45, 49, 63, 109, 123–25, 179
    death of, 105–6
    H.P.B.'s occult powers and, 77–80
    marriage of Helena Fadeyev and, 18–23, 27–29, 32–34
    second marriage of, 53, 55, 61, 75
    Yuri and, 89
Hahn, Vera von, *see* Zhelihovsky, Vera
Hahn-Hahn, Countess Ida, 23
Halleyburg College, 224
Harbottle, Thomas, 391
Harte, Richard, 412–13
Hartmann, Franz, 275, 280, 321, 339, 341, 344, 346–48, 355
    Coulomb controversy and, 289, 290, 293
    destruction of shrine by, 319–20, 329, 336–37, 343
Harvard University, 274
Hatha Yoga, 218
Hayden, Mrs., 68
Hayes, Rutherford B., 184
Henderson, Philip, 222, 223
Henley, William Ernest, 401
Hermetic literature, 72
Hermetic Theosophical Society, 292
Hilarion, 390, 466
Hindu Classical Dictionary (Dowson), 379
Hinduism, 73, 170, 181, 214, 417, 440
    Mahatma letters and, 245–46
    Theosophical Society and, 198–200, 206

Hints on Esoteric Theosophy (Hume), 254
History of Magic (Ennemoser), 158
Hitrovo, M., 329
Hodgson, Richard, 308, 347, 352, 354, 411, 448, 453, 466
  investigation carried out in India by, 335–45
  Report on Theosophy by, 362, 370, 393, 401, 428, 435
Holkar, Maharajah, 272
Holloway, Laura, 294, 308, 310, 312, 313, 317, 349, 394
Holmes, Jennie, 134–36
Holmes, Nelson, 134–36
Holt, Elizabeth, 104–6
Home, Daniel Dunglas, 73–74, 85, 129, 132–33, 164–65, 179, 368, 448
Home for Working Women, 447
Hong Kong *Daily Press*, 210
Hope, Lady Mary, 432
Houghton, Mr. and Mrs. Charles, 146
"How a Chela Found His Guru" (Ramaswamier), 259
Howe, Julia Ward, 261
Hubbe-Schleiden, William, 313, 355, 362, 364, 465–66
Huc, Abbe, 236
Hume, Allan Octavian, 211, 224–25, 239–44, 255, 259, 316, 319, 420
  Hodgson and, 343, 344
  in London, 389, 393
  Mahatma letters and, 229, 241–44, 257, 318
  pamphlet on Theosophical Society by, 247, 254
Hume, Joseph, 224
Hume, Maria Jane Burnby ("Minnie"), 225, 244, 246, 261, 343
Hume, Mary Anne ("Moggy"), 225–26, 240
Hyperboreans, 414

Ideal, The (Hahn), 28, 31, 34

Idyll of the White Lotus, The (Collins), 389
Imperishable Sacred Land, 414
"Important to Spiritualists" (Olcott), 140
Incidents in the Life of Madame Blavatsky (Sinnett), 370
Indian Brotherhood, *see* Secret Brotherhood
Indian Civil Service, 410
Indian Herald, 261
Indian Mirror, 218
Indian National Congress, 211, 440, 460
International Labor Congress, 432
Isadore, Metropolitan of Kiev, 75, 81–82
Isis Unveiled (Blavatsky), 205, 211, 298, 311, 321, 353, 356, 372, 376, 379, 382, 448, 453
  attacks on, 158, 233, 306, 363, 417
  French translation of, 285
  publication of, 173–76, 179
  reviews of, 179, 416
  writing of, 153, 158–63, 165, 168–74, 178, 184, 208, 245, 255, 354, 380, 391, 466
Isurenus, Polydorus, 139
Ivanof, Samoylo, 80
Ivins, William, 141, 154

Jacolliot, Louis, 158, 170
James, William, 238, 263, 336, 463
Jay Cooke and Company, 104
Jeffries, Augusta Sophia, 32, 37
Jennings, Hargrave, 158, 380
Jeypore, Maharaja of, 203
Jinarājadāsa, C., 444
Johnston, Charles, 392–93, 401, 403, 410–12, 446
Johnston, Vera (née Zhelihovsky), 373, 375, 407, 410–12, 446
Judaism, 416
Judge, Ella, 148, 216, 287–88
Judge, Frederick, 148
Judge, John, 177

Judge, William Quan, 148, 163,
177–78, 209, 216, 270, 308,
446–49, 456
  Besant and, 453, 458–59
  during Blavatsky–Olcott conflict,
409, 419–20
  in correspondence with Olcott,
198–99, 245
  at founding of Theosophical Society, 151, 154, 155
  H.P.B.'s letters to, 240, 376
  in India, 313–14, 319–20, 329,
447
  in Paris, 287–89, 291–92, 294,
311
Jung, Carl, 238, 468
*Juvenile Reflections Compiled for
My Children* (Zhelihovsky),
38

Kabbala Denudata (Rosenroth),
379
Kalmuck tribe, 28–30
Kappes (artist), 118, 125
Kardec, Allan, 94, 97, 305
Karma (Sinnett), 349
Katkov, Michael, 204, 209, 212,
294, 311, 314, 348
Kauffmann, Constantine Petrovitch,
50, 51
Keightley, Archibald, 293, 321,
382–83, 385–86, 391, 394–
97, 399, 401, 406, 438, 439,
445, 446
Keightley, Bertram, 313, 382–83,
385–86, 391–99, 401, 405,
406, 434, 438, 439, 444–46
Key to North American Birds
(Coues), 420
Key to Theosophy, The (Blavat-
sky), 418, 440
Khan, Amir Sher Ali, 198
Khandalavala, N. D., 272, 276
Kiddle, Henry A., 230, 269–70, 448
Kim (Kipling), 219
King, John, 110, 135–36, 138–39,
141, 144, 146, 153, 172, 311
King, Katie, 110, 134–35, 142
Kingsford, Anna B., 233, 276–79,
287, 292–93, 305, 309–10,
377–78, 407, 427
Kingsland, William, 437, 438
Kipling, Rudyard, 219, 220
Kiselev, Count Paul, 64, 75
Kiselev, Countess, 64
Kislingbury, Emily, 178, 181, 271,
372–73, 445, 446
Knowlton, Charles, 423
Koot Hoomi, Mahatma, 92, 170,
227–37, 239, 241–44, 250,
257–58, 261, 275, 280, 310,
316, 368, 377, 422, 452,
464–66
  Damodar and, 207, 267, 289
  French letter and, 303
  Judge and, 288
  Leadbeater and, 323–26, 444–45,
460
  letter to Massey from, 255
  letters to Sinnett from, 227–30,
232–34, 236–37, 242–44,
246–48, 259, 264, 269–70,
295, 310, 312, 322, 349, 353,
426–27, 464–66
  Mohini and, 287
  Olcott and, 264, 273–74, 291,
407, 409, 459
  Phoenix and, 266, 272
  portraits of, 264, 311–12, 314,
468
  Society for Psychical Research
investigation and, 306, 307,
343
Koot Hoomi Unveiled (Lillie), 311
Koucheleff Bezborrodke, Countess,
73
Krishnamachari, S., 258
Krishnamurti, Jiddu, 460
Krishnamurti, Nitya, 460
Kroll, Countess Alexandrine de, 73
Kuhlwein, Antonya Christianovna,
31–32, 37, 46, 69
Kuhlwein, Mr., 69
Kumaras, 415

Lane-Fox, St. George, 280, 285, 289, 315, 341
Lange, Baroness von, 53, 61, 75
Laws, The (Plato), 169
Leadbeater, Charles W., 292–93, 323–28, 330–31, 339, 341, 409, 444–45, 459–61
Leadbeater, Gerald, 444
Lebendorff, Tekla, 33, 41, 44, 45, 47–48, 77
Le Moyne, F. Julius, 166
Lemuria, 415, 416
Lenzburg (professor), 120
Leonard, Miss, 365–66, 372, 383
"Leopold," 467
Lermontov, Michael, 33, 46
Lévi, Eliphas, 158, 159, 312, 379
Leymarie, M. and Mme., 97
Liberal Catholic Church, 461
Liberal Christian, The (periodical), 147
Life Force, 413
Life Mutual Insurance Company of New York, 112
Light (weekly), 255, 269–70, 311, 318
Light of Asia (Arnold), 339, 439
Light on the Path (Collins), 390, 421
Lights and Shadows of Spiritualism (Home), 179
Lillie, Arthur, 270, 311, 323
Lippitt, General Francis J., 133, 136, 137, 143, 144
London *Daily News*, 429
London *Daily Telegraph*, 381, 405
London *Evening Standard*, 210, 278
London *Globe*, 210
London *Star*, 429, 443
London *Sun*, 429, 431, 432
London *Times*, 226, 318, 363
London University, 423
"Lost Canon of Proportion of the Egyptians, The" (Felt), 150
Louis, Chevalier, 149–50, 163
Louis Philippe, King of France, 20
Lucifer (magazine), 396–97, 403, 408, 418, 421, 427, 433–35, 437, 438
"Luminous Circle, The" (Blavatsky), 156
Lytton, Lord Edward, 208

M. Faciole and Company, 343
Machel, R. A., 442
Madras Christian College, 331
Madras Presidency College, 249
Maeterlinck, Maurice, 417–18
Magic and Mystery in Tibet (David-Neel), 172
Magnon, Madame, 105, 118, 120, 125, 143, 144
Maha-Chohan, 237, 287
Mahatma letters, 227–49, 257–58, 280, 307, 364, 407, 448, 464–66
    to Brown, 272
    Coulomb controversy and, 289, 313, 319
    French letter, 303, 370
    to Judge, 288
    to Olcott, 291, 409
    to Sinnett, 227–30, 232–34, 236–37, 240, 242–48, 253–54, 259, 264, 269–71, 295, 310, 312, 322, 349, 353, 394, 426–27, 464–66
    Society for Psychical Research investigation of, 309, 323, 337
Maitland, Edward, 226, 277, 293, 377–78, 407
Majji, 211–12
Man, Fragments of a Forgotten History (Holloway and Chatterji), 310
Manvantara, 412, 414
Marble, Mortimer, 187
Marie Antoinette, Queen of France, 467
Marquette, Lydia, 97
Marlborough, Duchess of, 460
Marryat, Ellen, 423
Mary, Queen of Scotland, 285

Masonry, 72
Massey, Charles C., 148–49, 181,
183, 193–94, 233, 254–55,
257, 270, 295, 305
Matin (newspaper), 294, 296
Matley, Frank, 325
Matley, James, 324, 325
Mavalankar, Damodar, 207–9, 218,
228, 243, 244, 249, 256, 287,
452
at Adyar, 260–61, 265, 267, 268,
280, 339
during Coulomb controversy,
289, 293, 313, 316, 319–20
in Ceylon, 214–15
death of, 342
family of, 212–14, 231
Hodgson's investigation and,
335–37, 343
on Punjab expedition, 272–73
Mead, George R. S., 404–5, 435,
438, 440, 445, 446, 450, 455,
456
Medallion (Hahn), 33
Melbourne University, 335
Memoirs of Gelesnobodsk (Hahn),
31
Mennell, Z., 419, 440, 441, 443,
454–55
Mentamon, Paulos, 65, 94
Metrovitch, Agardi, 75, 88, 89, 127,
157, 366, 367, 369, 375, 449
death of, 93–94
H.P.B.'s life with, 70–73, 90–92,
303, 349
Coulomb's knowledge of, 96,
205, 279, 299, 356
in Tiflis, 85–86
Meyendorff, Baron Nicholas, 85–
87, 89, 123, 132, 164, 180,
366–69, 449
Michener, Mrs. (clairvoyant), 143
Midford, Godolphin, 262
Mikado (Gilbert and Sullivan), 399
Miller, Captain, 68
Miller, Dr., 455
Mitchell, Belle, 182, 184
Modern American Spiritualism
(Britten), 149

Modern Priestess of Isis (Solov-
yov), 367
Modjeska, Helena, 390
Monsey (medium), 439
Montaigne, 379, 454
Moore, George, 403
More, Robert, 139
Morgan, Sir Henry, 110
Morgan, Henry Rhodes, 265–67,
316, 339, 345, 346, 408
Morgan, Mrs. Henry Rhodes, 265
Morgan, Mary Epplee, *see* Olcott,
Mary
Morial the Mahatma (Collins), 458
Morsier, Emile de, 294, 351, 352,
365
Morton, Mrs., 133
Morya, Mahatma (M.), 170, 236–
37, 246, 250, 256, 257, 278,
291, 310, 343, 353, 460,
464–66
Besant and, 433, 452
early messages to H.P.B. from,
181, 186
letters to Sinnett from, 243, 244,
259, 322
Olcott and, 205, 208, 209, 306,
341, 459
portraits of, 264, 311–12, 314
Moscheles, Ignaz, 44
Moscow *Chronicle*, 204
Moses, Stainton, 181, 233, 270, 305
Mr. Isaacs (Crawford), 261
Mr. Sludge, the "Medium"
(Browning), 74
Muller, Catherine Elise ("Helene
Smith"), 238, 466
Müller, Max, 158, 417
Murchison, Sir Roderick, 16
Musset, Alfred de, 401
"My Books" (Blavatsky), 453
Myers, Frederic, 305–8, 313, 379,
463
Mythologie de la Grèce Antique
(Decharme), 379

Napoleonic war (1815), 30
Narayan, 178

Nath, Darbhagiri ("Babaji"), 258–
  59, 265, 339, 346–48, 351–
  52, 354, 358, 361, 363–64,
  374–75
National Reformer (periodical),
  426
Navy Department, U.S., 112
Nehru, Jawaharlal, 459
Netherclift, Frederick George, 338,
  466
Nethercot, Arthur, 424, 430
New York *Daily Graphic*, 73, 114,
  118, 120, 122, 123, 125, 126,
  129, 131–33, 148, 183, 187–
  88
New York *Herald*, 179
New York *Star*, 106, 183
New York *Sun*, 102, 111, 114, 122,
  127, 128, 140, 156, 179, 185,
  204, 436, 447–49
New York Times, 179, 188, 416,
  460
New York *Tribune*, 111, 150, 457
New York *World*, 165
Nicholas I, Czar, 18–20, 41, 64, 75,
  125
Nicholas II, Czar, 82
Nights of Brahm, 413, 414
Nikolayevich, Grand Duke Mihail,
  47
Nogen, Jilbert de, 169

Oakley, Alfred J. *see* Cooper-Oak-
  ley, Alfred
Obolensky, Prince Konstantin Ivan-
  ovich, 15
Occult Room
  at Adyar, 262–65, 267–68, 275,
    280, 289, 329, 335–37
  in London, 442, 446
Occult Science in India (Jacolliot),
  170–71
Occult World (Sinnett), 220, 233,
  234, 269, 310, 349
O'Faolain, Sean, 404
Olcott, Bessie, 112
Olcott, Emmet, 186
Olcott, Henry Steel, 44, 93, 110–

  15, 126–32, 148, 295, 320,
    322–24, 343, 354–56, 366,
    376, 377, 379, 381, 426, 445,
    447–53
  break with Blavatsky, 350–51,
    371, 396, 407–12, 419–20,
    436–38, 450–51
  break with Spiritualism, 150,
    154–55
  in Brotherhood of Luxor, 141–42
  in Burma, 339, 342
  in Ceylon, 231–32, 239, 244, 245,
    256, 258, 268
  contacts in India, 181–82
  Coues and, 420
  death of, 459
  denounced by Home, 179
  departure for India, 182–89
  divorce of, 134
  at Elberfeld, 313, 314, 316–18
  in England, 275–76
  in first apartment with H.P.B.,
    166–68
  first meeting of H.P.B. and, 118–
    26
  at founding of Theosophical So-
    ciety, 151–52, 154–56
  French letter and, 303, 304
  H.P.B.'s ashes brought to India
    by, 456
  Holmes scandal and, 134–35
  in India
    Bombay, 195–200, 204–9, 212–
      17, 231–32, 245, 246
    Brown and, 272–74
    Calcutta, 248–49
    Karli Caves, 200–1
    Madras, 250–52, 260, 264–65,
      330–32, 335–37, 341, 343
    Punjab trip, 202–4
    Sinnett and, 209–12, 216–30
  John King and, 136
  during Kiddle controversy,
    269–71
  in London, 193–94, 292–93, 302,
    311, 321
  and marriage of H.P.B. and Be-
    tanelly, 137–39, 144–45, 177
  money sent to H.P.B. by, 347–48,

353, 372, 374, 383, 394
Palm and, 164–66, 176
return to Europe from India,
285–86, 291
Serapis' letters to, 145–47
Society for Psychical Research
and, 305–9, 335–37, 341,
343–46, 362–63
Wilder and, 173–74
during writing of *Isis Unveiled*,
157–63, 168–69, 171–72,
380, 466
Olcott, Mary (née Morgan), 112,
113, 134, 185, 189, 345
Olcott, Morgan, 112, 185
Olcott, Thomas, 111
Olcott, William Topping, 112, 185
Old Diary Leaves (Olcott), 113,
151
Old, Walter, 445, 446, 455
Oliver (author), 379
Oppenheim, Leon, 356–58, 370
Order of the Golden Dawn, 439
Oriental Library (Trubner), 343
Ouija Board, 136, 467
Our Corner (magazine), 427
Owen, Robert Dale, 133, 134
Oxford University, 405, 417

Pachiappa College, 330–31
Padshah, Sorab J., 280, 286, 288
Pal Mall Gazette, 323, 400, 425,
429, 456–57
Pali Text Society, 416
Palladino, Eusapia, 136
Pallandt, Baroness de, 432
Palm, Joseph Henry Louis Charles,
Baron de, 164–66, 176, 448
Pancoast, Seth, 141, 143, 154, 155,
175
Pan-Slavism, 84
Pasha, Nubar, 327
Pasteur, Louis, 378
Patanjali (author), 420
Path, The (magazine), 420
Patterson, George, 315, 337–38
Peebles, James M., 96, 120, 181

Peigneur, Henriette, 38
People of the Blue Mountains, The
(Blavatsky), 266, 315, 348
People From the Other World (Ol-
cott), 132, 142, 150, 164,
179
Peter II, Czar, 15
Peter the Great, Czar, 15, 31
Petri, Gus, 186–87, 193
Phallicism (Jennings), 380
Phillips, H. A., 120
Phoenix (newspaper), 264, 266, 272
Pillai, Keshava, 258–59
Pioneer (newspaper), 198, 210–12,
226, 227, 231, 253, 264, 444
Plato, 169, 173, 415
Plato and the Older Academy
(Zeller), 169, 173
Podmore, Frank, 306, 322
Pomar, Duchess de, 285
Popesco, Madame, 96
Poseidon, 415
Potemkin, Prince Gregory, 17
Praed, Rosa, 349
Pralaya, 413, 414
Pratt, Calvin E., 141
Pravda (newspaper), 182
Prince, Walter Franklin, 467
Proof Palpable of Immortality
(Sargent), 136
Pryse, James, 445
Psychische Studien (periodical),
132
Purānas, 246
"Purpose of Theosophy, The" (P.
Sinnett), 349
Pushkin, Alexander, 28, 47, 80
Pythagorean Triangle (Oliver), 379

Qabbala (Myers), 379

Ramaswamier, S. Ramabandra, 259
Rao, Shrivas, 267
Rawson, Alber Leighton, 64–66,
162–63, 167
Readers' Library, The, 28, 31

Rebus (journal), 245, 369
Recurrent Spontaneous Psychokinesis (RSPK), 80, 462
Religio-Philosophical Journal, 120, 133, 140, 164, 270, 411, 416, 421, 447–48, 457
Revue Theosophique, La, 418
Rhys, Ernest, 403
Roberts, Jane, 172
Robinson, James C., 154
Rockville, William, 236
Root Races, 414
Rosenkreutz, Christian, 72
Rosenroth, Knorr von, 379
Rosicrucianism, 72, 163, 170
Rosicrucians (Jennings), 158
Rounds, 414
Roussalkas, 25–26, 43, 146
Row, T. Subba, 249–51, 294, 332, 339, 344, 348, 350, 353, 372, 381, 394
Roy, Raja Ramohun, 248–49
Royal Asiatic Society, 416
Royal Geographical Society, 16
Rupsinghji, Prince Jarisinghji, 206, 280–81, 363–64
Rurik, Prince of Novgorod, 15
Russell, Edmund, 400, 412, 431
Russell, George W. ("AE"), 403–4, 410, 416
Russky Vyestnik, 296, 353, 367

Sacred Books of the East (Müller), 417
Salem witch trials, 113–14
Sand, George, 23, 33, 401
Sankariah, Dewan, 216–17
Sarasvati, Dayananda, *see* Dayananda, Swami
Sargent, Epes, 133, 136
Sassoon, Jacob, 272–73
Saturday Review, 233
Schmiechen, Hermann, 311–12, 314, 316, 355
Scholem, Gershom, 379
Schumann, Clara, 44
Schutze, Ernst, 466

Science (periodical), 416
Scott, Ross, 196, 225, 244, 246, 261
Sebir, Madame, 94–96, 205
Second Root Race, 414
Secret Brotherhood, 170, 180, 184, 199, 200, 212, 213, 225–27, 229, 238, 343, 345, 350, 378
    See also Koot Hoomi; Mahatma letters; Morya
Secret Doctrine, The (Blavatsky), 72, 169, 245, 311, 384, 396, 404, 406, 413–18, 452–54
    publication of, 413
    reviews of, 416–17, 425
    Stanzas of Dzyan and, 378–81, 395, 414
    writing of, 353–55, 362, 370, 372, 374, 376, 382, 391
Seevai, Hormusji, 225, 226, 343
Sellin, Professor, 361–63
Senzar language, 378, 414
Sepoy Mutiny, 69, 198, 224
"Seth," 172
Shakespeare, William, 136, 236, 380
Shankaracharya, 249
Shaw, George Bernard, 422, 424, 425, 429, 430
Short Cuts (magazine), 458
Siddons, Sara, 430
Sidgwick, Eleanor, 308
Sidgwick, Henry, 308, 322, 335
Sifra Di-Tseniutha, 379
Singh, Goolab, 204
Singh, Koot' Hoomi Lal, *see* Koot Hoomi
Sinnett, Alfred, 62, 63, 85, 88, 209–12, 218–30, 274, 278, 288, 307, 309, 316, 354, 362, 380, 382, 392, 424, 431, 444, 449
    as biographer of H.P.B., 54, 68–69, 89, 304, 355, 369–70, 375–77, 425, 436
    H.P.B.'s letters to, 85, 256, 266, 268, 276, 355, 365–68, 379
    London Lodge of Theosophical Society and, 286, 292, 305,

325, 377, 383, 393–94
Mahatma letters to, 227–30,
    232–34, 236–37, 240,
    242–48, 253–54, 259, 264,
    269–71, 295, 310, 312, 322,
    349, 353, 394, 426–27, 464–
    66
medical certificate sent to, 356–
    58
Pioneer edited by, 198, 210, 226,
    253, 264
at Simla, 216, 218–30, 239–44
Sinnett, Denny, 211, 444
Sinnett, Patience, 232, 233, 239,
    256, 349–50, 355
in India, 209–12, 216, 220–23,
    226, 264
in London, 276, 307, 394
Mahatma letters and, 246, 295
Siphra Dzeniuta, 378
Sixty Years of the Caucasian War
    (Fadeyev), 84
Skeleton Key to Mysterious Gates,
    see Isis Unveiled
"Ski," 193, 240, 254, 295
Smirnoff, E., 406–7
Smirnoff, Olga, 298–99, 314
Smith, Edward Sutton, 163
"Smith, Helene," 238, 466
Smithsonian Institution, 313, 420,
    448
Société Spirite, 94–96
Society for Psychical Research,
    305–9, 322–23, 353, 377,
    394, 411, 420, 457, 463
Report on Theosophy by, 361–62,
    383, 392–93, 401, 425, 428–
    29, 435
Solomon's Wisdom, 38, 39, 48
Solovyov, Serguey, 295
Solovyov, Vladimir, 295
Solovyov, Vsevolod, 295–97, 299,
    349, 351, 449
at Elberfeld, 314–15
H.P.B.'s letters to, 317–19, 323,
    329, 331, 332, 339, 347,
    368–69
Vera and, 302, 366–67, 372
in Würzburg, 354–55

"Some Account of My Intercourse
    with Madame Blavatsky"
    (Coulomb), 345
Song Celestial, The (Arnold), 439
Sorgho and Imphee, the Chinese
    and African Sugar-Canes
    (Olcott), 111
Sotheran, Charles, 150, 151, 155–
    56
Space, 413
Spencer, Herbert, 335
Spiritual Scientist (periodical),
    129, 140, 142
Spiritualism and Spiritualists, 95–
    96, 177, 285, 311, 462, 467
American, 97, 105, 107, 110,
    114–15, 119, 124, 126–27,
    132–36, 140, 142–44, 147,
    149, 152, 154–55, 164
English, 269, 321, 325, 382, 405,
    424
Home and, 73, 85
in Russsia, 77, 78, 82, 84
Spreti, Count and Countess von,
    313
Springfield Republican, 179
Stack, Herbert, 306
Stanhope, Lady Hester Lucy, 16
Stanzas of Dzyan, 378–79, 381,
    395, 414, 416, 418, 433
Stead, W. T., 400, 423, 425
Steiger, Isabelle de, 210–11, 277,
    286, 305, 311–12, 364–65,
    390
"Story of the Mystical, A" (Bla-
    vatsky), 156
Stray Feathers (journal), 224
Sturdy, E. T., 446
Sub-Races, 414
Sullivan, Arthur, 399
Sumangala, High Priest, 330
Sunyåsi, 202–3
Suvorov, Field Marshal Alexander,
    19
Swedenborg, Emanuel, 163, 382
Swift, Jonathan, 237

Tagore, Debendra Nath, 249
Tennyson, Alfred, Lord, 236

Terry, Luther, 261
Thackeray, William Makepeace, 236
Thackersey, Moolji, 181, 182, 195, 197, 199–204, 216, 306
Theophania Abiadjio (Hahn), 33
Theosophical Press Bureau, 458
Theosophical Publishing Company, 428
Theosophical Society, 135, 173, 205, 279, 318, 320, 324, 368, 376, 377
    American, 409–10, 420, 444, 448, 453, 459
    British, 254–55, 270–71, 277, 286–87, 292–93, 305–6, 308, 311, 321, 325, 377, 381–83, 385, 391, 397, 401, 405, 427–29, 435, 442
    See also Blavatsky Lodge; Esoteric Section
    in Ceylon, 215
    decline of, 174–75
    division of, 407–12, 450–51
    in Dublin, 393, 402–4
    founding of, 151–52, 154–56, 370
    in Germany, 361, 362
    in Holland, 240
    after H.P.B.'s death, 456–61, 468
    in India, 198–200, 204–9, 212, 216, 218–20, 223, 225, 230–33, 239, 241, 244, 247–53, 261, 315–16, 319, 331–32, 339, 341, 342, 344–46, 426
    Palm and, 164–65
    in Paris, 294, 296, 297, 299, 365, 369
    revival of, 181–82
    Society for Psychical Research Report on, 361–62, 383, 392–93, 401, 425, 428–29, 435
    in Sweden, 441
Theosophist (journal), 208, 212, 214, 215, 231, 254, 255, 259, 261, 264, 272, 275, 305, 311, 348, 353, 396, 408, 412, 419, 426–27
Theosophists, 134, 285, 322, 323, 392

    See also Theosophical Society
Theosophy, 72, 359, 400, 427, 444
    in *Isis Unveiled*, 168–69
    See also Theosophical Society
Third Root Race, 415
Three Sisters, The (Chekhov), 22
Through Afghanistan (Grodekoff), 212
Timaeus (Plato), 169
Time (periodical), 453
Times of India, 218, 228
Tolstoy, Leo, 35, 46
"Transactions of the Blavatsky Lodge," 419
Trinity College, 422
Trojan War, 417
Trubner (author), 343
"Truth about H. P. Blavatsky, The" (Hahn), 245, 369
Tulpas, 172
Tumene, Prince, 30
Tussaud, Madame, 194
Tynan, Katherine, 402, 411, 421
Tyndall (scientist), 236

Umballa (Hahn), 31
University College Hospital, 224
University of Moscow, 296
Upanishads, 246, 249
Upasika, 237, 239

Vanity Fair (Thackeray), 443
Vedic religion, 181
Veil of Isis, The, see Isis Unveiled
Victoria, Queen, 68, 224, 395
Vishnu Purana (Wilson), 379, 380
Vizianagram, Maharaja of, 211
Voice of the Silence, The (Blavatsky), 432–33, 435
Vorontzov, Prince Mihail, 45, 109
Vsevolodovich, Prince Michael, 15

Wachmeister, Countess Constance, 375, 389, 452
    at H.P.B.'s death, 454, 455
    in Inner Group, 446

in London, 397–98, 400, 407,
    412, 413, 428, 443, 445
at Ostend, 376–85
in Würzburg, 360–63, 365–66,
    368, 371–73
War Department, U.S., 112
Ward, Sam, 261
Washington *Evening Star*, 447
Webster, Forster, 466
Westbrook, R. B., 167, 168, 174–
    75, 447
Westminster School, 381
White, Andrew D., 153–54
White, Eliza, 134, 135
Whitney, William, 208
Wiggin, J. H., 147
Wilde, Constance, 405, 432
Wilde, Lady, 405
Wilde, Oscar, 307, 405, 432
Wilde, Willie, 405
Wilder, Alexander, 158, 173–76,
    187, 203, 354, 453
Wilson, E. V., 107
Wilson, W. H., 379, 380
Wimbridge, Edward, 184, 186,
    194–95, 201, 204, 208, 214–
    16, 218, 220, 231, 343
Winchell, Alexander, 379
Witchcraft on the Nilgiri (Mor-
    gan), 265
Witte, Alexander, 45
Witte, Andrey, 45
Witte, Katherine (née Fadeyev), 17,
    30, 36, 45–46, 49, 54, 55,
    81, 82, 87, 92, 93, 121
Witte, Serguey Yulyevich, 55, 81–
    85, 92–93
Witte, Yuli, 37, 45, 46, 73, 92
Wittgenstein, Prince Emile de, 449
Wolff, Hannah, 106–9, 120
Wood, Annie, *see* Besant, Annie
Wood, Emily, 423
Wood, Harry, 423
Wood, William, 422
Woodhull, Victoria, 107
Woolf, Mrs., 444
World Life (Winchell), 379

World's Judgment, The (Hahn), 33
"Worth, Patience," 467–68
Wright, Claude Falls, 392, 403,
    445, 446, 455
Wudhwan, Thakur of, 262, 280

Yahontov, Feodor, 76
Yahontov, General Nikolay de, 75
Yahontov, Rostislav, 76
Yeats, William Butler, 392, 400–5,
    410, 421, 439
Yoga Philosophy (Panlajali), 420
Yoga Vidya, 249, 254
Young Men's Christian Association,
    134
Yule, Mr. and Mrs., 108–9

Zanoni (Bulwer-Lytton), 67, 163,
    170, 209
Zeller, Edward, 169
Zenkowsky, O. I., 29
Zhelihovsky, Vera (née von Hahn),
    35, 48, 75–83, 87–88, 93,
    106, 123, 252–53, 399, 449
in adolescence, 51, 53, 54
article on H.P.B. published by,
    244–45, 369
birth of, 26
childhood of, 30, 32, 34, 36–39,
    44, 46
at Elberfeld, 373–75
first marriage of, 75–76
H.P.B.'s letters to, 90, 160–62,
    168, 171, 180, 194, 195, 232,
    244, 257, 309, 329, 355, 383,
    385, 393, 396, 399, 406, 418,
    419, 440–41, 443
London visits of, 407, 410, 411,
    446
Paris visit of, 294–95, 298–304
second marriage of, 82, 178
Solovyov and, 302, 366–67, 372
Zhelihovsky, Vladimir Ivanovich, 82
Zoharic writings, 379